PRINCIPLES OF MACRO-ECONOMICS

SECOND EDITION

PRINCIPLES OF MACRO-ECONOMICS

JOSEPH E. STIGLITZ

SECOND EDITION

STANFORD UNIVERSITY

W • W • NORTON & COMPANY • NEW YORK • LONDON

The text of this book is composed in Zapf Book
with the display set in Kabel
Composition by TSI
Manufacturing by Quebecor Hawkins
Book design by Antonina Krass
Cover painting: Laszlo Moholy-Nagy, *LIS*, 1922
Oil on canvas, 131 × 100 centimeters
Courtesy of the Kunsthaus, Zurich
Special thanks to Hattula Moholy-Nagy

Library of Congress Cataloging-in-Publication Data

Stiglitz, Joseph E.
Principles of macroeconomics / Joseph E. Stiglitz.—2nd ed.
p. cm.
Includes index.
1. Macroeconomics. I. Title.
HB172.5.S75 1996
339—dc20 95-21272
CIP

ISBN 0-393-96838-3 (pbk.)

W. W. Norton & Company, Inc., 500 Fifth Avenue, New York, N.Y. 10110
http://www.wwnorton.com
W. W. Norton & Company Ltd., 10 Coptic Street, London WCIA IPU

2 3 4 5 6 7 8 9 0

To Jane,
my harshest critic and best friend,
from whom I have learned the strengths and limits of economics;

and to
Julia, Jed, Michael, and Siobhan
in the hope, and belief, that a better understanding of economics
will lead to a better world for them to inherit.

ABOUT THE AUTHOR:

Internationally recognized as one of the leading economists of his generation, Joseph Stiglitz has made important contributions to virtually all of the major subdisciplines of economics: macroeconomics, monetary economics, public and corporate finance, trade, development, and industrial organization. After teaching at Yale, Princeton, and Oxford, in 1988 he accepted a position at Stanford University, where he has taught a wide variety of courses reflecting his broad interests, including Economics 1, one of the most popular courses on campus. In 1995, President Clinton asked him to serve as his chief economic adviser, appointing him Chairman of the Council of Economic Advisers and a member of the cabinet. In early 1997, Joseph Stiglitz will become the chief economist at the World Bank. Professor Stiglitz is the author and editor of hundreds of scholarly articles and books, including the best-selling undergraduate text *Economics of the Public Sector* (Norton) and, with Anthony Atkinson, *Lectures in Public Economics.* He is founding editor of the *Journal of Economic Perspectives,* established in 1987 to lower the barriers of specialization erected by other major economic journals, and a former vice president of the American Economic Association. Among his many prizes and awards, Professor Stiglitz has received the American Economic Association's John Bates Clark Award, given to the economist under forty who has made the most significant contributions to economics. Joe Stiglitz lives in Washington, D.C. with his wife and four children.

Contents in Brief

Part One | Introduction

Part Two | Full-Employment Macroeconomics

Part Three | Unemployment Macroeconomics

PART FOUR | DYNAMICS AND MACRO POLICY

PART FIVE | ISSUES IN MACROECONOMIC POLICY

Contents

Preface

Part One

Introduction

Chapter 1 The Automobile and Economics • 1

PART TWO

FULL-EMPLOYMENT MACROECONOMICS

CHAPTER 4 MACROECONOMIC GOALS AND MEASURES • 91

CHAPTER 5 MICROFOUNDATIONS • 118

CHAPTER 6 THE FULL-EMPLOYMENT MODEL • 150

CHAPTER 7 USING THE FULL-EMPLOYMENT MODEL • 177

PART THREE

UNEMPLOYMENT MACROECONOMICS

PART FIVE

ISSUES IN MACROECONOMIC POLICY

CHAPTER 17 GROWTH AND PRODUCTIVITY • 433

CHAPTER 18 DEFICITS AND DEFICIT REDUCTION • 463

CHAPTER 19 TRADE POLICY • 484

CHAPTER 20 ALTERNATIVE ECONOMIC SYSTEMS • 507

CHAPTER 21 DEVELOPMENT • 531

PREFACE

Introductory students should know the vitality of modern economics, and this book is intended to show it to them. When I set out to write the First Edition, I felt that none of the available texts provided an adequate understanding of the principles of *modern* economics—both the principles that are necessary to understanding how modern economists think about the world, and the principles that are required to understand current economic issues. Apparently, my feelings were shared by many, as indicated by the resounding success of the First Edition. Not only was the book widely adopted in colleges and universities throughout the world, it was also rapidly translated into many languages—from major editions in Spanish, German, Italian, Japanese, and Chinese, to small editions in countries such as Latvia. This Second Edition builds on the initiatives of its predecessor. With the benefit of a wealth of feedback from the market, I have made a painstaking effort to improve the book from cover to cover. I believe both students and their instructors will be pleased with the result.

This Second Edition is also informed by my recent professional activities. During the last two years I have enjoyed a direct role in U.S. policy making as Chairman of the President's Council of Economic Advisers and as a member of the cabinet. This experience reinforced my conviction that the traditional principles course is too far removed from our national policy concerns and the modern advances in economics that can illuminate them. Moreover, my service on the council afforded me the opportunity to discuss key economic problems with leaders throughout the world, both in the major industrialized countries, and in India, China, Russia, and elsewhere. It was thus with a unique perspective that I set to work on the revision during the last two years, carving out time on weekends and during countless hours before dawn.

Economics is the science of choice and writing a textbook involves many choices. As I began work on the Second Edition, I was convinced that the choices I had made in the First Edition—for instance, the attention to new topics such as technological change and finance, and the increased emphasis on international concerns—were moves in the right direction. However, I had become even more convinced that an understanding of these new topics had to be based on solid foundations in established fundamentals, such as the law of supply and demand, the theory of the firm, and traditional perspectives on unemployment, inflation, and economic growth. Thus, in the revision I simultaneously faced several challenges, not the least of which was to reinforce the exposition of the fundamentals at the same time as I strengthened the discussion of new topics.

As I began the revision, several of the dramatic changes that had loomed so large in the early 1990s seemed still to occupy center stage, but new issues and new perspectives had emerged. The Cold War has ended, with the political and economic system of Communism the clear loser. The economies of the former Soviet Union and Eastern Europe are making a slow and painful transition to market economies. The countries of East Asia have experienced unprecedented growth, in some cases at rates in excess of 10 percent, year after year; they have shown that development is indeed possible. Japan became an economic powerhouse, while Korea, Taiwan, and the other Asian "tigers" went from being poor, backward countries to major players in the international arena. Their growth was based on international trade; and trade throughout the world, including the United States, became increasingly important. Huge private capital flows helped finance the development of many countries as well as the huge deficits that the United States and other countries began to mount. When investors lost confidence in a country, as they did in Mexico in 1995, these same capital flows precipitated an economic crisis that quickly spread, and was only arrested through strong international cooperation.

The success of East Asia during the 1970s and 1980s stands out as an exception in a world economy facing disappointment; the countries of Africa saw their desperate economic conditions worsen. Beginning around 1973, growth in the industrialized countries, including the United States, slowed markedly. Europe, where unemployment rates in the 1960s had fallen to extremely low rates, saw them soar, often to double-digit levels, and stubbornly remain there; while in the United States, where growth had been benefiting all groups, but especially the poor, inequality increased, with those at the bottom actually seeing their living standards deteriorate.

Within the United States, the mid-1990s brought signs of a reversal of some of these trends. Unemployment and inflation rates fell to low levels that had not been seen for a quarter of a century. The poverty rate began to decline, and incomes of all groups, especially those at the bottom, began to rise. American manufacturing experienced rapid productivity growth, with matching success in the international arena—U.S. car production again became the largest in the world. But among many workers, anxiety remained high; while their real wages and incomes had begun to rise, they still had not recovered to their earlier peaks, and no one was sure these trends would continue. Overall productivity growth also remained below its previous levels. Though the soaring deficit was brought under control—it had been the largest experienced in the United States during peacetime, with the national debt quadrupling between 1981 and 1992—the long-run prospects appeared daunting; the aging of the baby boomers would put unprecedented strains on the Social Security and health care systems.

As the world has changed, expectations have changed as well. While there has been enormous improvement in the quality of air in cities like Pittsburgh and Gary, Indiana, and while Lake Erie has been rescued from becoming polluted to the point where life could not survive, our expectations about the environment have grown even faster; we have become increasingly aware of environmental costs. Longevity has increased, but our knowledge of how to prolong life has grown more rapidly, and rising medical costs have become a major political issue. The economic role of women has changed: not only have they taken a more active part in the labor force, there has been a revolution in expectations concerning the kinds of jobs women can hold.

And in virtually every one of the major issues facing the economy, there is a debate about the role of government. Government in the United States has grown enormously. Before World War II, government took less than one out of every five dollars; today it takes one out of three. Still, government in the United States is proportionately smaller than in most other industrialized countries. At one level, there is remarkable agreement about what the government should do: it has, for instance, a responsibility to help the economy remain at full employment with stable prices, to protect the environment, to support education, and to provide for the national defense. But how the government should fulfill its responsibilities in each of these areas is highly contentious. Issues concerning the responsibility, capability, and strategies of government in economics have come to the center of the political debate.

These are exciting issues and events, and they fill the front pages of our newspapers and the evening television news shows. Yet in the past, as a teacher of the introductory course in economics, I felt frustrated: none of the textbooks really conveyed this sense of excitement. Try as they might, none seemed to prepare students adequately for interpreting and understanding these important economic events.

As I thought about it more, one of the reasons for this became clear: the principles expounded in the classic textbook of Alfred Marshall of a hundred years ago, or that of Paul Samuelson, now almost fifty years old, were not the principles for today. The way we economists understand our discipline had changed to reflect the changing world, but the textbooks had not kept pace. Our professional discourse was built on a *modern* economics, but these new developments simply were not adequately reflected in any of the vast array of textbooks that were available to me as a teacher.

Indeed, changes in the economics discipline over the past half century have been as significant as the changes in world events. The basic competitive model of the economy was perfected in the 1950s. Since then, economists have gone beyond that model in several directions as they have come to better understand its limitations. Earlier researchers had paid lip service to the importance of incentives and to problems posed by limited information. However, it was only in the last two decades that real progress was made in understanding these issues. The 1996 Nobel Prize was awarded to two economists who pioneered our understanding of the role of information and incentives in the economy. Their work, and the work of others in this field, have found immediate applications. Both the collapse of the former Soviet bloc economies and the failure of the American S & L's can be viewed as consequences of the failure to provide appropriate incentives. A central question in the debate over growth and productivity has been, how can an economy provide stronger incentives for innovation? The debate over pollution and the environment centers around the relative merits of regulation and providing incentives not to pollute and to conserve resources.

The past fifty years have also seen a reexamination of the boundary between economics and business. Subjects like finance and management used to be relegated to business schools, where they were taught without reference to economic principles. Today we know that to understand how market economies actually work, we have to understand how firms finance and manage themselves. Tremendous insights can be gleaned through the application of basic economic principles, particularly those grounded in an understanding of incentives. Stories of corporate takeovers have been replaced on the front page by stories of bankruptcies as acquiring corporations have found themselves overextended. The 1990 Nobel Prize was awarded to three economists who had contributed most to the endeavor to integrate finance and economics. Yet the introductory textbooks had not yet built in the basic economics of finance and management.

We have also come to better appreciate the virtues of competition. We now understand, for instance, how the benefits of competition extend beyond price to competition for technological innovation. At the same time, we have come to see better why, in so many circumstances, competition appears limited. Again, as I looked over the available textbooks, none seemed to provide my students with a sense of this new understanding.

Samuelson's path-breaking textbook is credited with being the first to integrate successfully the (then) new insights of Keynesian economics with traditional microeconomics. Samuelson employed the concept of the neoclassical synthesis—the view that once the economy was restored to full employment, the old classical principles applied. In effect, there were two distinct regimes to the economy. In one, when the economy's resources were underemployed, macroeconomic principles applied; in the other, when the economy's resources were fully employed, microeconomic principles were relevant. That these were distinct and hardly related regimes was reflected in how texts were written and courses were taught; it made no difference whether micro was taught before macro, or vice versa. In the last few decades, economists came to question the split that had developed between microeconomics and macroeconomics. The profession as a whole came to believe that macroeconomic behavior had to be related to underlying microeconomic principles; there was one set of economic principles, not two. But this view simply was not reflected in any of the available texts.

This book differs from most other texts in several ways. Let me highlight some of the most prominent distinctions.

- Reflecting my recent involvement in policy making, throughout the text I have introduced examples to relate economic theory to recent policy discussions. In each chapter, there is a policy perspective box providing a vignette on one particular issue. These policy discussions both enliven the course and enrich the student's command over the basic material.
- Economists are a contentious lot, yet on most issues, differences between economists pale in comparison to differences between noneconomists. Indeed, there is a high degree of consensus among economists, and I have drawn attention to this throughout the book with 14 points of consensus in economics.
- The organization of the macroeconomic presentation has been changed to reflect more closely the microeconomic foundations of macroeconomics. It begins in Part Two with an analysis based on perfect markets—a full-employment model with perfectly flexible wages and prices. This model has the virtue of being pedagogically simple, and yet remarkably powerful. From there I move to the other extreme—and the focus of traditional macroeconomics—an unemployment model with rigid wages and prices (Part Three). This leads to a discussion of the dynamics of adjustment. Here I present the analysis of an economy in which wages and prices are neither perfectly flexible, nor perfectly rigid, and in which a principal concern is the rate of inflation (Part Four).
- One of the virtues of the new organization is that I can turn, in Chapter 7, to the important topics of economic growth and fiscal deficits, as applications of the full-employment model. Later, in Chapters 17 and 18, I return to consider economic growth and the deficit in greater detail. Students are eager to learn about these fundamental macroeconomic subjects, which are the focus of considerable attention in current policy debates.
- Throughout the book, I integrate the insights of modern advances in economics—such as those provided by endogenous growth theory, rational expectations, and theories of credit rationing and credit availability—with the more traditional topics. This approach lends insights into both the modern advances and the traditional perspectives.
- I have gone further to integrate international considerations into the macroeconomic analysis. For instance, after I set forth the full-employment model in Chapter 6, I use it to explain international capital flows and the determination of exchange rates in Chapter 7. Then, in presenting the models of unemployment (Part Three) and the dynamics of adjustment (Part Four), international dimensions are carefully addressed, especially in relation to monetary theory and policy.
- In addition to the extensive integration of international concerns throughout the book, I have added a new chapter on international trade policy (Chapter 19), focusing on various trade practices, including commercial policy, "fair trade" laws, and the role of bilateral trade agreements such as the North American Free Trade Agreement (NAFTA) and the World Trade Organization (WTO).

I emphasize in this book that most economic tasks are beyond the scope of any one individual. This lesson certainly applies to the writing and revision of a textbook. In writing the First Edition, I benefited greatly from the reactions of my students in the introductory courses at Princeton and Stanford who class-tested early drafts. Their enthusiastic response to the manuscript provided much-needed boosts to motivate me at several critical stages. The reception of the First Edition showed that the venture was well worth the effort. Similarly, the revision has benefited from the experience of the thousands of students who have used the book and their teachers who offered invaluable feedback.

This edition, and the previous, have benefited from numerous reviewers. The book has been improved immeasurably by their advice—some of which, quite naturally, was conflicting. In particular, I would like to thank Robert T. Averitt, Smith College; Mohsen Bahmani-Oskooee, University of Wisconsin, Milwaukee; H. Scott Bierman, Carleton College; John Payne Bigelow, University of Missouri; Bruce R. Bolnick, Northeastern University; Adhip Chaudhuri, Georgetown University; Michael D. Curley, Kennesaw State College; John Devereux, University of Miami; K. K. Fung, Memphis State; Christopher Georges, Hamilton College; Ronald D. Gilbert, Texas Tech University; Robert E. Graf, Jr., United States Military Academy; Glenn W. Harrison, University of South Carolina; Marc Hayford, Loyola University; Yutaka Horiba, Tulane University; Charles Howe, University of Colorado; Sheng Cheng Hu, Purdue University; Glenn Hubbard, Columbia University; Allen C. Kelley, Duke University; Michael M. Knetter, Dartmouth College; Stefan Lutz, Purdue University; Mark J. Machina, University of California, San Diego; Burton G. Malkiel, Princeton University; Lawrence Martin, Michigan State University; Thomas Mayer, University of California, Davis; Craig J. McCann, University of South Carolina; Henry N. McCarl, University of Alabama, Birmingham; John McDermott, University of South Carolina; Marshall H. Medoff, University of California, Irvine; Peter Mieszkowski, Rice University; W. Douglas Morgan, University of California, Santa Barbara; John S. Murphy, Canisius College; William Nielson, Texas A&M University; Neil B. Niman, University of New Hampshire; David H. Papell, University of Houston; James E. Price, Syracuse University; Daniel M. G. Raff, Harvard Business School; Christina D. Romer, University of California, Berkeley; Richard Rosenberg, Pennsylvania State University; Christopher J. Ruhm, Boston University; Suzanne A. Scotchmer, University of California, Berkeley; Richard Selden, University of Virginia; Andrei Shleifer, Harvard University; John L. Solow, University of Iowa; George Spiva, University of Tennessee; Mark Sproul, University of California at Los Angeles; Frank P. Stafford, University of Michigan; Raghu Sundaram, University of Rochester; Hal R. Varian, University of Michigan; Franklin V. Walker, State University of New York at Albany; James M. Walker, Indiana University; Andrew Weiss, Boston University; Gilbert R. Yochum, Old Dominion University.

It is a pleasure also to acknowledge the help of a number of research assistants. Many of them went well beyond the assigned tasks of looking up, assembling, and graphing data to providing helpful criticism of the manuscript. These include Edwin Lai, now at Vanderbilt University; Chulsoo Kim, now at

Rutgers University; Alexander Dyck, now at Harvard University; Patricia Nabti and Andres Rodriguez, now at University of Chicago; Marcie Smith; and Kevin Woodruff. I am particularly indebted to John Williams, who supervised and coordinated the final stages of preparation of the manuscript for the First Edition, and who assisted me on the entire preparation of the second. But John did more than this: he has been a sounding board for new ideas, new organizational structures, and new expositions.

I have been indeed fortunate in both editions in enlisting the help of individuals who combined a deep understanding of economics with an editor's fine honed pen: Timothy Taylor in the first edition and Felicity Skidmore in the second. Both have remarkable editorial skills; both have long been committed to the notion that it is important that modern economic ideas be communicated widely and that they *can* be, in a way that is both enlightening and enjoyable. Timothy, John, and Felicity all gave their energy and creativity to the enterprise, and the book is immeasurably better as a result.

This is the second book I have published with Norton, a company that reflects many of the aspects of organizational design that I discuss in the text. This book would not be nearly the one it is without the care, attention, and most important, deep thought devoted to my work by so many there. A few deserve special mention. Donald Lamm, chairman of the board at Norton, managed not only to keep the incentives straight within his firm, but also found time to read early drafts of the First Edition at several critical stages and offered his usual insightful suggestions. I cannot sufficiently acknowledge my indebtedness to Drake McFeely, who served as my editor on the First Edition (and succeeded Don Lamm as president of Norton) and Ed Parsons, who served as my editor on the Second Edition. Both have been concerned about the ideas *and* their presentation, and both have been tough, but constructive, critics. The work of Kate Barry, the manuscript editor, was as energetic as it was cheerful. All four made my work harder, so that readers of this book would have an easier time. Several others at Norton also deserve mention: Rosanne Fox for her outstanding proofreading, Ashley Deeks and Claire Acher, for their work on the photographs, Antonina Krass for the splendid design of the book, and Roy Tedoff and Jane Carter for coordinating its production. Finally, Stephen King, Steve Hoge, and Linda Puckette have contributed their unique talents in the creation of innovative electronic ancillaries for the text.

I owe a special thanks to those who prepared the ancillary materials that accompany the text. Given the fact that this book represents a departure from the standard mold of the past, the tasks they faced were both more important and more difficult. Their enthusiasm, insight, and hard work have produced a set of truly superb ancillaries: Lawrence Martin of Michigan State University prepared the print Study Guide and oversaw its transformation into an electronic counterpart, Ward Hanson of Stanford has developed an on-line version of the Instructor's Manual, and Alan Harrison of McMaster University prepared the test bank for the Second Edition.

It is common practice at this point in the preface to thank one's spouse and children, who have had to sacrifice so much (presumably time that the author would otherwise have spent with them). My debt goes beyond these commonplaces. My wife and children have motivated me, partly by the thirst for economic understanding they have evidenced by their questions about the rapidly changing economic scene, and partly by their challenging spirit—easy explanations, making heavy use of standard economics jargon, would not satisfy them. Moreover, in their perspective, the only justification for diverting my attention away from them and from my principal job as a teacher and researcher was the production of a textbook that would succeed in communicating the basic ideas of modern economics more effectively than those already available. I hope that what I—together with all of those who have helped me so much—have produced will please them.

OUTLINE FOR A SHORT COURSE

This book is suitable for short courses offered under a quarter system or other abbreviated schedules. Below I offer a provisional outline for such a short course, omitting several chapters. Naturally, to a large extent, *which* topics get omitted is a matter of taste. The following is my selection for a short course using fifteen chapters.

Chapter Number	Chapter Title
1	The Automobile and Economics
2	Basic Premises
3	The Price System
4	Macroeconomic Goals and Measures
5	Microfoundations
6	The Full-Employment Model
8	Overview of Unemployment Macroeconomics
9	Aggregate Demand
11	Money, Banking, and Credit
12	Monetary Theory
13	Fiscal and Monetary Policy
14	Inflation: Wage and Price Dynamics
16	Inflation vs. Unemployment: Approaches to Policy
17	Growth and Productivity
18	Deficits and Deficit Reduction

PART ONE

INTRODUCTION

These days economics is big news. If we pick up a newspaper or turn on the television for the prime-time news report, we are likely to be bombarded with statistics on unemployment rates, inflation rates, exports, and imports. How well are we doing in competition with other countries, such as Japan? Everyone seems to want to know. Political fortunes as well as the fortunes of countries, firms, and individuals depend on how well the economy does.

What is economics all about? That is the subject of Part One. Chapter 1 uses the story of the automobile industry to illustrate many of the fundamental issues with which economics is concerned. The chapter describes the four basic questions at the heart of economics, and how economists attempt to answer these questions.

Chapter 2 introduces the economists' basic model and explains why notions of property, profits, prices, and cost play such a central role in economists' thinking.

A fact of life in the modern world is that individuals and countries are interdependent. Even a wealthy country like the United States is dependent on foreign countries for vital imports. Chapter 3 discusses the gains that result from trade; why trade, for instance, allows greater specialization, and why greater specialization results in increased productivity. It also explains the patterns of trade—why each country imports and exports the particular goods it does.

Prices play a central role in enabling economies to function. Chapters 4 and 5 take up the question of what determines prices. Also, what causes prices to change over time? Why is water, without which we cannot live, normally so inexpensive, while diamonds, which we surely can do without, are very expensive? What happens to the prices of beer and cigarettes if the government imposes a tax on these goods? Sometimes the government passes laws requiring firms to pay wages of at least so much, or forbidding landlords to charge rents that exceed a certain level. What are the consequences of these government interventions?

Chapter 6 introduces two important realities: economic life takes place not in a single moment of time but over long periods, and life is fraught with risk. Decisions today have effects on the future, and there is usually much uncertainty about what those effects will be. How do economists deal with problems posed by time and risk?

Finally, Chapter 7 turns to the pervasive role of the government in modern economies. Its focus is on why the government undertakes the economic roles it does and on the economic rationale for government actions. It also describes the various forms that government actions might take and the changing roles of the government over time.

CHAPTER 1

THE AUTOMOBILE AND ECONOMICS

Imagine the world 100 years ago: no cars, airplanes, computers (and computer games!), movies—to say nothing of atomic energy, lasers, and transistors. The list of inventions since then seems almost endless.

Of all the inventions that have shaped the world during the past century, perhaps none has had so profound an effect as the automobile. It has changed how and where people work, live, and play. But like any major innovation, it has been a mixed blessing: traffic jams on the one hand, access to wilderness on the other. And the new opportunities it created for some were accompanied by havoc for others. Some occupations—such as blacksmiths—virtually disappeared. Others—such as carriage makers—had to transform themselves (into car body manufacturers) or go out of business. But the gains of the many who benefited from the new industry far outweighed the losses of those who were hurt.

The story of the automobile is familiar. But looking at it from the perspective of economics can teach us a great deal about the economic way of thinking.

KEY QUESTIONS

1. What *is* economics? What are the basic questions it addresses?
2. In economies such as that of the United States, what are the respective roles of government and the private, or "market," sector?
3. What are markets, and what are the principal markets that make up the economy?
4. Why is economics called a science?
5. Why, if economics is a science, do economists so often seem to disagree?

THE AUTOMOBILE: A BRIEF HISTORY

The idea of a motorized carriage occurred to many, in the United States and Europe, at roughly the same time. But ideas by themselves are not enough. Translating ideas into marketable products requires solving technical problems and persuading investors to finance the venture.

If you visit a museum of early cars, you will see that the technical problems were resolved in a variety of ways, by many people working independently. At the turn of the century, the area around Detroit was full of innovators developing cars—Ransom E. Olds, the Dodge brothers, and Henry Ford. The spirit must have been much like that of "Silicon Valley" (the area in California between San Francisco and San Jose) in the past quarter century, which has been at the center of computer technology development: a spirit of excitement, breakthroughs made, and new milestones reached. The various automobile innovators could draw upon a stock of ideas "floating in the air." They also had the help of specialized firms that had developed a variety of new technologies and skills: for example, new alloys that enabled lighter motors to be constructed and new techniques for machining that allowed for greater power, precision, and durability.

Henry Ford is generally given credit for having recognized the potential value of a vehicle that could be made and sold at a reasonable price. Before Ford, automobiles were luxuries, affordable only by the very rich. He saw the potential benefit from providing inexpensive transportation. After he introduced the Model T in 1909 at a "bargain" price of $900, he continued to cut the price—to $440 in 1914 and $360 in 1916. Sales skyrocketed from 58,000 in 1909 to 730,000 in 1916. Ford's prediction of a mass market for inexpensive cars had proved correct.

But success was neither sudden nor easy. To translate his idea into action

Ford had to put together a company to produce cars, figure out how to produce them cheaply, and raise the capital required to make all this possible.

Raising capital was particularly difficult, since the venture was extremely risky. Would Ford be successful in developing his automobile? Would someone else beat him to it? Would the price of a car be low enough for many people to buy it? If he was successful, would imitators copy his invention, robbing him of the mass market he needed to make money?

Ford formed a partnership to develop his first car. He was to supply the ideas and the work, while his partners supplied the funds. It took three partnerships before Ford produced a single car. The first two went bankrupt, with the financial partners in each case accusing Ford of spending all of his time developing ideas instead of acting on them.

But were the first two sets of partners treated unfairly? After all, they knew the risks. Ford could have entered each partnership in good faith and simply been unable to deliver.

But even in the third case, his partners were unhappy: They claimed he managed to garner for himself the lion's share of the profits. Ford may have argued that his ideas were far more important than the mere dollars that the financiers provided to carry them out.

Whatever the truth in Ford's case, the general problem of who contributes more in a partnership and who should get what share of any profits occurs often.

Ford's success was due as much to his ability to come up with innovative ways of providing incentives and organizing production as to his skill in solving technical problems. He demonstrated this ability with his original labor policies. He offered more than double the going wage and paid his workers the then princely sum of $5 a day. In exchange, Ford worked his employees hard; the moving assembly line he invented enabled him to set his workers a fast pace and push them to keep up. The amount produced per worker increased enormously. Still, it was clear that the high wages were ample compensation for the extra effort. Riots almost broke out as workers clamored for the jobs he offered. Ford had rediscovered an old truth: in some cases, higher wages for employees can repay the employer in higher productivity, through greater loyalty, harder work, and less absenteeism.

Ford's success in increasing productivity meant that he could sell his cars far more cheaply than his rivals could. The lower prices and the high level of sales that accompanied them made it possible for him to take full advantage of the mass production techniques he had developed. At one point, however, Ford's plans were almost thwarted when a lawyer-inventor named George Baldwin Selden claimed that Ford had infringed on his patent.

The U.S. government grants patents to enable inventors to reap the rewards of their innovative activity. These are generally for specific inventions, like a new type of braking system or transmission mechanism, not for general ideas. Ford's idea of an assembly line, for example, was not an invention that could be patented, and it was imitated by other car manufacturers. A patent gives the inventor the exclusive right to produce his invention for a limited time, thus helping to assure that inventors will be able to make some money from their successful inventions. Patents may lead to higher prices for these new products, since there is no competition from others making the same product. But the presumption is that the gains to society from the innovative activity more than compensate for the losses to consumers from the temporarily higher prices.

Selden had applied for, and been granted, a patent for a horseless, self-propelled carriage. He demanded that other car manufacturers pay him a royalty, which is a payment for the right to use a patented innovation. Ford challenged Selden's patent in court on the grounds that the concept of a "horseless, self-propelled carriage" was too vague to be patentable. Ford won. Providing cars to the masses at low prices made Ford millions of dollars and many millions of Americans better off, by enabling them to go where they wanted to go more easily, cheaply, and speedily.

Crisis in the American Automobile Industry

Today people think of computers and gene-splicing, not automobiles, as the new technologies. The story of the automobile is no longer emblematic of the latest technological breakthroughs. The changing fortunes of the American automobile industry during the past two decades are similar to those of many other parts of U.S. industry.

There were more than a hundred U.S. automobile manufacturers in the fall of 1903, twenty-seven of which accounted for more than 70 percent of the total sales of the industry. By the early 1960s, however, only three companies were responsible for 88 percent of U.S. auto sales. Of the car manufacturers that existed at the beginning of the century, many had gone bankrupt or given up on the automobile business, and the remainder had been agglomerated into or taken over by the dominant firms.

The most serious problems faced by the auto industry in the 1960s involved air pollution and automobile safety. To reduce pollution, the government regulated the amount of exhaust fumes a car could produce, and design changes followed. On the safety front, automobile companies quickly responded to demands for increased safety by providing seat belts.

This relatively rosy picture changed dramatically in 1973. That year, the Organization of Petroleum Exporting Countries (OPEC)—mainly countries in the Middle East—combined forces to hold down the supply of oil, create a scarcity, and thus push up its price. OPEC actually cut off all oil exports for a few tense weeks late in 1973. Its power was a surprise to many, including the American automobile industry. American cars then tended to be bigger and heavier than those in Japan and Europe. This was easily explained: incomes in the United States were higher; Americans could afford larger cars and the gasoline they guzzled. Also, Japan and Europe imposed much heavier taxes on gasoline than did the United States, encouraging consumers in those countries to buy smaller, more fuel-efficient cars.

The U.S. auto industry, thus, was ill-prepared for the higher gas prices caused by OPEC's move. But other countries, especially Japan, stood ready to

Figure 1.1 U.S. AUTOMOBILE IMPORTS FROM CANADA, JAPAN, AND GERMANY

Imports from Canada and Germany increased in the late 1960s. In the 1970s, however, imports from Japan rose sharply, and the Japanese manufacturers attained a powerful market position that they still enjoy today. *Source: Ward's Automotive Reports* (various years).

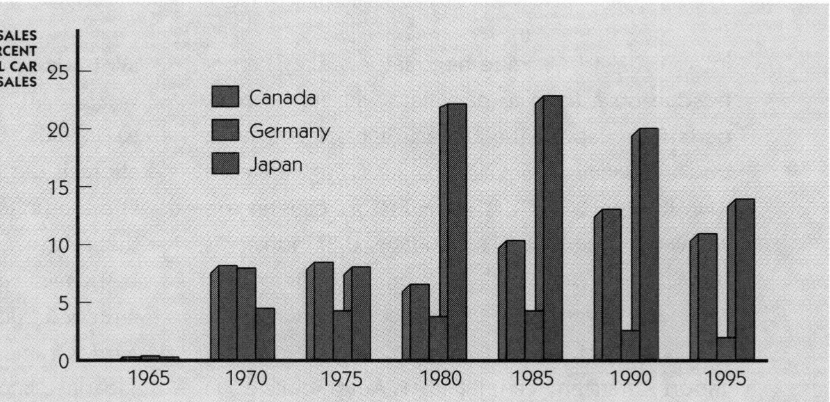

gain, with smaller, cheaper, and more fuel-efficient cars. Auto imports as a whole nearly doubled in the 1970s, from 15 percent of the total cars sold in the United States in 1970 to 27 percent by 1980, and they remained at a high level throughout the 1980s and into the 1990s. Figure 1.1 shows the dramatic increase in imports of new passenger cars from Canada, Germany, and especially Japan over the last thirty years.

It was clear that the Japanese firms were supplying what American consumers wanted, but the effect on the American automobile industry was devastating. Profits fell and workers were laid off.

Chrysler: Government to the Rescue

In the late 1970s, one firm, Chrysler, was on the verge of bankruptcy. The company did not have and could not borrow the cash to pay off loans that were due, so it asked for help from the government. In the ensuing debate about whether the government should save Chrysler, advocates of a bailout (rescue from financial ruin) painted a picture of unemployed workers and empty, wasted factories.

Critics of the bailout pointed out that the workers, machines, and buildings of a bankrupt company do not disappear. Instead, they can be hired by or sold to new companies under new management. Redeployment of resources was appropriate, critics argued, because the impending bankruptcy demonstrated that Chrysler management had failed to manage its resources well.

In the end, the government guaranteed some new loans for Chrysler. If Chrysler failed to pay back its loans, the government would do so with tax money. Because of this guarantee, Chrysler was able to obtain loans from private investors and banks, and at a relatively low rate of interest. Its subsequent

Policy Perspective: When Is a Truck a Car?

In April 1994 U.S. trade negotiator Mickey Kantor headed up a team to negotiate with its counterparts from Japan. The United States has a huge trade imbalance with Japan, importing far more than it exports. Of the many factors causing this imbalance, the one that infuriates U.S. industry is "unfair trade practices" or subtle actions by the Japanese government to restrict American sales. Rice is a good example. The Japanese refused to import American rice until 1994. Automobile parts are another example. Regulations—justified on safety grounds—restricted sales of replacement parts produced by firms other than the car's manufacturer. Only Toyota could make replacement parts for Toyota cars. But since almost all cars sold in Japan are made in Japan, this effectively kept out non-Japanese parts producers.

Part of Kantor's mission was to reduce such unfair trade practices, and he used the mini-van as a weapon. The mini-van may seem to have nothing to do with rice, but in the context of those negotiations it did. Why? Because importers of vehicles into the United States must pay a tariff (tax)—a tax that is higher on cars than on trucks.

The mini-van is currently taxed as a truck. But, is it really a truck? The mini-van is commonly built on a truck frame, but it hauls people, not goods. With Japanese imports accounting for 7 percent of the U.S. mini-van market, U.S. producers would be delighted to reduce their Japanese competition by getting the mini-van reclassified as a car and taxed as such. The higher tariff, of course, would raise the price of Japanese mini-vans to U.S. consumers and reduce their attractiveness in the U.S. market. The unspoken threat of such a reclassification was not lost on the Japanese.

success is an often-told tale, with the president of Chrysler, Lee Iacocca, claiming a large share of the credit for himself.

It turns out that the government had strong incentives to step in and help Chrysler. Not only was there concern about losing one of the three major firms in the automobile industry, but the government stood to lose money through an insurance program for workers' pensions set up several years before. This program guaranteed that even if a company went bankrupt, workers would still receive their pensions. Had Chrysler gone bankrupt, the government might have had to pay Chrysler workers hundreds of millions of dollars in pensions.

The government even ended up making money in bailing out Chrysler. In return for guaranteeing the loans, the government insisted that, in effect, it be granted some share of ownership in the firm. With the company's subsequent success, these shares turned out to be quite valuable.

Protection from Foreign Competition

The problems at Chrysler also existed in reduced form at General Motors and Ford. But in the early 1980s, all three began to make a recovery from the hard times of the 1970s, for several reasons. Unions dramatically reduced their wage demands. Smaller and more fuel-efficient cars were developed. And the government again stepped in, this time to help protect the industry from foreign competition. Again the concern was layoffs: in 1980, unemployment in Michigan, a major auto-producing state, had reached 12.6 percent (as contrasted with the total U.S. unemployment rate of 7.1 percent). Rather than imposing a tariff (tax) on car imports, the American government negotiated with the Japanese government to restrain Japan's automobile exports. Although the export limits were called voluntary, they were actually negotiated under pressure. If the Japanese had not taken the "voluntary" step of limiting exports, Congress probably would have passed a law forcing them to do so.

The reduced supply of Japanese cars led not only to increased sales of American cars, but to higher prices, both for Japanese and American cars. The American industry was subsidized not by the taxpayers in general but by those who bought cars, through these higher prices. The Japanese car manufacturers had little to complain about, since they too benefited from the higher prices. Had Japanese manufacturers gotten together and agreed to reduce their sales and raise prices, the action would have been viewed as a violation of U.S. antitrust laws, which were designed to enforce competition. But here the American government itself was encouraging less competition!

The Japanese responded in still another way to these restrictions. They decided to circumvent the limitations on their exports by manufacturing cars here in the United States. As shown in Figure 1.2, in 1995 more than one out of three cars produced in the United States is produced by foreign-owned firms. These are referred to as **transplants.** Honda, Mazda, Nissan, and Toyota could all claim that at least some of their cars were made in America.

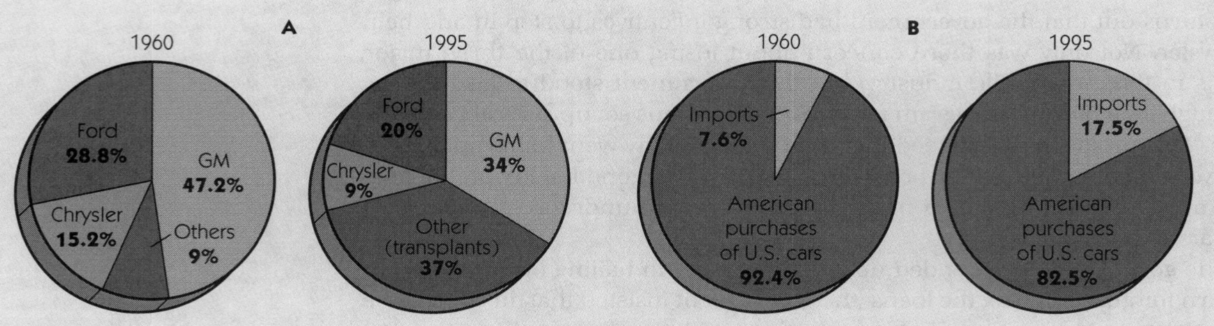

Figure 1.2 SHARES OF THE U.S. AUTOMOBILE MARKET

These pie charts show some of the changes in the U.S. auto market in recent decades. Panel A focuses on production, panel B on purchases. The charts in panel A show that production has remained concentrated. In 1960, the "other" firms were small American firms such as Studebaker and American Motors; in 1990, they were foreign-owned firms like Honda. The charts in panel B show the dramatic increase in imports. *Source: Ward's Automotive Reports* (various years).

THE REBIRTH OF THE AMERICAN AUTOMOBILE INDUSTRY

What would have happened had the automobile companies not been given the breather that the Japanese export restraints provided? We cannot tell. Perhaps they would have been forced to transform themselves more quickly. Perhaps one or more would have gone out of business. What we do know is that during the 1980s, the industry worked hard to compete effectively with its Japanese rivals. The different firms pursued different strategies.

General Motors, for instance, focused on automation, investing heavily in robots and other new equipment. Much of this turned out to be wasted. But GM did undertake a successful, major new venture—the Saturn project. In addition to innovations in product design and manufacturing, labor relations and marketing were improved. Worker participation in decision making was increased. And instead of the haggling that is typical of car purchases, Saturns were bought just like most other goods—at the prices on their stickers. The car generated so much customer loyalty that when the company invited owners to come to the factory in June 1994 to celebrate what was billed as its "homecoming," 44,000 people showed up.

THE HISTORY OF THE AUTOMOBILE IN STATISTICS

Figure 1.3 illustrates the history of U.S. car production. The ups and downs of the curve reflect the rise, fall, and recovery of the industry. Car production has

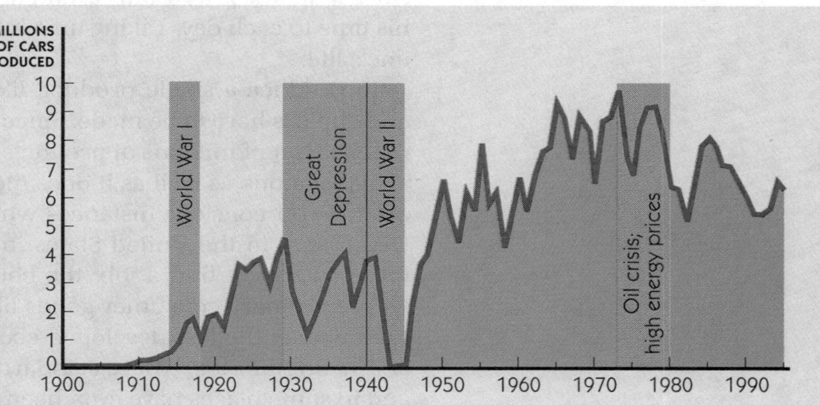

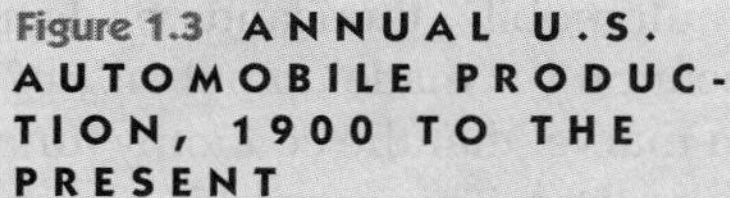
Figure 1.3 ANNUAL U.S. AUTOMOBILE PRODUCTION, 1900 TO THE PRESENT

Changes in U.S. automobile production have both reflected and influenced events in the U.S. economy and the world during the twentieth century. *Source: Ward's Automotive Reports* (various years).

been set against a backdrop of the major events affecting the economy as a whole. Different years are listed on the horizontal axis, while the number of cars built is provided on the vertical axis. Improvements in techniques of mass production led to the boom in sales early in this century. During the Great Depression of the 1930s, sales declined sharply, and civilian automobile production halted entirely during World War II. Production then rose during the boom of the 1950s and 1960s. In the 1970s, sharp increases in the price of gasoline helped trigger two worldwide recessions, reducing car sales. The U.S. economy recovered to a pattern of steady growth in the mid-1980s, halting, at least temporarily, the decline in automobile sales.

Heading into the economic downturn that began in 1990, the industry again showed its sensitivity to the health of the overall economy. Reduced confidence in the economy and lower incomes led consumers to put off purchasing cars. The reduced sales of cars, in turn, contributed to the slowdown of the economy. It was not until interest rates fell and the economy began to recover, in 1993, that automobile sales again began to recover; profits once again soared, reaching record levels.

WHAT IS ECONOMICS?

This narrative illustrates many facets of economics, but now a definition of our subject is in order. **Economics** studies how individuals, firms, governments, and other organizations within our society make **choices,** and how those choices determine the way the resources of society are used. **Scarcity** figures prominently in economics: choices matter because resources are scarce. Imagine an enormously wealthy individual who can have everything he wants. We might think that scarcity is not in his vocabulary—until we consider that time is a resource, and he must decide what expensive toy to devote his time to each day. Taking time into account, then, scarcity is a fact in everyone's life.

To produce a single product, like an automobile, thousands of decisions and choices have to be made. Since any economy is made up not only of automobiles but of millions of products, it is a marvel that the economy functions at all, let alone as well as it does most of the time. This marvel is particularly clear if you consider instances when things do not work so well: the Great Depression in the United States in the 1930s, when 25 percent of the work force could not find a job; the countries of the former Soviet Union today, where ordinary consumer goods like carrots or toilet paper are often simply unavailable; the less developed economies of many countries in Africa, Asia, and Latin America, where standards of living have remained stubbornly low, and in some places have even been declining.

The fact that choices must be made applies as well to the economy as a whole as it does to each individual. Somehow, decisions are made—by individuals, households, firms, and government—that together determine how the economy's limited resources, including its land, labor, machines, oil, and other natural resources, are used. Why is it that land used at one time for growing crops may, at another time, be used for an automobile plant? How was it that over the space of a couple of decades, resources were transferred from making horse carriages to making automobile bodies? that blacksmiths were replaced by auto mechanics? How do the decisions of millions of consumers, workers, investors, managers, and government officials all interact to determine the use of the scarce resources available to society? Economists reduce such matters to four basic questions concerning how economies function:

1. What is produced, and in what quantities? There have been important changes in consumption over the past fifty years. Spending for medical care, for example, was only 3.5 percent of total personal consumption in 1950. By 1995, more than one out of every seven dollars was spent on medical care. What can account for changes like these? The economy seems to spew out new products like videocassette recorders and new services like automated bank tellers. What causes this process of innovation? The overall level of production has also shifted from year to year, often accompanied by large changes in the levels of employment and unemployment. How can economists explain these changes?

In the United States, the question of what is produced, and in what quantities, is answered largely by the private interaction of firms and consumers, but government also plays a role. Prices are critical in determining what goods are produced. When the price of some good rises, firms are induced to produce more of that good, to increase their profits. Thus, a central question for economists is, why are some goods more expensive than others? And why have the prices of some goods increased or decreased?

2. How are these goods produced? There are often many ways of making something. Textiles can be made with hand looms. Modern machines enable fewer workers to produce more cloth. Very modern machines may be highly computerized, allowing one worker to monitor many more machines than was possible earlier. The better machines generally cost more, but they require less labor. Which technique will be used, the advanced technology or the labor-intensive one? Henry Ford introduced the assembly line. More recently, car manufacturers have begun using robots. What determines how rapidly technology changes?

In the U.S. economy, firms answer the question of how goods are produced, again with input from the government, which sets regulations and enacts laws that affect everything from the overall organization of firms to the ways they interact with their employees and customers.

3. For whom are these goods produced? In the United States, individuals who have higher incomes can consume more goods. But that answer only pushes the question back one step: What determines the differences in income and wages? What is the role of luck? of education? of inheritance? of savings? of experience and hard work? These questions are difficult to answer. For now, suffice it to say that while incomes are primarily determined by the private interaction of firms and households in the United States, government also plays a strong role, with taxes as well as programs that redistribute income.

Figure 1.4 shows the relative pay in a variety of different occupations. To judge by income, each physician receives five times as much of the economy's output as a firefighter, and seven times as much as a butcher.

4. Who makes economic decisions, and by what process? In a **centrally planned economy,** as the Soviet Union was, the government takes responsibility for virtually every aspect of economic activity. The government provides the answers to the first three questions. A central economic planning agency works through a bureaucracy to say what will be produced and by what method, and who shall consume it. At the other end of the spectrum are economies that rely primarily on the free interchange of producers and their customers

Figure 1.4 **WHO TAKES HOME AMERICA'S OUTPUT?**

This chart measures the earnings of a variety of professions relative to the wages of an average worker. Firefighters make 25 percent more than an average worker, while physicians make over six times as much.

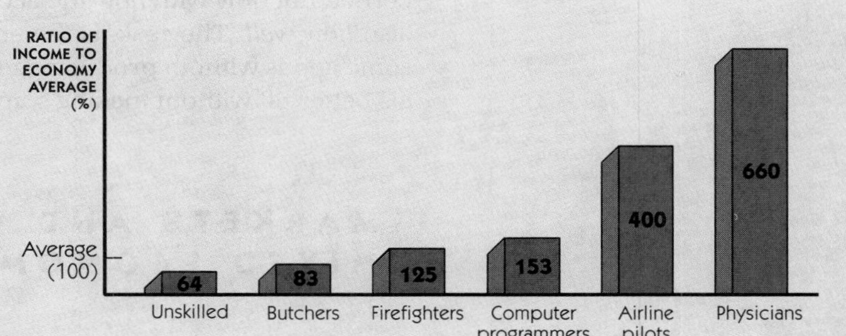

Basic Questions of Economics

1. What is produced, and in what quantities?
2. How are these goods produced?
3. For whom are these goods produced?
4. Who makes economic decisions, and by what process?

to determine what, how, and for whom. The United States, which lies near this latter end, has a **mixed economy;** that is, a mix between public (governmental) and private decision making. Within limits, producers make what they want; they use whatever method of production seems appropriate to them; and the output is distributed to consumers according to their income.

When economists examine an economy, they want to know to what extent economic decisions are made by the government, and to what extent they are made by private individuals. In the United States, while individuals for the most part make their own decisions about what kind of car to purchase, the government has inserted itself in a number of ways: it has taken actions that affect the import of Japanese cars, that restrict the amount of pollutants a car can produce, and that promote fuel efficiency and automobile safety.

A related question is whether economic decisions are made by individuals for their own interests or for the interest of an employer such as a business firm or government agency. This is an important distinction.We can expect people acting on their own behalf to make decisions that benefit themselves. When they act on behalf of organizations, however, a conflict of interest may arise. Observers often refer to corporations and governments as if they were a single individual. Economists point out that organizations consist, by definition, of a multitude of individuals and that the interests of these individuals do not necessarily coincide with one another or, for that matter, with the interests of the organization itself. Organizations bring a number of distinctive problems to the analysis of choice.

As you can see by their concern with decision making, economists are concerned not only with *how* the economy answers the four basic questions, but also *how well.* They ask, is the economy efficient? Could it produce more of some goods without producing fewer of others? Could it make some individuals better off without making some other individuals worse off?

MARKETS AND GOVERNMENT IN THE MIXED ECONOMY

The primary reliance on private decision making in the United States reflects economists' beliefs that this reliance is appropriate and necessary for economic efficiency; however, economists also believe that certain interventions by government are desirable. Finding the appropriate balance between the public and the private sectors of the economy is a central issue of economic analysis.

MARKETS

The economic concept of markets is used to include any situation where exchange takes place, though this exchange may not necessarily resemble the traditional village markets. In department stores and shopping malls, customers rarely haggle over the price. When manufacturers purchase the materials they need for production, they exchange money for them, not other goods. Most goods, from cameras to clothes, are not sold directly from producers to consumers. They are sold from producers to distributors, from distributors to retailers, from retailers to consumers. All of these transactions are embraced by the concepts of **market** and **market economy.**

In market economies with competition, individuals make choices that reflect their own desires. And firms make choices that maximize their profits; to do so, they must produce the goods consumers want, and they must produce them at lower cost than other firms. As firms compete in the quest for profits, consumers benefit, both from the kinds of goods produced and the prices at which they are supplied. The market economy thus provides answers to the four basic economic questions—what is produced, how it is produced, for whom it is produced, and how these decisions are made. And on the whole, the answers the market gives ensure the efficiency of the economy.

But the answer the market provides to the question of for whom goods are produced is one that not everyone finds acceptable. Like bidders at an auction, what market participants are willing and able to pay depends on their income. Some groups of individuals—including those without skills that are valued by the market—may receive such a low income that they could not feed and educate their children without outside assistance. Government provides the assistance by taking steps to increase income equality. These steps, however, often blunt economic incentives. While welfare payments provide an important safety net for the poor, the taxation required to finance them may discourage work and savings. If the government takes one out of three or even two dollars that an individual earns, that individual may not be inclined to work so much. And if the government takes one out of two or three dollars a person earns from interest on savings, the person may decide to spend more and save less. Like the appropriate balance between the public and private sectors, the appropriate balance between concerns about equality (often referred to as **equity concerns**) and efficiency is a central issue of modern economics.

THE ROLE OF GOVERNMENT

The answers to the basic economic questions that the market provides on the whole ensure efficiency. But in certain areas the solutions appear inadequate to many. There may be too much pollution, too much inequality, and too little concern about education, health, and safety. When the market is not perceived to be working well, people often turn to government.

The government plays a major role in modern economies. We need to understand both what that role is and why government undertakes the activities that it does. The story of the automobile provides several instances. Early on, George Baldwin Selden was almost able to use government-created patent laws to change the course of the industry. In the late 1970s, government loan guarantees enabled Chrysler to survive. The automobile industry was helped by government restrictions on Japanese imports but probably hurt by government regulations concerning pollution. The strength of the auto unions, reflected in their success in raising wages to high levels, was partly a result of the rights that federal legislation had granted to them. Later on we will see more ways in which government policy has affected industry.

The U.S. government sets the legal structure under which private firms and individuals operate. It regulates businesses to ensure that they do not discriminate by race or sex, do not mislead customers, are careful about the safety of their employees, and do not pollute air and water. In some industries, the government operates like a private business: the government-owned Tennessee Valley Authority (TVA) is one of the nation's largest producers of electricity; most children attend government-owned public schools; and most mail is still delivered by the government-owned post office. In other cases, the government supplies goods and services that the private sector does not, such as providing for the national defense, building roads, and printing money. Government programs provide for the elderly through Social Security (which pays income to retired individuals) and Medicare (which funds medical needs of the aged). The government helps those who have suffered economic dislocation, through unemployment insurance for those temporarily unemployed and disability insurance for those who are no longer able to work. The government also provides a safety net of support for the poor, particularly children, through various welfare programs.

One can easily imagine a government controlling the economy more directly. In countries where decision-making authority is centralized and concentrated in the government, government bureaucrats might decide what and how much a factory should produce and set the level of wages that should be paid. Various European governments run steel companies, coal mines, and the telephone system. At least until recently, governments in countries like the former Soviet Union and China attempted to control practically all major decisions regarding resource allocation.

THE THREE MAJOR MARKETS

The market economy revolves around exchange between individuals (or households), who buy goods and services from firms, and firms, which take **inputs,** the various materials of production, and produce **outputs,** the goods and services that they sell. In thinking about a market economy, economists focus their attention on three broad categories of markets in which individu-

Close-up: A Failed Alternative to the Mixed Economy

While the mixed economy now is the dominant form of economic organization, it is not the only possible way of answering the basic economic questions. Beginning in 1917, an experiment in almost complete government control was begun in what became the Soviet Union.

What was produced in such an economy, and in what quantities? Government planners set the targets, which workers and firms then struggled to fulfill.

How were these goods produced? Again, since government planners decided what supplies would be delivered to each factory, they effectively chose how production occurred.

For whom were these goods produced? The government made decisions about what each job was paid, which affected how much people could consume. In principle, individuals could choose what to buy at government-operated stores, at prices set by the government. But in practice, many goods were unavailable at these stores.

Who made economic decisions, and by what process? The government planners decided, basing the decisions on their view of national economic goals.

At one time, all this planning sounded very sensible, but as former Soviet premier Nikita Khrushchev once said, "Economics is a subject that does not greatly respect one's wishes." Many examples of Soviet economic woes could be cited, but two will suffice. In the shoe market, the Soviet Union was the largest national producer in the world. However, the average shoe was of such low quality that it fell apart in a few weeks, and inventories of unwanted shoes rotted in warehouses. In agriculture, the Soviet government had traditionally allowed small private plots. Although the government limited the time farmers could spend on these plots,

publicly run farming was so unproductive that the 3 percent of Soviet land that was privately run produced about 25 percent of the total farm output.

Today the standard of living in the former Soviet Union is not only below that in industrialized nations like the United States and those of Western Europe, but it is barely ahead of developing nations like Brazil and Mexico. Workers in the Soviet Union shared a grim one-liner: "We pretend to work and they pretend to pay us."

The collapse of the Soviet Union was, to a large extent, the result of the failure of its economic system. Much of this text is concerned with explaining why mixed economies work as well as they do.

als and firms interact. The markets in which firms sell their outputs to households are referred to collectively as the **product market.** Many firms also sell goods to other firms; the outputs of the first firm become the inputs of the second. These transactions too are said to occur in the product market.

On the input side, firms need (besides the materials that they buy in the product market) some combination of labor and machinery with which their goods can be produced. They purchase the services of workers in the **labor market.** They raise funds, with which to buy inputs, in the **capital market.** Traditionally, economists have also highlighted the importance of a third input, land, but in modern industrial economies, land is of secondary importance. For most purposes, it suffices to focus attention on the three major markets listed here, and this text will follow this pattern.

As Figure 1.5 shows, individuals participate in all three markets. When individuals buy goods or services, they act as **consumers** in the product market. When people act as **workers,** economists say they "sell their labor services" in the labor market. When individuals buy shares of stock in a firm or lend money to a business, economists note that they are participating in the capital market, and refer to them as **investors.**

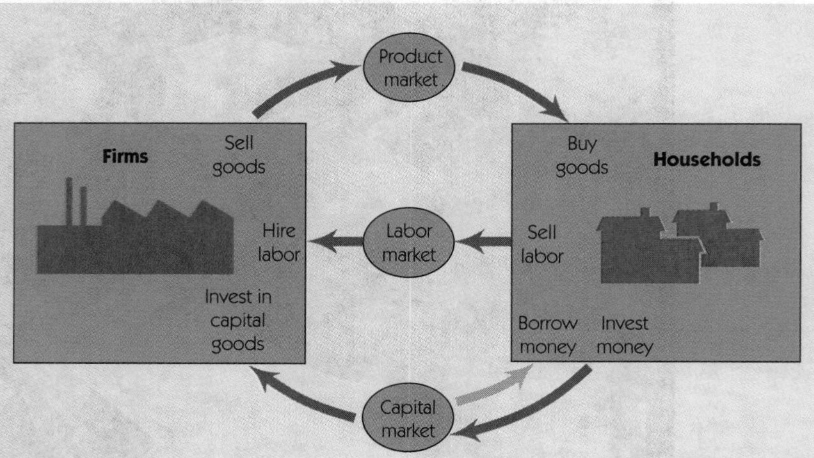

Figure 1.5 THE THREE MARKETS

To economists, people wear different hats: they are usually consumers in the product market, workers in the labor market, and borrowers and lenders in the capital market.

TWO CAVEATS

Terms in economics often are similar to terms in ordinary usage, but they can have special meanings. The terms **markets** and **capital** illustrate the problem.

Though the term "market" is used to conjure an image of a busy **marketplace,** there is no formal marketplace for most goods and services. There are buyers and sellers, and economists analyze the outcome *as if* there were a single marketplace in which all the transactions occurred.

Moreover, economists often talk about the "market for labor" as if all workers were identical. But workers obviously differ in countless ways. In some cases, these differences are important. We might then talk about the "market for skilled workers," or "the market for plumbers." But in other cases—such as when we are talking about the overall state of the economy and focusing on the unemployment rate (the fraction of workers who would like jobs but cannot get them)—these differences can be ignored.

When newspapers refer to the capital market, they mean the bond traders and stockbrokers and the companies they work for on Wall Street and other financial districts. When economists use the term capital market they have in mind a broader concept. It includes all the institutions concerned with raising funds (and, as we will see later, sharing and insuring risks), including banks and insurance companies.

The term "capital" is used in still another way—to refer to the machines and buildings used in production. To distinguish this particular usage, in this book we refer to machines and buildings as **capital goods.** Capital markets thus refers to the markets in which funds are raised, borrowed, and lent. **Capital goods markets** refers to the markets in which capital goods are bought and sold.

MICROECONOMICS AND MACROECONOMICS: THE TWO BRANCHES OF ECONOMICS

The detailed study of product, labor, and capital markets is called **microeconomics.** Microeconomics ("micro" is derived from the Greek word meaning "small") focuses on the behavior of the units—the firms, households, and individuals—that make up the economy. It is concerned with how the individual units make decisions and what affects those decisions. By contrast, **macroeconomics** ("macro" comes from the Greek word meaning "large") looks at the behavior of the economy as a whole, in particular the behavior of such aggregate measures as overall rates of unemployment, inflation, economic growth, and the balance of trade. The aggregate numbers do not tell us what any firm or household is doing. They tell us what is happening in total, or on average.

It is important to remember that these perspectives are simply two ways of looking at the same thing. Microeconomics is the bottom-up view of the economy; macroeconomics is the top-down view. The behavior of the economy as a whole is dependent on the behavior of the units that make it up.

The automobile industry is a story of both micro- and macroeconomics. It is a story of microeconomic interactions of individual companies, investors, and labor unions. It is also a story of global macroeconomic forces like oil shortages and economic fluctuations. When auto companies laid off workers in the late 1970s, their problems boosted the overall unemployment rate. The recession of the early 1990s brought heavy reductions in car sales. When the recovery occurred, auto sales grew rapidly.

THE SCIENCE OF ECONOMICS

Economics is a **social science.** It studies the social problem of choice from a scientific viewpoint, which means that it is built on a systematic exploration of the problem of choice. This systematic exploration involves both the formulation of theories and the examination of data.

A **theory** consists of a set of assumptions (or hypotheses) and conclusions derived from those assumptions. Theories are logical exercises: *if* the assumptions are correct, *then* the results follow. If all college graduates have a better chance of getting jobs and Ellen is a college graduate, then Ellen has a better chance of getting a job than a nongraduate. Economists make predictions with their theories. They might use a theory to predict what will happen if a tax is increased or if imports of foreign cars are limited. The predictions of a theory are of the form "If a tax is increased and if the market is competitive, then output will decrease and prices will increase."

In developing their theories, economists use models. To understand how economists use models, consider a modern car manufacturer trying to design a new automobile. It is extremely expensive to construct a new car. Rather than creating a separate, fully developed car for every engineer's or designer's conception of what she would like to see the new car be, the company uses models. The designers might use a plastic model to study the general shape of the vehicle and to assess reactions to the car's aesthetics. The engineers might use a computer model to study the air resistance, from which they can calculate fuel consumption and a separate model for judging the car's comfort.

Just as engineers construct different models to study particular features of a car, so too economists construct models of the economy—in words or equations—to depict particular features of the economy. An economic model might describe a general relationship ("When incomes rise, the number of cars purchased increases"), describe a quantitative relationship ("When incomes rise by 10 percent, the number of cars purchased rises, on average, by 12 percent"), or make a general prediction ("An increase in the tax on gasoline will decrease the demand for cars").

DISCOVERING AND INTERPRETING RELATIONSHIPS

A **variable** is any item that can be measured and that changes. Prices, wages, interest rates, quantities bought and sold, are all variables. What interests economists is the connection between variables. When economists see what appears to be a systematic relationship among variables, they ask, could it have arisen by chance, or is there indeed a relationship? This is the question of **correlation.**

Economists use statistical tests to measure and test correlations. Consider the problem of deciding whether a coin is biased. If you flip a coin 10 times and get 6 heads and 4 tails, is the coin a fair one? Or is it weighted to heads? Statistical tests will say that the result of 6 heads and 4 tails could easily happen by chance, so the evidence does not prove that the coin is weighted. This does not prove that it is *not* slightly weighted. The evidence is just not strong enough for either conclusion. But if you flip a coin 100 times and get 80 heads, statistical tests will tell you that the possibility of this happening by blind chance with a fair coin is extremely small. The evidence supports the assertion that the coin is weighted.

A similar logic can be used on correlations in economic data. People with more education tend to earn higher wages. Is the connection merely chance? Statistical tests show whether the evidence is too weak for a conclusion, or whether it supports the existence of a systematic relationship between education and wages.

CAUSATION VERSUS CORRELATION

Economists would like to accomplish more than just asserting that different variables are indeed correlated. They would like to conclude that changes in one variable *cause* the changes in the other variable. The distinction between correlation and **causation** is important. If one variable "causes" the other, then changing one variable necessarily will change the other. If the relationship is just a correlation, this may not be true.

Earlier, we saw that Japanese imports increased for more than a decade after 1973 and sales of U.S. cars decreased. The two variables were negatively correlated. But did that prove that increased Japanese sales caused the decreased American sales? If the decline in U.S. car production during this period was because American companies were producing large gas guzzlers that people no longer wanted, reducing Japanese car sales might not increase the sales of U.S.-made cars. In short, if there was a common cause to both changes—increased oil prices leading to increased sales of Japanese cars and decreased sales of U.S. cars—then these trends would be reversed only when American companies started to produce fuel-efficient cars.

In some cases, the *direction* of causation is not clear: did high Japanese sales cause low U.S. sales, or vice versa? For instance, it might have turned out, upon closer investigation, that the true explanation of decreased sales of U.S. cars was strikes that caused production shortages; when U.S. cars were not available, consumers turned to Japanese cars. To tell which explanation is valid—whether high Japanese sales cause low U.S. sales, whether low U.S. sales cause high Japanese sales, or whether both are caused by a third factor—requires closer examination of, for example, the circumstances in which the two variables moved in directions different from those normally observed.

EXPERIMENTS IN ECONOMICS

Many sciences use laboratory experiments to test alternative explanations, since experiments allow the scientist to change one factor at a time and see what happens. But the economy is not a chemistry lab. Instead, economics is like astronomy, in that both sciences must use the experiments that nature provides. Economists look for situations in which only one factor changes, and study the consequences of changing that factor. A change in the income tax system is an example of a natural experiment. But nature is usually not kind to economists; the world does not hold still. As the tax system changes, so do other features of the economy, and economists often have a difficult time deciding whether changes are the result of the new tax system or of some other economic change. Sometimes they can use what is called **econometrics,** the branch of statistics developed to analyze the particular measurement problems that arise in economics.

In a few cases, economists have engaged in social experiments. For example, they have given a selected group of individuals a different income tax schedule or welfare program from that faced by another, otherwise similar, group. In recent years, a major new branch of economics, called **experimental economics,** has analyzed certain aspects of economic behavior in a controlled, laboratory setting. One way of seeing how individuals respond to risk, for example, is to construct a risky situation in such a setting and force individuals to make decisions and act on them. By varying the nature of the risk and the rewards, one can learn about how individuals will respond to different risks in real life situations. Similarly, different kinds of auctions can be simulated in a controlled laboratory setting to see how buyers respond. Lessons learned from such auctions have already been used by government in designing some of the auctions it conducts. Both social and laboratory experiments have provided economists with valuable insights concerning economic behavior.

But even with all available tools, the problem of finding a variety of correlations between several different types of data and having to discern which connections are real and which are only apparent is a difficult one. Economists' interest in these questions is motivated by more than just curiosity. Often important policy questions depend on what one believes is really going on. Whether a country thinks it worthwhile to pour more resources into higher education may depend on whether it believes that the differences in wages observed between those with and without a college education are largely due to the skills and knowledge acquired during college, or whether they are mainly related to differences in ability between those who make it through college and those who do not.

The important lessons to remember here are (1) the fact of a correlation does not prove a causation; (2) the way to test different explanations of causation is to hold all of the factors constant except for one, and then allow that one to vary; (3) data do not always speak clearly, and sometimes do not allow any conclusions to be drawn.

WHY ECONOMISTS DISAGREE

Economists are frequently called upon to make judgments on matters of public policy. Should the government reduce the deficit? Should inflation be reduced? If so, how? In these public policy discussions, economists often disagree. They differ in their views of how the world works, in their *description* of the economy, in their predictions of the consequences of certain actions. And they differ in their values, in how they evaluate these consequences.

When they describe the economy, and construct models that predict either how the economy will change or the effects of different policies, they are engaged in what is called **positive economics.** When they evaluate alternative policies, weighing up the various benefits and costs, they are engaged in what is called **normative economics.** Positive economics is concerned with what "is," with describing how the economy functions. Normative economics deals with what "should be," with making judgments about the desirability of various courses of action. Normative economics makes use of positive economics. We cannot make judgments about whether a policy is desirable unless we have a clear picture of its consequences. Good normative economics also tries to be explicit about precisely what values or objectives it is incorporating. It tries to couch its statements in the form "If these are your objectives . . . , then this is the best possible policy."

Consider the normative and positive aspects of the proposal to restrict imports of Japanese cars. Positive economics would describe the consequences: the increased prices consumers have to pay; the increased sales of American cars; the increased employment and increased profits; the increased pollution and oil imports, because American cars on average are less fuel efficient than Japanese cars. In the end, the question is, *should there be restraints on imports of Japanese cars?* This is a normative question: Normative economics would weigh these various effects—the losses of the consumers, the gains to workers, the increased profits, the increased pollution, the increased oil imports—to reach an overall judgment. Normative economics develops systematic frameworks within which these complicated judgments can be conducted in a systematic way.

Close-up: Economists Agree!

Try the following six statements out on your classmates or your family to see whether they, like the economists surveyed, disagree, agree with provisos, or agree:

	Percentage of economists who		
	Disagree	Agree with provisos	Agree
1. Tariffs and import quotas usually reduce general economic welfare.	6.5%	21.3%	71.3%
2. A ceiling on rents reduces the quantity and quality of housing available.	6.5%	16.6%	76.3%
3. The cause of the rise in gasoline prices that occurred in the wake of the Iraqi invasion of Kuwait is the monopoly power of large oil companies.	67.5%	20.3%	11.4%
4. The trade deficit is primarily a consequence of the inability of U.S. firms to compete.	51.5%	29.7%	18.1%
5. Cash payments increase the welfare of recipients to a greater degree than do transfers-in-kind of equal cash value.	15.1%	25.9%	58.0%

Among the general population, these are controversial questions. You will find many people who believe that restricting foreign imports is a good thing; that government regulation of rents has few ill effects; that the trade deficit is mainly caused by the inability of U.S. companies to compete; that government should avoid giving cash to poor people (because they are likely to waste it); and that oil companies are the cause of higher oil prices.

But when professional economists are surveyed, there is broad agreement that many of those popular answers are misguided. The percentages listed above are from a survey carried out by economists at Weber State University and Brigham Young University in 1990. Notice that healthy percentages of economists apparently believe that most import quotas are economically harmful; that government control of rents does lead to adverse consequences; that oil companies are not to blame for higher oil prices; that the trade deficit is not caused by the competitive problems of individual companies; that cash payments benefit the poor more than direct (in-kind) transfers of food, shelter, and medical care.

Sources: Richard M. Alston, J. R. Kearl, and Michael B. Vaughan, "Is There a Consensus Among Economists in the 1990s?" *American Economic Review* (May 1992).

Disagreements Within Positive Economics

Even when they describe how the economy works, economists may differ for two main reasons. First, economists differ over what is the appropriate model of the economy. They may disagree about how well people and firms are able to perceive and calculate their self-interest, and whether their interactions take place in a competitive or a noncompetitive market. Different models will produce different results. Often the data do not allow us to say which of two competing models provides a better description of some market.

Second, even when they agree about the appropriate theoretical model, economists may disagree about quantitative magnitudes, which will cause their predictions to differ. They may agree, for instance, that reducing the tax on interest income will encourage individuals to save more, but they may produce different estimates about the amount of the savings increase. Again, many of these disagreements arise because of inadequate data. We may have considerable data concerning savings in the United States over the past century. But institutions and economic conditions today are markedly different from those of fifty or even ten years ago.

Disagreements Within Normative Economics

There are generally many consequences of any policy, some beneficial, some harmful. In comparing two policies, one may benefit some people more, another may benefit others. One policy is not unambiguously better than another. It depends on what you care more about. A cut in the tax on the profits from the sale of stocks might encourage savings, but at the same time, most of the benefits accrue to the very wealthy; hence, it increases inequality. A reduction in taxes to stimulate the economy may reduce unemployment, but it may also increase inflation. Even though two economists agree about the model, they may make different recommendations. In assessing the effect of a tax cut on unemployment and inflation, for instance, an economist who is worried more about unemployment may recommend in favor of the tax cut, while the other, concerned about inflation, may recommend against it. In this case, the source of the disagreement is a difference in values.

But while economists may often seem to differ greatly among themselves, in fact they agree more than they disagree: their disagreements get more attention than their agreements. Most importantly, when they do disagree, they seek to be clear about the source of their disagreement: 1) to what extent does it arise out of differences in models, 2) to what extent does it arise out of differences in estimates of quantitative relations, and 3) to what extent does it arise out of differences in values? Clarifying the sources of and reasons for disagreement can be a very productive way of learning more.

CONSENSUS ON THE IMPORTANCE OF SCARCITY

Most of what we have discussed in this chapter fits within the areas on which there is broad consensus among economists. This includes the observation that the U.S. economy is a mixed economy and that there are certain basic questions that all economic systems must address. We highlight the most important points of consensus throughout the book. Our first consensus point concerns scarcity. It is the most important point of consensus in this chapter.

1 Scarcity

There is no free lunch. Having more of one thing requires giving up something else. Scarcity is a basic fact of life.

REVIEW AND PRACTICE

SUMMARY

1. Economics is the study of how individuals, firms, and governments within our society make choices. Choices are unavoidable because desired goods, services, and resources are inevitably scarce.

2. There are four basic questions that economists ask about any economy. (1) What is produced, and in what quantities? (2) How are these goods produced? (3) For whom are these goods produced? (4) Who makes economic decisions, and by what process?

3. The United States has a mixed economy; there is a mix between public and private decision making. The economy relies primarily on the private interaction of individuals and firms to answer the four basic questions, but government plays a large role as well. A central question for any mixed economy is the balance between the public and private sectors.

4. The term "market" is used to describe any situation where exchange takes place. In America's market economy, individuals, firms, and government interact in product markets, labor markets, and capital markets.

5. Economists use models to study how the economy works and to make predictions about what will happen if something is changed. A model can be expressed in words or equations, and is designed to mirror the essential characteristics of the particular phenomena under study.

6. A correlation exists when two variables tend to change together in a predictable way. However, the simple existence of a correlation does not

prove that one factor causes the other to change. Additional outside factors may be influencing both.

7. Positive economics is the study of how the economy works. Disagreements within positive economics center on the appropriate model of the economy or market and the quantitative magnitudes characterizing the models. Normative economics deals with the desirability of various actions. Disagreements within normative economics center on differences in the values placed on the various costs and benefits of different actions.

KEY TERMS

centrally planned economy	**labor market**	**theory**
mixed economy	**capital market**	**correlation**
market economy	**capital goods**	**causation**
product market	**microeconomics**	**positive economics**
	macroeconomics	**normative economics**

REVIEW QUESTIONS

1. Why are choices unavoidable?

2. How are the four basic economic questions answered in the U.S. economy?

3. What is a mixed economy? Describe some of the roles government might play, or not play, in a mixed economy.

4. Name the three main economic markets, and describe how an individual might participate in each one as a buyer and seller.

5. Give two examples of economic issues that are primarily microeconomic, and two examples that are primarily macroeconomic. What is the general difference between microeconomics and macroeconomics?

6. What is a model? Why do economists use models?

7. When causation exists, would you also expect a correlation to exist? When a correlation exists, would you also expect causation to exist? Explain.

8. "All disagreements between economists are purely subjective." Comment.

PROBLEMS

1. Characterize the following events as microeconomic, macroeconomic, or both.
   (a) Unemployment increases this month.

(b) A drug company invents and begins to market a new medicine.
(c) A bank loans money to a large company but turns down a small business.
(d) Interest rates decline for all borrowers.
(e) A union negotiates for higher pay and better health insurance.
(f) The price of oil increases.

2. Characterize the following events as part of the labor market, the capital market, or the product market.
(a) An investor tries to decide which company to invest in.
(b) With practice, the workers on an assembly line become more efficient.
(c) The opening up of the economies in Eastern Europe offers new markets for American products.
(d) A big company that is losing money decides to offer its workers a special set of incentives to retire early, hoping to reduce its costs.
(e) A consumer roams around a shopping mall, looking for birthday gifts.
(f) The federal government needs to borrow more money to finance its level of spending.

3. Discuss the incentive issues that might arise in each of the following situations. (Hint: Remember the history of the automobile industry at the start of this chapter.)
(a) You have some money to invest, and your financial adviser introduces you to a couple of software executives who want to start their own company. What should you worry about as you decide whether to invest?
(b) You are running a small company, and your workers promise that if you increase their pay, they will work harder.
(c) A large industry is going bankrupt and appeals for government assistance.

4. Name ways in which government intervention has helped the automobile industry in the last two decades, and ways in which it has injured the industry.

5. The back of a bag of cat litter claims, "Cats that use cat litter live three years longer than cats that don't." Do you think that cat litter actually causes an increased life expectancy of cats, or can you think of some other factors to explain this correlation? What evidence might you try to collect to test your explanation?

6. Life expectancy in Sweden is 78 years; life expectancy in India is 61 years. Does this prove that if an Indian moved to Sweden he would live longer? That is, does this prove that living in Sweden causes an increase in life expectancy, or can you think of some other factors to explain these facts? What evidence might you try to collect to test your explanation?

CHAPTER 2

BASIC PREMISES

Everyone thinks about economics, at least some of the time. We think about money (we wish we had more of it) and about work (we wish we had less of it). But there is a distinctive way that economists approach economic issues, and one of the purposes of this course is to introduce you to that way of thinking. This chapter begins with a basic model of the economy. We follow this with a closer look at how individuals and firms make choices in situations where they are faced with scarcity. In Chapters 3 and 5, we study ways in which individuals, firms, and government interact with one another, and how those interactions "add up" to determine how society's resources are allocated. To set the stage for these later chapters, this chapter concludes with a discussion of the most basic economic interactions—trade—both among individuals and nations.

KEY QUESTIONS

1. What is the basic competitive model of the economy?
2. What are incentives, property rights, prices, and the profit motive, and what roles do these essential ingredients of a market economy play?
3. What alternatives for allocating resources are there to the market system, and why do economists tend not to favor these alternatives?
4. What are some of the basic techniques economists use in their study of how people make choices? What are the various concepts of costs that economists use?
5. Why is trade (exchange) mutually beneficial?
6. What are the similarities and differences between trade (exchange) between individuals within a country and trade between countries?

THE BASIC COMPETITIVE MODEL

Though different economists employ different models of the economy they all use a basic set of assumptions as a point of departure. The economist's basic competitive model has three components: assumptions about how consumers behave, assumptions about how firms behave, and assumptions about the markets in which these consumers and firms interact. The model ignores government, because we need to see how an economy without a government might function before we can understand the role of government.

RATIONAL CONSUMERS AND PROFIT-MAXIMIZING FIRMS

Scarcity, which we encountered in Chapter 1, implies that individuals and firms must make choices. Underlying much of economic analysis is the basic assumption of **rational choice,** that people weigh the costs and benefits of each possibility. This assumption is based on the expectation that individuals and firms will act in a consistent manner, with a reasonably well-defined notion of what they like and what their objectives are, and with a reasonable understanding of how to attain those objectives.

In the case of an individual, the rationality assumption is taken to mean that he makes choices and decisions in pursuit of his own self-interest. Different people will, of course, have different goals and desires. Sally may want to drive a Porsche, own a yacht, and have a large house; to attain those objectives, she knows she needs to work long hours and sacrifice time with her family. Andrew is willing to accept a lower income to get vacations and more leisure throughout the year.

Economists make no judgments about whether Sally's preferences are "better" or "worse" than Andrew's. They do not even spend much time asking why different individuals have different views on these matters, or why tastes change over time. These are important questions, but they are more the province of psychology and sociology. What economists are concerned about are the consequences of these different preferences. What decisions can they expect Sally and Andrew, rationally pursuing their respective interests, to make?

In the case of firms, the rationality assumption is taken to mean that firms operate to maximize their profits.

COMPETITIVE MARKETS

To complete the model, economists make some assumptions about the places where self-interested consumers and profit-maximizing firms meet: markets. Economists begin by focusing on the case where there are many buyers and sellers, all buying and selling the same thing. You might picture a crowded farmers' market to get a sense of the number of buyers and sellers—except that you have to picture everyone buying and selling just one good. Let's say we are in Florida, and the booths are all full of oranges.

Each of the farmers would like to raise his prices. That way, if he can still sell his oranges, his profits go up. Yet with a large number of sellers, each is forced to charge close to the same price, since if any farmer charged much more, he would lose business to the farmer next door. Profit-maximizing firms are in the same position. In an extreme case, if a firm charged any more than the going price, it would lose *all* of its sales. Economists label this case **perfect competition.** In perfect competition, each firm is a **price taker,** which simply means that because it cannot influence the market price, it must accept that price. The firm takes the market price as given because it cannot raise its price without losing all sales, and at the market price it can sell as much as it wishes. Even if it sold ten times as much, this would have a negligible effect on the total quantity marketed or the price prevailing in the market. Markets for agricultural goods would be, in the absence of government intervention, perfectly competitive. There are so many wheat farmers, for instance, that each farmer believes that he can grow and sell as much wheat as he wishes and have no effect on the price of wheat. (Later in the book, we will encounter markets with limited or no competition, like monopolies, where firms can raise prices without losing all their sales.)

On the other side of our farmers' market are rational individuals, each of whom would like to pay as little as possible for her oranges. Why can't she pay less than the going price? Because the seller sees another buyer in the crowd who will pay the going price. Thus, the consumers also take the market price as given, and focus their attention on other factors—their taste for oranges, primarily—in deciding how many to buy.

This model of consumers, firms, and markets—rational, self-interested consumers interacting wtih rational, profit-maximizing firms, in competitive markets where firms and consumers are both price takers—is the **basic**

competitive model. The model has one very strong implication: if actual markets are well described by the competitive market, then the economy will be efficient—resources are not wasted, it is not possible to produce more of one good without producing less of another, and it is not even possible to make anyone better off without making someone else worse off. These results are obtained without government.

Virtually all economists recognize that actual economies are not *perfectly* described by the competitive model, but most still use it as a convenient benchmark—as we will throughout this book. We will also point out important differences between the predictions of the competitive model and observed outcomes, which will guide us to other models that provide a better description of particular markets and situations. Economists recognize too that, while the competitive market may not provide a *perfect* description of some markets, it may provide a good description—with its predictions matching actual outcomes well, though not perfectly. As we shall see, economists differ in their views about how prevalent are the markets that the basic competitive model describes, and how well alternative models do in rectifying the deficiencies of the competitive model in particular cases.

Ingredients in the Basic Competitive Model

1. Rational, self-interested consumers
2. Rational, profit-maximizing firms
3. Competitive markets with price-taking behavior

PRICES, PROPERTY RIGHTS, AND PROFITS: INCENTIVES AND INFORMATION

For market economies to work efficiently, firms and individuals must be informed and have incentives to act on available information, produce efficiently, work, save, and invest. Indeed, incentives can be viewed as at the heart of economics. Without incentives, why would individuals go to work in the morning? Who would undertake the risks of bringing out new products? Who would put aside savings for a rainy day? There is an old expression about the importance of having someone "mind the store." But without incentives, why would anyone bother?

Market economies provide information and incentives through *prices, profits,* and *property rights.* Prices provide information about the relative scarcity of different goods. The **price system** ensures that goods go to those individuals who are most willing and able to pay for them. Prices convey information to firms about how individuals value different goods.

The desire for profits motivates firms to respond to the information provided by prices. By producing what consumers want in the most efficient way, in ways that least use scarce resources, they increase their profits. Similarly, rational individuals' pursuit of self-interest induces them to respond to prices: they buy goods which are more expensive—relatively more scarce—only if they provide commensurately greater benefits.

For the **profit motive** to be effective, firms need to be able to keep at least some of their profits. Households, in turn, need to be able to keep at least some of what they earn or receive as a return on their investments. (The return on their investments is simply what they receive back in excess of what they invested. If they receive back less than they invested, the return is negative.) There must, in short, be **private property,** with its attendant **property rights.** Property rights include both the right of the owner to use the property as she sees fit and the right to sell it.

These two attributes of property rights give individuals the incentive to use property under their control efficiently. The owner of a piece of land tries to figure out the most profitable use of the land; for example, whether to build a store or a restaurant. If he makes a mistake and opens a restaurant when he should have opened a store, he bears the consequences: the loss in income. The profits he earns if he makes the right decisions—and the losses he bears if he makes the wrong ones—give him an incentive to think carefully about the decision and do the requisite research. The owner of a store tries to make sure that her customers get the kind of merchandise and the quality of service they want. She has an incentive to establish a good reputation, because if she does so, she will do more business and earn more profits.

The store owner will also want to maintain her property—which is not just the land anymore, but includes the store as well—because she will get more for it when the time comes to sell her business to someone else. Similarly, the owner of a house has an incentive to maintain *his* property, so that he can sell it for more when he wishes to move. Again, the profit motive combines with private property to provide incentives.

How the Profit Motive Drives the Market System

In market economies, incentives are supplied to individuals and firms by prices, profits, and property rights.

Incentives versus Equality

While incentives are at the heart of market economies, they come with a cost: inequality. Any system of incentives must tie compensation with performance. Whether through differences in luck or ability, performance of different individuals will differ. In many cases, it will not be possible to identify why performance is high. The salesperson may claim that the reason his sales are high is superior skill and effort, while his colleague may argue that it is dumb luck.

If pay is tied to performance, there will inevitably be some inequality. And the more closely compensation is tied to performance the greater the inequality. The fact that the greater the incentives, the greater the resulting inequality is called the **incentive-equality trade-off.** If society provides greater incentives, total output is likely to be higher, but there will also probably be greater inequality.

One of the basic questions facing society in the choice of tax rates and welfare systems is how much would incentives be diminished by an increase in tax rates to finance a better welfare system and thus reduce inequality? What would be the results of those reduced incentives?

Consensus on Incentives

Incentives, prices, profits, and property rights are central features of any economy, and highlight an important area of consensus among economists. This brings us to our second point of consensus:

2 Incentives

Providing appropriate incentives is a fundamental economic problem. In modern market economies, profits provide incentives for firms to produce the goods individuals want, and wages provide incentives for individuals to work. Property rights also provide people with important incentives, not only to invest and to save, but to put their assets to the best possible use.

RATIONING

The price system is only one way of allocating resources, and a comparison with other systems will help to clarify the advantages of markets. When individuals get less of a good than they would like at the terms being offered, the good is said to be **rationed.** Different rationing schemes are different ways of deciding who gets society's scarce resources.

Rationing by Queues Rather than supplying goods to those willing and able to pay the most for them, a society could give them instead to those most willing to wait in line. This system is called **rationing by queues,** after the British term for lines. Tickets are often allocated by queues, whether they are for movies, sporting events, or rock concerts. A price is set, and it will not change no matter how many people line up to buy at that price. (The high price that scalpers can get for "hot" tickets is a good indication of how much more than the ticket price people would be willing to pay.)

Rationing by queues is thought by many to be a more desirable way of supplying medical services than the price system. Why, it is argued, should the rich—who are most able to pay for medical services—be the ones to get better or more medical care? Using this reasoning, Britain provides free medical care to everyone on its soil. To see a doctor there, all you have to do is wait in line. Rationing medicine by queues turns the allocation problem around: since the value of time for low-wage workers is lower, they are more willing to wait, and therefore they get a disproportionate share of (government-supplied) medical services.

In general, rationing by queues is an inefficient way of distributing resources because the time spent in line is a wasted resource. There are usually ways of achieving the same goal within a price system that can make everyone better off. Returning to the medical example, if some individuals were allowed to pay for doctors' services instead of waiting in line, more doctors could be hired with the proceeds, and the lines for those unable or unwilling to pay could actually be reduced.

Rationing by Coupons Most governments in wartime use **coupon rationing.** People are allowed so many gallons of gasoline, so many pounds of sugar, and so much flour each month. To get the good, you have to pay the market price *and* produce a coupon. The reason for coupon rationing is that without coupons prices might soar, inflicting a hardship on poorer members of society.

Coupon systems take two forms, depending on whether coupons are tradable or not. Coupons that are not tradable give rise to the same inefficiency that occurs with most other nonprice systems—goods do not in general go to the individuals who are willing and able to pay the most. There is generally room for a trade that will make all parties better off. For instance, I might be willing to trade some of my flour ration for some of your sugar ration. But in a nontradable coupon system, the law prohibits such transactions. When coupons cannot be legally traded, there are strong incentives for the establishment of a **black market,** an illegal market in which the proscribed trades occur.

OPPORTUNITY SETS

We have covered a lot of ground so far in this chapter. We have seen the economist's basic model, which relies on competitive markets. We have seen how prices, the profit motive, and private property supply the incentives that drive a market economy. And we have gotten our first glimpse at why economists believe that market systems, which supply goods to those who are willing and able to pay the most, provide the most efficient means of allocating what the economy produces. They are far better than the nonprice rationing schemes that have been employed. It is time now to return to the question of choice. Market systems leave to individuals and firms the question of what to consume. How are these decisions made?

For a rational individual or firm, the first step in the economic analysis of any choice is to identify what is possible—what economists call the **opportunity set,** which is simply the group of available options. If you want a sandwich and you have only roast beef and tuna fish in the refrigerator, then your opportunity set consists of a roast beef sandwich, a tuna fish sandwich, a strange sandwich combining roast beef and tuna fish, or no sandwich. A ham sandwich is out of the question. Defining the limitations facing an individual or firm is a critical step in economic analysis. One can spend time yearning after the ham sandwich, or anything else outside the opportunity set, but when it comes to making choices and facing decisions, only what is within the opportunity set is relevant.

BUDGET AND TIME CONSTRAINTS

Constraints limit choices and define the opportunity set. In most economic situations, the constraints that limit a person's choices—that is, those constraints that actually are relevant—are not sandwich fixings, but time and money. Opportunity sets whose constraints are imposed by money are referred to as **budget constraints;** opportunity sets whose constraints are prescribed by time are called **time constraints.** A billionaire may feel that his choices are limited not by money but by time; while for an unemployed worker, time hangs heavy—lack of money rather than time limits his choices.

Table 2.1 ALFRED'S OPPORTUNITY SET

Cassettes	CDs
0	10
2	9
4	8
6	7
8	6
10	5
12	4
14	3
16	2
18	1
20	0

The budget constraint defines a typical opportunity set. Consider the budget constraint of Alfred, who has decided to spend $100 on either cassette recordings or compact discs. A CD costs $10, a cassette $5. So Alfred can buy 10 CDs or 20 cassettes; or 9 CDs and 2 cassettes; or 8 CDs and 4 cassettes. The various possibilities are set forth in Table 2.1. And they are depicted graphically in Figure 2.1:[1] along the vertical axis, we measure the number of cassettes purchased, and along the horizontal axis, we measure the number of CDs. The line marked B_1B_2 is Alfred's budget constraint. The extreme cases, where Alfred buys only CDs or only cassettes, are represented by the points B_1 and B_2 in the figure. The dots between these two points, along the budget constraint, represent the other possible combinations. The cost of each combination of CDs and cassettes must add up to $100. The point actually chosen by Alfred is labeled *E*, where he purchases 4 CDs (for $40) and 12 cassettes (for $60).

Alfred's budget constraint is the line that defines the outer limits of his opportunity set. But the whole opportunity set is larger. It also includes all points below the budget constraint. This is the shaded area in the figure. The budget

[1]See the Chapter appendix for help in reading the graphs.

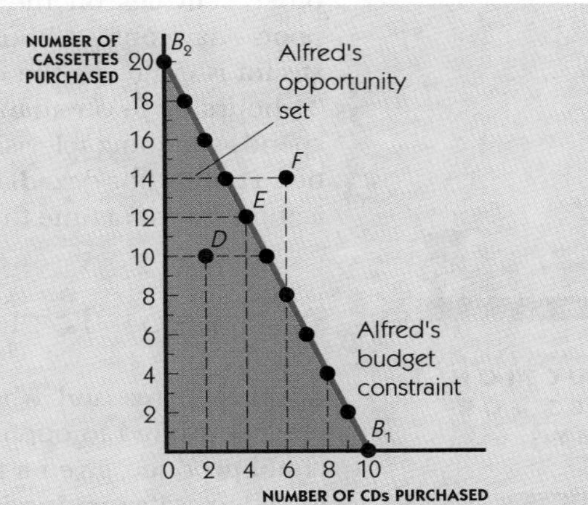

Figure 2.1 ALFRED'S BUDGET CONSTRAINT

The budget constraint identifies the limits of an individual's opportunity set between CDs and cassettes. Points B_1 and B_2 are the extreme options, where he chooses all of one and none of the other. His actual choice is point *E*. Choices from the shaded area are possible, but less attractive than choices actually on the budget constraint.

constraint shows the maximum number of cassettes Alfred can buy for each number of CDs purchased, and vice versa. Alfred is always happiest when he chooses a point on his budget constraint rather than below it. To see why, compare the points *E* and *D*. At point *E*, he has more of both goods than at point *D*. He would be even happier at point *F*, where he has still more cassettes and CDs, but that point, by definition, is unattainable.

Figure 2.2 depicts a time constraint. The most common time constraint simply says that the sum of what an individual spends her time on each day—including sleeping—must add up to 24 hours. The figure plots the hours

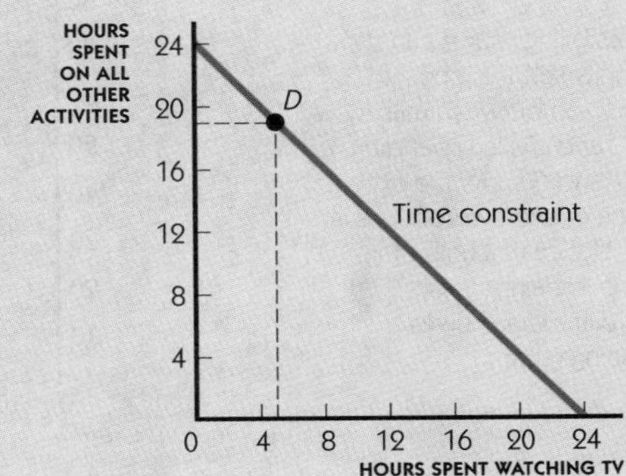

Figure 2.2 AN OPPORTUNITY SET FOR WATCHING TV AND OTHER ACTIVITIES

This opportunity set is limited by a time constraint, which shows the trade-off a person faces between spending time watching television and spending it on other activities. At 5 hours of TV time per day, point *D* represents a typical choice for an American.

spent watching television on the horizontal axis and the hours spent on all other activities on the vertical axis. People—no matter how rich or how poor—have only 24 hours a day to spend on different activities. The time constraint is quite like the budget constraint. A person cannot spend more than 24 hours or fewer than zero hours a day watching TV. The more time she spends watching television the less time she has available for all other activities. Point *D* (for dazed) has been added to the diagram at 5 hours a day—this is the amount of time the typical American chooses to spend watching TV.

THE PRODUCTION POSSIBILITIES CURVE

Table 2.2 **PRODUCTION POSSIBILITIES FOR THE ECONOMY**

Guns (millions)	Butter (millions of tons)
100	0
90	40
70	70
40	90
0	100

Business firms and whole societies face constraints. They too must make choices limited to opportunity sets. The amounts of goods a firm or society could produce, given a fixed amount of land, labor, and other inputs, are referred to as its **production possibilities.**

As one commonly discussed example, consider a simple description of a society in which all economic production is divided into two categories, military spending and civilian spending. Of course, each of these two kinds of spending has many different elements, but for the moment, let's discuss the choice between the two broad categories. For simplicity, Figure 2.3 refers to military spending as "guns" and civilian spending as "butter." The production of guns is given along the vertical axis, the production of butter along the horizontal. The possible combinations of military and civilian spending—of guns and butter—is the opportunity set. Table 2.2 sets out some of the possible combinations: 90 million guns and 40 million tons of butter, or 40 million guns and

Figure 2.3 **THE GUNS AND BUTTER TRADE-OFF**

A production possibilities curve can show society's opportunity set. This one describes the trade-off between military spending ("guns") and civilian spending ("butter"). Points *F* and *G* show the extreme choices, where the economy produces all guns or all butter. Notice that unlike the budget and time constraints, the production possibilities line curves, reflecting diminishing returns.

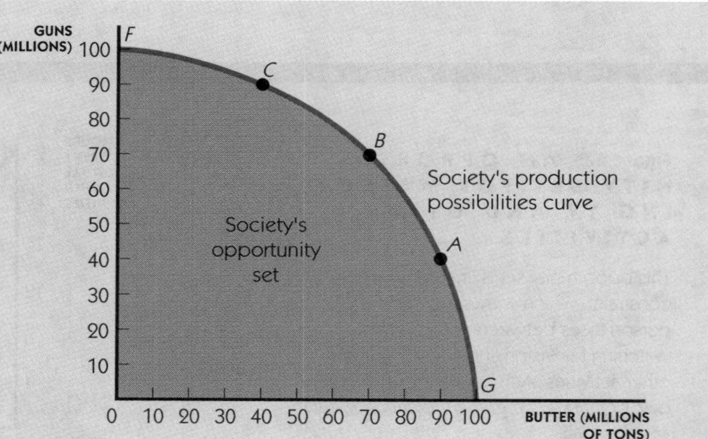

90 million tons of butter. These possibilities are depicted in the figure. In the case of a choice involving production decisions, the boundary of the opportunity set—giving the maximum amount of guns that can be produced for each amount of butter and vice versa—is called the **production possibilities curve.**

The importance of the guns-butter trade-off can be seen dramatically by looking back at Figure 1.3, which shows that during World War II, car production plummeted almost to zero as the automobile factories were diverted to the production of tanks and other military vehicles.

When we compare the individual's opportunity set and that of society, reflected in its production possibilities curve, we notice one major difference. The individual's budget constraint is a straight line, while the production possibilities curve bows outward. There is a good reason for this. An individual typically faces fixed **trade-offs:** if Alfred spends $10 more on CDs (that is, he buys one more CD), he has $10 less to spend on cassettes (he can buy two fewer cassettes).

On the other hand, the trade-offs faced by society are not fixed. If a society produces only a few guns, it will use those resources—the men and machines—that are best equipped for gun making. But as society tries to produce more and more guns, doing so becomes more difficult; it will increasingly have to rely on those who are less good at producing guns. It will be drawing these resources out of the production of other goods, in this case, butter. Thus, when the economy increases its production of guns from 40 million a year (point *A*) to 70 million (*B*), butter production falls by 20 million tons, from 90 million to 70 million tons. But if production of guns is increased further, to 90 million (*C*), an increase of only 20 million, butter production has to decrease by 30 million tons, to only 40 million tons. For each increase in the number of guns, the reduction in the number of tons of butter produced gets larger. That is why the production possibilities curve is curved.

In another example, assume that a firm owns land that can be used for growing wheat but not corn, and land that can grow corn but not wheat. In this case, the only way to increase wheat production is to move workers from the cornfields to the wheat fields. As more and more workers are put into the wheat fields, production of wheat goes up, but each successive worker increases production less. The first workers might pick the largest and most destructive weeds. Additional workers lead to better weeding, and better weeding leads to higher output. But the additional weeds rooted up are smaller and less destructive, so output is increased by a correspondingly smaller amount. This is an example of the general principle of **diminishing returns.** Adding successive units of any input such as fertilizer, labor, or machines to a fixed amount of other inputs—seeds or land—increases the output, or amount produced, but by less and less.

Table 2.3 shows the output of the corn and wheat fields as labor is increased in each field. Assume the firm has 6,000 workers to divide between wheat production and corn production. Thus, the second and fourth columns together give the firm's production possibilities, which are depicted in Figure 2.4.

Table 2.3 **DIMINISHING RETURNS**

Labor in cornfield (no. of workers)	Corn output (bushels)	Labor in wheat field (no. of workers)	Wheat output (bushels)
1,000	60,000	5,000	200,000
2,000	110,000	4,000	180,000
3,000	150,000	3,000	150,000
4,000	180,000	2,000	110,000
5,000	200,000	1,000	60,000

INEFFICIENCIES: BEING OFF THE PRODUCTION POSSIBILITIES CURVE

There is no reason to assume that a firm or an economy will always be on its production possibilities curve. Any inefficiency in the economy will result in a point such as *A* in Figure 2.4, below the production possibilities curve. One of the major quests of economists is to look for instances in which the economy is inefficient in this way.

Whenever the economy is operating below the production possibilities curve, it is possible for us to have more of every good—more wheat and more corn, more guns and more butter. No matter what goods we like, we can have more of them. That is why we can unambiguously say that points below the

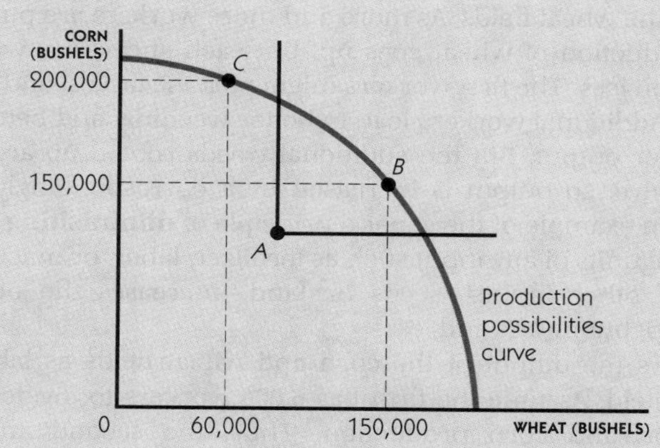

Figure 2.4 THE WHEAT AND CORN TRADE-OFF

This production possibilities curve shows that as wheat production increases, it becomes necessary to give up larger and larger amounts of corn. Or to put the same point a different way, as corn production falls, the resulting increase in wheat production gets smaller and smaller. Point *A* illustrates an inefficient outcome in this opportunity set. Any point on or inside the production possibilities curve is in the opportunity set.

production possibilities curve are undesirable. But this does not mean that every point on the production possibilities curve is better than any point below it. Compare points *A* and *C* in Figure 2.4. Corn production is higher at *C*, but wheat production is lower. If people do not like corn very much, the increased corn production may not adequately compensate them for the decreased wheat production.

There are many reasons why the economy may be below the production possibilities curve. If land better suited for the production of corn is mistakenly devoted to the production of wheat, the economy will operate below its production possibilities curve. If some of society's resources—its land, labor, and capital goods—are simply left idle, as happens when there is a depression, the economy operates below the production possibilities curve.

COST

The beauty of an opportunity set like the budget constraint, the time constraint, or the production possibilities curve is that it specifies the cost of one option in terms of another. If the individual, the firm, or the society is operating on the constraint or curve, then it is possible to get more of one thing only by sacrificing some of another. The "cost" of one more unit of one good is how much you have to give up of the other.

Economists thus think about cost in terms of trade-offs within opportunity sets. Let's go back to Alfred choosing between CDs and cassettes in Figure 2.1. The trade-off is given by the **relative price,** the ratio of the prices of CDs and cassettes. In our example, a CD cost $10, a cassette $5. The relative price is $10 ÷ $5 = 2; for every CD Alfred gives up, he can get two cassettes. Likewise, societies and firms face trade-offs along the production possibilities curve, like the one shown in Figure 2.3. There, point *A* is the choice where 40 million guns and 90 million tons of butter are produced. The trade-off can be calculated by comparing points *A* and *B*. Society can have 30 million more guns by giving up 20 million tons of butter.

Trade-offs are necessary because resources are scarce. If you want something, you have to pay for it; you have to give up something. If you want to go to the library tomorrow night, you have to give up going to the movies. If a sawmill wants to make more two-by-four beams from its stock of wood, it will not be able to make as many one-by-four boards.

OPPORTUNITY COSTS

If someone were to ask you right now what it costs to go to a movie, you would probably answer, "Seven dollars," or whatever you paid the last time you went to the movies. But with the concept of trade-offs, you can see that a *full* answer is not that simple. To begin with, the cost is not the $7 but what that $7 could otherwise buy. Furthermore, your time is a scarce resource that must be figured into the calculation. Both the money and the time represent opportunities forgone in favour of going to the movie, or what economists refer to as the **opportunity cost** of the movie. To apply a resource to one use means that it cannot be put to any other use. Thus, we should consider the next-best, alternative use of any resource when we think about putting it to any particular use. This next-best use is the formal measurement of opportunity cost.

Some examples will help to clarify the idea of opportunity cost. Consider a student, Sarah, who enrolls in college. She thinks that the check for tuition and room and board represents the costs of her education. But the economist's mind immediately turns to the job she might have had if she had not enrolled in college. If Sarah could have earned $15,000 from September to June, this is the opportunity cost of her time, and this forgone income must be added to the university bills in calculating the total economic cost of the school year.

Now consider a business firm that has bought a building for its headquarters that is bigger than necessary. If the firm could receive $3 per month in rent for each square foot of space that is not needed, then this is the opportunity cost of leaving the space idle.

The analysis can be applied to the government as well. The federal government owns a vast amount of wilderness. In deciding whether it is worthwhile to convert some of that land into a national park, the government needs to take into account the opportunity cost of the land. The land might be used for growing timber or for grazing sheep. Whatever the value of the land in its next-best use, this is the economic cost of the national park. The fact that the government does not have to buy the land does not mean that the land should be treated as a free good.

Thus, in the economist's view, when rational firms and individuals make decisions—whether to undertake one investment project rather than another, whether to buy one product rather than another—they take into account *all* of the costs, the full opportunity costs, not just the direct expenditures.

SUNK COSTS

Economic cost includes costs, as we have just seen, that noneconomists often exclude, but it also ignores costs that noneconomists include. If an expenditure has already been made and cannot be recovered no matter what choice is made, a rational person would ignore it. Such expenditures are called **sunk costs.**

To understand sunk costs, let's go back to the movies, assuming now that you have spent $7 to buy a movie ticket. You were skeptical about whether the movie was worth $7. Half an hour into the movie, your worst suspicions are realized: the movie is a disaster. Should you leave the movie theater? In making that decision, the $7 should be ignored. It is a sunk cost; your money is gone whether you stay or leave. The only relevant choice now is how to spend the next 90 minutes of your time: watch a terrible movie or go do something else.

Or assume you have just purchased a fancy laptop computer for $2,000. But the next week, the manufacturer announces a new computer with twice the power for $1,000; you can trade in your old computer for the new one by paying an additional $400. You are angry. You feel you have just paid $2,000 for a computer that is now almost worthless, and you have gotten hardly any use out of it. You decide not to buy the new computer for another year, until you have gotten at least some return for your investment. Again, an economist would say that you are not approaching the question rationally. The past decision is a sunk cost. The only question you should ask yourself is whether the extra power of the fancier computer is worth the additional $400. If it is, buy it. If not, don't.

MARGINAL COSTS

The third aspect of cost that economists emphasize is the extra costs of doing something, what economists call the **marginal costs.** These are weighed against the (additional) **marginal benefits** of doing it. The most difficult decisions we make are not whether to do something or not. They are whether to do a little more or a little less of something. Few of us waste much time deciding whether or not to work. We have to work; the decision is whether to work a few more or a few less hours. A country does not consider whether or not to have an army; it decides whether to have a larger or smaller army.

Jim has just obtained a job for which he needs a car. He must decide how much to spend on the car. By spending more, he can get a bigger and more luxurious car. But he has to decide whether it is worth a few hundred (or thousand) marginal dollars for a larger car or for extra items like fancy hubcaps, power windows, and so on.

Polly is thinking about flying to Colorado for a ski weekend. She has three days off from work. The air fare is $200, the hotel room costs $100 a night, and the ski ticket costs $35 a day. Food costs the same as at home. She is trying to decide whether to go for two or three days. The *marginal* cost of the third day is $135, the hotel cost plus the cost of the ski ticket. There are no additional

BASIC STEPS OF RATIONAL CHOICE

Identify the opportunity sets.

Define the trade-offs.

Calculate the costs correctly, taking into account opportunity costs, sunk costs, and marginal costs.

Policy Perspective: Policy at the Margin

Investment tax credits have been a popular tool of policymakers. With a 10 percent investment tax credit, a firm that invests $100 million—say in the construction of a new factory—gets a credit against its taxes of $10 million. The government is in effect paying 10 percent of the investment. In 1993, the Clinton administration proposed a new form of tax credit, one that would have rewarded businesses for increasing the amount they spent on new investment over what they had spent the previous year. This proposal differs from the usual investment tax credit, which rewards all new investment equally (including the vast amount that would have been invested anyway). The Clinton proposal, which Congress failed to pass, makes good economic sense. Since it focuses on the additional (marginal) dollar, which is the focus of a business's investment decision, it gets more bang for the tax buck.

Here is the logic. As we have seen, an investment tax credit that allows firms to reduce their tax bill by 10 percent of their investment expenditures effectively reduces the cost of investment by 10 percent. This is a strong incentive to invest. But it comes at a high cost, because most of the investment would have been undertaken anyway. If, for example, the economy would have undertaken $750 billion of investment, and the tax credit increases this to $810 billion, the cost of the $60 billion in increased investment is $81 billion in lost federal revenue.

The proposal that lost in the 1993 Congress, in contrast, was a net investment tax credit. The intent of this, as noted, is to reward only investment that would not have happened without the credit. How do we know what that is? We don't. But an acceptable if imperfect substitute is to provide the credit on investment increases over the previous year. In terms of the previous example, suppose that last year's investment was in fact $700 billion—an imperfect estimate of the $750 billion that would have occurred without the tax credit. Since it is only the marginal cost that is relevant to investment decision makers, a 10 percent net investment tax credit will increase investment to $810 billion, as before. But because the credit is only paid on $110 billion ($810 billion minus $700 billion), the Treasury loses only $11 billion ($110 billion × 10 percent)—$70 billion less than the revenues lost from the regular investment tax credit.

The 1993 Congress may have dropped the ball on the investment tax credit. But it did focus on policy at the margin when it renewed a provision that makes increases in research and development (R & D) expenditures eligible for a 20 percent tax credit.

transportation costs involved in staying the third day. She needs to compare the marginal cost with the additional enjoyment she will have from the third day.

People, consciously or not, think about the trade-offs at the margin in most of their decisions. Economists, however, bring them into the foreground. Like opportunity costs and sunk costs, marginal analysis is one of the critical concepts that enable economists to think systematically about alternative choices.

Using Economics: Using Marginal Analysis to Set Safety Standards

For the past decades, the government has taken an active role in ensuring auto safety. It sets standards that all cars must meet. For instance, the car must be able to withstand a side collision with a car approaching at a particular velocity. One of the most difficult problems the government faces is deciding what those standards should be. It recently considered tightening standards for withstanding side collisions on trucks. The government calculated that the higher standards would result on average in 79 fewer deaths per year. It calculated that to meet the higher standards would increase the cost of an automobile by $81. (In addition, the heavier trucks would use more fuel.) In deciding whether to impose the higher standard, it used marginal analysis. It looked at the *additional* lives saved and at the *additional* costs.

Trade and Exchange

Individuals differ in their endowments (what they own and their abilities) and in their preferences (what they like). As a result of these differences, there is an opportunity for trades that benefit all parties to the trade. Kids trading baseball cards learn the basic principles of exchange. One has two Ken Griffey, Jr. cards, the other has two Barry Bonds cards. A trade will benefit both of them. The same lesson applies to countries. Nigeria has more oil than it can use, but it does not produce enough food to feed its populace. The United States has more wheat than Americans can consume, but needs oil. Trade can benefit both countries.

Voluntary trade involves only winners. If the trade would make a loser of any party, that party would choose not to trade. Thus, a fundamental consequence of voluntary exchange is that it benefits everyone involved.

"FEELING JILTED" IN TRADE

In spite of the seemingly persuasive argument that individuals only voluntarily engage in trade if they think they will be better off as a result, people often walk away from a deal believing they have been hurt. It is important to understand that when economists say that a voluntary trade makes the two traders better off, they do not mean that it makes them both happy.

Imagine, for example, that Frank brings an antique rocking chair to a flea market to sell. He is willing to sell it for $100 but hopes to sell it for $200. Helen comes to the flea market planning to buy such a chair, hoping to spend only $100, but willing to pay as much as $200. They argue and negotiate, eventually settle on a price of $125, and make the deal. But when they go home, they both complain. Frank complains the price was too low, and Helen that it was too high.

From an economist's point of view, such complaints are self-contradictory. If Frank *really* thought $125 was too low, he would not have sold at that price. If Helen *really* thought $125 was too high, she would not have paid the price. Economists argue that people reveal their preferences not by what they say, but by what they do. If one voluntarily agrees to make a deal, one also agrees that the deal is, if not perfect, at least better than the alternative of not making it.

Two common objections are made to this line of reasoning. Both involve Frank or Helen "taking advantage" of the other. The implication is that if a buyer or a seller can take advantage, then the other party may be a loser rather than a winner.

The first objection is that either Frank or Helen may not really know what is being agreed to. Perhaps Helen recognizes the chair is an antique, but by neglecting to tell Frank, manages to buy it for only $125. Perhaps Frank knows the rockers fall off but sells the chair without telling this to Helen, thus keeping the price high. In either case, lack of relevant information makes someone a loser after the trade.

The second objection concerns equitable division of the **gains from trade.** Since Helen would have been willing to pay as much as $200, anything she pays less than that is **surplus,** the term economists use for a gain from trade. Similarly, since Frank would have been willing to sell the chair for as little as $100, anything he receives more than that is also surplus. The total dollar value of the gain from trade is $100—the difference between the maximum price Helen was willing to pay and the minimum price at which Frank was willing to sell. At a price of $125, $25 of the gain went to Frank, $75 to Helen. The second objection is that such a split is not fair.

Economists do not have much patience with these objections. Like most people, they favor making as much information public as possible, and they think vendors and customers should be made to stand behind their promises. But economists also point out that second thoughts and "If only I had known" are not relevant. If Frank sells his antique at a flea market instead of having it valued by reputable antique dealers, he has made a voluntary decision to save his time and energy. If Helen buys an antique at a flea market instead of going to a reputable dealer, she knows she is taking a risk.

The logic of free exchange, however, does not say that everyone must express happiness with the result. It simply says that when people choose to make a deal, they prefer making it to not making it. And if they prefer the deal, they are by definition better off *in their own minds* at the time the transaction takes place.

The objections to trade nonetheless carry an important message: most exchanges that happen in the real world are considerably more complicated than the Frank-Helen chair trade. They involve problems of information, estimating risks, and expectations about the future. These complications will be discussed throughout the book. So without going into too much detail at the moment, let's just say that if you are worried that you do not have the proper information to make a trade, shop around, get a guarantee or expert opinion, or buy insurance. If you choose to plunge ahead without these precautions, don't pretend you didn't have other choices. Like those who buy a ticket in a lottery, you know you are taking a chance.

Economic Relations as Exchanges

Individuals in our economy are involved in masses of voluntary trades. They "trade" their labor services (time and skills) to their employer for dollars. They then trade dollars with a multitude of merchants for goods (like gasoline and groceries) and services (like plumbing and hair styling). The employer trades the goods it produces for dollars, and trades those dollars for labor services. Even your savings account can be viewed as a trade: you give the bank $100 today in exchange for the bank's promise to give you $105 at the end of the year (your original deposit plus 5 percent interest).

TRADE BETWEEN COUNTRIES

Why is it that people engage in this complex set of economic relations with others? The answer is that people are better off as a result of trading. Just as individuals *within* a country find it advantageous to trade with one another, so too do countries find trade advantageous. Just as it is impossible for any individual to be self-sufficient, it is impossible for a country to be self-reliant without sacrificing its standard of living. The United States has long been part of an international economic community. This participation has grown in recent decades increasing the interdependence between the United States and its trading partners. How has this affected the three main markets in the U.S. economy?

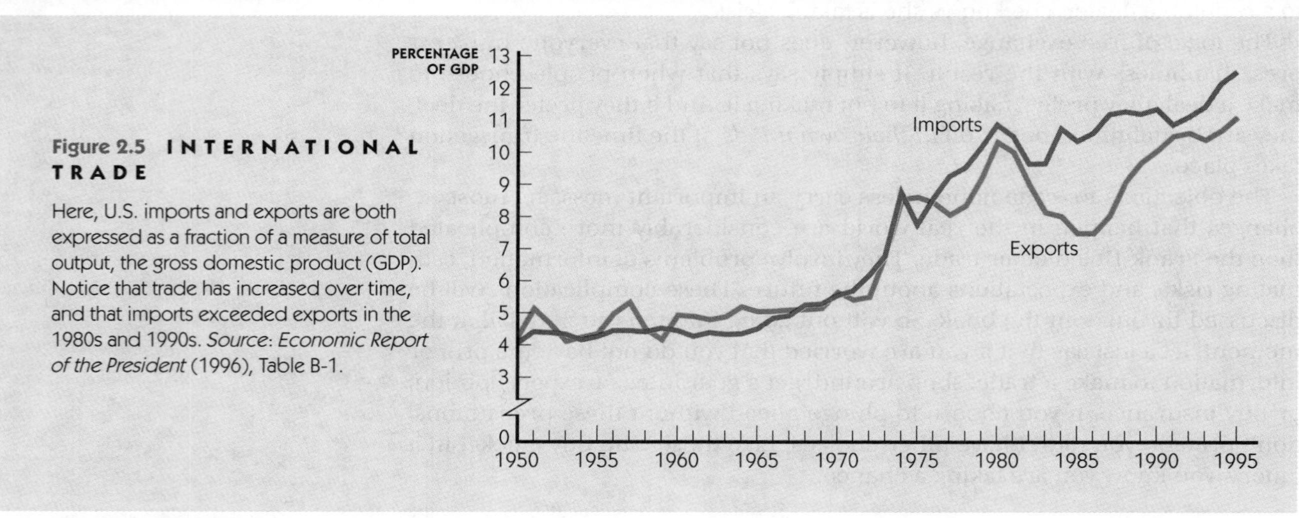

Figure 2.5 INTERNATIONAL TRADE

Here, U.S. imports and exports are both expressed as a fraction of a measure of total output, the gross domestic product (GDP). Notice that trade has increased over time, and that imports exceeded exports in the 1980s and 1990s. *Source: Economic Report of the President* (1996), Table B-1.

Interdependence in the Product Market Foreign-produced goods are commonplace in U.S. markets. In the 1990s, for instance, more than a quarter of the cars sold in the United States were **imported** (imports are goods produced abroad but bought domestically), along with a third of apparel items, a third of the oil, and virtually all of the diamonds. Many of the minerals essential for the U.S. economy must also be imported from abroad. At the same time, U.S. farmers **export** almost two-fifths of the agricultural goods they produce (exports are goods produced domestically but sold abroad), including almost three-fourths of the wheat and one-third of the cotton.

Imports have grown in recent decades, not only in dollars, but also as a percentage of overall production. Exports have grown almost commensurately. Figure 2.5 shows how exports and imports have grown relative to the nation's total output: as a percentage of national output, both have more than doubled over the last twenty-five years. Smaller countries are typically even more dependent on international trade than the United States. Britain and Canada import a quarter of their goods, France a fifth.

Earnings from abroad constitute a major source of income for some of our largest corporations; exports account for 45 percent of sales for Boeing, 20 percent for Hewlett-Packard, and 12 percent for Ford.

Interdependence in the Labor Market International interdependence extends beyond simply the shipping of goods between countries. More than 99 percent of the U.S. citizens either immigrated here from abroad or are descended from people who did. Though the flow of immigrants, relative to the size of the population, has slowed since its peak at the turn of the century, it is still substantial, numbering in the millions every year. Today many rural American areas are dependent upon foreign-born doctors and nurses. Half of the engineers currently receiving doctorates at American universities are foreign-born. The harvests of many crops are highly dependent on migrant laborers from Mexico.

The nations of Europe have increasingly recognized the benefits that result from this international movement of workers. One of the important provisions of the treaty establishing the European Union, an agreement among most countries within Western Europe, allows for the free flow of workers within the member countries.

Interdependence in the Capital Market The United States has become a major borrower from abroad, but the country also invests heavily overseas. In 1995, for example, U.S. private investors owned approximately $2.5 trillion of assets (factories, businesses, buildings, loans, etc.) in foreign countries, while foreign investors owned $2.8 trillion of assets in the United States. American companies have sought out profitable opportunities abroad, where they can use their special skills and knowledge to earn high returns. They have established branches and built factories in Europe, Japan, Latin America, and elsewhere in the world.

Just as the nations of Western Europe have recognized the advantages that follow from the free flow of goods and labor among their countries, so too have they recognized the gains from the free flow of capital. Funds can be invested where they yield the highest returns. Knowledge and skills from one country can be combined with capital from another to produce goods that will be enjoyed by citizens of all countries. Though the process of liberalizing the flow of goods, labor, and capital among countries of the European Union has been going on for more than twenty years, 1992 was the crucial year when all remaining barriers were officially removed.

MULTILATERAL TRADE

Many of the examples to this point have emphasized two-way trade. Trade between two individuals or countries is called **bilateral trade.** But exchanges between two parties is often less advantageous than trade between several parties, called **multilateral trade.** Such trades are observed between sports teams. The New York Mets send a catcher to the St. Louis Cardinals, the Cardinals send a pitcher to the Los Angeles Dodgers, and the Dodgers send an outfielder to the Mets (see Figure 2.6A). No two of the teams was willing to make a two-way trade, but all can benefit from the three-way swap.

Countries function in a similar way. Japan has no domestic oil; it imports oil from Arabian countries. The Arabian countries want to sell their oil, but they want wheat and food, not the cars and television sets that Japan can provide. The United States can provide the missing link by buying cars and televisions from Japan and selling food to the Arab nations. Again, this three-way trade, shown in Figure 2.6B, offers gains that two-way trade cannot. The scores of nations active in the world economy create patterns far more complex than these simplified examples.

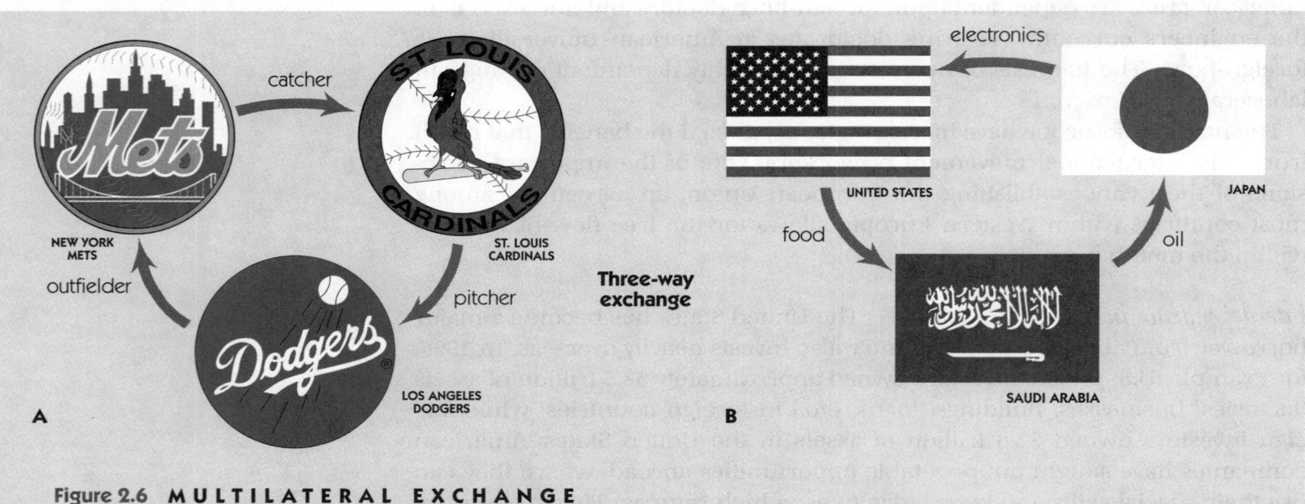

Figure 2.6 MULTILATERAL EXCHANGE

Panel A shows a multilateral, three-way trade between baseball teams. Notice that no two of the teams have the ingredients for a mutually beneficial exchange. Panel B illustrates a multilateral exchange in international trade.

Figure 2.7 illustrates the construction of a Ford Escort in Europe, and dramatizes the importance of multilateral and interconnected trade relations. The parts that go into an Escort come from all over the world. Similar diagrams could be constructed for many of the components in the diagram; the aluminum alloys may contain bauxite from Jamaica, the chrome plate may use chromium from South Africa, the copper for wiring may come from Chile.

Multilateral trade means that trade between any two participants may not balance. In Figure 2.6B, the Arab countries send oil to Japan but get no goods (only yen) in return. No one would say that the Arab countries have an unfair trade policy with Japan. Yet some congressional representatives, newspaper columnists, and business executives complain that since the United States imports more from a particular country (often Japan) than it exports to that country, the trade balance is "unfair." A misguided popular cliché says that "trade is a two-way street." But trade in the world market involves hundreds of possible streets between nations. While there are legitimate reasons to be concerned with the overall U.S. trade deficit, there is no reason why U.S. exports and imports with any particular country should be balanced.

COMPARATIVE ADVANTAGE

We have so far focused on exchanges of existing goods. But clearly, most of what is exchanged must first be produced. Trade allows individuals and countries to concentrate on what they produce best.

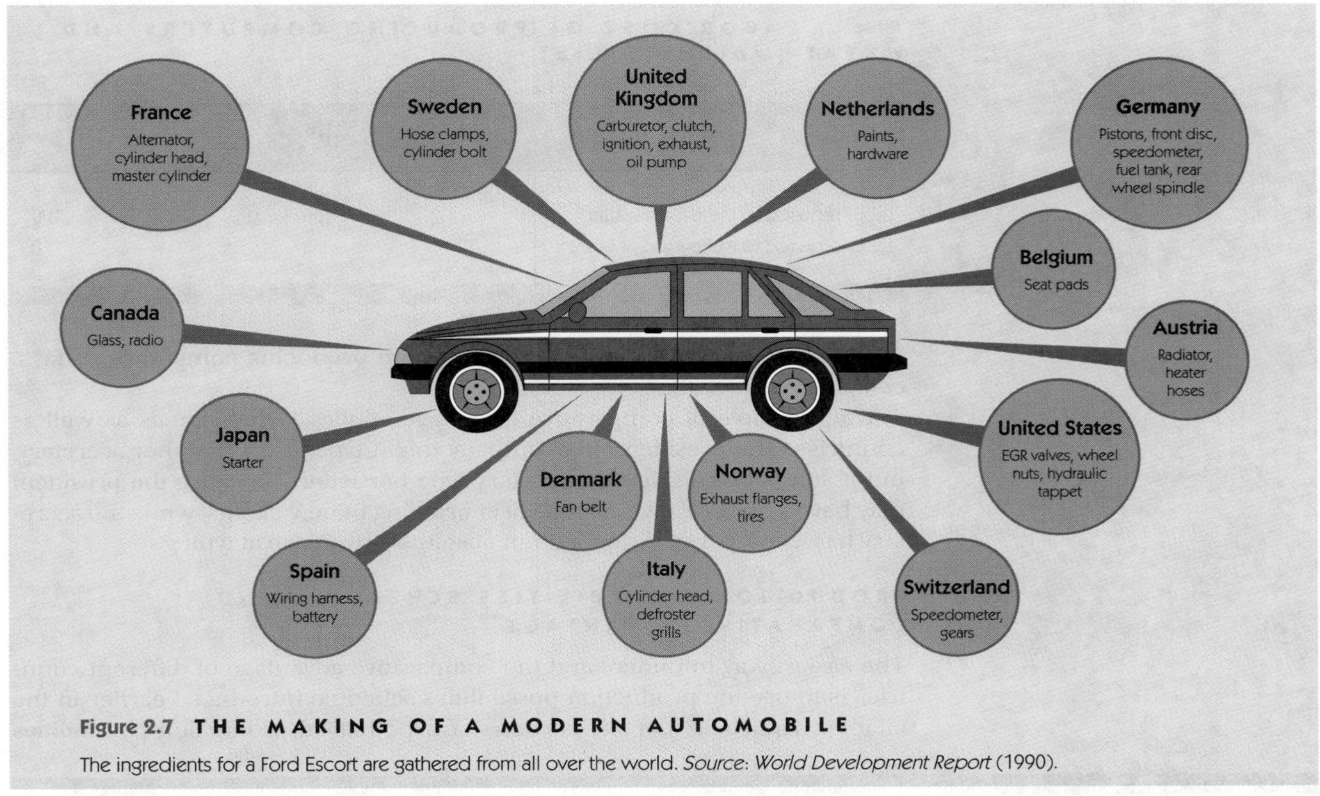

Figure 2.7 THE MAKING OF A MODERN AUTOMOBILE

The ingredients for a Ford Escort are gathered from all over the world. *Source: World Development Report* (1990).

Some countries are more efficient at producing almost all goods than other countries. The possession of superior production skills is called having an **absolute advantage,** and these advanced countries are said to have an absolute advantage over the others. How can the countries with disadvantages successfully engage in trade? The answer lies in the principle of **comparative advantage,** which states that individuals and countries specialize in producing those goods in which they are *relatively,* not absolutely, more efficient.

To see what comparative advantage means, let's say that both the United States and Japan produce two goods, computers and wheat. The amount of labor needed to produce these goods is shown in Table 2.4. (These numbers are all hypothetical.) The United States is more efficient (spends fewer worker hours) at making both products. America can rightfully claim to have the most efficient computer industry in the world, and yet it imports computers from Japan. Why? The *relative* cost of making a computer (in terms of labor used) in Japan, relative to the cost of producing a ton of wheat, is low, compared with the United States. That is, in Japan, it takes 15 times as many hours (120/8) to produce a computer as a ton of wheat; in the United States, it takes 20 times as many hours (100/5) to produce a computer as a ton of wheat.

Table 2.4 LABOR COST OF PRODUCING COMPUTERS AND WHEAT (worker hours)

	United States	Japan
Labor required to make a computer	100	120
Labor required to make a ton of wheat	5	8

While Japan has an absolute *dis*advantage in producing computers, it has a *comparative* advantage.

The principle of comparative advantage applies to individuals as well as countries. The president of a company might type faster than her secretary, but it still pays to have the secretary type her letters, because the president may have a comparative advantage at bringing in new clients, while the secretary has a comparative (though not absolute) advantage at typing.

PRODUCTION POSSIBILITIES SCHEDULES AND COMPARATIVE ADVANTAGE

The easiest way to understand the comparative advantage of different countries is to use the production possibilities schedule introduced earlier in the chapter. Figure 2.8 depicts portions of hypothetical production possibilities

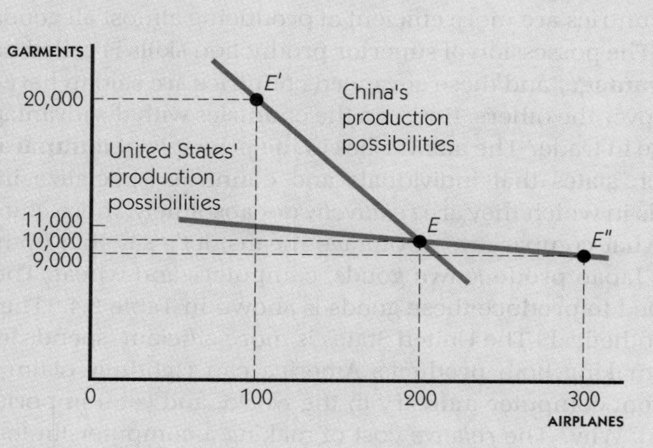

Figure 2.8 EXPLOITING COMPARATIVE ADVANTAGE

The production possibilities curves for China and the United States, each manufacturing two commodities, garments and airplanes, illustrate the trade-offs at different levels of production. Point *E* shows the current level of production for each country; *E' and E''* illustrate production decisions that better exploit each country's comparative advantage. When China decreases its production of airplanes by 100, its production of garments goes up by 10,000; while when the United States increases its production of airplanes by 100, its production of garments goes down by only 1,000. Thus, the shift from *E* to *E'* and *E''* leads to an overall increased production of garments by 9,000.

Close-up: The Comparative Advantage of the United States

What is the U.S. comparative advantage? Looking at the strengths of the United States in comparison with the rest of the world, one thinks of high technology. With over three-fourths of the world living in poor countries, without access even to the capital required for manufacturing, it would seem that these countries would have a *comparative* advantage in agriculture. Thus agriculture would be an area in which the United States had a comparative disadvantage. This intuitive answer is half right. The United States does export high technology products, like computing equipment, aircraft and aircraft engines, industrial organic chemicals, plastics and resins, and pharmaceuticals (drugs). In addition, the United States receives two billion dollars in payments from other countries using its patents.

But the United States is also a major exporter of agricultural goods, dominating world exports of wheat, corn, and cereals. It also exports rice, dairy products, and a host of other agricultural commodities.* For some commodities, this is a consequence of governmental intervention overruling the workings of the market: the costs of production of dairy products exceeds what is received on the international market, with the taxpayer making up the difference through subsidies to exports. In most cases, however, the United States has a true comparative advantage: American farmers substitute sophisticated knowledge of farming, using skilled labor, advanced seeds, fertilizers, pesticides, and equipment instead of unskilled labor.

*The seemingly paradoxical observation that the United States was exporting less-capital-intensive goods, and importing more-capital-intensive goods, was first noted by Nobel Prize-winning economist Wassily Leontief, in a famous paper written in 1953. It is referred to as the Leontief paradox in his honor.

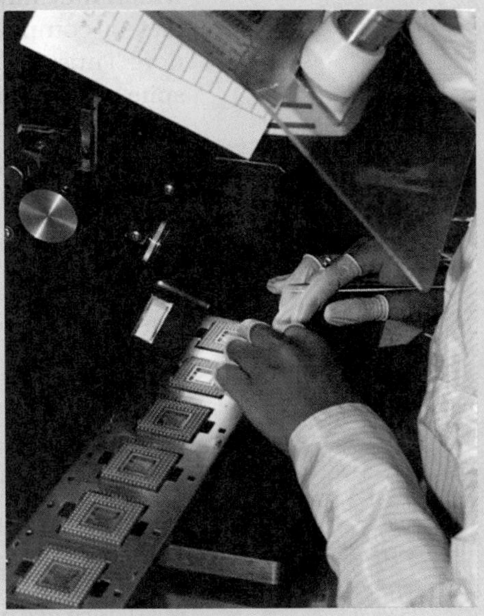

schedules for two countries, China and the United States, producing two commodities, textiles (garments) and airplanes. In both schedules, point *E* represents the current level of production. Let us look at what happens if each country changes its production by 100 airplanes.

China has a comparative advantage in producing textiles. If it reduces its airplane production by 100, its textile production can be increased by 10,000 garments. This trade-off between airplanes and garments is called the **marginal rate of transformation.** By contrast, if the United States reduces its airplane production by 100 airplanes, its textile production can be increased by only 1,000 garments. Conversely, if it increases its airplane production by 100, it will have to reduce its garment production by only 1,000 garments. We can now see why the world is better off if each country exploits its comparative advantage. If China moves from E to E' (decreasing airplane production by 100), 10,000 more garments can be produced. If the United States at the same time increases its airplane production by 100, from E to E'', only 1,000 fewer garments will be produced. In the new situation, the world production of airplanes is unchanged, but world production of garments has increased by 9,000. So long as the production trade-offs differ—that is, so long as the marginal rates of transformation differ—it pays for China to specialize increasingly in textiles, and the United States to specialize increasingly in airplanes. Notice that the analysis only requires knowledge about the production trade-offs. We do not need to know how much labor or capital is required in either country to produce either airplanes or garments.

Though it pays countries to increase production and export of goods in which they have a comparative advantage and to import goods in which they have a comparative disadvantage, this may not lead to complete specialization. Thus, the United States continues to be a major producer of textiles, in spite of heavy imports from the Far East. This does not violate the principle of comparative advantage: not all textiles require the same skill and expertise in manufacturing. Thus, while China may have a comparative advantage in inexpensive textiles, the United States may have a comparative advantage in higher quality textiles. At the same time, the comparative advantage of other countries is so extreme in producing some goods that it does not pay for the United States to produce them at all: TVs, VCRs, and a host of other electronic gadgets, for example.

CONSENSUS ON THE BENEFITS OF TRADE

There is broad agreement among economists on the benefits derived from trade. This provides the basis of our third consensus point.

3 Trade

There are gains from voluntary exchanges. Whether between individuals or across national borders, all can gain from voluntary exchange. Trade allows parties to specialize in those activities in which they have a comparative advantage.

REVIEW AND PRACTICE

SUMMARY

1. The economists' basic model consists of rational, self-interested individuals and profit-maximizing firms, interacting in competitive markets.

USING ECONOMICS: CALCULATING THE GAINS FROM TRADE

Problem: Using the earlier example of Japan and the United States, producing wheat and computers, calculate the trade-offs and show the gains from specialization. Assume that both countries have 240,000 worker hours, initially divided equally between producing wheat and computers.

Solution: First, draw the production possibilities curves, as in the figure below. Since the costs (in worker hours) of producing each unit of each commodity are fixed, the production possibilities schedule is a straight line. If the United States used all its labor to produce computers, it would produce 2,00 computers; if it used all its labor to produce wheat, it would produce 48,000 tons of wheat. If Japan used all its labor to produce computers, it would produce 2,000 computers; if it used all its labor to produce wheat, it would produce 30,000 tons of wheat.

In both curves, use point *A* to mark the current point of production, at which labor is equally divided between computers and wheat.

Next, calculate the slope of the production possibilities curve, giving the trade-offs: in the United States, increasing wheat output by 1,000 tons leads to a reduction of computers by 50, while reducing wheat output by 1,000 tons in Japan leads to an increase in computers of 66 2/3. Thus, each shift of wheat production by 1,000 tons from Japan to the United States increases world computer production by 16 2/3.

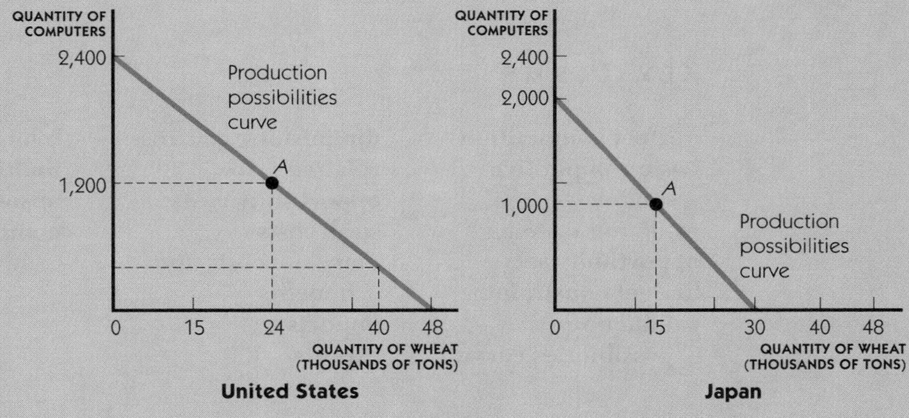

2. The profit motive and private property provide incentives for rational individuals and firms to work hard and efficiently.

3. Society often faces choices between efficiency, which requires incentives that enable people or firms to receive different benefits depending on their performances, and equality, which requires people to receive more or less equal benefits.

4. The price system is one way of allocating goods and services. Other, less efficient, methods include rationing by queue and by coupon.

5. An opportunity set illustrates what choices are possible. Budget constraints and time constraints define individuals' opportunity sets. Both show the trade-offs of how much of one thing a person must give up to get more of another.

6. A production possibilities curve defines a firm or society's opportunity set, representing the possible combinations of goods that the firm or society can produce. If a firm or society is producing below its production possibilities curve, it is said to be inefficient, since it could produce more of either good (or both goods) without producing less of the other.

7. The opportunity cost is the cost of using any resource. It is measured by looking at the next-best, alternative use of that resource.

8. A sunk cost is a past expenditure that cannot be recovered, no matter what choice is made in the present. Thus, rational decision makers ignore them.

9. Most economic decisions concentrate on choices at the margin, where the marginal (or extra) cost of a course of action is compared with its extra benefits.

10. Both individuals and countries gain from voluntary trade. The principle of comparative advantage asserts that countries should export the goods with *relatively* low production costs.

KEY TERMS

perfect competition
basic competitive model
rationing systems
opportunity sets
budget constraint
production possibilities curve
diminishing returns
relative price
opportunity costs
sunk costs
marginal costs and benefits
imports
exports
bilateral trade
multilateral trade
absolute advantage
comparative advantage

REVIEW QUESTIONS

1. What are the essential elements of the basic competitive model?

2. Explain the roles of prices, profits, incentives, and private property in a market economy.

3. Why might government policy to make the distribution of income more equitable lead to less efficiency?

4. List advantages and disadvantages of rationing by queue and by coupon. If the government permitted a black market to develop, might some of the disadvantages of these systems be reduced?

5. What are some of the opportunity costs of going to college? What are some of the opportunity costs a state should consider when deciding whether to widen a highway?

6. Give two examples of a sunk cost, and explain why they should be irrelevant to current decisions.

7. How is marginal analysis relevant in the decision about which car or which house to purchase? After deciding the kind of car to purchase, how is marginal analysis relevant?

8. Why are all voluntary trades mutually beneficial?

9. Describe the advantage of multilateral trade over bilateral trade.

10. Does a country with an absolute advantage in a product necessarily have a comparative advantage in that product?

PROBLEMS

1. Consider a lake in a state park where everyone is allowed to fish as much as he wants. What outcome do you predict? Might this problem be averted if the lake were privately owned and fishing licenses were sold?

2. Suppose an underground reservoir of oil may reside under properties owned by several different individuals. As each well is drilled, it reduces the amount of oil that others can take out. Compare how quickly the oil is likely to be extracted in this situation with how quickly it would be extracted if one person owned the property rights to drill for the entire pool of oil.

3. Most universities do not allocate dormitory rooms using the price system—with the most attractive room going to the student willing to pay the most. Rather, they use a lottery system, with the most attractive room going to the student getting the lowest lottery number. Discuss the merits of the alternative systems. Should universities allow students to trade or sell their lottery numbers?

Radios, television broadcasters, cellular telephones, and beepers all use part of the electromagnetic spectrum to send their signals. The spectrum is a scarce resource. Having the right to broadcast may be worth millions of dollars. It used to be that, in effect, the spectrum was allocated among qualified applicants by a lottery. In recent years, the spectrum has been allocated by auctions, with those who bid the most getting the right to use the spectrum. Discuss the relative merits of the two systems. Does it make a difference whether the winners of the lottery can sell the spectrum that has been awarded to them? Is your attitude towards using lotteries different for allocating the spectrum and allocating dormitory rooms?

4. During times of war, governments often impose coupon rationing. What are the advantages of allowing people to buy and sell their coupons? What are the disadvantages?

5. Kathy, a college student, has $20 a week to spend; she spends it either on junk food at $2.50 a snack, or on gasoline at $1 per gallon. Draw Kathy's opportunity set. What is the trade-off between junk food and gasoline? Now draw each new budget constraint she would face if

(a) a kind relative started sending her an additional $10 per week;
(b) the price of a junk food snack fell to $2;
(c) the price of gasoline rose to $1.20 per gallon.

In each case, how does the trade-off between junk food and gasoline change?

6. Why is the opportunity cost of going to medical school likely to be greater than the opportunity cost of going to college? Why is the opportunity cost of a woman with a college education having a child greater than the opportunity cost of a woman with just a high school education having a child?

7. Bob likes to divide his recreational time between going to movies and listening to compact discs. He has twenty hours a week available for recreation; a movie takes two hours, and a CD takes one hour to listen to. Draw his "time budget constraint." Bob also has a limited amount of income to spend on recreation. He has $60 a week to spend on recreational activities; a movie costs $5, and a CD costs $12. (He never likes to listen to the same CD twice.) Draw his budget constraint. What is his opportunity set?

8. Four players on a Little League baseball team discover that they have each been collecting baseball cards, and they agree to get together and trade. Is it possible for everyone to benefit from this agreement? Does the fact that one players starts off with many more cards than any of the others affect your answer?

9. David Ricardo illustrated the principle of comparative advantage in terms of the trade between England and Portugal in wine (port) and wool. Suppose that in England it takes 120 laborers to produce a certain quantity of wine, while in Portugal it takes only 80 laborers to produce that same quantity. Similarly, in England it takes 100 laborers to produce a certain quantity of wool, while in Portugal it takes only 90. Draw the opportunity set of each country, assuming that each has 72,000 laborers. Assume that each country commits half its labor to each product in the absence of trade, and designate that point on your graph. Now describe a new production plan, with trade, that can benefit both countries.

APPENDIX: READING GRAPHS

Whether the old saying that a picture is worth a thousand words under- or overestimates the value of a picture, economists find graphs extremely useful.

For instance, look at Figure 2.9; it is a redrawn version of Figure 2.1, showing the budget constraint—the various combinations of CDs and cassettes he

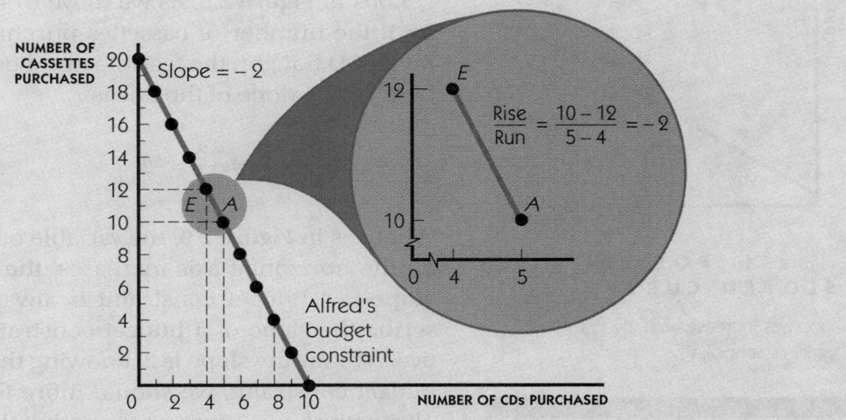

Figure 2.9 READING A GRAPH: THE BUDGET CONSTRAINT

Graphs can be used to show the relationship between two variables. This one shows the relationship between the variable on the vertical axis (the number of cassettes Alfred can buy) and the variable on the horizontal axis (the number of CDs).

The slope of a curve like the budget constraint gives the change in the number of cassettes that can be purchased as Alfred buys one more CD. The slope of the budget constraint is negative.

can purchase—of an individual, Alfred. More generally, a graph shows the relationship between two variables, here, the number of CDs and the number of cassettes that can be purchased. The budget constraint gives the maximum number of cassettes that can be purchased, given the number of CDs that have been bought.

In a graph, one variable (here, CDs) is put on the horizontal axis and the other variable on the vertical axis. We read a point such as *E* by looking down to the horizontal axis and seeing that it corresponds to 4 CDs, and by looking across to the vertical axis and seeing that it corresponds to 12 cassettes. Similarly, we read point *A* by looking down to the horizontal axis and seeing that it corresponds to 5 CDs, and by looking across to the vertical axis and seeing that it corresponds to 10 cassettes.

In the figure, each of the points from Table 2.1 has been plotted, and then a curve has been drawn through those points. The "curve" turns out to be a straight line in this case, but we still use the more general term. One advantage of the curve over the table is that we can read off from the graph points on the budget constraint that are not in the table.

Sometimes, of course, not every point on the graph is economically meaningful. You cannot buy half a cassette or half a CD. For the most part, we ignore these considerations when drawing our graphs; we simply pretend that any point on the budget constraint is actually possible.

SLOPE

In any diagram, the amount by which the value along the vertical axis increases from a change in a unit along the horizontal axis is called the **slope,** just like the slope of a mountain. Slope is sometimes described as "rise over

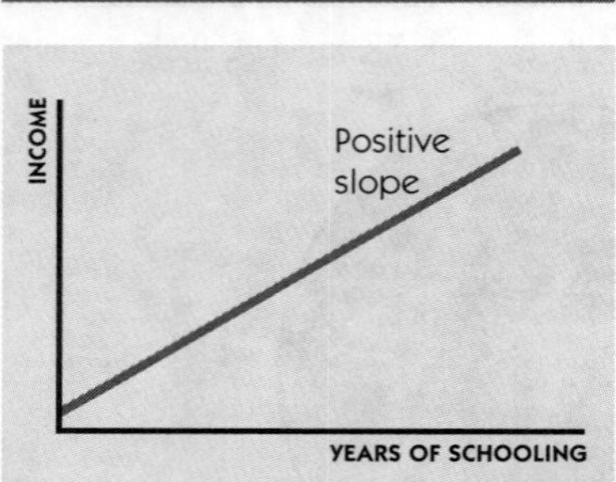

Figure 2.10 POSITIVELY SLOPED CURVE

Incomes increase with the number of years of schooling.

run," meaning that the slope of a line can be calculated by dividing the change on the vertical axis (the "rise") by the change on the horizontal axis (the "run").

Look at Figure 2.9. As we move from E to A, increasing the number of CDs by 1, the number of cassettes purchased falls from 12 to 10. For each additional CD bought, the feasible number of cassettes that can be purchased falls by 2. So the slope of the line is

$$\frac{\text{rise}}{\text{run}} = \frac{10 - 12}{5 - 4} = \frac{-2}{1} = -2.$$

When, as in Figure 2.9, the variable on the vertical axis falls when the variable on the horizontal axis increases, the curve, or line, is said to be **negatively sloped.** A budget constraint is always negatively sloped. But when we describe the slope of a budget constraint, we frequently omit the term "negative." We say the slope is 2, knowing that since we are describing the slope of a budget constraint, we should more formally say that the slope is negative 2. Alternatively, we sometimes say that the slope has an absolute value of 2.

Figure 2.10 shows the case of a curve that is **positively sloped.** The variable along the vertical axis, income, increases as schooling increases, giving the line its upward tilt from left to right.

In later discussions, we will encounter two special cases. A line that is very steep has a very large slope; that is, the increase in the vertical axis for every unit increase in the horizontal axis is very large. The extreme case is a perfectly vertical line, and we say then that the slope is infinite (Figure 2.11, panel A). At the other extreme is a flat, horizontal line; since there is no increase in the vertical axis no matter how large the change along the horizontal, we say that the slope of such a curve is zero (panel B).

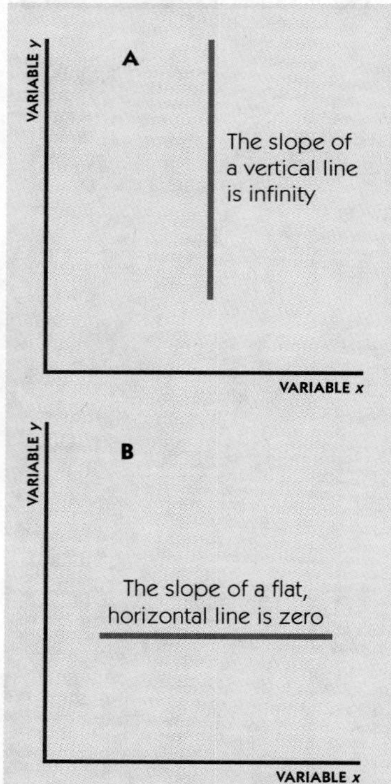

Figure 2.11 LIMITING CASES

In panel A, the slope of a vertical line is infinite. In panel B, the slope of a horizontal line is zero.

Figures 2.9 and 2.10 both show straight lines. Everywhere along the straight line, the slope is the same. This is not true in Figure 2.12, which repeats the production possibilities curve shown originally in Figure 2.3. Look first at point E. Panel B of the figure blows up the area around E, so that we can see what happens to the output of guns when we increase the output of butter by 1 (ton). From the figure, you can see that the output of guns decreases by 1 (million). Thus, the slope is

$$\frac{\text{rise}}{\text{run}} = \frac{69 - 70}{71 - 70} = -1 \text{ (million guns/tons of butter).}$$

Now look at point A, where the economy is producing more butter. The area around A has been blown up in panel C. Here, we see that when we increase butter by 1 more ton, the reduction in guns is greater than before. The slope at A is

$$\frac{\text{rise}}{\text{run}} = \frac{38 - 40}{91 - 90} = -2 \text{ (million guns/tons of butter).}$$

With curves such as the production possibilities curve, the slope differs as we move along the curve.

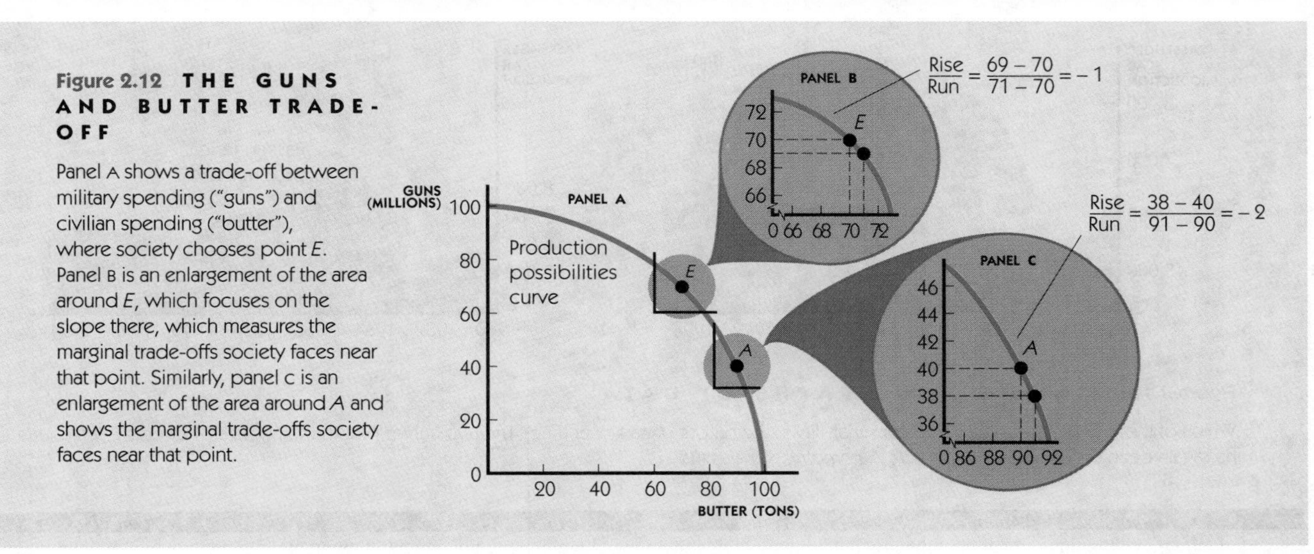

Figure 2.12 THE GUNS AND BUTTER TRADE-OFF

Panel A shows a trade-off between military spending ("guns") and civilian spending ("butter"), where society chooses point *E*. Panel B is an enlargement of the area around *E*, which focuses on the slope there, which measures the marginal trade-offs society faces near that point. Similarly, panel C is an enlargement of the area around *A* and shows the marginal trade-offs society faces near that point.

INTERPRETING CURVES

Look at Figure 2.13. Which of the two curves has a larger slope? The one on the left appears to have a slope that has a larger absolute value. But look carefully at the axes. Notice that in panel A, the vertical axis is stretched relative to

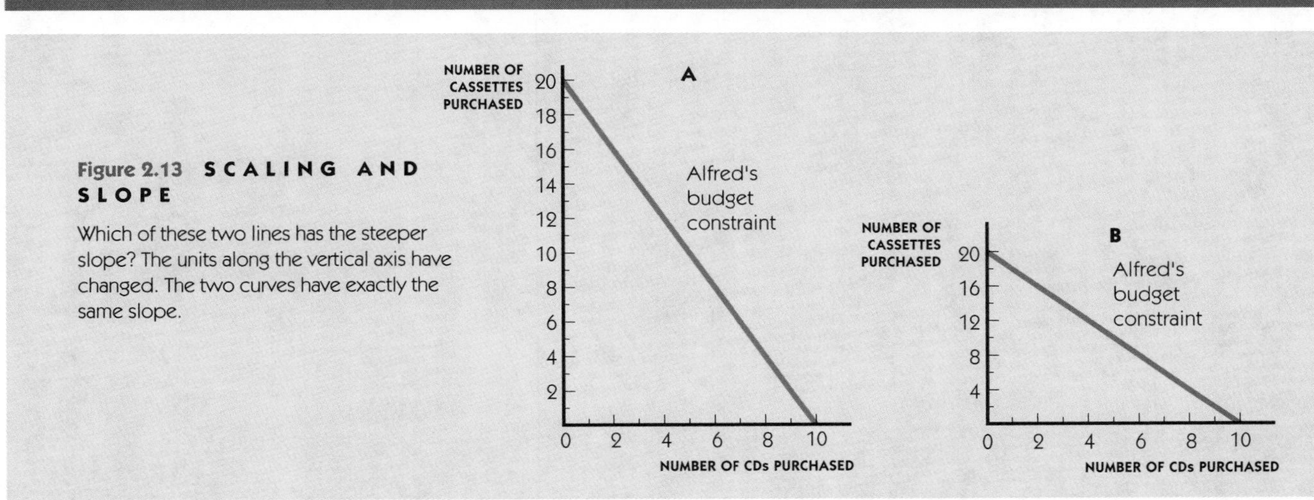

Figure 2.13 SCALING AND SLOPE

Which of these two lines has the steeper slope? The units along the vertical axis have changed. The two curves have exactly the same slope.

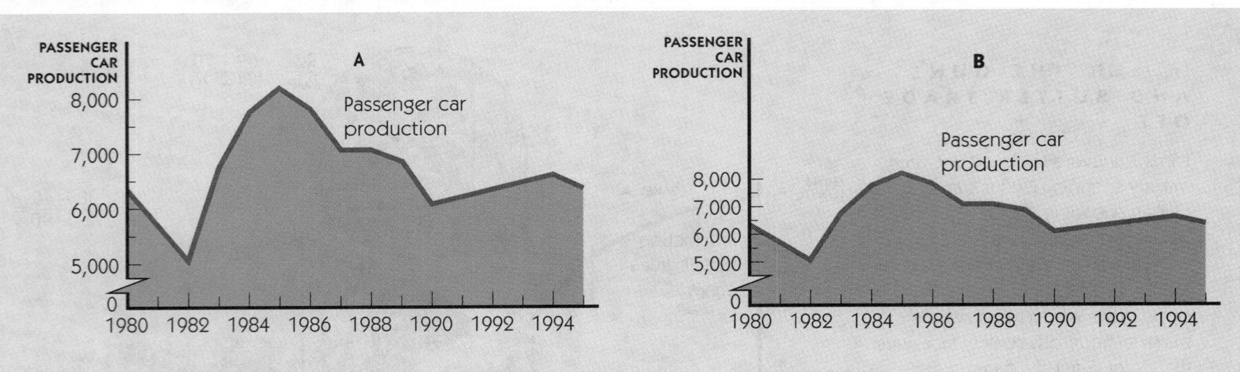

Figure 2.14 **SCALING AND GRAPHS OF DATA**

Which of these two curves shows greater variability in the output of cars over time? The two curves plot the same data. The vertical scale has again been changed. *Source*: *Ward's Automotive Reports* (1991).

panel B. The same distance that represents 20 cassettes in panel B represents only 10 cassettes in panel A. In fact, both panels represent the same budget constraint. They have exactly the same slope.

This kind of cautionary tale is as important in looking at the graphs of data that were common in Chapter 1 as it is in looking at the relationships presented in this chapter. Compare, for instance, panels A and B of Figure 2.14. Which of the two curves exhibits more variability? Which looks more stable? Panel B appears to show that car production does not change much over time. But again, a closer look reveals that the axes have been stretched in panel A. The two curves are based on exactly the same data, and there is really no difference between them.

CHAPTER 3

THE PRICE SYSTEM

In the previous chapter, we presented the basic competitive model of the economy—profit-maximizing firms interacting with rational consumers in competitive markets. In this model, prices played a crucial role. Prices, for instance, determined what producers received from selling their products; when prices increased, they had greater incentives to produce more. Prices are one way participants in the economy communicate with one another. Assume a drought hits the country, reducing drastically the supply of corn. Households will need to reduce their consumption of corn or there will not be enough to go around. But how will they know this? Suppose newspapers across the country ran an article informing people they would have to eat less corn because of a drought. What incentive would they have to pay attention to it? How would each family know how much it ought to reduce its consumption? As an alternative to the newspaper, consider the effect of an increase in the price of corn. The higher price conveys all the relevant information. It tells families corn is scarce at the same time as it provides incentives for them to consume less of it. Consumers do not need to know anything about why corn is scarce.

This chapter asks, how are prices in competitive markets determined? And what causes them to change? Understanding the causes of changes in prices and being able to predict their occurrence is not just a matter of academic interest. One of the events that precipitated the French Revolution was the rise

KEY QUESTIONS

1. What is meant by demand? Why do demand curves normally slope downward? On what variables, other than price, does the quantity demanded depend?
2. What is meant by supply? Why do supply curves normally slope upward? On what variables, other than price, does the quantity supplied depend?
3. Why do economists say that the equilibrium price occurs at the intersection of the demand and supply curves?
4. How do shifts in the demand and supply curves affect the equilibrium price?
5. How do we measure the magnitude by which demand or supply changes in response to a change in price?
6. What happens when prices do not adjust to the level at which demand equals supply?

in the price of bread, for which the people blamed the government. Large price changes have also given rise to recent political turmoil in several countries, including Morocco, the Dominican Republic, Russia, and Poland.

Noneconomists see much more in prices than the impersonal forces of supply and demand. It was the landlord who raised the rent on the apartment; it was the oil company or the owner of the gas station who raised the price of gasoline. These people and companies *chose* to raise their prices, says the noneconomist, in moral indignation. True, replies the economist, but there must be some factor that made these people and companies believe that a higher price was not a good idea yesterday, but is today. And economists point out that at a different time, these same impersonal forces can force the same landlords and oil companies to cut their prices. Economists see prices, then, as symptoms of underlying causes. They focus on the forces of demand and supply behind the price changes.

DEMAND

Economists use the concept of **demand** to describe the quantity of a good or service that a household or firm chooses to buy at a given price. It is important to understand that economists are concerned not just with what people desire, but with what they choose to buy given the spending limits imposed by their budget constraint and given the prices of various goods. In analyzing demand, the first question they ask is how the quantity of a good purchased by an individual changes as the price changes, keeping everything else constant.

THE INDIVIDUAL DEMAND CURVE

Think about what happens as the price of candy bars changes. At a price of $5.00, you might never buy one. At $3.00, you might buy one as a special treat. At $1.25, you might buy a few, and if the price declined to $.50, you might buy a lot. The table in Figure 3.1 summarizes the weekly demand of one individual, Roger, for candy bars at these different prices. We can see that the lower the price, the larger the quantity demanded. We can also draw a graph that shows the quantity Roger demands at each price. The quantity demanded is measured along the horizontal axis, and the price is measured along the vertical axis. The graph in Figure 3.1 plots the points.

A smooth curve can be drawn to connect the points. This curve is called the **demand curve.** The demand curve gives the quantity demanded at each price. Thus, if we want to know how many candy bars a week Roger will demand at a price of $1.00, we simply look along the vertical axis at the price $1.00, find the corresponding point *A* along the demand curve, and then read down to the horizontal axis. At a price of $1.00, Roger buys 6 candy bars each week. Alternatively, if we want to know at what price he will buy just 3 candy bars, we look along the horizontal axis at the quantity 3, find the corresponding point *B* along the demand curve, and then read across to the vertical axis. Roger will buy 3 candy bars at a price of $1.50.

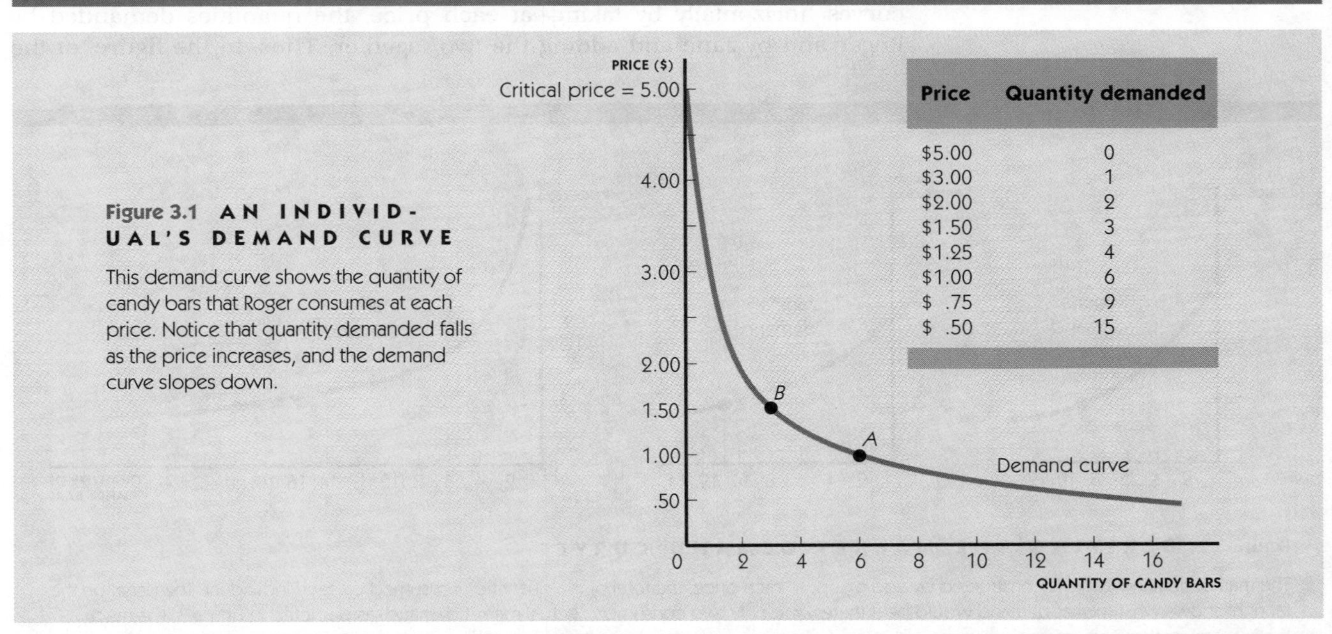

Price	Quantity demanded
$5.00	0
$3.00	1
$2.00	2
$1.50	3
$1.25	4
$1.00	6
$ .75	9
$ .50	15

Figure 3.1 AN INDIVIDUAL'S DEMAND CURVE

This demand curve shows the quantity of candy bars that Roger consumes at each price. Notice that quantity demanded falls as the price increases, and the demand curve slopes down.

As the price of candy bars increases the quantity demanded decreases. This can be seen from the numbers in Figure 3.1, and in the shape of its demand curve, which slopes downward from left to right. This relationship is typical of demand curves and makes common sense: the cheaper a good is (the lower down we look on the vertical axis), the more of it a person will buy (the farther right on the horizontal axis); the more expensive, the less a person will buy.

DEMAND CURVE

The demand curve gives the quantity of the good demanded at each price.

THE MARKET DEMAND CURVE

Suppose there was a simple economy made up of two people, Roger and Jane. Figure 3.2 illustrates how to add up the demand curves of these two individuals to obtain a demand curve for the market as a whole. We "add" the demand curves horizontally by taking, at each price, the quantities demanded by Roger and by Jane and adding the two together. Thus, in the figure, at the

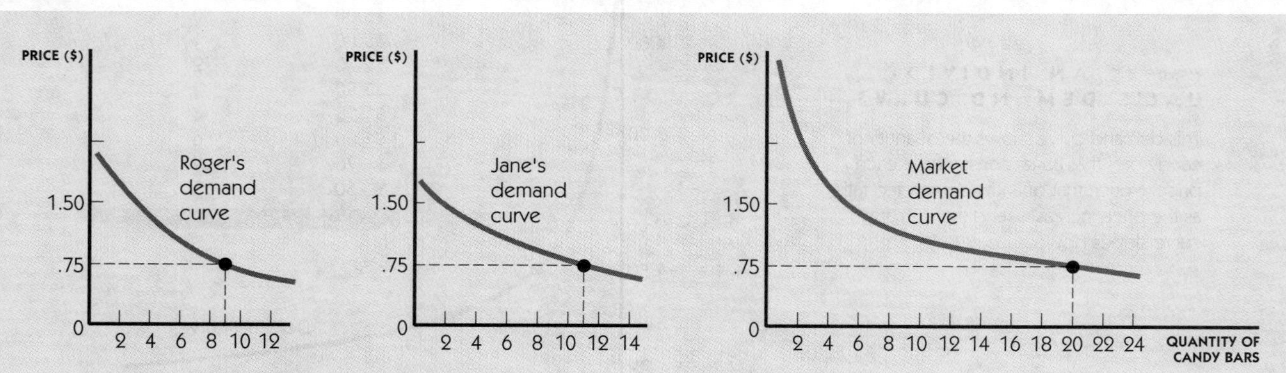

Figure 3.2 DERIVING THE MARKET DEMAND CURVE

The market demand curve is constructed by adding up, at each price, the total of the quantities consumed by each individual. The panel on the far right shows what market demand would be if there were only two consumers. Actual market demand, as depicted in Figure 3.3, is much larger because there are many consumers.

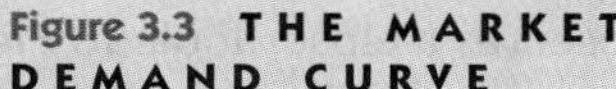

Figure 3.3 THE MARKET DEMAND CURVE

The market demand curve shows the quantity of the good demanded by all consumers in the market at each price. The market demand curve is downward sloping, for two reasons: at a higher price, each consumer buys less, and at high enough prices, some consumers decide not to buy at all—they exit the market.

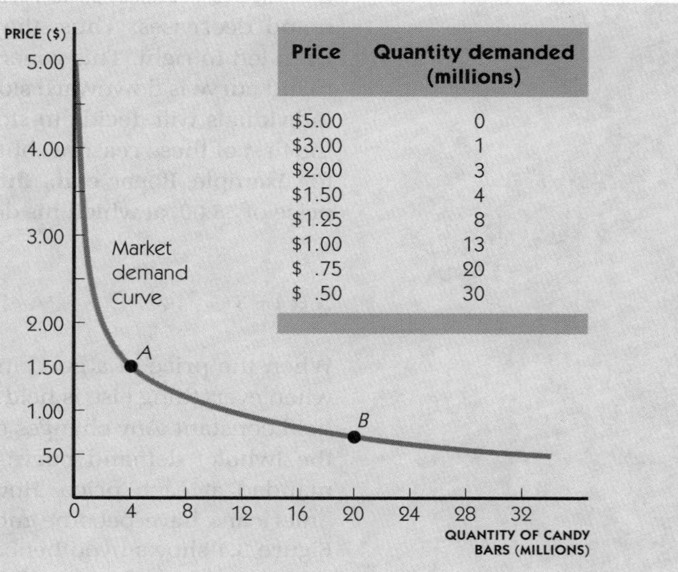

Price	Quantity demanded (millions)
$5.00	0
$3.00	1
$2.00	3
$1.50	4
$1.25	8
$1.00	13
$ .75	20
$ .50	30

price of $.75, Roger demands 9 candy bars and Jane demands 11, so that the total market demand is 20 candy bars. The same principles apply no matter how many people there are in the economy. The **market demand curve** gives the total quantity of the good that will be demanded at each price. Figure 3.3 summarizes the information for our example of candy bars; it gives the total quantity of candy bars demanded by everybody in the economy at various prices. If we had a figure like Figure 3.1 for each person in the economy, we would construct Figure 3.3 by adding up, at each price, the total quantity of candy bars purchased. Figure 3.3 tells us, for instance, that at a price of $3.00 per candy bar, the total market demand for candy bars is 1 million candy bars, and that lowering the price to $2.00 increases market demand to 3 million candy bars.

Figure 3.3 depicts the same information in a graph as well as a table. As with Figure 3.1, price lies along the vertical axis, but now the horizontal axis measures the quantity demanded by everyone in the economy. Joining the points in the figure together, we get the market demand curve. If we want to know what the total demand for candy bars will be when the price is $1.50 per candy bar, we look on the vertical axis at the price $1.50, find the corresponding point *A* along the demand curve, and read down to the horizontal axis; at that price, total demand is 4 million candy bars. If we want to know what the price of candy bars will be when the demand equals 20 million, we find 20 million along the horizontal axis, look up to find the corresponding point *B* along the market demand curve, and read across to the vertical axis; the price at which 20 million candy bars are demanded is $.75.

Notice that just as when the price of candy bars increases, the individual's demand decreases, so too when the price of candy bars increases, market demand decreases. Thus, the market demand curve also slopes downward from left to right. This general rule holds both because each individual's demand curve is downward sloping and because as the price is increased, some individuals will decide to stop buying altogether. We have already examined the first of these reasons, but the second deserves a closer look. In Figure 3.1, for example, Roger **exits the market**—consumes a quantity of zero—at the price of $5.00, at which his demand curve hits the vertical axis.

SHIFTS IN DEMAND CURVES

When the price of a good increases, the demand for that good decreases—when everything else is held constant. But in the real world, everything is not held constant. Any changes other than the price of the good in question shift the (whole) demand curve—that is, change the amount that will be demanded at each price. How the demand curve for candy has shifted as Americans have become more weight conscious provides a good example. Figure 3.4 shows hypothetical demand curves for candy bars in 1960 and in 1995. We can see from the figure, for instance, that the demand for candy bars at a price of $.75 has decreased from 20 million candy bars (point E_{1960}, the original equilibrium) to 10 million (point E_{1995}), as people have reduced their "taste" for candy.

Figure 3.4 SHIFTS IN THE DEMAND CURVE

A leftward shift in the demand curve means that a lesser amount will be demanded at every given market price.

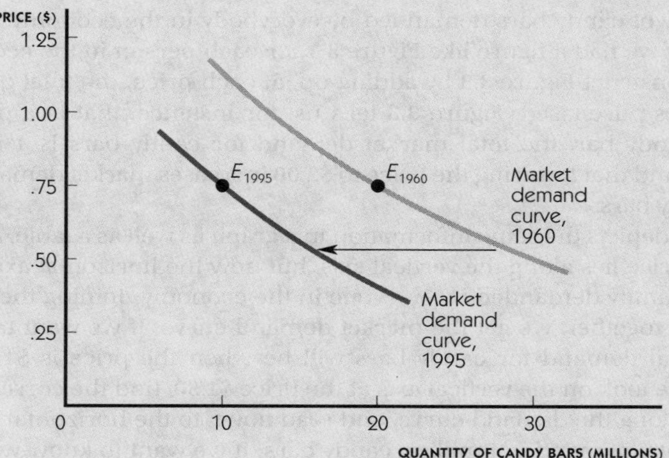

SOURCES OF SHIFTS IN DEMAND CURVES

Two of the factors that shift the demand curve—changes in income and in the price of other goods—are specifically economic factors. As an individual's income increases, she normally purchases more of any good. Thus, rising incomes shift the demand curve to the right, as illustrated in Figure 3.5. At each price, she consumes more of the good.

Changes in the price of other goods, particularly closely related goods, will also shift the demand curve for a good. For example, when the price of margarine increases, some individuals will substitute butter. Butter and margarine are thus **substitutes.** When people choose between butter and margarine, one important factor is the relative price, that is, the ratio of the price of butter to the price of margarine. A decrease in the price of butter and an increase in the price of margarine both decrease the relative price of butter. Thus, both induce individuals to substitute butter for margarine. Thus an increase in the price of margarine shifts the demand curve for butter to the right.

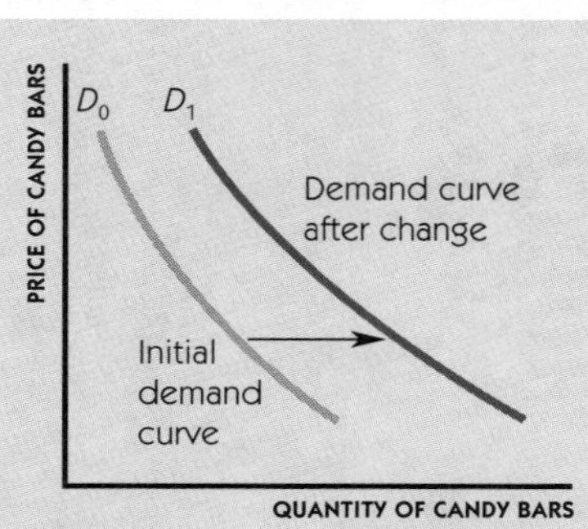

Figure 3.5 A RIGHTWARD SHIFT IN THE DEMAND CURVE

If, at each price, there is an increase in the quantity demanded, then the demand curve will have shifted to the right, as depicted. An increase in income, an increase in the price of a substitute, or a decrease in the price of a complement can cause a rightward shift in the demand curve.

Sometimes, however, an increase in a price of other goods has just the opposite effect. Consider an individual who takes sugar in her coffee. In deciding on how much coffee to demand, she is concerned with the price of a cup of coffee *with* sugar. If sugar becomes more expensive, she will demand less coffee. For this person, sugar and coffee are **complements;** that is, an increase in the price of one *decreases* the demand for the other. A price increase of sugar shifts the demand curve of coffee to the left. (At each price, the demand for coffee is less.) Similarly a *decrease* in the price of sugar shifts the demand curve for coffee to the right.

Noneconomic factors can also shift market demand curves. The major ones are changes in tastes and in composition of the population. The candy example shown earlier was a change in taste. Other taste changes over the past decade in the United States include a shift from hard liquor to wine and from fatty meats to low-cholesterol foods.

Population changes that shift demand curves are often related to age. The consequences of these population changes are referred to as **demographic effects.** Young families with babies purchase disposable diapers. The demand for new houses and apartments is closely related to the number of new households, which in turn depends on the number of individuals of marriageable age. The U.S. population has been growing older, on average, both because life expectancies are increasing and because birthrates fell somewhat after the baby boom that followed World War II. So there has been a shift in demand away from diapers and new houses.

Sometimes demand curves shift as the result of new information. The shifts in demand for alcohol and meat—and even more so for cigarettes—are related to improved consumer information about health risks.

Changes in the availability of credit also can shift demand curves—for goods like cars and houses that people typically buy with the help of loans. When banks, for example, increase the interest rate charged on loans or reduce the availability of credit, the demand curves for cars and houses shift.

Finally, what people think will happen in the future can shift demand curves. If people think they may become unemployed, they will reduce their spending. In this case, economists say that their demand curve depends on expectations.

SOURCES OF SHIFTS IN MARKET DEMAND CURVES

A change in income
A change in the price of a substitute
A change in the price of a complement
A change in the composition of the population
A change in tastes
A change in information
A change in the availability of credit
A change in expectations

SHIFTS IN A DEMAND CURVE VERSUS MOVEMENTS ALONG A DEMAND CURVE

The distinction between changes that result from a *shift* in the demand curve and changes that result from a *movement along* the demand curve is crucial to understanding economics. A movement along a demand curve is simply the change in the quantity demanded as the price changes. Figure 3.6A shows a movement along the demand curve from point *A* to point *B; given a demand curve,* at lower prices, more is consumed. Figure 3.6B shows a shift in the demand curve to the right; *at a given price,* more is consumed. Quantity demanded again increases from Q_0 to Q_1, but the price stays the same.

In practice, both effects are often present. Thus, in panel C of Figure 3.6, the movement from point *A* to point *C*—where the quantity demanded has been increased from Q_0 to Q_2—consists of two parts: a change in quantity demanded resulting from a shift in the demand curve (the increase in quantity from Q_0 to Q_1), and a movement along the demand curve due to a change in the price (the increase in quantity demanded from Q_1 to Q_2).

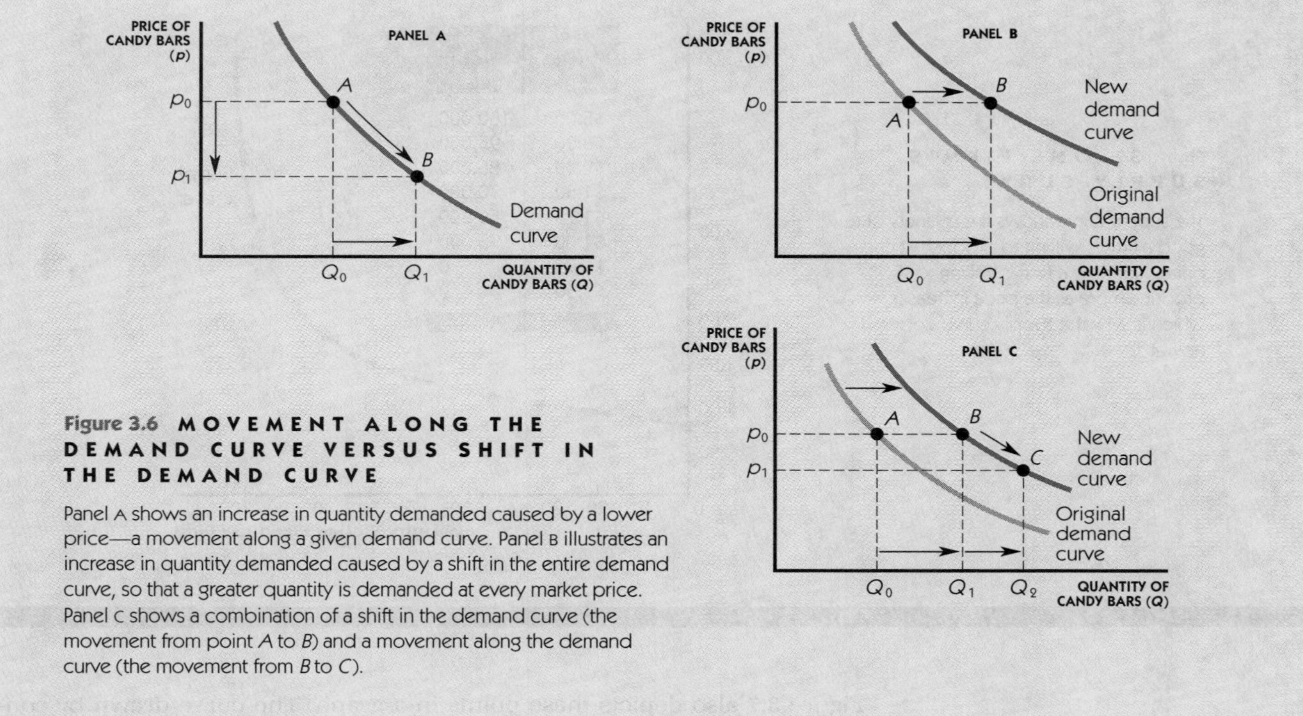

Figure 3.6 MOVEMENT ALONG THE DEMAND CURVE VERSUS SHIFT IN THE DEMAND CURVE

Panel A shows an increase in quantity demanded caused by a lower price—a movement along a given demand curve. Panel B illustrates an increase in quantity demanded caused by a shift in the entire demand curve, so that a greater quantity is demanded at every market price. Panel C shows a combination of a shift in the demand curve (the movement from point *A* to *B*) and a movement along the demand curve (the movement from *B* to *C*).

SUPPLY

Economists use the concept of **supply** to describe the quantity of a good or service that a household or firm would like to sell at a particular price. Supply in economics refers to such seemingly disparate choices as the number of candy bars a firm wants to sell and the number of hours a worker is willing to work. As with demand, the first question economists ask is how does the quantity supplied change when price changes, keeping everything else the same?

Figure 3.7 shows the number of candy bars that the Melt-in-the-Mouth Chocolate Company would like to sell, or supply to the market, at each price. As the price rises, so does the quantity supplied. Below $1.00, the firm finds it unprofitable to produce. At $2.00, it would like to sell 85,000 candy bars. At $5.00, it would like to sell 100,000.

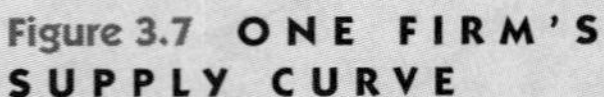

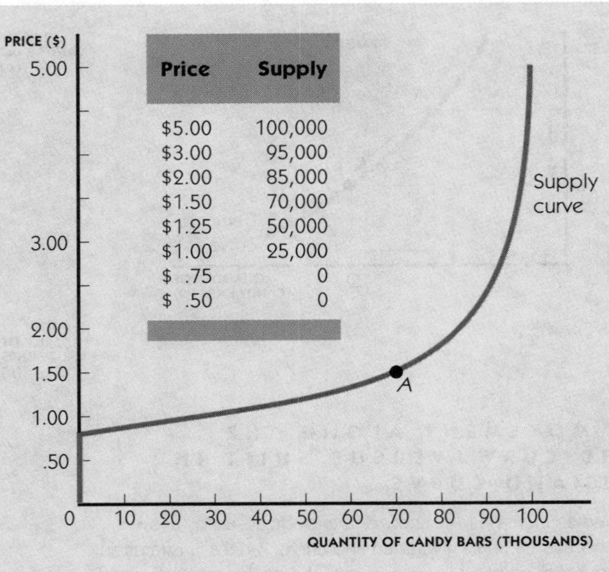

Price	Supply
$5.00	100,000
$3.00	95,000
$2.00	85,000
$1.50	70,000
$1.25	50,000
$1.00	25,000
$ .75	0
$ .50	0

Figure 3.7 ONE FIRM'S SUPPLY CURVE

The supply curve shows the quantity of a good a firm is willing to produce at each price. Normally a firm is willing to produce more as the price increases, which is why the supply curve slopes upward.

Figure 3.7 also depicts these points in a graph. The curve drawn by connecting the points is called the **supply curve.** It shows the quantity that Melt-in-the-Mouth will supply at each price, holding all other factors constant. As with the demand curve, we put the price on the vertical axis and the quantity supplied on the horizontal axis. Thus, we can read point *A* on the curve as indicating that at a price of $1.50 the firm would like to supply 70,000 candy bars.

In direct contrast to the demand curve, the typical supply curve slopes upward from left to right; at higher prices, firms will supply more. This is because higher prices yield suppliers higher profits—giving them an incentive to produce more.

SUPPLY CURVE

The supply curve gives the quantity of the good supplied at each price.

MARKET SUPPLY

The **market supply** of a good is simply the total quantity that all the firms in the economy are willing to supply at a given price. Similarly, the market supply of labor is simply the total quantity of labor that all the households in the economy are willing to supply at a given wage. Figure 3.8 tells us, for instance, that at a price of $2.00, firms will supply 70 million candy bars, while at a price of $.50, they will supply only 5 million.

Figure 3.8 also shows the same information graphically. The curve joining the points in the figure is the **market supply curve.** The market supply curve gives the total quantity of a good that firms are willing to produce at each price. Thus, we read point *A* on the market supply curve as showing that at a price of $.75, the firms in the economy would like to sell 20 million candy bars.

As the price of candy bars increases, the quantity supplied increases, other things equal. The market supply curve slopes upward from left to right for two reasons: at higher prices, each firm in the market is willing to produce more; and at higher prices, more firms are willing to enter the market to produce the good.

The market supply curve is calculated from the supply curves of the different firms in the same way that the market demand curve is calculated from the demand curves of the different households: at each price, we add horizontally the quantities that each of the firms is willing to produce.

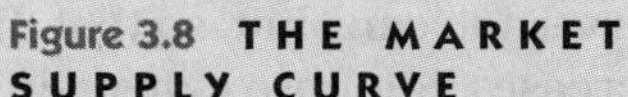

Figure 3.8 THE MARKET SUPPLY CURVE

The market supply curve shows the quantity of a good all firms in the market are willing to supply at each price. The market supply curve is normally upward sloping, both because each firm is willing to supply more of the good at a higher price and because higher prices entice new firms to produce.

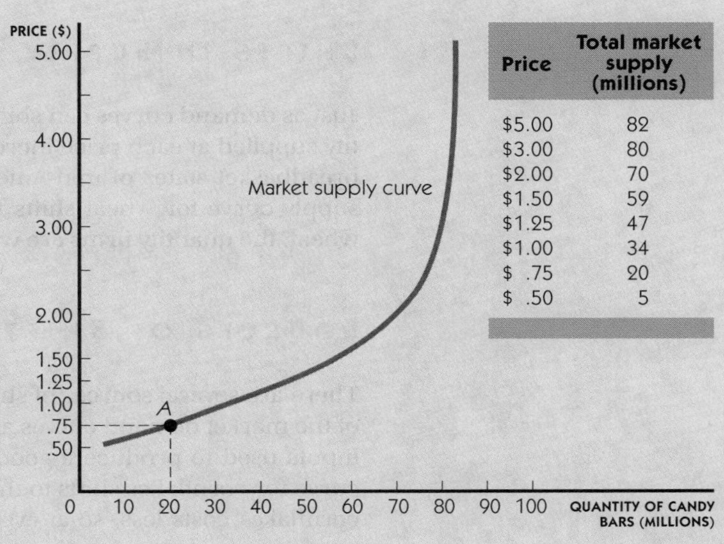

Price	Total market supply (millions)
$5.00	82
$3.00	80
$2.00	70
$1.50	59
$1.25	47
$1.00	34
$ .75	20
$ .50	5

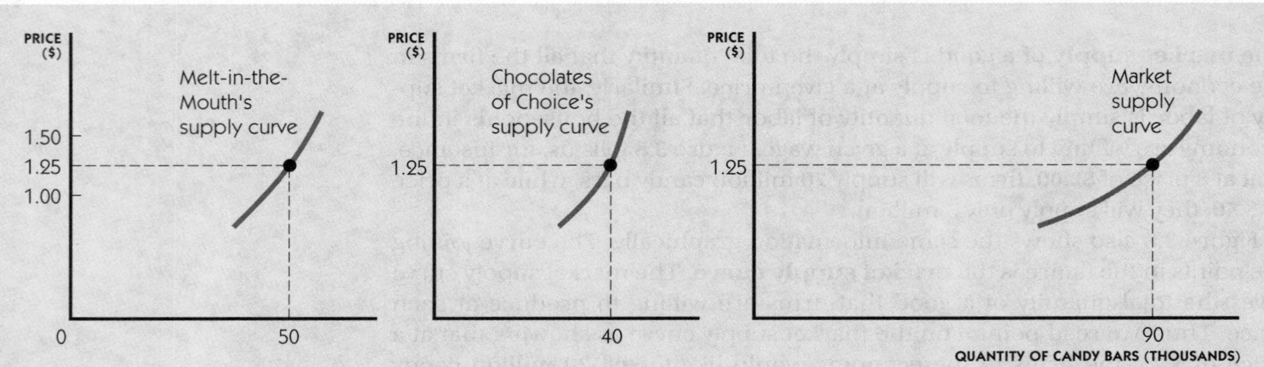

Figure 3.9 DERIVING THE MARKET SUPPLY CURVE

The market supply curve is constructed by adding up the quantity that each of the firms in the economy is willing to supply at each price. It shows what market supply would be if there were only two producers. Actual market supply, as depicted in Figure 3.8, is much larger because there are many producers.

Figure 3.9 shows how this is done in a market with only two producers. At a price of $1.25, Melt-in-the-Mouth Chocolate produces 50,000 candy bars, while the Chocolates of Choice Company produces 40,000. So the market supply is 90,000 bars.

SHIFTS IN SUPPLY CURVES

Just as demand curves can shift, supply curves too can shift, so that the quantity supplied at each price increases or decreases. Suppose a drought hits the breadbasket states of mid-America. Figure 3.10 illustrates the situation. The supply curve for wheat shifts to the left, which means that at each price of wheat, the quantity firms are willing to supply is smaller.

SOURCES OF SHIFTS IN SUPPLY CURVES

There are several sources of shifts in market supply curves, just as in the case of the market demand curves already discussed. One is changing prices of the inputs used to produce a good. As corn becomes less expensive, the supply curve for cornflakes shifts to the right, as illustrated in Figure 3.11. Producing cornflakes costs less, so at every price, firms are willing to supply a greater quantity.

Another source of shifts is changes in technology. The technological improvements in the computer industry over the past two decades have led to a

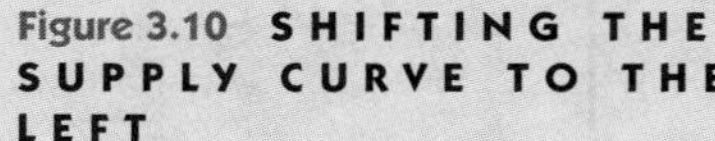

Figure 3.10 SHIFTING THE SUPPLY CURVE TO THE LEFT

A drought or other disaster (among other possible factors) will cause the supply curve to shift to the left, so that at each price, a smaller quantity is supplied.

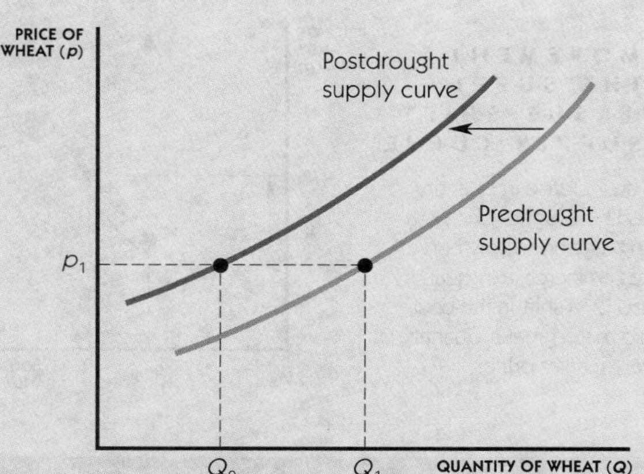

rightward shift in the market supply curve. Yet another source of shifts is nature. The supply curve for agricultural goods may shift to the right or left depending on weather conditions, insect infestations, or animal diseases.

Reduction in the availability of credit may curtail firms' ability to borrow to obtain inputs needed for production, and this too will induce a leftward shift in the supply curve. Finally, changed expectations can also lead to a shift in the supply curve. In early 1996, U.S. oil importers *expected* that the oil embargo against Iraq would be partially lifted; this would increase supplies and lower prices. In anticipation of this price decrease, they reduced their purchases of oil, using up inventories. When the embargo failed to be lifted, there was a scarcity: expectations had led to a leftward shift in the supply curve and oil prices soared.

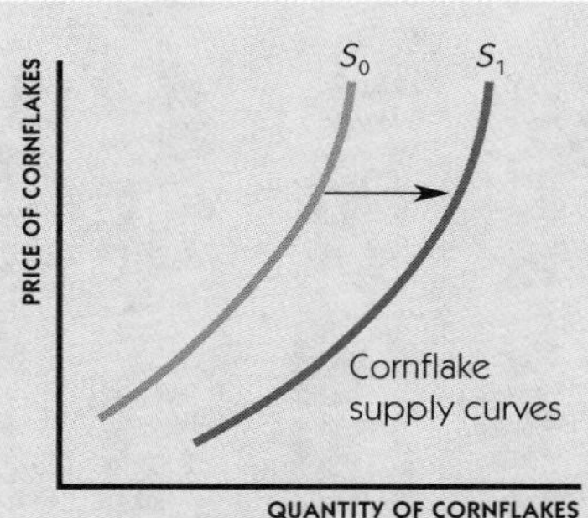

Figure 3.11 SHIFTING THE SUPPLY CURVE TO THE RIGHT

An improvement in technology or a reduction in input prices (among other possible factors) will cause the supply curve to shift to the right, so that at each price, a larger quantity is supplied.

Sources of Shifts in Market Supply Curves

A change in the prices of inputs
A change in technology
A change in the natural environment
A change in the availability of credit
A change in expectations

Figure 3.12 MOVEMENT ALONG THE SUPPLY CURVE VERSUS SHIFT IN THE SUPPLY CURVE

Panel A shows an increase in quantity supplied caused by a higher price—a movement along a given supply curve. Panel B illustrates an increase in quantity supplied caused by a shift in the entire supply curve, so that a greater quantity is supplied at every market price.

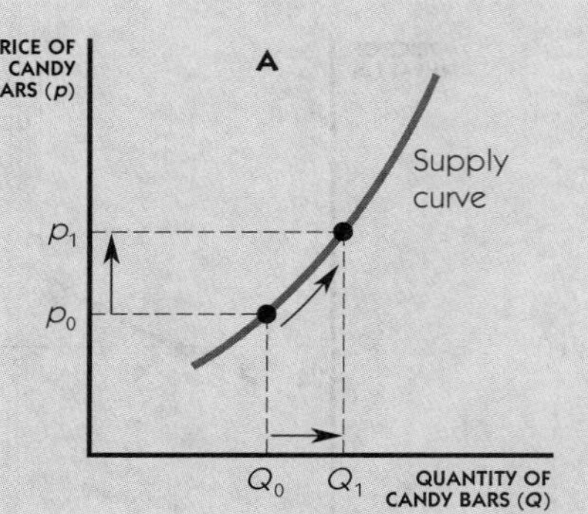

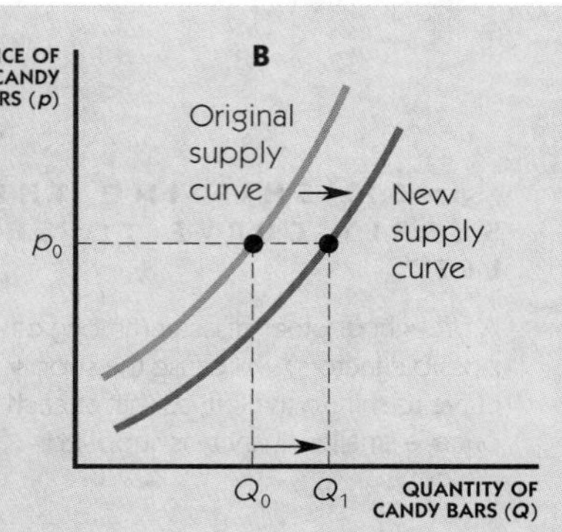

SHIFTS IN A SUPPLY CURVE VERSUS MOVEMENTS ALONG A SUPPLY CURVE

Distinguishing between a movement *along* a curve and a *shift* in the curve itself is just as important for supply curves as it is for demand curves. In Figure 3.12A, the price of candy bars has gone up, with a corresponding increase in quantity supplied. Thus, there has been a movement along the supply curve.

By contrast, in Figure 3.12B, the supply curve has shifted to the right, perhaps because a new production technique has made it cheaper to produce candy bars. Now, even though the price does not change, the quantity supplied increases. The quantity supplied in the market can increase either because the price of the good has increased, so that for a *given supply curve,* the quantity produced is higher; or because the supply curve has shifted, so that at a *given price,* the quantity supplied has increased.

LAW OF SUPPLY AND DEMAND

This chapter began with the assertion that supply and demand work together to determine the market price in competitive markets. Figure 3.13 puts a market supply curve and a market demand curve on the same graph to show how this happens. The price actually paid and received in the market will be determined by the intersection of the two curves. This point is labeled E_0, for equilibrium, and the corresponding price ($.75) and quantity (20 million) are called, respectively, the **equilibrium price** and the **equilibrium quantity.**

Since the term **equilibrium** will recur throughout the book, it is important to understand the concept clearly. Equilibrium describes a situation where

Figure 3.13 SUPPLY AND DEMAND EQUILIBRIUM

Equilibrium occurs at the intersection of the demand and supply curves, at point E_0. At any price above E_0, the quantity supplied will exceed the quantity demanded, the market will be out of equilibrium, and there will be excess supply. At any price below E_0, the quantity demanded will exceed the quantity supplied, the market will be out of equilibrium, and there will be excess demand.

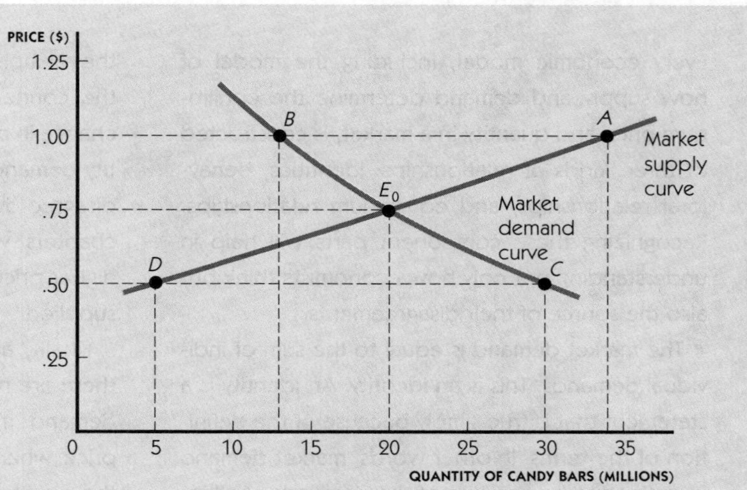

there are no forces (reasons) for change. No one has an incentive to change the result—the price or quantity in the case of supply and demand.

Physicists also speak of equilibrium in describing a weight hanging from a spring. Two forces are working on the weight. Gravity is pulling it down; the spring is pulling it up. When the weight is at rest, it is in equilibrium, with the two forces just offsetting each other. If one pulls the weight down a little bit, the force of the spring will be greater than the force of gravity, and the weight will spring up. In the absence of any further intrusions, the weight will bob back and forth and eventually reach its equilibrium position.

An economic equilibrium is established in the same way. At the equilibrium price, consumers get precisely the quantity of the good they are willing to buy at that price, and producers sell precisely the quantity they are willing to sell at that price. Neither producers nor consumers have any incentive to change.

But consider the price of $1.00 in Figure 3.13. This is not an equilibrium price. First find $1.00 on the vertical axis. Now look across to find point *A* on the supply curve, and read down to the horizontal axis; point *A* tells you that a price of $1.00, firms want to supply 34 million candy bars. Now look at point *B* on the demand curve. Point *B* shows that at a price of $1.00, consumers only want to buy 13 million candy bars. Like the weight bobbing on a spring however, this market will work its way back to equilibrium, in the following way. At a price of $1.00, there is **excess supply.** As producers discover that they cannot sell as much as they would like at this price, some of them will lower their prices slightly, hoping to take business from other producers. When one producer lowers prices, his competitors will have to respond, for fear that they will end up unable to sell their goods. As prices come down, consumers

Close-up: The Structure of Economic Models

Every economic model, including the model of how supply and demand determine the equilibrium price and quantity in a market, is constructed of three kinds of relationships: identities, behavioral relationships, and equilibrium relationships. Recognizing these component parts will help in understanding not only how economists think but also the source of their disagreements.

The market demand is equal to the sum of individual demands. This is an identity. An identity is a statement that is true simply because of the definition of the terms. In other words, market demand is *defined* to be the sum of the demands of all individuals. Similarly, it is an identity that market supply is equal to the sum of the supplies of all firms; the terms are defined in that way.

The demand curve represents a relationship between the price and the quantity demanded. Normally, as prices rise, the quantity of a good demanded decreases. This is a description of how individuals behave, and is called a behavioral relationship. The supply curve for each firm is also a behavioral relationship.

Economists may disagree over behavioral relationships. They may agree about the direction of the relationship but disagree about the strength of the connection. For any given product, does a change in price lead to a large change in the quantity demanded or a small one? But they may even disagree over the direction of the effect. As later chapters will discuss, in some special cases a higher price may actually lead to a *lower* quantity supplied.

Finally, an equilibrium relationship exists when there are no forces for change. In the supply and demand model, the equilibrium occurs at the price where the quantity demanded is equal to the quantity supplied. An equilibrium relationship is not the same as an identity. It is possible for the economy to be out of equilibrium, at least for a time. Of course, being out of equilibrium implies that there are forces for change pushing toward the equilibrium. But an identity must always hold true at all times, as a matter of definition.

Economists usually agree about what an equilibrium would look like, but they often differ on whether the forces pushing the markets toward equilibrium are strong or weak, and thus on whether the economy is typically close to equilibrium or may stray rather far from it.

will also buy more, and so on until the market reaches the equilibrium price and quantity.

Similarly, assume that the price is lower than $.75, say $.50. At the lower price, there is **excess demand:** individuals want to buy 30 million candy bars (point *C*), while firms only want to produce 5 million (point *D*). Consumers unable to purchase all they want will offer to pay a bit more; other consumers, afraid of having to do without, will match these higher bids or raise them. As prices start to increase, suppliers will also have a greater incentive to produce more. Again the market will tend toward the equilibrium point.

To repeat for emphasis: at equilibrium, no purchaser and no supplier has an incentive to change the price or quantity. In competitive market economies actual prices tend to be the equilibrium prices, at which demand equals supply. This is called the **law of supply and demand.** Note: this law does not mean that at every moment of time the price is precisely at the intersection of the demand and supply curves. As with the example of the weight and the spring, the market may bounce around a little bit when it is in the process of adjusting. What the law of supply and demand does say is that when a market is out of equilibrium, there are predictable forces for change.

USING DEMAND AND SUPPLY CURVES

The concepts of demand and supply curves—and market equilibrium as the intersection of demand and supply curves—constitute the economist's basic model of demand and supply. This model has proven to be extremely useful. It helps explain why the price of some commodity is high, and that of some other commodity is low. It also helps *predict* the consequences of certain changes. Its predictions can then be tested against what actually happens. One of the reasons that the model is so useful is that it gives reasonably accurate predictions.

Figure 3.14 repeats the demand and supply curve for candy bars. Assume, now, however, that sugar becomes more expensive. As a result, at each price, the amount firms are willing to supply is reduced. The supply curve shifts to the left, as in panel A. There will be a new equilibrium, at a higher price and a lower quantity of candy consumed. Alternatively, assume that Americans become more health conscious, and as a result, at each price fewer candy bars are consumed: the demand curve shifts to the left, as shown in panel B. Again, there will be a new equilibrium, at a lower price and a lower quantity of candy consumed. This illustrates how changes in observed prices can be related either to shifts in the demand curve or shifts in the supply curve.

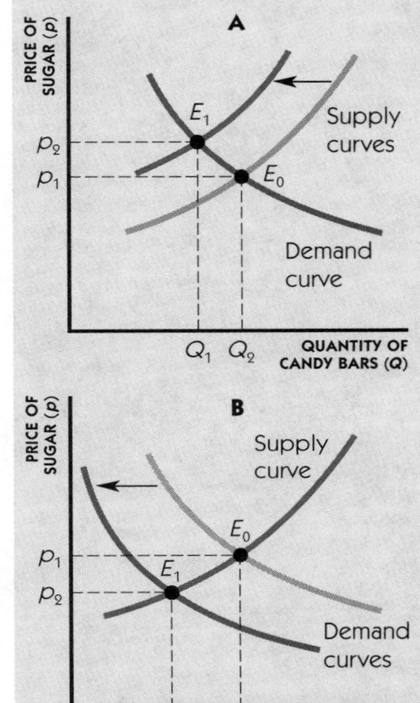

Figure 3.14 USING SUPPLY AND DEMAND CURVES TO PREDICT PRICE CHANGES

Initially the market for candy bars is in equilibrium at E_0. An increase in the cost of sugar shifts the supply curve to the left, as shown in panel A. At the new equilibrium, E_1, the price is higher and the quantity consumed is lower. A shift in taste away from candy results in a leftward shift in the demand curve as shown in panel B. At the new equilibrium, E_1, the price and the quantity consumed is lower.

CONSENSUS ON THE DETERMINATION OF PRICES

The law of supply and demand plays such an prominent role in economics that there is a joke about teaching a parrot to be an economist simply by teaching it to say "supply and demand." That prices are determined by the law of supply and demand is one of the most long-standing and widely accepted ideas of economists. It forms our fourth point of consensus.

4 Prices

In competitive markets, prices are determined by the law of supply and demand. Shifts in the demand and supply curves lead to changes in the equilibrium price. Similar principles apply to the labor and capital markets. The price for labor is the wage, and the price for capital is the interest rate.

QUANTIFYING THE EFFECTS OF PRICE CHANGES

So far, we have observed that the equilibrium price is determined by the intersection of the demand and supply curves, and that shifts in either the demand or the supply curve result in changes in the equilibrium price. The magnitude of the price change depends on the shape of the demand and supply curves.

THE PRICE ELASTICITY OF DEMAND

Figure 3.15 illustrates that a given shift in the supply curve has a large effect on price and a small effect on quantity if the demand curve is relatively steep; and a small effect on price and a large effect on quantity if the demand curve is relatively flat. When the demand curve is steep, a given change in price has a relatively small effect on quantity demanded; when the demand curve is flat, a given change in price has a large effect on quantity demanded. More formally, the sensitivity of demand to price changes is measured by the **price elasticity of demand** (for short, the price elasticity or the elasticity of demand). The price elasticity of demand is defined as the percentage change in the quantity demanded divided by the percentage change in price. In mathematical terms,

$$\text{elasticity of demand} = \frac{\text{percent change in quantity demanded}}{\text{percent change in price}}.$$

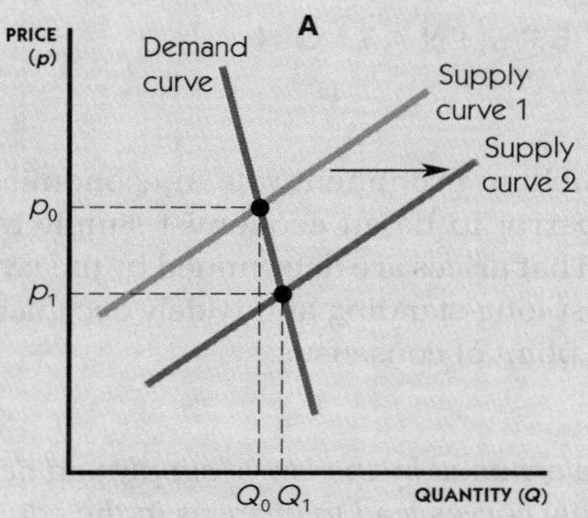

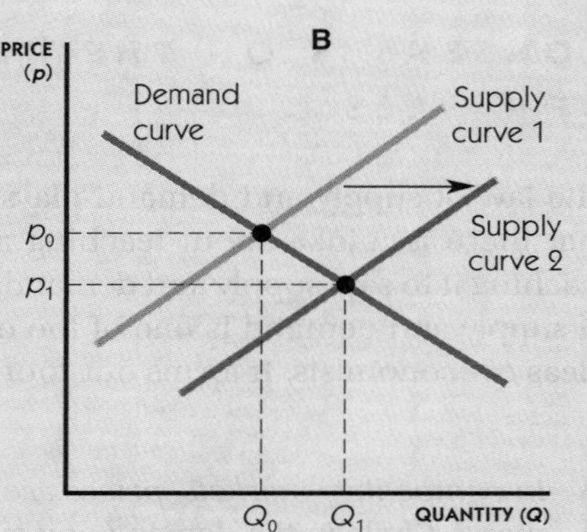

Figure 3.15 DIFFERENT EFFECTS ON PRICE OF A SHIFT IN THE SUPPLY CURVE

Panel A shows the effect of a shift in the supply curve when the demand curve is relatively steep. Panel B shows the effect when the demand curve is relatively flat. The change in the equilibrium price is greater when the demand curve is relatively steep (panel A).

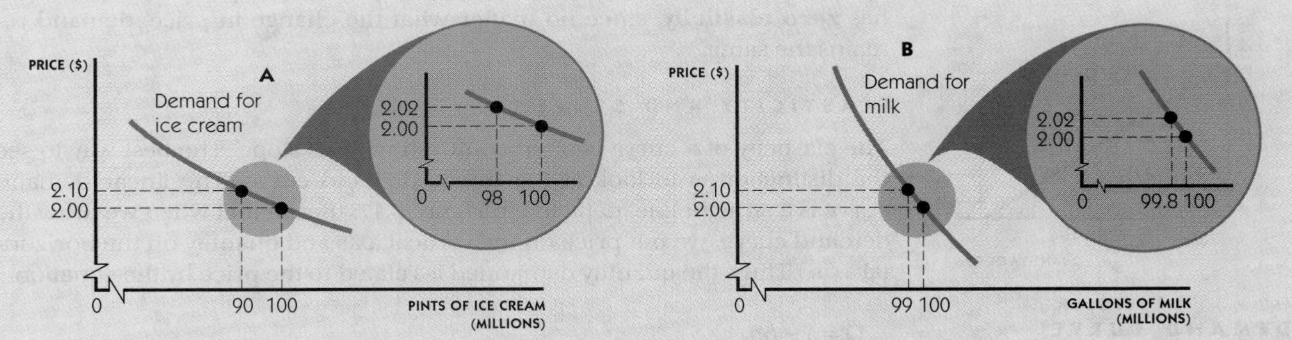

Figure 3.16 ELASTIC VERSUS INELASTIC DEMAND CURVES

Panel A shows a hypothetical demand curve for ice cream. Note that quantity demanded changes rapidly with fairly small price changes, indicating that demand for ice cream is elastic. The telescoped portion of the demand curve shows that a 1 percent rise in price leads to a 2 percent fall in quantity demanded. Panel B shows a hypothetical demand curve for milk. Note that quantity demanded changes very little, regardless of changes in price, meaning that demand for milk is inelastic. The telescoped portion of the demand curve shows that a 1 percent rise in price leads to a .2 percent fall in quantity demanded.

If the quantity demanded changes 8 percent in response to a 2 percent change in price, then the elasticity of demand is 4.

(Price elasticities of demand are really *negative* numbers; that is, when the price increases, quantities demanded are reduced. But the convention is to simply refer to the elasticity as a number with the understanding that it is negative.)

It is easiest to calculate the elasticity of demand when there is just a 1 percent change in price. Then the elasticity of demand is just the percent change in the quantity demanded. In the telescoped portion of Figure 3.16A, we see that increasing the price of ice cream from $2.00 a pint to $2.02—a 1 percent increase in price—reduces the demand from 100 million pints to 98 million, a 2 percent decline. So the price elasticity of demand for ice cream is 2.

By contrast, assume that the price of milk increases from $2.00 a gallon to $2.02 (again a 1 percent increase in price), as shown in the telescoped portion of Figure 3.16B. This reduces demand from 100 million gallons per year to 99.8 million. Demand has gone down by .2 percent, so the price elasticity of demand is therefore .2. Larger values for price elasticity indicate that demand is more sensitive to changes in price. Smaller values indicate that demand is less sensitive to price changes. When the price elasticity is less than one, we say that the demand is inelastic; when the price is greater than one, we say that the demand is elastic. Demand for necessities, like food, is typically inelastic while demand for luxuries, like perfume, is typically elastic.

There are two extreme cases. A flat demand curve is perfectly horizontal. We say that such a demand curve is perfectly elastic, or has **infinite elasticity,** since even a slight increase in the price results in demand dropping to zero. By contrast, a demand curve that is perfectly vertical is perfectly inelastic, or has **zero elasticity,** since no matter what the change in price, demand remains the same.

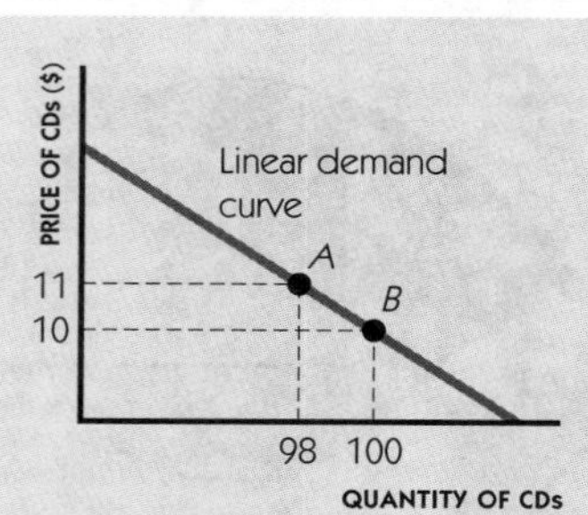

Figure 3.17 LINEAR DEMAND CURVE

The linear demand curve is a straight line; it is represented algebraicly by the equation $Q = a - bp$. The slope of the demand curve is a constant. However, the elasticity varies with output. At low outputs (high prices) it is very high. At high outputs (low prices) it is very low.

ELASTICITY AND SLOPE

The elasticity of a curve is often confused with its slope. The best way to see the distinction is to look at the **linear** demand curve. The linear demand curve is a straight line, depicted in Figure 3.17. (Recall that when we draw the demand curve, we put price on the vertical axis and quantity on the horizontal axis.) Thus, the quantity demanded is related to the price by the equation

$$Q = a - bp.$$

If $a = 100$, and $b = 2$, at a price of 1, $Q = 98$; at a price of \$2, $Q = 96$; at a price of \$3, $Q = 94$, and so forth. While the slope is constant, the elasticity is not. When $p = \$1$, a 1 percent price increase to \$1.01 reduces Q by .02, so the elasticity is $.02/98$ or approximately .0002. When the price is \$20, $Q = 60$. A 1 percent price increase to \$20.20 lowers Q by .4, so the elasticity is $.4/60$, or .0067.

THE DETERMINANTS OF THE ELASTICITY OF DEMAND

One of the important determinants of the elasticity of demand is the availability of substitutes. An important determinant of the degree of substitutability is the length of time to make an adjustment. Because it is always easier to find substitutes and to make other adjustments when you have a longer time to make them, the elasticity of demand is normally larger in the *long run*—in the period in which all adjustments can be made—than it is in the *short run,* when at least some adjustments cannot be made. Figure 3.18 illustrates the

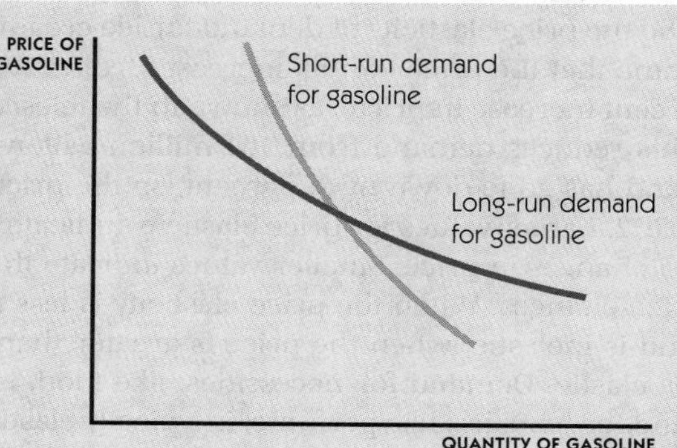

Figure 3.18 ELASTICITY OF DEMAND OVER TIME

Demand curves tend to be inelastic in the short run, when there is little time to adapt to price changes, but more elastic in the long run.

difference in shape between short-run and long-run demand curves for gasoline.

The sharp increase in oil prices in the 1970s provides an outstanding example. The short-run price elasticity of gasoline was .2 (a 1 percent increase in price led to only a .2 percent decrease in quantity demanded), while the long-run elasticity was .7 or more; the short-run elasticity of demand for fuel oil was .2, and the long-run elasticity was 1.2. In the short run, consumers were stuck with their old gas-guzzling cars, their drafty houses, and their old fuel-wasting habits. In the long run, however, consumers bought smaller cars, became used to houses with slightly lower temperatures, installed better insulation in their homes, and turned to alternative energy sources. The long-run demand curve was therefore much more elastic (flat) than the short-run curve. Indeed, the long-run elasticity turned out to be much larger than anticipated.

How long is the long run? There is no simple answer. It will vary from product to product. In some cases, adjustments can occur rapidly; in other cases, they are very gradual. As old gas guzzlers wore out, they were replaced with fuel-efficient compact cars. As furnaces wore out, they were replaced with more efficient ones. New homes are now constructed with more insulation, so that gradually, over time, the fraction of houses that are well insulated is increasing.

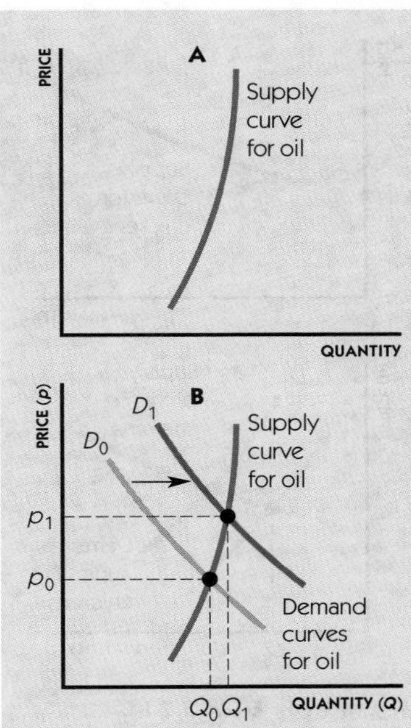

Figure 3.19 INELASTIC SUPPLY CURVE

Panel A shows the supply curve for oil. It is inelastic: quantity supplied increases only a small amount with a rise in price. Panel B shows the effect of a shift in the demand curve for oil. The change in price is large and the change in the quantity supplied is small.

THE PRICE ELASTICITY OF SUPPLY

Supply curves normally slope upward. As with demand curves, they are steep in some cases and flat in others. The degree of steepness reflects sensitivity to price changes. A steep supply curve, like the one for oil in Figure 3.19A, means that a large change in price generates only a small change in the quantity firms want to supply. Panel B of Figure 3.19 shows a shift in the demand curve for oil, which results in a large change in price, but little change in the quantity supplied. A flatter curve, like the one for chickens in Figure 3.20A, means that a small change in price generates a large change in supply. In Figure 3.20B, a shift in the demand curve for chickens results in a small change in price and a large change in the quantity supplied. Just as with demand, economists have developed a precise way of representing the sensitivity of supply to prices in a way that parallels the one already introduced. The **price elasticity of supply** is defined as the percentage change in quantity supplied divided by the percentage change in price (or the percentage change in quantity supplied corresponding to a price change of 1 percent).

$$\text{elasticity of supply} = \frac{\text{percentage change in quantity supplied}}{\text{percentage change in price}}.$$

The elasticity of supply of oil is low—an increase in the price of oil will not have a significant effect on the total supply. The elasticity of supply of chickens is high, as President Nixon found out when he imposed price controls in August 1971. When the price of chicken was forced lower than the market

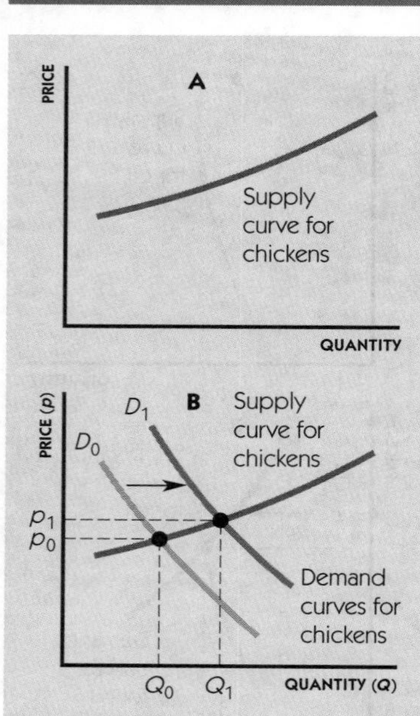

Figure 3.20 ELASTIC SUPPLY CURVE

Panel A shows a supply curve for chickens. It is elastic: quantity supplied increases substantially with a rise in price. Panel B shows the effect of a shift in the demand curve for chickens. The change in price is small and the change in the quantity supplied is large.

equilibrium price, less than 10 percent lower, farmers found it was simply unprofitable to produce chickens and sell them at that price; there was a large decrease in the quantity supplied, and the result was huge shortages.

As is the case with demand, if a 1 percent increase in price results in more than a 1 percent increase in supply, we say the supply curve is elastic. If a 1 percent increase in price results in less than a 1 percent increase in supply, the supply curve is inelastic. In the extreme case of a vertical supply curve—where the amount supplied does not depend at all on price—the curve is said to be perfectly inelastic, or to have *zero* elasticity; and in the extreme case of a horizontal supply curve, the curve is said to be perfectly elastic, or to have *infinite* elasticity.

The supply elasticity may differ at different points of the supply curve (just as the demand elasticity may differ at different points on the demand curve). Figure 3.21 shows a typical supply curve in manufacturing. An example might be ball bearings. At very low prices, plants are just covering their operating costs. Some plants shut down. In this situation, a small increase in price elicits a large increase in supply. The supply curve is relatively flat (elastic). But eventually, all machines are being worked, and factories are also working all three shifts. In this situation, it may be hard to increase supply further, so that the supply curve becomes close to vertical (inelastic). That is, however much the price increases, the supply will not change very much.

SHORT RUN VERSUS LONG RUN

Economists distinguish between the responsiveness of supply to price in the short run and in the long run, just as they do with demand. The long-run supply elasticity is greater than the short-run. We define the short-run supply curve as the supply response *given the current stock of machines and buildings.* The long-run supply curve assumes that firms can adjust the stock of machines and buildings.

Figure 3.21 CHANGING ELASTICITY ALONG A SUPPLY CURVE

When output is low and many machines are idle, a small change in price can lead to a large increase in quantity produced, so the supply curve is flat and elastic. When output is high and all machines are working close to their limit, it takes a very large price change to induce even a small change in output; the supply curve is steep and inelastic.

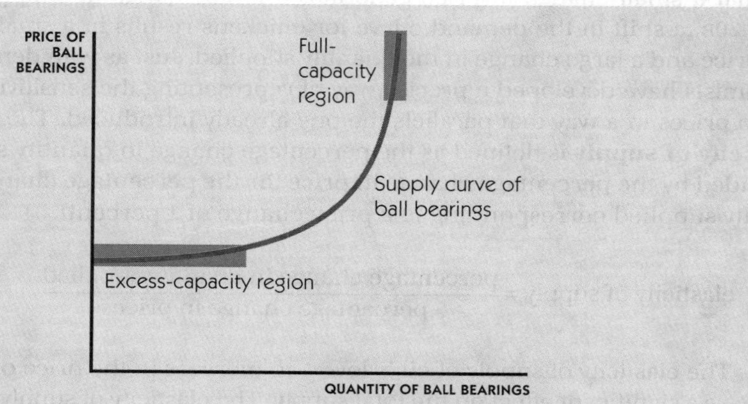

Farm crops are a typical example of a good whose supply in the short run is not very sensitive to changes in price; that is, the supply curve is steep (inelastic). After farmers have done their spring planting, they are committed to a certain level of production. If the price of their crop goes up, they cannot go back and plant more. If the price falls, they are stuck with the crop they have. In this case, the supply curve is relatively close to vertical, as illustrated by the steeper curve in Figure 3.22.

The long-run supply curve for many crops, in contrast, is very flat (elastic). A relatively small change in price can lead to a large change in the quantity supplied. A small increase in the price of soybeans relative to the price of corn may induce many farmers to shift their planting from corn and other crops to soybeans, generating a large increase in the quantity of soybeans. This is illustrated in Figure 3.22 by the flatter curve.

Earlier, we noted the response of consumers to the marked increase in the price of oil in the 1970s. The long-run demand elasticity was much higher than the short-run. So too for supply. The higher prices drove firms, both in the United States and abroad in places like Canada, Mexico, and the North Sea off the coast of Great Britain, to explore for more oil. Though the alternative supplies could not be increased much in the short run (the short-run supply curve was inelastic, or steep), in the long run new supplies were found. Thus, the long-run supply elasticity was much higher (the supply curve was flatter) than the short-run supply elasticity.

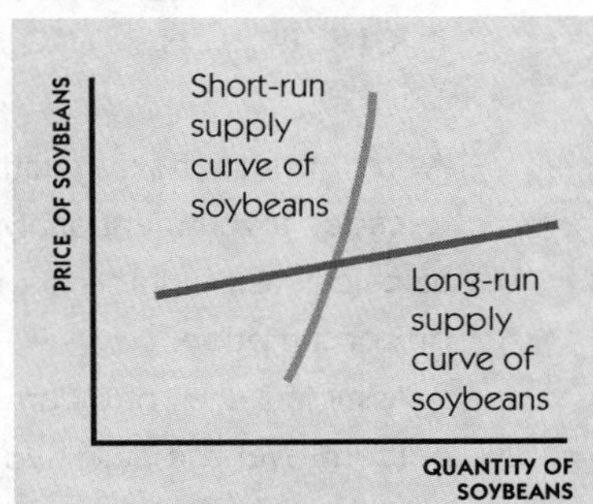

Figure 3.22 ELASTICITY OF SUPPLY OVER TIME

Supply curves may be inelastic in the short run and very elastic in the long run, as in the case of agricultural crops like soybeans.

SHORTAGES AND SURPLUSES

The law of supply and demand works so well in a developed modern economy most of the time that everyone can take it for granted. If you are willing to pay the "market price"—the prevailing price of the good, determined by the intersection of demand and supply—you can obtain almost any good or service. Similarly, if a seller of a good or service is willing to charge no more than the market price, he can always sell what he wants to.

When the price is set so that demand equals supply—so that any individual can get as much as she wants at that price, and any supplier can sell the amount he wants at that price—economists say that the market **clears.** But when the market does not clear, there are shortages or surpluses. A **shortage** means that people would like to buy something, but they simply cannot find as much of it as they would like to buy for sale at the going price. A **surplus** means that sellers would like to sell their product, but they cannot sell as much of it as they would like at the going price. The problem is that the "going price" is not the market equilibrium price.

At various times and for various goods, markets have not cleared. There have been shortages of apartments in New York; in 1973, there was a shortage of gasoline, with cars lined up in long lines outside of gasoline stations. Farm surpluses have plagued both Western Europe and the United States.

Using Economics: Calculating Responses to Oil Price Changes

As oil prices have fluctuated during the past decade, government analysts have repeatedly had to calculate the implications of those changes for oil consumption.

Assume prices of oil are expected to rise by 10 percent over the next two years. What will this do to the consumption of oil in the United States, if the elasticity of demand is .7? An elasticity of demand of .7 means that a 1 percent increase in price reduces demand by .7 percent. So a 10 percent increase in price will reduce demand by 7 percent. If the initial level of demand is 100 million barrels, demand will fall to 93 million.

What happens to total expenditures? If the initial price was $20 a barrel, total expenditures initially were $2 billion. Now, with a price of $22 a barrel (a 10 percent increase from $20), they have gone up to $22 × 93 million = $2.04 billion.

What happens to imports? The United States imports oil from abroad, and because the price of each barrel it imports has increased, it is worse off. But this is partly offset by the decreased use of oil. Assume the United States produces 50 million barrels, and that production remains unchanged. Initially, it imported 50 million barrels, but now, it imports only 43 million. U.S. expenditures on imports actually fall: before the expenditures were 50 million × $20 = $1 billion; now they are 43 million × $22 = $946 million.

In the long run, the elasticity of demand is greater, so the reduction in consumption is larger. If the long-run elasticity is 1, then consumption falls to 90 million barrels, and expenditures remain unchanged. Imports fall to 40 million barrels, with a value of $880 million.

Unemployment is a type of surplus, when people who want to work find that they cannot sell their labor services at the going wage.

In some markets, like the stock market, the adjustment of prices to shifts in the demand and supply curves tends to be very rapid. In other cases, such as in the housing market, the adjustments tend to be sluggish. When price adjustments are sluggish, shortages or surpluses may appear as prices adjust.

When the market is not adjusting quickly toward equilibrium, economists say that prices are **sticky.** Even in these cases, the analysis of market equilibrium is useful. It indicates the direction of the changes—if the equilibrium price exceeds the current price, prices will tend to rise. Moreover, the rate at which prices fall or rise is often related to the gap, at the going price, between the quantity demanded and the quantity supplied.

POLICY PERSPECTIVE: THE 1996 FARM BILL

For decades, the government has attempted to provide a safety net for farmers, ensuring that they would not be ravaged by low prices. Because demand and supply curves for agricultural products are highly inelastic, slight changes in supply caused by good weather can cause large decreases in price. Over the years, this protection has taken on a variety of forms. One was to provide a minimum price. Typically, this was set above the equilibrium price, resulting in huge surpluses, which the government purchased at a huge cost to taxpayers. To reduce these costs, planting limitations were imposed on farmers participating in the program. And eligibility to participate in the program was restricted to farmers who had previously participated in it. Thus, to receive support prices for corn, one had to keep one's land planted in corn. These policies reduced farmers' responses to price signals, and contributed to environmental degradation, because farmers could not rotate their crops or allow their land to remain fallow without losing eligibility for benefits.

The 1996 Farm Bill marked a major transformation of agricultural policy, by substituting fixed payments for price supports and allowing far more flexibility in planting. It was hoped that market forces would lead to a more efficient allocation of resources—but critics worried that the reduction of the safety net would present problems down the road, if farm prices should plummet, as they occasionally do. The question was, would farmers avail themselves of the opportunities provided by today's markets to insure themselves against these contingencies?

REVIEW AND PRACTICE

SUMMARY

1. An individual's demand curve gives the quantity demanded of a good at each possible price. It normally slopes down, which means that the person demands a greater quantity of the good at lower prices and a lesser quantity at higher prices.

2. The market demand curve gives the total quantity of a good demanded by all individuals in an economy at each price. As the price rises, demand falls, both because each person demands less of the good and because some people exit the market.

3. A firm's supply curve gives the amount of a good the firm is willing to supply at each price. It is normally upward sloping, which means that firms supply a greater quantity of the good at higher prices and a lesser quantity at lower prices.

4. The market supply curve gives the total quantity of a good that all firms in the economy are willing to produce at each price. As the price rises, supply rises, both because each firm supplies more of the good and because some additional firms enter the market.

5. The law of supply and demand says that in competitive markets, the equilibrium price is that price at which quantity demanded equals quantity supplied. It is represented on a graph by the intersection of the demand and supply curves.

6. A demand curve *only* shows the relationship between quantity demanded and price. Changes in tastes, in demographic factors, in income, in the prices of other goods, in information, in the availability of credit, or in expectations are reflected in a shift of the entire demand curve.

7. A supply curve *only* shows the relationship between quantity supplied and price. Changes in factors such as technology, the prices of inputs, the natural environment, expectations, or the availability of credit are reflected in a shift of the entire supply curve.

8. It is important to distinguish movements along a demand curve from shifts in the demand curve, and movements along a supply curve from shifts in the supply curve.

9. The price elasticity of demand describes how sensitive the quantity demanded of a good is to changes in the price of the good. When demand is inelastic, an increase in the price has little effect on quantity demanded; when demand is elastic, an increase in the price has a large effect on quantity demanded. Demand for necessities is usually quite inelastic; demand for luxuries is elastic.

10. The price elasticity of supply describes how sensitive the quantity supplied of a good is to changes in the price of the good. If price changes do not induce much change in supply, the supply curve is very steep and is said to be inelastic. If the supply curve is very flat, indicating that price changes cause large changes in supply, supply is said to be elastic.

11. The extent to which a shift in the supply curve is reflected in price or quantity depends on the shape of the demand curve. The more elastic the demand, the more a given shift in the supply curve will be reflected in changes in equilibrium quantities and the less it will be reflected in

changes in equilibrium prices. The more inelastic the demand, the more a given shift in the supply curve will be reflected in changes in equilibrium prices and the less it will be reflected in changes in equilibrium quantities. Likewise, the extent to which a shift in the demand curve is reflected in price or quantity depends on the shape of the supply curve.

12. Demand and supply curves are likely to be more elastic in the long run than in the short run. Therefore a shift in the demand or supply curve is likely to have a larger price effect in the short run and a larger quantity effect in the long run.

13. Price rigidity or stickiness implies that prices may not instantaneously adjust to the market clearing level. If the equilibrium price is higher than the current price, prices will tend to rise. The size of the gap between the quantity demanded and the quantity supplied affects the rate at which prices fall or rise.

KEY TERMS

demand curve
substitute
complement
demographic effects
supply curve
equilibrium price
excess supply
excess demand
price elasticity of demand
price elasticity of supply
infinite elasticity of demand
zero elasticity of demand
market clearing
sticky prices

REVIEW QUESTIONS

1. Why does an individual's demand curve normally slope down? Why does a market demand curve normally slope down?

2. Why does a firm's supply curve normally slope up? Why does a market supply curve normally slope up?

3. What is the significance of the point where supply and demand curves intersect?

4. Explain why, if the price of a good is above the equilibrium price, the forces of supply and demand will tend to push the price toward equilibrium. Explain why, if the price of the good is below the equilibrium price, the market will tend to adjust toward equilibrium.

5. Name some factors that could shift the demand curve out to the right.

6. Name some factors that could shift the supply curve in to the left.

7. What is meant by the elasticity of demand and the elasticity of supply? Why do economists find these concepts useful?

8. Is the slope of a perfectly elastic demand or supply curve horizontal or vertical? Is the slope of a perfectly inelastic demand or supply curve horizontal or vertical? Explain.

9. Under what condition will a shift in the demand curve result mainly in a change in quantity? in price?

10. Under what condition will a shift in the supply curve result mainly in a change in price? in quantity?

11. Why do the elasticities of demand and supply tend to change from the short run to the long run?

12. Why do sticky prices lead to shortages and surpluses?

PROBLEMS

1. Imagine a company lunchroom that sells pizza by the slice. Using the following data, plot the points and graph the demand and supply curves. What is the equilibrium price and quantity? Find a price at which excess demand would exist and a price at which excess supply would exist, and plot them on your diagram.

Price per slice	Demand (number of slices)	Supply (number of slices)
$1	420	0
$2	210	100
$3	140	140
$4	105	160
$5	84	170

2. Suppose a severe drought hit the sugarcane crop. Predict how this would affect the equilibrium price and quantity in the market for sugar and the market for honey. Draw supply and demand diagrams to illustrate your answers.

3. Imagine that a new invention allows each mine worker to mine twice as much coal. Predict how this will affect the equilibrium price and quantity in the market for coal and the market for heating oil. Draw supply and demand diagrams to illustrate your answer.

4. Americans' tastes have shifted away from beef and toward chicken. Predict how this change affects the equilibrium price and quantity in the market for beef, the market for chicken, and the market for roadside hamburger stands. Draw supply and demand diagrams to illustrate your answer.

5. During the 1970s, the postwar baby boomers reached working age, and it became more acceptable for married women with children to work. Predict how this increase in the number of workers is likely to affect the equilibrium wage and quantity of employment. Draw supply and demand curves to illustrate your answer.

6. Suppose the price elasticity of demand for gasoline is .2 in the short run and .7 in the long run. If the price of gasoline rises 28 percent, what effect on quantity demanded will this have in the short run? in the long run?

7. Imagine that the short-run price elasticity of supply for a farmer's corn is .3, while the long-run price elasticity is 2. If prices for corn fall 30 percent, what are the short-run and long-run changes in quantity supplied? What are the short- and long-run changes in quantity supplied if prices rise by 15 percent? What happens to the farmer's revenues in each of these situations?

8. Assume that the demand curve for hard liquor is highly inelastic and the supply curve for hard liquor is highly elastic. If the tastes of the drinking public shift away from hard liquor, will the effect be larger on price or on quantity? If the federal government decides to impose a tax on manufacturers of hard liquor, will the effects be larger on price or on quantity? What is the effect of an advertising program that succeeds in discouraging people from drinking? Draw diagrams to illustrate each of your answers.

9. Imagine that wages (the price of labor) are sticky in the labor market, and that a supply of new workers enters that market. Will the market be in equilibrium in the short run? Why or why not? If not, explain the relationship you would expect to see between the quantity demanded and supplied, and draw a diagram to illustrate. Explain how sticky wages in the labor market affect unemployment.

PART TWO

FULL-EMPLOYMENT MACRO-ECONOMICS

"Peace and prosperity" is the slogan on which many political candidates have run for office, and the failure to maintain prosperity has led to many a government's defeat. There is widespread belief among the citizenry that government is responsible for maintaining the economy at full employment, with stable prices, and for creating an economic environment in which growth can occur. This belief is reflected in the Full Employment Act of 1946, which stated that "it is the continuing policy and responsibility of the Federal Government to use all practicable means . . . to promote maximum employment, production, and purchasing power."

Although most economists still agree with these sentiments, there are dissenting views. Some claim that the government has relatively little power to control most of the fluctuations in output and employment; some argue that, apart from isolated instances such as the Great Depression of the 1930s, neither inflation nor unemployment is a major *economic* problem (though they obviously remain political problems); and some believe that government has been as much a cause of the problems of unemployment, inflation, and slow growth as part of their solution. We will explore these various interpretations in greater depth in the chapters that follow.

The problems of unemployment, inflation, and growth relate to the performance of the entire economy. Earlier in the book, we learned how the law of supply and demand operates in the market for oranges, apples, or other goods. At any one time, one industry may be doing well, another poorly. Yet to understand the forces that determine how well the economy as a whole is doing, we want to see beyond the vagaries that affect any particular industry. This is the domain of macroeconomics. Macroeconomics focuses not on the output of single products like orange juice or peanut butter, nor on the demand for masons or bricklayers or computer programmers. Rather, it is concerned with the characteristics of an entire economy, such as the overall level of output, the total level of employment, and the stability of the overall level of prices. What accounts for the "diseases" that sometimes affect the economy—the episodes of massive unemployment, rising prices, or economic stagnation—and what can the government do, both to prevent the onset of these diseases and to cure them once they have occurred?

Macroeconomic *theory* is concerned with what determines the level of employment and output as well as the rate of inflation and the overall growth rate of the economy; while macroeconomic *policy* focuses on what government can do to stimulate employment, prevent inflation, and increase the economy's growth rate.

We begin our study of macroeconomics in Chapter 4 by learning the major statistics used to assess the state of the economy—the rates of unemployment, inflation, and growth. Chapters 5 and 6 then build on the microeconomic analysis of Part Two to construct an *aggregate* model of the economy. Chapter 5 uses the demand and supply curves introduced in Chapter 3 to show how equilibrium in the labor market determines the wage rate, equilibrium in the product market determines prices, and equilibrium in the capital market determines interest rates. It goes on to show how all markets are interrelated, and that there is a circular flow in the economy, with income that households receive from firms—in the form of wages for their labor or as a return to the capital they invest—flowing back to firms in the form of purchases of goods, or additional investments.

Chapter 6 uses these microfoundations as building blocks to construct an aggregate model. In this basic aggregate model, we assume there is full employment. The rate of growth is determined, in part, by the level of investment that emerges from the market equilibrium. And changes in the price level (and the rate of inflation) are determined by changes in the money supply.

International trade plays an increasingly important role in the U.S. economy. Exports have been expanding far faster than the economy as a whole has been growing. And the United States has been borrowing annually billions of dollars from abroad. Thus, international economic relations affect both the product and capital markets, as Chapter 6 also discusses.

One of the most frequently discussed issues of the U.S. economy in the last few years has been the soaring trade deficit and the soaring fiscal deficit—the huge excess of federal expenditures over taxes, reaching almost 5 percent of the economy's output in 1992. Chapter 7 uses the full-employment model of Chapter 6 to address these and several important questions. It shows, for instance, that to a large extent, the trade deficit is a *consequence* of the fiscal deficit, and that another consequence of the fiscal deficit is lower economic growth.

CHAPTER 4

Macroeconomic Goals and Measures

Just as doctors take a patient's temperature to help them determine just how sick the patient is, economists use statistics to get a quantitative measure of the economy's performance. This chapter introduces the major statistics that summarize the overall condition of the economy. In studying these measures, economists look for patterns. Are good years regularly followed by lean years? Does inflation usually accompany high employment levels? If they find patterns, they ask why.

This chapter also discusses problems of measurement that affect almost every economic variable. When the rate of unemployment or inflation changes by a few tenths of a percent it often means little, just as there is rarely cause for alarm when a person's temperature changes by a tenth of a degree. But over time, the statistics describing the economy may change more dramatically. When unemployment statistics show an increase from 5 percent to 10 percent (that is, a change from one out of twenty workers without jobs to one out of ten), few would doubt that there has been a sizable increase in unemployment.

The sections below discuss unemployment, inflation, and growth, and explain how each is measured.

KEY QUESTIONS

1. What are the main objectives of macroeconomic policy?
2. How are unemployment, output, growth, and inflation measured?
3. What are some of the central problems in measuring these variables?

THE THREE MACROECONOMIC ILLS

Chapter 1 characterized the economy in terms of a set of interconnected labor, product, and capital markets. The diagram often referred to as the circular flow diagram in Figure 1.5 shows firms obtaining labor and capital from households and using it to produce goods, which are then sold to households, who buy the goods with the income they earn providing labor and capital to firms. Given these interconnections, it is not surprising that problems in one part of the economy may be manifested in other parts. The symptoms in one part may indicate disease elsewhere in the system.

Later chapters will enable us to understand the entire system. Here we focus on the symptoms, each of which is most closely associated with a particular part of the system.

In the 1992 presidential election campaign, two slogans struck a responsive chord: "It's the economy, stupid!" and "Jobs, Jobs, Jobs." America was entering the third year of an economic slowdown. Even though by historical standards, the **unemployment rate** was not very high—one out of thirteen workers was without a job—many faced the threat of unemployment, and anxiety levels were high. And even this level of unemployment represented a significant departure from the basic competitive model, which assumes that all resources—including labor—are fully employed, with demand equaling supply.

Two years later, policymakers began to worry about another problem: **inflation,** or rising prices. These price increases were, again by historical standards, moderate, about 2 to 4 percent a year. But policymakers feared the rate of inflation would grow. Only fifteen years earlier, inflation had hit double digit levels (13.3 percent in 1979). Still, the U.S. experience has been tame compared to that in other countries. In Ukraine, the inflation rate recently hit 10,000 percent a year! Inflation—the continual increase in prices month to month—means the demand and supply of goods in the product market are not in equilibrium at a stable price level.

Although we may focus on unemployment or inflation at any given moment, the real long-run concern is living standards. In the early 1970s, average Americans expected not only their children to enjoy better living standards, but also expected their own incomes to rise continually over time—a pattern that had held true for more than a century. But things started unraveling around 1973. Average family incomes stagnated, and those at the lower part of the income distribution fell, sometimes dramatically. The problem was inadequate **economic growth.** It was partly due to insufficient amounts of money going from the capital market to fund new investments and new innovations.

These three ills, unemployment, inflation, and lack of growth, are the diseases that macroeconomists are constantly trying to fight, with varying degrees of success.

THREE GOALS OF MACROECONOMIC POLICY

Full employment
Low inflation
Rapid growth

GROWTH

For generations, Americans had simply taken for granted that each generation would be better off than the previous one, and for decades Americans had presumed that their firms would be the most competitive and productive in the world. The continued increases in productivity (output per hour) provided the basis for continued increases in standards of living. Beginning around 1973, doubts arose concerning these expectations. The rate of increase in productivity slowed down: from around 3 percent per year from 1950 to 1973, to about 1 percent per year from 1973 to 1995. These changes were reflected in slow growth of standards of living for ordinary Americans.

In comparing countries, as well as comparing output within the same country over time, we have to adjust for differences in population. **Output per capita** simply divides total output by the population. As Figure 4.1 shows, Japan and several other countries of East Asia in the past two decades experienced far more rapid growth in output per capita than the United States. For years, Americans could take comfort in the idea that they were simply catching up. But by the 1980s, in some industries productivity in Japan exceeded that in the United States.

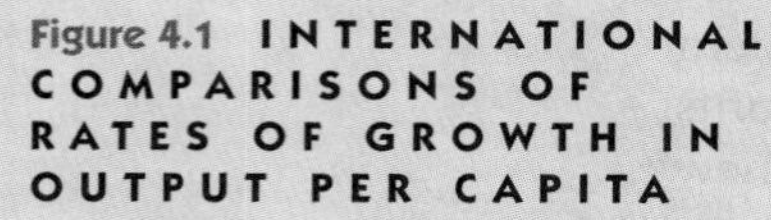

Figure 4.1 INTERNATIONAL COMPARISONS OF RATES OF GROWTH IN OUTPUT PER CAPITA

Other countries have been growing more rapidly in recent decades than the United States.

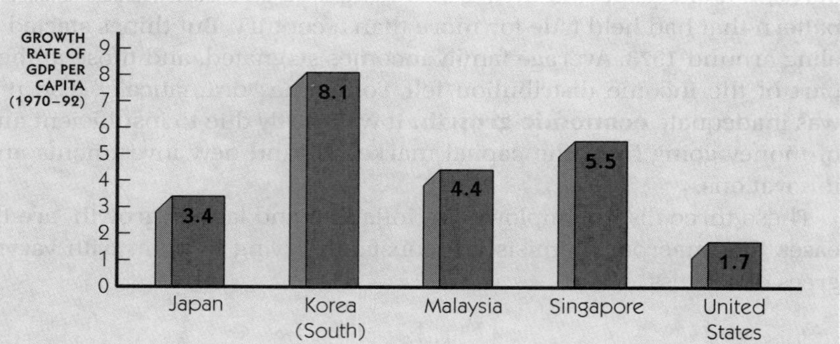

MEASURING OUTPUT

The output of the economy consists of millions of different goods. We could report how much of each good the economy produced: 1,362,478 hammers, 473,562,382 potatoes, 7,875,342 wristwatches, and so forth. Such data may be useful for some purposes, but they do not provide us with the information we want. If next year the output of hammers goes up by 5 percent, the output of potatoes goes down by 2 percent, and the output of wristwatches rises by 7 percent, has total output gone up or down? And by how much?

We need a single number that summarizes the output of the economy. But how do we add up the hammers, potatoes, wristwatches, and billions of other products produced in the economy? We do this by adding the money value of all the final goods (goods that are not used to make other goods) produced and arriving at a single number that encapsulates the production of the economy. This number is called the **gross domestic product,** or **GDP.** It is the standard measure of the output of an economy, and sums up the total money value of the goods and services produced by the residents of a nation during a specified period. GDP includes everything from buttons to air travel, and from haircuts to barrels of oil. It makes no difference whether the production takes place in the public or private sector, or whether the goods and services are purchased by households or by government.[1]

There is one problem with using money as a measure of output. The value of a dollar changes over time. Candy bars, books, movie tickets, hammers, all cost more today than they did ten years ago. Another way of saying this is that a dollar does not buy as much as it did ten years ago. We do not want to be misled into believing that the output is higher when in fact only prices have risen.

[1]We use prices not only because they are a convenient way of making comparisons, but also because prices reflect how consumers value different goods. If the price of an orange is twice that of an apple, it means an orange is worth twice as much (at the margin) as an apple.

To keep the comparisons of different years straight, economists adjust GDP for changes in the average level of prices. Unadjusted GDP is known as **nominal GDP.** The term **real GDP** is used for inflation-adjusted GDP figures, which are truer year-to-year measures of what the economy actually produces. To calculate real GDP, economists simply take the nominal value of GDP—the money value of all the goods and services produced in the economy—and divide it by a measure of the price level. Thus, real GDP is defined by the equation

$$\text{real GDP} = \frac{\text{nominal GDP}}{\text{price level}}.$$

If nominal GDP has risen 3 percent in the past year but inflation has also increased prices by 3 percent, then real GDP is unchanged.

Another way of thinking about real GDP is to ask, what would GDP be if prices had remained unchanged; that is, simply add up the number of apples produced today times the price of apples (in the "base" year, a year which is used as a point of reference) plus the number of oranges produced today times the price of oranges (in the base year). This calculation gives the *real value* of GDP today using base year prices.

This approach encounters a problem when *relative* prices change dramatically. If the price of computers should fall rapidly as the output of computers increases—as has happened over the past two decades—then real output, using an earlier base year, such as 1987, will look like it is increasing very rapidly. When the base year is changed—as is done periodically—the growth of the economy will appear to diminish suddenly; in the *new* base year, computer prices are lower so each computer "counts" for less in GDP. Of course, the growth of the economy did not really diminish; it was only that our yardstick distorted the picture.

To avoid this problem, the Bureau of Economic Analysis, the government agency responsible for the GDP numbers, changed its methodology in January 1996. It now provides a measure which is called the **chain-weighted real GDP.** It uses 1995 prices to calculate real income in 1996; 1996 prices to calculate real income in 1997; and so forth. This measure allows us to say how much GDP would have grown this year, if prices had remained unchanged at last year's levels. If output in 1997 is 3 percent higher than output in 1996, and output in 1996 is 2 percent higher than that in 1995, then 1997 output is 5 percent higher than 1995 output.

POTENTIAL GDP

GDP measures how much the economy actually produces. But sometimes the economy is capable of producing more than it actually does. Another measure, **potential GDP,** indicates what the economy *could* produce if labor and machines were used fully to their capacity.

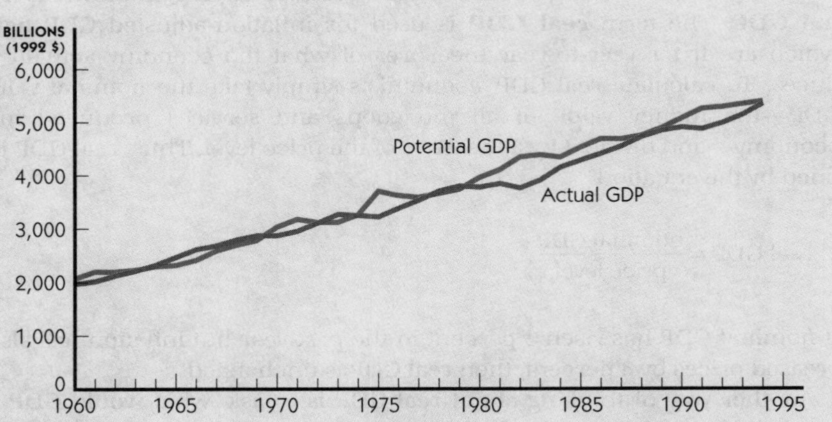

Figure 4.2 POTENTIAL AND ACTUAL GDP

Potential GDP measures how much the economy would produce if it used all its resources. Actual GDP shows what the economy actually produces. Notice that both have been growing over time. *Source: ERP* (1996), Tables B-2, B-50.

Figure 4.2 shows how potential (real) GDP and actual (real) GDP have increased over the past quarter century.[2] Output does not grow smoothly, and there have been periods in which actual output has been far below potential output. The jagged progression in the figure shows the effect of short-term fluctuations around an upward trend. Sometimes these fluctuations represent only a slowdown in the rate of growth; sometimes output actually falls. The dips in real GDP from 1971 to 1973, from 1980 to 1981, and from 1990 to 1991 represent periods when U.S. economic output actually declined. Strong upward fluctuations are called **booms,** and downward ones are called **recessions.** Severe downturns are referred to as **depressions.** The last depression, called the Great Depression because of its length and depth, began in 1929. The economy did not fully recover from it until World War II. While there is no technical definition of a boom, a recession is said to have occurred when GDP falls for at least two consecutive quarters. (For statistical purposes, the year is divided into quarters.)

The economy's fluctuations are sometimes referred to as **business cycles.** But the term cycle suggests a degree of regularity that is not really present. Though it is true that every so often the economy has a downturn, the time between one **trough** (the bottom of a recession) and another, or one **peak** (the top of a boom) and another, is highly variable, from just a few years, to as many as eight. Indeed, the likelihood of a downturn in the economy after, say, five years from the previous trough is no greater than three years from the

[2]Figure 4.2 shows actual GDP exceeding potential GDP in a few years. How is this possible, if potential GDP really measures what the economy *could* produce? The answer is that the estimates of potential GDP are based on assumptions about normal levels of unemployment and on the fact that even when the economy is quite strong, some capacity is not fully utilized. In fact, for short spurts of time, such as when a country goes to war, actual GDP can exceed estimates of potential GDP by a considerable amount.

Figure 4.3 CAPACITY UTILIZATION

Capacity utilization measures the fraction of machines and buildings that are actually in use. Notice that the figure fluctuates between about 70 and 90 percent as the economy moves between booms and recessions. *Source: ERP* (1996), Table B-50.

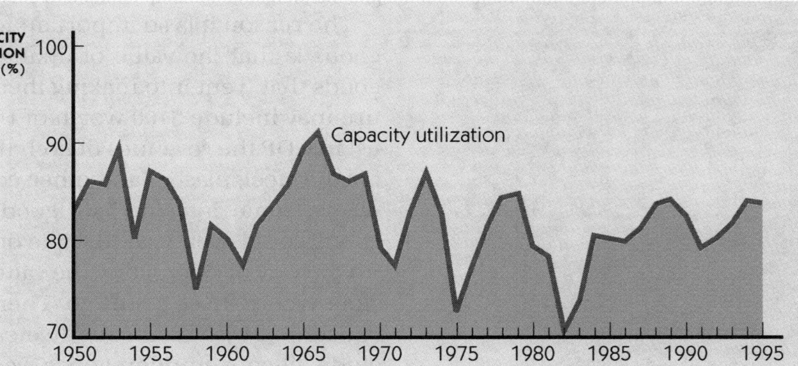

previous trough, and even sophisticated statistical models cannot predict accurately the next turning point in the economy.

In recessions the economy operates well below its potential. Unemployment is high and a large fraction of machines remain idle. Figure 4.3 shows the percentage of America's industrial capacity that was utilized for the past several decades. The figures vary from slightly more than 70 percent of industrial capacity in a recession to over 90 percent of industrial capacity in a boom. (Because some machines are being repaired and maintained, while other are idle because they are not suited for the economy's current structure, the economy never shows a 100 percent capacity utilization rate.) Low-capacity utilization, like unemployment of workers, represents a waste of scarce economic resources.

MEASURING GDP: THE VALUE OF OUTPUT

There are three approaches to measuring GDP (whether real or nominal), each of which yields the same result. Two concentrate on output data. The third—relying on the fact that the value of output all becomes income to someone—uses income figures to obtain a measure of output.

THE FINAL GOODS APPROACH

On the face of it, measuring GDP is a straightforward task, albeit massive. One gathers together the dollar values of all goods and services sold in a country, and then adds them up. Unfortunately, matters are not this simple, because it is first necessary to distinguish between final goods and intermediate goods. Final goods—like automobiles, books, bread, and shoes—are sold to consumers. Intermediate goods are used to produce outputs—such as coal when used to make steel, or apples when used to make applesauce. A good such as an apple can be either a final or an intermediate good, depending on how it is used. The **final goods approach** to GDP adds up the total dollar value of goods and services produced, categorized by their ultimate users.

The reason it is so important to distinguish between final and intermediate goods is that the value of final goods *includes* the value of the intermediate goods that went into making them. When Ford sells a car for $12,000, that figure may include $100 worth of Uniroyal tires. It would be double counting to list in GDP the revenues of both the car maker and the tire producer. Likewise for the steel, plastic, and other components that go into the car. In fact, cases where some intermediate goods are used to produce other intermediate goods could even lead to triple or quadruple counting.

One way of calculating the value of the final goods of the economy is to consider where those goods go. There are four possibilities. Some final goods are consumed by individuals—we call this aggregate **consumption** (and we include all consumption goods, regardless of where they are produced). Some are used by firms to build buildings and make machines—this is called aggregate **investment** (again, we include all investment goods, regardless of where they are produced). Some are purchased by government, and are called **government spending.** And, some of the goods, called **exports,** go abroad. If we didn't import (that is, buy from abroad) any goods, then GDP would simply consist of goods that went for private consumption, private investment, to the government, or for export. But not all consumption, investment, or government purchases is produced at home. We, therefore, need a final step to get GDP by this method. We have to subtract the amount imported. Thus,

$$\text{GDP} = C + I + G + X - M$$

where C = consumption, I = investment, G = government purchases, X = exports, and M = imports. The difference between exports and imports is referred to as **net exports.** This equation is an **identity,** that is, it is always true (by definition) that GDP equals consumption plus investment plus government expenditures plus net exports.

GDP equals consumption plus investment plus government expenditures plus exports minus imports.

THE VALUE-ADDED APPROACH

A second way to calculate the value of GDP is to study the intermediate goods directly. The production of most items occurs in several stages. Consider the automobile. At one stage in its production, iron ore, coal, and limestone are mined. At a second stage, these raw materials are shipped to a steel mill. A third stage finds a steel company combining these ingredients to make steel.

Policy Perspective: A Slowdown in Economic Growth?

In early 1996, a controversy broke out over whether the U.S. economy could grow faster than it had been growing over the last twenty years. Growth since 1973 had been markedly slower than in the 1950s and 1960s. While the policy discussion focused on how to make the economy grow faster, economists pointed out that some of the apparent slowdown might only be a statistical artifact, arising from well-known measurement problems.

MEASURING QUALITY CHANGES

With many products, such as computers, quality changes almost every year. GDP statisticians try to make adjustments for changes in quality. For example, when antipollution devices were first required in automobiles in the early 1970s, the price of cars rose. The national income accountants decided that the increased cost was a quality improvement and effectively added to real output: consumers were buying a better car. But in some sectors, such as the financial and health sectors and the computer industry, the adjustments may be inadequate. The real growth of GDP is accordingly understated, and because these sectors are expanding rapidly, the magnitude of the understatement may be larger today than it was thirty years ago.

MEASURING GOVERNMENT SERVICES

The standard GDP calculation measures price and quantity at the point of sale. But what about goods that are not sold, at least not directly?

One important category of such goods is government-produced services. Imagine that state government bureaucrats become more efficient and are able to process automobile registrations faster. This might mean that the state can hire fewer workers to do the same job. But GDP statistics simply reflect the number of hours worked by government officials, not the actual value of what they produce. If the government becomes more efficient, measured GDP might go down, even though actual output—the number of registrations—increases. In this case, the conventional GDP measure would again understate the real growth of the economy.

MEASURING NONMARKETED GOODS

Nonmarketed goods and services, like housework done by family members, present similar problems. The statistics underestimate the true level of production in the economy, because they ignore such economic activity. For example, if one spouse stays at home and cleans and cooks, that would not be measured in GDP. However, if that spouse leaves home to take a job and hires someone else to do the cleaning and cooking, then both the spouse and the housekeeper would be measured in GDP.

If, in this way, more and more previously nonmarketed goods and services become part of the economy's measured output, then measured growth will overstate the actual growth of the economy.

Finally, the steel and other inputs, such as rubber and plastics, are combined by the automobile firm to make a car. The difference in value between what the automaker pays for intermediate goods and what it receives for the finished cars is called the firm's **value added.**

Value added = firm's revenues − cost of intermediate goods. GDP can be measured by calculating the value added at each stage of production.

GDP = sum of value added of all firms.

THE INCOME APPROACH

The third method used to calculate GDP involves measuring the income generated by selling products, rather than the value of the products themselves. This is known as the **income approach.** Firms do five things with their revenues. They pay for labor, they pay interest, they buy intermediate goods, they pay indirect taxes such as excise taxes, and they enjoy what is left over as profits.

Revenues = wages + interest payments + cost of intermediate inputs + indirect taxes + profits.

But we already know that the firm's value added is its revenue minus the cost of intermediate goods. Therefore, value added = wages + interest payments + indirect taxes + profits. And since the value of GDP is equal to the sum of the value added of all firms, GDP must also equal the sum of the value of all wage payments, interest payments, taxes, and profits for all firms:

GDP = wages + interest payments + indirect taxes + profits.

People receive income from wages, from capital, and from profits of the firms they own (or own shares in). Thus, the right-hand side of this identity is just the total income of all individuals plus government revenue from indirect taxes. This is an extremely important result, one economists use frequently, so it is worth highlighting: *aggregate output equals aggregate income.*

Differences between Individual Incomes and National Income The notion of income used above to calculate GDP differs slightly from the way individuals commonly perceive income, and it is important to be aware of the distinction.

First, people are likely to include in their view of income any capital gains they earn. **Capital gains** are increases in the value of assets, and accordingly do not represent production (output) in any way. The national income accounts used to calculate GDP, which are designed to focus on the production of goods and services, do not include capital gains.

Second, profits that are retained by a firm are included in national income, but individuals may not perceive these retained profits as part of their own income. Again, this is because the GDP accounts measure the value of production, and profits are part of the value of production, whether those profits are actually distributed to shareholders or retained by firms.

COMPARISON OF THE FINAL GOODS AND INCOME APPROACHES

Earlier we learned how to break down the output of the economy into four categories—consumption, investment, government expenditures, and net exports. We break down the income of the economy into three categories—

Table 4.1 **TWO APPROACHES TO U.S. GDP, 1995**

Final goods	Billions $	Income	Billions $
Consumption	4,923.4	Employee compensation	4,209.4
Investment	1,067.5	Profits, rents, interest, etc.	2,442.5
Government expenditures	1,358.5	Indirect taxes	595.9
Net exports	–101.7	Total	7,247.8
Total	7,247.8		

payments to workers, consisting mainly of wages; payments to owners of capital, including profits, interest, and rents; and taxes. As Table 4.1 shows, the value of GDP is the same whether calculated in output or income terms: in 1995, U.S. GDP was approximately $7,248 billion.

That the value of output is equal to the value of income—that GDP measured either way is identical—is no accident. It is a consequence of the circular flow of the economy. What each firm receives from selling its goods must go back somewhere else into the economy—as wages, profits, interest, or taxes. The income to households flows back in turn either to firms—in consumption goods households purchase or in savings, which eventually are used to purchase plant and equipment by firms—or to government, in the form of taxes or newly issued government bonds. Similarly, the money spent by the government must have come from somewhere else in the economy—either from households or corporations in the form of taxes, or through borrowing.

ALTERNATIVE APPROACHES TO MEASURING NATIONAL OUTPUT

Measuring output of final goods

Value of final output:

Consumption + Investment + Government Expenditures + Net Exports

Sum of value added in each stage of production

Measuring income

Employee compensation + Profits, Rents, Interest + Indirect taxes

Output = Income

ALTERNATIVE MEASURES OF OUTPUT

The U.S. government has used GDP as its main statistical measure of output since 1991. Before then, **gross national product (GNP)** was used. Gross national product is a measure of the incomes of residents of a country, including income they receive from abroad (wages, returns on investment, interest payments), but subtracting similar payments made to those abroad. By contrast, GDP ignores income received from or paid overseas. It is thus a measure of the goods and services actually produced *within* the country. GDP was the standard measure of output used by most European countries, in which trade had traditionally been far more important than in the United States. As international trade became more important for the United States, it was natural for the country to switch. Besides, the switch made comparisons with the performance of other countries easier.

The treatment of machines and other capital goods (buildings) is another problem in measuring national output. As machines are used to produce output, they wear out. Worn-out machines are a cost of production that should be balanced against total output.

As an example, consider a firm that has a machine worth $1,000 and uses that machine, with $600 of labor, to produce $2,000 worth of output. Furthermore, assume that at the end of the year the machine is completely worn out. The firm then has a *net* output of $400: $2,000 minus the labor costs *and* minus the value of the machine that has worn out.

The reduction in the value of the machine is called the machine's **depreciation.** Since machines wear out at all sorts of different rates, accounting for how much the machines in the economy have depreciated is an extremely difficult problem. The GDP figures take the easy road and make no allowance for depreciation. The term "gross" in "gross domestic product" should serve as a reminder that the statistic covers all production. Economists sometimes use a separate measure that includes the effects of depreciation, called **net domestic product (NDP),** which subtracts an estimate of the value of depreciation from GDP:

$$\text{NDP} = \text{GDP} - \text{depreciation}.$$

The problem is that economists have little confidence in the estimates of depreciation. For this reason they usually use the GDP figure as the measure of the economy's output. Since GDP, GNP, and NDP go up and down together, for most purposes, it does not much matter which one you use as long as you are consistent.

MEASURING THE STANDARD OF LIVING

GDP tells something about the overall level of a nation's economic activity, the goods and services produced in market transactions. But it is only part of the measure of a society's overall well-being. Other social indicators are often employed for this, such as literacy rates (the percentage of the population that can read or write), infant mortality rates (the fraction of infants that die), and life expectancy.

GDP does not reflect environmental degradation which may accompany economic growth. And GDP statistics may be misleading: consider a poor country that decides to harvest its hardwood forests to increase its income. These forests take centuries to grow. Harvesting the forest increases the measured output of the economy, but decreases the country's assets. The output is not sustainable. The United Nations is creating a new set of national accounts, called **Green GDP,** which attempts to incorporate some of the effects on the environment and natural resources. In the above example, Green GDP would subtract from conventional GDP the decrease in the natural resource base. Policymakers would then know that the conventionally measured increase in GDP from cutting down the hardwood forest is short-lived. It is based not on an addition to society's wealth, but rather a subtraction from it.

UNEMPLOYMENT

While increasing living standards is the central economic goal over the long run, when the economy goes into a downturn, unemployment becomes a source of immediate concern. To an economist, unemployment represents an underutilization of resources. People who are willing and able to work are not being productively employed. To the unemployed individuals and their families, unemployment represents economic hardship and changes in their way of life. If a person is unemployed for a long time, he will be unable to meet his current expenses—like utilities and rent—and will have to move to cheaper housing and reduce other aspects of his standard of living.

Unemployment not only costs individuals their paychecks, it can deal a powerful blow to their self-respect. Unemployed workers in today's urban America cannot fall back on farming or living off the land as they might have done in colonial times. Instead, they and their families may be forced to choose between poverty and the bitter taste of government or private charity. Many of these families break up under the strain.

Unemployment presents different problems for each age group of workers. For the young, having a job is necessary for developing job skills, whether they are technical skills or such basic work prerequisites as punctuality and responsibility. Persistent unemployment for them not only wastes valuable human resources today but also reduces the future productivity of the labor force. Individuals fail to obtain critical on-the-job training that improves their skills, and to develop work habits that improve their on-the-job productivity. Furthermore, young people who remain unemployed for an extended period are especially prone to becoming alienated from society and turning to antisocial activities such as crime and drug abuse.

For the middle-aged or elderly worker, losing a job poses different problems. Despite federal and state prohibitions against age discrimination, employers are often hesitant to hire an older worker. They may fear she is more likely than a younger person to become sick or disabled. They may worry about being able to "teach old dogs new tricks." If older workers are unemployed for long periods of time, they may have lost some of their skills. Even if the unemployed older worker succeeds in getting a job, it often entails reduced wages and lower status than in her previous job and may make less than full use of her skills. The toll of such changes is a heavy burden of stress on the dislocated worker and her family.

In addition to these personal losses, unemployment poses heavy costs for communities. If people in a town are thrown out of work—say, because a big employer closes down or decides to move—everyone else in town is likely to suffer as well, since there will be fewer dollars circulating to buy everything from cars and houses to gasoline and groceries. As more unemployment results in fewer people paying local taxes, the quality of schools, libraries, parks, and police can be threatened.

Unemployment may also reinforce racial divisions in society as a whole. The rate of unemployment for blacks is generally more than twice that for whites. During the 1980s and early 1990s, among blacks between the ages of sixteen and nineteen who were just beginning to look for work, unemployment averaged 37 percent, nearly reaching 50 percent in the recession years of 1982 to 1983.

Unemployment represents a tragedy for the individual and the family, a source of dislocation and stress for a community, and a waste of productive resources for society as a whole.

The Magnitude of the Problem

Living in the midst of the approximately 125 million people who get up and go to work every morning is a fluctuating group of several million healthy people who do not. During the recession year of 1991, 8.5 million people were out of work, and one-fourth of those people were jobless for fifteen weeks or more. From the standpoint of the economy as a whole, the potential production of workers who cannot find jobs is a major loss. One calculation puts the loss in output from the high unemployment of the early 1980s at between $122 billion and $320 billion a year, for a per capita loss of between $500 and somewhat more than $1,300.[3] In other words, using the latter number, every man, woman, and child in the United States would have had (on average) an additional $1,300 to spend if the unemployed workers had been gainfully employed.

Unemployment Statistics

In the United States, unemployment data are collected by the Department of Labor, which surveys a representative mix of households and asks each whether a member of the household is currently seeking employment. The

[3]A. Blinder, *Hard Heads, Soft Hearts* (Reading, Mass.: Addison-Wesley, 1987).

unemployment rate is the ratio of the number seeking employment to the total labor force. If there are 120 million Americans employed and 10 million say they are looking for a job but cannot find one, then the total labor force is 130 million, and the

$$\text{unemployment rate} = \frac{\text{number unemployed}}{\text{labor force}}$$

$$= \frac{\text{number unemployed}}{\text{number employed} + \text{number unemployed}}$$

$$= \frac{10 \text{ million}}{120 \text{ million} + 10 \text{ million}} = 7.7 \text{ percent.}$$

Figure 4.4 plots the unemployment rate for the United States since 1960. The figure illustrates two facts. First, unemployment is persistent. Second, the level of unemployment can fluctuate dramatically. In the worst days of the Great Depression, over one quarter of the U.S. labor force was unemployed. The unemployment rate among those who worked in manufacturing was even worse—at one point, one out of three workers in manufacturing had lost their jobs. As recently as 1983, the unemployment rate in the United States was nearly 10 percent. The level of unemployment in the early 1990s, at 5.4 to 7.4 percent, while much lower than that of the early 1980s, is still higher than the rate that prevailed in the mid-1960s, around 4 percent.

Unemployment in other countries has often been worse than in the United States (Figure 4.5). In European countries, it reached over 10 percent during much of the 1980s, and in many developing countries over 20 percent.

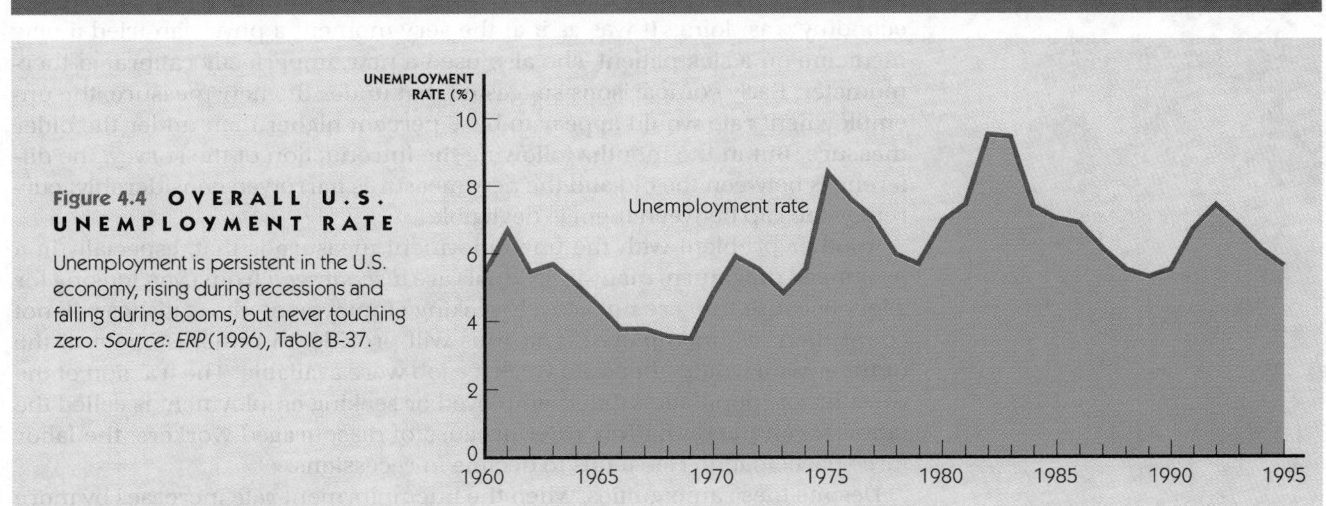

Figure 4.4 OVERALL U.S. UNEMPLOYMENT RATE

Unemployment is persistent in the U.S. economy, rising during recessions and falling during booms, but never touching zero. *Source: ERP* (1996), Table B-37.

Figure 4.5 INTERNATIONAL UNEMPLOYMENT COMPARISONS

In other developed countries, the unemployment rate is often much higher than has been observed in the United States in recent years. *Source: ERP* (1996), Table B-105.

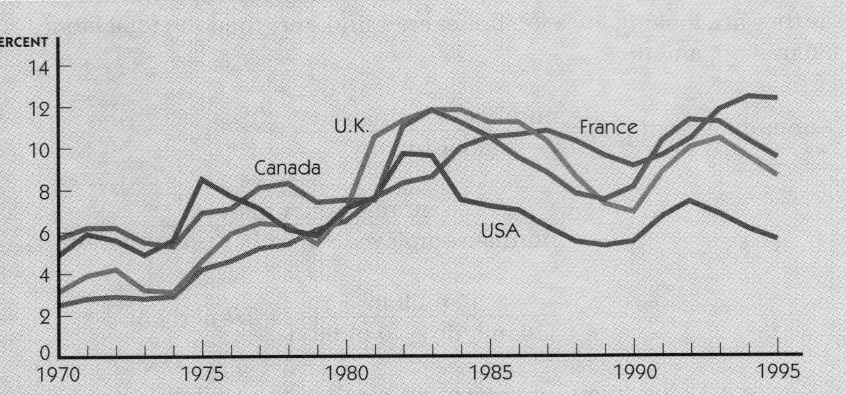

PROBLEMS WITH THE UNEMPLOYMENT STATISTICS

Unemployment statistics are supposed to measure the number of workers who are actively seeking employment but cannot find a job. Information is obtained from a survey of households, and the results of such survey often depend on how the survey is conducted. For instance, in January 1994, the Bureau of Labor Statistics changed the manner in which it conducted its monthly survey. The timing could not have been worse: the economy was pulling out of a recession and a major policy initiative, the 1993 deficit reduction, was just going into effect. Policymakers wanted to know how the economy was doing. It was as if at the very moment a physician tried a new medicine on a sick patient, she also used a new, imperfectly calibrated thermometer. Early comparisons suggested that under the new measure, the unemployment rate would appear to be .6 percent higher than under the older measure. But in the months following the introduction of the survey, the differences between the old and the new measures narrowed considerably; currently, the gap between them is negligible.

Another problem with the unemployment measure is that, especially in a prolonged downturn, many individuals are *discouraged* from even looking for a job. Because they are not actively seeking employment, the statistics will not count them as unemployed, and thus will provide an underestimate of the number who would choose to work if a job were available. The fraction of the working age population that is employed or seeking employment is called the **labor force participation rate.** Because of discouraged workers, the labor force participation rate tends to decline in recessions.

Despite these ambiguities, when the unemployment rate increases by more than a trivial amount, it is safe to conclude that the economy has slowed down. Some individuals have been laid off and have not found new jobs, and firms may have slowed down the pace at which they hire new workers.

FORMS OF UNEMPLOYMENT

Economists distinguish between different kinds of unemployment. Right before Christmas, there is a huge demand for retail salespeople to work in department stores and shopping malls across the country. In many parts of the country, construction slows down in the winter because of the climate. For the same reason, tourism often increases in the summer, and so does the number of jobs that cater to tourists. The supply of labor also increases in the summer, as high school and college students enter the labor force on a temporary basis. Unemployment that varies with the seasons is called **seasonal unemployment.** Since these movements in employment and unemployment reflect normal seasonal patterns, the unemployment rate you see reported on the news is adjusted according to the average amount of seasonal unemployment. These adjustments are called seasonal adjustments. Thus, if, on average, the unadjusted unemployment rate is normally .4 percent higher in the summer than at other times, the seasonally adjusted unemployment rate for July will be the measured unemployment rate minus .4 percent.

While workers in construction, agriculture, and tourism regularly face seasonal unemployment, other workers become unemployed only as part of a normal transition from one job to another. This kind of unemployment is referred to as **frictional unemployment.** If people could move from job to job instantaneously, there would be no frictional unemployment. In a dynamic economy such as America's, with some industries growing and other declining, there will always be movements from one job to another, and hence there will always be frictional unemployment.

Most bouts of unemployment are short-lived; the average person who loses a job is out of work for only three months. However, about 10 percent of the jobless have been unemployed for more than six months. This kind of long-term unemployment often results from structural factors in the economy, and is called **structural unemployment.** Substantial structural unemployment is found quite often side by side with job vacancies, because the unemployed lack the skills required for the newly created jobs. For example, there may be vacancies for computer programmers, while construction workers are unemployed. By the same token, there may be job shortages in those parts of the economy that are expanding (as in the Sunbelt) and unemployment in areas that are suffering decline (as in Michigan during the period of decline in demand for U.S. cars).

Unemployment that increases when the economy goes into a slowdown and decreases when the economy goes into a boom is called **cyclical unemployment** and is the fundamental concern of this part of the book. Government policy is particularly interested in reducing both the frequency and magnitude of this kind of unemployment, by reducing the frequency and magnitude of the recessions that give rise to it. Government also seeks to reduce its impact, by providing unemployment compensation for those temporarily thrown out of work.

As the economy goes into a recession, the demand for labor—the number of hours to be worked—decreases; if the decreased demand were spread uniformly among all workers, the social disruption would be limited; but in

FORMS OF UNEMPLOYMENT

Seasonal
Frictional
Structural
Cyclical

fact, most workers have a slight reduction in work, while a few workers simply lose their jobs. And unskilled workers and minorities are especially likely to become unemployed. Unemployment rates among these groups often soar in a downturn.

INFLATION

In the 1920s, the years of silent pictures, a movie ticket cost a nickel. By the late 1940s, in the heyday of Hollywood, the price was up to $.50. By the 1960s, the price of a movie was $2.00, and now it is over $7.00. This steady price rise is no anomaly. Most other goods have undergone similar increases over time. This increase in the general level of prices is called inflation. While unemployment tends to be concentrated in certain groups within the population, everyone is affected by inflation. Thus, it is not surprising that when inflation becomes high, it almost always rises to the top of the political agenda.

It is not inflation if the price of only one good goes up. It *is* inflation if the prices of *most* goods go up. The **inflation rate** is the rate at which the *general level* of prices increases.

MEASURING INFLATION

If the prices of all goods rose by the same proportion, say by 5 percent, over a period of a year, measuring inflation would be easy: the rate of inflation for that year would be 5 percent. The difficulties arise from the fact that the prices of different goods rise at different rates, and some goods even decline in price. Over the past twenty years, while the price of fruits and vegetables has increased by 220 percent, the price of gasoline by 138 percent, and the price of medical care by 383 percent, the price of computers has declined by over 90 percent. To determine the change in the overall price level, economists calculate the *average* percentage increase in prices. But since some goods loom much larger in the typical consumer's budget than others, this calculation must reflect the relative purchases of different goods. A change in the price of housing, for example, is much more important than a change in the price of pencils. If the price of pencils goes down by 5 percent but the price of housing goes up by 5 percent, the overall measure of the price level should go up.

Economists have a straightforward way of reflecting the differing importance of different goods. They ask, what would it cost consumers to purchase the same bundle of goods this year that they bought last year? If, for example, it cost $22,000 in 1996 to buy what it cost consumers only $20,000 to purchase in 1995, we say that prices, *on average,* have risen by 10 percent. Such results are frequently expressed in the form of a **price index,** which, for ease of comparison, measures the price level in any given year relative to a common base year.

The price index for the base year is, by definition, 100. The price index for any other year is calculated by taking the ratio of the price level in that year to the price level in the base year and multiplying it by 100. For example, if 1995 is our base year and we want to know the price index for 1996, we first calculate the ratio of the cost of a certain bundle of goods in 1996 ($22,000) to the cost of the same bundle of goods in 1995 ($20,000), which is 1.1. The price index in 1996 is therefore $1.1 \times 100 = 110$. The index of 110, using 1995 as a base, means that prices are 10 percent higher, on average, in 1996 than in 1995.

There are several different price indices, each using a different bundle of goods. To track the movement of prices that are important to American households, the government collects price data on the bundle of goods that represents how the average household spends its income. This index is called the **consumer price index,** or CPI. To determine this bundle, the government, through the Bureau of Labor Statistics of the Department of Labor, conducts a Consumer Expenditure Survey, which is updated once a decade or so.

THE AMERICAN EXPERIENCE WITH INFLATION

As we have learned, the inflation rate is the percentage increase in the price level from one year to the next. Figure 4.6 shows the inflation rate for the United States during this century. Three interesting features stand out.

First, prices were relatively stable for much of the century, with the inflation rate under 5 percent except in three periods: around World War I, around World War II, and during the period 1973–1981. Indeed, from the start of the twentieth century until the early 1960s, average inflation ran at only about 1 percent per year.

Second, prices can actually come down. During the recession that followed World War I, prices fell by more than 15 percent, and in the Great Depression of the 1930s by more than 30 percent. It may seem hard to believe in an era when inflation seems the ever-present threat, but at the end of the nineteenth century, the concern was **deflation,** which is a steady decline of the price

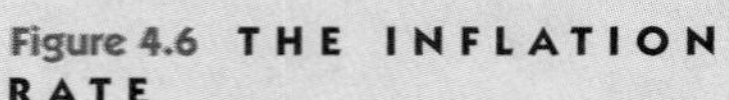

Figure 4.6 THE INFLATION RATE

The inflation rate is the percentage increase in the price level in a given year. Notice that inflation was low through most of the early part of this century (although high during World Wars I and II), rose sharply in the 1970s, and then fell somewhat in the 1980s. *Sources: ERP* (1996), Table B-60; *Historical Statistics of the United States.*

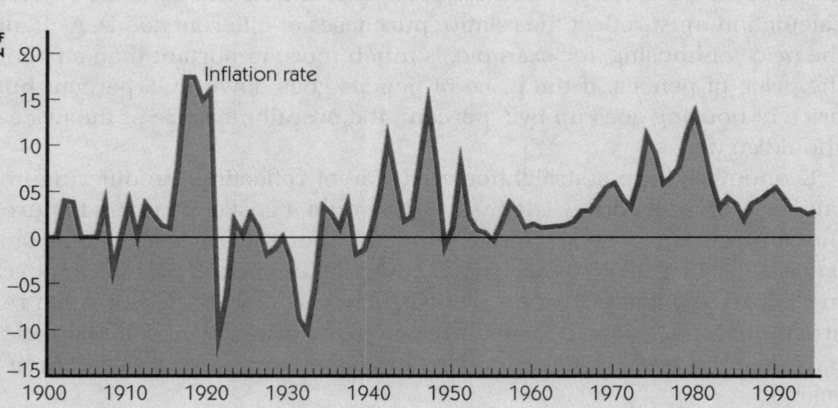

level. Borrowers at that time who were in debt and had not anticipated the fall in prices found that the dollars they had to pay back were worth far more than the dollars that they had borrowed. They were as upset about this as investors (lenders) are today when inflation makes the value of the dollars they get back from an investment or loan worth less than the value of the dollars they originally put in.

Finally, while prices on average have been stable and there have even been periods of price decline, there have also been a few periods of high inflation, when prices increased rapidly. The most notable recent episode was in the late 1970s and early 1980s. In 1980 alone, prices rose by more than 13 percent.

The Importance of Inflation

In modern economies, much has been done to ease the pain of inflation. For workers, rising levels of prices are usually accompanied by higher wages, and if a worker faces higher prices but has commensurately more money in her pocket, she is just as well off. The U.S. government has taken steps to adjust the income of retirees to changes in the price level. Most significant, Social Security payments are now "indexed," that is, adjusted, to keep up with changes in the cost of living.

Why, then, does fighting inflation rank so high as a priority in economic policy? There seem to be three answers.

The first is that some groups still suffer. Anyone whose income does not adjust fully is made worse off by increases in the price level. Second, when the rate of inflation suddenly increases, those who have lent money find that the dollars they are being paid back with are worth less. Thus, creditors (those

Using Economics: Calculating the Consumer Price Index

Encapsulating the movements of masses of prices into an index provides an easy way to look at price trends over time. Suppose that in 1990 the average American family spent \$1,000 per month to buy a basket of goods. Assume that in 1996 it cost \$1,200 to buy the same basket. Then the price index for 1996 is just the ratio of the cost in 1996 to the cost in 1990, times 100. That is,

$$\text{CPI for 1996} = 1{,}200/1{,}000 \times 100 = 120.$$

The advantage of an index is that once there is an index number for any given year, we can compare it with any other year. The CPI for 1973 was 44, and for 1994 it was 148. Between those years, the index rose by 104, so the increase was

$$100 \times 104/44 = 236 \text{ percent.}$$

On average, prices rose by 236 percent from 1973 to 1994.

The figure below shows the level of the consumer price index from 1900 to the present, using 1983 as the base year. For example, prices in 1920 were 20 percent of what they were in 1983.

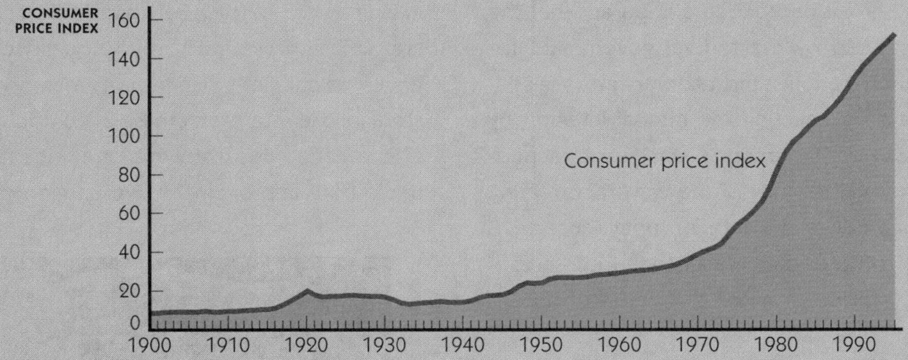

Source: ERP (1996), Table B-56.

who lend money) are worse off, while debtors are better off. When the inflation rate varies, both borrowing and lending become riskier.

Third, many feel that something is fundamentally wrong with the economy when what cost \$1 five years ago costs \$2 today. Sometimes these observers are right. Inflation can reflect gross errors in government economic policy, such as spending that is far in excess of revenues, or excessive provision of credit. But frequently inflation gets the blame when something else is the underlying problem. The steep increase in oil prices in 1973 set off a worldwide inflationary spiral. With Americans paying more to the oil-exporting countries, the United States was, in a sense, poorer. Someone had to take a cut. Furthermore, the worldwide economic downturn set off by the 1973 oil price rise made the cut that had to be taken that much larger. Thus, workers' real

Policy Perspective: The Price Index Makes a Difference!

Price indices have increasingly come to play an important role in economic life, in spite of the dry, technical flavor that seems to pervade most discussion of them. The Social Security benefits of the elderly increase with the cost of living index, and tax brackets and tax exemptions also change with the index. If the index overstates the cost of living (rate of inflation) increases, the real benefits (purchasing power) of the elderly increase, and real inflation-adjusted tax revenues decrease. Both distortions increase the budget deficit of the government—the first by increasing the outlays, the second by reducing the receipts of government.

By early 1994, it had become apparent that the price index used by the federal government for adjusting both benefits and tax brackets was seriously flawed—overstating the rate of inflation by between .5 and 1.5 percent a year. Several scheduled changes will go part of the way in correcting those errors. But in the interim, until those revisions are instituted, the Treasury will lose an estimated $100 billion or more as a result of the biased index.

The upward bias stems from three problems. The first is the "fixed basket problem." Price indices are generally calculated by comparing how much it costs to purchase a particular market basket of goods that represents an average consumer's expenditure pattern. But expenditure patterns change steadily over time, while the market basket is revised only infrequently (for instance, 1997 will be the first revision since 1982 through 1984). As people buy more of the goods which have become relatively less expensive, and less of the goods which have become relatively more expensive, the index increasingly overweights goods whose prices are rising.

The second major problem is "quality adjustments." New products, which can do new and better things than older products, constantly enter the market. To compare the prices of the new products with the old, some quality adjustment must be made. If the price goes up by 10 percent, but the product lives longer and does better than the old one, in a real sense the price increase is less than 10 percent and may even be a price reduction. The quality adjustments may sometimes be easy: one machine can do what two machines did before. But usually the comparisons are difficult. If we measure the quality of computers by calculations per minute, memory, and disk storage, the rate of decrease in computer prices is phenomenal. But even this does not fully reflect the quality improvement. We can do things with

the computer now that were unimaginable twenty-five years ago at any price. And how do we treat a new drug that cures a previously incurable disease? The Bureau of Labor Statistics tries to make adjustments for quality. But the consensus is that these adjustments are imperfect and result in an overestimate in the inflation rate of between a few tenths of a percent to more than 1 percent.

A third set of problems is technical, having to do with the way the data are collected and the details of the calculation.

But many economists believe that the scheduled revisions will not fully eliminate the CPI bias. They argue that, as a result, Social Security and taxes should be indexed to the CPI rate of inflation minus 1 or .5.

wages fell. They blamed inflation for their declining standard of living. But inflation was not really the culprit—higher oil prices were.

As the economy has adapted to inflation, economists have increasingly debated about how concerned we should be about moderate rates of inflation—the 3 to 6 percent inflation that has occurred regularly during the past few decades. They worry that the cures for moderate inflation may be worse than the disease. Still, most economists think that double-digit inflation levels, at the very least, are symptomatic of some kind of malfunction in the economy. Certainly there is a consensus that the kinds of rapid inflation experienced in Israel and some Latin American countries are extremely disruptive to the economy.

Alternative Measures of Inflation

The consumer price index is one measure of inflation, based on what the average consumer pays. Other price indices can be calculated using different market baskets. A different measure of prices is the **producer price index,** which measures the average level of prices of goods sold by producers. This index is useful because it gives us an idea of what will happen to consumer prices in the near future. Usually, if producers are receiving higher prices from their sales to wholesalers, eventually retailers will have to charge higher prices. This will be reflected in a higher consumer price index.

Earlier in the chapter we observed that real GDP is nominal GDP adjusted for the price level. The price index we use for calculating real GDP is called the **GDP deflator.** It represents a comparison between what it would cost to buy the total mix of goods and services within the economy today and in a base year. In other words, the GDP deflator is a weighted average of the prices of different goods and services, where the weights represent the importance of each of the goods and services in GDP.

CONNECTING THE THREE MAJOR VARIABLES

Often the major macroeconomic variables move together in systematic ways. For example, when the economy is in a recession, as it was in 1982, unemployment tends to be higher, inflation tends to be lower, and growth comes to a standstill. These connections make sense. After all, when the economy is suffering tough times, businesses reduce their output, lay off workers, and do not hire new workers. In addition, businesses that are having a hard time selling products in a competitive market are less likely to raise prices.

FLOWS AND STOCKS

GDP, GNP, and NDP are all measures of output *per year.* Rate measurements such as these are called **flows.** When a news report says, "The quarterly GDP statistic, just released, shows that GDP was $4 trillion per year," it does not mean that $4 trillion of goods and services was produced during the quarter. Rather, it means that $1 trillion was produced during the quarter, so that if that rate of production were maintained for a whole year, the total value of goods and services would be $4 trillion.

Flow statistics need to be contrasted with **stock** statistics, which measure an item at a single point in time. Among the most important stocks is the capital stock—the total value of all the buildings and machines that underlie the productive potential of the economy.

The relationships between stocks and flows are simple. The stock of capital at the end of 1996, for example, consists of the stock of capital at the end of 1995 plus or minus the flows into or out of this stock during 1996. Investment is the flow into the capital stock. Depreciation is the flow out of the capital stock.

Similarly, we can look at the *number* of unemployed individuals as a stock. This number at the end of 1996 consists of the number at the end of 1995 plus or minus the flows into or out of the unemployment pool during 1996. Layoffs, firings, resignations, and new entry into the labor force can be thought of as flows into the unemployment pool; new hires represent flows out of the unemployment pool.

REVIEW AND PRACTICE

SUMMARY

1. The three central macroeconomic policy objectives of the government are low unemployment, low inflation, and high growth. Macroeco-

nomics studies how these aggregate variables change as a result of household and business behavior, and how government policy may affect them.

2. Productivity has not been increasing as rapidly in the United States in the last two decades as it had earlier.

3. Gross domestic product (GDP) is the typical way of measuring national output. Real GDP adjusts GDP for changes in the price level.

4. GDP can be calculated in three ways: the final goods approach, which adds the value of all final goods produced in the economy; the value-added approach, which adds the difference between firms' revenues and costs of intermediate goods; and the income approach, which adds together all income received by those in the economy. All three methods give the same answer.

5. Unemployment imposes costs both on individuals and on society as a whole, which loses what the unemployed workers could have contributed and ends up supporting them in other ways.

6. Seasonal unemployment, such as construction in areas with harsh winters, occurs regularly depending on the season. Frictional unemployment results from people being in transition between one job and another. Structural unemployment refers to the unemployment generated as the structure of the economy changes, with the new jobs being created having requirements different from the old jobs being lost. Cyclical unemployment increases or decreases with the level of economic activity.

7. The inflation rate is the percentage increase of the price level from one year to the next. U.S. inflation was low through most of the early part of this century, rose sharply in the 1970s and early 1980s, and then fell somewhat in the later 1980s and early 1990s. In different countries at different times, inflation has sometimes been very high, with prices increasing by factors of tens or hundreds in a given year.

8. The amount of inflation between two years is measured by the percentage change in the amount it would cost to buy a given basket of goods in those years. Different baskets define different price indexes, such as the consumer price index and the producer price index.

9. Many macroeconomic variables seem to move together in systematic ways. For example, in a boom, unemployment tends to fall, inflation tends to rise, and productivity tends to rise. In a recession, the reverse happens.

10. Economists distinguish between flows—such as output per year—and stocks—such as the stock of capital.

KEY TERMS

unemployment rate
inflation
gross domestic product (GDP)
nominal GDP
real GDP

chain-weighted real GDP
potential GDP
business cycles
boom
recession
trough
peak
value added
capital gains
gross national product (GNP)
depreciation
net domestic product (NDP)
Green GDP
labor force participation rate
seasonal unemployment
frictional unemployment
structural unemployment
cyclical unemployment
consumer price index
deflation
producer price index
GDP deflator
flows
stocks

REVIEW QUESTIONS

1. What are the three main goals of macroeconomic policy?

2. What is the difference between nominal GDP, real GDP, and potential GDP?

3. What is the difference between the final outputs approach to measuring GDP, the value-added approach, and the income approach?

4. What is the difference between GDP, GNP, and NDP?

5. What has happened in the last two decades to the rate of change of productivity?

6. What is the difference between frictional unemployment, seasonal unemployment, structural unemployment, and cyclical unemployment?

7. When there is a reduction in the number of hours worked in the economy, is this normally shared equally by all workers? Are workers in some groups more impacted by increased unemployment than those in other groups?

8. When the prices of different goods change at different rates, how do we measure the rate of inflation?

9. Are all groups of people affected equally by inflation? Why or why not?

PROBLEMS

1. Which would you expect to fall fastest in a recession, real GDP or potential GDP? Could potential GDP rise while real GDP fell?

2. Geoffrey spends his allowance on three items: candy, magazines, and renting VCR movies. He is currently receiving an allowance of $30 per month, which he is using to rent 4 movies at $2 apiece, buy 10 candy bars

at $1 apiece, and purchase 4 magazines at $3 apiece. Calculate a Geoffrey price index (GPI) for this basket of goods, with the current price level equal to 100, in the following cases.

(a) The price of movies rises to $3.

(b) The price of movies rises to $3, and the price of candy bars falls by $.20.

(c) The price of movies rises to $3, the price of candy bars falls by $.20, and the price of magazines rises to $4.

3. An increase in the consumer price index will often affect different groups in different ways. Think about how different groups will purchase items like housing, travel, or education in the CPI basket, and explain why they will be affected differently by increases in components of the CPI. How would you calculate an "urban CPI" or a "rural CPI"?

4. Given the information below about the U.S. economy, how much did real U.S. GDP grow between 1965 and 1975? between 1975 and 1985?

	1965	1970	1975	1980	1985	1990	1995
Nominal GDP (billions)	$700	$1,000	$1,600	$2,700	$4,000	$5,500	$7,000
Consumer price index	100	115	160	250	320	415	480

5. Much of this chapter has discussed how economists adjust the data to find what they want to know—for example, by adjusting for inflation or dividing by the population level. What adjustments might you suggest for analyzing education expenditures? Social Security expenditures?

6. Firms typically do not fire workers quickly as the economy goes into a recession—at least not in proportion to the reduction in their output. How might you expect output per worker and output per hour to move over the business cycle?

CHAPTER 5

MICROFOUNDATIONS

Chapter 4 took up the key objectives of macroeconomic policy—growth, full employment, and stable prices—and the way in which success in reaching each of these objectives is gauged. In Chapter 6, we begin to look specifically at what determines such aggregate variables as the economy's output and employment levels. The behavior of these macroeconomic variables is determined by the actions of the millions of households and firms that make up the economy. Accordingly, an understanding of macroeconomics begins with microeconomics. Earlier chapters discussed how prices are determined in competitive markets by the intersection of demand and supply curves. This chapter rounds out that discussion.

First, we look at how households and firms interact in product, labor, and capital markets. We then survey the economy as a whole, from the perspective of the basic competitive model first introduced in Chapter 2. However, many economists believe that the basic competitive model provides an incomplete description of the economy. Most important, the model assumes that in every market, demand equals supply. When applied to the labor market, this assumption means that there is no unemployment. Since one of the main concerns in macroeconomics is what determines the unemployment rate and why there are periods in which it is persistently high, we must go beyond the basic competitive model. Accordingly, the final section of this chapter points out the discrepancies between modern economies and the basic competitive model. This lays the groundwork for the analysis of such central macroeconomic phenomena as unemployment and inflation, to which we will turn in Parts Three and Four.

KEY QUESTIONS

1. How are the demand and supply curves for goods and services derived? for labor? for capital?
2. How does the basic competitive model provide answers to the questions of what will be produced and in what quantities, how it will be produced, and for whom it will be produced?
3. How are the various parts of the economy tied together?
4. What are the most important limitations of the basic competitive model? Why may markets by themselves not result in economic efficiency?

HOUSEHOLDS IN THE BASIC COMPETITIVE MODEL

In the basic competitive model, rational households interact with profit-maximizing firms in competitive markets. The supply and demand curves introduced in Chapter 3 give us a framework for analyzing this interaction. Here and in the next section, we explore the determinants of the demand and supply curves—why they have the shapes they do, and what causes the curves to shift. This section takes the perspective of households, while the next one gives the firm's viewpoint. The principles developed here will be applied to each of the markets that make up the economy: product, labor, and capital. After looking at the decisions of households and firms, we will look at the market equilibrium, how firms and households interact in all three markets, and the implications of these interactions for the economy as a whole.

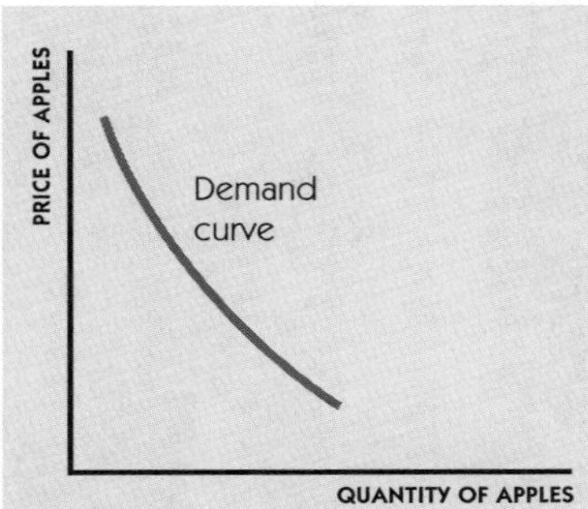

Figure 5.1 DOWNWARD-SLOPING DEMAND CURVE

As the price of any good (here, apples) rises, the demand for the good decreases.

THE HOUSEHOLD'S CONSUMPTION DECISION

As we saw in Chapter 2, individuals face a budget constraint. They have a certain amount of money to spend; they can only consume more of one good by consuming less of another. The trade-off is given by relative prices. If the price of apples is twice that of oranges, by giving up one apple, an individual can get two oranges.

Chapter 3 suggested that normally, demand curves are downward sloping, as shown in Figure 5.1; that is, as the price rises, people consume less of a good. There are two reasons for this. First, as the price of apples increases, apples become less attractive relative to oranges and other goods. To get one more apple, Alfred must give up more oranges, so Alfred substitutes oranges (and other fruits) for apples. The reduction in demand resulting from the

Using Economics: Income Elasticities

In Chapter 3 we introduced the concept of price elasticity: the percentage change in demand from a 1 percent increase in price. Economists use an analogous concept of income elasticity to quantify income effects: the income elasticity is the percentage change in demand from a 1 percent increase in income.

As an economy grows, it will normally import more goods. Governments often want to know how much will imports be rising. The answer is provided by the income elasticity of demand for the imported goods. In the United States, for instance, many imports consist of luxury goods, for which the income elasticity is large; accordingly a 1 percent increase in income may lead to a more than 1 percent increase in imports. If U.S. incomes increase from \$6 trillion to \$6.3 trillion per year—that is, by 5 percent—and imports are \$600 billion, and the income elasticity of imported goods is 1.2, then imports will be expected to rise by 6 percent, or by \$36 billion. If foreigners' income is expected to rise by only 3 percent and U.S. exports are \$500 billion per year, and if the foreign income elasticity for imports is slightly smaller, at say 1, then as a result of their increased income, they will buy \$15 billion more of U.S. goods (3 percent × \$500 billion × income elasticity of demand). Under these circumstances, the trade deficit—the gap between exports and imports—would (if nothing else changed) be expected to rise by \$21 billion (\$36 billion more imports –\$15 billion more exports).

change in the relative price—to get one more apple, Alfred must give up more oranges—is called the **substitution effect.**

Second, if Alfred spends all or even part of his income on apples, he is worse off when the price of apples increases. He simply cannot buy what he bought before. He is, in this sense, poorer, just as he would be if his income had been reduced. If we define **real income** as what an individual's income will buy (rather than simply the money received), Alfred's real income has been reduced. When this happens, he spends less on almost every good.[1] The reduction in Alfred's demand for apples resulting from the reduction in real income is called the **income effect.** Both the income and substitution effects lead Alfred to demand fewer apples when the price increases. This is why the demand curve for apples is depicted as downward sloping: at higher prices, fewer apples are demanded.

Chapter 3 identified a number of factors, such as income, tastes, and demographics, that affected the market demand curve. Most importantly, demand in one market is affected by prices determined in other markets. The price of oranges will have an effect on the demand for apples, for instance. On a broader level, the intertwining of markets is a central feature of macroeconomic analysis; for instance, an increase in wages (as a result of a shift in the

[1]There are some exceptions. A good for which the demand decreases as income increases is said to be *inferior,* while goods for which demand increases as income increases are said to be *normal.*

SUBSTITUTION AND INCOME EFFECTS

Substitution effect: The reduction in demand resulting from the change in the relative price; the individual substitutes less expensive products for more expensive ones.

Income effect: The reduction in demand resulting from the reduction in real income that occurs when the price of any good rises.

demand or supply curves of labor) increases the income workers have to spend, and thus affects the demand curve for each and every good. Figure 5.2 shows that an increase in income, or a change in tastes or the prices of other goods, may lead to a shift in the demand curve for a good.

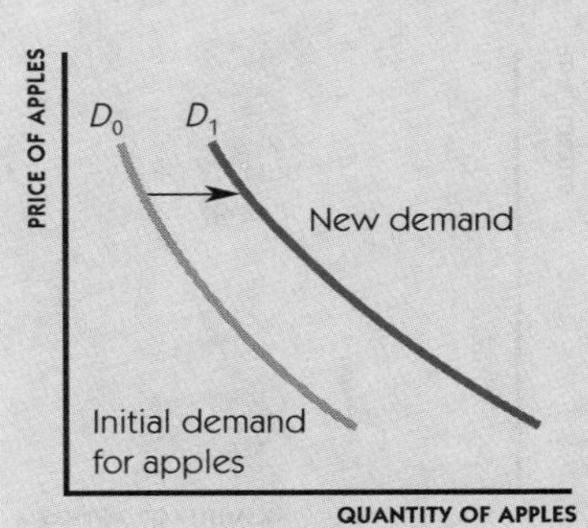

Figure 5.2 SHIFTS IN DEMAND CURVES

Changes in income, tastes, or the prices of other goods may lead to a shift in the demand curve for a good.

THE HOUSEHOLD'S SAVING DECISION

The same kind of analysis applies to Alfred's decision about how much to save. We can think of a decision about how much to save as a decision about how much to consume now and how much to consume in the future. If Alfred reduces his consumption (with a fixed income), he has money left over, which he saves. He takes this savings and puts it in the bank (or invests it some other way), and receives a return of *r* (the interest rate). If *r* is 10 percent, then for every dollar of reduced consumption today, he gets $1.10 in the future. Thus, $1.10 is the *relative* price of consumption today versus consumption in the future.

What is the effect of an increase in the interest rate? If Alfred saves nothing —he takes his current income and simply consumes it—then the interest rate has no effect. If he does save, he has more to consume in the future. He is better off. Earlier, we learned that when an individual's income goes down, she normally consumes less of all goods. Likewise, when Alfred is better off, he normally consumes more of every good; this means, in our example, that he consumes more now and more in the future. This is the income effect of higher interest rates. Alfred consumes more now, which implies that he saves less.

On the other hand, an increase in the interest rate means that for each dollar of consumption Alfred gives up today, he gets more consumption in the future; the trade-off has changed. This is the substitution effect, and the substitution effect of higher interest rates leads Alfred to consume less today and more in the future. Thus, an increase in the interest rate has an income effect leading to lower savings and a substitution effect leading to more savings. The net effect is ambiguous, though most studies indicate that, on average, the substitution effect slightly outweighs the income effect: savings increase

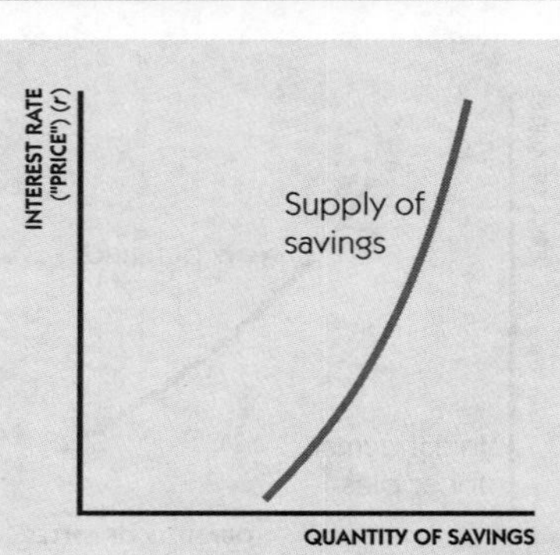

Figure 5.3 THE SUPPLY CURVE FOR SAVINGS

The supply of savings rises slightly with increases in the interest rate. The substitution effect slightly exceeds the income effect.

slightly. Figure 5.3 shows the supply of savings as a slightly upward-sloping curve.

EXPECTATIONS

To an economist, a decision about whether to consume today or consume five years from now is just like a decision about whether to consume apples or oranges. Alfred looks at his preferences and his opportunity set, and especially the trade-offs. The trade-offs are given by relative prices—here determined by the interest rate. But there is one important difference. In making his decisions about the future, Alfred must form expectations: how much he will want to set aside for the future may depend upon what he expects his future wage will be, or what the price of his favorite goods will be.

INVESTING

Having decided how much to save, Alfred now faces a new problem: what to do with his savings. He has a number of choices. For instance, he could put his money in a bank account. Alternatively, he could buy a certificate of deposit, which is a promise from the bank to pay him, in addition to the money he has invested (the principal) a specified amount of interest in, say, six months or a year. Other options include corporate stocks and corporate or government bonds. In evaluating his alternatives, Alfred looks at several characteristics of each asset: the **expected return** (what he expects to get on average), the risk, the tax advantages, and how costly it would be for him to sell the asset quickly, should he need to do so (technically called the **liquidity**).

In making his investment decisions, again expectations play a key role. If Alfred believes that a new smog-reducing technology will make living in Los Angeles much more attractive in ten years, he believes that the price of land will increase ten years from now. But if land is expected to have a high value ten years from now, it will have a high value nine years from now—since if it did not, investors would recognize that by buying the land cheaply and holding it for just one year, they would make an enormous capital gain. But, reasoning backwards, if land is expected to have a high value nine years from now, it will have a high value eight years from now, and so on. The point is an event which is believed to have a large effect on increasing values ten years from now will be reflected in the price *today*. The demand for assets today, and thus the price today, reflects expectations of events which will affect uses in the future, and hence demands in the future. Just as different markets within the economy today are linked together, so are markets over time linked together.

Risk arises whenever there is uncertainty about the returns. If an oil company is successful and finds oil, investing in the company can yield huge returns. But if it does not find oil, not only may there be no returns, the amount invested may not be recovered. High-tech companies are similarly engaged in risky research ventures: if their research pays off, investors will be repaid many times what they invested. But in many cases, the companies' research does not pay off, or someone else beats them to the patent office. Then, investors lose everything they have invested. Some stocks are less risky—food businesses tend to do well no matter how the economy is doing. There is little downside risk, but neither is there the great upside potential of the high-tech companies.

THE HOUSEHOLD'S LABOR SUPPLY DECISION

We can use the same basic reasoning that we have employed to analyze the demand for apples and the supply of savings to discuss how much Alfred decides to work. Of course, in some jobs, Alfred may have no choice; if he wants to work for Grinding Grinders, he may have to work a sixty-hour week, while if he wants to work for Easy Riding Stables, his work week may be only thirty hours. But the number of hours he wants to work will affect which job he chooses; and economists believe that, by and large, employers respond to preferences of workers. If workers, on average, want shorter work weeks, then over time, work weeks will get shorter. In fact, the work week is considerably shorter today than it was at the beginning of the century.

The question is, what determines how much Alfred would like to work? Again, we need to look at Alfred's opportunity set. If he works less, his income will be lower; he will not be able to consume as much as he otherwise could. In making his decision, he looks at the trade-off, the benefit of the extra leisure and the cost of the reduced amount of goods he can buy. This trade-off is given by the wage he receives. The wage is the price of labor. The **real wage** is the nominal wage divided by the average price of the goods a person buys (as reflected, for instance, in the consumer price index). Thus, the real wage tells us how much extra consumption Alfred can have if he works an hour more.

What happens when real wages increase? Again, there is an income effect. Alfred is better off and so would like to consume more of every good; viewing leisure as a "good," he wants more leisure—that is, he wants to work less. On the other hand, the higher wage has changed the trade-off. For every hour of leisure he gives up, he now gets, for example, $20 of extra consumption rather than $10. The substitution effect causes him to want to work more. Again, the net effect is ambiguous. Most studies show that the income and substitution effects are almost precisely balanced, so that the labor supply curve appears to be fairly steep, as depicted in Figure 5.4.

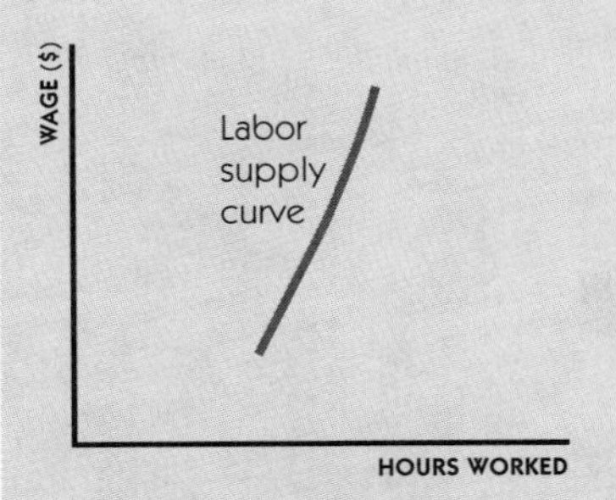

Figure 5.4 THE LABOR SUPPLY CURVE

The supply of labor increases with the wage, but only slightly. The income and substitution effects are almost just balanced.

FIRMS IN THE BASIC COMPETITIVE MODEL

Competitive firms maximize their profits.[2] Profits are just revenues minus costs. Revenues are the price of a good times the quantity sold of the good.

[2]Alternatively, we can describe firms as maximizing their market value; to do that, they must maximize their profits. They may, of course, be willing to give up some profits today if they think profits in the future will be increased by enough to compensate.

The firm in the basic competitive model believes that it has no effect on price —it takes the market price as given. For instance, any wheat farmer believes that the price of wheat will be unaffected by the amount of wheat he sells.

THE FIRM'S SUPPLY DECISION

In deciding how much to produce, the firm in the competitive model compares the extra revenue it receives from producing one more unit of output—the price—with the extra cost, which is called the **marginal cost.** When price exceeds marginal cost, the firm gains more than the increased costs; it pays to expand output. By contrast, if marginal cost exceeds price, it pays to contract output. The firm produces at the level where price equals marginal cost. This is the profit-maximizing level of output.

Here is another way of looking at the firm's decision. Figure 5.5 shows the firm's total costs of producing each level of output. Total costs increase as the firm produces more. The figure also shows the company's total revenue curve. The firm's profit at any level of output is simply the difference between the two at that level of output. The slope of the total revenue curve measures the increase in revenues when output increases by a unit, called the **marginal revenue.** In competitive markets, a firm's total revenue increases in proportion to output. The total revenue curve is thus a straight line through the origin, with a slope equal to the market price: marginal revenue (the extra revenue from selling one more unit) equals price. The slope of the total cost curve (the extra cost from producing one more unit) is the marginal cost. As long as marginal revenue is higher than marginal cost, profits are increasing. Profits are maximized when the two curves have the same slope; that is, when marginal revenue (price) equals marginal cost.

We learn more about the firm's production decision by looking more closely at its costs. The firm's **average costs,** total costs divided by output, are shown in Figure 5.6. The average cost curve is U-shaped. It heads downward

Figure 5.5 THE FIRM'S REVENUE AND COST CURVES

In competitive markets, a firm's total revenues increase in proportion to the output sold. Its total costs also increase with output. Profits are the difference between the two. They are maximized at Q^*, where the slope of the total revenue curve—which equals the price—and the slope of the total cost curve are the same. The slope of the total cost curve is the marginal cost.

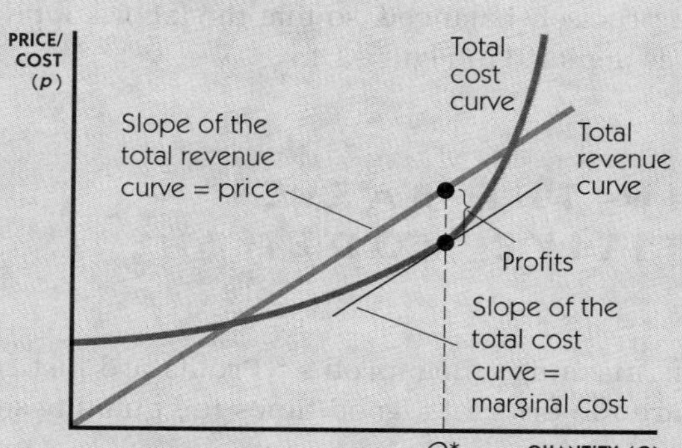

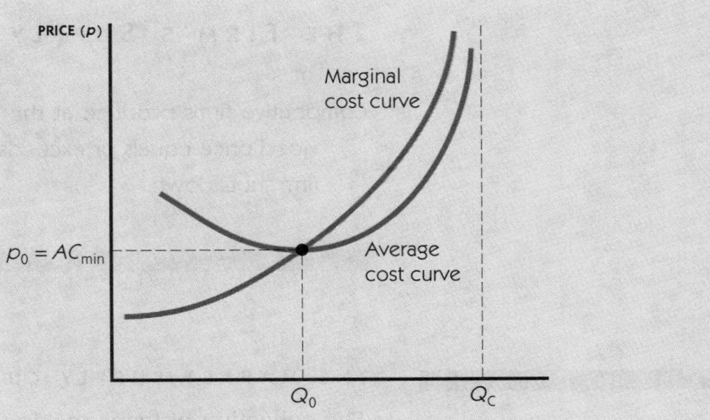

Figure 5.6 THE FIRM'S AVERAGE COST CURVE
The typical firm faces a U-shaped average cost curve. Marginal costs increase with output. The marginal cost curve intersects the average cost curve at the bottom of the U-shaped average cost curve. The output at this point is denoted by Q_0, and the average cost by AC_{min}. The maximum output the firm can produce is Q_c. It is prohibitively expensive to produce beyond this point.

at low levels of output because there are certain costs a firm must pay just to remain in operation. It has to pay rent, pay its top management, and so forth. These are referred to as **fixed** or **overhead costs.** If these were the only costs, then average costs would decline rapidly as output increases. There are other costs, however, called **variable costs,** and not only do these increase as output increases, but they often increase faster than output, at least beyond a certain point. In the short run, the firm cannot immediately expand the number of machines and workers. To produce more, it has to work two or three shifts, and must work its machines and workers at full speed. This is expensive. Thus, its average costs start to increase. This explains why the typical firm has a U-shaped average cost curve.

Figure 5.6 also shows the firm's marginal costs. In the figure, marginal costs are initially relatively flat. If the firm wishes to expand production, it simply hires more workers and buys more raw materials. But as we just saw, after some point it becomes more expensive to produce an extra unit. Marginal costs start to increase. Eventually the firm may find that it simply cannot increase its output beyond a certain level. The marginal cost curve in the figure intersects the average cost curve at its lowest price. This is no accident. When marginal costs—the costs of producing an extra unit—exceed the average costs, the marginal costs are pulling up the average, so average costs are rising. When marginal costs are below average costs, marginal costs are pulling down the average, so average costs are falling.

Once we understand the average cost curve, we can add an important qualification to the statement above that the firm in the competitive model produces at the point where price equals marginal cost. It does so only *so long as it covers costs*—that is, so long as price equals or exceeds average costs (ignoring sunk costs). If price is below average costs, the firm shuts down. Thus, the firm's supply curve is its marginal cost curve in the region where price exceeds minimum average costs; otherwise, the firm supplies zero.

THE FIRM'S SUPPLY DECISION

Competitive firms produce at the output at which price equals marginal costs, provided price equals or exceeds average costs. If price is below average costs, the firm shuts down.

THE MARKET SUPPLY CURVE

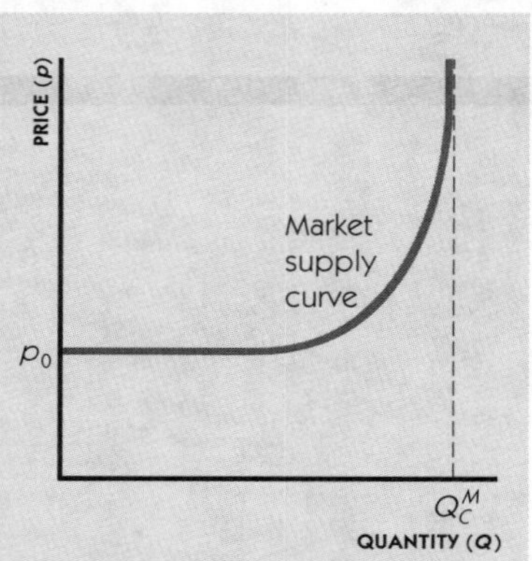

Figure 5.7 THE MARKET SUPPLY CURVE

The figure illustrates a typical shape, with a horizontal portion at price p_0 and an upward-sloping portion beyond that. There is some total capacity of the industry: it simply cannot produce at output beyond Q_C^M.

The collection of firms making the same product is called an **industry.** The industry or market supply curve, as we saw in Chapter 3, is found simply by adding up the supply curves of each of the firms in the industry. Figure 5.7 shows a typical shape, with a horizontal portion at price p_0 and an upward-sloping portion beyond that. In the figure, the industry simply cannot produce at an output beyond Q_c^M; this point is referred to as the total **capacity** of the industry.

The reason that the market supply curve has this shape can be seen if we return to the cost curves illustrated in Figure 5.6. Assume all firms have the same average cost curves, with minimum average cost equal to AC_{min} and the corresponding output equal to Q_0. Then, when the price is $p_0 = AC_{min}$, each firm is indifferent between not operating and operating at Q_0. If there are N firms, then industry output at price p_0 is somewhere between 0, when all shut down, and $N \times Q_0$, when all operate. Above p_0, the market supply is simply the sum of the amounts supplied by each of the firms, all of which will be operating.

The Effect of Wage Increases on the Market Supply Curve The amount the industry is willing to supply depends, of course, not just on the price it receives, but on what it must pay for labor and other inputs. Implicitly, we have assumed throughout the analysis so far that those are fixed.

An increase in wages (or the price of any other input) shifts *all* of the cost curves—total, average, and marginal—upward. Figure 5.8A illustrates the effects on average and marginal costs. As a result, the supply curve of the industry shifts, as depicted in panel B.

THE FIRM'S DEMAND FOR LABOR AND CAPITAL

The firm's production decision is intimately tied to its demand for labor. At each level of wages and prices, we can calculate the amount firms are willing to supply. But we can also calculate their demand for labor. As the wage increases

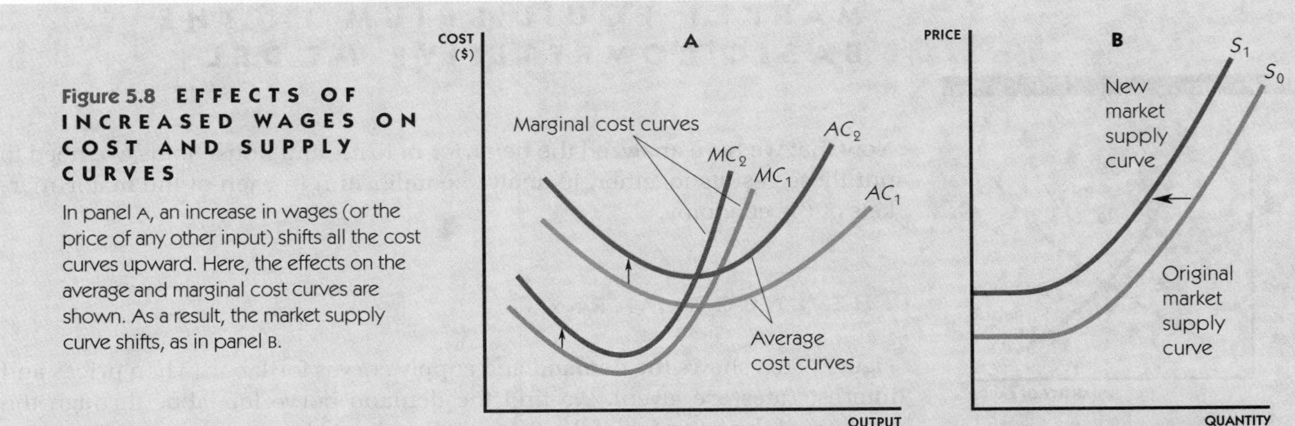

Figure 5.8 EFFECTS OF INCREASED WAGES ON COST AND SUPPLY CURVES

In panel A, an increase in wages (or the price of any other input) shifts all the cost curves upward. Here, the effects on the average and marginal cost curves are shown. As a result, the market supply curve shifts, as in panel B.

at a given price level, firms' demand for labor will decrease, for two reasons. First, the upward shift in the marginal cost curve means that firms will wish to produce less. With lower levels of production, they will demand less labor. But in addition, if wages increase, labor becomes more expensive relative to other inputs. Firms will thus substitute, where possible, other inputs for labor. In some cases, this may be easy; for instance, some industries can use more machines, or more expensive machines, which require fewer workers to run them. In other cases, it is more difficult.

We can immediately extend this analysis to the industry, and then to the whole economy: as wages increase (at fixed prices), the total amount of labor demanded by all firms together—the market demand for labor—decreases.

Figure 5.9 shows a firm's demand curve for labor, which is downward sloping. It is drawn under the assumption of a given price of output. If the price of output increases, firms will want to produce more; and at the higher level of output, they will want more labor. The demand curve for labor will shift to the right, as depicted in the figure.

Exactly the same kind of analysis applies to the demand for capital.[3] As the interest rate—the price of using capital—increases, firms' demand for capital decreases; each firm produces less and each firm substitutes other inputs, such as labor, for capital, which has become more expensive.

WAGE

New demand for labor

Old demand for labor

QUANTITY OF LABOR

Figure 5.9 THE FIRM'S DEMAND CURVE FOR LABOR

As wages increase, the amount of labor demanded by firms decreases. The demand curve for labor shifts to the right when the price of the good produced by the firm increases.

[3]Recall the discussion of Chapter 1, which pointed out that the term "capital" is used in two different ways: it refers to capital goods—plant and equipment—and to the funds used to purchase these capital goods. Here, we are referring to the latter, to the supply of "funds" made available to firms by households and to the demand for funds by firms to finance their investment.

MARKET EQUILIBRIUM IN THE BASIC COMPETITIVE MODEL

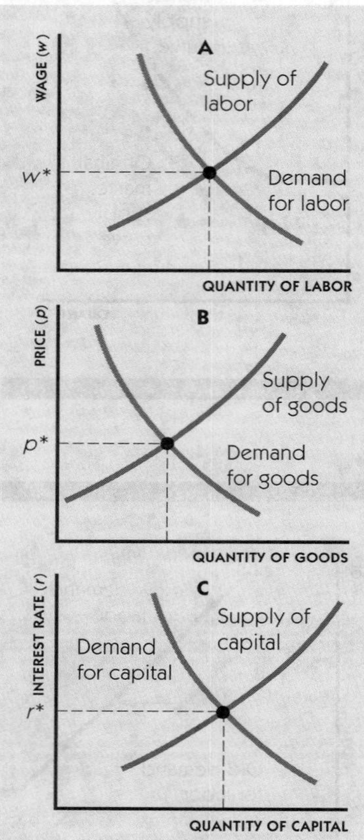

Figure 5.10 MARKET EQUILIBRIUM

In panel A, the equilibrium wage is at the intersection of the demand and supply curves for labor (when prices and interest rates are given). In panel B, the equilibrium price level is given by the intersection of the demand and supply curves for goods (when wages and interest rates are given). Panel C shows the equilibrium interest rate at the intersection of the demand and supply curves for capital (when wages and prices are given).

Now that we have analyzed the behavior of firms and households, we need to put these results together, to analyze equilibrium in each of the major markets of the economy.

THE LABOR MARKET

Figure 5.10A shows the demand and supply curves for labor (when prices and interest rates are given). We find the demand curve for labor through the analysis of the behavior of the firm, as described above, and the supply curve of labor through an analysis of the household's labor supply decision. The intersection gives the equilibrium wage. When the demand for labor equals the supply of labor, we say that the labor market **clears.** By definition, in the basic competitive model, there is no unemployment, since the wage is set at the level at which the demand for labor equals the supply.

THE PRODUCT MARKET

Figure 5.10B shows the demand and supply curves for goods (when wages and interest rates are given). The demand curve is derived from the household's consumption decision, and the supply curve from the firm's production decision. This aggregate view of the product market incorporates demand and supply curves for each of the many products produced in the economy, and closer inspection would reveal a myriad of product markets, one for each good in the economy. The intersection of the demand and supply curves for any individual good gives its equilibrium price, as we saw in Chapter 3. When we talk about the product market as a whole, with an aggregate demand and supply curve, we say that the intersection of the demand and supply curves gives the equilibrium **price level.**

THE CAPITAL MARKET

Figure 5.10C shows the demand and supply curves for capital, derived from the supply of savings by households and the demand for funds by firms to finance new investment. As we saw earlier, we can think of the interest rate as the price of funds; for instance, higher interest rates mean that households have to give up more future consumption if they wish to increase current consumption by a dollar. The intersection of the demand and supply curves gives the equilibrium interest rate.

GENERAL EQUILIBRIUM

The **general equilibrium** of the economy is the situation in which *all* markets are in equilibrium (or all markets clear); that is, the demand for each good equals its supply, the demand for each kind of labor equals its supply, and the demand for capital equals its supply. We call such a situation an equilibrium because when all markets clear, there is no incentive for prices—including the price of labor (the wage) and the price of capital (the interest rate)—in any market to change.

THE INTERRELATEDNESS OF MARKETS

It is important to recognize that all markets are interrelated: what goes on in one market may have repercussions throughout the economy. Consider, for instance, a tax that firms must pay on each worker hired. Figure 5.11 shows the initial effect of the tax. The tax means that the wage received by a worker is less than the cost of labor to the firm, which includes both the wage and tax. At each wage received by the worker, w, the cost of the worker to the firm has gone up by the amount, t, so the demand for labor decreases. The demand curve shifts to the left. As the figure illustrates, the wage received by the worker accordingly goes down, from w_0 to w_1, and the total cost of the worker to the firm, $w_1 + t$, goes up. But this is not the end of the story.

Lower wages received by households result in their demanding fewer goods; the demand curve for each product shifts to the left. Higher wages paid by firms result in firms' being willing to supply less output at any given price; the supply curve for each product shifts to the left. Output is reduced, and normally the price will change.

Figure 5.11 EFFECT OF A TAX ON LABOR

The tax means that the wage received by a worker is less than the cost of labor to the firm, which includes the tax. As a result of the tax, the wage received by the worker normally goes down, and the total cost of labor to the firm normally goes up. These are, however, only the initial effects. These wage changes give rise to changes in the product and capital markets, and the resulting changes in interest rates and prices have reverberations back on the demand and supply curves for labor, and hence on the equilibrium wage rate.

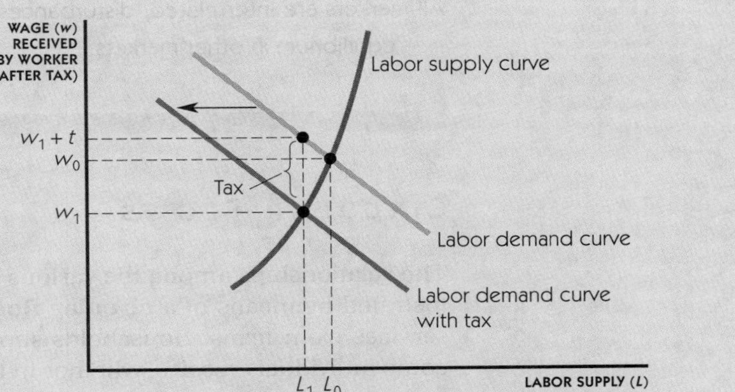

If, for instance, the price level increases, this will have ramifications back on the labor market. At higher prices, households' real wages—the extra goods workers can buy as a result of working an hour more—will be lower, and they will be willing to supply less labor. At higher prices, firms will, at each wage, be willing to produce more, and hence will demand more labor. The wage rate—both the wage paid by firms and the wage received by workers—will thus increase. We then need to trace the effect of this wage increase back on the product market.

The labor market is not the only market to be disturbed. The capital market will also be affected. As firms expand or contract production, they will demand more or less capital. As wages increase, firms will substitute capital for labor, since labor has become relatively more expensive. Accordingly, the demand curve for capital shifts. At the same time, if workers' income is reduced, they are likely to reduce their savings, so the supply curve of capital also shifts. As the demand and supply curves of capital shift, the interest rate changes, and this too has effects, both on the product market (since households' incomes and firms' cost curves are thereby affected) and on the labor market (for the same reasons).

The process continues. Eventually the economy settles down to a new equilibrium. General equilibrium analysis takes all of these interactions into account.

GENERAL EQUILIBRIUM

The general equilibrium of the economy occurs when all markets clear. The demand for labor equals the supply; the demand for each good equals its supply; and the demand for capital equals the supply.

All markets are interrelated; disturbances to one market have consequences for the equilibrium in other markets.

CIRCULAR FLOWS

The relationships among the various parts of the economy are sometimes illustrated by means of a **circular flow** diagram. Households buy goods and services from firms. Households supply labor and capital to firms. The income individuals receive, whether in the form of wages or the return on their savings, is spent to buy the goods that firms produce.

Figure 5.12 depicts this circular flow for a simplified economy in which there are no savings (and therefore no capital), no government, and no foreign trade. Firms hire labor from households and sell goods to households.

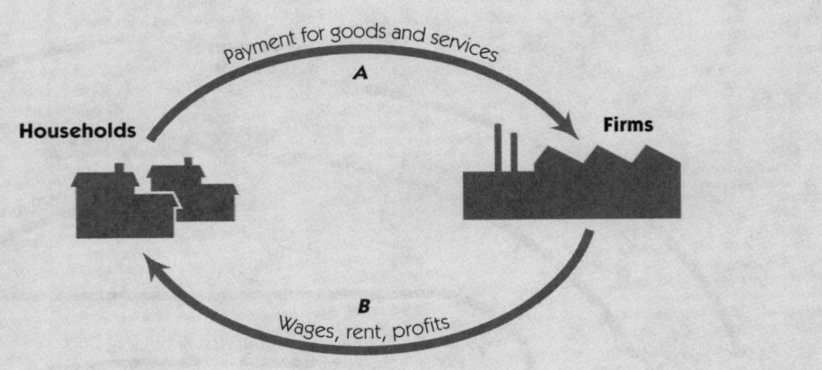

Figure 5.12 A SIMPLE CIRCULAR FLOW DIAGRAM

In this simple circular flow diagram, only labor and product markets and only the household and firm sectors are represented. It can be analyzed from any starting point. For example, funds flow from households to firms in the form of purchases of goods and services. Funds flow from firms to households in the form of payments for the labor of workers and profits paid to owners.

The income they receive from selling their products goes to pay their workers, and anything left over is paid out to households as profits.

A circular flow can be analyzed from any starting point, but let's start on the upper arrow (at point *A*), moving from left to right. Consumers pay money to firms to buy their goods and services, and this money then flows back through the firms to households at *B* in the form of wages, rents on land, and profits. Not only is the circular flow diagram useful in keeping track of how funds flow through the economy, it also enables us to focus on certain balance conditions, which must always be satisfied. Thus, in the figure, the income of households (the flow of funds from firms) must equal the expenditures of households (the flow of funds to firms).

Figure 5.13 expands the depiction of circular flow in several ways. First, savings and capital are included. Here, some of the funds that flow from the firm to the household are return on capital (interest on loans, dividends on equities), while some of the funds that flow from the household to the firm are savings, which go to purchase machines and buildings. In addition, firms retain some of their earnings and use them to finance investment.

The diagram is expanded further to include funds flowing into and out of the government. Now households and firms have both additional sources of funds and additional places where funds go. Some households receive money from the government (like Social Security and welfare payments); some sell their labor services to the government rather than private firms; and some receive interest on loans to the government (U.S. government bonds). And there is now an important additional outflow: part of household income goes to the government, in the form of taxes. Similarly, firms have additional sources of inflow in the sales of goods and services they make to the government and in government subsidies to firms, and an additional outflow in the taxes they must pay to the government.

Just as the flow of funds into and out of households and firms must balance, the flow of funds into the government must balance the flow of funds

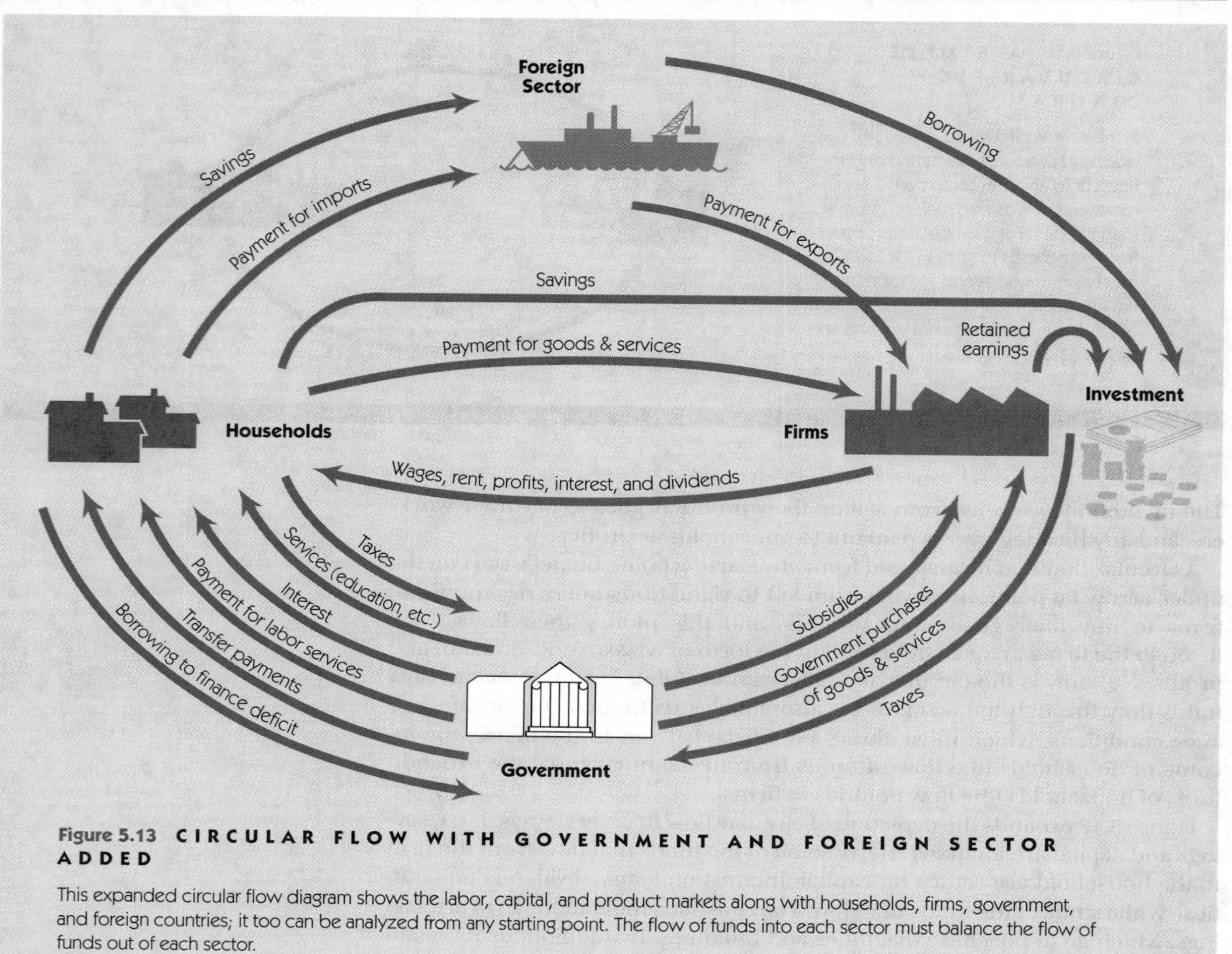

Figure 5.13 CIRCULAR FLOW WITH GOVERNMENT AND FOREIGN SECTOR ADDED

This expanded circular flow diagram shows the labor, capital, and product markets along with households, firms, government, and foreign countries; it too can be analyzed from any starting point. The flow of funds into each sector must balance the flow of funds out of each sector.

out.[4] Funds go out as purchases of goods and services from firms, purchases of labor services from households, and payments of interest to households on the government debt. Funds also go out as direct flows to households, for Social Security, welfare payments, and so forth (called "transfer payments" in the diagram), and to firms as subsidies. Funds flow into the government from taxes on both households and firms. When there is a deficit—that is, when

[4]We ignore here the possibility that the government can simply pay for what it obtains by printing money. In the United States, the government always finances any shortfall in revenue by borrowing.

the government spends more than it collects in taxes—as there has been in recent years, funds go into the government as borrowings from households. The government finances the difference between what it spends and what it raises in taxes by borrowing (in our diagram, from households).

Figure 5.13 also includes the flow to and from foreign countries. Firms sell goods to foreigners (exports) and borrow funds from foreigners. Households buy goods from foreigners (imports) and invest funds in foreign firms. Again, there must be a balance in the flow of funds: U.S. exports plus what the country borrows from abroad (the flow of funds from abroad) must equal its imports plus what it lends abroad (the flow of funds to other countries).[5]

The flow of funds diagram is useful as a way of keeping track of the various relationships in the economy. The various balance conditions that make up the diagram are basically identities. Identities, as we know, are statements that are always true; they follow from the basic definitions of the concepts involved. Household income, for example, must equal expenditures on goods plus savings (the flow of funds to firms).

The interconnections and balance conditions making up circular flow analysis are the same as those that arise in the competitive equilibrium model discussed earlier in the chapter. Even if the economy were not competitive, however, the interrelationships and balance conditions of the circular flow diagram would still be true. The circular flow diagram is useful, for it reminds us that whether the economy is competitive or not, if one element of a balance changes, some other element *must* change.

Let's put the circular flow diagram to work. Consider a reduction in the personal income tax, such as occurred in 1981 under President Reagan. The flow of funds into the government was reduced. The circular flow diagram reminds us that if flows in and out are to remain balanced, then either some other flow into the government must be increased or some flow out of the government must be decreased. That is, either some other tax flow must be increased, government borrowing must increase, or government expenditures must decrease.

THE ROLE OF GOVERNMENT

In the basic competitive model, we ignored government, arguing that before we can understand what government does, we must first understand how markets without government function. The government is important: in the United States, federal government expenditures amount to a fifth of GDP, and total government expenditures amount to 36 percent. In other countries, government is an even larger part of the economy: in Sweden and Italy expenditures equal or exceed 50 percent of GDP.

[5]This condition can be put another way: the difference between U.S. imports and exports must equal the net flow of funds from abroad (the difference between what the country borrows from abroad and what it lends).

What is the rationale for all of this government activity? What does the government do? What should the government do? In recent years, the last question has been at the center of extensive political debate.

The Efficiency of Markets

Behind this debate is one of the most fundamental ideas in economics: competitive markets are efficient. Firms have an incentive to lower costs to the minimum level possible, and to produce the goods that consumers want. As we saw in Chapter 3, prices guide firms in their production decisions and households in their consumption decisions.

Adam Smith argued that in competitive economies, the public interest is best served by individuals pursuing their own self-interest. As he put it:

> Man has almost constant occasion for the help of his brethren, and it is in vain for him to expect it from their benevolence only. He will be more likely to prevail if he can interest their self-love in his favor, and show them that it is for their own advantage to do for him what he requires of them. . . . It is not from the benevolence of the butcher, the brewer, or the baker, that we expect our dinner, but from their regard to their own interest. We . . . never talk to them of our own necessities but of their advantages.[6]

Smith's insight was that individuals work hardest to help the overall economic production of society when their efforts help themselves. He argued that an "obvious and simple system of liberty" provided the greatest opportunities for people to help themselves and thus, by extension, to create the greatest wealth for a society.

Smith used the metaphor of the **"invisible hand"** to describe how self-interest led to social good: "He intends only his own gain, and he is in this as in many other cases led by an invisible hand to promote an end which was no part of his intention . . . By pursuing his own interest he frequently promotes that of the society more effectually than when he really intends to promote it."

Economics has progressed considerably since Adam Smith, but his fundamental argument still has great appeal. Competitive markets ensure that the economy operates along its production possibilities curve: given the economy's inputs, more of one good can only be produced by decreasing production of other goods. The economy produces the goods that consumers want. Production simultaneously takes into account the trade-offs individuals are willing to make (how many apples they are *willing* to give up to get one more orange) and the trade-offs the production possibilities curve gives the economy (how many apples *have* to be given up to get one more orange).

Moreover, competitive markets ensure that goods get to the right people. As we saw in Chapter 2, if individuals do not like the particular mix of goods they have, they can trade; exchange will continue until no further mutually advantageous trades are feasible.

[6]*The Wealth of Nations*, (1776), Book 1, Chapter 2.

As a result, in competitive markets, no one can be made better off without someone else being made worse off. An economy with this property is said to be **Pareto efficient**—a term named after the great Italian economist of the early twentieth century Vilfredo Pareto.

LIMITATIONS OF THE BASIC COMPETITIVE MODEL

While the basic model provides a good starting point for economic analysis, under some circumstances it may not provide a good description of the economy. In this book, we will be particularly concerned with the problem of unemployment. Periodically, the economy is plagued with high levels of unemployment, so the assumption that all markets—including the labor market—are clearing seems, at times, inappropriate.

When markets fail to correspond to the theoretical ideal of the basic competitive model, there is said to be a market failure. When there is a **market failure,** the economy is not Pareto efficient. Certain government interventions *might* make some individuals better off without making others worse off. In the remaining chapters of this book, we will spend considerable time understanding the causes of large-scale unemployment and related macroeconomic market failures. Many of the explanations for unemployment are related to other ways in which market economies differ from the assumptions of the competitive equilibrium model. The remaining pages of this chapter take up the most important of these differences.

IMPERFECTIONS OF COMPETITION

The basic competitive model begins with the assumption that there are so many buyers and sellers in each market that each firm and each individual believes that it has no effect on the equilibrium price. We say that firms and households are **price takers.** In particular, the amount produced by any firm has a negligible effect on the market price.

In many markets, firms do seem to have an effect on the price. They are **price makers.** This is true of many of the goods we buy—from automobiles to film, brand-name cereals, beer, and soft drinks. The production decision of a price maker determines the price it receives; alternatively, such a firm picks a price, and the price it picks determines how much it can sell. The difference between the price-taking firms of the basic competitive model and the price-making firms of imperfect competition can be represented by the demand curves they face. With perfect competition, firms face a horizontal demand curve. They can sell as much as they want at the going market price. With imperfect competition, firms face a downward-sloping demand curve.

The basic rule for determining how much firms produce is still that firms increase production as long as the extra (or marginal) revenue of producing

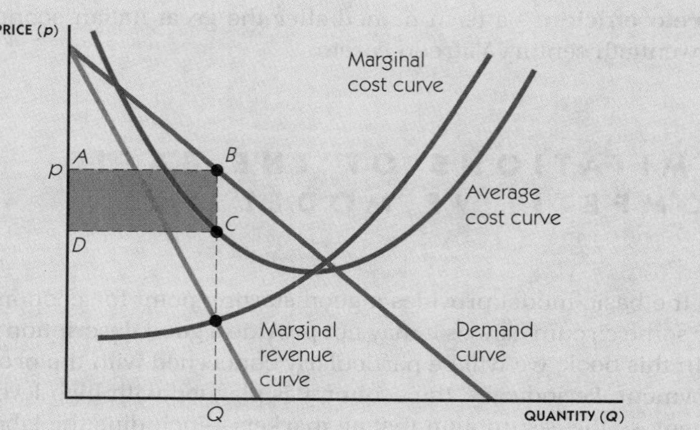

Figure 5.14 IMPERFECT COMPETITION

In markets with a single firm or sufficiently few firms so that there is imperfect competition, firms face downward-sloping demand curves. They set marginal revenue equal to marginal cost. Profits are the difference between (price and average costs) times the quantity produced, the area *ABCD*.

one more unit exceeds the marginal cost. Profit maximizing entails setting marginal revenue equal to marginal cost. The important difference between perfect and imperfect competition is that with its downward-sloping demand curve, if the imperfectly competitive firm increases its output, price falls. The extra revenue the firm receives (its marginal revenue) is less than the price at which it sells the last unit, because in order to sell that last unit, the firm had to lower the price on all the other units it sold.

Thus, in Figure 5.14, the marginal revenue curve is below the demand curve, and the equilibrium output is that at which marginal revenue equals marginal cost. The profits per unit sold are the difference between the price and average costs. Total profits are shown in the figure as the rectangle *ABCD*, the difference between price and average costs times the quantity produced.

The extreme case of imperfect competition is no competition. A firm that faces no competitors is called a **monopolist.** There are relatively few industries with only one firm. At one time, Kodak was a virtual monopolist in the photographic film industry, as was the Aluminum Company of America in the aluminum industry.

When there are a few firms in an industry, it is called an **oligopoly.** The analysis of oligopolies is complicated by the fact that the extra revenue a firm receives from selling an extra unit depends in part on how the company's rivals react. Firms must consider rivals' possible reactions when they make decisions such as whether to produce more or to advertise more.

In between oligopolies and perfect competition is a situation called **monopolistic competition,** where there are sufficiently many firms in an industry so that no firm worries about the reactions of rivals to any action it takes. At the same time, however, there are sufficiently few firms so that each one faces a downward-sloping demand curve for its product. With monopolistic competition, barriers to entry (such as the costs of entering a market) are low enough that profits may be driven to zero, but still firms are not price takers.

In most markets in modern economies, competition is not perfect. A firm that raises its price does not lose all of its customers, as would be the case in the perfectly competitive model. There are several reasons for this, the most important of which is the fact that the products of different firms are slightly different from one another. There is **product differentiation.** The automobile made by Ford is slightly different from the one made by General Motors, and likewise throughout most of the major industries in the United States.

The differences may be real or simply perceived. They may be as simple as the differences in location of several gasoline stations, or as complex as the differences between two separate computers. The differences may be related to differences in the quality of products, or they may arise from brand loyalty or firm reputations. As will be discussed briefly later in this chapter, developing new and better products, different from those produced by other firms, is one of the main ways in which firms compete in modern economies. In the basic competitive model, however, firms only compete on price.

In labor markets, competition is also often limited. In many industries, workers do not compete actively against one another but rather work together, through unions. Together, they threaten to refuse to work for a firm unless the firm raises its wages; that is, they use their market power to extract higher wages by threatening a strike. Of course, their market power is limited by the fact that the employer may turn to nonunion workers. For example, in 1991, the United Automobile Workers struck Caterpillar, a major producer of heavy machinery such as that used in road building, and the firm threatened to replace its employees with nonunion workers. After Caterpillar proceeded to carry out its threat, the strike was quickly settled.

For the present purposes, it is important to note that the ability of unions to extract higher wages depends on the ability of firms to pay higher wages. When a firm has profits resulting from monopoly power, then it can pay higher wages. When the firm operates in a highly competitive industry, if it pays higher wages, it cannot compensate by charging higher prices.

As illustrated in Figure 5.15, the role of unions has been declining markedly in the United States for the past forty years. In fact, within the private sector,

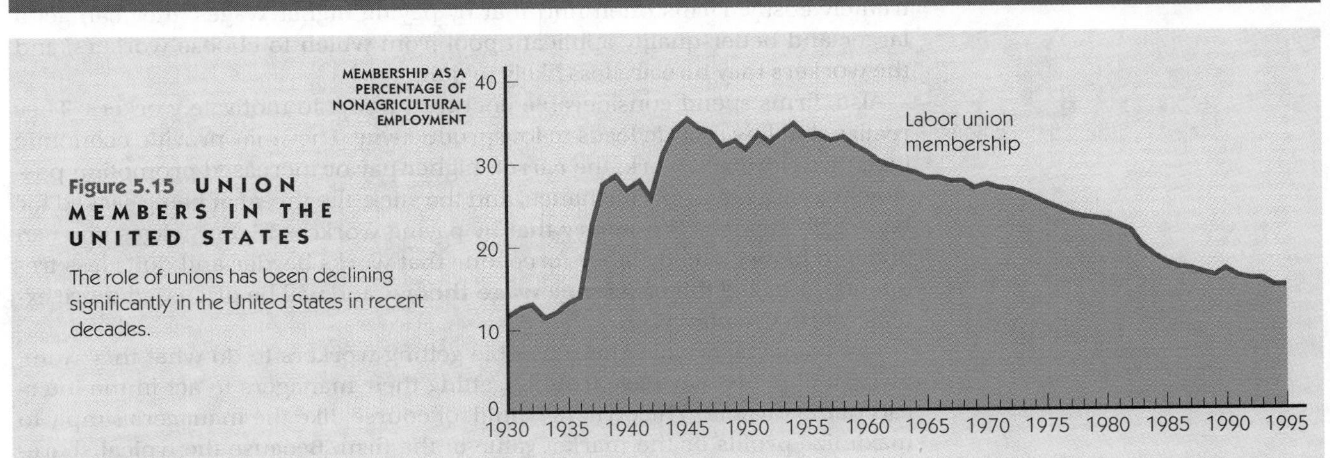

Figure 5.15 UNION MEMBERS IN THE UNITED STATES

The role of unions has been declining significantly in the United States in recent decades.

the decline has been even more marked; the major area of growth of unionization is among public employees. Part of this decline is attributed to the increased competition faced by such traditionally highly unionized sectors as automobiles and steel. And employment in these sectors has declined, some claim, partly as a result of the high wages the unions have won for their workers. In most European countries, however, unions remain powerful and play a major role in setting wages.

Imperfect Information

An important assumption of the basic competitive model is that households are well informed. They have good information about the products they buy. They know the prices at which they can acquire each good at each store. They have good information about the firms in which they invest. Similarly, firms have good information about potential employees. Firms know each worker's abilities. They can costlessly monitor what workers are doing and ensure that they do as they are told. It is clear that these assumptions are not quite correct; households and firms both face limited or, as economists say, **imperfect information**. This fact has important implications for how each of the markets in the economy functions.

In the product market, imperfect information provides an additional reason why each firm faces a downward-sloping demand curve. If firm A lowers its price below that of its rival, firm B, it does not instantly gain all of B's customers. Customers may not know that firm A has lowered its prices; even if they do, they may not be sure that the product being sold by A, or the services it provides in conjuction with the product, are of the same quality as the product sold by B. Thus, imperfect information leads to imperfect competition.

In the labor market, a firm must spend considerable resources trying to screen various applicants, to find out which are best suited for the firm. Even then, it will not be perfectly successful. Some of the workers it hires will turn out to be unsuitable. Thus, in many jobs, hiring and training workers is extremely costly. Firms often find that by paying higher wages, they can get a larger and better-quality applicant pool from which to choose workers, and the workers they hire are less likely to quit.

Also, firms spend considerable energy in trying to motivate workers. They realize that low morale leads to low productivity. They may provide economic incentives for hard work: the carrot, higher pay or increased promotion possibilities with better performance, and the stick, the threat of being sacked for bad performance. The theory that by paying workers higher wages one can obtain a higher-quality labor force, one that works harder and quits less frequently, is called the **efficiency wage theory,** and will be discussed more extensively in Chapter 15.

Just as managers may have trouble getting workers to do what they want, owners of firms may have trouble getting their managers to act in the interests of the owners. The owners would, of course, like the managers simply to maximize profits or the market value of the firm. Because the typical shareholder has her wealth spread out among many firms, she may not care much about the risks incurred by the firm. That is why she simply wants the firm to maximize its profit or market value; and one of the assumptions of the basic competitive model is that firms maximize profits.

But the shareholders do not themselves make the decisions concerning what the firm does. They must rely on those who manage the firm, and the managers may not do what is in the interests of the shareholders; that is, they may not maximize profits or market value. For instance, a manager's welfare is closely tied with that of the firm. If the firm goes bankrupt, he has a good chance of being out of a job, and other firms may be reluctant to hire him; even if the firm does not go bankrupt, if it does badly, the manager's pay is likely to suffer. Therefore, managers may take too few risks. Another possibility is that they may use their position to enhance their life-style rather than the profits of the firm; they may use corporate jets not so much to improve productivity, but perhaps to fly around to vacation spots also owned by the firm.

There are, in fact, some checks on managerial discretion. A manager who does not take actions that maximize the value of the firm under her charge may find that her firm is threatened with a takeover. Or shareholders may revolt and elect a board that fires the management. But both of these checks provide only imperfect discipline.

Finally, information problems have a major effect on how capital markets work. To take one example, consider a firm that wishes to borrow money. Normally, you might think that if, at the going interest rate, some potential borrower cannot obtain all the funds he wants, all he needs to do is offer to pay a higher interest rate. Lenders would prefer to receive the higher interest rate, and it would seem that no one is precluded from the market. But this does not seem to work, and for a simple reason. Lenders worry that if they charge a higher interest rate, their expected returns will actually decrease because the chance of default will increase. At higher interest rates, safer investors find that it does not pay to borrow. A disproportionate number of those willing to borrow at high rates are high-flyers—people who are undertaking high-risk projects that, if successful, will yield high returns, more than enough to cover the interest charge. But if the projects fail, they simply go bankrupt, and the lender is left "holding the bag."

Thus, the relationship between expected returns to the lender and the interest rate charged may look like the curve in Figure 5.16. In this case, there is an optimal interest rate, r^*, at which the bank's expected return is maximized. If at that interest rate the demand for funds exceeds the supply, lenders will not be willing to lend at a higher interest rate, because they know that their expected returns will actually be lower if they do so. In this situation, economists say there is **credit rationing.** Some borrowers are rationed in the amount of credit they can obtain. The capital market does not clear.

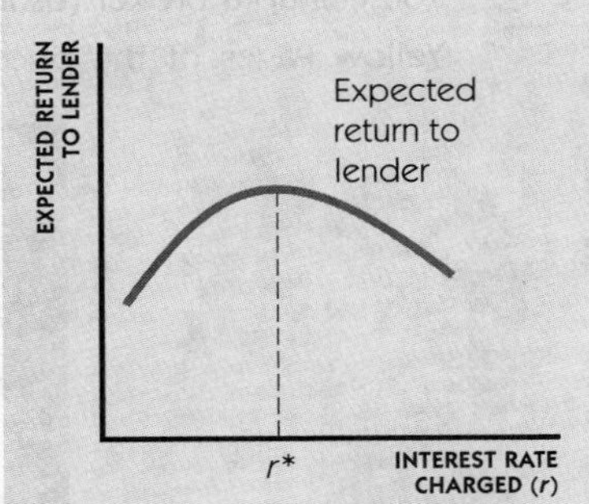

Figure 5.16 EXPECTED RETURNS FROM LENDING

Increasing the interest rate charged may actually lead to lower expected returns, as the best risks decide not to apply for loans and those who do borrow undertake riskier projects.

MISSING MARKETS

The basic competitive model assumes that there are competitive markets for all goods and services; the only reason a market for a good might not exist is if, at the minimum cost of producing it, demand is zero. In fact, many markets are missing; among the most important of these are the markets that would provide insurance against the various risks that households and firms face

Close-up: Automobile Brokers and Imperfect Information

A broker is someone who arranges contracts between two parties. In older times, marriage brokers brought together prospective couples. Stockbrokers bring together buyers and sellers of stocks. Car brokers bring together buyers and sellers of cars.

In every case, though, a broker is someone whose job exists only because of imperfect information. After all, why can't a person just go out and choose a spouse or a stock or a car? The obvious problem is that many different varieties are available, and it costs time and energy and money to collect the information to make an informed decision. A good broker is out there in the market all the time, keeping track of what is going on. Having a relatively small number of people keeping track of buyers and sellers is certainly more efficient than having all buyers and sellers duplicating one another's efforts.

Consider how car brokers work, for example. You call up a broker (usually they are listed in the Yellow Pages of the phone book) and describe what sort of car you want—make, model, year, accessories. The broker then finds you the best deal.

Working as a broker may seem like a funny way to make a living. How can someone get paid for shopping for cars? The answer is that shopping for a car involves time and the energy of confronting dealers and haggling over price. Even if the buyer spends several days or weeks shopping, it is not clear she will find the best deal. Paying a knowledgeable broker will certainly save time and energy, and might result in a cheaper price too. A good broker will know the sales representative's typical commission or the "preparation fee" that dealers receive for getting a car ready to sell. By taking factors like this into account, the broker can often negotiate a better price.

Not everyone will need or want an automobile broker. But for those who feel their information about the car market is extremely imperfect, a broker may be a wise choice.

Source: "A Better Way to Buy a Car?" *Consumer Reports*, September 1989, pp. 593–95.

(such as unemployment or crop failure). Government has stepped in to provide a variety of insurance programs, partly because, at least at the time the programs were initiated, the private sector did not.

TECHNOLOGICAL CHANGE

The basic competitive model proceeds under the assumption that every firm has a given technology, a given way of converting inputs into outputs. There is a given array of products that are produced. In fact, the development of new products and less expensive ways of producing old products is an essential part of modern industrial economies; the fact that modern economies do these things so well is often cited as one of their greatest virtues.

Because the basic competitive model ignores technological change, it cannot address fundamental issues: Why has productivity increased less rapidly in recent years? Why does productivity seem to increase faster in some countries than in others?

Moreover, in sectors of the economy in which technological change is important, there is a limited number of firms. Each faces a downward-sloping demand curve. It is a price maker, not a price taker. These are the characteristics of imperfect competition. Nevertheless, competition is keen—it involves the race to develop new products and better production methods, so that one company can undercut its rivals.

Government's interest in promoting technological progress often conflicts with its interest in promoting competition. If a firm is to be willing to spend its funds to do research and develop new products, it must be able to get a return from any inventions that are the fruit of that research. Governments therefore grant patents, giving an inventor the exclusive right to an invention for a period of seventeen years. The losses from the reduction in competition for this limited period are thought to be outweighed by the gains from the spur to innovation that the patent provides.

Even with a good patent system, there may be insufficient spur to innovation. Firms seldom capture all the benefits that accrue from their inventive activity. Other firms see what they have done, learn from it, and use it as a basis for producing still better products. Customers benefit. Innovation in the computer industry has made faster and faster computers available at lower and lower prices. And in the long run, workers benefit as well, as the improved technology becomes reflected in higher wages. Economists say these are *externalities* associated with innovation.

EXTERNALITIES AND PUBLIC GOODS

Externalities occur when the actions of a household or firm generate benefits or costs to other households or firms without compensation. For example, a factory that releases toxic fumes into the air generates a negative externality for those who breath the air. Innovations, on the other hand, are often thought to produce positive externalities. Whenever there are externalities, markets will not be efficient, since people will not take into account either all the benefits or all the costs of their actions.

There are some instances where a good can be enjoyed by everyone—that is, no one can be excluded from its benefits—and in which there is in fact no

Close-up: IBM—From the Edge of Monopoly to the Edge of Competition

IBM committed itself to computers in the 1950s, and rapidly asserted its dominance in the business of large "mainframe" computers. IBM machines were often the most technologically advanced, and in the few cases where they might not have been the best, they still had an extraordinary reputation for great service and support. Back in the days when computers were more than a little mysterious to most of their users, that reputation mattered a lot.

IBM was never a literal monopoly. Throughout the 1960s and 1970s, competition came from firms like Control Data, Honeywell, Sperry Univac, Burroughs, and NCR. But by 1980, IBM still had over 80 percent of the world market for mainframe computers. It was common for the company's sales to grow every year by double-digit percentages.

But by the early 1990s, its market share had slipped dramatically. In 1990, it had only 15 percent of the fastest-growing segment of the market, personal computers. Upstarts—Apple, Compaq, Dell, AST—as well as foreign producers—NEC and Toshiba—dominated the market. IBM was forced to make dramatic cutbacks. For the first time in its history, there were massive layoffs. It engaged in large-scale restructuring, trying to make itself "nimble" enough to compete in the fast-moving market. Less than two decades after the Justice Department had tried to break up IBM, charging that it was too close to a monopoly, it was scrambling for market share.

Joseph Schumpeter, one of the great economists of the twentieth century, focused on the importance of technological change. He described it as resulting in a process of *creative destruction,* as new firms and industries put constant pressure on the old. IBM's struggle is a real world example of Schumpeter's vision of markets with dominant firms only able to maintain their position temporarily in the face of intense technological competition from new entrants.

reason to exclude anyone, since there are no extra costs associated with an additional individual enjoying the good. National defense is an example: if the United States is protected, everybody in the country benefits, and there are no additional costs incurred when an additional baby is born. Such goods are called pure public goods, and will not be supplied, or will be undersupplied, by private markets.

Adjustments

The basic competitive model focuses on the *equilibrium* of the economy, the state of the economy in which there are no forces for change, where the supply for each good equals the demand—that is, where all markets clear.

Of course, the economy is always changing. One year, the price of oil may rise as a war in the Middle East reduces the supply. Another year, exports may decline as foreign customers face an economic downturn. Technological progress in the Japanese car industry may have a direct and obvious impact on American producers (and customers). There is a constant need for prices—including the price of labor (the wage) and the price of capital (the interest rate)—to change. Earlier, we saw how what happens in one market can, and normally will, have repercussions in other markets.

Imagine that the economy is initially in an equilibrium and then is disturbed, say by a large increase in the price of imported oil. The task of finding the new equilibrium prices for the millions of other goods and services in the economy is an extraordinarily difficult one. The adjustments do not occur overnight; in some cases, they may take weeks, months, perhaps stretch out to years. In the meanwhile, some markets may not be in equilibrium: demand may not equal supply (markets may not clear).

INCOME DISTRIBUTION

Even if all the conditions of the basic competitive model were satisfied, this would only mean that the economy was efficient. The resulting distribution of income might be totally unacceptable. Those with few skills might receive a wage that is below what they need to survive.

Behind the macroeconomic objectives of stable prices, full employment, and high growth lie other concerns, including the distribution of income. To a large extent, the goals may be complementary. Reducing unemployment is of particular benefit to the poor, since lack of jobs is one of the main causes of poverty. Eliminating those market failures that give rise to unemployment will, at the same time, make the distribution of income more equitable.

While generally, high rates of growth are thought to benefit everyone, this presumption has come to be questioned. Many of the benefits of growth since the 1970s seem to have gone to those in the upper part of the income distribution. Real wages of the unskilled remain unchanged, or are actually lower today than they were then. This experience has convinced many that the government needs to take a more active stance, not only in preventing unemployment, but in ensuring that the fruits of growth would be shared by all.

GOVERNMENT FAILURES

Whenever there is a market failure, there is a potential role for government. But government, like markets, often departs from the ideal: governments are subject to imperfections of information. They often do not fully anticipate all the consequences of their actions. Thus, they did not fully anticipate the devastating effects that superhighways had on urban centers, as it facilitated the flight to the suburbs. Nor did they anticipate the extent to which reforms in mental institution policies would lead to homelessness in cities. They often do not fully anticipate private sector responses to government actions. For instance, in 1990, the government required drug companies to provide drugs to the government at the lowest price sold on the market. The government had observed that drug companies sold drugs to some customers at prices below those at which they were selling drugs to the government under the Medicare program, and calculated that it could save billions of dollars by taking advantage of these discounts. But the drug companies canceled all discounts, recognizing that it did not pay to discount at all if they had to give the government a discount every time they gave someone else a discount. As a result, instead of saving the government money, the legislation wound up costing other people who purchase drugs more money.

Both bureaucrats and politicians are motivated in part at least by private incentives, which may lead them to take actions which are not in the public interest. The political process itself encourages politicians to think more about how votes will be affected by their actions than about any broader concept of public interest.

As a result of increased recognition of these government failures, there is increased interest in ascertaining how they can be reduced, for instance, by more extensive use of performance measures and by encouraging more competition within the public sector and between the public and private sectors. In certain areas, such as the postal service, productivity in the public sector has increased rapidly.

Today, in addressing the proper role of government, economists not only ask is there a market failure, but also whether government—recognizing its limitations—is likely to remedy those market failures.

THE BASIC MODEL COMPARED WITH THE REAL WORLD: A SUMMARY

If the real world matched up to the assumptions of the basic model of perfectly competitive markets, then markets could be given free rein. They would supply efficient outcomes. If an outcome seemed inequitable, society simply would redistribute initial wealth and let markets take care of the rest.

In the two centuries since Adam Smith first enunciated the view that markets ensure economic efficiency, economists have investigated the model with great care. Nothing they have discovered has shaken their belief that markets are, by and large, the most efficient way to coordinate an economy. However, they have found significant departures between modern economies and the competitive model. Few would go so far as to condemn the model totally for its flaws; its insights are simply too powerful. Rather, most economists use the basic competitive model as the starting point for building a richer, more complete model that recognizes the following qualifications.

1. Most markets are not as competitive as those envisioned by the basic model.
2. The basic model simply ignores technological change. It tells us about the striving for efficiency that occurs as consumers and firms meet in competitive markets, but it assumes that all firms operate with a given technology. Competition in the basic model is over price, yet in the real world, a primary focus of competition is the development of new and better products and the improvements in production, transportation, and marketing that allow products to be brought to customers at lower costs and thus at a

lower price. This competition takes place not between the multitude of small producers envisaged in the basic competitive model, but often between industrial giants like Du Pont and Dow Chemical, and between the industrial giants and upstarts, like IBM and the slew of small computer firms that eventually took away a major share of the computer market. Changes in technology lie behind economic growth, one of the principal concerns of macroeconomics.

3. The individuals and firms envisioned in the basic model have easy and inexpensive access to the information they need in order to operate in any market they enter. Buyers know what they are buying, whether it is stocks or bonds, a house, a car, or a refrigerator. Firms know perfectly the productivity of each worker they hire, and when a worker goes to work for a firm, he knows precisely what is expected of him in return for his promised pay.

   We have already encountered instances in which information problems are important and may fundamentally affect how markets work. In the following chapters, we will see other instances in which imperfect information and the other market imperfections to which imperfect information gives rise help to explain a variety of macroeconomic phenomena. We will see, for instance, in Chapter 14 how lack of information about the quality of people applying for jobs may make firms worry that if they lower the wages they pay, they will obtain a lower-quality work force; and that lack of information about the consequences of changing prices may result in prices being sticky, which partly explains the slow adjustment of the economy to equilibrium.

4. The basic model assumes that the costs of bringing a good to the market accrue fully and completely to the seller, and that the benefits of consuming a good go fully and completely to the buyer. Earlier in this chapter, however, we encountered the possibility of externalities, which are extra costs or benefits that do not figure in the individual's or firm's calculation.

5. The basic model answers the question "What goods will be produced, and in what quantities?" by assuming that all desired goods that *can* be brought to market *will* be brought to market. Trees that bloom in gold coins and tablets that guarantee an eternal youth are out of the question. But if customers want to buy green hair coloring, cancer-causing tobacco products, or life insurance policies overladen with extras, then producers can be expected to supply such goods. There are, however, some important markets that are missing. The most obvious example already given, is the firm that wants to borrow money but cannot, even at high interest rates.

   Imperfections in the capital market—the inability to obtain funds—play, as we will see, an important role in economic fluctuations. When firms cannot obtain funds to produce or to invest, production, investment, and employment all suffer. And, as in the recession that began in 1990, firms often attribute cutbacks in production and investment to an inability to obtain funds.

6. In the basic model, all markets hover at or near equilibrium. That is, they

THE BASIC MODEL VERSUS THE REAL WORLD

The basic model	The real world
1. All markets are competitive.	1. Most markets are *not* characterized by the degree of competition envisioned in the basic model.
2. Technological know-how is fixed and cannot change.	2. Technological change is a central part of competition in modern industrial economies.
3. Firms, consumers, and any other market participants have easy access to information that is relevant to the markets in which they participate.	3. Good information may be impossible to come by, and in most cases is costly to obtain. In many markets, buyers of products know less than the sellers.
4. Sellers bear the full and complete costs of bringing goods to market, and buyers reap the full benefit.	4. Externalities mean that market transactions may not accurately account for costs and benefits and the private market provides an inadequate supply of public goods.
5. All desired markets exist.	5. Some markets may not exist, even though goods or services in that market might be provided at a cost consumers would be willing to pay.
6. There is no involuntary unemployment.	6. There is involuntary unemployment. Adjustments may be slow, so that even if markets eventually clear, unemployment may persist for extended periods of time.
7. Competitive markets provide an efficient allocation of resources.	7. Efficiency is not enough. The income distribution generated by the market may be socially unacceptable.

clear: supply meets demand at the market price. Decades of evidence, however, suggest that labor markets often do not clear. Workers sometimes want to supply their labor services at the market wage, but cannot do so. The Great Depression of the 1930s is the most dramatic example of large-scale unemployment. During that period, unemployment rates rose as high as 25 percent of those willing and able to work.

7. Even if markets are efficient, the way they allocate resources may appear to be socially unacceptable; there may be massive pockets of poverty, or other social needs may remain unmet. Income distribution is a major concern of modern societies and their governments.

REVIEW AND PRACTICE

SUMMARY

1. An increase in the price of a good reduces a person's demand for that good both because of the income effect (the higher price makes the individual worse off, and because she is worse off, she reduces her consumption) and because of the substitution effect (the good is now more expensive *relative* to other goods, so she substitutes other goods).

2. An increase in the interest rate has an ambiguous effect on savings and current consumption. The income effect leads to more current consumption (reduced savings), but the substitution effect leads to less current consumption. The net effect on savings is probably slightly positive.

3. An increase in the wage rate has an ambiguous effect on labor supply. Individuals are better off, and so the income effect leads to more leisure (less work). But the substitution effect—the increased consumption from working an additional hour—leads to more work. In practice, the two effects probably just offset each other.

4. The typical firm has a U-shaped average cost curve. It produces at the level where price equals marginal cost, so long as price equals or exceeds average costs. The market supply curve is found by adding the supply curves of each of the firms in an industry. The typical shape is relatively horizontal when output is very low, but close to vertical as capacity is reached.

5. General equilibrium analysis stresses that all markets are interrelated. Equilibrium occurs when demand equals supply for every good and service and every input; the labor, capital, and product markets clear.

6. The circular flow diagram shows the flow of funds among the various parts of the economy.

7. Under certain ideal conditions, competitive markets are Pareto efficient: no one can be made better off without making someone else worse off. The economy operates along its production possibilities schedule, produces the goods individuals want, and ensures that goods are allocated efficiently among individuals.

8. There are some important limitations to the basic competitive model, which explain why sometimes markets fail to produce efficient outcomes. Among these are imperfections of competition, imperfections of informa-

tion, and externalities. Competitive markets may also spend too little on developing new technologies, may be slow in adjusting to new situations, and may fail to distribute income in an egalitarian way.

KEY TERMS

substitution effect
real income
income effect
expected return
liquidity
real wage
marginal cost
marginal revenue
average costs
fixed or **overhead costs**
variable costs
circular flow
Pareto efficiency
monopoly
oligopoly
monopolistic competition
product differentiation
imperfect information
efficiency wage theory
credit rationing

REVIEW QUESTIONS

1. Use the concepts of income and substitution effects to explain why demand curves for goods are normally downward sloping. Why may increases in the interest rate not lead to much more saving? Why may increases in the wage rate not lead to a much greater amount of work done?

2. What are some of the important factors individuals take into account in deciding how to invest their savings?

3. Why are average cost curves often U-shaped?

4. How is the level of output of a firm determined? What is the effect of an increase in wages on the market supply curve?

5. Why is the demand curve for labor by firms downward sloping?

6. Why may what happens in one market have effects on other markets? Illustrate with an example.

7. What is a circular flow diagram, and what do we learn from it.

8. Describe various aspects of the efficiency of competitive markets. What is meant by Pareto efficiency?

9. How is output determined in a monopoly? What are some forms that imperfect competition takes?

10. What are the most important reasons that competitive markets may not yield efficient outcomes?

PROBLEMS

1. Assume Alfred has $10,000, which he can either consume today or save and consume next year. If the interest rate is 10 percent, how much can

he consume next year if he consumes nothing now? Draw a budget constraint, with "Consumption today" on the horizontal axis and "Consumption next year" on the vertical. Show how the budget constraint shifts if the interest rate increases to 20 percent. Use the budget constraint diagram to discuss the income and substitution effects of the increase in the interest rate.

2. Assume now that Alfred has no income this year, but next year will come into an inheritance of $11,000. The bank is willing to lend money to Alfred at a 10 percent interest rate. Draw his budget constraint. Show how the budget constraint shifts if the interest rate the bank charges increases to 20 percent. Why can you be certain that as a result of the higher interest rate, his consumption this year will go down? (Hint: Explain why the income and substitution effects now both work in the same direction.)

3. If Alfred saves an extra dollar today and invests it at 7 percent interest, how much extra consumption can he have in thirty years' time?

4. Draw Alfred's budget constraint between leisure and consumption, assuming he can work 2,000 hours a year and his wage is $10 an hour. Show how his budget constraint changes if his wage increases to $15 an hour. Use the diagram to discuss income and substitution effects.

5. Use demand and supply diagrams for the labor, product, and capital markets to trace out the effects of immigrant workers. Look first at the labor market—what does the increase in the supply of labor do to the equilibrium wage? Explain how the resulting lower wage will shift the demand and supply curves for goods and for capital. Describe how these changes in price and interest rates will affect the demand and supply curves for labor.

6. Use the extended circular flow diagram, with the foreign sector included, to trace out the possible consequences of the following:

(a) a law requiring that businesses raise the wages of their employees;
(b) a decision by consumers to import more and save less;
(c) an increase in government expenditure financed by a corporate income tax;
(d) an increase in government expenditure without an accompanying increase in taxes.

7. For each of the programs listed below, discuss what market failures might be given as reasons for implementing the program:

(a) automobile safety belt requirements;
(b) regulations on automobile pollution;
(c) unemployment compensation;
(d) Medicare (medical care for the aged);
(e) Medicaid (medical care for the indigent);
(f) federal deposit insurance;
(g) federally insured mortgages;
(h) law requiring lenders to disclose the true rate of interest they are charging on loans (truth-in-lending law);
(i) urban renewal.

CHAPTER 6

THE FULL-EMPLOYMENT MODEL

If we look at history in decades, the market economy creates jobs for almost all who seek them. In the 1980s, for example, the American labor force increased by 19 million people, and the number of people employed increased by the same amount. But sometimes the markets fail, as is evident when one out of ten, one out of five, or even (during the Great Depression) one out of four job seekers cannot find jobs. Yet every period in which the market has failed to create enough jobs for those who seek them has been followed by a period in which the economy catches up. Thus, while the economy stalled from 1991 to 1992, creating only 1 million jobs, in the two and a half years from January 1993 until July 1995, more than 7 million new jobs were created.

The economic theories in the next part of the book explain why there are important episodes in which markets fail to create enough jobs and what the government can do about them. In this part of the book, we will see how the economy works in the long run—when it creates jobs at the rate of new entry into the labor force. We focus on the aggregate behavior of the economy—on movements of such macroeconomic variables as output and wages—when resources are fully employed. We show how competitive markets, when they work well, help explain the vitality of the American economy. No government official can calculate where to place the 7 million new workers who are expected to enter the labor force between 1996 and the year 2000. Indeed, if anyone from the president on down, had been asked where all the new entrants

KEY QUESTIONS

1. In an economy operating at full employment, what determines real wage, level of output, and investment?
2. How is the economy affected by government expenditures and international trade? When government increases its expenditures, but raises taxes to pay for the increased expenditures, what happens to investment? How might the answer differ between a small country like Switzerland and a large country like the United States?
3. How are markets in the economy interlinked?

would find jobs in the 1993 to 1994 growth spurt, no one would have known the precise answer, though they could have pointed to particular parts of the economy that would be the most likely sources of job growth. But they would have said, on the basis of past experience, that somehow, somewhere, the economy would create the jobs. The economic theories that we explore in this and the following chapters help explain this job growth.

MACROECONOMIC EQUILIBRIUM

The model we employ here is the basic competitive model described in earlier chapters. In it, large numbers of households and firms interact in the labor, product, and capital markets. Households supply labor to firms that use the labor to produce goods and compensate workers by paying them wages. Households also save, and those savings finance firms' investments such as the plant and equipment that firms need to produce. For the use of their funds, households receive interest and dividends from firms. With the income they earn from working and the return they earn from their savings, households buy the products that firms produce.

Two key lessons emerge from the basic competitive model. First, all markets are interrelated. What goes on in one market has an impact on others. The demand for labor, for instance, depends on the level of output (the product market). Second, wages, interest rates, and prices adjust to equate demand and supply. In this part of the book, we continue to focus on product, labor, and capital markets, and to assume that the adjustments in wages, interest rates, and prices are sufficiently rapid that, for practical purposes, all markets are always in equilibrium. That is, they all clear, with demand equal to supply. This assumption is not only a convenient starting point, but it gives us powerful insights into some of the basic macroeconomic questions. We began the chapter with the observation that *somehow* the economy creates jobs for the millions of new entrants into the labor force each year. It has done

Close-up: The Birth of the Micro–Macro Division

Today even noneconomists have heard the terms "microeconomics" and "macroeconomics." But economists did not actually begin thinking in those terms until the 1930s, when the global economy suffered the collapse that became known as the Great Depression. In the United States, the economy shrank 30 percent from 1929 to 1933; the unemployment rate hit 25 percent in 1933. Attention shifted to what determined aggregate variables like the unemployment rate and GDP.

John Maynard Keynes expressed the general idea when he wrote in 1936: "The division of Economics . . . is, I suggest, between the Theory of the Individual Industry or Firm and of the rewards and the distribution of a given quantity of resources on the one hand, and the Theory of Output and Employment *as a whole* on the other hand."

The first known written use of the words "microeconomic" and "macroeconomic" was by P. de Wolff, a little-known economist at the Netherlands Statistical Institute. In a 1941 article, de Wolff wrote: "The micro-economic interpretation refers to the relation . . . for a single person or family. The macro-economic interpretation is derived from the corresponding relation . . . *for a large group of persons or families (social strata, nations, etc.).*"

In the 1960s and 1970s, many economists became concerned that macroeconomic thinking had strayed too far from its microeconomic roots. Interestingly, some of the most important economic work of the last twenty years—which will be described in the following chapters—has sought to break down that wall and explain how rational, well-informed consumers and profit-maximizing firms can work together in a way that sometimes creates unemployment, inflation, or fluctuations in growth.

Source: Hal R. Varian, "Microeconomics," in Eatwell, Milgate, and Newman, eds., *The New Palgrave: A Dictionary of Economics* (1987), 3:461–63.

this without any government official or private individual managing the whole process. The magic of the market—the adjustment of wages and prices equilibrating the labor market—guides this process, and the model we present here explains how this happens.

The analysis here differs in one important way from the kind of microeconomic analysis we have seen previously. In macroeconomics, we focus on aggregates, on total output, rather than the output of individual products. We focus on total employment, and on average prices, which we refer to as the price level. We also proceed as if there is a single good being produced or a single kind of labor. That is, we can picture the economy as if all firms produced the same commodity and all workers are identical. In looking at these aggregates, we ignore the richness of the microeconomic detail we dealt with earlier. Hidden behind an increase in the price level are a myriad of changes in relative prices. Some prices have gone up faster than this average, some have gone up more slowly, some may have even decreased. The basic premise of macroeconomics is that we can say a great deal about the aggregates without inquiring into the smaller details.

THE LABOR MARKET

By assumption, in the basic competitive model, all markets clear. In the labor market, the fact that the demand for labor equals the supply implies that there is full employment. No worker who wishes to get a job (for which she is qualified) at the going market wage will fail to get one. Adjustments in wages ensure that this will occur. Of course, when economists say that there is full employment of the labor force—that the demand for labor is equal to the supply—there is still a small amount of unemployment. As we learned in Chapter 4, there is always some frictional unemployment in modern economies, as workers in transition between jobs, or just entering the labor force search for new positions. Thus, full employment should not be equated with an unemployment rate of zero.

The assumption of zero unemployment, while it is clearly unrealistic, is a useful simplification, particularly for studying changes in the economy in periods in which unemployment is relatively low, or for comparing the economy at different periods in which unemployment was low, such as 1989 and 1995.

In the aggregate labor market, the relationship between wages (w) and the price level (P) is very important. Economists distinguish between real and nominal wages. The real wage, as we learned in Chapter 5, is the nominal wage adjusted for increases in the price level. Dividing the nominal wage by the price level gives us the real wage, or w/P. This means that if wages and the price level change together, the real wage will remain the same. For example, suppose that nominal wages and the price level both increase by 2 percent during the course of a year. The real wage would be exactly the same as it was at the beginning of the year, because the increase in the nominal wage would be offset by a proportional increase in prices. Alternatively, if the price level is held constant, changes in the nominal wage represent changes in the real wage, and if the nominal wage is held constant while the price level increases (or decreases), the real wage will fall (or rise).

Figure 6.1 shows the aggregate labor market, with the real wage (w/P) on the vertical axis, the quantity of labor (L) on the horizontal axis, and the aggregate demand and supply curves for labor. With a given set of machines and technology, the aggregate demand for labor depends on the wages firms must pay, the prices firms receive for the goods they produce, and the prices they have to pay for other inputs, including raw materials and machines. Holding the prices of goods and inputs constant, the aggregate demand curve traces out the quantity of labor demanded by firms at different wages. At lower wages, the quantity of labor demanded is greater. There are two reasons for this. First, as wages fall relative to the cost of machines, it pays firms to substitute workers for machines. Second, as the wage falls, labor becomes relatively less expensive compared with the price of the goods it produces (so at the old level of employment, the value of the marginal product of the last unit of labor hired would exceed the wage), and again employers will hire more workers.

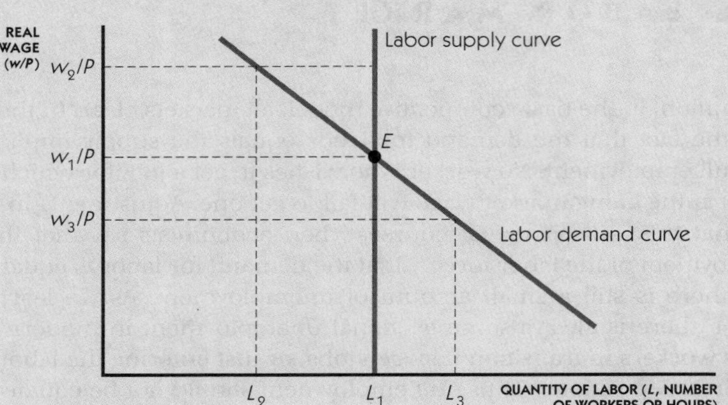

Figure 6.1 EQUILIBRIUM IN THE LABOR MARKET

Equilibrium in the labor market is at the intersection of the aggregate demand and supply curves for labor. If the real wage is above w_1/P where demand equals supply, there will be unemployment, putting pressure on wages to fall as workers compete to offer their services. Below w_1/P there will be excess demand for labor, which will put pressure on wages to rise.

Thus, the demand curve for labor slopes down, as shown in the diagram.

The figure also shows an aggregate labor supply curve. To simplify matters, we assume that labor supply is inelastic.[1] That is, individuals are either in the labor force, working a full (forty-hour) work week, or they are not. They do not enter and exit the market as wages go up and down, nor do they reduce or increase the hours they work in response to such changes. One advantage of making the assumption that the hours worked per week is fixed is that we can put *either* the number of hours worked (per week) or the number of workers hired on the horizontal axis of the figure. The demand and supply of labor hours (per week) is simply forty times the demand and supply of workers.

Basic supply and demand analysis implies that market equilibrium should occur at the intersection of the demand and supply curves, point *E*. The reason for this is simple: if the wage happens to be above the equilibrium wage w_1/P, say at w_2/P, the demand for labor will be L_2, much less than the supply, L_1. There will be an excess supply of workers. Those without jobs, who want jobs, will offer to work for less than the going wage, bidding down the wages of those already working. The process of competition will lead to lower wages, until eventually demand again equals supply. Likewise, if the wage is lower than w_1/P, say at w_3/P, firms in the economy will demand more labor than is supplied. Competing with one another for scarce labor services, they will bid the wage up to w_1/P.

[1]Recall the definition of elasticity from Chapter 3: the percentage change in quantity divided by the percentage change in price. Thus, an inelastic labor supply means that a 1 percent increase in wages results in a small percentage increase in supply. A perfectly inelastic labor supply curve is vertical: that means the labor supply does not change at all when wages increase.

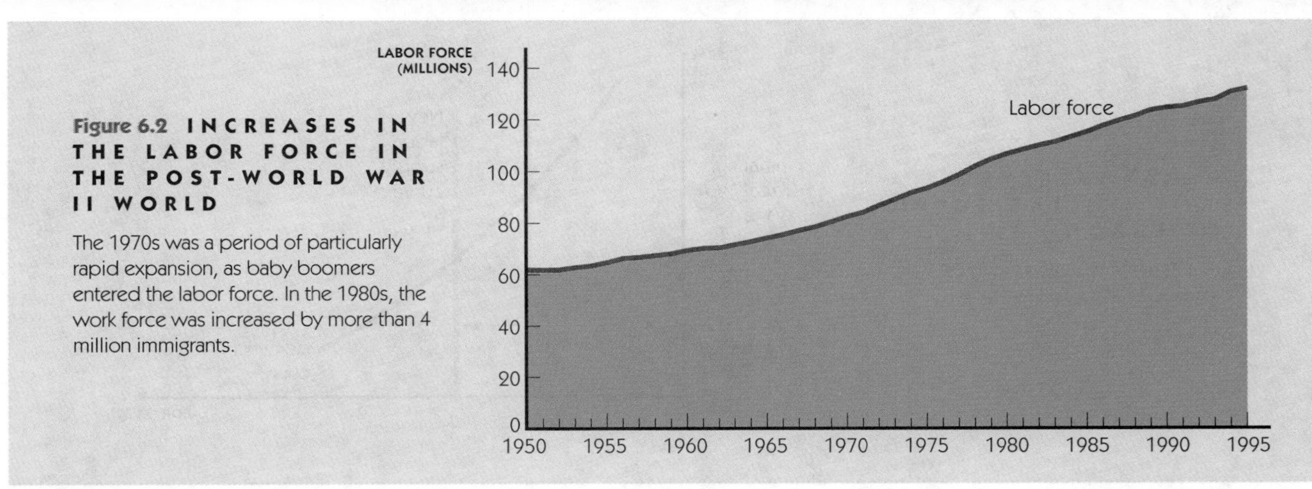

Figure 6.2 INCREASES IN THE LABOR FORCE IN THE POST-WORLD WAR II WORLD

The 1970s was a period of particularly rapid expansion, as baby boomers entered the labor force. In the 1980s, the work force was increased by more than 4 million immigrants.

SHIFTS IN THE DEMAND AND SUPPLY OF LABOR

The basic competitive model makes clear predictions of the consequences of shifts in the demand and supply of labor. Consider first shifts in the supply curve of labor. This can occur because there are more young people reaching working age than there are old people retiring, or because of new immigrants, or because of social changes which lead more women to join the labor force. Figure 6.2 shows the increase in the labor force over the last forty-five years. It shows, in particular, a rapid expansion in the 1970s. The consequences of such a large shift in the labor supply curve are depicted in Figure 6.3. The supply curve (here depicted as vertical) shifts to the right. The equilibrium real wage falls. The economy responds to the lower wages by creating more jobs. The wages (the price of labor) indicate to firms that labor is less scarce, in a sense, than it was before, and so firms should economize less in the use of labor.

Consider now the effects of a shift in the demand curve for labor. First consider the case of a decrease in investment leading to a reduction in the quantity of machines available for use by workers. This reduces the productivity of workers, thereby shifting the demand curve for labor to the left, as depicted in panel A of Figure 6.4. For a given real wage, firms want to hire fewer workers than before.

Panel B depicts the effects of technological progress on the demand for labor. Workers are more productive and the labor demand curve shifts to the right.

These examples suggest that increases in investment and improvements in technology imply an increase in the demand for labor represented by a

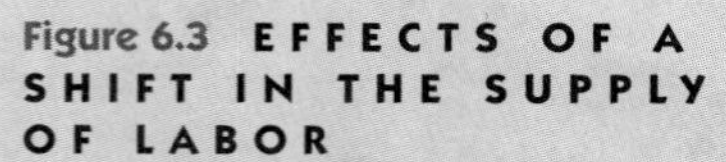

Figure 6.3 EFFECTS OF A SHIFT IN THE SUPPLY OF LABOR

A shift of the supply curve to the right leads to a fall in real wages.

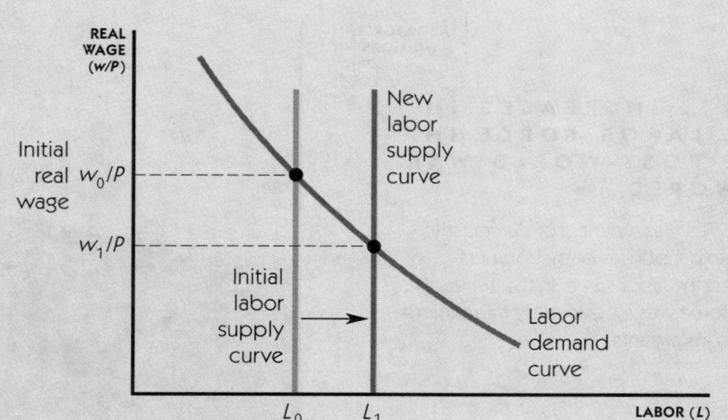

rightward shift in the labor demand curve. Although this is generally true, it may be the case that the demand for some types of labor, especially unskilled labor, actually declines with investment in new machines and technology, while the demand for skilled workers may increase. In this case, the labor market is really made up of two markets: that of skilled and that of unskilled workers. An increase in investment or technology may increase the demand

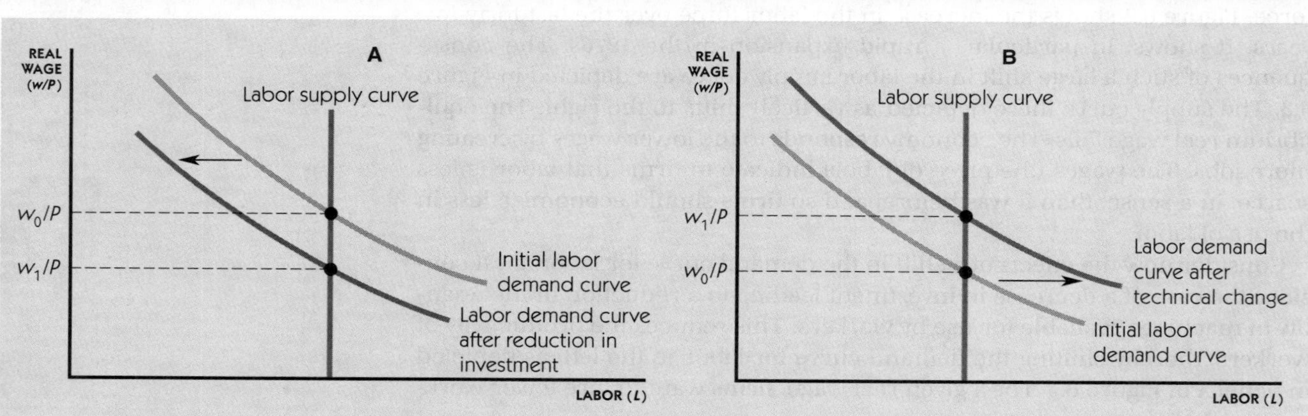

Figure 6.4 EFFECTS OF CHANGES IN INVESTMENT AND TECHNOLOGY

New investment or technological change shifts the demand curve for labor. Panel A shows a reduction in investment. Workers have fewer machines to work with, and the demand curve for labor shifts to the left, lowering real wages. Panel B shows an improvement in technology. The demand curve shifts to the right, as workers' marginal productivity increases, leading to higher real wages.

for skilled workers as in panel B, but decrease the demand for unskilled workers as in panel A. This represents one of the cases where merely studying the market for all labor is not sufficient to understand an interesting macroeconomic phenomenon—the increase in wage inequality based on skill levels.

LABOR MARKET EQUILIBRIUM

Real wages adjust to equate labor demand with labor supply.

A rightward shift in labor supply lowers the real wage, inducing firms to create additional jobs equal to the increased labor supply.

Technological change or new investment induces changes in the real wage, so that all workers remain fully employed. The real wage adjusts to equate supply and demand.

THE PRODUCT MARKET

Just as the real wage adjusts to ensure that the demand for labor equals the supply, so too—in our basic competitive model—prices adjust to ensure that the demand for goods equals the supply.

AGGREGATE SUPPLY

At any point in time, the economy has a certain capital stock, a set of machines and buildings that, together with labor and materials, produces output. If more workers are hired, output increases. The relationship between employment and output is called the **short-run production function,** depicted in Figure 6.5. There are diminishing returns. As more workers are hired, output goes up, but at a diminishing rate. The most productive machines are used first; if more labor is put to work, it is assigned to older and less productive machines.

We have been assuming that there is a fixed supply of labor. With this fixed supply of labor, the economy has a certain productive capacity, also referred to as the potential GDP or the **full-employment level of output.** This level of output is also referred to as the **aggregate supply.** It represents the amount of goods that firms would be willing to supply, given their plant and equipment, assuming wages and prices are flexible, and adjust so that everyone is fully employed.

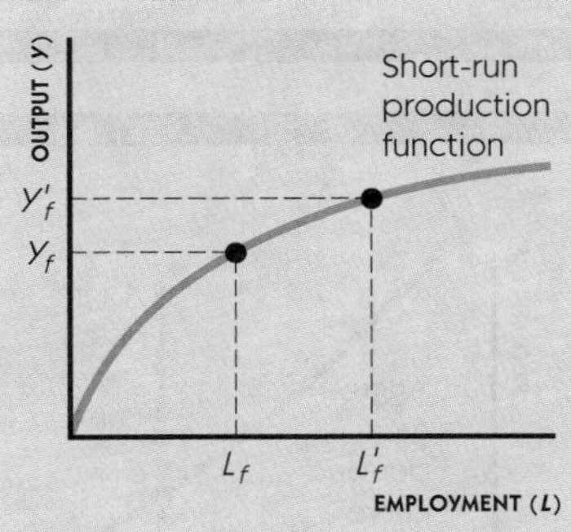

Figure 6.5 SHORT-RUN PRODUCTION FUNCTION

In the short run, with given technology and a given set of plant and equipment, as more labor is employed, output increases, but with diminishing returns. (Each successive increase in input results in smaller increases in output.) L_f is the full-employment level of employment, so Y_f is the full-employment level of output. An increase in the labor supply generates a movement along the short-run production function; the full-employment level of output will increase to Y_f'.

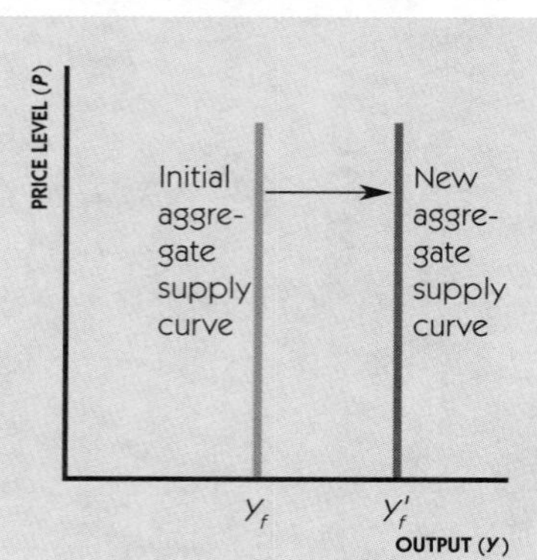

Figure 6.6 AGGREGATE SUPPLY CURVE

If real wages adjust to clear the market, the aggregate supply curve is vertical. If the labor force grows, the aggregate supply curve shifts to the right.

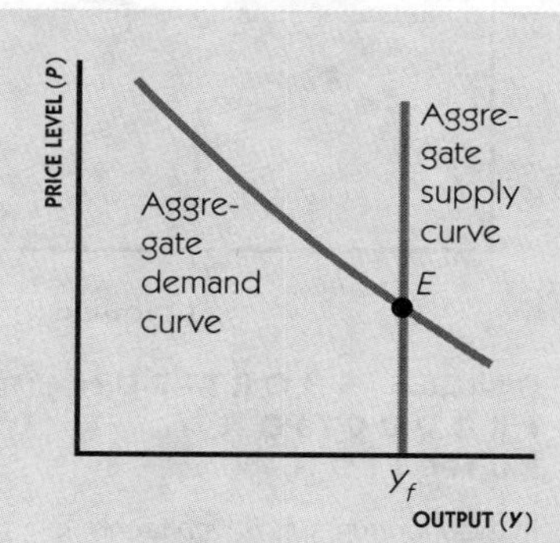

Figure 6.7 AGGREGATE DEMAND CURVE

The aggregate demand curve is downward sloping. Equilibrium in the product market occurs at the intersection of the aggregate demand and supply curves.

Output can occasionally exceed capacity: for short spurts, such as during wars, output can be increased further, by deferring maintenance, running machines three shifts, and so forth.

If the labor supply increases, even with a fixed stock of machines, the capacity of the economy increases. This is a movement along the short-run production function. Figure 6.5 shows that if employment increases from L_f to L_f', then output increases from Y_f to Y_f'.

The **aggregate supply curve** gives the level of aggregate supply at each price level. Note that if real wages adjust to clear the labor market, then the level of aggregate supply does not depend at all on price. Thus, Figure 6.6 depicts the aggregate supply curve (sometimes referred to as the **long-run aggregate supply curve,** since it is based on the long-run assumption that labor markets clear) as vertical. We have seen that an increase in the labor force leads to a shift in the aggregate supply curve to the right, as depicted.[2]

AGGREGATE DEMAND AND EQUILIBRIUM OUTPUT

Aggregate demand is the sum total of the goods and services demanded by all the households and firms in the economy and by government—plus foreigners wishing to buy the country's goods and services. In Chapter 4, we divided aggregate output into four components: consumption, investment, government expenditures, and (net) exports. Analyses of aggregate demand thus focus on identifying the demand for each of these components.

The **aggregate demand curve** gives the quantity of goods and services demanded at each price level, and has the shape of the demand curves encountered in Chapter 3. In particular, it is downward sloping, as depicted in Figure 6.7. The reason for this can be seen by focusing on consumption, which accounts for 70 percent of aggregate demand. Households' demand for real consumption (that is, consumption, taking into account changes in the price level) depends on their real wealth. When individuals are wealthier, they purchase more goods. An important part of individuals' wealth is their money and other financial assets denominated in dollars, for instance, government savings bonds promising to pay $100 in ten years. When the price level increases, the real value of these assets decreases. Households' real wealth thus decreases and hence their consumption decreases. Higher price levels will be associated with lower levels of consumption and lower levels of aggregate demand, as depicted in the figure.[3]

The equilibrium, the intersection of the aggregate demand and supply curves, determines the price level and output. Since we know that, in equilibrium, demand equals supply, and supply is fixed at Y_f, equilibrium output equals Y_f.

[2]Later, we will see how technological change and investment shift the short-run production function out, and even with a fixed labor supply, also shift the aggregate supply curve to the right.

[3]Later, we will see that there are other reasons why the aggregate demand curve may have the shape depicted.

PRODUCT MARKET EQUILIBRIUM

In equilibrium, output is equal to the full-employment level of output, that is, the output which can be generated by the available labor force working with the given set of plant and equipment.

Increases in the labor supply (rightward shifts in the labor supply curve), increases in the stock of plant and equipment as a result of net investment, and technological change all increase the full-employment level of output.

THE CAPITAL MARKET

We turn now to the capital market. Equilibrium in the capital market requires that savings (the supply of funds) equal investment (the demand for funds). Our analysis of each builds on the microfoundations discussed in Chapter 5.

SAVINGS

The most important determinants of savings are income and interest rates. Each year, families have to decide how much of their income they spend on current consumption, and how much they save for future consumption, for retirement, for emergencies, to pay for their children's college education, or to buy a new car or a new home. On average, families with higher incomes spend more and save more. Of course, what is relevant is how much income households have to spend; this is called their **disposable income**—their income after taxes. Thus, when the government increases taxes, it reduces disposable income, and when disposable income is reduced, household savings will be reduced.

In this chapter, we assume that the stock of plant and equipment as well as the labor supply are given. With wages and prices adjusting to ensure that the labor market clears, aggregate output is fixed. We now make use of an important result from Chapter 4: we saw there that national income equals aggregate output. The money that is used to purchase goods has to go into somebody's pockets, and thus becomes income. If aggregate output is given, so is aggregate income. Here, we also assume that taxes are fixed, so that with aggregate income given, so is aggregate disposable income.

With taxes fixed, our focus is on the interest rate, which is the return on savings. Figure 6.8 shows two different possibilities. In panel A, savings increase

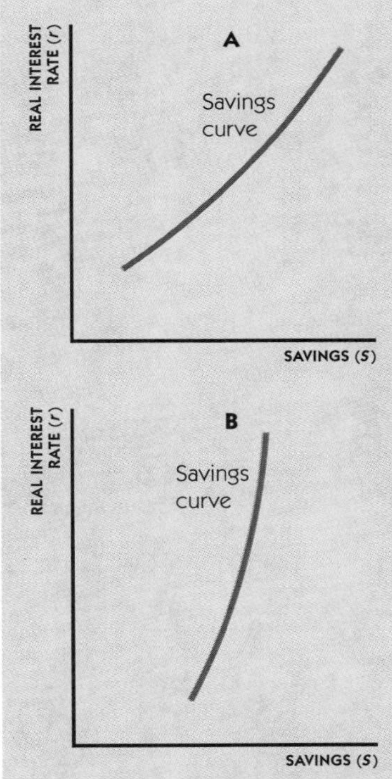

Figure 6.8 SAVINGS AND THE REAL INTEREST RATE

Different savings curves are shown in panels A and B. In panel A, savings increase with the interest rate. In panel B, savings are only slightly sensitive to the interest rate, a relationship which is supported by empirical evidence.

significantly with the interest rate, while in panel B, savings respond only slightly to changes in the interest rate. Empirical studies suggest that savings are only slightly sensitive to interest rates, that is, the savings curve is almost vertical—it looks more like panel B than panel A. For simplicity, in the rest of the chapter we depict the savings curve as completely inelastic—that is, as a vertical straight line.

But doesn't a higher interest rate provide greater incentives to save? Yes, but at higher interest rates, individuals who save are better off, and as a result, consume more, and save less. This is the income effect, in contrast to the incentive or substitution effect. The two effects pull in opposite directions, and essentially offset each other. That is why savings are not very sensitive to the interest rate.

Of course, when individuals look at the return to savings, they take into account inflation—the fact that a dollar in the future may buy less than a dollar today. Thus the relevant interest rate for savings is the *real* interest rate, which is just the nominal interest rate minus the rate of inflation. If the nominal interest rate is 10 percent, and the rate of inflation is 4 percent, then the real interest rate is 6 percent. As in the macroeconomic analysis of the labor and product markets, where we ignore differences between the variety of wages and prices, here we ignore the differences between the various interest rates at play in the economy. We simply refer to the interest rate in general.

INVESTMENT

Economists use the word investment in two different ways. Households think of the stocks and bonds they buy as investments—**financial investments.** These financial investments provide the funds for firms to buy capital goods—machines and buildings. The purchases of new machines and buildings represent firms' investments, referred to as **capital goods investments.** In macroeconomics, when we refer to investments, it is to capital, not financial, investments.

Firms invest in order to increase their capacity to produce, enabling them to produce more goods. They expect returns from the sale of these extra goods to cover the cost of additional workers and raw materials required to increase production, as well as the cost of the funds to finance the investment, leaving them with a profit.

There are thus two key determinants of investment: firms' expectations concerning the future, which we will assume for now to be fixed, and the interest rate. Many firms borrow to finance their investment. The cost of these funds—what they have to pay the bank for using its funds—is the interest rate. Since a firm pays back a debt with dollars that have less purchasing power due to inflation, the relevant cost of funds is the real interest rate.

The higher the interest rate, the fewer investment projects are profitable—that is, the fewer the projects which, after paying the bank its interest, will yield a return to the investor sufficient to compensate him for the risks he undertakes. Even if the firm is flush with cash, the interest rate matters. The interest rate then becomes the opportunity cost of the firm's money, what it could have obtained if, instead of making the investment, it had simply decided to lend the money to the government or some other firm.

The **investment function** gives the level of (real) investment at each value of the real interest rate. The investment function slopes downward to the right: investment increases as the real interest rate decreases. This is depicted in Figure 6.9, which shows the real interest rate on the vertical axis and the real investment level on the horizontal axis.

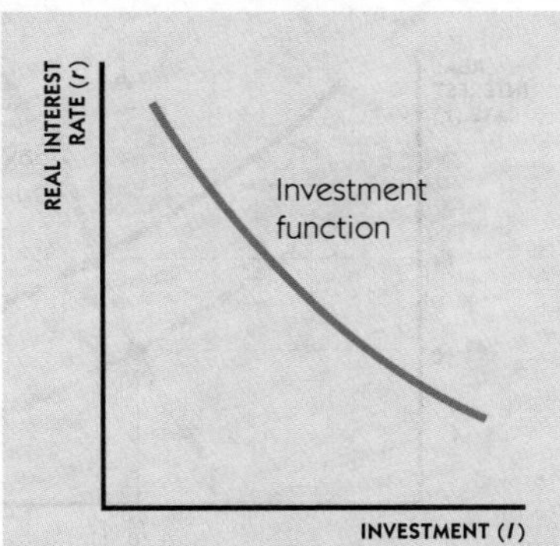

Figure 6.9 THE INVESTMENT FUNCTION

The investment function slopes downward to the right, tracing out the levels of real investment at different real interest rates. As the interest rate falls, investment increases.

There is another way of seeing why the interest rate matters: while the firm puts out money today to buy machines, the returns it receives, in increased profits, do not occur until the future. A dollar received in the future is not worth as much as a dollar today, because of the time value of money: a dollar today could have been put in the bank and earned interest; if the interest rate is 7 percent, in ten years, the dollar will have doubled to $2. We thus say that the **present discounted value** of $2 ten years from now is a dollar. (The present discounted value of a dollar in the future is what someone would be willing to pay today for that dollar.) An increase in the interest rate reduces the present discounted value of future dollars. At a 14 percent interest rate, a dollar put in the bank today has doubled to $2 in five years and quadrupled to $4 in ten years. Thus, a dollar in ten years is worth only a quarter, while at 7 percent it is worth fifty cents. An investment is undertaken if the present discounted value of (expected) profits is more than the cost; with an increase in the interest rate, fewer investments meet this criterion. The aggregate level of investment thus decreases.

EQUILIBRIUM IN THE CAPITAL MARKET

The equilibrium real interest rate is the rate at which savings equal investment, depicted in Figure 6.10. Panels A and B show the effect of an increased demand for investment at each real interest rate. In panel A, both the equilibrium real interest rate and the equilibrium level of savings and investment are increased, while in panel B, only the equilibrium real interest rate is changed.

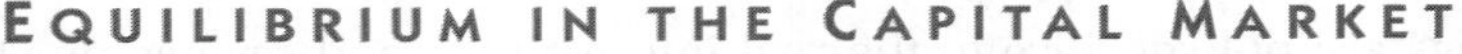

CAPITAL MARKET EQUILIBRIUM

In equilibrium, savings equal investment.

Increases in savings (shifts to the right in the savings curve) lead to lower real interest rates and higher levels of investment.

Shifts to the right in the investment schedule lead to higher real interest rates, but unchanged or higher levels of investment.

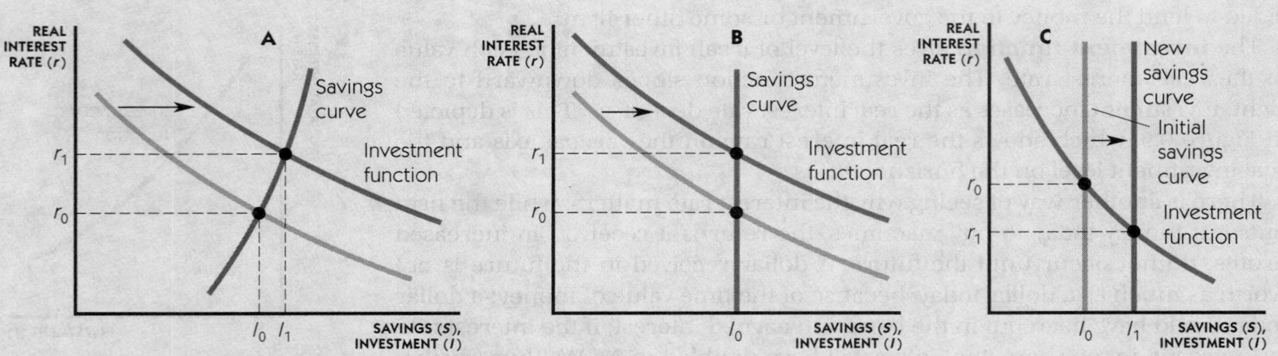

Figure 6.10 EQUILIBRIUM IN THE CAPITAL MARKET

Equilibrium requires the demand for funds (investment) equal the supply (savings). The level of desired investment decreases as the real interest rate increases.

We assume the economy is at full employment. In panel A, savings increase slightly with increases in the real interest rate. In panels B and C, savings are not interest sensitive, so the savings curve is a vertical straight line. The equilibrium level of investment is simply equal to the full employment level of savings.

A shift in the investment function—so that at every real interest rate the demand for investment is increased—is depicted in panels A and B. In panel A, investment is increased from I_0 to I_1, while in panel B, with inelastic savings, the only effect is to increase the real interest rate from r_0 to r_1, leaving investment (and savings) unchanged. Panel C shows a rightward shift in the savings curve. The level of savings increases at each real interest rate, resulting in a decrease of the real interest rate from r_0 to r_1, and an increase in investment from I_0 to I_1.

Because savings are not sensitive to the real interest rate, and savings must equal investment, investment remains unchanged. By contrast, a rightward shift in the savings curve, so that at every real interest rate savings increase, results in a reduction in the real interest rate and an increase in investment (panel C). Because the savings curve is almost vertical, the shift in the savings curve translates to a corresponding change in investment.

THE GENERAL EQUILIBRIUM

We can now describe the general equilibrium of the economy, the real wages, price level, and interest rate at which the labor, product, and capital markets all clear:

The real wage adjusts to ensure the demand for labor equals the supply. This determines the equilibrium real wage. The price level adjusts to ensure that aggregate demand equals aggregate supply, which in turn is equal to the full-employment level of output. Thus, equilibrium output is equal to potential GDP, the output which the labor supply, working with the available capital

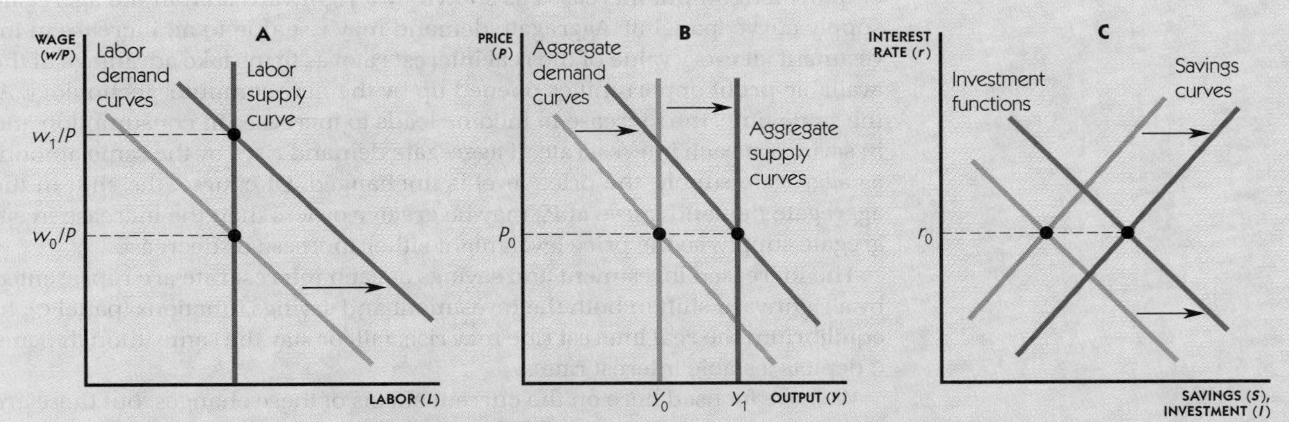

Figure 6.11 EFFECTS OF INTRODUCING PERSONAL COMPUTERS INTO THE ECONOMY

Panel A depicts the labor market. Personal computers increase the marginal product of workers, resulting in a rightward shift of the labor demand curve and an increase in the equilibrium real wage from w_0 to w_1. Panel B depicts the product market. With the increased productivity of workers, the aggregate supply curve shifts to the right. Output increases from Y_0 to Y_1. If aggregate demand increases (due to an increase in investment and an increase in consumption from higher incomes) the aggregate demand curve will shift to the right. If at P_0 the increase in aggregate demand is the same as the increase in aggregate supply, the price level will remain at P_0. Panel C depicts the capital market. Investment increases as firms purchase computers, and savings increase as a result of increased income. Both the investment and savings curves shift to the right. There may be no net effect on the interest rate (r_0), as shown here.

stock, can produce. Finally, the real interest rate adjusts to ensure that, at this full-employment level of output, savings are equal to investment.[4]

Using the General Equilibrium Model

The general equilibrium model is useful because it allows us to understand the effects of various changes in the economy—from the market in which these changes originate to all the other markets in the economy.

Consider the effect of the introduction of personal computers to the economy. The marginal product of workers increases, causing a shift in the demand curve for labor to the right. The equilibrium real wage increases as shown in Figure 6.11, panel A.

[4]We can, in fact, show that if savings are equal to investment at the full-employment level of output, then aggregate demand equals aggregate supply at that level of output.

In our simplified model with no government and no foreign trade, there are two sources of aggregate demand, investment and consumption:

$Y^d = C + I.$

Since national output *always* equals national income, full-employment output, Y_f, equals full-employment income, and full-employment incomes are either saved or consumed:

$Y_f = C + S$ or $S = Y_f - C.$ (cont'd. on p. 164)

Given the greater productivity of workers and the fixed labor supply, full-employment output increases as shown by a rightward shift in the aggregate supply curve (panel B). Aggregate demand may rise due to an increase in investment (at every value of the real interest rate) as firms take advantage of the available profit opportunities opened up by the new computer technology. At the same time, the increase in income leads to increases in consumption and in savings at each interest rate. If aggregate demand rises by the same amount as aggregate supply, the price level is unchanged. Of course, the shift in the aggregate demand curve at P_0 may be greater or less than the increase in aggregate supply, so the price level might either increase or decrease.

The increased investment and savings at each interest rate are represented by a rightward shift in both the investment and savings functions (panel C). In equilibrium the real interest rate may rise, fall, or stay the same (though panel C depicts a stable interest rate).

We have focused here on the current effects of these changes, but there are important future effects. In the future, there will be more plant and equipment. The economy's future capacity will increase. Thus, not only are all markets linked today, but markets today are linked with markets in the future.

EXTENDING THE BASIC FULL-EMPLOYMENT MODEL

Macroeconomics is concerned with policy: what are the impacts, for instance, of increasing government expenditure or increasing the money supply. The basic full-employment aggregate model can incorporate government expenditures, money, and international trade, and thus be used to address these policy questions.

GOVERNMENT

Introducing government into the analysis affects both the product market and the capital market. In the product market, government expenditures add to aggregate demand, but taxes reduce disposable income and thus subtract from aggregate demand. In the capital market, an increase in taxes to fund in-

---

Thus, when desired investment (as reflected in the investment schedule) equals full-employment savings,

$$I = S^d,$$

where we use the superscript to remind us that this is the desired level of savings, then from the second equation,

$$I = Y_f - C.$$

Substituting the fourth equation back into the first equation gives

$$Y^d = C + I = C + Y_f - C = Y_f;$$

thus, aggregate demand equals full-employment output, the aggregate supply. There is equilibrium in the product market.

USING ECONOMICS: QUANTIFYING IMPACTS ON INVESTMENT OF INCREASED GOVERNMENT EXPENDITURES MATCHED BY INCREASED TAXES

Increased government expenditures, even when matched by increased taxes, crowd out private investment. It is easy to quantify the effect. Assume the government increases government expenditure by $100 billion and increases taxes on individuals by $100 billion. With higher taxes, individuals have a lower income, and so—at any interest rate—they save less. For simplicity, assume that for each extra hundred dollars of after-tax income, individuals save ten dollars. Thus, the increased $100 billion of taxes reduces savings by $10 billion. For simplicity, assume that savings are completely insensitive to the interest rate, that is, the savings curve is a vertical straight line. Then, if savings equal investment, and savings are reduced by $10 billion, so is investment. In the new equilibrium, aggregate output is unchanged (at the full-employment level); government expenditures are increased by $100 billion, offset by a reduction of consumption of $90 billion and of investment by $10 billion.

If savings have a slight positive elasticity, then as interest rates rise, there will be increased savings. Thus, investment will be greater and consumption less than if savings are totally insensitive to the interest rate.

creased government expenditures affects savings, investment, and the interest rate. In Figure 6.12, the reduction in disposable income from taxes shifts the savings curve to the left, reducing equilibrium savings, from S_0 to S_1. With an unchanged investment schedule, the equilibrium interest rate rises and the equilibrium investment level falls.

Figure 6.12 GOVERNMENT EFFECTS ON THE CAPITAL MARKET

Government taxes reduce disposable income and savings, resulting in a leftward shift of the savings curve from S_0 to S_1. The equilibrium interest rate rises from r_0 to r_1, and the investment level falls.

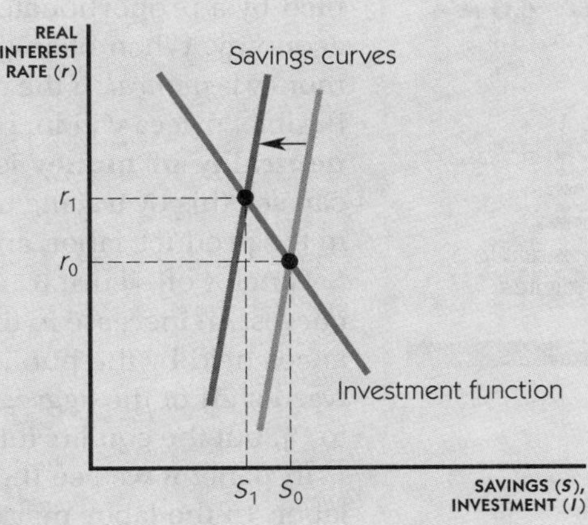

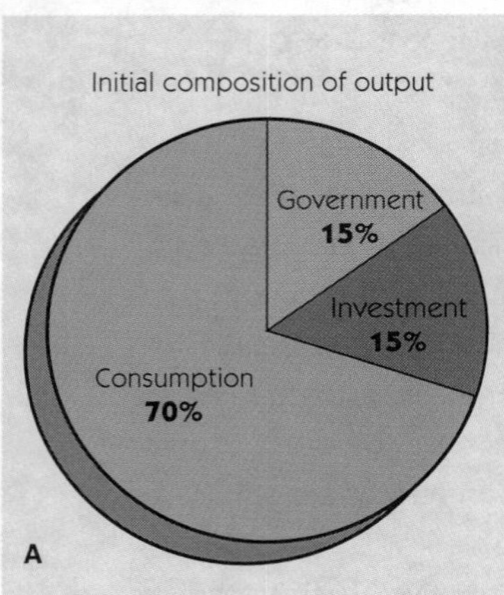

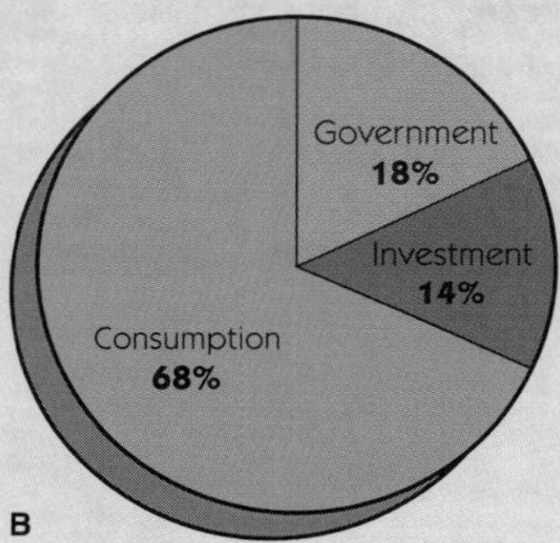

Figure 6.13 EFFECT OF AN EQUAL INCREASE IN GOVERNMENT EXPENDITURES AND TAXES ON THE COMPOSITION OF OUTPUT

An increase in government expenditure financed by an increase in taxes leads to a decrease in consumption and investment. Government expenditure is said to crowd out private expenditure.

Government also affects the composition of output. Figure 6.13 shows how an increase in government expenditure matched with an increase in taxes changes the composition of output. The total size of the pie is unchanged; we assume that the economy remains at full employment. Thus, the effect of government is simply to change how the pie is divided. Investment and consumption are both lowered—or **crowded out**—to make room for increased government expenditures. Even if government increases taxes by an amount to pay fully for the increased expenditure—in our example, by 3 percent of GDP—consumption is reduced by less, as individuals adjust in part by reducing savings.

THE MONEY SUPPLY

Government may also play a role in the economy by changing the amount of money in circulation. This is done through monetary policy, a subject we will consider later in the book. For now, it is important to understand the consequences of changes in the money supply for the full-employment model.

By and large, economists agree that in a full-employment economy, money affects the price level, but little else. In particular, it does not affect the quantity of goods produced or the number of workers employed. We can use an imaginative example to understand the point. Suppose that instantaneously, the entire supply of money in the economy was increased by a multiple of ten. In effect, we have tacked a zero onto the money supply. Dollar bills are now worth \$10; five-dollar bills are now worth \$50; ten-dollar bills are now worth \$100; your checking account of \$250 is now worth \$2,500, and so on. Stores, acting perfectly efficiently, and knowing that the money supply has multiplied by ten, would increase their prices tenfold. Thus, the actual amount of goods and services produced and consumed would be the same; there would be no real effect. The only difference would be the numbers on the bills, bank statements, and price tags.

The lesson is more general: an increase in the supply of money accompanied by a proportionate increase in the price level has no real effects on the economy. When changing the money supply has no real effects we say that money is *neutral.* If the economy is at full employment and prices are perfectly flexible, prices will increase proportionally with the money supply. Thus, the **neutrality of money** is a basic property of the full-employment model. We can see this by tracing through the effects of an increase in the money supply in the product, labor, and capital markets, as shown in Figure 6.14.

Panel A of Figure 6.14 shows the aggregate supply and aggregate demand curves. An increase in the money supply represents an increase in money balances held by the public, so private wealth increases. This results in a rightward shift of the aggregate demand curve. The price level increases from P_0 to P_1, but the equilibrium level of output remains at Y_0.

In panel B we see the aggregate supply and aggregate demand curves for labor. In the labor market, the increase in the price level will be matched by an increase in the nominal wage, from w_0 to w_1, so that the real wage remains at its original level, $w_0/P_0 = w_1/P_1$. At this real wage, the demand for labor continues to equal its supply. Thus the effect on the labor market of an increase in

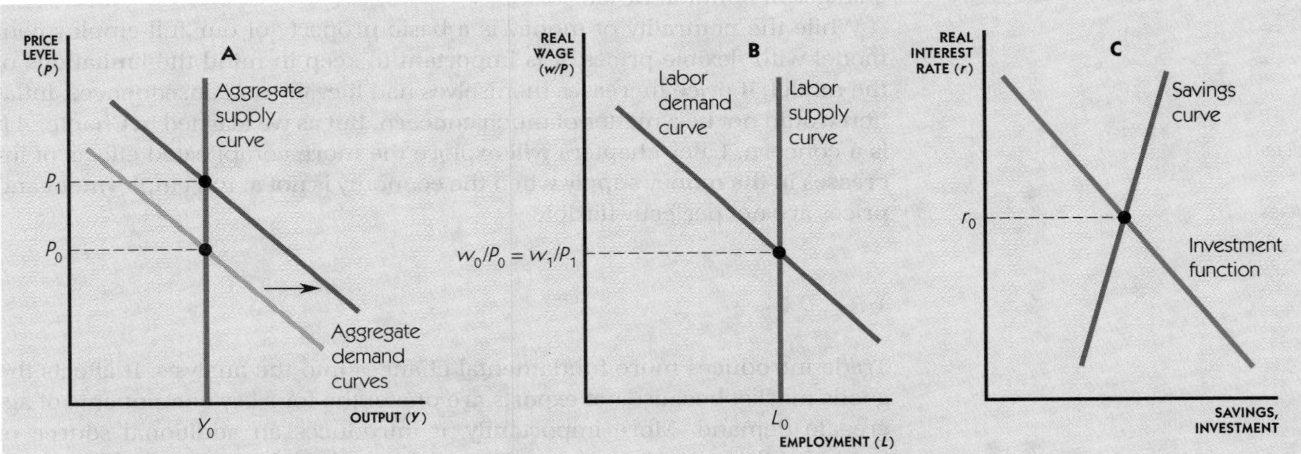

Figure 6.14 EFFECTS OF AN INCREASE IN THE MONEY SUPPLY

Panel A shows the product market. The increase in the money supply results in a rightward shift of the aggregate demand curve. The price level rises from P_0 to P_1, and the equilibrium level of output remains at Y_0. Panel B shows the labor market. The nominal wage (w) increases in proportion to the increase in the price level, so that the real wage is unaffected. Panel C shows the capital market. The savings and investment curves giving the *real* levels of those variables remain unchanged. The real interest rate, r_0, is unaffected.

the price level is simply a proportionate increase in the nominal wage. There are no real effects—the equilibrium real wage and the equilibrium level of employment L_0 are not affected.

In the capital market, real savings and investment both depend on the real interest rate, which is not affected by the increase in the price level. Accordingly, in panel C, neither the savings curve nor the investment function shifts. At each real interest rate, *nominal* savings and investment would increase by an amount exactly proportional to the increase in the money supply. Why? Because households and firms must increase the dollar amount of savings and investment in order to maintain the value of savings and investment relative to the higher price level. But panel C shows the levels of *real* savings and investment at each real interest rate. The equilibrium real interest rate, r_0, remains the same. The overall result once again displays the neutrality of money because there are no real effects in the capital market. Only the *nominal* levels of savings and investment change in proportion to the change in the price level.

The neutrality of money highlights the important distinction economists make between real and nominal phenomena. As we have seen here and in earlier chapters, in referring to nominal variables, such as nominal GDP and nominal wages, we mean the current money value of those variables, that is, the value *without* adjustments for changes in the price level. As this example shows, our full-employment model with flexible prices makes a perfect distinction between real and nominal phenomena. Relationships between real variables—which are the focus of the model—are completely independent of changes in nominal variables.

While the neutrality of money is a basic property of our full-employment model with flexible prices, it is important to keep in mind the limitations of the model. If price increases themselves had literally no consequences, inflation would not be a matter of much concern. But as we learned in Chapter 4 it is a concern. Later chapters will explore the more complicated effects of increases in the money supply when the economy is not at full employment and prices are not perfectly flexible.

TRADE

Trade introduces more fundamental changes into the analysis. It affects the goods market because net exports are one of the four key components of aggregate demand. More importantly, it introduces an additional source of funds for financing investment. The savings schedule depicted so far is the domestic source of funds. If investment, the demand for funds, exceeds domestic savings, firms can borrow abroad.

We say that an economy which trades with other countries and borrows from and lends to other countries is an **open economy.** A small open economy like Switzerland faces an essentially horizontal supply curve of funds at a given real interest rate. If Switzerland pays a slightly higher interest rate than that paid in other countries, those with capital divert their funds to Switzerland. If Switzerland pays slightly less than the interest rate available in other countries (adjusted, of course, for risk) it can obtain no capital. Those who have capital in Switzerland can take their funds and invest them abroad. For a small country, the interest rate is determined by the international capital market. Effectively, such a country takes the interest rate as fixed. This is shown in Figure 6.15, where the interest rate is fixed at r^*. A fixed interest rate, in turn, means that the level of investment is fixed, at I^* in Figure 6.15. A short-

Figure 6.15 SUPPLY OF SAVINGS IN A SMALL OPEN ECONOMY

In a small open economy, the real interest rate, r^*, is determined by the international capital market. That in turn determines the level of investment, I^*. In the figure, savings are assumed to be fixed, unaffected by the interest rate. If domestic savings equal S_0, the shortfall, B_0, is made up by borrowing from abroad. A reduction in savings to S_1 leads to increased borrowing, B_1, but leaves investment unchanged.

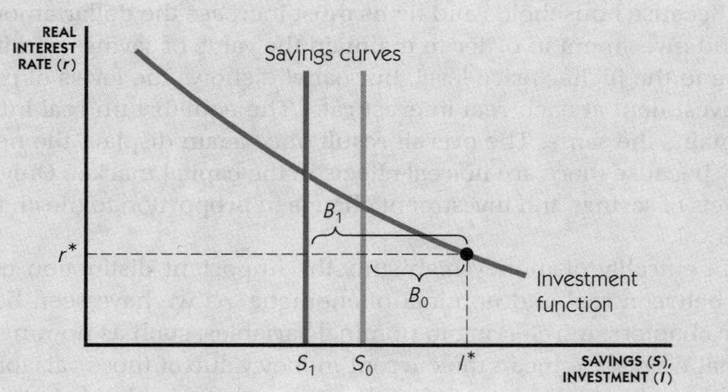

Policy Perspective: A Global Capital Shortage?

No sooner had the world economy begun showing signs of recovery from the recession of the early 1990s than the newspapers sounded a new alarm: a global capital shortage.

Of course, economists are reluctant to refer to shortages, because they recognize that prices (here interest rates) adjust to demand and supply. What was really worrying people was the possibility that the world's savings curve was shifting left and the world's investment curve was shifting right—and the combination was driving up real interest rates. The reason for the anxiety was not hard to see. In the space of a year, real interest rates rose from 1 percent to 4 percent, far higher than the average real interest rates that had prevailed over the first nine decades of the century (between .5 percent and 1.5 percent).

And several factors suggested that the situation might not be simply a temporary aberration. First, national savings rates in Europe, the United States, and Japan were all down significantly from what they had been a decade or so earlier—on average by perhaps 4 percent of GDP. Second, Eastern Europe and Russia represented a vast area of potential investment that was at last opening up to the world's capital market. And the reforms required to make these economies more hospitable to foreign investment were occurring, albeit at a slower pace than had been anticipated. Third, many less developed countries that had previously discouraged foreign investment were now actively seeking it. While these emerging markets remained small on the scale of the world capital market, they represented an enormous potential increase in demand. Some of the fastest-growing countries, like Singapore and China, have managed to sustain savings rates roughly commensurate with their high investment rates (exceeding 25 percent of GDP). But in South Asia and Latin America, investment demand could easily exceed savings by a substantial amount.

It is too soon to tell whether the higher real

interest rates are to remain a feature of the world's capital market in coming decades. If so, American firms will have to pay higher real interest rates. Higher real interest rates in turn will lead to lower levels of investment, unless a rightward shift of the investment curve offsets the higher real interest rates. (Such a shift of the investment curve could arise if technological change and new business practices sufficiently increased the returns to new investment.)

fall (B_0) between the level of savings and that level of investment is funded by borrowing from abroad. A reduction in the amount of savings increases the amount of foreign borrowing (B_1), but leaves investment unaffected.

This result contrasts markedly with our earlier result for a **closed economy,** one in which there was no foreign borrowing or lending. There, we noted that lower savings (a shift to the left in the savings curve) result in less investment. There is a similar contrast in the effect of an increase in government expenditure matched by an increase in taxes. In a closed economy, increased taxes reduce household and thus national savings, and hence, reduce investment. In an open economy, investment is unchanged.

Though investment is unaffected, the increased foreign borrowing has consequences for the future. In the future, interest will have to be paid to foreigners on this debt, and this will lower future standards of living, much as the lower level of investment would have. These effects will be discussed at greater length in the next chapter.

THE U.S. ECONOMY

The United States is an open economy. But it is such a large part of the world scene, that—unlike in the case of a small country like Switzerland—changes in the U.S. savings function affect the international interest rate, with global ramifications. The U.S. economy represents about one-quarter of world output and one-fifth of world savings. Thus, a shift to the left in the U.S. savings function (so less is saved at each interest rate) raises world real interest rates and leads to less investment in the United States. Because the full impact is spread throughout the world, the effect on U.S. investment is far less than it would be if the United States were a closed economy.

The discussion so far has assumed that the world's capital markets are fully integrated. However, the world capital market is far from fully integrated. Individuals know more about what is going on in their own country than what is going on abroad. American investors require slightly higher return on foreign investments to compensate them for this increased risk. In recent years, with the greater flow of information, the magnitude of this risk premium—the extra return they must earn—has decreased. But it is still the case that capital does not flow perfectly freely, so that interest rates are not equalized and a decrease in U.S. savings is not made up fully by an increased flow of capital from abroad.

Policy Perspective: Improving the International Capital Markets

NAFTA, the North American Free Trade Agreement, eliminated all trade barriers in North America. During the national discussion leading up to the ratification of NAFTA, Vice President Al Gore debated Ross Perot, who opposed the agreement. One of Perot's most notable lines referred to "a giant sucking sound," as Mexico attracted investment and jobs out of the United States. He conveyed an image of Mexico attracting thousands of factories with its cheap labor, leaving hundreds of thousands of Americans without jobs. His predictions proved wrong, partly because the slight reduction in tariffs has negligible effects. Moreover, labor-intensive firms (that is, firms that required a lot of unskilled labor) were already in the process of shifting operations to abroad, for instance to Malaysia, China, and Korea; NAFTA might induce some of these firms to move to Mexico, but was unlikely to have much effect on the overall flow.

But Perot was correct in emphasizing an important aspect of NAFTA: it was not only a trade agreement, but also an investment agreement. Increasingly, countries have recognized the importance not only of free trade, but also of open capital markets, where capital can flow to wherever returns are highest. By allowing the free flow of capital, world GDP is increased. If the return to investment in one country is 8 percent and in another it is 24 percent, a billion dollars invested in the second country yields an extra $160 million a year. Moreover, trade and investment flows are often interlinked. American firms investing, say, in Asia often turn to other firms in the United States to supply parts and components.

International investment agreements focus on two issues. The first is called national treatment. American firms investing abroad should not be discriminated against; they should be given exactly the same treatment that the country's own firms receive. The second is called reciprocity. Foreign governments should extend to our firms the same treatment that we extend to theirs. While there is general agreement about the first principle, the second is more contentious. For instance, formerly, Japan did not allow American banks to open up branches in certain rural areas; and Japan requires rigorous testing of automobile parts from sources other than the original car manufacturer before they can be used by repair shops. National treatment says that these practices are permissible, so long as Japanese firms are subjected to the same requirements. Similarly, the United States used to have a law forbidding banks from opening up branches in more than one state. Again, under national treatment, such restrictions would be permissible, if applied uniformly. Often, however, national treatment can still result in effective discrimination. Almost all cars sold in Japan are Japanese, so that the Japanese manufacturers can supply parts for repair shops; but the testing process is so long that American parts firms are effectively precluded from the market. The greater openness of the U.S. economy, including the relative absence of regulations, means that foreign firms find it easier to enter the United States than American firms find it to open shop abroad. Reciprocity is required to restore a level playing field.

However, less developed countries often argue persuasively that the kinds of regulations that are appropriate for more developed countries would not be appropriate for them. International agreements working towards harmonization of regulations is the way that principles of national treatment and reciprocity can be reconciled.

How much does U.S. investment decrease as a result of a shift to the left of the U.S. savings curve by, say, $1 billion? Early estimates, for the decades immediately following World War II, suggested that U.S. investment would decrease by $800 million to $1 billion—by almost the full amount of the change in savings. Current estimates indicate that the effect would be much smaller, somewhere between $350 and $500 million.

OPEN ECONOMY INVESTMENT

The United States is a large open economy. Reductions in the U.S. savings rate are reflected in increases in the real interest rate internationally (and therefore in the United States), and reduced levels of investment. But the effects on investment in the United States are smaller than would be the case if the economy were closed.

CONSENSUS IN MACROECONOMICS

Macroeconomic issues are often front and center in newspapers and nightly newscasts on television. There is good reason for this. As we learned in Chapter 4, the macroeconomic problems of unemployment, slow growth, and inflation have substantial, widespread consequences. With modest productivity gains, the concern is with slow economic growth; when the unemployment rate increases, the focus is on impending recession; when the consumer price index goes up faster, attention shifts to inflation. These problems, and the ways to address them, are often hotly debated, giving rise to controversy. In this context, the views of economists often appear to be contradictory, and the old saw about how any two economists will give you three opinions may seem true. But in fact, there is remarkable consensus among economists about basic macroeconomic principles. In this chapter we have encountered our fifth and sixth points of consensus:

5 Effects of Government Expenditures at Full Employment

When the economy is at full employment, and the economy is closed, increases in government expenditures must come at the expense of private consumption and/or investment. Even when matched with increases in taxes, such increases crowd out private investment, since the increased taxes will normally lead to a reduction in savings. If the economy is open, government expenditures lead to increased foreign borrowing, but in the United States, the increased borrowing does not fully offset the reduced savings, so investment is decreased.

6 Neutrality of Money

At full employment, an increase in the money supply only leads to a proportionate increase in prices and wages, with no real consequences.

LOOKING FORWARD

This chapter has used the basic competitive model to analyze the full-employment macroeconomic equilibrium of the economy. We have seen how real wages adjust to ensure that the demand for labor always equals the supply, even in the face of changes in technology and new investments which might replace workers. We have seen how prices and interest rates adjust in the face of shifts in the demand for investment so that the economy continues to produce at its productive capacity and so that savings continue to equal investment at the full-employment level of output.

In the long run, wages, prices, and interest rates do adjust in much the manner described here. In the short run, however, they may not. If they did adjust to shifts instantaneously, then the full-employment model would not only be a good description of how the economy in the long run is able to create enough new jobs to match the increase in labor supply, but it would also be a good description of the economy in the short run. But wages and prices in particular may be sticky, that is, fail to adjust to the market-clearing levels. This has profound implications for how the economy behaves in the short run, as we shall see in the following two parts. First, however, we take a closer look at some of the important implications of our full-employment model.

REVIEW AND PRACTICE

SUMMARY

1. Macroeconomic equilibrium focuses on equilibrium levels of aggregates: employment, output, and investment. In a full-employment competitive equilibrium, each is determined by equating demand and supply. Full employment is attained as a result of flexible wages and prices.

2. The real wage equates the demand for labor with the supply of labor. Increases in the labor supply are reflected in lower real wages, which induce firms to create additional jobs to match the increased supply.

3. The full-employment level of output is that level of output which the economy can produce with its given stock of plant and equipment, when labor is fully employed. It will increase with increases in the labor supply.

4. The price level adjusts to equate aggregate demand to aggregate supply.

5. The real interest rate (which takes account of inflation) equates investment and savings. The desired level of investment decreases with increases in the real interest rate. Savings depend on disposable income and the real interest rate. With flexible wages and prices, labor is fully employed, so output is always at the full-employment level. Since aggregate output equals national income, if taxes are fixed, disposable income will be fixed. Hence, in a full-employment economy the interest rate is the main variable of concern in determining savings. Savings increase slightly with increases in the real interest rate.

6. In a closed economy, government expenditures, when paid for by increases in taxes, crowd out consumption and investment. In a small open economy, investment is unchanged and foreign borrowing increases. The United States is a large open economy—with effects somewhere between a closed economy and a small open economy.

7. Shifts to the left in the savings curve lead to reduced investment in a closed economy, and to increased foreign borrowing in a small open economy.

8. All the markets in the economy are interlinked. Changes in one market have effects on all other markets.

9. In a full-employment economy with perfectly flexible wages and prices, money is neutral: increases in the money supply are simply reflected in increases in prices.

Key Terms

short-run production function
full-employment level of output
aggregate supply curve
aggregate demand curve
disposable income
financial investments
capital goods investments
investment function
present discounted value
crowding out
neutrality of money
open economy
closed economy

Review Questions

1. How do competitive markets with flexible wages and prices ensure that labor is always fully employed? What induces firms to create just the right number of additional jobs to match an increase in the number of workers?

2. Describe the effects of shifts in the labor supply curve on equilibrium real wages and potential GDP (full-employment level of output).

3. What determines the economy's productive capacity or aggregate supply or potential GDP? How does aggregate supply increase when labor supply increases?

4. What is the aggregate demand curve? Why is it downward sloping? Why is the aggregate supply curve vertical? What determines the price level?

5. What is the investment schedule? Why does investment decrease when the real interest rate increases? What role do expectations play in investment?

6. What determines the level of savings? Explain why, if taxes are fixed, disposable income in a full-employment economy is fixed. Explain why savings may not be very sensitive to the real rate of interest.

7. How is the equilibrium rate of interest determined?

8. How do government expenditures matched by taxes affect the market equilibrium?

9. What difference does it make whether the economy is closed or open? Illustrate by examining the effects of an increase in government expenditure.

10. How does the U.S. economy differ from a closed economy? from a small open economy such as Switzerland?

PROBLEMS

1. In the text, we assumed that the labor supply did not depend on the real wage. Assume that at higher real wages, more individuals wish to work. Trace through how each of the steps in the analysis has to be changed. (Show the equilibrium in the labor market. What happens to real wages, employment, GDP, and savings if the labor supply curve shifts to the right?)

2. An increase in capital resulting from an increase in investment allows a given number of workers to produce more. Show the effect on the short-run production function and the full-employment level of output.

3. Firms hire workers up to the point where the real wage equals the marginal product of labor, the extra output that an extra worker produces. Explain why the slope of the short-run production function is the marginal product of labor. Explain why, with diminishing returns, an increase in the real wage leads to a lower level of demand for labor. Draw an example of a shift outward in the short-run production function, caused by technological change, which causes (at any real wage) the demand for labor to decrease; to increase.

4. Explain how income and substitution effects offset each other in the

supply curve of labor; in the supply curve for savings. Is it possible for an improvement in technology to lead to a lower real wage?

5. Trace through how the effects of a change in one market—such as an increase in the supply of labor—has effects on other markets. How was it possible for there to be a large increase in the labor supply, such as occurred during the 1970s and 1980s, and yet real wages changed relatively little.

6. Trace through the effects of an increase in taxes without a corresponding increase in government expenditures, or an increase in government expenditures without a corresponding increase in taxes.

7. What are some of the reasons that, even in an open economy, investment and savings might be highly correlated.

8. "Even if, in an open economy, a decrease in savings does not decrease investment, future generations are worse off." Discuss.

9. Consider a closed economy initially in equilibrium with $400 billion in savings (investment) and a real interest rate of 4 percent. Households save 10 percent of their $4 trillion income. The government imposes a $100 billion additional tax on households, used to finance $100 billion additional government expenditures. If the interest elasticity of savings is zero, and if a 10 percent increase in the real interest rate (from 4 to 4.4 percent) decreases investment by 2.6 percent, what are the new equilibrium level of investment, savings, and the real interest rate? Show that if the interest elasticity of savings is .1 (so an increase of the interest rate to 4.4 percent generates $4 billion in increased savings), the new equilibrium entails the real interest rate rising by 7 percent, to 4.28 percent. What happens to investment in this case?

CHAPTER 7

USING THE FULL-EMPLOYMENT MODEL

The federal budget deficit ballooned during the 1980s and emerged from being a problem that mainly interested economists and political pundits into the national spotlight. By the 1992 presidential election, public opinion polls were persistently ranking the huge deficits among the central problems facing the country. In this chapter we use the model developed in Chapter 6 to elucidate the consequences of the deficit. Another big problem in the 1980s was the huge trade deficit; every year we imported billions of dollars more than we exported. The full-employment model can also be used to help us understand the trade deficit, and how it might be affected by various policies.

In Chapter 4, we described the three fundamental economic problems of growth, unemployment, and inflation. By assumption, the full-employment model of Chapter 6 cannot directly shed light on the problem of unemployment, though in the next chapter we will explain how simply by changing one of the critical assumptions of that model, there can be unemployment. In the last chapter we saw how the full-employment model provides us with useful insights into inflation—with the price level increasing in proportion to the money supply. In this chapter, we also show how the full-employment model provides us with useful insights into the problem of growth.

KEY QUESTIONS

1. What are the consequences of the huge fiscal deficits of the 1980s?
2. What gave rise to the huge trade deficits of the 1980s and 1990s? What are their consequences?
3. How do deficits affect economic growth? What are some other policies that can help promote growth?

THE DEFICIT

When the government spends more than it receives in taxes and other revenues in any given year, it has a deficit, often referred to as the **fiscal deficit,** to distinguish it from the gap between imports and exports, which is called the trade deficit. It must borrow to finance the deficit. In 1981, taxes were cut, but expenditures were not cut commensurately. Figure 7.1 shows the result-

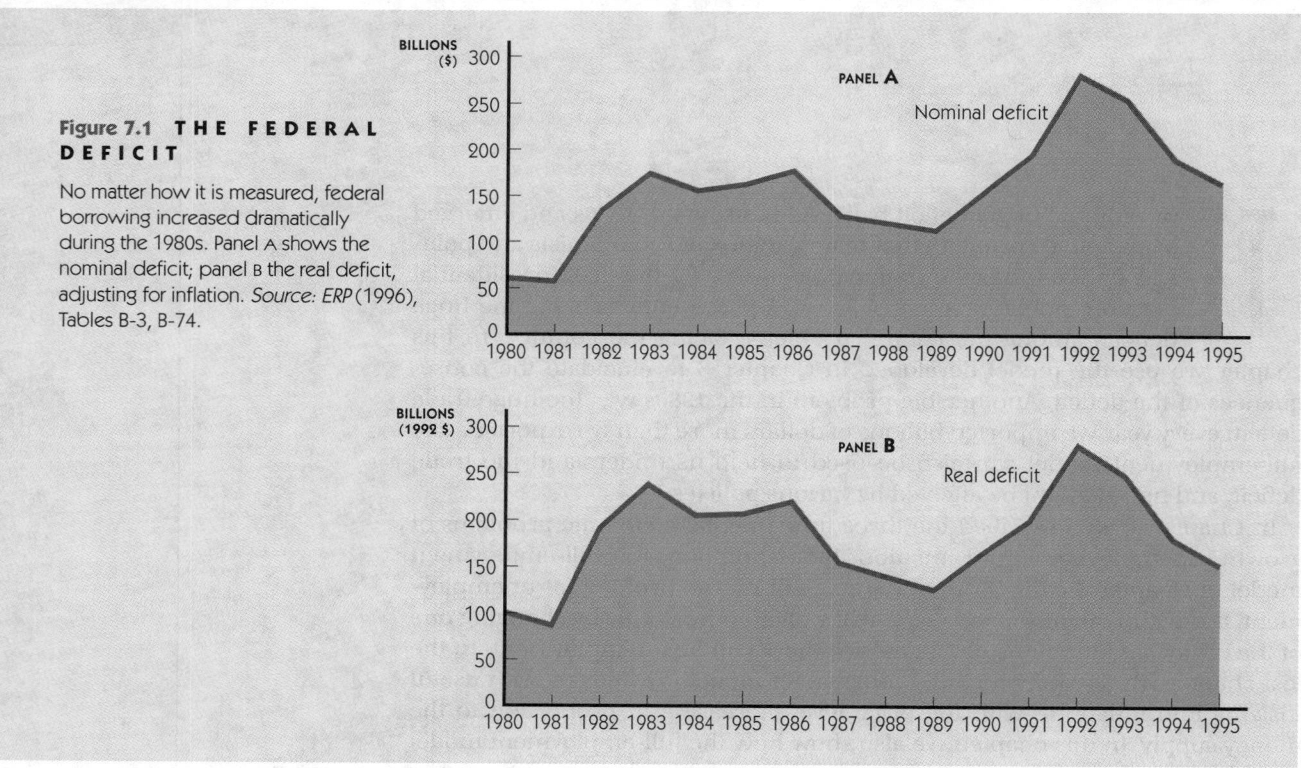

Figure 7.1 THE FEDERAL DEFICIT

No matter how it is measured, federal borrowing increased dramatically during the 1980s. Panel A shows the nominal deficit; panel B the real deficit, adjusting for inflation. *Source: ERP* (1996), Tables B-3, B-74.

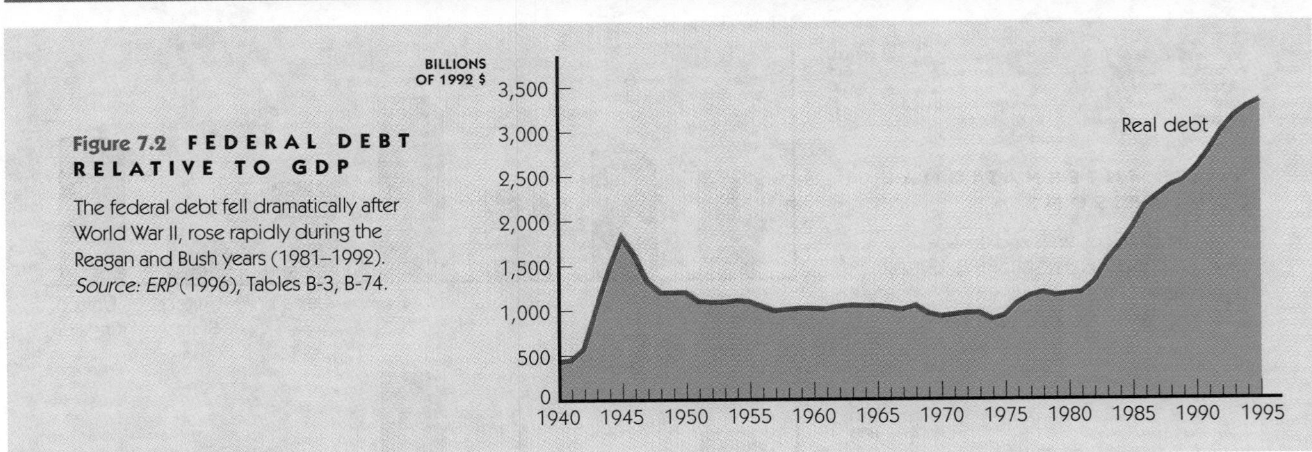

Figure 7.2 FEDERAL DEBT RELATIVE TO GDP

The federal debt fell dramatically after World War II, rose rapidly during the Reagan and Bush years (1981–1992). *Source: ERP* (1996), Tables B-3, B-74.

ing increase in the deficit. In twelve years, from 1981 to 1992, the federal deficit more than quadrupled, from $60 billion to $280 billion. Even adjusting for inflation, the increase in the deficit was dramatic. These represented the first major peacetime deficits in the country's history.

The **federal debt** is the cumulative amount that the government owes. Figure 7.2 shows that the federal debt, after falling dramatically after World War II, rose rapidly during the Reagan and Bush years.

The Clinton administration managed to bring the deficit as a percentage of GDP down from 4.9 percent in 1992 to 1.6 percent in 1996. As a result of these efforts, even by 1995, neither the deficits nor the debt are as large as those of many European countries or Canada—as Figure 7.3 illustrates.

In Chapter 18 we will discuss at greater length some of the political and economic events that gave rise to the deficit, as well as the debates about precisely how deleterious the deficit is for the economy's well-being. Here, we use the model of Chapter 6 to give us a qualitative picture of the consequences. In Chapter 6 we discussed the effects of an increase in government expenditures matched with an increase in taxes. Here, we look at the effect of an increase in government expenditures not matched with an increase in taxes. (The same results hold for a decrease in taxes—as in 1981—unmatched with a decrease in expenditures.) Our earlier analysis identified the openness of the economy as a critical determinant. We examine the two extreme cases—a closed economy and a small open economy—remembering that the U.S. economy lies between these extremes.

A CLOSED ECONOMY

If the government increases its expenditures without increasing taxes, it must borrow the difference.[1] Now private savings, S_p, has two purposes—to

[1]It used to be that some governments simply printed money to pay for the difference. Today, within developed countries, printing money to finance deficits is more the exception than the rule.

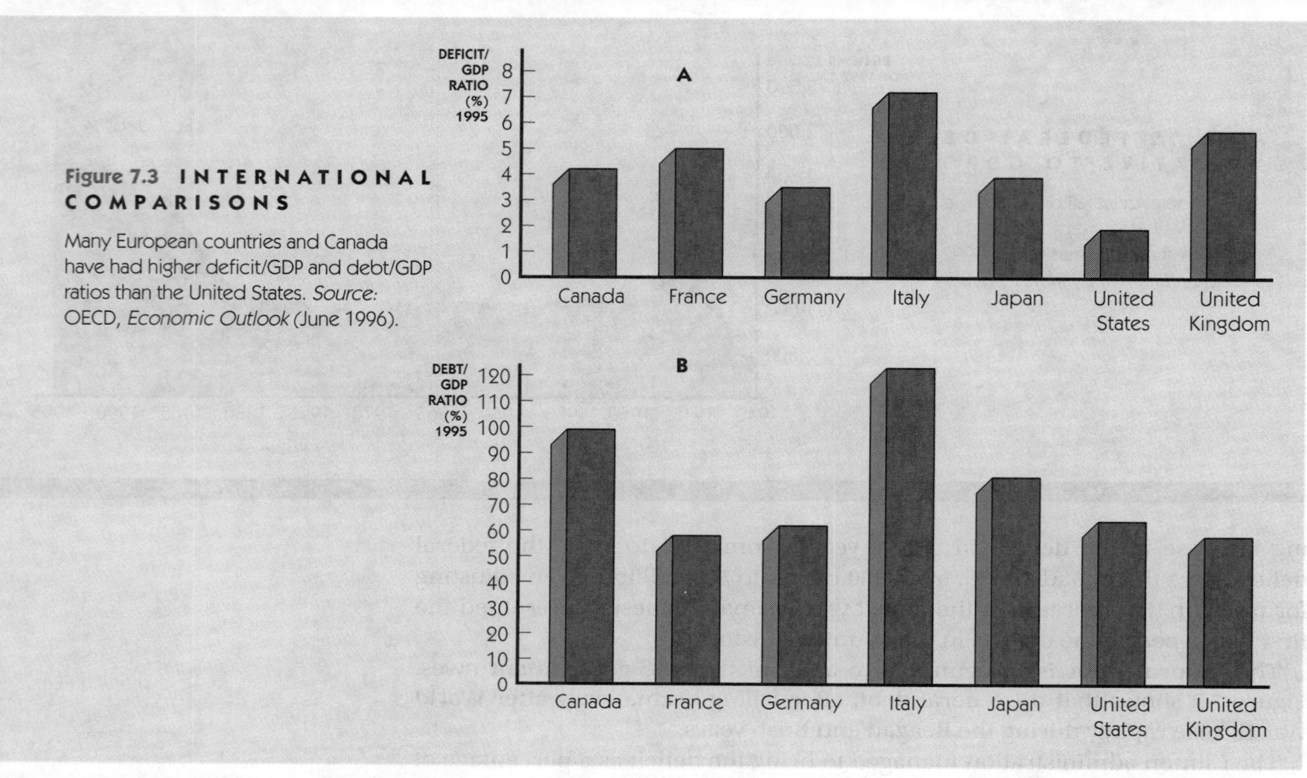

Figure 7.3 INTERNATIONAL COMPARISONS

Many European countries and Canada have had higher deficit/GDP and debt/GDP ratios than the United States. *Source:* OECD, *Economic Outlook* (June 1996).

finance the deficit, D, and to finance investment, I:

$$S_p = D + I.$$

Alternatively, we can think of the deficit as **negative public savings**

$$D = -S_g.$$

From this perspective, we can rewrite the first equation as

$$S_p - D = I$$

or

$$S = S_p + S_g = I.$$

National savings, S, consisting of private (household and business) savings, S_p, plus government savings, S_g, equal investment.

In Figure 7.4, the increased deficit is reflected as a shift to the left of the savings curve, decreasing the equilibrium level of investment and increasing the

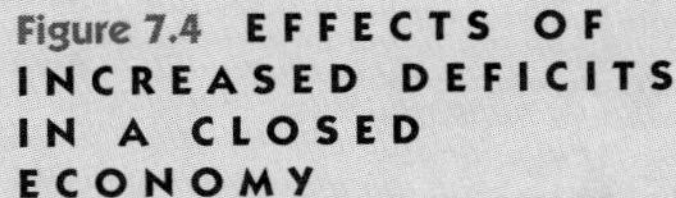

Figure 7.4 EFFECTS OF INCREASED DEFICITS IN A CLOSED ECONOMY

Increased deficits reduce national savings. With a leftward shift in the savings curve, the equilibrium level of interest rates is higher and the equilibrium level of investment is lower.

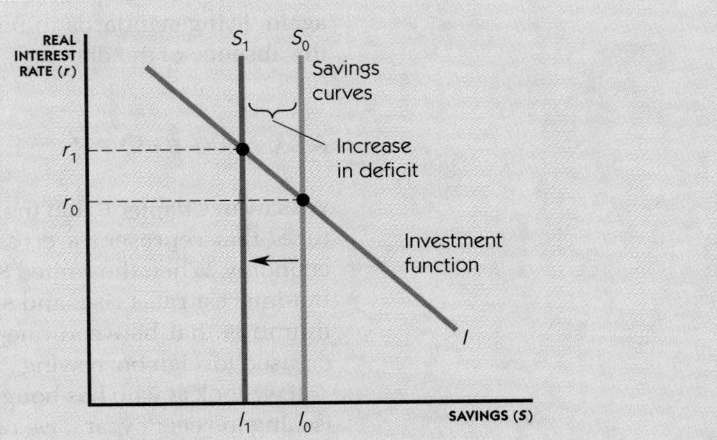

equilibrium real interest rate. Because investment is lower, output and living standards in the future will be lower.

A Small Open Economy

The difference between an open economy and a closed economy is that when national savings are reduced in an open economy, it can turn to other countries to finance its investment. Figure 7.5 shows the increased deficit reducing national savings, and shifting the savings curve to the left. The leftward shift leaves investment unchanged—this is determined simply by the international

Figure 7.5 EFFECTS OF INCREASED DEFICITS IN AN OPEN ECONOMY

Increased deficits shift the national savings curve to the left. Investment is unaffected, but foreign borrowing increases.

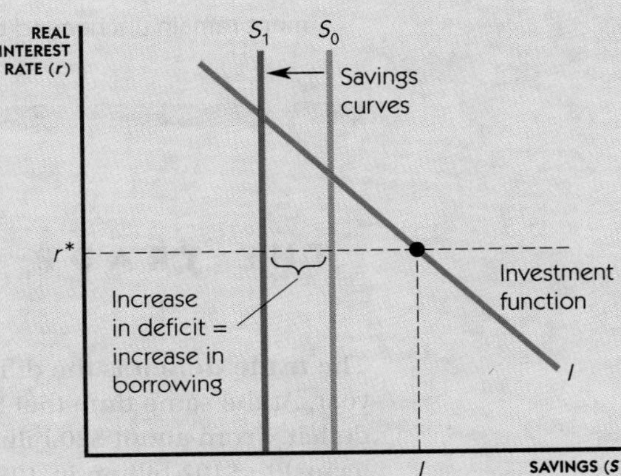

real interest rate. But it increases borrowing from abroad—in future years the country will be poorer as it has to pay interest on this indebtedness. Once again, living standards in the future are lower than they would have been in the absence of the deficit.

A Large Open Economy

We saw in Chapter 6 that the United States is a large open economy—with features that represent a cross between a closed economy and a small open economy. When the United States has a deficit, it borrows more from abroad, but interest rates rise, and some investment is crowded out. A rough rule of thumb is that between one-third and one-half of the deficit is offset by increased foreign borrowing.

If we look at who has bought the additional bonds the government has been issuing in recent years, we note that some but not all of the higher deficit has been financed by foreigners. But the consequences are equally or even more disturbing if foreigners do not *directly* finance the deficit. A high deficit can lead to increased foreign indebtedness directly as the government borrows directly from abroad, or it can increase foreign debt indirectly by sopping up available domestic savings so that Americans no longer have the money to invest in U.S. businesses and foreigners come in to fill the gap. Some economists have described the latter situation by saying that government borrowing can *crowd in* foreign investment.

In a closed economy, an increase in government expenditure not accompanied by an increase in taxes (or a decrease in taxes, not accompanied by a corresponding decrease in government expenditures) results in higher interest rates and decreased investment, while in a small, open economy, interest rates and investment remain unchanged but foreign borrowing increases.

THE TRADE DEFICIT

The **trade deficit** is the difference between imports and exports in any given year. At the same time that the budget deficit was exploding, so was the trade deficit. From about $20 billion a year from 1977 to 1982, it soared (in nominal terms) to $102 billion in 1984, $142 billion in 1987, and back down to $96 billion in 1995—though as a percentage of GDP, it declined from 3 percent in 1987 to 1.4 percent in 1995.

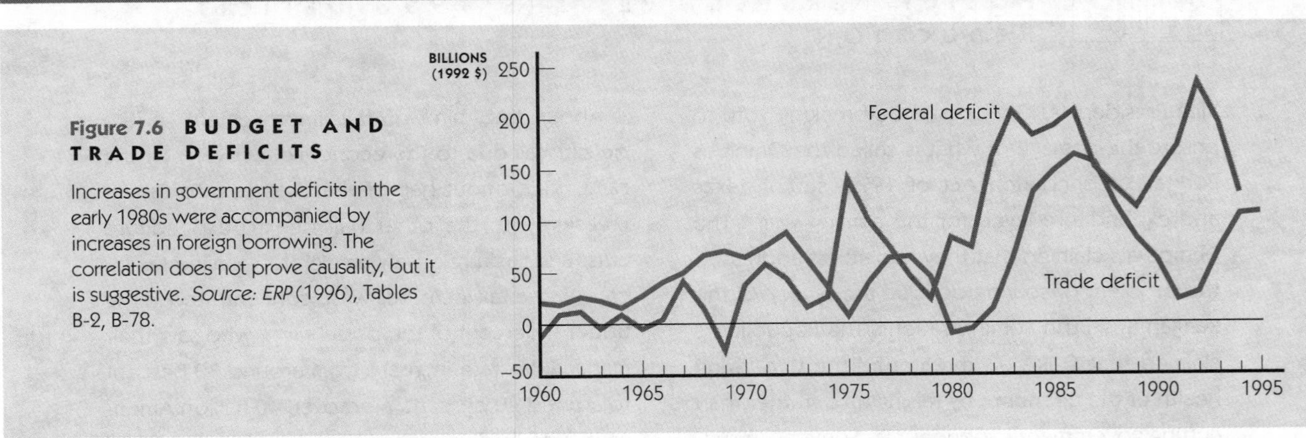

Figure 7.6 BUDGET AND TRADE DEFICITS

Increases in government deficits in the early 1980s were accompanied by increases in foreign borrowing. The correlation does not prove causality, but it is suggestive. *Source: ERP* (1996), Tables B-2, B-78.

Figure 7.6 shows the trade and federal deficits. The two have moved together. This is no accident: the two are in fact closely related. The reason for this we already noted: for an open economy, an increase in government expenditure not matched by an increase in taxes (or a decrease in taxes, not matched by a reduction in government expenditures) results in an increased deficit and increased foreign borrowing. We will now see why increased foreign borrowing implies an increase in the trade deficit.

Capital Flows

To see the relationship between foreign borrowing and the trade deficit, we first need to see the links between trade flows and capital flows. Let's trace what happens when an American buys a German car. It seems like a simple matter: he pays good American dollars to his dealer. His dealer buys the car—in dollars—from an importer. The importer buys the car from the German manufacturer, who wants to be paid in German marks. For the importer, this is no problem: he goes to a bank, say in Germany, and exchanges his dollars for marks. But the bank won't just hold those dollars. It will sell them, either to someone wanting to purchase U.S. goods or to someone wanting to invest in a dollar-denominated asset.

We call the money coming into the United States to buy investments, to be deposited in U.S. banks, to buy U.S. government bonds, or to lend to Americans for any reason—including buying a German car—**capital inflows.** U.S. dollars going to other countries for similar purposes are called **capital outflows.** For most purposes, we are interested in **net capital inflows,** the inflows minus the outflows.

As we have seen, every dollar an American spends to buy a foreign import eventually comes back, either to buy American exports or to buy an investment in the United States. We can express this relation by a simple equation:

Policy Perspective: The 1993 Deficit Reduction

Vice President Al Gore cast a tie-breaking vote to ensure the passage of what is called the Omnibus Budget Reconciliation Act of 1993, setting taxes and expenditure levels for the coming years. The Democrats claimed that they had at last addressed the problem of soaring deficits, the legacy of the Reagan and Bush administrations. The Republicans claimed that OBRA 93 threatened the underlying health of the economy, by raising taxes rather than cutting government expenditures. Some even suggested that the deficit would become worse: that the reduced economic activity resulting from the increased taxes would actually lead to reduced tax revenues.

As it turned out, the deficit reduction was genuine. While the deficit had been projected to increase without OBRA 93 to as much as $350 billion by 1996, the actual deficit, after OBRA 93 was implemented, was about $140 billion. The economy had a healthy recovery, and this by itself contributed significantly to the deficit reduction. The Clinton administration, of course, said that the deficit reduction, by restoring confidence in the economy and leading to reduced interest rates, spurred investment and the recovery; critics claimed that the recovery was based on the underlying strength of the American economy, and had occurred in spite of the tax increase.

About one-third of the improvement in the deficit was due to the economic recovery. Of the remainder, about half of that was due to tax increases, with the other half due to expenditure cuts. Besides a relatively moderate gasoline tax increase, the tax increases were concentrated in the upper 2 percent of the population, who saw their marginal tax rate increase from around 30 percent to around 40 percent. Moreover, 40 million Americans—families with incomes below $28,000—had an effective tax decrease. Still, a large percentage of Americans believed that they had a tax increase. This belief contributed strongly to demands for a middle-class tax cut.

imports into the United States = exports + capital inflows.

Subtracting exports from both sides of this equation, we obtain the basic trade identity:

trade deficit = imports − exports = capital inflows.

Thus, a trade deficit and an inflow of foreign capital are two ways of saying the same thing. This can be put another way: the only way that American consumers and businesses can import more from abroad than they export abroad is if foreigners are willing to make up the difference by lending to or investing in the United States.

In a world of multilateral trade, the accounts between any particular country and the United States do not have to balance. Assume Japan and Europe are in trade balance and the United States and Europe are in trade balance, but Japanese investors like to put their money into Europe and Europeans like to invest in the United States. Europe has zero net capital inflows with a positive capital inflow from Japan offset by a capital outflow to the United States. In this situation, the U.S. trade deficit with Japan is offset by a capital inflow from Europe. But what must be true for any country is that total imports minus total exports (the trade deficit) equal total capital inflows.

The basic trade identity can describe a capital outflow as well as a capital inflow. In the 1950s, the United States had a substantial trade surplus, as the country exported more than it imported. Europe and Japan did not receive enough dollars from selling exports to the United States to buy the imports that they desired, and they borrowed the difference from the United States. There was a net capital outflow from America, which gradually accumulated. Japan now exports more than it imports, with the difference equal to its capital outflows.

Exchange Rates

If a country borrows more (or less) from abroad, the **exchange rate** ensures that net imports adjust. The exchange rate tells how much of one currency exchanges for a given amount of another. For instance, in October 1995, one dollar could be exchanged for approximately 100 yen. Exchange rates may change rapidly. In 1992 a dollar was worth 126 yen. At the beginning of 1995, a dollar was worth only 100 yen. It then fell to only about 85 yen in March: a fall in value of 15 percent in three months. When the dollar has become less valuable relative to the yen, we say it has **depreciated;** the yen has become more valuable—it has **appreciated.**

The exchange rate is thus a price—the relative price of two currencies. Like any price, the exchange rate is determined by the laws of supply and demand. For simplicity, let us continue to focus on the exchange rate between the dollar and the yen (ignoring the fact that, in the world trading system, all exchange markets are interlinked). Figure 7.7 depicts the market for dollars in terms of the exchange rate with the yen. The exchange rate in yen per dollar is on the vertical axis, and the quantity of U.S. dollars is on the horizontal axis. The supply curve for dollars represents the quantity of dollars supplied by Americans to purchase Japanese goods and to make investments in Japan. At higher exchange rates—when the dollar buys more yen—Americans will supply higher quantities of dollars. The supply curve for dollars thus slopes upward to the right. The demand curve for dollars represents the dollars

Figure 7.7 EQUILIBRIUM IN THE MARKET FOR DOLLARS

The exchange rate is the relative price of two currencies. The equilibrium exchange rate, e_e, occurs at the intersection of the supply and demand curves for dollars.

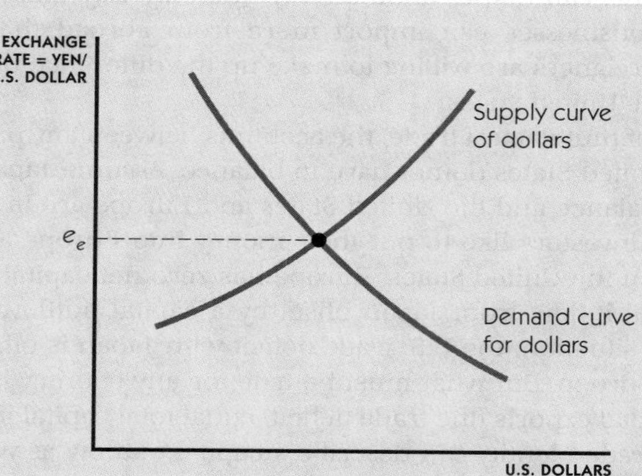

demanded by the Japanese to purchase American products and to make investments in the United States. At higher exchange rates—when it takes more yen to buy one dollar—the Japanese demand lower quantities of dollars, resulting in a demand curve which slopes downward to the right. The equilibrium exchange rate, e_e, lies at the intersection of the supply and demand curves for dollars.

Now we can see how the exchange rate connects the flow of capital and goods between countries. We continue with the case of the United States and Japan. Suppose the United States wants to borrow more from Japan. Higher U.S. interest rates will attract more Japanese investment to the United States. Japanese demand for dollars increases at each exchange rate, shifting the demand curve for dollars to the right, as depicted in Figure 7.8. The higher interest rates will also make Japanese investments relatively less attractive to American investors, who will therefore increase their investments at home. Americans will be willing to supply fewer dollars at each exchange rate, shifting the supply curve for dollars to the left. These shifts in the supply and demand curves for dollars cause the exchange rate to rise from e_0 to e_1—the dollar appreciates and the yen depreciates.[2] Since the dollar can now buy more Japanese products, U.S. imports increase (Japanese exports increase). Changes in the exchange rate thus ensure that the trade deficit moves in tandem with foreign borrowing.

The Savings-Investment Identity

We can now return to the issue discussed at the beginning of this section, where we saw that in the 1980s, both the trade and fiscal deficit increased.

[2]Later, in Chapter 14, we shall see that matters are somewhat more complicated. Investors have to take into account expectations concerning changes in the exchange rates as well.

Figure 7.8 EXCHANGE RATE EFFECTS OF INCREASED FOREIGN BORROWING

The equilibrium exchange rate is e_0 before the increase in U.S. borrowing from Japan. Higher interest rates in the United States attract Japanese investment to the U.S., shifting the demand curve for U.S. dollars to the right. At the same time, more Americans decide to invest in the U.S. rather than abroad, represented by a shift to the left of the supply curve for dollars. The exchange rate rises from e_0 to e_1. At the higher exchange rate, the dollar buys more yen, so U.S. imports of Japanese products increase. Conversely, U.S. exports decrease.

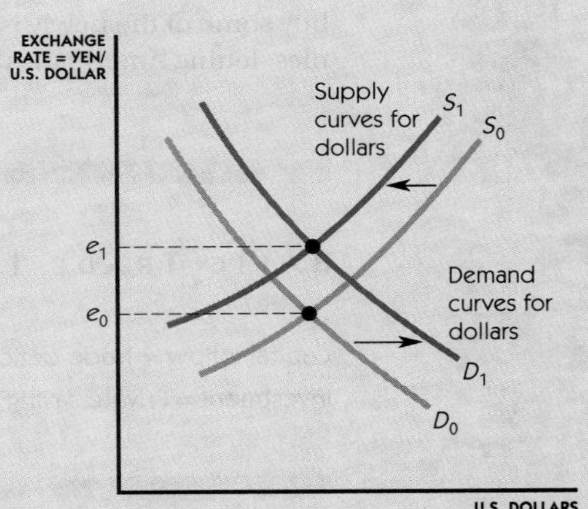

The fact that they moved together was no accident: as the United States needed to borrow more to finance the increased deficit, interest rates increased. The higher interest rates attracted foreign investors; the foreign borrowing helped finance the deficit. But at the same time, the dollar appreciated (from increased demand for dollars to invest in the United States), which reduced exports and increased imports, and hence increased the U.S. trade deficit.

The relationship between the fiscal deficit and the trade deficit (or foreign borrowing) can be seen another way using the savings and investment identity:

private (household and business) savings + capital flows (borrowing) from abroad = investment in machines and equipment + federal budget deficit.

Private savings and capital flows from abroad can be thought of as the "sources" of funds; and investment and budget deficits can be thought of as the uses of funds. A slightly different approach is to think of the fiscal deficit as dissaving, or negative savings. Just as when a household spends less than its income it is saving, and when it spends more than its income it is dissaving, so too with government. The savings-investment identity can thus be rewritten:

private savings + government savings + capital flows from abroad = investment.

The savings-investment identity says that if there is an increase in the deficit and if private savings and investment are unchanged, capital flows from abroad must increase and foreigners must end up holding more American assets. But the identity does not specify which assets they will hold. They may buy some of the newly issued government bonds or they may buy U.S. companies, letting Americans use their savings to buy the newly issued bonds.

BASIC TRADE IDENTITIES

Capital inflow = Trade deficit

Investment = Private saving + Government savings + Capital inflows

WHY TRADE DEFICITS ARE A PROBLEM

Borrowing from abroad is not necessarily bad, any more than borrowing in general is necessarily bad. In its first century, America borrowed heavily from abroad. For most of this century, the United States has loaned more money to foreign countries and investors than it has borrowed. This pattern is typical. In the early stages of development, countries borrow to build up their economies, and repay the loans with a portion of their economic gains. More mature economies typically lend capital.

The enormous U.S. trade deficits in the 1980s reversed this pattern. Just as when the government borrows year after year the cumulative budget deficits lead to a high level of government debt, when the country borrows from abroad year after year, the cumulative trade deficits (cumulative capital inflows) also lead to a high level of debt to foreigners.

The effect of the trade deficits of the 1980s was to convert the United States from the world's largest creditor nation at the beginning of the 1980s to the world's largest debtor nation by the end of the 1980s. The sum of U.S. indebtedness equals the combined amount owed by the three huge Latin American debtor countries, Mexico, Brazil, and Argentina. Figures on how much private parties in one country owe or have borrowed from another country are not fully reliable, yet it is clear that the U.S. debt is huge and growing.

Figure 7.9 shows that in the mid-1980s the United States slipped from being a creditor nation to being a debtor nation. At the beginning of the decade, the net international investment position of the United States—the value of all of America's assets abroad plus what others owe it minus the value of all assets within the United States owned by foreigners minus what it owes others—was positive.[3] But the cumulative effect of the trade deficits was to make this posi-

[3]One has to be careful about interpreting the figures. Critics of such figures point out that many of the assets that the United States owns abroad have greatly increased in value since it obtained those assets, but the data do not adequately reflect these increases. Still, there is little doubt about the general picture—there is a definite deterioration in America's net investment position.

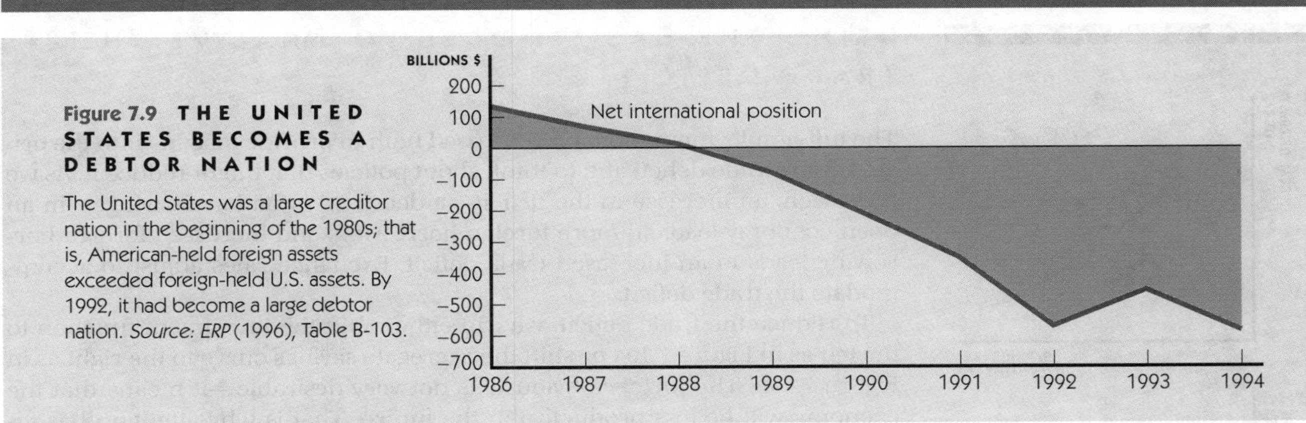

Figure 7.9 THE UNITED STATES BECOMES A DEBTOR NATION

The United States was a large creditor nation in the beginning of the 1980s; that is, American-held foreign assets exceeded foreign-held U.S. assets. By 1992, it had become a large debtor nation. *Source: ERP* (1996), Table B-103.

tion negative by the end of the decade. As a result, the U.S. economy will have to pay interest, dividends, and profits to foreign investors each year. The effects are readily apparent: for the first time since World War I, America is sending more dollars abroad in payment of interest and dividends than it is receiving.

The consequences for the nation are little different from those you would experience if you borrowed a large amount from the bank. In the future, unless you used the borrowed funds to make an investment that yielded a return at least equal to the interest you had to pay, you would be unable to consume as much as you would otherwise, because you must pay the bank interest as well as the principal. Consider this rough calculation: if the nation's debt to foreign investors reaches $1 trillion by the year 2000 and the average rate of interest is 6 percent, the interest payments alone work out to over $200 for every man, woman, and child in the United States *every year*.

LONG-RUN CONSEQUENCES OF PERSISTENT TRADE DEFICITS

Increased foreign indebtedness, leading eventually to

Increased interest and dividend payments abroad, and if foreign borrowing is not used to finance additional investments that yield returns sufficient to pay the increased interest and dividend payments,

Lower living standards

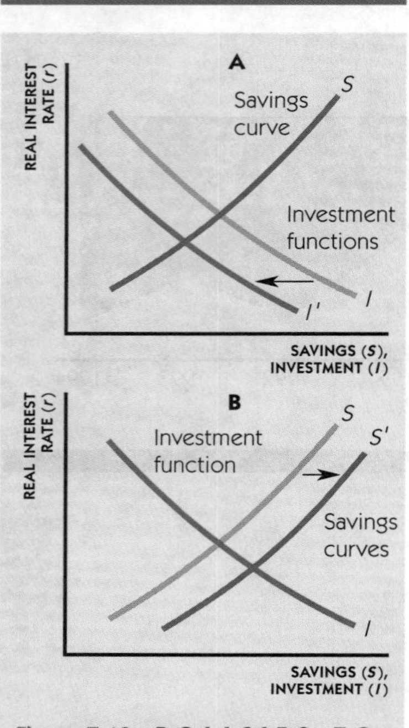

Figure 7.10 POLICIES TO REDUCE THE TRADE DEFICIT

The trade deficit can be reduced either by shifting the investment function to the left (panel A) or the savings function to the right (panel B).

USING THE BASIC MODEL TO ANALYZE THE TRADE DEFICIT

The full-employment model can be used both to provide insights into the origins of the trade deficit and to think about policies that might reduce it. As we have seen, an increase in the deficit—a decrease in national savings—in an open economy leads to more foreign borrowing; and increased foreign borrowing leads to an increased trade deficit. Exchange rates adjust to accommodate the trade deficit.

To reduce the trade deficit, we can either shift the investment function to the left as in Figure 7.10A or shift the aggregate savings curve to the right as in Figure 7.10B. The former obviously is not very desirable—it means that the economy will be less productive in the future. That is why attention has focused on shifting the aggregate savings curve. There are two ways to do this: either increase government savings (reduce the deficit) or increase private savings.

REDUCING THE TRADE DEFICIT

Increase private savings
Reduce the fiscal deficit
Reduce investment

GROWTH

The full-employment model can also be used to analyze policies that might promote economic growth. There are three keys to increased growth: (1) a more productive labor force—the result of improved education and training; (2) more and better capital—the result of increased investment in plant and equipment and investment in **infrastructure,** such as roads and airports; and (3) technological progress—partially the result of public and private expenditures on research and development. Expenditures in all three categories are referred to as **investments,** which are expenditures made today that reap benefits in the future. Investments in people are often called **human capital.** All three of these investments shift future short-run production func-

Figure 7.11 **INCREASING THE ECONOMY'S PRODUCTIVE POTENTIAL**

Improved education and training, the result of investments in people, more and better capital, the result of investments in plant and equipment, and improved technology, the result of investments in research and development and technology, all shift the short-run production function out, so that the level of output produced by any level of employment is increased.

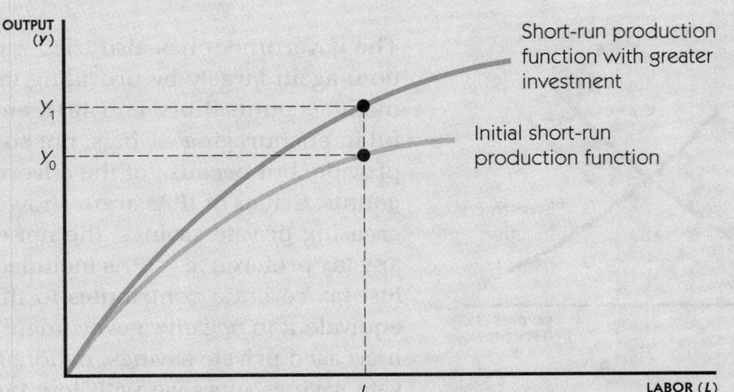

tions out, as depicted in Figure 7.11, so that the level of output that can be obtained at any level of employment is increased.

In a closed economy, there are basically two ways to increase investment: shift the investment function or the savings function to the right.

STIMULATING INVESTMENT

Governments have used tax policy as a way of shifting the investment function, as illustrated in Figure 7.12. With an **investment tax credit,** firms can subtract a fraction of the cost of the investment from their taxes, so that, in effect, the government is paying part of the cost of the investment. For example, with a 10 percent investment tax credit, a machine costing $100 results in a reduction in tax payments of $10, so the net cost of the machine is only $90. Naturally, the firm will invest more.

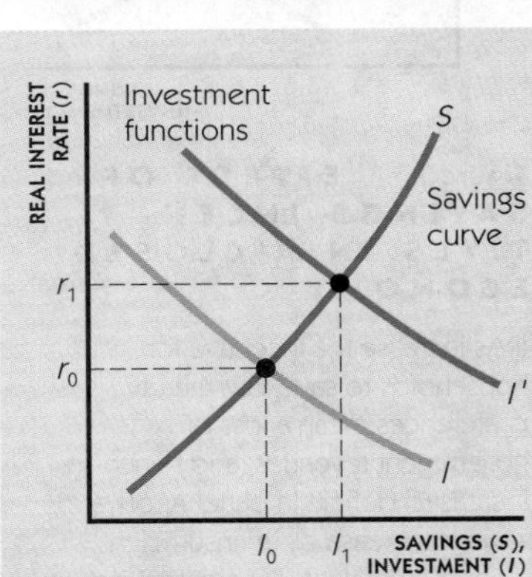

Figure 7.12 **EFFECT OF INVESTMENT TAX CREDIT IN A CLOSED ECONOMY**

An investment tax credit shifts the investment schedule to the right, resulting in a higher equilibrium interest rate and more investment. The higher level of investment increases the rate of growth, at least in the short run.

Another way that the government encourages investment through the tax system is through **accelerated depreciation.** When a firm buys a machine that lasts, say, ten years, in calculating its taxable income it is allowed to deduct 10 percent of the cost of the machine each year, to reflect the fact that over time, the machine is becoming worth less and less. The deduction is called a **depreciation allowance.** In 1981, the government passed a law allowing firms to accelerate their depreciation. Thus, they might be able to pretend that a machine that lasted ten years only lasted five, deducting 20 percent of the value in each of the first five years of its life. This meant that taxes they paid in the first five years were lower. Obviously, a dollar today is worth far more than a dollar five years from now: with accelerated depreciation, the present discounted value of the tax reductions associated with depreciation allowances is greatly increased. This makes investments more attractive, shifting the investment function to the right.

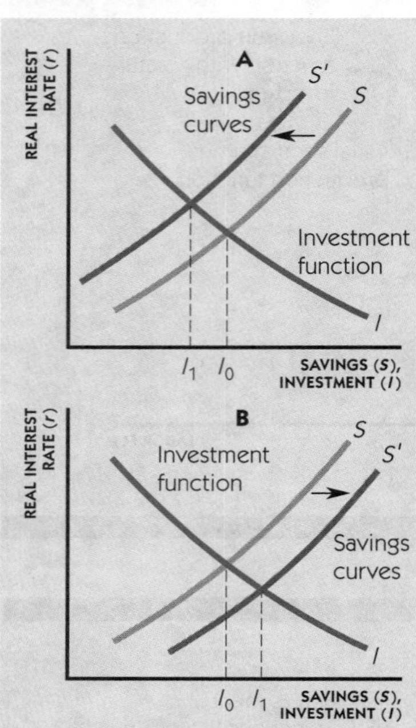

Figure 7.13 EFFECT OF SAVINGS INCENTIVES IN A CLOSED ECONOMY

IRAs increase the incentive for households to save, but the tax preferences mean a loss of government revenues, and hence an increased deficit. In panel A, private savings increase by an insufficient amount to offset the increased deficit, so that the aggregate savings curve shifts to the left. Investment is actually lowered. In panel B, the increased private savings more than offset the increased deficit; the aggregate savings curve shifts to the right, leading to lower interest rates, increased investment, and higher growth.

STIMULATING SAVINGS

The government has also tried a variety of ways of shifting the savings function, again largely by providing tax preferences, including individual retirement accounts (IRAs) and 401K and 403B plans. IRAs may have been successful in encouraging savings, not so much because of the extra incentives they provide, but because of the advertising that banks did to recruit new IRA accounts. Critics of IRAs argue, however, that even if IRAs have succeeded in increasing private savings, the net effect on national savings is negative. With any tax preference—IRAs included—government loses tax revenues, and the lost tax revenue contributes to the deficit. And the deficit, we have seen, is equivalent to *negative* government savings. If the lost tax revenue exceeds the increased private savings, national savings actually decrease. How much private savings increase with low taxes depends on the **interest elasticity of savings,** that is, if the after-tax interest rate (what savers care about) is increased by 1 percent, by what percentage do savings increase? Most estimates suggest that savings are relatively inelastic, that is, lowering the tax rate to zero—and thus increasing the after-tax return substantially—will not induce even an individual facing a 40 percent marginal tax rate to save much more. The reason is simple: if he is saving for his retirement, the amount he has to save, to provide any level of retirement income, will be reduced as the after-tax interest rate increases.[4] If savings are relatively inelastic, then the increase in private savings is insufficient to offset the increased deficit, and national savings are reduced. Figure 7.13 illustrates the two possible cases.

REDUCING THE DEFICIT

We saw earlier that reducing the deficit is equivalent to shifting the aggregate savings curve to the right. But we need to emphasize that the net effect on growth depends on how the deficit is cut. In Figure 7.14 we illustrate a case where deficit reduction actually leads to lower growth. As we saw earlier, the shift in the aggregate savings curve to the right leads to lower interest rates and increased private investment. This shifts the economy's future short-run production function out to *0P'*. But if the government reduces the deficit by cutting back on productive public investments, such as research, investments in education, or infrastructure, the future short-run production function shifts in, to *0P"*—below where it was before the deficit reduction. If private savings is responsive to after-tax interest rates, as in Figure 7.13, a dollar of deficit reduction does not, in general, result in an increase of private invest-

[4]Higher interest rates mean that savers are better off, so they consume more today. This is the income effect. At the same time, a higher after-tax interest rate increases the incentive to save; this is the substitution effect—for every dollar of consumption forgone today, the individual can consume more dollars of consumption in the future. The income and substitution effects largely offset each other.

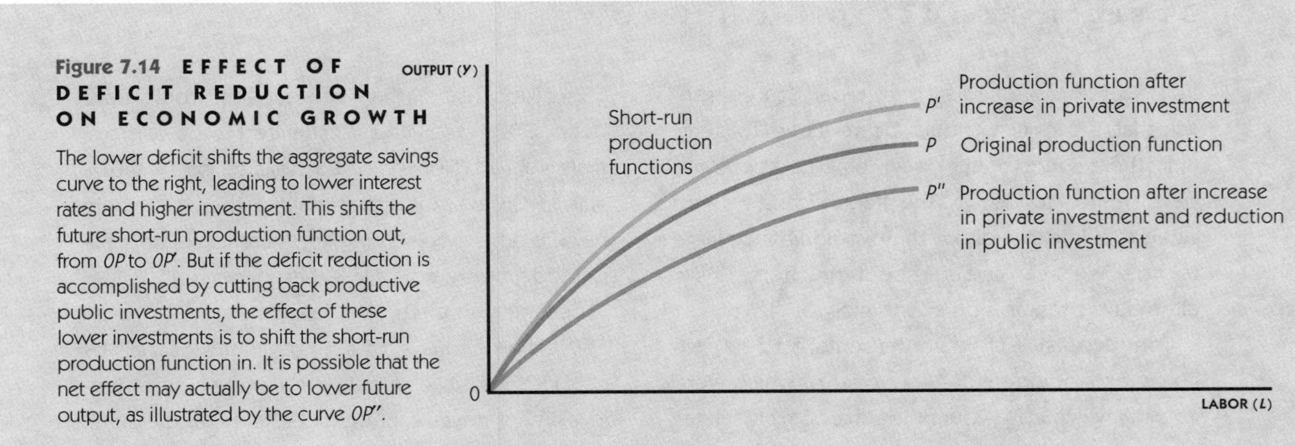

Figure 7.14 EFFECT OF DEFICIT REDUCTION ON ECONOMIC GROWTH

The lower deficit shifts the aggregate savings curve to the right, leading to lower interest rates and higher investment. This shifts the future short-run production function out, from *OP* to *OP'*. But if the deficit reduction is accomplished by cutting back productive public investments, the effect of these lower investments is to shift the short-run production function in. It is possible that the net effect may actually be to lower future output, as illustrated by the curve *OP''*.

ment by a dollar (because the investment function is downward sloping[5]). Thus, even if public investment is *less* productive than private investment, deficit reduction attained through investment reduction can lower economic growth. And there is evidence that public investments in education, research, and infrastructure may actually yield higher marginal returns than private investment.

Open Economy

In an open economy, investment may differ from domestic savings, since the country can always borrow to finance its investment. By the same token, changes in domestic savings need not equal changes in investment. For a small open economy, with a perfectly elastic supply of funds at the international interest rate, r^*, the level of investment is determined by that interest rate.

In a large open economy like the United States, however, savings and investment tend to move together, with increases in savings leading to increases in investment, but not on a dollar-for-dollar basis. As we have noted, today most estimates suggest that an increase in domestic savings by a dollar increases investment by between 35 and 50 cents.

If a small open economy wishes to increase its growth rate, it focuses its attention on shifting its investment function; changes in the savings curve only affect the amount it borrows from abroad (though, as we have seen, this will have important consequences for the economy's future well-being).

[5]Only if the investment function were a horizontal straight line would a shift in an upward-sloping savings curve to the right by a dollar result in an increase in investment by a dollar.

Using Economics: Estimating the Effect of Deficit Reduction on Growth

In 1995 there seemed to be a bipartisan consensus that the deficit should be reduced to zero. Still, there were sharp disagreements about the best way to reduce it. The Republicans wanted deep cuts in expenditure that would finance large tax cuts. What can one say about the effects of the alternative programs on economic growth?

Consider first a program that entailed $200 billion in expenditure cuts—a quarter of which were cuts in investment. Assume the economy manages to remain at full employment, and there are no tax cuts, so consumption remains unchanged. Based on historical experience, the $200 billion increased national savings will result in $100 billion increased private investment. (For the economy to remain at full employment when government expenditures decrease by $200 billion, and consumption is unchanged, if investment increases by $100 billion, net exports must increase by $100 billion. Exchange rates must change to accommodate the increase in net exports and interest rates must change to generate the increased investment.*) Thus, aggregate investment increases by $50 billion per year (private investment increases by $100 billion, offset by a reduction of $50 billion in public investment). The $50 billion per year, cumulated over ten years, assuming no depreciation, yields at the end of a decade $500 billion more capital, which, with a return of approximately 7 percent, will mean that national income will be $35 billion higher than it otherwise would have been. GDP in ten years is estimated to be approximately $10 billion (in 1995 dollars), so that GDP will be .35 percent higher than it otherwise would have been, representing an increase in the expected growth rate of less than .1 percent.

Consider an alternative plan that had an extra $50 billion annually of tax cuts, financed half by cuts in public investments and half by cuts in noninvestment government expenditures, and assume labor supply is unchanged. The extra $50 billion in tax cuts—because they are fully financed by expenditure cuts—leaves public savings unchanged. But since a household's disposable income has increased by the amount of the tax cut, its savings increase. Typically, an increase in household income of $50 billion yields an increase in savings of somewhat less than $5 billion. An increase in national savings of $5 billion generates an extra $2.5 billion in private investment. Thus aggregate investment (public plus private) is reduced by $22.5 billion. Thus, almost half of the gain in growth from the original deficit reduction package is lost with the tax cuts that are partially financed by reductions in public investment.

*This analysis assumes that the savings rate is not sensitive to the interest rate. If lowering the interest rate leads to reduced savings—and increased consumption—then the requisite adjustments in investment and net exports will be accordingly reduced.

CONSENSUS IN MACROECONOMICS

From this chapter emerges a seventh point of consensus in macroeconomics:

7 Growth

Increases in standards of living require increases in productivity; increases in productivity require expenditures on research and development, investments in new technology, plant, equipment, and infrastructure, and increases in the skills of the labor force.

In a closed economy, investment can be increased either by shifting the investment curve to the right (such as by an investment tax credit) or the savings curve to the right (such as by preferential tax treatment). Some preferential tax treatments may actually lower national savings, since the induced private savings are less than the increased deficit. Similarly, deficit reduction, in a closed economy, will result in increased private investment, but if the deficit reduction is attained through reducing public investment, future output and living standards may actually be reduced.

REVIEW AND PRACTICE

SUMMARY

1. The early 1980s were marked by a surge in the size of federal budget deficits in the United States, leading to marked increases in the national debt. Beginning in 1993, the deficit began to be substantially reduced.

2. In a closed economy, increases in the deficit lead to lower private investment and increased interest rates. The net effect of reductions in the deficit depend on how it is reduced. If generated by reductions in public investment, growth is likely to be reduced, as the increased private investment is unlikely to be sufficient to offset the reduced public investment.

3. In a small open economy, increases in the deficit have no effect on investment, but lead to increased foreign indebtedness and larger trade deficits. Cumulative increases in foreign indebtedness will make future citizens worse off, as they have to pay interest on the foreign indebtedness.

4. The large increases in the trade deficit that began in the 1980s were largely explained by the large increases in the fiscal deficit which began at that time. The trade deficit must equal capital inflows. Policy options for reducing the U.S. trade deficit and foreign borrowing include decreasing investment (a bad idea for long-term growth), increasing household and business savings (a good idea if the government could do it), or reducing the federal deficit.

5. The savings-investment identity for an open economy says that the sum of private savings, capital flows from abroad, and government savings is equal to investment. This identity implies that a change in any one factor must also involve offsetting changes in other factors.

6. Increases in investments in human capital, plant and equipment, infrastructure, and improved technology all shift out the short-run production curve, increasing the full-employment output of the economy and the economy's rate of growth. Investment can be stimulated either through investment tax credits or accelerated depreciation, or, in a closed economy, by increasing the rate of savings through tax preferences. Because of a low interest elasticity of savings, tax preferences may not be very effective.

Key Terms

fiscal deficit
trade deficit
capital flows (capital outflow, inflow)
exchange rates
depreciate
appreciate
investment tax credit
accelerated depreciation
depreciation allowance
interest elasticity of savings
infrastructure
human capital

Review Questions

1. What happened to the size of the budget deficits in the 1980s? What is the relationship between the deficit and the level of the debt?

2. What are the consequences of an increased deficit for private investment in an open economy and in a closed economy?

3. Why do the consequences for growth of deficit reduction depend on whether the deficit reduction is accomplished by cutting government investment, by cutting government consumption expenditures, or by raising taxes?

4. What happened to the trade deficit during the 1980s? How did the foreign indebtedness of the U.S. economy change during the 1980s? What is the relationship between these two changes?

5. What is the relationship between the trade deficit and an inflow of foreign capital?

6. What is the relationship between the trade deficit and the fiscal deficit?

7. What is the exchange rate? How is it determined? What role do adjustments in the exchange rate play in ensuring that capital inflows equal the trade deficit?

8. What are the consequences of persistent trade deficits?

9. What is the savings-investment identity for an open economy?

10. How may government stimulate investment and savings?

11. How do efforts to increase economic growth differ in a small open economy compared to a large open economy?

PROBLEMS

1. Suppose a certain country has private savings of 6 percent of GDP, foreign borrowing of 1 percent of GDP, and a balanced budget. What is its level of investment? If the budget deficit is 1.5 percent of GDP, how does your answer change?

2. Why does it make a difference if a country borrows abroad to finance the expansion of its railroads, or to finance increased Social Security benefits for the elderly?

3. Assume investments in human capital yield a return of 15 percent, private investments yield a total return of 10 percent, and public investments in research yield a return of 25 percent. Assume the deficit is $100 billion per year, and the government wishes to eliminate it. What will be the impact on economic growth of a deficit reduction package which consists of reducing Medicare expenditures by $50 billion, education expenditures by $40 billion, and research expenditures by $10 billion?

4. The primary deficit is defined as the difference between government expenditures *excluding interest payments* and tax revenues; it represents what the deficit would have been, has the government not inherited any debt. The table below shows the primary deficit over time. (A negative deficit means the government is running a surplus.) Discuss why the concept of a primary deficit may or may not be useful or relevant.

Year	Primary deficit	Actual deficit
1980	21.3	73.8
1985	82.8	212.3
1990	37.2	221.4
1995	–68.4	163.8

5. If the economy is growing at 5 percent per year, and the debt/GDP ratio is 50 percent, what is the critical value of the deficit/GDP ratio, such that if the deficit/GDP ratio exceeds that number, the debt/GDP ratio will increase, and if the deficit/GDP ratio falls short of that number, the debt/GDP ratio decreases.

6. U.S. foreign indebtedness is greater than that of Mexico, Brazil, and Argentina combined. But does this necessarily mean that the United States has a larger debt problem than those countries? Why or why not? Can you think of a situation in which an individual with debts of larger value may actually have less of a debt problem?

7. If Congress were to pass a law prohibiting foreigners from buying U.S. Treasury bills, would this prevent government borrowing from leading to capital inflows? Discuss.

8. Japan had large trade surpluses during the 1980s. Would this cause Japan to be a borrower or a lender in international capital markets?

9. If a nation borrowed $50 billion from abroad one year and its imports were worth $800 billion, what would be the value of its exports? How does the answer change if, instead of borrowing, the nation loaned $100 billion abroad?

10. Since other countries benefit from exporting their products to the United States, why shouldn't the U.S. government charge them for the privilege of selling in the United States?

PART THREE

UNEMPLOYMENT MACROECONOMICS

Part Two explored full-employment macroeconomics. The basic assumption there was that the economy operates as envisioned in the basic competitive model: prices, wages, and interest rates adjust quickly and fully to ensure that all markets clear. Most importantly, the demand for labor equals the supply of labor. The assumption may be unrealistic, but the model is instructive. We saw how deficits crowd out investment and increase foreign borrowing, and we got to look more closely at economic growth.

The full-employment model needs to be modified to take up two further, fundamental macroeconomic questions: unemployment and inflation. In this part, we take up unemployment, reserving inflation for Part Four. Over the long run, as we have seen, the economy has managed to create jobs to keep pace with the increasing number of workers. But in the short run, mismatches between demand and supply not only give rise to public outcries, but are among the most important determinants of the fates of elected officials. Today, government is viewed as having the responsibility for keeping the economy on an even keel, which means avoiding the pitfalls of excessive unemployment.

Here, in Part Three, we examine the problem of maintaining the economy at full employment. The most fundamental difference in our analysis in this part of the book is that we drop the assumption that wages and prices instantaneously adjust to clear all markets. For simplicity, we will assume that they do not adjust at all, that they are fixed. In Part Four, we will take up the in-between case, exploring how wages and prices adjust, and why they often change so slowly.

Chapter 8 provides an overview of the macroeconomics of unemployment, and introduces some of the basic concepts. The next two chapters focus on the product market. Chapter 9 looks at aggregate demand—which, as we will see, in situations of unemployment, determines the level of aggregate output. Chapter 10 looks more closely at two of the most important components of aggregate demand, consumption and investment.

Chapters 11–12 then focus on the capital market, and the links between that market and the product market. We begin with a discussion, in Chapter 11, of money. Chapter 12 then discusses monetary theory—how changes in the supply of money and the availability of credit affect the level of economic activity, and how government changes the supply of money and credit availability. Chapter 13 puts the entire unemployment model with fixed prices and wages together, focusing on how fiscal and monetary policy can be used to restore the economy to full employment. To reach a better understanding of the roles these two alternative policy instruments play, it contrasts both their consequences and the difficulties that are faced in using them effectively.

CHAPTER 8

Overview of Unemployment Macroeconomics

People worry about jobs. They worry about layoffs. If they are laid off, they worry about how long it will take to get another job. In all market economies, there is some unemployment. In a dynamic economy, some firms and industries are shrinking—jobs are being lost—at the same time that new jobs are being created. It takes time for individuals to switch from one job to another. But at times, as we saw in Chapter 4, the unemployment rate becomes very high. Labor markets do not clear: the demand for labor is much less than the supply. In such situations, governments take on the responsibility of reducing the unemployment rate—not necessarily to zero, but at least to a low level.

We have seen how all markets of the economy are interlinked. The labor market is linked to the product market and the product market to the capital market. The labor market is particularly sensitive to changes in the product market: if output goes down, so too will the demand for labor. If real wages adjust too slowly, there will be unemployment. In this chapter, we do not ask why they adjust slowly—that is a question postponed until Part Four. We focus instead on the consequences. After a few words about the nature of macroeconomic models, we discuss the labor market, then the product market, and finally the capital market. The chapter closes by applying the framework to discuss some recent macroeconomic events.

Key Questions

1. How do economists analyze what determines levels of aggregate output and employment in the short run, when wages and prices are fixed?
2. What causes shifts in the aggregate demand and supply curves for labor? Why may unemployment result if wages fail to adjust in response to these shifts?
3. What is the aggregate demand curve? What happens when the price level is fixed at a level at which aggregate demand is less than aggregate supply? What are the consequences of a shift in the aggregate demand curve in these circumstances?
4. How can we use aggregate demand curves to interpret some of the major macroeconomic episodes of the past fifty years?

More About Macroeconomic Models

Part Two developed the full-employment macroeconomic model. The critical assumption of Part Two was that wages and prices adjust so that all markets—including the labor market—clear: there is no unemployment. The basic way in which this part differs from Part Two is that here, we are concerned about the problem of unemployment. The basic explanation for unemployment is that wages do not adjust quickly enough to shifts in either the demand or supply curve for labor, so that *at least for a while, and sometimes for extended periods of time,* the demand for labor at market wages and prices may be less than the supply. In this part of the book, to simplify matters, we assume wages and prices are fixed; that is, they do not adjust at all. Economists say that such wages and prices are **rigid.** The results are much the same as they would be if they adjusted slowly—that is, adjusted in the direction required by market clearing, but too slowly to ensure that the demand and supply for, say, labor were equated. While some prices—such as those on the stock market—adjust quickly, others—wages in particular—adjust slowly. Unions, for instance, often sign three-year contracts, and even nonunionized firms let workers know their wages at the beginning of the year, and are reluctant to lower wages quickly in response to either the availability of cheaper labor elsewhere or a decrease in the demand for their products. At the bottom, minimum wage laws prevent employers from lowering wages, even if they wanted to. Over the last fifteen years, much of Europe has had much higher rates of unemployment, and this is widely attributed, in part at least, to their greater wage rigidity.

The fact that slow adjustments can lead to persistent unemployment is one of the reasons that macroeconomists focus so much on dynamics—how, and in particular, *how fast* things change. In Part Four of the book, we will describe the dynamics of the economy, focusing in particular on price and wage adjustments. We will analyze how and how fast the economy adjusts.

This part of the book focuses on the short run, a time span that might range from a week or a month up to a few years. Although investment is occurring in the economy, we assume the net change in the capital stock is so small in the short term that it can be ignored. Except when we focus explicitly upon *changes* in government actions, we will also assume that tax rates, levels of expenditures, and the money supply are all fixed.

THE LABOR MARKET

Since unemployment is our key concern in this part of the book, our discussion naturally begins with the labor market. In Chapter 6, we described equilibrium in the labor market as the intersection of the aggregate demand and supply curves for labor. Both depended on real wages. We are assuming now that prices are fixed, so we do not have to distinguish between nominal and real wages.

In the earlier discussion of the labor market, we simplified the analysis in two ways. We assumed that each worker supplied exactly 40 hours of labor—no more and no less—per week, and that real wages did not affect aggregate supply.[1] Thus, the aggregate labor supply curve was vertical. Wages were flexible, so that they adjusted to equate demand and supply, to w_1/P in Figure 8.1.

But what happens if wages do not adjust quickly? Assume, for some reason, that the demand curve for labor suddenly shifts to the left, so that at each

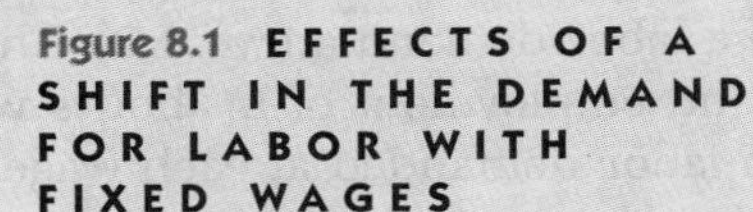

Figure 8.1 EFFECTS OF A SHIFT IN THE DEMAND FOR LABOR WITH FIXED WAGES

Equilibrium in the labor market is at the intersection of the aggregate demand and supply curves for labor. If the demand for labor decreases and the wage is fixed, employed labor decreases from L_1 to L_2.

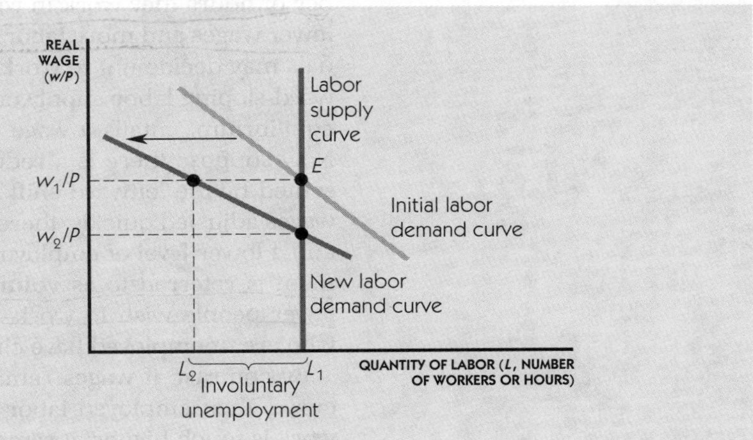

[1]The fact that each worker works 40 hours means that we can put on the horizontal axis either the number of workers or the number of hours worked.

wage, fewer workers are demanded. At the old equilibrium wage, w_1/P, the supply for labor exceeds the demand. However, if the wage is stuck at the original level, w_1/P—above the wage at which the demand for labor equals the supply—firms will still only hire the amount demanded. More workers will be willing to work than can get jobs at that wage. Those without jobs will be involuntarily unemployed. In Figure 8.1 the demand for labor will only be L_2, while the supply is L_1. The distance between these two points measures the amount of involuntary unemployment. At this high wage, the supply of labor exceeds the demand.

Involuntary unemployment arising from reductions in the demand for labor (combined with wage rigidity) would be much less of a social problem if the impact could be spread over the entire population. Even if the demand for labor were reduced by 10 percent and wages did not fall, the consequences would be limited if each worker worked 10 percent fewer hours. The problem in that case would be *underemployment*. Each person in the economy might work only 36 hours per week, when she wished to work 40 hours.

In the modern industrial economy, the problem is different. Most workers continue to work the same, or only a slightly reduced, number of hours when the labor market goes out of equilibrium, but an unfortunate few will find no full-time job at all at the going wage. This is the problem of unemployment. Whenever the supply of labor exceeds the demand at the going wage, there will be "rationing"—some individuals will not be able to sell all the labor they would like. But the impact of this rationing is not evenly spread in the economy; some workers will manage to sell little if any of their labor services, while others will be fully employed. Many of the social problems associated with a reduced demand for labor result from the fact that the economic burden is so concentrated.

The analysis is little different if we assume an upward-sloping, rather than vertical, labor supply curve. This would mean that workers change the number of hours they work in response to wage changes, supplying less labor at lower wages and more labor at higher wages. And at low wages, some individuals may decide not to work at all. Consider Figure 8.2, which shows an upward-sloping labor supply curve and a labor demand curve, LD_1. The initial equilibrium, entails a wage of w_1/P and employment of L_1 (hours worked). Now suppose there is a reduction in labor demanded at each wage, represented by the leftward shift of the labor demand curve from LD_1 to LD_2. If wages adjusted quickly, there would be a new equilibrium with wages at w_2/P and a lower level of employment at L_2. In this case, the reduction in employment is referred to as **voluntary unemployment.** At the lower wage w_2/P fewer people wish to work—those who wish to work have jobs, and those who are unemployed have chosen not to work.

By contrast, if wages remain at w_1/P after the shift of the labor demand curve, then employed labor falls to L_3. At this wage, the number willing to work is much higher: it remains at L_1. The workers who cannot get jobs represent **involuntary unemployment.** They are willing and able to work at the going wage, w_1/P, but simply cannot find jobs.

Most economists believe that the individual's labor supply curve, while not perfectly inelastic (or vertical), is relatively inelastic, and that much of the re-

Figure 8.2 THE EFFECTS OF A SHIFT IN THE DEMAND FOR LABOR WITH FIXED WAGES AND ELASTIC LABOR SUPPLY

If wages do not fall when the demand for labor shifts to the left, involuntary unemployment results. If wages adjust, employment decreases, but this is a voluntary change.

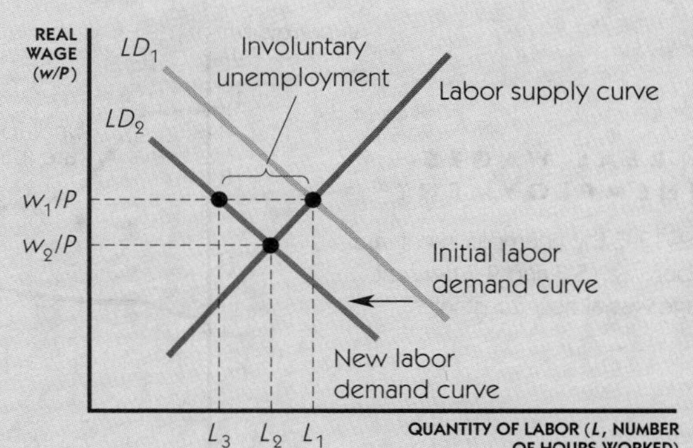

sponsiveness of the aggregate labor supply to wages comes from decisions to participate in the labor force (rather than in the desired number of hours worked per week). Moreover, as we have noted, when demand for labor is less than the supply, the shortfall usually takes the form mostly of reduction in employed workers, rather than hours worked per worker. For simplicity, in the following analysis, we shall assume that the hours worked per worker are fixed, and reductions in the demand for labor hours are translated directly into reductions in employment.

Unemployment and Wage Rigidities

If we look at data on real wages—the wage adjusted for changes in the price level—we see that wages vary little with economic conditions. Figure 8.3 plots the real wage and unemployment rate during 1982 through 1994. During that period the unemployment rate fluctuated between 5.3 and 9.7 percent, yet the real wage was almost constant. Even in the Great Depression, with massive unemployment, real wages did not fall, or fell very little.

Given the relatively small changes in real wages, the magnitude of the changes in employment cannot be explained by movements along a fixed, steep labor supply curve. Then how can we account for such large changes in employment?

There are but two possibilities. One is that the labor market always remains in equilibrium. Thus, the labor supply curve is not only not fixed, but shifts dramatically—in a way just offsetting shifts in the labor demand curve—so that in spite of large variations in employment, real wages remained unchanged. Few economists accept this account. Even if there are sudden, dramatic shifts in the labor supply curve, it is hard to believe they would occur in just the right amount to offset shifts in the labor demand curve.

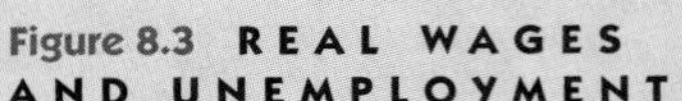

Figure 8.3 REAL WAGES AND UNEMPLOYMENT

During 1982–1995 the unemployment rate fluctuated between 5.3 and 9.7 percent. The real wage was almost constant.

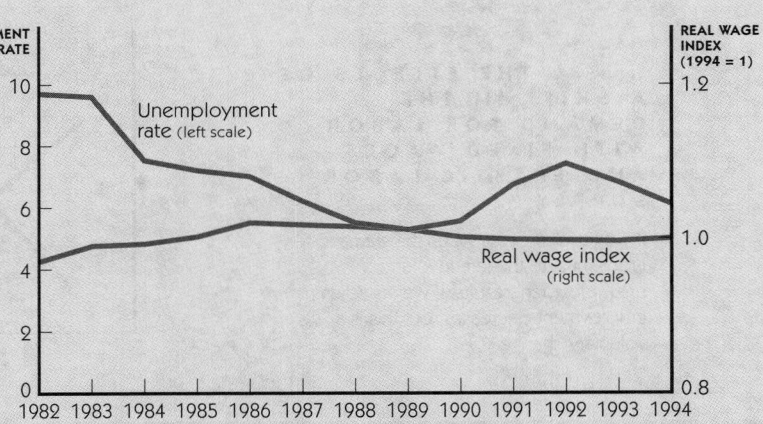

Economists have focused their attention on the other possible explanation: at least at times, demand for labor is less than supply—the labor market is not in equilibrium. How does such a situation arise? First, there is a shift in the demand curve for labor, as we illustrated in Figures 8.1 and 8.2. Such shifts can occur fairly rapidly, mainly because of changes in output. Second, wages fail to fall enough to restore equilibrium (where demand for labor equals supply), resulting in involuntary unemployment. Because there is widespread agreement over this explanation, we may present it as our eighth point of consensus:

8 Unemployment

Unemployment is typically generated by shifts in the aggregate demand curve for labor when wages fail to adjust. The shifts in the aggregate demand curve for labor typically arise from changes in aggregate output.

Unemployment and the Aggregate Supply of Labor

While most unemployment arises from sudden leftward shifts in the demand curve for labor, occasionally large rightward shifts in the supply curve for labor can also give rise to unemployment, as illustrated in Figure 8.4. Normally, aggregate labor supply changes only slowly, such as through demographic changes or changes in labor force participation rates. But there are circumstances in which aggregate supply can shift dramatically in a short span of time. For instance, in the early 1990s, Israel was faced with a flood of Jewish immigrants from Russia, increasing its labor force by more than 10 percent. In the short run, real wages did not adjust quickly enough, and unemployment rose. Remarkably, within five years, the unemployment rate was

Figure 8.4 UNEMPLOYMENT AND THE AGGREGATE SUPPLY OF LABOR

Unemployment may arise from rightward shifts of the aggregate supply curve for labor, when wages fail to adjust. The initial equilibrium wage is w_0/P, at the intersection of the aggregate demand curve for labor and the initial aggregate supply curve for labor (LS_0). The aggregate supply curve for labor then shifts from LS_0 to LS_1. The real wage remains at w_0/P, where the quantity of labor demanded, L_0, is less than the quantity of labor supplied, resulting in unemployment.

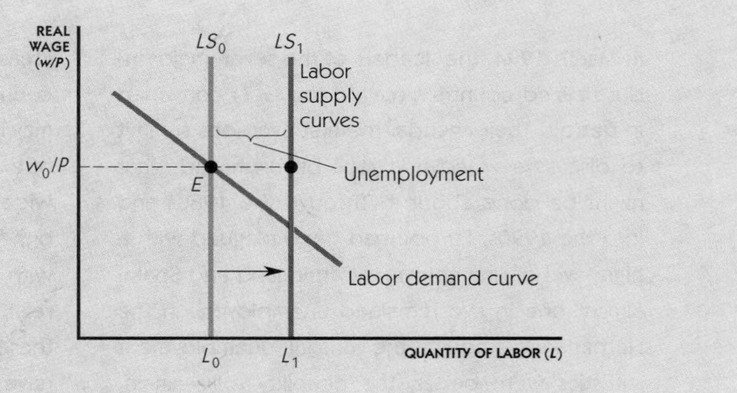

back down—though the adjustment seems to have been more through a compensating shift in the aggregate demand curve for labor than a lowering of the real wage. Another instance of *potentially* rapid shifts in the labor supply curve are associated with changes in tax laws, which might induce a smaller or larger fraction of the population to join the labor force—though in practice such changes appear to take place more gradually.

BASIC ISSUES IN THE ANALYSIS OF UNEMPLOYMENT

1. What causes shifts in the demand curve for labor?
2. Why do wages fail to adjust?

THE PRODUCT MARKET IN THE SHORT RUN

To understand unemployment we must understand what causes changes in output. Thus, we now turn to the product market. Later, in Part Four, we will return to another basic issue of unemployment—what causes real wages to adjust slowly.

Close-up: G-7 and the Worldwide Jobs Problem

In March 1994, the leaders of the seven major industrialized countries (called the G-7) convened in Detroit. Their agenda: the first ever jobs summit to discuss a worldwide jobs problem and what might be done about it. Through the 1980s and into the 1990s, Europe had been plagued with a high level of unemployment. In Ireland and Spain, almost one in five remained unemployed. In the Netherlands, though the official unemployment statistics were better, the disability rolls—again, one in five—disguised what was really going on; more generous disability benefits and an absence of tight screening led many who were thrown out of jobs to apply for disability rather than unemployment benefits. The United States was beginning to control unemployment, but in many other countries unemployment remained a problem, as the figure on the next page indicates.

All countries agreed that the major source of the problem was with low-skilled and unskilled workers. The demand curve for these workers had not shifted to the right enough to offset the increased supply of such workers—and in some countries, the demand curve for these workers may have even shifted to the left. Though a variety of explanations have been put forward, the most widely accepted focus is on changes in technology, which have increased the demand for those with skills (such as the ability to use computers) relative to those without skills. The responses to these shifts in labor supply and demand curves have varied from country to country. In the United States, real wages of unskilled labor fell. In Europe, higher minimum wages helped prevent such a drop in real wages at the bottom of the skill distribution. Real wages of those employed in Europe increased over the 1970s through the 1990s by about 2 percent per year, in contrast to the virtual stagnation in the United States.

While the focus of attention was on unskilled workers, in Europe the problem seemed to be more widespread. Total job creation in the private sector in the first half of the 1990s was virtually nil—in contrast to the United States where more

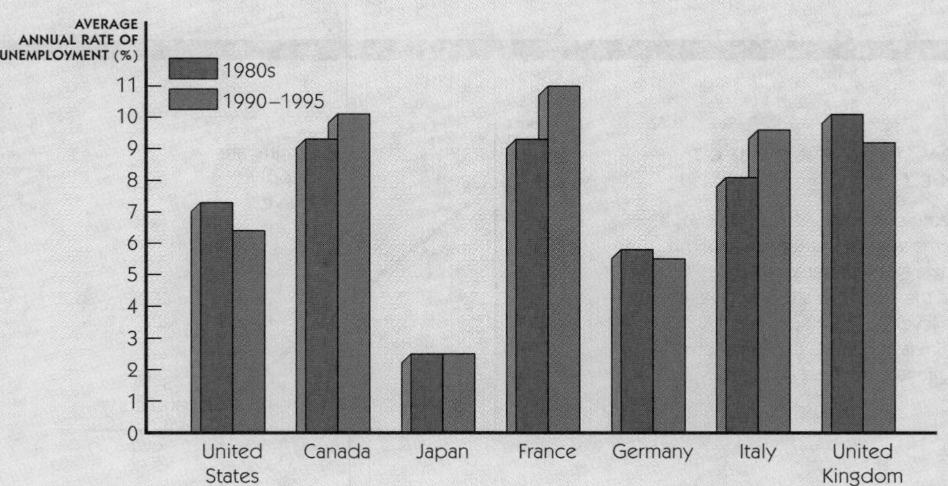

than seven million jobs were created in the private sector from 1993 through 1995. While there is no universally accepted explanation of Europe's poor job performance, one widely held view focuses on their more rigid labor markets, in which it is harder for firms to fire workers. But the flip side of greater job security is that firms become more nervous about taking on more workers.

Thus, in Europe fewer people had jobs, but those that did did better. The European solution involved greater inequality among the unskilled workers (higher wages versus no wages) and a loss of economic efficiency, as human resources were vastly underutilized.

Just as the demand and supply curves for labor were the basic tools for analyzing the labor market, the aggregate supply and demand curves for goods provide the framework for analyzing the product market. Recall the graph of the product market from Chapter 6. Redrawn here as Figure 8.5, it shows the vertical aggregate supply curve and the downward-sloping aggregate demand curve intersecting at point *E*. As we know from Chapter 6, the aggregate supply curve defines the economy's full-employment level of output, denoted as Y_s. At point *E* the economy is at full employment at the price level, P_0.

Like the assumption of fixed wages in our short-run analysis of the labor market, we assume that prices are fixed in the short-run analysis of the product market. In the short run, prices change little in response to movements of the aggregate demand and supply curves. Automobile manufacturers, for instance, typically change their prices only when new models come out. There are costs to changing prices—such as those of printing new catalogues and price lists—and risks—if a firm raises its price and its rival does not, it might price itself out of the market and lose customers. While there are a few markets, such as the stock market or the market for gold, in which prices adjust to shifts in the demand and supply curves on a daily or faster basis, for most

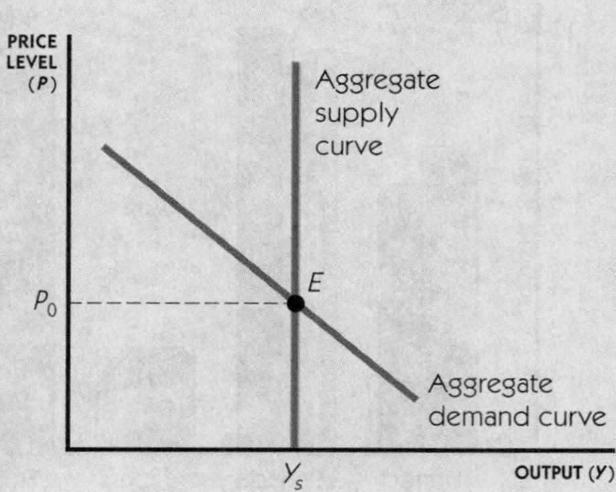

Figure 8.5 THE PRODUCT MARKET

The full-employment level of output, Y_s, is given by the vertical aggregate supply curve. The aggregate demand curve intersects the aggregate supply curve, at the price level P_0. Full-employment equilibrium is at point E, the intersection of the aggregate demand and supply curves.

goods and services, whether sold by producers, wholesalers, or retailers, there is considerable price rigidity.

Consider what happens in the short run if aggregate demand shifts to the left, as depicted in Figure 8.6. At price level P_0, firms will produce only the quantity that they can sell, the quantity Y_1, below the full-employment level of output. One result of the reduced output will be a decrease in the demand for labor. Because of fixed wages in the labor market, this results in involuntary unemployment. Eventually, prices and wages may adjust, and if the aggregate demand curve remains in its new position (AD_1), the economy may move down the aggregate demand curve toward the future full-employment equi-

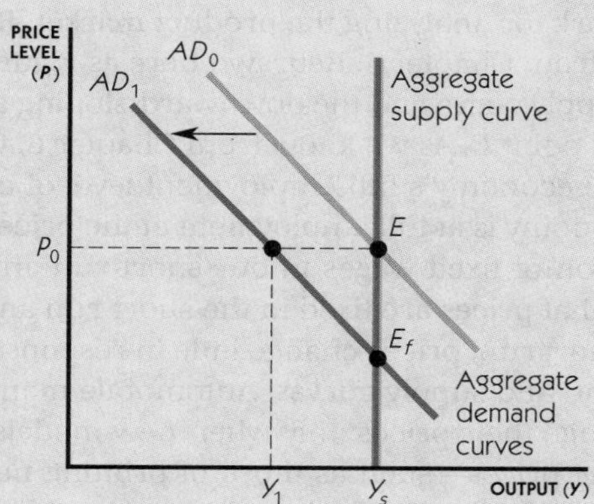

Figure 8.6 OUTPUT BELOW CAPACITY

With the price level fixed at P_0, if the aggregate demand curve shifts to the left, the economy will fall below the full-employment level of output, Y_s. Output will be given by the aggregate demand curve at P_0, the level of output, Y_1. Eventually, if the aggregate demand curve remained at AD_1, the economy will move down the aggregate demand curve toward the future full-employment equilibrium, E_f.

Figure 8.7 EXCESS DEMAND

If the aggregate demand curve shifts to the right (from AD_0 to AD_1), aggregate demand will exceed the economy's capacity to produce at P_0. There will be excess demand and upward pressure on prices. Eventually, the economy will move up the aggregate supply curve toward the future full-employment equilibrium at E_f.

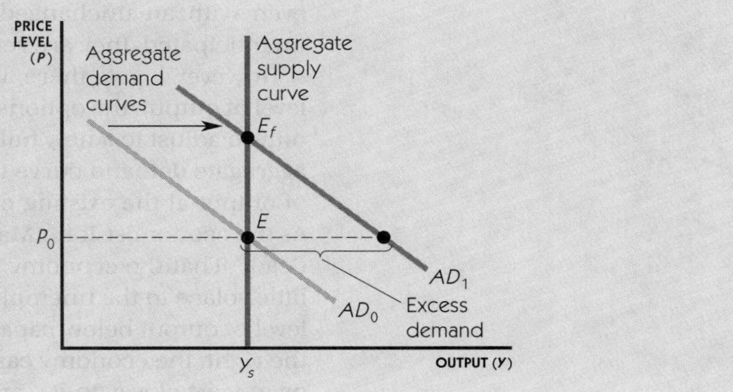

librium, E_f. But this process of adjustment is beyond the scope of our concern here. In the short run, which may span a year or more, the economy will be stuck at P_0, with output below capacity and involuntary unemployment.

Another scenario is also possible, and is illustrated in Figure 8.7. What happens if the aggregate demand curve shifts to the right, when the economy is initially in equilibrium at full employment? At price level P_0, demand exceeds supply, output is limited by aggregate supply (Y_s), and there is upward pressure on prices, anticipating the economy's eventual movement up the aggregate supply curve toward the future full-employment equilibrium, E_f. Under such circumstances the problem is not unemployment, but inflation, a subject we will consider in detail in later chapters. For now, the point to remember is that inflation becomes a concern when demand exceeds supply at a given price level; unemployment is the opposite problem, when demand at a given price level is less than the full-employment supply, Y_s.

THE ECONOMY BELOW CAPACITY

The economy may fall below the full-employment level of output for any number of reasons. Anything that decreases the demand (at a given price level) for consumption, investment, government expenditures, or net exports can give rise to a leftward shift in the aggregate demand curve, bringing the economy to a level of output below the full-employment level. For instance, an economic downturn in Mexico, Japan, or Europe will decrease their demand for American goods, decreasing our exports to them at any price level. Or, if businesses lose confidence in the future, they will be less willing to invest. Such unexpected shifts in the aggregate demand curve are referred to as **demand shocks.**

Occasionally, shifts in the supply schedule can also give rise to excess capacity—a wave of immigration faster than the economy can absorb or improvements in technology that increase the economy's productive capacity, even with an unchanged labor supply. When such shifts are sudden and unanticipated, they are referred to as **supply shocks.**

However it gets there, when the economy falls below the full-employment level of output, the options for policymakers are clear: either wait for the economy to adjust to a new full-employment equilibrium, or take action to shift the aggregate demand curve to the right, reestablishing the full-employment level of output at the existing price level. Policymakers have tended to take action. As the economist John Maynard Keynes once said: "In the long run, we are all dead." That the economy will resume full employment in the long run offers little solace to the unemployed. Figure 8.8 depicts the economy beginning at a level of output below capacity at Y_0. By shifting the aggregate demand curve to the right, the economy can be brought to the full-employment level of output, or at least closer to it—and faster than if markets were allowed to adjust on their own.

Anything that increases the demand (at a given price level) for consumption, investment, government expenditures, and net exports may lead to a rightward shift in the aggregate demand curve. One option for government is to increase its expenditures. For instance, by increasing defense expenditures, aggregate demand at each price level would increase, shifting the aggregate demand curve to the right. With excess capacity in the economy, this would result in increased output.

Raising government expenditures in response to involuntary unemployment is an act of **fiscal policy.** By fiscal policy, economists refer to changes in government expenditures and taxes directed at improving macroeconomic performance, including increasing output when there is excess capacity. Economists sometimes refer to a government effort to stimulate the economy through fiscal policy as a **fiscal stimulus.**

Figure 8.8 ATTAINING FULL EMPLOYMENT

At price level P_0, if the government can shift the aggregate demand curve enough to the right, the economy can be moved to operate at full capacity. When the aggregate demand curve shifts from AD_0 to AD_1, output increases from Y_0 to Y_1. With the aggregate demand curve, AD_2, the economy attains the full-employment equilibrium at P_0.

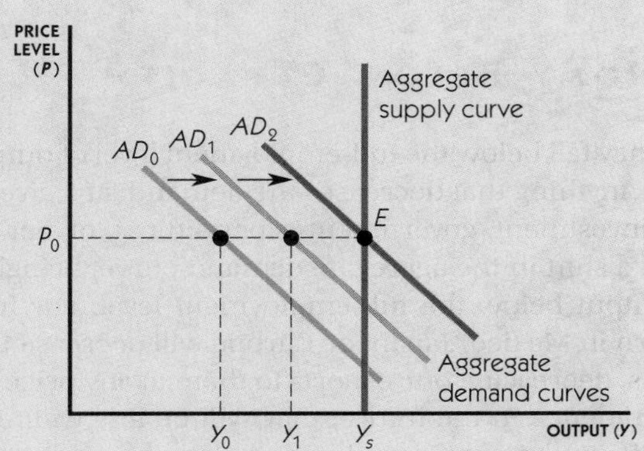

Figure 8.9 INCREASING AGGREGATE SUPPLY

At the current price level P_0, aggregate demand is less than Y_s, so that an increase in the economy's productive capacity has no effect on output in the short run.

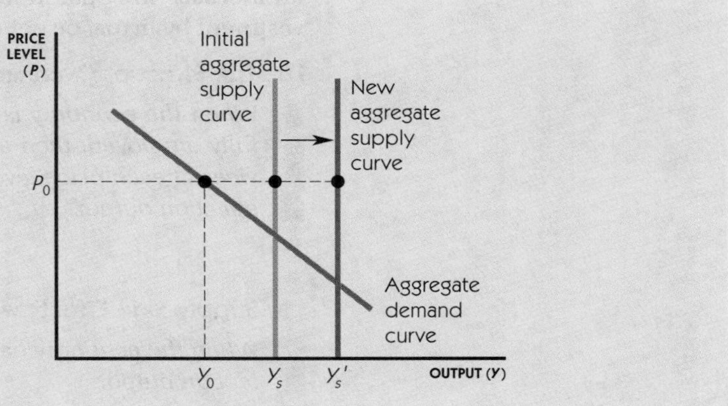

THE SUPPLY SIDE OF THE MARKET

So far we have focused on the demand side of the market, and shifts in aggregate demand. What effect do increases in aggregate supply have on involuntary unemployment when the economy is below capacity?

Increased capacity of the economy may result from new investment or new technology. This shifts Y_s to the right. Figure 8.9 shows a rightward shift of the aggregate supply curve when the economy is initially below capacity at the price level, P_0. The result is only an increase in the amount by which aggregate supply exceeds aggregate demand at P_0. There is no effect on output.

On the other hand, when there is excess demand for goods (see Figure 8.7), an increase in aggregate supply will reduce the magnitude of the excess demand for goods, and thus the magnitude of the inflationary pressures. This was part of the rationale for the "supply-side" policies of the early 1980s, in which lower taxes were supposed to lead to increased labor supply and increased investment. As it turned out, the supply-side effects were small, and were overwhelmed by demand effects arising out of monetary policy.

THREE MORE POINTS OF CONSENSUS

The important results of this analysis of aggregate demand and supply can be summarized in our ninth, tenth, and eleventh points of consensus.

9 Stimulating the Economy when It Is Below Capacity

When the economy has excess capacity, an increase in aggregate demand at each price level results in an increase in aggregate output, with relatively little effect on prices.

The increase in aggregate demand can, of course, come from any source: an increase in consumption by households, expenditure by government, investment by firms, or net exports.

10 The Effect of Overstimulating the Economy

When the economy is close to capacity, with most machines and workers fully employed, then a further increase in the demand for goods and services at each price level results in upward pressure on prices and has little effect on output.

11 Supply-Side Effects when There Is Excess Capacity

When the economy has excess capacity, increases in capacity have little effect on output.

LINKS WITH THE CAPITAL MARKET

We have now discussed the labor and product markets, two of the three central markets of the economy. These are both linked to the capital market in important ways.

In the capital market, interest rates are influenced by **monetary policy**—the actions of the **Federal Reserve Board,** which is the government agency responsible for controlling the money supply and interest rates. The Federal Reserve can lower and raise interest rates, with important consequences for the product and labor markets. Consider first the product market. Low interest rates may encourage home construction and investment, leading to a higher demand for goods and a higher level of output. If the Federal Reserve detects a lull in economic activity, it may choose to lower the interest rate. Figure 8.10 shows the effect of lower interest rates on the product market. There is a rightward shift of the aggregate demand curve. If the economy is initially operating with excess capacity, the shift in the aggregate demand curve leads to an increase in aggregate output. We could then trace through the effects on the labor market: higher aggregate output leads to a higher level of employment.

On the other hand, if the Federal Reserve is worried that the inflation rate is about to increase, it typically raises the interest rate. A situation with inflationary pressure is typically one where, at the current price level, aggregate demand exceeds the economy's full-employment level of output, as we depicted earlier in Figure 8.7. A higher interest rate dampens the level of aggregate demand—at each price, the quantity of investment that firms wish to make is reduced, so that the aggregate demand curve shifts to the left. If the Federal Reserve Board's assessment of the economic situation is correct, then the leftward movement of the aggregate demand curve simply decreases the upward pressure on prices, without having much effect on output. But if it increases

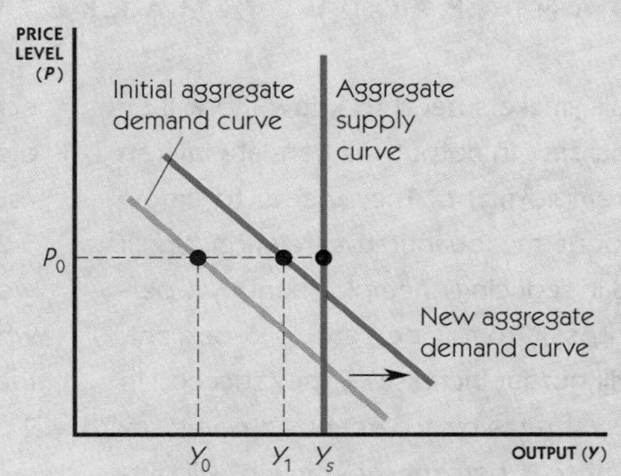

Figure 8.10 THE LINK BETWEEN THE CAPITAL MARKET AND THE PRODUCT MARKET

Lower interest rates lead to increased investment. This in turn leads to a rightward shift in the aggregate demand curve. If the economy is initially operating with excess capacity, aggregate output increases.

interest rates too far, it will shift the aggregate demand curve too much to the left, so that aggregate demand at the current price level P_0 will be less than Y_s: output will fall and unemployment will increase.

We have thus come full circle: all the markets of the economy are interconnected. So too are all the major policy concerns. The Federal Reserve may stimulate the economy by cutting the interest rate. On the other hand, aggressive action to contain inflation by restraining the economy—by raising the interest rate—discourages investment, and may lead to lower growth. If the Federal Reserve acts excessively aggressively, it may overshoot, lowering output and inducing unemployment. Rather than just curtailing inflation, it may actually push the economy into a recession. Later chapters will pursue these links, as well as the trade-offs for policymakers.

INTERDEPENDENCIES AMONG MARKETS

Changes in the capital market—such as lower interest rates—have immediate and direct impacts on the product market, shifting the aggregate demand curve.

Changes in the product market—such as increased aggregate demand—have impacts on the labor market, shifting the demand curve for labor.

Using Economics: Quantifying Links between Labor and Product Markets

Economic policymakers need to know more than just that an increase in output will translate into an increase in employment. They need to know something about the quantitative relationship: If they succeed in reducing unemployment by 1 percentage point, say from 7 percent to 6 percent, how much will output increase? If they succeed in reducing interest rates by 1 percentage point, say from 4 percent to 3 percent, how much will output increase? In making their calculations, they often use simple rules of thumb, based on historical experience. The most famous of these is called Okun's law, after Arthur Okun, who served as chairman of the Council of Economic Advisers under President Johnson. He calculated that the percentage increase in output was approximately twice the percentage decrease in the unemployment rate. Thus, lowering the unemployment rate from 7 percent to 6 percent will increase output by 2 percent.

Thus, in early 1996, there was widespread support for the view that the Federal Reserve Board should lower interest rates, given the absence of any inflationary pressures. This would stimulate economic growth. In February 1996, the unemployment rate stood at 5.5 percent. If lower interest rates succeeded in lowering unemployment to 5.2 percent, then, according to Okun's law, output would increase by approximately .6 percent (over what it otherwise would have been). Given that the economy had been forecast to grow at about 2 percent for the year, this represented a substantial increase in the growth rate *for that year.*

Okun's law can also be used in reverse. In early 1993, the unemployment rate stood at slightly more than 7 percent. Policymakers wanted to know how much would output have to increase in order to get the unemployment rate down to 6 percent. Okun's law gave them an answer: it would have to grow by about 2 percent *more* than the amount by which output would increase simply from the increase in productivity and the increase in employment that would result from the increased labor force with a *fixed* unemployment rate. With GDP at the time of approximately $6.5 trillion, this meant that aggregate demand would have to be increased by an additional amount of approximately $130 billion.

Macroeconomic Lessons from the Postwar Period

The wide areas of macroeconomic consensus have been developed in part through a series of hardlearned lessons in the decades following World War II. The brief historical sketches that follow highlight some of the major policy discussions of the period.

THE KENNEDY TAX CUT

In 1963, the unemployment rate seemed to be stuck at an unacceptably high level, 5.5 percent. Ten years before it had been 2.8 percent. By 1959, it was 5.3 percent. President Kennedy's economic advisers believed that a cut in the individual income tax would cause households to consume more. This in turn would lead to a rightward shift in the aggregate demand curve. A shift in the aggregate demand curve, Kennedy's advisers believed, would result in increased output—not higher prices. This is because they believed that the economy had excess capacity, that productive workers and machines were lying idle. As a result, the shift in the aggregate demand curve would be translated into increases in output, as shown in Figure 8.11.

Increases in output, as we have learned, imply increases in employment. The predictions of Kennedy's advisers turned out to be correct. Unemployment fell to 4.4 percent in 1965 and stayed under 4 percent for the rest of the 1960s. In addition, real GDP grew at the remarkable average rate of 5.5 percent from 1964 to 1966.

THE REAGAN PROGRAM

When President Reagan took office in 1981, there was a widespread view that something should be done to stop inflation, which was high and appeared to be moving higher. Paul Volcker, chairman of the Federal Reserve Board, is generally given credit for doing so—though in the process he caused the worst recession in the postwar period. The Fed took strong actions to tighten the availability of credit and to raise interest rates—interest rates reached

Figure 8.11 THE KENNEDY TAX CUT

The 1963 tax cut shifted the aggregate demand curve to the right and increased output from Y_0 to Y_1.

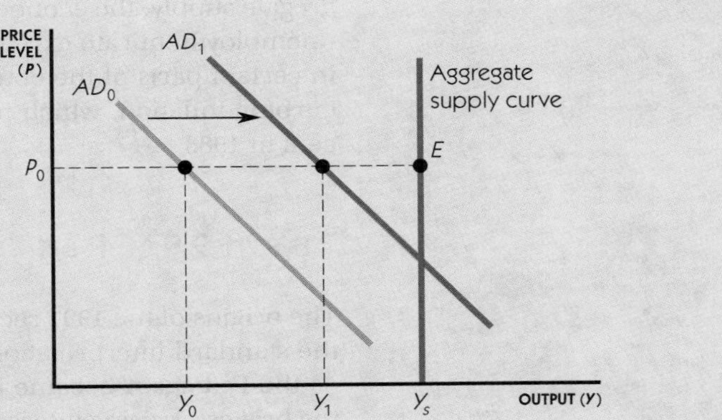

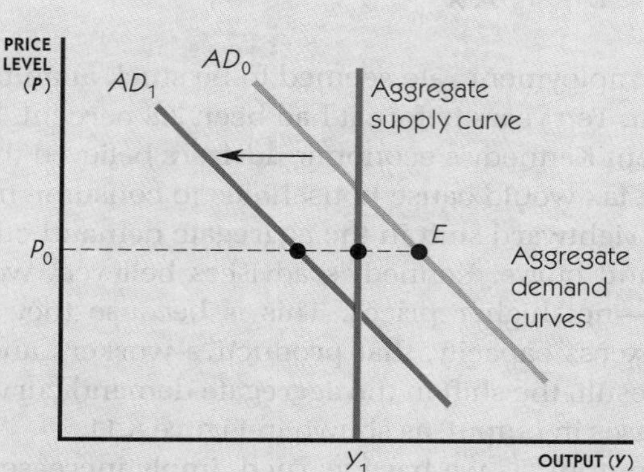

Figure 8.12 MONETARY POLICY CONTROLS INFLATION BUT CAUSES A RECESSION

Beginning in the late 1970s and early 1980s, the Federal Reserve Board, worried about runaway inflation, acted to restrict credit and thus consumption and investment. The resulting leftward shift in the aggregate demand curve caused a major recession. The effects were so strong that they more than offset the increased expansionary effects from the 1981 tax cut. The downward price pressures did, however, serve to reduce the pace of inflation.

record levels in excess of 20 percent before Volcker deemed inflation defeated. (How the Fed does this and the broader impact of such measures will be the subject of Chapters 11 and 12.) As a result of the Fed's actions, firms cut back their investments, and households cut back their purchases of items like cars and houses. Interestingly, at the same time that the Fed was taking these actions to restrict aggregate demand, fiscal policy was stimulating the economy. Reagan cut taxes, without cutting expenditures an offsetting amount. But the contractionary effect of higher interest rates more than offset the expansionary effect of lower taxes, and the aggregate demand curve shifted to the left, as shown in Figure 8.12. There, the initial upward pressure on prices is reflected by aggregate demand exceeding aggregate supply at the initial price level P_0 in the original situation. But the leftward shift in the aggregate demand curve was so large that at P_0, aggregate demand was much less than aggregate supply: the economy was thrown into a major recession. The national unemployment rate exceeded 11 percent, and climbed as high as 20 percent in certain parts of the country. However, the recession did have the effect of curbing inflation, which fell from around 13 percent in 1980 to just 3.2 percent in 1983.

THE 1991 RECESSION

The origins of the 1991 recession remain somewhat controversial. In perhaps the standard interpretation, inflation increased gradually from 1989 to 1991. As the Fed again became increasingly worried about inflation, it stepped on the brakes—raising interest rates. The large leftward shift in the aggregate demand curve had the predictable effect of lowering equilibrium output. But when the Fed subsequently loosened interest rates—lowering them to 3 percent—to restart the economy, the impacts were smaller, and took longer to

Policy Perspective: The Role of Economic Data

Because it takes time for policy changes to have an effect, policymakers would like to have a crystal ball. If, without some action, the economy would go into a recession in six months, changes need to be made today. But policymakers not only don't have a crystal ball to see into the future—they often don't even know precisely where the economy is today, or was even yesterday. It takes time for reliable economic data gauging the strength of the economy to be produced. The most rapidly produced data are those on employment. Employment data for each month are collected in the second week of the month, and then published in the first week of the next month. Other important data series take weeks to be produced. And even when the data are first made available, the numbers are preliminary and subject to large adjustments.

The data on output published in 1991 indicated that the economic downturn was a very mild one. But over four years later, in January 1995, revised data were published. These data showed that the downturn was far more severe than had previously been realized. Many pundits suggested that had the data been available, the Fed would have taken stronger action, the economy would have recovered more quickly, and the outcome of the election would have been different. Others are more skeptical. The Fed uses a whole variety of economic indicators, of which output is only one. Still, better and more timely data would help policymakers make more informed decisions in a more timely way.

take effect, than it had anticipated. The slow recovery is often thought to have contributed to President Bush's defeat in 1992.

Two factors complicate this story. The Persian Gulf War, beginning in August 1990 with Iraq's invasion of Kuwait, almost coincided with the recession; the sudden increase in oil prices is sometimes given credit for stalling out the economy. Most observers, however, note that the slowdown of the economy had actually set in slightly before. Still, the economic disruption of the war may have contributed to the downturn.

Secondly, when President Bush came into office, he found a fragile banking system. Part of it—the savings and loan associations—was on the verge of bankruptcy, and required a bailout costing taxpayers upward of $150 billion. Lax enforcement of regulations during the preceding years had contributed to the debacle. Regulators, worried about repeating the mistake, became overzealous, and banks were forced to cut back on lending to marginal borrowers. And the weakened financial shape of banks in many parts of the country made them less willing to make loans that they considered in any way risky. The result was a cutback in lending, which shifted the aggregate demand curve to the left. Whether this shift by itself would have thrown the economy into a recession is debatable, but what is clear is the weakened financial condition of the banks made them less willing and able to respond to the easing of the Fed, and this accounts in part for why it was unable to engineer a recovery with the speed that it would have liked.

DEFICIT REDUCTION TO STIMULATE THE ECONOMY

The final episode which we will discuss was a drama played out in 1993 and 1994. Clinton took office on a promise to restart the economy. Clinton's 1993 budget, which narrowly passed Congress, included about $250 billion of expenditure cuts and $250 billion of tax increases over the following five years, for a total deficit reduction of $500 billion. Many economists were worried: both expenditure cuts and tax increases reduce aggregate demand. Potentially, they could have made the economic downturn even worse. But there was another effect: the lower demand for borrowing (and the anticipated decreases in future years) led to lower interest rates, and the lower interest rates stimulated investment. The *net* effect was a shift in the aggregate demand curve to the right. The economy took off. Indeed, in a span of two years, more than five million new jobs were created.

Notice that both in this episode and that at the beginning of the Reagan administration, interest rate effects overwhelmed fiscal policy effects. In the former case, high interest rates led to a recession, even though fiscal policy was expansionary; in the more recent case, low interest rates led to recovery, even though fiscal policy was contractionary.

As is so often the case, the evidence is consistent with more than one interpretation: some believe that what really happened was a normal recovery from an economic downturn. If anything, the deficit reduction dampened the recovery, rather than causing it. In this interpretation, the dampening effects of expenditure cuts and tax increases more than offset the stimulating effect of increased investment due to lower interest rates, but the economy's momentum of recovery overcame the government's policy.

REVIEW AND PRACTICE

SUMMARY

1. Unemployment macroeconomics assumes that wages and prices are fixed in the short run.

2. To explain unemployment, we need to explain why the aggregate labor market does not clear. If real wages do not adjust to shifts in the aggregate supply and demand curves for labor, and either the demand curve for labor shifts to the left or the supply curve for labor shifts to the right, then the quantity of labor supplied will exceed the quantity demanded at the prevailing wage, and there will be involuntary unemployment.

3. The demand curve for labor shifts because of a fall in the production of goods by firms, as a result of a decrease in the demand for their products at each price level.

4. In the product market, if aggregate demand at a given price level is less than the economy's full-employment output (capacity), output will be limited by aggregate demand. Shifting the aggregate demand curve to the right will increase output and employment, and may restore the economy to full employment.

5. If, at a given price level, aggregate demand exceeds aggregate supply, output will be limited by aggregate supply, and there will be upward pressure on prices.

6. All markets in the economy are interrelated. Thus disturbances in the product market have consequences for the labor market, and disturbances in the capital market have consequences for the product market. For instance, when there is involuntary unemployment, lower interest rates may result in increased investment, increasing output and employment.

KEY TERMS

voluntary unemployment
involuntary unemployment
demand shocks
supply shocks
fiscal policy
fiscal stimulus
monetary policy
Federal Reserve Board

REVIEW QUESTIONS

1. If the labor market always cleared, would there be any unemployment? What does it mean for the labor market not to clear? What gives rise to unemployment?

2. If the labor market always cleared, can there be variations in the level of employment?

3. What inferences do you draw from the following two facts?
   (a) The labor supply curve is relatively inelastic.
   (b) Large variations in employment coexist with relatively small variations in real wages.

4. What might shift the aggregate demand curve for labor?

5. If prices are rigid, and at a level *above* that at which aggregate demand equals supply, what will be the level of output? What will happen if the aggregate demand curve shifts to the left? To the right? If the aggregate supply curve shifts to the left? To the right?

6. If prices are rigid, and at a level *below* that at which aggregate demand equals supply, what will be the level of output? What will happen if the aggregate demand curve shifts to the left? To the right? If the aggregate supply curve shifts to the left? To the right?

7. What are some of the ways in which the various markets of the economy are interlinked?

8. Use the aggregate demand and supply curve framework to describe some of the major macroeconomic episodes of the postwar period.

PROBLEMS

1. In the 1970s, a large number of new workers entered the U.S. economy from two main sources. The baby boom generation grew to adulthood and the proportion of women working increased substantially. If wages adjust, what effect will these factors have on the equilibrium level of wages and quantity of labor? If wages do not adjust, how does your answer change? In which case will unemployment exist? Draw a diagram to explain your answer. What is the effect of the increased labor supply on the product market? Illustrate your answer diagrammatically.

2. Soon after Iraq invaded Kuwait in August 1990, many firms feared that a recession would occur. Anticipating a lack of demand for their goods, they began cutting back on production. If wages adjust, what will happen to the equilibrium level of wages and employment? If wages do not adjust, how does your answer change? In which case will unemployment exist?

3. In early 1995, Mexico faced a financial crisis, which led to a major economic downturn in that country. Exports to Mexico exceed those to any other country except Canada. If nothing else had happened, what effect would you expect this to have on the aggregate demand curve and on the level of national output in the short run, at a given price level?

4. In the early 1990s, there was a massive wave of Russian immigrants into Israel. Yet, within a few years, unemployment returned to normal levels and real wages had not fallen. Using aggregate demand and supply curves for goods and labor, explain how this could have occurred. (Hint: new immigrants generate additional demand for goods as well as additional supplies of labor.)

5. When Bill Clinton became president in early 1993, the unemployment rate was in excess of 7 percent. There was worry about the speed of economic recovery. He proposed—but Congress rejected—a small "stimulus" package, consisting mainly of increased investment. Show diagrammatically what this might have done to the aggregate demand curve and the level of output at a given price level. Critics worried that the government would have had to borrow more money to pay for the additional expenditures, and that this would drive up interest rates, discouraging private investment. If this happened, show what would have happened to the aggregate demand curve and the level of output at a given price level.

6. While for the most part, macroeconomics focuses on aggregate employment, ignoring distinctions among different categories of workers, it sometimes focuses on broad categories, such as skilled and unskilled

workers. Assume, for simplicity, that there are just these two categories, and that for the most part, they cannot be substituted for each other.

(a) Draw demand and supply curves for skilled and unskilled workers, marking the initial equilibrium in each market.

(b) Assume now that there is a technological change which increases the demand for skilled labor at each wage, while it shifts the demand curve for unskilled labor to the left. If wages do not adjust, can there be vacancies of one type of labor at the same time there is unemployment of another type?

CHAPTER 9

AGGREGATE DEMAND

In Chapter 8 we learned that the major cause of unemployment was a shift in the demand curve for labor, without a commensurate fall in the real wage. We also learned that the major cause of a shift in the demand curve for labor was a reduction in aggregate output. Thus, to understand events in the labor market, we must understand the product market—what determines the level of output and its changes.

The objective of this and the following chapters is to answer that question, focusing on those circumstances where supply imposes no constraints—that is, where there is excess capacity of machines and unemployment of labor. In this simple scenario, output is determined entirely by aggregate demand.

The task of this chapter is to explain what determines the level of aggregate demand at any particular set of wages and prices, what causes changes in aggregate demand, and why output can be so volatile.

KEY QUESTIONS

1. When the economy has excess capacity, what determines the aggregate level of output?
2. What are the components of aggregate expenditures?
3. How do consumption and imports increase with income?
4. Why, if investment or government expenditures or exports increase by a dollar, does aggregate output increase by more than a dollar? What determines the amount by which it increases?

INCOME-EXPENDITURE ANALYSIS

Let us return for a moment to the aggregate demand and supply framework that we introduced in Chapter 8, focusing on a situation where the economy has a large excess capacity. Figure 9.1 shows the aggregate demand and supply curves, with the price level P_0 such that there is a large excess supply: at P_0, aggregate demand is much less than the economy's capacity to produce. In this situation, a shift in the aggregate demand curve, from AD_0 to say AD_1, leads to an increase in aggregate output, from Y_0 to Y_1.

But what determines the level of aggregate demand at each price level? And what determines changes in this level of demand? Recall the four components of aggregate output and demand: consumption, investment, government expenditures, and net exports. Aggregate demand at any price level is

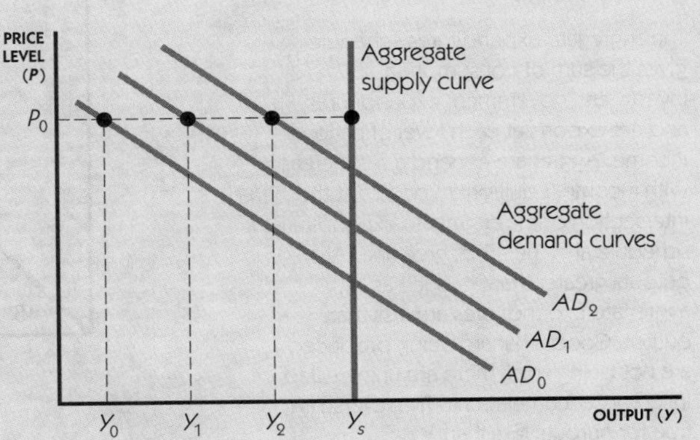

Figure 9.1 SHIFTS IN THE AGGREGATE DEMAND CURVE WHEN THERE IS EXCESS SUPPLY

When the economy has excess capacity, shifts in the aggregate demand curve result in different levels of output at the fixed price level P_0.

just the sum of consumption, investment, government expenditures, and net exports demanded at that price level. We can think of this demand as the expenditures in four parts of the economy: households on consumer goods, firms on investment goods, government on public goods and services, and foreigners on net exports.

The trick to solving for the equilibrium level of output, and the equilibrium level of aggregate demand, is the **aggregate expenditures schedule.** The term aggregate expenditures refers to the total of expenditures on consumption, investment, government goods and services, and net exports. The aggregate expenditures schedule traces out the relationship, at a fixed price level, between aggregate expenditures and national income—the aggregate income of everyone in the economy. It is depicted in Figure 9.2, where the vertical axis measures aggregate expenditures and the horizontal axis measures national income.

The aggregate expenditures schedule has three critical properties. First, it is upward sloping—as national income goes up, so do aggregate expenditures. Changes in other variables (like interest rates, tax rates, and exchange rates) cause the aggregate expenditures schedule to shift up or down, and they may even change the slope.

Second, as income increases by a dollar, aggregate expenditures increase by less than a dollar. The reason for this is that consumers save some of their increased income. Figure 9.2 also shows a line through the origin at a 45-degree angle. The slope of this line is unity. All along this line, a one-dollar change in the horizontal axis (income) is matched by a one-dollar change in the vertical axis (aggregate expenditures). By contrast, the aggregate expendi-

Figure 9.2 THE AGGREGATE EXPENDITURES SCHEDULE AND INCOME-EXPENDITURE ANALYSIS

The aggregate expenditures schedule gives the sum of consumption, investment, government expenditures, and net exports at each level of national income. Aggregate expenditures increase with income. Equilibrium occurs at the intersection of the aggregate expenditures schedule and the 45-degree line. At outputs greater than Y^*, such as Y_1, aggregate expenditures are less than output. Goods that are being produced are not being sold; there are unintended inventory accumulations. The reverse is true for outputs less than Y^*.

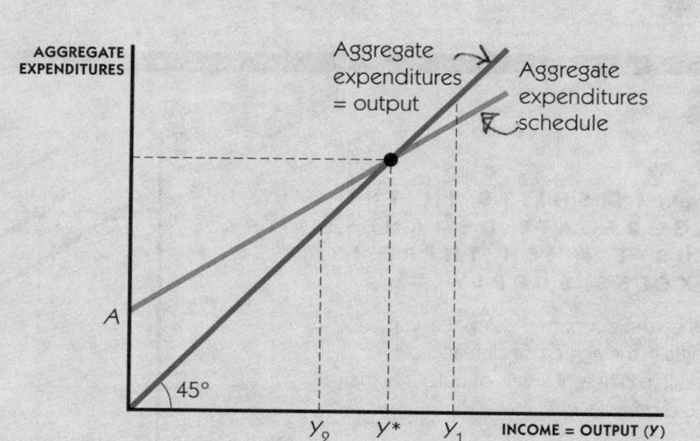

tures schedule is flatter than the 45-degree line since aggregate expenditures increase less than dollar for dollar with increased income.

Third, even if national income were zero, aggregate expenditures would remain positive. This is reflected in the fact that the aggregate expenditures schedule intercepts the vertical axis at a positive level, point *A*. (We will discuss the reasons for this later in the chapter.)

The facts that (a) the aggregate expenditures schedule is flatter than the 45-degree line through the origin and (b) aggregate expenditures are positive, even when income is zero, imply that the aggregate expenditures schedule intersects the 45-degree line, as seen in the figure.

What is the relationship between the aggregate expenditures schedule and the aggregate demand schedule discussed in the last chapter? The aggregate expenditures schedule shows expenditures, at each level of price and income; the aggregate demand curve shows aggregate demand (or expenditures) at each level of price—when the level of income has been adjusted to its (short-run) equilibrium level. This brings us to our central question: What determines the (short-run) equilibrium level of output, when there is excess capacity? Besides the aggregate expenditure schedule, we need two more concepts for our analysis.

The National Income-Output Identity

National income is equal to national output (as shown in Chapter 4). This reflects the fact that when a good is purchased, the money that is paid must eventually wind up as someone's income—as wages, in the pockets of workers in the firm that produced the good (or of workers who produced the intermediate goods that were used in the production of the final good); as interest payments, in the pockets of those who have lent the firm money; or as profits, in the pockets of the owners of the firm. For simplicity, we will assume that the residents of the country neither receive money (net) from abroad nor pay money (net) to abroad, so GNP and GDP coincide. If Y is used to represent national income, this identity can be written

$$\text{GDP} = \text{national income} = Y.$$

This identity is our second necessary concept. It allows us to interpret the horizontal axis in Figure 9.2 in two different ways. We can say the aggregate expenditures schedule gives the level of expenditures at each level of national *income*. We can also say it gives the level of expenditures at each level of national *output*.

Equilibrium Output

Normally, firms will only produce what they believe they can sell. This means that the total output produced by all firms will equal the total demand for output. This is our third necessary concept, and it can be put another way. In equilibrium, aggregate expenditures, which we denote by *AE*, must equal aggregate output (GDP). Since aggregate output equals national income (Y), we have the simple equation

$$AE = \text{GDP} = Y.$$

In Figure 9.2, the 45-degree line through the origin is labeled "Aggregate expenditures = output." The line traces all points where the vertical axis (aggregate expenditures) equals the horizontal axis (national income, which equals aggregate output).

Equilibrium lies at the point on the aggregate expenditures schedule that also satisfies the aggregate-expenditures-equal-output condition. That is, equilibrium occurs at the intersection of the aggregate expenditures schedule and the 45-degree line. The corresponding equilibrium value of aggregate output is denoted by Y^*.

The analysis that determines equilibrium output by relating income (output) to aggregate expenditures is called **income-expenditure analysis.** We can see that Y^* is the equilibrium in two different ways. The first way is to note that it is the only point that satisfies the two conditions for equilibrium. In equilibrium, everything produced must be purchased. Thus, aggregate expenditures must be equal to national output (income), as represented by the 45-degree line. In equilibrium, the level of aggregate expenditures must also be what households, firms, and government want to spend in total at that level of national income, given by the aggregate expenditures schedule.

The second way is to consider what happens at a level of income Y_1, in excess of Y^*. At that point, the aggregate expenditures schedule lies below the 45-degree line. What households, firms, and government would like to spend at that level of national income, as reflected in the aggregate expenditures schedule, is less than national income (output). More goods are being produced than individuals want to buy. Some of the goods, like strawberries, cannot be stored. They simply spoil. The goods that can be stored go into inventories.

Economists distinguish between **planned inventories** and **unplanned inventories.** Firms choose to have some inventory on hand because it makes business more efficient. Planned inventories are considered an investment, and their buildup is therefore counted as part of investment spending in the aggregate expenditures schedule. Unplanned inventories are simply the goods firms are producing but cannot sell. In Figure 9.2, at Y_1, above the 45-degree line, firms find that unplanned inventories are piling up—they are producing goods that cannot be sold, which are either spoiling or increasing inventories beyond the desired level. They respond by cutting back production until they reach Y^*. At Y_2, the aggregate expenditures schedule lies above the 45-degree line. Households, firms, and government are spending more than national income (output). They are, in other words, purchasing more than the economy is producing. This is possible because firms can sell out of inventories. With planned inventories being depleted, firms increase production until equilibrium is restored, with output (income) again equal to Y^*.

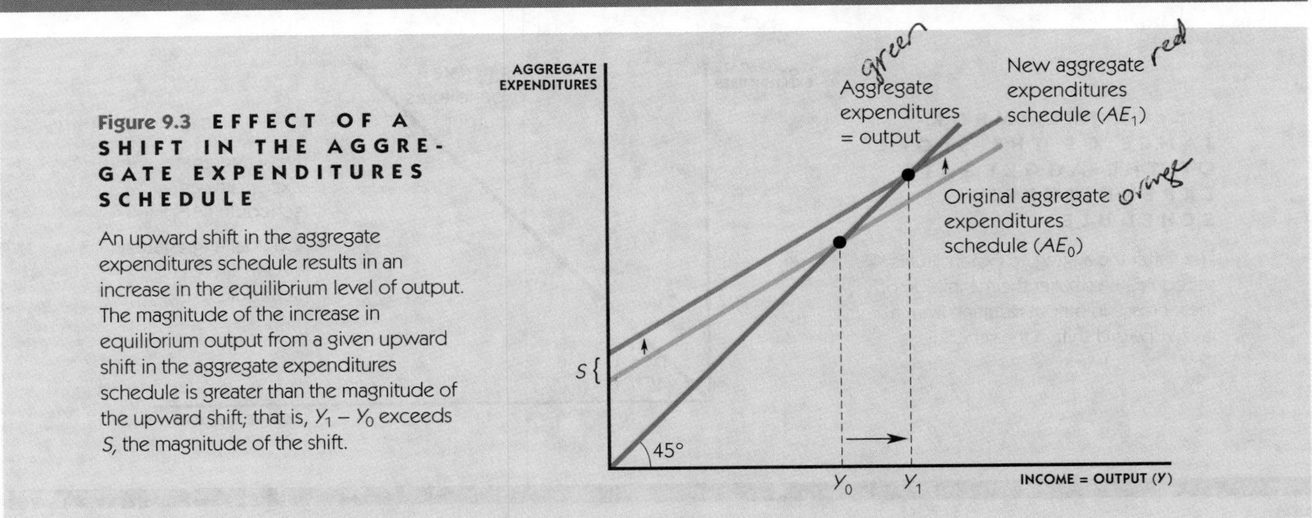

Figure 9.3 EFFECT OF A SHIFT IN THE AGGREGATE EXPENDITURES SCHEDULE

An upward shift in the aggregate expenditures schedule results in an increase in the equilibrium level of output. The magnitude of the increase in equilibrium output from a given upward shift in the aggregate expenditures schedule is greater than the magnitude of the upward shift; that is, $Y_1 - Y_0$ exceeds S, the magnitude of the shift.

SHIFTS IN THE AGGREGATE EXPENDITURES SCHEDULE

The aggregate expenditures schedule can shift through a variety of changes in the economy that lead households, firms, and government to decide, *at each level of income,* to spend more or less. Figure 9.3 shows what happens if the level of aggregate expenditures increases at each level of national income by the amount S. The new aggregate expenditures schedule is denoted by AE_1.

INCOME-EXPENDITURE ANALYSIS

1. Equilibrium output is at the point where the aggregate expenditures schedule equals output (income).
2. Upward shifts in the aggregate expenditures schedule result in increases in equilibrium output. The increases in equilibrium output are larger than the initial shift in the aggregate expenditures schedule. How much larger depends on the slope of the aggregate expenditures schedule. The steeper the slope, the greater the increase.

Figure 9.4 THE IMPORTANCE OF THE SLOPE OF THE AGGREGATE EXPENDITURES SCHEDULE

The flatter the aggregate expenditures schedule, the smaller the magnitude of the increase in output resulting from a given upward shift in the schedule.

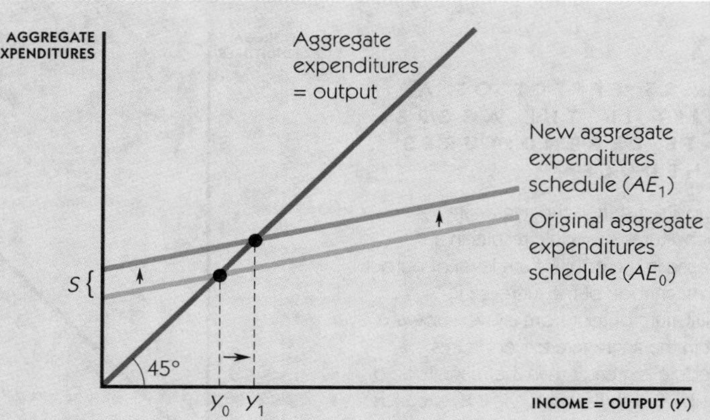

The equilibrium output increases from Y_0 to Y_1, *which is greater than the amount S.* How much greater depends on the slope of the aggregate expenditures schedule. In Figure 9.4, the aggregate expenditures schedule shifts up by the same amount it did in Figure 9.3, but the aggregate expenditures schedule is flatter. Consequently, the increase in equilibrium output is much smaller.

MATHEMATICAL FORMULATION

We can describe the equilibrium using simple algebra. The aggregate expenditures equation can be written:

$$AE = b + cY,$$

where b is the vertical intercept of the aggregate expenditures schedule (the value of AE when $Y = 0$); and c is the slope of the aggregate expenditures schedule (an increase in Y of \$1 increases AE by \$$c$). The fact that the slope is less than 45 degrees implies that c is between 0 and 1. Equilibrium requires aggregate expenditures to equal income—which, under our simplifying assumptions, equals Y:

$$AE = Y.$$

Substituting the second equation into the first equation yields

$$Y = b + cY,$$

which can be solved for Y:

$$Y = b/(1 - c).$$

An upward shift in the aggregate expenditures schedule corresponds to an increase in b, say to $b + 1$. Then Y increases by an amount $1/(1 - c)$. Since c is less than 1, $1/(1 - c)$ is greater than 1. If $c = .9$, then $1 - c = .1$ and $1/(1 - c) = 10$, so that an upward shift in the aggregate expenditures schedule by \$1 increases GDP by \$10. This basic property is called the multiplier. Later in the chapter we will take a closer look at it.

A LOOK FORWARD

We have just learned two of the central principles of macroeconomics: (1) shifts in the aggregate expenditures schedule determine changes in the equilibrium output of the economy, and (2) the magnitude of those changes is greater than the magnitude of the shift up or down in the aggregate expenditures schedule and increases with the slope of the aggregate expenditures schedule. The remainder of this chapter explores the implications of these principles. Two questions are addressed.

The first question is: What determines the slope of the aggregate expenditures schedule—that is, the extent to which aggregate expenditures increase as income increases? As we have seen, the greater that slope, the larger the increase in output from any upward shift in the schedule. The second question is: What causes shifts in the aggregate expenditures schedule? And what, if anything, can the government do to shift the schedule? The possibilities for government are an important issue. In the last chapter, we saw that unemployment is created when there is a shift in the demand curve for labor without a corresponding downward adjustment of wages. The primary reason for a shift in the demand curve for labor is a change in the equilibrium level of output. When output is low, the demand for labor is low. If government can increase the equilibrium level of output by somehow shifting the aggregate expenditures schedule, then it can increase the level of employment.

To answer these questions, we need to take a closer look at each of the four components of aggregate expenditures: (1) consumption goods, such as food, television sets, or clothes, all of which are purchased by consumers; (2) investment in capital goods, machines or buildings that are bought by firms to help them produce goods; (3) government purchases, both goods and services bought for current use (public consumption) and goods and services like buildings and roads, bought for the future benefits they generate (public investment); and (4) net exports. We say net exports, because we have to subtract from the value of goods sold abroad the value of those goods and services bought by U.S. households, businesses, and government that are produced abroad, that is, imports.

Using AE for aggregate expenditures, C for consumption spending, I for investment spending, G for government spending, and E for net exports, we can set out the components of aggregate expenditures in equation form:

$$AE = C + I + G + E.$$

This equation is nothing more than a definition. It says that consumption spending, investment spending, government spending, and net exports add up to aggregate expenditures. Net exports is sometimes written as $X - M$, where X stands for exports and M for imports. These symbols represent near-astronomical numbers for the U.S. economy. In 1995, AE was $7,248 billion, of which C was $4,923 billion (67.9% of AE), I was $1,067 billion (14.7% of AE), G was $1,359 billion (18.8% of AE), X was $805 billion, and M was $906 billion (so E was −1.4% of AE). We now take a brief look at each of these categories.

CONSUMPTION

Table 9.1 **RELATIONSHIP BETWEEN INCOME AND CONSUMPTION**

Income	Consumption
$ 5,000	$ 6,000
10,000	10,500
20,000	19,500
30,000	28,500

The most important determinant of consumption is income. On average, families with higher incomes spend more. Table 9.1 shows the relationship between consumption and income for a hypothetical family. The same information is depicted graphically in Figure 9.5A, with the amount of consumption given along the vertical axis and income along the horizontal axis. The upward slope of the line indicates that consumption for this family increases as income does. The relationship between a household's consumption and its income is called its **consumption function.** Every family has different consumption patterns because the tastes and circumstances of families differ, but the pattern shown in Table 9.1 is typical.

Table 9.2 **AGGREGATE CONSUMPTION AND NATIONAL INCOME** (billions of dollars)

National income	Consumption (C)
$ 1,000	$ 1,050
2,000	1,950
3,000	2,850
4,000	3,750
6,500	6,000
10,000	9,150
20,000	18,150

Aggregate consumption is the sum of the consumption of all the households in the economy. Just as when a typical family's income rises its consumption increases, when the total income of the economy rises, aggregate consumption increases. For purposes of macroeconomics, it is the **aggregate consumption function,** the relationship between aggregate consumption and aggregate income, that is of importance. And the measure of income that is important is disposable income, or what people have after paying taxes. But because we are assuming no government for the moment, disposable income equals national income. The relationship between aggregate consumption and national income is given in Table 9.2, and the aggregate consumption function is depicted graphically in Figure 9.5B.

THE MARGINAL PROPENSITY TO CONSUME

The amount by which consumption increases when disposable income increases by a dollar is called the **marginal propensity to consume** (MPC). For the United States as a whole, the marginal propensity to consume in recent

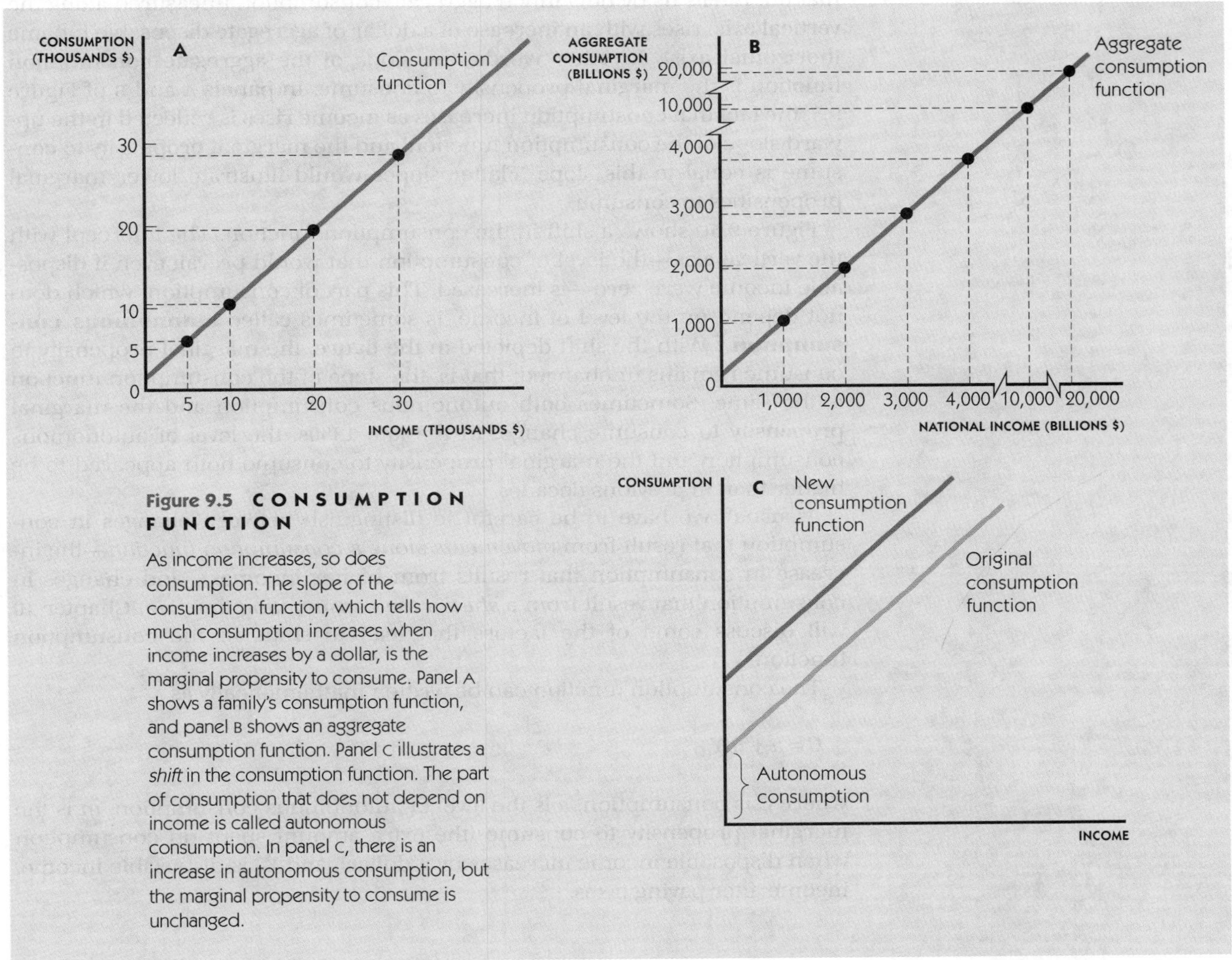

Figure 9.5 CONSUMPTION FUNCTION

As income increases, so does consumption. The slope of the consumption function, which tells how much consumption increases when income increases by a dollar, is the marginal propensity to consume. Panel A shows a family's consumption function, and panel B shows an aggregate consumption function. Panel C illustrates a *shift* in the consumption function. The part of consumption that does not depend on income is called autonomous consumption. In panel C, there is an increase in autonomous consumption, but the marginal propensity to consume is unchanged.

years has been somewhere between .9 and .97. That is, of each extra dollar of income households receive, they spend on average between 90 and 97 percent.[1] If aggregate income increases by $100 billion, then aggregate consumption will increase by between $90 and $97 billion. In the hypothetical consumption function illustrated in Figure 9.5B, the marginal propensity to consume is .9: when disposable income goes up by $1 trillion, aggregate consumption goes up by $900 billion.

[1]In the late 1980s, consumption was sometimes as high as 97 percent of household income. More recently, consumption has been somewhat lower. These statistics give the *average* ratio of consumption to disposable income. The *marginal* propensity to consume is somewhat smaller.

The slope of the aggregate consumption function conveys important information. It tells us by how much aggregate consumption (measured along the vertical axis) rises with an increase of a dollar of aggregate disposable income (horizontal axis). In other words, the slope of the aggregate consumption function is the marginal propensity to consume. In panels A and B of Figure 9.5, the fact that consumption increases as income rises is reflected in the upward slope of the consumption function, and the marginal propensity to consume is equal to this slope. Flatter slopes would illustrate lower marginal propensities to consume.

Figure 9.5C shows a shift in the consumption function. The intercept with the vertical axis—the level of consumption that would prevail even if disposable income were zero—is increased. This part of consumption, which does not depend on the level of income, is sometimes called **autonomous consumption.**[2] With the shift depicted in the figure, the marginal propensity to consume remains unchanged; that is, the slope of the consumption function is the same. Sometimes both autonomous consumption and the marginal propensity to consume change. In the late 1980s, the level of autonomous consumption and the marginal propensity to consume both appeared to be higher than in previous decades.

As usual, we have to be careful to distinguish between changes in consumption that result from *movements along a consumption function*—the increase in consumption that results from higher incomes—and changes in consumption that result from a *shift in the consumption function*. Chapter 10 will discuss some of the factors that lead to shifts in the consumption function.

The consumption function can be written mathematically as

$$C = a + mY_d,$$

where C is consumption, a is the level of autonomous consumption, m is the marginal propensity to consume (the extra amount spent on consumption when disposable income increases by a dollar), and Y_d is disposable income, income after paying taxes.

The Marginal Propensity to Save

Individuals have to either spend or save each extra dollar of disposable income, so savings and consumption are mirror images of each other. The definition "income = consumption plus savings" tells us that when disposable income rises by a dollar, if aggregate consumption increases by 90 cents, aggregate savings increase by 10 cents. The higher level of savings stemming from an extra dollar of income is called the **marginal propensity to save** (*MPS*). This is the counterpart to the marginal propensity to consume, and the

[2]People can consume even when their income is zero by using up savings.

two must always sum to one:

marginal propensity to save + marginal propensity to consume = 1.

The high marginal propensity to consume today means that there is a low marginal propensity to save. Fifty years ago, the marginal propensity to consume was smaller than it is today, somewhere between .8 and .9; of each extra dollar of disposable income, between 80 and 90 cents was spent on consumption. By the same token, the marginal propensity to save was larger; between 10 and 20 cents of each extra dollar of disposable income went into savings.

INVESTMENT

We now turn to the second major component of GDP—investment. Investment varies greatly from year to year, and, as we learned in Chapter 6, depends on the level of interest rates. Now, however, our focus is on the relationship between aggregate expenditures and national income as described by the aggregate expenditures schedule. We assume the level of investment is unrelated to the level of income this year. This assumption is made largely to simplify the analysis, but it also reflects the view that investment is primarily determined by firms' estimates of the economic prospects over the future. Accordingly, investment levels are not greatly affected by what happens this year and, in particular, not greatly affected by the level of national income. (See Table 9.3.) We can now analyze equilibrium output in a simplified economy

Table 9.3 SOME COMPONENTS OF AGGREGATE EXPENDITURES (billions of dollars)

Disposable income (Y_d)	Consumption expenditures (C)	Investment spending (I)	Total aggregate expenditures
$ 1,000	$ 1,050	$500	$ 1,550
2,000	1,950	500	2,450
3,000	2,850	500	3,350
4,000	3,750	500	4,250
6,500	6,000	500	6,500
10,000	9,150	500	9,650
20,000	18,150	500	18,650

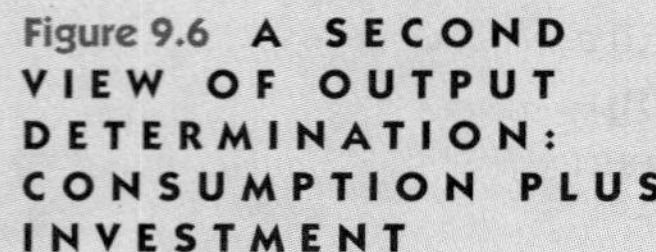

Figure 9.6 A SECOND VIEW OF OUTPUT DETERMINATION: CONSUMPTION PLUS INVESTMENT

Investment is fixed, so the aggregate expenditures schedule is a fixed amount above the consumption function alone. The slope of $C + I$ is the same as that of the consumption function; it is just the marginal propensity to consume.

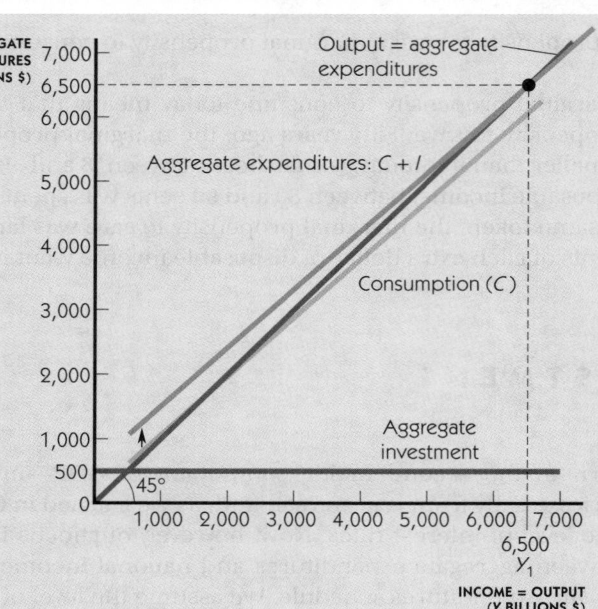

with no government and no foreign trade. Aggregate expenditures thus consist only of consumption and investment.

Table 9.3 combines the information from Table 9.2 with a fixed level of investment, $500 billion. Because we have assumed away government—both taxes and expenditures—disposable income is the same as national income. The table shows the level of aggregate expenditures for various levels of national income. Aggregate expenditures consist of the sum of consumption and investment, shown in the fourth column of the table and plotted in Figure 9.6. Because we assume investment does not depend on current income, the slope of the upper line in the figure is exactly the same as the slope of the consumption function: as income increases, aggregate expenditures increase by the same amount that consumption does, that is, by the marginal propensity to consume. The slope of the aggregate expenditures schedule is still the marginal propensity to consume. The equilibrium—the intersection of the aggregate expenditures schedule and the 45-degree line—is at Y_1 ($6,500 billion).

THE MULTIPLIER

One of the fundamental insights of income-expenditure analysis is that factors shifting the aggregate expenditures schedule will have a compound effect on output. Consider, for instance, an upward shift in the aggregate expenditures schedule induced by an increase in investment of $1 billion. We continue to

USING ECONOMICS: CALCULATING EQUILIBRIUM OUTPUT

Equilibrium output can be calculated as follows. Since

$$C = a + mY$$

and

$$AE = C + I = a + mY + I,$$

and since in equilibrium, aggregate expenditures equal income,

$$AE = Y,$$

we have

$$Y = a + mY + I,$$

or

$$Y = \frac{a + I}{1 - m}.$$

As a numerical example, let a = \$2 trillion, I = \$1 trillion, and $m = \frac{1}{2}$. When we substitute all these, we get Y = \$6 trillion.

assume that the marginal propensity to consume (MPC) is .9. The first-round effect of the extra investment spending, shown in Table 9.4, is straightforward: output increases by \$1 billion as firms purchase capital goods. This is only the beginning, however. The value of this increased output is distributed to the members of the economy as income, in the form of either higher wages, higher interest payments, of higher profits that become income to the firms' owners. Given that the marginal propensity to consume is .9, this will lead consumption demand to increase by .9 × \$1 billion = \$900 million. This second-round effect creates a \$900 million increase in output and thus income, which in turn brings on a third-round increase of consumption of .9 × \$900 million = \$810 million. In the next round, output is increased by .9 × \$810,000, then by .9 times that amount, then by .9 times that amount, and so on. In this example, when all the increases are totaled, a \$1 billion increase in investment will lead to a \$10 billion rise in equilibrium output.

Unfortunately, the multiplier process also works in reverse. Just as an increase in investment leads to a multiple increase in national output, a decrease in investment leads to a multiple decrease in national output. In our example, with an *MPC* of .9, if investment decreases by \$1 billion, national output will decrease by \$10 billion. The relationship between any change in investment expenditures and the resulting eventual change in national output is called the investment multiplier, or just **multiplier** for short. An increase in government expenditures or net exports has a similar multiplier effect.

In our simple model, with no trade and no government, the multiplier has a simple mathematical form: $\frac{1}{1 - MPC}$. As we learned earlier, any income an individual does not consume is saved, and an increase of income by a dollar must be spent either on consumption or on savings. Therefore,

$1 - MPC = MPS$, the marginal propensity to save.

Table 9.4 EFFECTS OF AN INCREASE IN INVESTMENT OF \$1 BILLION (millions of dollars)

First round	\$ 1,000
Second round	900
Third round	810
Fourth round	729
Fifth round	656
Sixth round	590
Seventh round	531
Eighth round	478
Ninth round	430
Tenth round	387
Eleventh round	349
Sum of twelfth and successive rounds	\$ 3,140
Total increase	\$10,000

Policy Perspective: A Little Stimulus Can Go a Long Way

The basic lesson of the multiplier is that a little stimulus can go a long way—at least a longer way than it would without the multiplier. In 1993, with the economy still in an economic downturn, and unemployment in excess of 7 percent, newly elected President Clinton argued for a small stimulus package, consisting largely of investments, of approximately \$16 billion. Sixteen billion dollars in a six trillion dollar economy seems like a small number—about a quarter of one percent. But with a multiplier of 2, that could add \$32 billion to national output. A \$32 billion increase in output in turn would lop off two- to three-tenths of a percentage point from the unemployment rate—not enough by itself to bring the economy's unemployment rate down to the target of 6 percent or below, but enough to speed the recovery and show that the administration was doing something about the slowdown which by then had lasted close to two years. Indeed, the small size was viewed as a virtue: it posed little threat of overheating the economy, should the economy's recovery take hold on its own faster than had been forecast.

This result allows us to rewrite the basic formula for the multiplier:

$$\text{multiplier} = \frac{1}{1 - MPC} = \frac{1}{MPS}.$$

In other words the multiplier is the reciprocal of the marginal propensity to save. If the marginal propensity to consume is .9, the marginal propensity to save is 1 − .9 = .1, and the multiplier is 10.

Using Economics: Calculating the Multiplier

Earlier, we showed that

$$Y = \frac{a + I}{1 - m}.$$

To see the multiplier, assume that I increases by a dollar. Now

$$Y_1 = \frac{a + I + 1}{1 - m}.$$

The change in Y, $Y_1 - Y$ is found by subtraction:

$$Y_1 - Y = \frac{1}{1 - m}.$$

The smaller m, the marginal propensity to consume, is the flatter the aggregate expenditures schedule is, and the smaller the multiplier is. If $m = .9$, the multiplier is 10. If $m = .8$, the multiplier is 5.

THE MULTIPLIER

An increase in investment leads to an increase in output that is a multiple of the original increase.

The multiplier equals $1/(1 - MPC)$, or $1/MPS$.

GOVERNMENT AND TRADE

The basic operation of the multiplier is unchanged when government and foreign trade are included in the analysis. Changes in government expenditure and net exports lead, through a multiplier, to larger changes in equilibrium output. But, as we will see, the effects of government and trade change the size of the multiplier.

THE EFFECTS OF GOVERNMENT

Government serves as a double-edged sword in the macroeconomy: its spending increases aggregate expenditures at the same time that its taxes reduce the amount of people's income. Let us take taxes first. Since consumption depends on individuals' disposable income—the amount of income they have available to spend after paying taxes—government taxes also reduce consumption.

Total income equals total output, denoted by Y. Disposable income is simply total income minus taxes, T:

$$\text{disposable income} = Y - T.$$

Taxes do two things. First, since at each level of national income disposable income is lower with taxes, consumption is lower. Taxes shift the aggregate expenditures schedule down. Second, when taxes increase with income, the multiplier is lower (the slope of the aggregate expenditures schedule is smaller). This is because taxes typically go up with income. When total income increases by a dollar, therefore, consumption increases by less than it otherwise would, since a fraction of the increased income goes to government.

Without taxes, when investment goes up by a dollar, income rises by a dollar, which leads to an increase in consumption determined by the marginal propensity to consume. This increase in consumption then sets off the next round of increases in national income. If, when income goes up by a dollar,

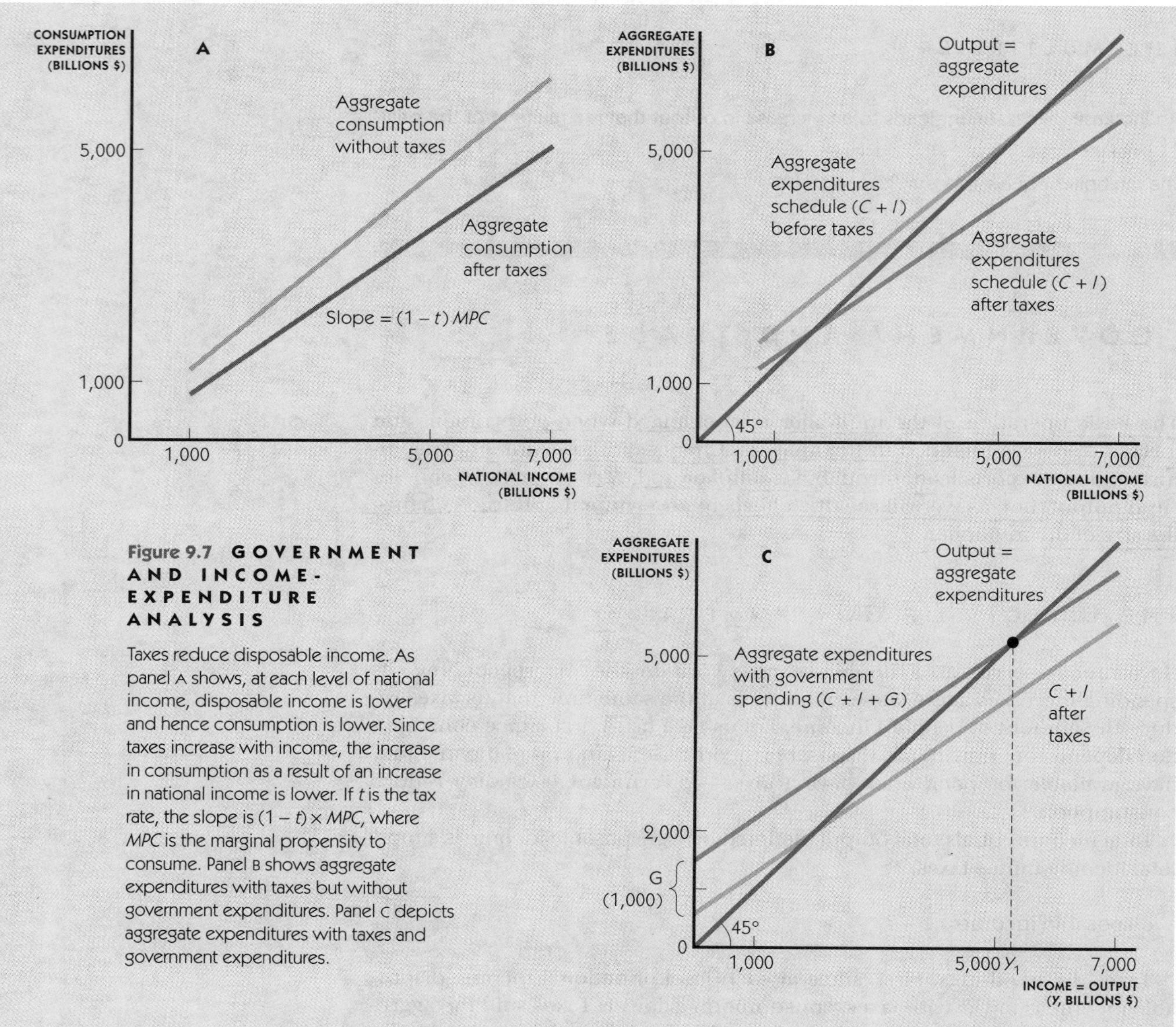

Figure 9.7 GOVERNMENT AND INCOME-EXPENDITURE ANALYSIS

Taxes reduce disposable income. As panel A shows, at each level of national income, disposable income is lower and hence consumption is lower. Since taxes increase with income, the increase in consumption as a result of an increase in national income is lower. If t is the tax rate, the slope is $(1 - t) \times MPC$, where MPC is the marginal propensity to consume. Panel B shows aggregate expenditures with taxes but without government expenditures. Panel C depicts aggregate expenditures with taxes and government expenditures.

government tax collections increase by 25 cents, then disposable income increases by only 75 cents. So the increase in consumption with taxes is one quarter smaller than it is without. In other words, the consumption function is flatter, as shown in panel A of Figure 9.7. Because the slope of the aggregate consumption function is flatter, the slope of the aggregate expenditures schedule is flatter, as illustrated in panel B. And because the slope of the aggregate expenditures schedule is flatter, the multiplier is smaller.

How about government spending? The answer to this question would be simpler if the government's expenditures moved in lockstep with its revenues. However, the government can spend more than it raises in taxes, by borrowing. When annual government expenditures exceed tax revenues, there is a **deficit.** There is some debate about the effects of deficits. Here we make the simplifying assumption that the deficit itself (as opposed to the spending imbalance that created the deficit) has no *direct* effect on either consumption or investment.

We also assume that government expenditures do not increase automatically with the level of income; they are assumed to be fixed, say at $1,000 billion. Thus, while taxes shift the aggregate expenditures schedule down and flatten it, government expenditures shift the aggregate expenditures schedule up by the amount of those expenditures, as shown in panel C of Figure 9.7. In this panel, the upward shifts in the aggregate expenditures schedule from government expenditures have been superimposed on the downward shifts in the aggregate expenditures schedule from taxes depicted in panel B. Note that the contributions of investment, *I* (which, in the example of Figure 9.7, are still assumed to be $500 billion), and government expenditures, *G,* raise the schedule but do not change its slope. The slope in panel C is the same as in panel B. Equilibrium again occurs at the intersection of the aggregate expenditures schedule and the 45-degree line. Increased government expenditures can have a powerful effect in stimulating the economy. But if the economy is in a serious recession, the government may have to increase expenditures a great deal to raise output to the full-employment level.

THE EFFECTS OF INTERNATIONAL TRADE

The analysis so far has ignored the important role of international trade. This is appropriate for a closed economy, an economy that neither exports nor imports, but not for an open economy, one actively engaged in international trade. Today the United States and other industrialized economies are very much open economies.

International trade can have powerful effects on national output. To begin with, exports expand the market for domestic goods. In recent years, the American economy has exported goods and services amounting to approximately 10 percent of national output. For smaller countries, exports amount to a much larger percentage of output: 26 percent for the United Kingdom and 12 percent for Japan, for instance.

But just as exports expand the market for domestic goods, imports decrease it. Therefore, imports and exports affect the aggregate expenditures schedule in different ways. In recent years, net exports—the appropriate concept when looking at the overall effect on aggregate expenditures—have turned sharply negative in the United States. That is to say, imports have exceeded exports. In the late 1980s, net exports amounted to *minus* 2 to 3 percent of U.S. GDP. Trade not only has increased in size relative to the economy, but net exports have changed dramatically, as illustrated in Figure 9.8.

Figure 9.8 **U.S. NET EXPORTS SINCE 1950**

U.S. net exports were generally positive through the 1950s and 1960s, before turning sharply negative in the 1980s. *Source: ERP* (1996), Table B-1.

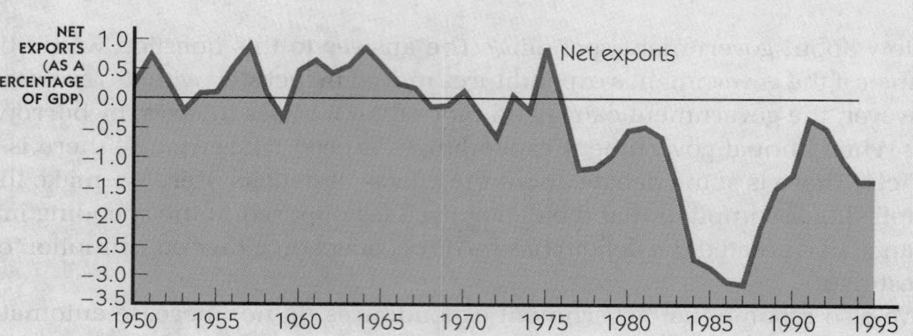

IMPORTS

When households' incomes rise, they not only buy more American-made consumer goods, they also buy more goods from abroad. We can illustrate an **import function** in much the same way that we illustrated a consumption function. (We have assumed investment and government expenditures to be fixed here, so for now there is no schedule relating either of these to income.) The import function shows the levels of imports corresponding to different levels of income. Table 9.5 shows hypothetical levels of imports for different

USING ECONOMICS: PUTTING GOVERNMENT INTO THE EQUATION

When we add government, the equation for aggregate expenditures becomes

$$AE = C + I + G = a + mY_d + I + G,$$

where Y_d is disposable income. For simplicity, we assume a given fraction, t, of income is paid in taxes, so

$$Y_d = Y(1 - t).$$

Hence, in equilibrium, with aggregate expenditures equaling income

$$AE = Y = a + mY(1 - t) + I + G$$

or

$$Y = \frac{a + I + G}{1 - m(1 - t)}.$$

Hence,

$$\text{multiplier} = \frac{1}{1 - m(1 - t)}.$$

If $m = .8$ and $t = .25$, the multiplier $= 2.5$. By contrast, the multiplier without taxes is 5, twice as large. The reason that the multiplier is larger without taxes than with is simple. Without taxes every dollar of extra income translates into 80 cents of extra expenditure. With taxes, when income goes up by a dollar, consumption increases by only $.8 \times (1 - .25) = 60$ cents.

Figure 9.9 THE IMPORT FUNCTION

Imports (*M*) increase steadily as disposable income (*Y*) rises. The slope of the import function is equal to the marginal propensity to import.

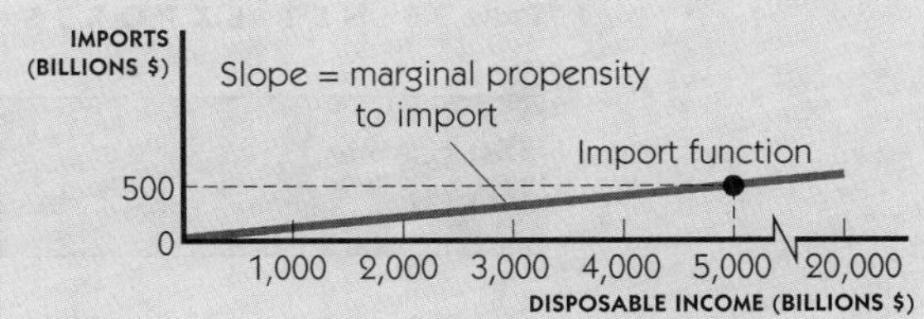

levels of income. For simplicity, we assume that imports are bought by consumers and that, accordingly, it is disposable income that determines their level. The import function is depicted in Figure 9.9.

Imports increase with income. The **marginal propensity to import** gives the amount of each extra dollar of income spent on imports. If the marginal propensity to import is .1, then if income goes up by $1,000, imports go up by $.1 \times \$1{,}000 = \$100$. In Figure 9.9, the marginal propensity to import is given by the slope of the import function.

Table 9.5 IMPORTS AND DISPOSABLE INCOME (billions of dollars)

Disposable income	Imports
$ 1,000	$ 100
2,000	200
3,000	300
4,000	400
5,000	500
10,000	1,000
20,000	2,000

EXPORTS

What foreigners buy from the United States depends on the income of foreigners and not directly on income in the United States. Exports may also depend on other factors, such as the marketing effort of American firms and the prices of American goods relative to those of foreign goods. Our focus here is to determine output in the United States. For simplicity, we assume that these other factors are fixed and do not depend on what happens in the United States. In particular, we assume that foreigners' incomes do not depend significantly on incomes in the United States. Hence, the level of exports is taken as fixed at $400 billion.

Exports minus imports (net exports) is sometimes referred to as the **balance of trade.** Net exports at each level of national income are given in Table 9.6. At very low levels of income, net exports are positive. That is to say, exports exceed imports. As income increases, imports increase, with exports remaining unchanged. Eventually imports exceed exports; the balance of trade becomes negative.

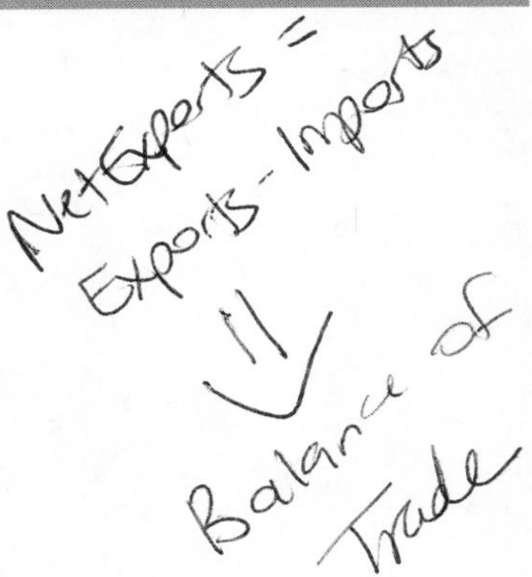

Trade, like taxes, has the effect of flattening the aggregate expenditures schedule. This is because as income increases, some of it goes to buy foreign goods rather than domestically produced goods. Hence, aggregate expenditures—spending for goods produced within the country—increase by a smaller amount. In a closed economy, when income increases by a dollar aggregate expenditures increase by the marginal propensity to consume. In an open economy, when income increases by a dollar, aggregate expenditures increase by the marginal propensity to consume *minus* the marginal propensity to import. The difference between the two can be thought of as the marginal propensity to consume domestically produced goods.

This can be seen in Table 9.7, which calculates, for different levels of national

Table 9.6 **NET EXPORTS** (billions of dollars)

Disposable income	Exports	Imports	E (exports – imports)
$ 1,000	$400	$ 100	$ 300
2,000	400	200	200
3,000	400	300	100
4,000	400	400	0
5,000	400	500	–100
10,000	400	1,000	–600
20,000	400	1,800	–1,400

income, the level of disposable income, consumption, investment, government expenditures, and net exports. Every time aggregate income increases by $1,333 billion, disposable income increases by only $1,000 billion; and while consumption increases by $900 billion, net exports *fall* (because imports increase) by $100 billion, so the net increase in aggregate expenditures is only $800 billion. In a closed economy with government, aggregate expenditures would have increased by $900 billion.

At an income of $5,333 billion (a disposable income of $4,000 billion), net exports are zero. At higher levels of income, net exports are negative. At lower levels, they are positive. Thus, trade increases aggregate expenditures at lower levels of national income, and decreases aggregate expenditures at higher lev-

Table 9.7 **AGGREGATE EXPENDITURES SCHEDULE**
(billions of dollars)

Income	Disposable income	Consumption	Investment	Government	Net exports	Aggregate expenditures
$ 1,333	$ 1,000	$ 1,050	$500	$1,000	$ 300	$ 2,850
2,666	2,000	1,950	500	1,000	200	3,650
4,000	3,000	2,850	500	1,000	100	4,450
5,125	3,844	3,609	500	1,000	16	5,125
5,333	4,000	3,750	500	1,000	0	5,250
13,333	10,000	9,150	500	1,000	–600	10,050
26,666	20,000	18,150	500	1,000	–1,400	18,250

Note: The numbers in the table are constructed under the following assumptions: a tax rate of .25, a marginal propensity to consume of .9, and a marginal propensity to import of .1.

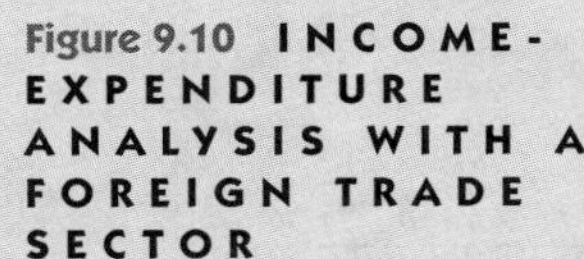

Figure 9.10 INCOME-EXPENDITURE ANALYSIS WITH A FOREIGN TRADE SECTOR

Adding a fixed level of exports raises the aggregate demand function. But adding imports makes the slope of the function flatter, since some of national income is now going to buy products produced outside the country. The multiplier is reduced.

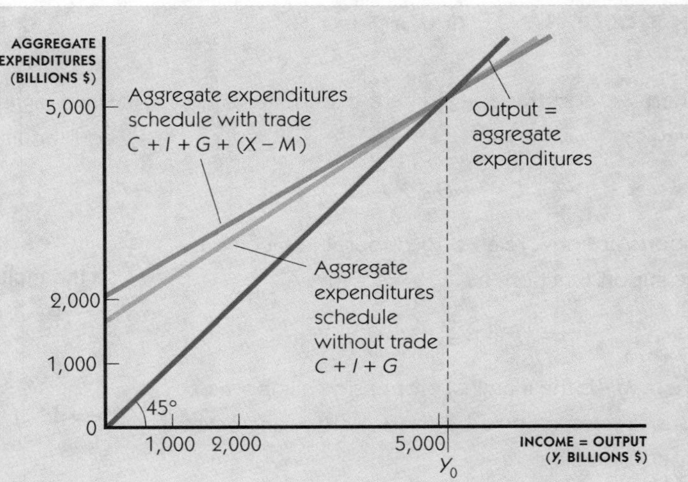

els of national income. At low levels of income, the stimulation provided by exports more than offsets the losses from imports; at higher levels of income just the opposite happens.

In Figure 9.10, the income-expenditure analysis diagram is again used to show how the level of output is determined. As before, the equilibrium condition that output equals aggregate expenditures, $Y = AE$, is represented by the 45-degree line. The aggregate expenditures schedule now adds all of its components: $C + I + G + (X - M)$. The slope of this line is even flatter than in Figure 9.7C. This is because, as income increases, net exports—one of the components of aggregate expenditures—actually decrease. Equilibrium again occurs at the intersection of the aggregate expenditures schedule and the 45-degree line, the output level Y_0 (equal to $5,125) in the figure.

We know that whenever the aggregate expenditures schedule is flattened, the multiplier is lowered. To see precisely how this works in the case of trade, think again about how the multiplier works through various rounds in the economy. The first-round effect of the increase in investment is augmented by the second-round effect of the rise in consumption induced by the higher income of those producing the investment goods. This is augmented by the third-round effect of the increase in consumption induced by the higher income of those involved in producing the second round. And so on. But now, when investment rises by $1 billion, the second-round effect is only the increase in consumption of domestically produced goods. If the marginal propensity to consume is .9, the tax rate is .25, and the marginal propensity to import is .1, the increase in *domestically produced* consumption goods is $600 million (not $675 million, as it would be without trade, or $900 million, as it would be without taxes or trade).[3] Not only is the second-round effect

[3]Of the $1 billion, the government takes 25 percent, leaving households with $750 million. Households consume 90 percent of this amount, but 10 percent of their income is spent on imports, so 80 percent of

USING ECONOMICS: PUTTING INTERNATIONAL TRADE INTO THE EQUATION

When we add trade, aggregate expenditures are given by

$$AE = C + I + G + X - M.$$

Imports are now related to disposable income by the import function

$$M = MPI \times Y_d,$$

where *MPI* is the marginal propensity to import; exports are assumed to be fixed. Hence, aggregate expenditures are

$$AE = a + mY(1 - t) + I + G + X - MPI(1 - t)\,Y.$$

Since aggregate expenditures equal income, in equilibrium

$$Y = \frac{a + I + G + X}{1 - (1 - t)\,(m - MPI)},$$

so the multiplier is

$$\frac{1}{1 - (1 - t)\,(m - MPI)}.$$

If $t = .25$, $m = .8$, $MPI = .1$, then the multiplier is

$$\frac{1}{1 - .75\,(.8 - .1)} = 2.1,$$

much smaller than in the absence of trade (2.5).

smaller, the third-round effect is also smaller. The increase of \$600 million in the second round leads to increased consumption of domestically produced goods of \$360 million in the third round.

If more of the income generated on each successive round is not spent on goods produced within the country, the multiplier will be smaller. When income generated in one round of production is not used to buy more goods produced within the country, economists say there are **leakages.** In a closed economy there are two leakages: savings and taxes. In an open economy there are three leakages: savings, taxes, and imports.

BACK TO THE AGGREGATE DEMAND CURVES

We began the chapter with an aggregate demand and supply schedule. The objective of this chapter was to show how at any price level aggregate demand—and equilibrium output—is determined. We can use the analysis to *derive* the aggregate demand curve simply by asking, what happens to aggregate demand—and equilibrium output—when the price level changes? To answer that question, all we have to ascertain is, how does the aggregate expenditures schedule shift when the price level increases or decreases? When

their income is spent on domestically produced consumer goods. The increase in demand for domestically produced consumer goods is $.8 \times \$750$ million = \$600 million.

Figure 9.11 DERIVING THE AGGREGATE DEMAND CURVE

Panel A shows the effect of an increase in the price level from P_0 to P_1 on the aggregate expenditures schedule. It decreases equilibrium output from Y_0 to Y_1. Panel B traces out the equilibrium values of aggregate demand (and output) corresponding to different price levels.

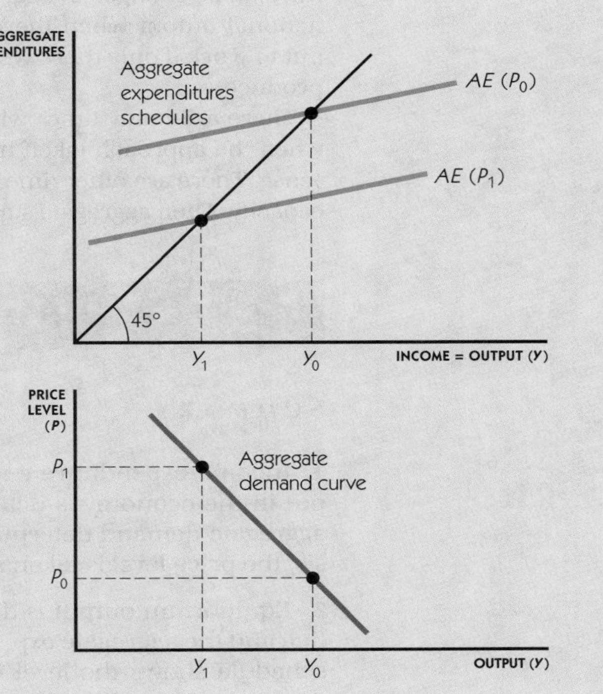

the price level rises, at each level of income, consumers will consume less, since the real value of their bank balances will have decreased. Also, if *current* price levels are higher relative to (fixed beliefs about) *future* price levels, then households may ***substitute*** against current consumption (which has become relatively expensive) for future consumption. In either case, the aggregate expenditures schedule shifts down, as depicted in Figure 9.11, and equilibrium output falls. Thus, while Y_0 is the point on the aggregate demand schedule corresponding to P_0, Y_1 is the point on the aggregate demand schedule corresponding to P_1. Later chapters will explore more fully how changes in the price level shift the aggregate expenditures schedule.

LIMITATIONS OF THE INCOME-EXPENDITURE APPROACH

This chapter has analyzed the determination of national output by focusing exclusively on the aggregate expenditures schedule, which underlies the aggregate demand curve. But what happened to aggregate supply? Isn't that important too?

Recall that aggregate demand rules the roost when there is excess capacity. That is, changes in aggregate demand alone determine what happens to national output when there are idle machines and workers that could be put to work if only there were sufficient demand to purchase the goods they produce.

There are many times when there is excess capacity in the economy, and when the approach taken here, ignoring capacity constraints, makes perfect sense. There are other times, however, when the economy is working close to capacity. Then aggregate supply has to be brought into the picture.

REVIEW AND PRACTICE

SUMMARY

1. Income-expenditure analysis shows how the equilibrium level of output in the economy is determined when there is excess capacity, so that aggregate demand determines the level of output. Throughout the analysis, the price level is taken as fixed.

2. Equilibrium output is determined by the intersection of the 45-degree line and the aggregate expenditures schedule. The aggregate expenditures schedule shows the level of aggregate expenditures at each level of national income, while the 45-degree line represents the points where aggregate expenditures equal output (income).

3. Shifts in the aggregate expenditures schedule give rise to changes in the equilibrium level of output. The magnitude of the increase in output resulting from an upward shift in the aggregate expenditures schedule depends on the slope of the schedule. Much of macroeconomic analysis focuses on what determines the slope of the aggregate expenditures schedule, what causes shifts in the schedule, and how government can shift the schedule.

4. Aggregate expenditures are the sum of consumption, investment, government expenditures, and net exports. Net exports are the difference between exports and imports.

5. Consumption increases as disposable income increases, and the relationship between income and consumption is called the consumption function. The amount by which consumption increases when disposable income increases by a dollar is called the marginal propensity to consume (*MPC*). The amount by which savings increase when disposable income increases by a dollar is called the marginal propensity to save (*MPS*). Since all income must be saved or consumed, the sum of the *MPC* and *MPS* must be 1.

6. The multiplier is the factor by which a change in investment or government expenditures must be multiplied to get the resulting change in

national output. In a simple model without government spending, taxes, or net exports, the multiplier for changes in investment is $1/(1 - MPC)$, or $1/MPS$.

7. Government spending increases aggregate expenditures, and taxes reduce disposable income and therefore consumption. When taxes increase with income, consumption increases by less than it otherwise would, since a fraction of the increased income goes to government. The aggregate expenditures schedule is flatter, and the multiplier is smaller.

8. Exports increase aggregate demand, and imports reduce aggregate demand. Imports increase with income, but exports are determined by factors in other countries. Trade flattens the aggregate expenditures schedule, because as income increases some of it goes to buy foreign rather than domestic goods. As a result, the multiplier is smaller.

9. The aggregate expenditures schedule is used to derive the equilibrium level of output at each price level (assuming that there is excess capacity in the economy). As the price level increases, the aggregate expenditures schedule shifts down and equilibrium output decreases. The aggregate demand curve then traces out the equilibrium level of output at each price level.

KEY TERMS

aggregate expenditures schedule
income-expenditure analysis
planned and **unplanned inventories**
consumption function
marginal propensity to consume
autonomous consumption
marginal propensity to save
multiplier
import function
marginal propensity to import
balance of trade

REVIEW QUESTIONS

1. What is the aggregate expenditures schedule? What are the components of aggregate expenditures?

2. How is the equilibrium level of output determined? Why are points on the aggregate expenditures schedule above the 45-degree line not sustainable? Why are points on the aggregate expenditures schedule below the 45-degree line not sustainable?

3. What is a consumption function? What determines its slope? What is an import function? What determines its slope?

4. What is the consequence of a shift in the aggregate expenditures schedule? Give examples of what might give rise to such a shift.

5. Illustrate the difference between a change in consumption resulting

from an increase in income with a given consumption function and a change in consumption resulting from a shift in the consumption function.

6. Why is the sum of the marginal propensity to save and the marginal propensity to consume always 1?

7. Show that the magnitude of the effect of a given shift in the aggregate expenditures schedule on equilibrium output depends on the slope of the aggregate expenditures schedule. What determines the slope of the aggregate expenditures schedule? How is it affected by taxes? by imports?

8. How can changes of a certain amount in the level of investment or government spending have a larger effect on national output? What is the multiplier?

9. What is the relationship between the aggregate expenditures schedule and the aggregate demand curve? How does the aggregate expenditures schedule shift when the price level increases? How can the aggregate demand curve be derived?

PROBLEMS

1. In the economy of Consumerland, national income and consumption are related in this way:

National income	$1,500	$1,600	$1,700	$1,800	$1,900
Consumption	$1,325	$1,420	$1,515	$1,610	$1,705

Calculate national savings at each level of national income. What is the marginal propensity to consume in Consumerland? What is the marginal propensity to save? If national income rose to $2,000, what do you predict consumption and savings would be?

2. To the economy of Consumerland add the fact that investment will be $180 at every level of output. Graph the consumption function and the aggregate expenditures schedule for this simple economy. What determines the slope of the aggregate expenditures schedule? What is the equilibrium output?

3. Calculate the first four rounds of the multiplier effect for an increase of $10 billion in investment spending in each of the following cases:
   (a) a simple consumption and investment economy where the *MPC* is .9;
   (b) an economy with government but no foreign trade, where the *MPC* is .9 and the tax rate is .3;
   (c) an economy with an *MPC* of .9, a tax rate of .3, and a marginal propensity to import of .1.

4. If, at each level of disposable income, savings increase, what does this imply about what has happened to the consumption function? What will be the consequences for the equilibrium level of output?

5. Use the income-expenditure analysis diagram to explain why a lower level of investment, government spending, and net exports all have similar effects on the equilibrium level of output.

6. In a more stable economy (where national output is less vulnerable to small changes in, say, exports), government policy is less effective (changes in government expenditures do not do much to stimulate the economy); in a less stable economy, government policy is more effective. Explain why there is a trade-off between the stability of the economy and the power of government policy.

CHAPTER 10*

CONSUMPTION AND INVESTMENT

Now that we have developed the overall framework of income-expenditure analysis, we take a closer look at two of the components of aggregate expenditures, consumption and investment. Examining them will help us understand both why the level of economic activity fluctuates and what policies the government might pursue to reduce those fluctuations or to stimulate the economy.

*This chapter may be skipped or taken up after subsequent chapters without loss of continuity.

KEY QUESTIONS

1. Why may current consumption not be very dependent on current income, and what implications does this have for the use of tax policy to stimulate the economy?
2. What other factors determine the level of aggregate consumption?
3. What are "consumer durables," and why are expenditures on them so volatile?
4. What are the major determinants of the level of investment? What role do variations in real interest rates and the availability of credit play? What role is played by changing perceptions of risk and the ability and willingness to bear risk?
5. Why is the variability in investment and expenditures on consumer durables so important?

CONSUMPTION

The consumption function presented in Chapter 9 said that the demand for goods and services by households is determined by the level of disposable income. As disposable income goes up, so does consumption. Knowing this year's disposable income, then, an economist can use the consumption function to predict this year's consumption spending.

This simple consumption function, often referred to as the Keynesian consumption function, is a good starting point, as Figure 10.1 illustrates. Income varies from year to year, and so does consumption. If they moved in lockstep as the simple consumption function predicts, a straight line could be drawn through all the points in the figure. The relationship is remarkably close to the linear relationship predicted by the theories. Still, economists have sought to develop even better predictors of consumption.

FUTURE-ORIENTED CONSUMPTION FUNCTIONS

In the decades after Keynes's time, many economists questioned his notion that current consumption depends primarily on current income. They argued that individuals, in making consumption decisions, look at total income over their lifetime, averaging good years with bad, and recognizing that income typically increases with experience.

Nobel laureate Franco Modigliani, for instance, emphasized that people save for retirement. He called this motive **life-cycle savings,** to convey the notion that individuals will save during their working years so they will not have to curtail their consumption after they retire. Milton Friedman, also a

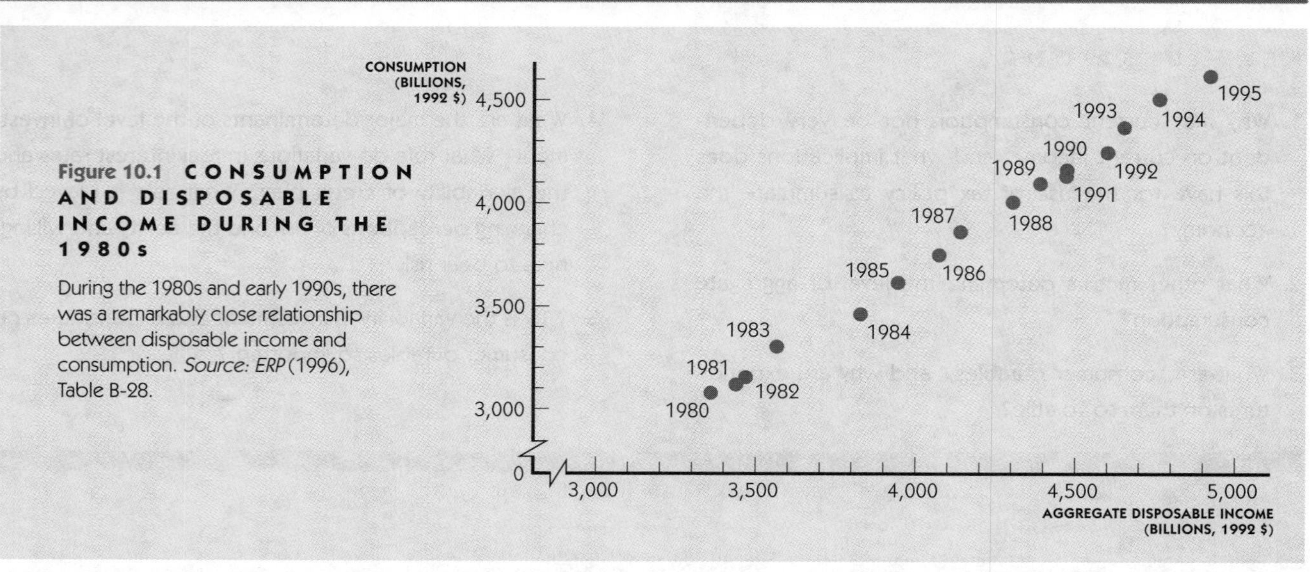

Figure 10.1 CONSUMPTION AND DISPOSABLE INCOME DURING THE 1980s

During the 1980s and early 1990s, there was a remarkably close relationship between disposable income and consumption. *Source: ERP* (1996), Table B-28.

Nobel laureate, emphasized how the future affects consumption today by pointing out that people save in good years to carry them through bad years. His view is called the **permanent income hypothesis.** Permanent income is a person's average income over her lifetime. Friedman stressed that consumption depends not so much on current income as on total lifetime income, averaging good years with bad. While Modigliani emphasized the role of savings in smoothing consumption between working and retirement years, Friedman emphasized its role in smoothing consumption between good and bad years. Underlying both views is the notion that people like their consumption patterns to be stable.

These future-oriented theories of savings and consumption yield different consequences from the basic Keynesian or traditional theory that consumption simply depends on this year's income. Consider an individual who happens to get a windfall gain in income one year—perhaps he wins $1 million in the state lottery. If the marginal propensity to consume is .9, the Keynesian consumption function predicts that he will consume $900,000 of his winnings that year. The future-oriented consumption theories suggest that the lucky winner will spread the extra income over a lifetime of consumption. Similarly, if the government temporarily lowers taxes for one year, the future-oriented consumption theories predict that a taxpayer will not dramatically increase consumption in that year but will spread over his lifetime the extra consumption that the one-year tax reduction allows. Thus, they suggest that *temporary* tax changes will be much less effective in stimulating consumption than the Keynesian model predicts.

Figure 10.2 compares the future-oriented consumption function and the Keynesian consumption function for the household. Suppose a household were to have a onetime increase in its disposable income. If consumption responds according to the Keynesian consumption function, it will increase from C_0 to C_1 as shown in panel A.

The future-oriented theories predict that consumption will not change very much. We can see this in two different ways. Panel B shows consumption depending on average disposable income over a person's lifetime. Now the change in this year's income from Y_0 to Y_1 has little effect on average disposable income, and hence little effect on consumption. Panel C put this year's disposable income on the horizontal axis, as does panel A. The difference in slope between the consumption functions in panels A and C reflects the difference between Keynes's views and those of the future-oriented theorists. Consumption, in the latter view, is not very sensitive to current disposable income, which is why the line is so flat.

The principle that consumption depends not just on income this year but also on longer-run considerations holds at the aggregate level as well. Figure 10.3 shows the implications of future-oriented theories for aggregate expenditures and the determination of equilibrium output. Since the relationship between changes in today's income and changes in consumption is weaker than in the Keynesian model, the aggregate expenditures schedule is now much flatter, that is, increases in current income lead to relatively small changes in consumption and aggregate expenditures. This in turn has strong implications for the multiplier. An increase in, say, investment, which shifts the aggregate expenditures schedule up, increases equilibrium output by an amount only slightly greater than the original increase in investment. The multiplier is very small.

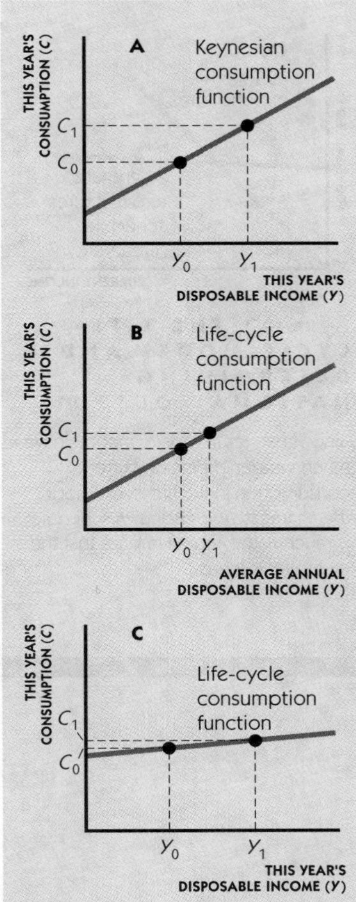

Figure 10.2 EFFECT OF A TEMPORARY INCOME CHANGE IN THE LIFE-CYCLE MODEL

With the Keynesian consumption function, panel A, a temporary change in income results in a large change in consumption. In the life-cycle model, panel B, a temporary change in income has only a small effect on average annual income over a lifetime, and thus leads to only a small change in consumption. Panel C shows how the life-cycle model predicts that consumption will react in response to *this year's income*. Since consumption does not change by much, the life-cycle consumption function is very flat.

WEALTH AND CAPITAL GAINS

The future-oriented consumption theories suggest not only that current income is relatively unimportant in determining consumption but also that variables Keynes ignored may be important. For instance, wealthier people consume more (at each level of current income). Since consumption is related to wealth, changes in consumption will be affected by changes in wealth.

The distinction between income and wealth as a determinant of consumption is important. It corresponds to the distinction between flows and stocks. Flows are measured as "rates." Both income and consumption are flow variables. They are measured as dollars *per year*. Wealth is a stock variable.[1] It is measured simply by the total value ("dollars") of one's assets. Future-oriented theories emphasize that there is no reason that an individual's current consumption should be related to his current income. What he consumes should be related to how well off he is, and that is better measured by his wealth.[2]

[1]Other stock variables in macroeconomics include capital stock; other flow variables include the interest rate.

[2]Future-oriented theories take an expansive view of what should be included in wealth: they include *human capital*, the present discounted value of future wage income. (See Chapter 6 for a definition of present discounted value.)

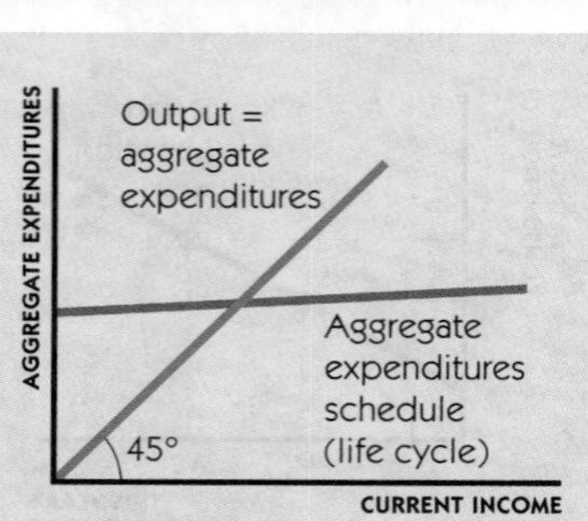

Figure 10.3 THE LIFE-CYCLE MODEL AND DETERMINING NATIONAL OUTPUT

Since changes in today's income have much weaker effects on current consumption in the life-cycle model, the aggregate expenditures schedule is much flatter, which implies that the multiplier is lower.

Capital gains, or changes in the value of assets, change an individual's wealth. Thus, these theories predict that when stock or real estate prices rise in value and people expect this change to last for a long time, individuals who own these assets will increase their level of consumption. They will do so because their overall wealth has grown, even if they do not immediately receive any income from the increase in value.

There is some evidence to support this view. Many economists believe that the stock market crash of 1929, which preceded the Great Depression, contributed to that Depression by generating a downward shift in the consumption function. On the other hand, when the stock market fell by over 22 percent on a single day in October 1987, consumption did not decline sharply in the way one might have expected. People responded only slightly to this capital loss. One reason for this is that individuals respond to changes in wealth only slowly, and in 1987 their consumption had not yet fully responded to the increases in stock market prices that had occurred during the preceding few years. A prolonged and persistent decline in the stock market might, however, have an extremely depressing effect on consumption.

RECONCILING CONSUMPTION THEORY WITH FACTS

The permanent income and life-cycle hypotheses contain large elements of truth. Families do save for their retirement, so life-cycle considerations are important. And households do smooth their consumption between good years and bad, so permanent income considerations are relevant. Even so, household consumption appears to be more dependent on current income than either theory would suggest. There are two reasons for this, durable goods and credit rationing. Each plays an important role in consumption.

DURABLE GOODS

Goods such as cars, refrigerators, and furniture are called **durable goods.** Purchasing a durable good is like an investment decision, because such goods are bought for the services they render over a number of years. Decisions to postpone purchasing a durable good have quite different consequences from decisions not to buy food or some other nondurable. If you do not buy strawberries today, you will have to do without them. But not buying a durable does not mean you will do without. It simply means you may have to make do with the services provided by an older durable. The costs of postponing the purchase of a new car are often relatively low; you can make do with an old car a little bit longer.

When a household's income is temporarily low, rather than borrowing to purchase durables, the household simply postpones the purchase. Similarly, if a worker worries about losing his job, he may cut back durable purchases. Figure 10.4 traces the purchases of durables as a percentage of disposable income during the postwar period. These fluctuations in purchases of durables, together with the variations in investment, seem to account for much of the variation in economic activity over the business cycle. Variations in the

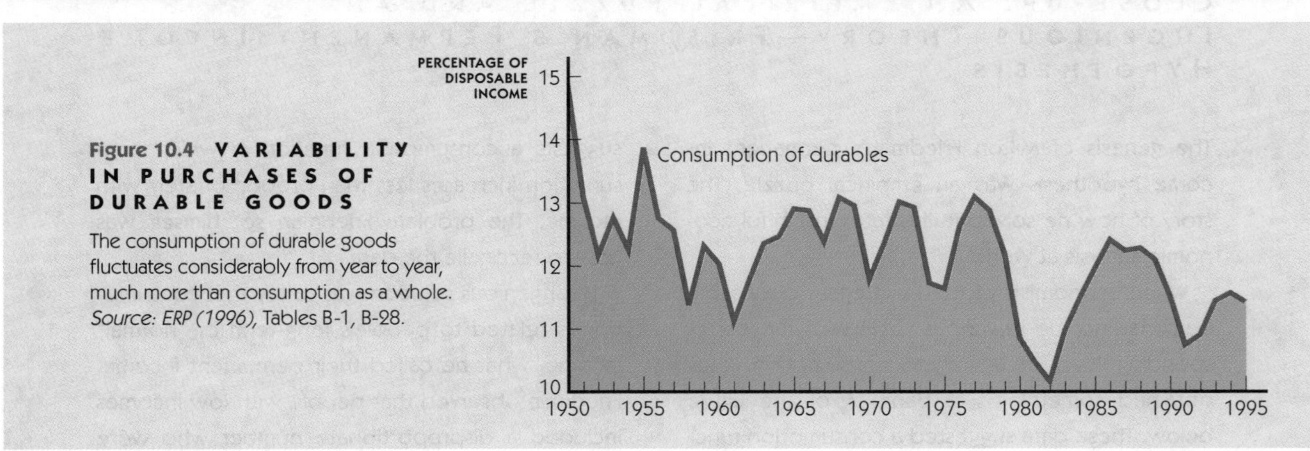

Figure 10.4 VARIABILITY IN PURCHASES OF DURABLE GOODS
The consumption of durable goods fluctuates considerably from year to year, much more than consumption as a whole.
Source: ERP (1996), Tables B-1, B-28.

services provided by durable goods—and hence in true consumption—are much smaller.

CREDIT RATIONING

Empirical studies show that even nondurable consumption expenditures seem more dependent on current income than the future-oriented theories suggest. These theories, in particular the permanent income hypothesis, assume that when an individual has a bad year, he can maintain his consumption at a steady level. They assume, in other words, either that the household has a large stock of savings to draw on while its income is temporarily low, or that the household can easily borrow.

For many people, neither of these conditions is true. Most individuals, even in the United States, have few liquid assets upon which to draw. They may have considerable savings tied up in a pension scheme, but they cannot draw upon these until they retire. They may have some equity in their house, but the last thing they want to do is sell their home. Moreover, it is precisely in times of need, when a person is unemployed or a business is doing badly, that banks are least forthcoming with funds. (As the saying goes, banks only lend to those who don't need the money!)

Credit rationing occurs when people are unable to obtain funds at the market rate of interest, because of the risks associated with lending to them. Many people are credit rationed. For those who have no assets and are credit rationed, cutting back on consumption when income declines is not a matter of choice. For these individuals, consumption depends heavily on current income.

If people were not credit rationed, short-term unemployment would not be as important a problem as it appears to be. The suffering caused by temporary layoffs would be much less. To see why, we need to look again at the concept of total wealth. Assume, for instance, that Evan will work for forty years,

Close-up: An Empirical Puzzle and an Ingenious Theory—Friedman's Permanent Income Hypothesis

The genesis of Milton Friedman's permanent income hypothesis was an empirical puzzle. The story of how he solved it illustrates insightful economic analysis at work.

When economists plotted aggregate disposable personal income in various years with the corresponding level of aggregate consumption, they obtained something like panel A of the figure below. These data suggested a consumption function in which consumption increases proportionately with income. But, when economists plotted the consumption of different income groups against their current income for any particular year, they obtained something more like panel B. This suggests a consumption function in which consumption increases less than proportionately with income. The problem Friedman set himself was how to reconcile the data.

His ingenious solution was to say that consumption is related to people's long-term or "normal" income, what he called their permanent income. Friedman observed that people with low incomes included a disproportionate number who were having unusually bad years. And correspondingly, those with very high incomes included a disproportionate number having unusually good years. Those having a bad year did not reduce their consumption proportionately; those having a particu-

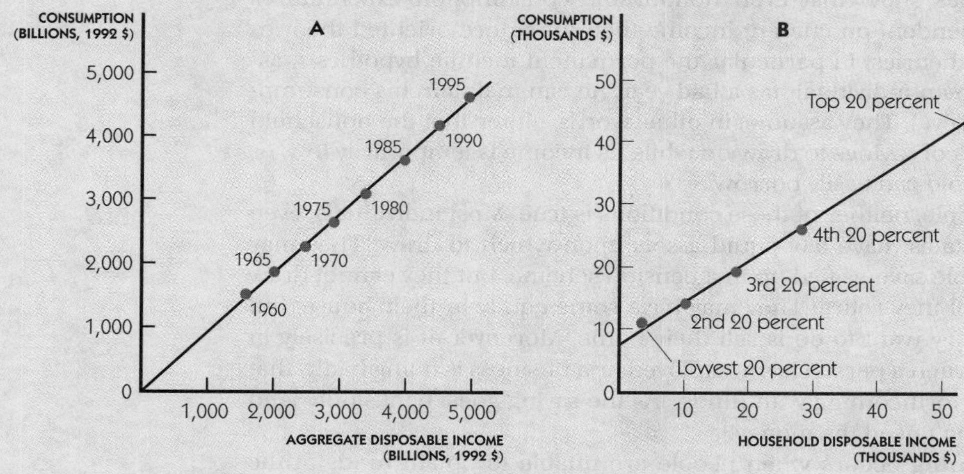

Panel A shows that as income has increased over time, consumption has increased almost in proportion. Panel B illustrates the fact that individuals with higher income increase their consumption somewhat less than proportionately, especially at the highest income levels. *Sources: ERP* (1995), Table B-28; *Consumer Expenditure Survey* (1988).

larly good year did not increase their consumption proportionately. Friedman was thus able to explain how, over time, aggregate consumption could rise in proportion to income for the population as a whole, even though the consumption of any particular household increased less than proportionately with current income.

Stanford University economist Robert Hall has pointed out an unsettling consequence of the permanent income hypothesis. If the level of consumption a person chooses depends on permanent income, which incorporates all information about what future *expected* income will be, changes in consumption are related only to *unexpected* changes. By definition, unexpected changes are random and unpredictable. Thus, the permanent income theory predicts that changes in consumption are largely random and unpredictable—not good news for economists trying to understand and forecast such patterns.

that his initial salary is $25,000 per year, that his salary increases in real terms at 5 percent per year, and that 5 percent is the real rate of interest. Then the present discounted value of his lifetime earnings is $1 million. This is his wealth, assuming that he has no unexpected windfall, no inheritance from his great-aunt, and no other assets. Imagine that Evan loses his job and is unemployed for half a year. At first glance, that looks like a personal calamity. But upon closer inspection, we see that it represents a loss of only a bit more than 1 percent of his lifetime wealth.

If Evan could borrow six months' pay, he would have no trouble paying it back, and the period without work would be no tragedy—his life-style would be constrained, but insignificantly. Since he would have to cut expenditures by only a bit more than 1 percent, cutting out a few movies, a fancy restaurant meal or two, and a few other activities would do the trick. However, for most people, losing a job for half a year would in fact be a major disaster—not because of the reduction in total lifetime wealth, but because most individuals face important constraints on the amount they can borrow. Without a job, they cannot obtain loans, except possibly at very high interest rates. Because of these credit constraints, for most lower- and many middle-income individuals, the traditional Keynesian consumption function is all too relevant. When their current income is reduced, their consumption is necessarily reduced.

Macroeconomic Implications of Consumption Theories

The alternative theories of consumption we have explored so far have two sets of macroeconomic implications. First, the future-oriented theories of consumption, in arguing that consumption does not depend heavily on current income, maintain that the aggregate expenditures schedule is flat and therefore the multiplier is low. This is both good news and bad news for the economy. It is good news because a small multiplier means that decreases in the level of investment lead to much smaller decreases in the level of national income than they would if the multiplier were large. It is bad news because it

Policy Perspective: A Quick Stimulus in the Face of an Impending Election Tests the Future-Oriented Theories

In late 1991 and early 1992, as the presidential election neared and the economy remained stubbornly stuck in an economic downturn, President Bush decided the economy needed a quick stimulus. He did two things.

First, he reduced IRS tax-withholding rates (which postponed payment of taxes without altering the amount of ultimate tax liability). With more money in their pockets, he hoped people would spend more, even though the day of reckoning was only postponed. This provided a clear test of the future-oriented theories. Disposable income was increased in 1992, but permanent income was not changed in any way. If the future-oriented theories were correct, there should have been no effect. In fact, there was a significant positive effect on consumption.

Second, government departments were required to increase the pace of their spending. Again, total spending (over the course of the year) would not be changed, but outlays would be made at a faster pace. This could give a temporary boost to the economy.

Many derided these actions as gimmicks, but they seemed to work—though not fast enough for the president. The economy had a strong fourth quarter in 1992, too late to have much effect on voters.

means that government efforts to stimulate the economy through temporary reductions in taxes—or to dampen an overheated economy through temporary increases in taxes—will be less effective than if the multiplier were larger.

Second, by identifying other determinants of consumption, future-oriented theories help explain why the ratio of consumption to disposable income may shift from year to year. Expectations concerning future economic conditions, changes in the availability of credit, or variations in the price of houses or shares of stock are among the factors that can give rise to such shifts in the consumption function. These shifts in turn give rise to larger variations in the equilibrium level of national output. Indeed, they help explain how a slight downturn in economic activity can become magnified. With a downturn, consumers may lose confidence in the future. They worry about layoffs, and cut back on purchases of durables. At the same time, banks, nervous about the ability of borrowers to repay loans should the downturn worsen, become more restrictive. Even those adventurous souls willing to buy a new car in the face of the uncertain future may find it difficult to find a bank willing to lend to them. The net effect is a downward shift in the consumption function, exacerbating the initial decline in national income.

DETERMINANTS OF CONSUMPTION

1. Keynesian consumption function: stresses the dependence of consumption on current disposable income
2. Future-oriented consumption theories: stress the dependence of consumption on total lifetime wealth and the role of savings in smoothing consumption
   a. Life-cycle theory: stresses the importance of savings for retirement
   b. Permanent income theory: stresses the role of savings in smoothing consumption between good and bad years
   c. Implications
      i. Consumption not very dependent on current income: small multipliers
      ii. Consumption sensitive to capital gains and losses
3. Explanations of why consumption seems to be more dependent on current income than future-oriented theories predict
   a. Durable goods
   b. Credit constraints

INVESTMENT

Variations in the level of investment are probably the principal cause of variations in aggregate expenditures, and hence in national output. Just how volatile investment is can be seen in Figure 10.5. In recent years, investment has varied from 13 to 18 percent of GDP.

The investment spending relevant for aggregate expenditures includes three broad categories. The first is firms' purchases of new capital goods, which includes, besides buildings and machines, the automobiles, cash registers, and desks that firms use. These make up the **plant and equipment** portion of overall investment. Firms also invest in **inventories** as they store their output in anticipation of sales or store the raw materials they will need to produce more goods. The third investment category consists of households' purchases of new homes. The purchases of previously owned capital goods or houses do not count, because they do not increase output. Households' financial investments such as stocks and bonds are a related but different concept. Usually when an individual buys, say, a share of stock, she buys it from someone else. She makes an investment, but someone else makes a "disinvestment." There is simply a change in who owns the economy's assets. There is, however, a close relationship between investment in new capital goods and the capital market in general: when firms issue new shares or borrow funds

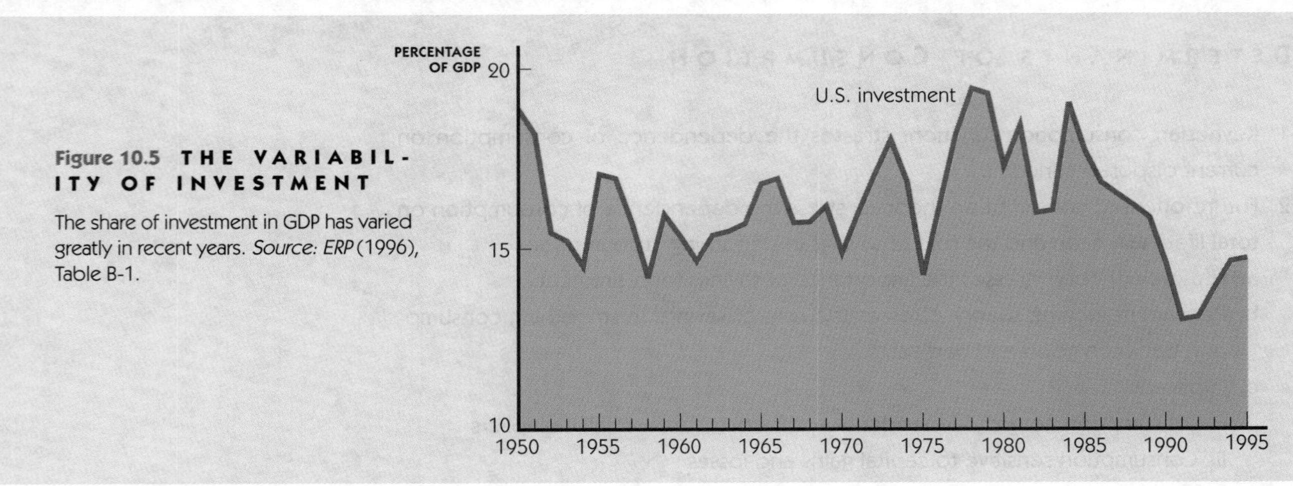

Figure 10.5 THE VARIABILITY OF INVESTMENT

The share of investment in GDP has varied greatly in recent years. *Source: ERP* (1996), Table B-1.

by issuing bonds, they procure the resources with which to purchase new capital goods. (In this way, financial investments and capital investments—with which we are concerned here—are closely linked.)

We restrict our focus in this discussion to business investment, which includes two of our three major investment categories: plant and equipment, and inventories. The third major investment category—consumers' demand for new housing—is best analyzed as a very long-lived durable good, using the principles governing the demand for durable goods developed earlier in this chapter.

Three questions concern us here. What determines the level of business investment? Why is it so variable? And how does government influence it? We direct these questions first to plant and equipment investment and then to inventory investment.

Investment in Plant and Equipment

To undertake an investment, firms must believe that the expected future returns will be large enough to compensate them for the risks of the investment. Moreover, firms are aware that a dollar in the future is worth less than a dollar today; if they have a dollar this year, they can put it in the bank and get back the dollar *with interest* next year. As the interest rate rises, future dollars are worth less relative to today's dollars. That means there will be fewer projects with future returns large enough to offset forgone interest. To put it another way, think of the firm as having to borrow the money for the investment project. Higher interest rates increase the cost of undertaking the project. Fewer projects will have a sufficiently high return to pay these higher interest costs. Thus, higher interest rates lead to lower levels of investment. The rela-

Close-up: The Corporate Veil

When firms have money left over after paying all their bills, they can either use the funds to pay dividends to stockholders or retain the earnings and invest them. Retained earnings, which can be thought of as a firm's savings, are more than triple the savings of households.

When a firm saves through retained earnings, the future profits of the firm should be higher as it begins to receive a return from this investment. Anticipation of these higher profits should raise the price of shares of stock in the firm, and shareholders should accordingly feel wealthier.

Strictly rational shareholders would treat the increased stock value due to retained earnings just as if they had saved the money themselves. Thus, they will incorporate this wealth gain into their *overall* savings decisions. But will they? Only if they are fully informed about and fully understand what happens inside the corporation—they see through the "corporate veil," as economists would say. Recent economic theories emphasize the consequences for the economy if shareholders have only blurry vision through the veil.

Much more than idle curiosity motivates this discussion. The extent to which people see through the veil affects the size of the multiplier—the factor by which an initial change in spending is transformed into a larger change in aggregate demand. Assume that firms increase their investment, but finance the additional investment with retained earnings, forgoing an increase in dividends. If people perceive only that their dividends have not increased—without fully realizing that the corporation is putting their money into productive investments—they may reduce their consumption and the total increase in aggregate demand resulting from the increase in investment will be much smaller than predicted by traditional Keynesian theory.

The Tax Reform Act of 1986 provided a test of the corporate veil theory. This act reduced taxes levied on individuals and increased taxes on corporations by a corresponding amount (roughly $120 billion over a five-year period). Those who believed people can see through the corporate veil argued that the increase in disposable income would have little effect, since people would realize that total tax burdens were unchanged. However, consumption did increase somewhat, implying that a corporate veil does exist.

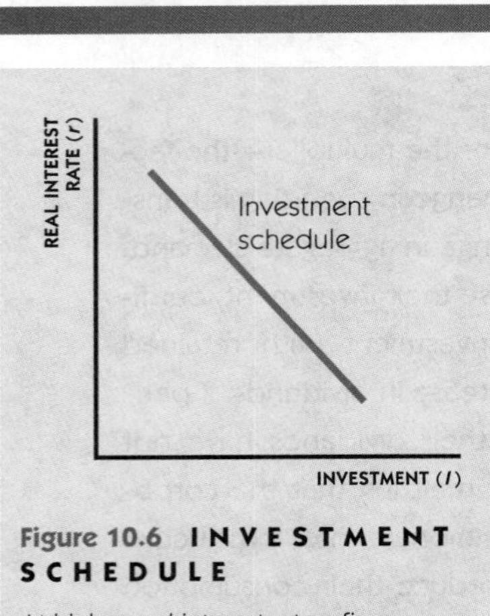

Figure 10.6 INVESTMENT SCHEDULE

At higher real interest rates, firms are willing to invest less.

tionship between interest rates and investment is the investment schedule introduced in Chapter 6, and is depicted as the downward-sloping curve in Figure 10.6. Of course, what matters for investment is the real interest rate, the cost of funds taking into account the effect of inflation. If the *nominal* interest rate increases but future prices increase in an offsetting way, firms' investment will be unaffected. (The real interest rate is the nominal interest rate minus the rate of inflation.) And, of course, what matters for long-term investments is the long-term real interest rate—over the period of the investment.

EXPECTATIONS AND RISK

Perhaps the hardest part of the firm's investment decision is predicting future returns. In some cases, there are **technological risks**—the firm may be using a new technology which could prove unreliable. In most cases, there are **market risks.** Will there be a market for the product? At what price will it sell? What wage will workers demand in the future? What will be the price of electricity and other inputs? The firm has no crystal ball: it has to make an educated guess, recognizing that there is uncertainty.

Typically, firms insist on being compensated for bearing risks. There are three major determinants of the amount that firms require to compensate them for bearing risks: the magnitude of the risks, their ability to share the risks, and their willingness to bear the risks. When the economy goes into a recession, typically firms perceive that the risks of investing are greater. The primary way that firms share risks is through the stock market. In companies whose share are widely held, large numbers of individuals share risks. When the stock market is booming, firms find it easy to issue new shares and thus to spread risks more widely. Finally, the ability and willingness of firms to bear risks depends on their own financial strength. If their net worth has been eroded by a series of losses, and if they have had to borrow to remain afloat, their ability and willingness to bear risks will be reduced.

THE ACCELERATOR

One of the most important determinants of expectations of returns to investment is future sales. When sales are up today, firms may expect future sales to be high, and perhaps even increasing. With high and increasing sales, firms will want to have more capital—that is, they want to invest more. Thus, an increase in government expenditures today not only gives rise to an even larger increase in output through the multiplier, but to a still larger increase, as the higher output generates more investment, which further stimulates the economy. The fact that increases in output beget further increases in output as a result of increased investment is referred to as the **accelerator.**

AVAILABILITY OF FUNDS

There is one more important determinant of investment. The analysis so far has assumed that firms can borrow funds, if they wish to, at the market rate of interest. Particularly in economic downturns, many firms *claim* they cannot borrow as much as they would like. When they cannot borrow, they must resort to **retained earnings**—their profits, less what they pay out to shareholders in dividends—to finance their investment.

For instance, in the 1992 economic downturn, many builders claimed that they could not obtain funds to continue their construction activities. Banks simply would not lend to them. At that time, many banks had been badly hurt by high defaults. With their capital eroded, they were less willing to bear the risks of lending. Even if they had wanted to, bankers said that bank regulators prohibited them from making many loans that had previously been made. However, some banks—and many economists—argued that the issue was not banks' unwillingness to make loans. The problem was a shortage of good borrowers, and an unwillingness of many borrowers to pay an interest rate commensurate with banks' perceptions of the riskiness of the loans.

In fact, most firms—even those that can easily borrow—finance most of their investments out of retained earnings. But even if they cannot borrow from banks, large firms have two other sources of funds—they can issue new shares on the stock market, or they can issue new bonds on the bond market. But typically, in an economic downturn, the stock market does not fare well, so that firms would have a hard time issuing new shares; current owners would have to give up a large share of their firm—more than they think it is worth—to raise a limited amount of funds. And the bond market is likely to be no more friendly, requiring what the borrower may feel is an exorbitant interest rate to compensate them for what they perceive as the high risk of lending in the midst of a recession. Thus, as a practical matter, particularly in an economic downturn, many firms view the availability of funds as a major constraint on their investment.

RECESSIONS

As the economy goes into a recession, typically the investment schedule shifts to the left, as depicted in Figure 10.7. Expectations of profits decrease, risks appear larger, the ability to share risks is decreased, and the ability and willingness to bear risks is reduced. Moreover, firms that are not able to borrow and have to use retained earnings to finance investment, have fewer funds available for investment. And banks—with their capital base eroded from higher defaults and with a perception of a greater risk of default for new loans—may be less willing to make loans. Under these circumstances, even large changes in (real) interest rates may be unable to generate much additional investment.

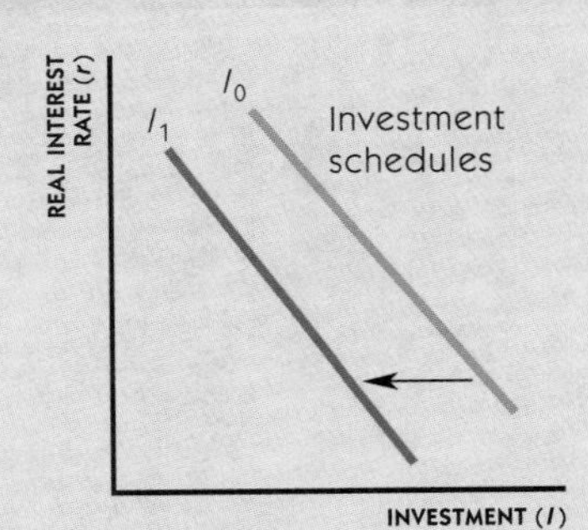

Figure 10.7 THE EFFECT OF A RECESSION ON INVESTMENT

As the economy enters a recession, expectations of profits decrease, the ability to share risks decreases, and the availability of financing decreases. This leads to a shift in the investment schedule to the left.

Why Investment May Be Low in Recessions

Low expectations of future profits

Banks unwilling to lend and low firm profits make it impossible for firms to finance investment projects

Perceptions of greater risk and lower ability to bear risk make banks less willing to lend and firms less willing to invest

USING ECONOMICS: OFFSETTING FISCAL CONTRACTION WITH LOWER INTEREST RATES

Upon assuming office in 1993, the Clinton administration faced two economic problems: reducing the deficit and stimulating the economy to lower the unemployment rate. It proposed a five-year $500 billion deficit reduction package, roughly divided evenly between tax increases and expenditure reductions. Assume it proposed lowering expenditures in 1993 by $50 billion and raising taxes by $50 billion. How much would interest rates have had to fall just to offset the contractionary effects of fiscal policy?

The tax increase was concentrated on the upper 2 percent of the population, whose marginal propensity to consume may be slightly lower than the average for the economy. If the marginal propensity to consume is .9, then fiscal policy would have reduced aggregate demand a total of $95 billion ($45 billion reduced consumption plus $50 billion reduced government expenditures).

It was estimated that a .1 percentage point reduction in interest rates would increase investment by $10 billion. Thus, long-term interest rates would have to fall by .95 percentage points just to offset fiscal policy.

Clinton tried to "backload" the deficit reduction: more of the expenditure cuts were imposed in later years, so that the fiscal drag on the economy in 1993 would be smaller. It was hoped that long-term interest rates would respond to the long-term commitment of credible deficit reduction. In fact, long-term interest rates fell by one percentage point from 7.3 to 6.3, and investment increased substantially.

Combined with increasing exports, aggregate demand increased sufficiently to reduce the unemployment rate from 7.3 percent at the end of 1992 to 6.4 percent at the end of 1993.

A LOOK AT THE DATA

There is considerable evidence that lowering interest rates does stimulate investment. Some kinds of investment—such as investment in housing—are viewed to be more interest sensitive than others (such as inventories, which we will discuss shortly). When, for instance, interest rates increased in late 1994, there was a quick reduction in the number of new housing starts. By the same token, when interest rates fell in early 1995, housing construction quickly picked up.

While interest rates are an important determinant of investment, they are not the only determinant: as we have seen, changes in expectations, perceptions of risk, and willingness to bear risk may all shift the investment schedule. Indeed, in certain periods of time, most of the variations in investment appear related to these other variables. Figure 10.8 illustrates this. Panel A shows investment and long-term real interest rates for 1954 through 1969; panel B shows the same for 1930 through 1995. Two observations emerge: there have been long periods of time (such as the 1950s and 1960s) when real interest rates varied little—from slightly below 2 percent to slightly below 3

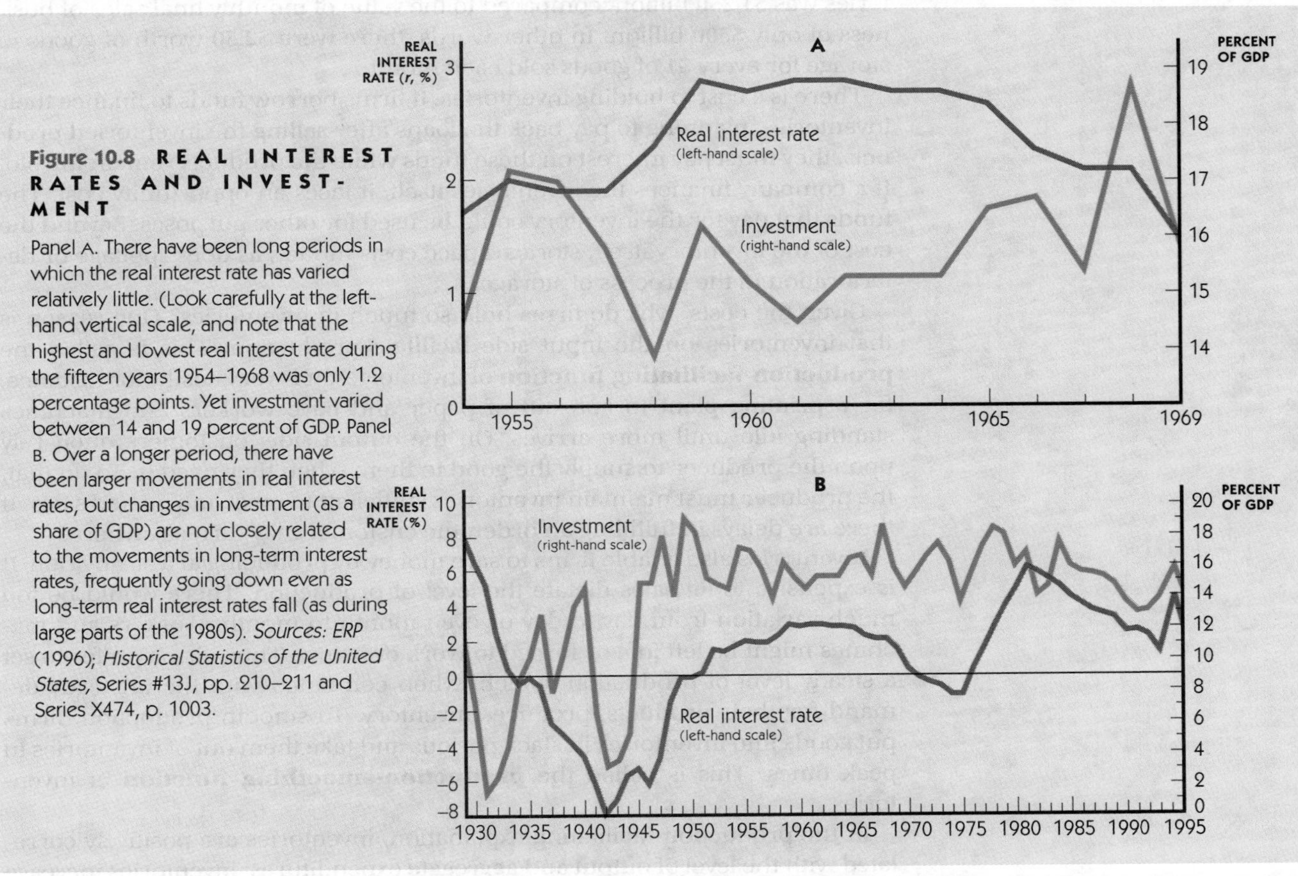

Figure 10.8 REAL INTEREST RATES AND INVESTMENT

Panel A. There have been long periods in which the real interest rate has varied relatively little. (Look carefully at the left-hand vertical scale, and note that the highest and lowest real interest rate during the fifteen years 1954–1968 was only 1.2 percentage points. Yet investment varied between 14 and 19 percent of GDP. Panel B. Over a longer period, there have been larger movements in real interest rates, but changes in investment (as a share of GDP) are not closely related to the movements in long-term interest rates, frequently going down even as long-term real interest rates fall (as during large parts of the 1980s). *Sources: ERP* (1996); *Historical Statistics of the United States*, Series #13J, pp. 210–211 and Series X474, p. 1003.

percent. Almost none of the volatility in investment in this period can be attributed to interest rate changes. In the early 1980s, real interest rates were substantially higher than in the 1960s, yet investment (relative to GDP) was not substantially lower.

We now know why investment in plant and equipment can be volatile: changes in expectations, availability of funds, a firm's net worth, as well as interest rates can affect investment. Indeed, Keynes thought firms' investment decisions were so unpredictable as to be based on "animal spirits."

INVENTORY INVESTMENT

One of the most volatile components of investment are inventories—the materials that are held in storage either awaiting use in production or for sale to customers.

Inventories are typically very large. In 1995, for example, the value of inventories was $1,250 billion, compared to the value of monthly final sales of business of only $500 billion. In other words, there were $2.50 worth of goods in storage for every $1 of goods sold each month.

There is a cost to holding inventories. If firms borrow funds to finance their inventories, planning to pay back the loans after selling the inventoried products, they must pay interest on these funds while the products remain unsold. If a company finances the inventories itself, it faces an opportunity cost. The funds that pay for the inventory could be used for other purposes. Beyond the cost of the inventory itself, storage space costs money, as does spoilage or deterioration in the process of storage.

Given the costs, why do firms hold so much in inventories? One reason is that inventories on the input side facilitate production. This is called the **production-facilitating function** of inventories. It is very costly, for instance, for a printing plant to run out of paper and have workers and machines standing idle until more arrives. On the output side, customers often rely upon the producer to supply the good to them when they need it. To do that, the producer must maintain inventories sufficient to meet anticipated sales. If there are delays in fulfilling an order, the customer may turn elsewhere.

Inventories also enable firms to save money by producing at a steady rate. It is expensive to let sales dictate the level of production. There would be too much variation from day to day or even month to month. Workers and machines might be left idle or forced to work overtime. Thus, firms prefer to set a steady level of production, which, when combined with the unsteady demand for their products, produces inventory. To smooth production, firms put goods into inventories in slack periods and take them out of inventories in peak times. This is called the **production-smoothing function** of inventories.

In the production-facilitating explanation, inventories are positively correlated with the level of output and aggregate expenditures: inventories increase when the level of output is high. In the production-smoothing explanation, inventories are negatively correlated with aggregate expenditures: they go up when expenditures go down. This pattern would seem to suggest that inventories reduce fluctuations in national output, by allowing firms to keep an even level of production.

In fact, however, rather than serving to dampen business fluctuations, inventories seem to exacerbate them. Inventories vary far more than output, and as was mentioned earlier, they seem to be a major contributing factor to fluctuations in aggregate expenditures. This is true even for inventories of consumer goods, which should serve a particularly smoothing role.

One reason for the variability of investment in inventories may again be the risk-averse behavior of firms and the availability of credit. When the economy enters a recession, firms often find that their net worth is decreased. They are less willing to make any kind of investment, including inventory investment. Where possible, they would like to "disinvest," or convert their assets back into cash. By far, the easiest kind of disinvestment is to sell off inventories. When a business faces credit rationing, it may be forced to sell its inventories to raise the requisite capital. And even if it is not yet forced to sell off its inventories, it

CLOSE-UP: JUST-IN-TIME INVENTORY MANAGEMENT

Simmons is the firm that makes the well-known "Beautyrest" mattress. But in the mid-1980s, the company was anything but relaxed. Its costs were high enough to threaten its financial stability. It was operating a network of 19 manufacturing facilities and 67 warehouses, linked together by 128 truck tractors and 250 trailers. The company's freight bill alone was 6 percent of total sales, and inventory costs were high. The solution? A "just-in-time" manufacturing system. Simmons would only produce *after* receiving an order.

Simmons reorganized the company to eliminate all its warehouses, five of its plants, and 43 of its trucks.

The Simmons plan was based on the just-in-time inventory system pioneered by Toyota in 1972. The idea was to hold inventories to a bare minimum by providing inputs only when they were immediately needed. The system spread throughout Japanese industry during the rest of the 1970s. During the 1980s, it was adopted in the United States, with big companies like General Motors, IBM, Hewlett-Packard, General Electric, and Black and Decker among those who tried it first.

Besides saving on the costs of carrying inventory, just-in-time systems help companies modernize in other ways. *The Economist* magazine described it this way: "A favorite analogy is with water in a river. When the level of water falls, rocks start to appear. The rocks can be removed rather than hit." In other words, carrying big inventories can allow a company to cover up a variety of other organizational problems. Thinking about how to cut inventories can be a powerful tool for overall efficiency.

The widespread adoption of just-in-time systems may have significant effects on macroeconomic stability. For instance, within two weeks of the beginning of a strike at two GM brake plants in March 1995, GM's entire production was brought to a halt: there were no inventories of brakes, and without brakes, no cars could be constructed. More than 200,000 workers were laid off.

At the same time, the overall stability of the economy may be enhanced. Under standard systems with large inventories, when sales dip, a business may cut down purchases and production drastically while inventories are depleted. A business with just-in-time inventories will reduce purchases only a little, and will cut production just by the amount of the reduction in sales.

Sources: The Economist, April 25, 1987, p. 68; Richard J. Schonberger, "The Transfer of Japanese Manufacturing Management Approaches to U.S. Industry," *Academy of Management Review* (1982) 7:479–87; "Bringing JIT's Benefits to the Bottom Line," *Traffic Management* (November 1991), p. 57.

may fear future credit rationing and, in anticipation, seek to reduce its inventories.

UNINTENDED INVENTORY ACCUMULATIONS

Often, as the economy goes into a recession, inventories build up "involuntarily." Retail stores, for instance, make orders based on expected sales; if the sales fail to materialize, the store holds the unsold merchandise as "inventories." This unintended inventory accumulation can feed back quickly into production, as stores reduce their factory orders in response to their larger than desired inventories. Lower orders lead quickly to a cutback in production. The cutbacks in production as firms try to restore inventories to normal size relative to sales are referred to as "inventory corrections." Cyclical variability induced by inventories are called inventory cycles.

POLICIES TO STIMULATE INVESTMENT

While the government cannot control all of the determinants of investment, it has a variety of instruments that may affect it. If the business community is convinced of the government's commitment to economic stability, businesses may perceive less risk and be more willing to invest. But predicting, let alone controlling, the psychology of business executives is at best a tricky business.

The government can change the tax code to make investment more attractive. It can, for instance, provide an **investment tax credit.** With an investment tax credit, a fraction (say 6 percent) of the amount spent on investment is deductible from the tax bill. It is *as if* the government were paying 6 percent of the cost of the machine (for corporations and individuals who have sufficiently large tax liabilities). Temporary tax changes can be particularly effective; a temporary tax credit has the same effect as a sale: a firm that buys a machine during the period of the temporary tax credit saves money, just as it would if the firm temporarily lowered its price. The effects of such temporary tax changes are more predictable than the effects of policies aimed at changing the psychological climate. But temporary tax changes are a cumbersome tool, requiring action by Congress and the president. Temporary tax changes may also distort how resources are allocated, though the macroeconomic gains—in higher levels of output—may well be worth the microeconomic losses from these distortions.

For the most part, however, the government relies on monetary policy, which affects both the availability of credit and the terms on which firms can borrow. Firms raise funds through the capital market. How and when the government, through monetary authorities, affects the capital market (interest rates and availability of credit) are important, complex questions that we will explore in the next three chapters. For now, it is worth noting once again the interrelationships among all the pieces of the macroeconomic puzzle. What goes on in the product market (the determination of the equilibrium level of output) affects the labor market (the level of unemployment in the economy), and what goes on in the capital market (interest rates and the availability of credit) affects investment and thus the product market.

WAYS OF STIMULATING INVESTMENT

1. Increasing business confidence: government demonstrating a commitment to maintaining high levels of employment and output
2. Lowering the cost of investment: subsidies to investment through the tax system
3. Increasing the availability of credit or making it available on more attractive terms (monetary policy)

REVIEW AND PRACTICE

SUMMARY

1. The Keynesian consumption function stresses the importance of current disposable income in determining consumption. In contrast, future-oriented consumption theories focus on an individual's total wealth, including what he will receive as income over his entire life; savings serves to smooth consumption. Thus, the life-cycle hypothesis says that people save during their life so that they can spend after retirement. The permanent income hypothesis argues that people save in good years to offset the bad years.

2. In the traditional (Keynesian) consumption function, the government could manipulate this year's consumption by changing this year's tax rate. In the future-oriented theories, temporary tax reductions would have a limited effect in stimulating consumption, since people are considering a longer horizon than this year for their consumption decisions.

3. Both the life-cycle and permanent income models predict that consumption will depend on lifetime wealth, and that changes in wealth (including capital gains) will therefore affect consumption.

4. Household consumption appears to be more dependent on current income than either the life-cycle or permanent income theory suggests. Consumers can easily postpone the purchase of durables when current income falls. Also, limitations on their ability to borrow (credit rationing) may keep the consumption of many people with little savings close to their current income.

5. Future-oriented theories of consumption suggest that the aggregate expenditures schedule is flat and the multiplier is low.

6. Variations in the level of investment are probably the principal reason for variations in total aggregate expenditures. The three main categories of investment are firms' purchases of plant and equipment, firms' increase or decrease of inventories, and households' purchases of new homes.

7. While investment depends on the real rate of interest, historically, much if not most of the variation in investment is attributed to other factors, such as changes in expectations, perceptions of risk, and willingness and ability to bear risk, all of which shift the investment schedule.

8. As income increases, investment tends to increase, partly because expectations of future sales increases, partly because as GDP increases, profits increase, increasing the availability of funds for investment. The relationship between income and investment is called the accelerator.

9. Most firms finance most of their investment out of retained earnings. When firms cannot borrow, or raise money in the stock market—or can do so only at very unattractive terms—firms may perceive lack of availability of funds as limiting their investment.

10. Investment is low in a recession because of low expectations of future profits, an unwillingness of banks to lend, a lack of profits, which makes it impossible for firms to finance investment projects on their own, and perceptions of greater risk and a lower ability to bear risk, which make banks less willing to lend and firms less willing to invest.

11. Inventories both serve to facilitate production and smooth production. Variations in inventory accumulation contribute to the economy's fluctuations; a slight unanticipated downturn in the economy leads to unintended inventory accumulation, and as firms cut back orders to reverse this unintended inventory accumulation, output falls.

12. Government can stimulate investment by increasing business confidence, especially through a demonstrated commitment to maintain the economy at high levels of employment and output, by subsidizing investment through the tax system, and by lowering interest rates and increasing the availability of credit.

KEY TERMS

life-cycle savings
permanent income hypothesis
durable goods
accelerator
retained earnings
production-facilitating function
production-smoothing function
investment tax credit (ITC)

REVIEW QUESTIONS

1. What is the difference between the Keynesian model of consumption, the life-cycle model, and the permanent income model?

2. Why do the life-cycle and permanent income hypotheses predict that temporary tax changes will have little effect on current consumption?

3. What factors affect consumer expenditures on durables? Why are these expenditures so volatile?

4. How will the existence of credit rationing make consumption more dependent on current income than the future-oriented consumption theories would suggest?

5. What are the principle forms of investment? Why does the level of investment depend on the real interest rate? What are other important determinants of the level of investment in plant and equipment? Historically, what role have these various determinants played in variations in the level of investment?

6. What is the accelerator, what gives rise to it, and what are its consequences?

7. What are the possible sources of funds for firms that wish to invest? Why might availability of funds play an important role in investment?

8. Why does investment tend to fall in a recession?

9. Why do firms hold inventories? What are the costs and benefits of holding inventories? What are unintended inventory accumulations, and what role do they play? Why might inventory investment be as volatile as it is?

10. How can government stimulate investment?

PROBLEMS

1. Under which theory of consumption would a temporary tax cut have the largest effect on consumption? Under which theory would a permanent rise in Social Security benefits have the largest effect on consumption? Under which theory would permanently higher unemployment insurance benefits have the largest effect on consumption? Explain.

2. Which theory of consumption predicts that aggregate savings will depend on the proportion of retired and young people in the population? What is the relationship? Which theories predict that consumption will not vary a great deal according to whether the economy is in a boom or recession? Why?

3. If the government made it easier for people to borrow money, perhaps by enacting programs to help them get loans, would you expect consumption behavior to become more or less sensitive to current income? Why?

4. How would you predict that a crash in the stock market would affect the relationship between consumption and income? How would you predict that rapidly rising prices for homes would affect the relationship between consumption and income? Draw shifts in the consumption function to illustrate. How do your predictions differ depending on whether the consumer is a Keynesian, life-cycle, or permanent income consumer?

5. A company that expects the long-term real interest rate to be 3 percent is considering a list of projects. Each project costs $10,000, but they vary in the amount of time they will take to pay off, and in how much they will pay off. The first will pay $12,000 in two years; the second, $12,500 in three years; the third, $13,000 in four years. Which projects are worth doing? If the expected interest rate was 5 percent, does your answer change? You may assume that prices are stable.

6. Take the projects in problem 5 and reevaluate them, this time assuming that inflation is at 4 percent per year and the payoffs are in nominal dollars at the time they occur. Are the projects still worth doing?

7. Draw a diagram to show how investment is affected in each of the following situations.
   (a) The government passes an investment tax credit.
   (b) Businesses believe the economic future looks healthier than they had previously thought.
   (c) The government reduces the real interest rate.

8. Imagine that the government raises personal income taxes, but also enacts an investment tax credit for a corresponding amount. Describe under what circumstances this combination of policies would be most effective in stimulating aggregate demand. Consider differing theories of consumption, and the choice between permanent and temporary changes in the tax code.

9. Explain how purchasing a durable good is like an investment. How might an increase in the interest rate or a change in credit availability affect the demand for durables?

10. Explain why if most inventories were held for reasons of production smoothing, inventory accumulation would actually serve to stabilize the economy. Why do economists focus on movements in inventories of consumption goods to argue that there are important factors other than production smoothing that determine patterns of inventory holding? What is one possible explanation of the observed pattern?

Why would you expect the desired level of inventory holdings to increase with the level of output? Explain why this accelerator relationship might contribute to economic instability. How would you expect changes in the rate of interest, changes in the costs of storage, and innovations in inventory management techniques to affect the desired inventory-sales ratio?

APPENDIX: THE INVESTMENT-SAVINGS IDENTITY

We typically think of savings and investment together. Both are virtues: "A penny saved is a penny earned." Increased investment enhances the future productivity of the economy. It has frequently been suggested that Americans should encourage savings, the presumption being that savings are automatically converted into investment.

When a *closed* economy is operating along its production possibilities curve, with all resources fully utilized, increased savings—reduced consumption—mean that more capital goods can be produced. Then savings and investment will move together. But when the economy is operating below its production possibilities curve, increased savings—reduced consumption—may simply push the economy further below that curve.

In *open* economies, savings and investment do not have to change together even when the economy is on its production possibilities curve. This is because the economy can undertake investment, even when there is little domestic saving, by borrowing from abroad.

The income-expenditure analysis of Chapter 9 focused on the relationship between aggregate expenditures and income. Equilibrium occurs when aggregate expenditures equal national income. An alternative way of describing how national output is determined focuses on savings and investment. We look at a simple model first, in which disposable income equals national income. For this to be the case, we assume that taxes are zero and all of a firm's profits are paid out as dividends. To simplify further, we assume there are no government savings or dissavings, or any flow of funds from abroad. Later we will loosen up these assumptions to get a fuller picture.

By definition individuals can either spend their income today or save:

$$\text{income} = \text{consumption} + \text{savings}. \tag{10.1}$$

With no government purchases or net exports, we know from the components of aggregate expenditures that firms can produce only two kinds of goods: consumer goods and investment goods. Thus, output, Y, can be broken into its two components:

$$Y = \text{consumption} + \text{investment}. \tag{10.2}$$

These two identities can be combined to form a new one. Since the value of national output equals national income,

$$Y = \text{income}, \tag{10.3}$$

we can use the right-hand side of (10.1) and (10.2) to get

$$\text{consumption} + \text{savings} = \text{consumption} + \text{investment}. \quad (10.4)$$

Subtracting consumption from both sides of the equation yields

$$\text{savings} = \text{investment}. \quad (10.5)$$

One way to understand this identity is to think of firms as producing a certain amount of goods, the value of which is just equal to the income of the individuals in the economy (because everything firms take in they pay out as income to someone). The income that is not consumed is, by definition, saved. On the output side, firms either sell the goods they produce or put them into inventory for sale in future years. Some of the inventory buildup is planned, because businesses need inventories to survive. Some of it is unplanned—businesses may be surprised by an economic downturn that spoils their sales projections. Both intended and unintended inventory buildups are considered investment. Thus, the goods that are not consumed are, by definition, invested.

This identity (10.5) can be transformed into an equation determining national output, once it is recognized that in equilibrium firms will cut back production if there is unintended inventory accumulation. Because firms will cut back, in equilibrium the amount companies invest is the amount they wish to invest (including inventories), given current market conditions. The equilibrium condition, then, is that

$$\text{investment} = \text{desired investment}. \quad (10.6)$$

Now switch over to the savings side of the identity (10.5). The consumption function presented earlier tells how much people wish to consume at each level of income. But since what is not consumed is saved, the consumption function can be transformed into a savings function, giving the level of savings at each level of income. Savings is income minus consumption:

$$\text{savings} = \text{income } (Y) - \text{consumption}. \quad (10.7)$$

Figure 10.9 shows the savings function. The slope of this curve, the amount by which savings increase with income, is the marginal propensity to save, which is 1 minus the marginal propensity to consume.

Since savings must equal investment, and in equilibrium investment must equal desired investment, then in equilibrium

$$\text{savings} = \text{desired investment}. \quad (10.8)$$

The figure shows a fixed level of desired investment, I_1. Desired investment is horizontal because investment is assumed to be unaffected by the level of income. Equilibrium occurs at the intersection of the desired investment curve and the savings curve, point E.

Figure 10.9 THE SAVINGS FUNCTION AND NATIONAL INCOME

As income increases, the amount individuals desire to save increases. The amount by which savings increase as the result of a $1 increase in income—the slope of the savings function—is called the marginal propensity to save. In equilibrium, savings equal desired investment. Thus, equilibrium occurs at the intersection of the savings function and the level of investment.

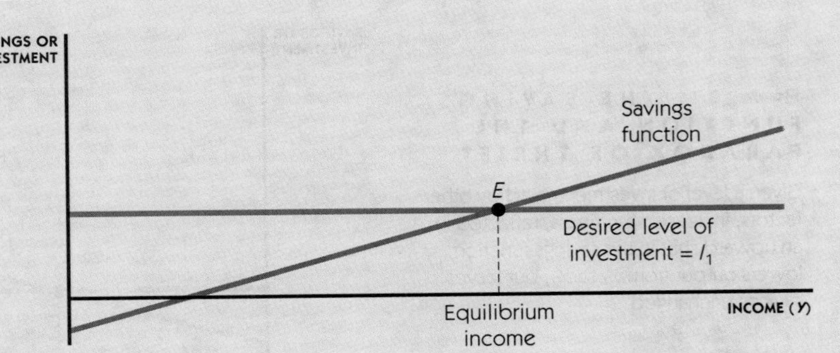

As with income-expenditure analysis, savings-investment analysis shows how an increase in investment leads to an increase in output that is a multiple of itself. Figure 10.10 shows that as investment shifts up from I_1 to I_2, the equilibrium shifts from E_1 to E_2, and output increases from Y_1 to Y_2. The change in output is again larger than the change in investment, ΔI. This should not surprise us, since income-expenditure analysis and savings-investment analysis are two ways of looking at the same thing.

The Paradox of Thrift We can use a similar diagram to illustrate what may seem a paradoxical result. When the economy's resources are not fully employed, an increase in thrift—the level of savings at each level of income—may have no effect at all on the equilibrium level of savings or investment. The

Figure 10.10 USING THE SAVINGS-INVESTMENT DIAGRAM

A shift in investment from I_1 to I_2 leads to an increase in output from Y_1 to Y_2; the increase in output is a multiple of the original increase in investment.

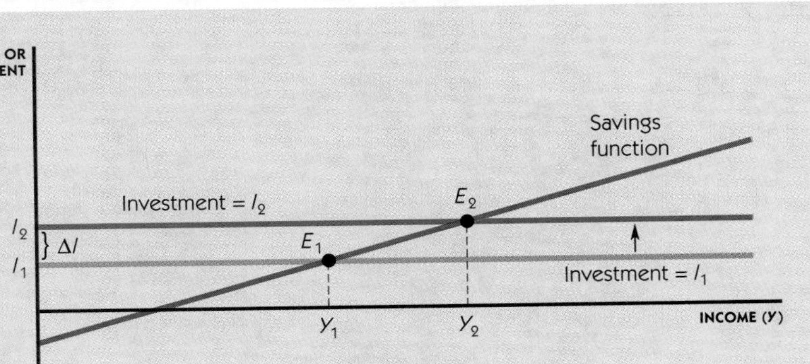

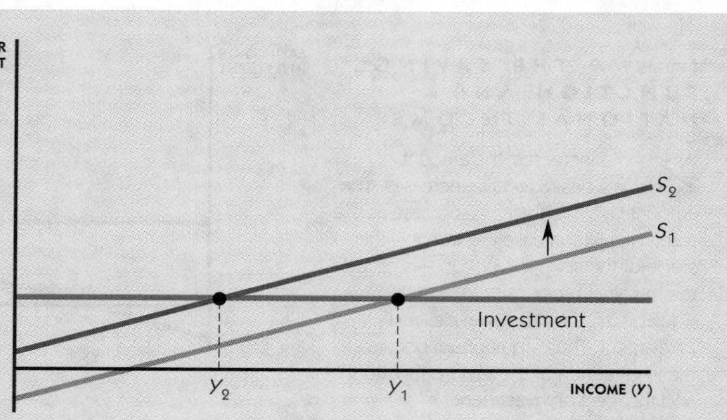

Figure 10.11 THE SAVINGS FUNCTION AND THE PARADOX OF THRIFT

Given a level of investment fixed by other factors, increased thriftiness, reflected in an upward shift in the savings function, lowers output from Y_1 to Y_2, but leaves savings unchanged.

only effect of greater thrift is to lower national income and output. Figure 10.11 shows the effect of an upward shift in the savings function—at each level of income, savings are higher. But in equilibrium, savings equal investment. With investment fixed, savings, in equilibrium, must also be fixed. To attain that level of savings (equal to the level of investment), income must be lowered from Y_1 to Y_2.

CHAPTER 11

Money, Banking, and Credit

Some say money is the root of all evil. Some say money makes the world go 'round. Actually, money does not *do* anything, in and of itself. Part of the economy is made up of real people working with real machines to make goods that satisfy needs directly. Money for the most part is just paper and a ledger mark in a bank account. It satisfies needs only indirectly, when it is spent.

In Chapter 6 we encountered the principle of money neutrality. At full employment, an increase in the money supply only leads to a proportionate increase in prices and wages, with no real consequences. Yet controlling the supply of money is considered such an important function of government that failure to exercise that control properly has been blamed not only for inflations, but also for depressions. In the short run, the economy may deviate significantly from full employment, and under such conditions monetary policy may affect output and employment substantially.

We have emphasized that all markets are interlinked. Fluctuations in aggregate output cause fluctuations in employment. Changes in aggregate output can be traced to changes in the level of aggregate demand, which in turn can be related to changes in the level of investment. Investment depends on interest rates and other aspects of the capital market.

So it is to the capital market that we now turn. We will see in this and the next two chapters how government can—through monetary policy—affect interest rates and the availability of credit, and thus the level of investment in

Key Questions

1. What *is* money? What economic functions does it serve?
2. What is meant by the money supply, and how is it measured?
3. What institutions in our economy are responsible for controlling the money supply and determining monetary policy?
4. How do modern economies create money through the banking system? How do monetary authorities affect the creation of money and the availability of credit? How do they, in other words, affect the supply of money and credit?

the short term. This chapter will explain what money is, what it does, and why it is so important. The following two chapters will show how, why, and when monetary policy affects the level of economic activity.

Money Is What Money Does

We use the term "money" to mean much more than just currency and coins. When someone asks how much money you make, he means what is your income. When someone says, "He has a lot of money," she means he is wealthy, not that he has stashed away lots of currency. When someone accuses corporations of being "interested only in making money," she means they are interested only in making profits.

Economists define money by the functions it serves, and we must look at these functions before we can develop a formal definition of money.

Money as a Medium of Exchange

Money's first function is to facilitate trade—the exchange of goods or services for mutual benefit. This is called the **medium of exchange** function of money. Trade that occurs without money is called **barter.** Barter involves a direct exchange of one good or service for another. Two families agree to take turns baby-sitting for each other, or a doctor and a lawyer agree to trade consultations. Nations sometimes sign treaties phrased in barter terms. A certain amount of oil, for example, might be traded for a certain amount of machinery or weapons.

Barter works best in simple economies. One can imagine an old-style farmer bartering with the blacksmith, the tailor, the grocer, and the doctor in his small town. For simple barter to work, however, there must be a **double-coincidence of wants.** That is, one individual must have what the other wants, and vice versa. Henry has potatoes and wants shoes, Joshua has an extra pair of shoes and wants potatoes. Bartering can make them both happier. But if Henry has firewood and Joshua does not need any of that, then bartering for Joshua's shoes requires one or both of them to go searching for more people in the hope of making a multilateral exchange. Money provides a way to make multilateral exchange much simpler. Henry sells his firewood to someone else for money and uses the money to buy Joshua's shoes. The convenience of money becomes even clearer when one considers the billions of exchanges that take place in a modern economy.

Any easily transportable and storable good can, in principle, be used as a medium of exchange. And a wide variety of items have served that function. Indeed, the item chosen as "money" can be thought of as a social convention. The reason you accept money in payment for what you sell is that others will accept it for things you want to buy. Different cultures in different times have used all sorts of items as money. American Indians used wampum, South Sea Islanders used cowrie shells. In World War II prisoner-of-war camps and in many prisons of today, cigarettes serve as a medium of exchange.

For a long time, gold was the major medium of exchange. However, the value of a gold coin depends on its weight and purity, as well as on the supply and demand for gold in the gold market. It would be expensive to weigh and verify the quality of gold every time you engaged in a transaction. So one of the functions of governments, right up until the twentieth century, was to mint gold coins, certifying their weight and quality. But because gold is soft, it wears thin with use. Criminals have also profited by shaving the edges off gold coins. The ridges on U.S. dimes and quarters are a carryover from coins developed to deter this practice.

Today all the developed countries of the world use paper (printed by the government specially for this purpose) as well as metal coins for currency. However, most business transactions use not currency but checks drawn on banks, credit cards whose balances are paid with checks, or funds wired from one bank to another. Economists consider checking account balances to be money, just as currency is, because they are accepted as payment at most places and thus serve the medium of exchange function. Since most people have much more money in their checking accounts than they do in their wallets, it should be evident that the economists' measure of the money supply is much larger than the amount of coins and other currency in circulation.

Money as a Store of Value

People will only be willing to exchange what they have for money if they believe they can later exchange the money for the goods or services they want. Thus, for money to serve its role as a medium of exchange, it must hold its value, at least for a short while. This function is known as the **store of value** function of money. There was a time when governments feared that paper money by itself would not be accepted in the future and so paper money was not as good a store of value as gold. People had confidence in paper dollars only because they were backed by gold (if you wished, you used to be able to exchange your paper dollars for gold).

Today, however, all major economies have **fiat money**—money that has value only because the government says it has value and because people are willing to accept it in exchange for goods. The dollar bill in your pocket recognizes this need for security with its message: "This note is legal tender for all debts, public and private." The fact that it is legal tender means that if you owe someone $100, you have fully discharged that debt if you give her a hundred-dollar bill.

There are many other stores of value. Gold, which is no longer "money" because it no longer serves as a medium of exchange, nevertheless continues to serve as a store of value. In India, for instance, people hold much of their savings in the form of gold. Land, corporate stocks and bonds, oil and minerals—all are stores of value. None of them is perfectly safe, in the sense that you cannot be precisely sure what they can be exchanged for in the future. But currency, checking account balances, and other forms of money are not a perfectly safe store of value either. If prices change, then what you can buy with the dollars in your pocket or bank account will change.

MONEY AS A UNIT OF ACCOUNT

In performing its roles as a medium of exchange and a store of value, money serves a third purpose. It is a way of measuring the relative values of different goods. This is the **unit of account** function of money. If a banana costs 25 cents and a peach 50 cents, then a peach is worth twice as much as a banana. A person who wishes to trade bananas for peaches can do so at the rate of two bananas for one peach. Money thus provides a simple and convenient yardstick for measuring relative market values.

Imagine how difficult it would be for firms to keep track of how well they were doing without such a yardstick. The ledgers might describe how many of each item the firm bought or sold. But the fact that the firm sold more items than it purchased would tell you nothing about how well that firm was doing. You need to know the value of what the firm sells relative to the value of what it purchases. Money provides the unit of account, the means by which the firm and others take these measurements.

We are now ready for the economic definition of **money.** Money is anything that is generally accepted as a medium of exchange, a store of value, and a unit of account. Money is, in other words, what money does.

MEASURING THE MONEY SUPPLY

The quantity of money is called the **money supply,** a stock variable like the capital stock. Most of the other variables discussed in this chapter are stock variables as well, but they have important effects on the flow variables (like the level of economic activity, measured as dollars *per year*).

Close-up: When Atlanta Printed Money

In the nineteenth and early twentieth centuries, in the rural South and West, there was often a shortage of cash for everyday transactions. Workers could not shop for food or clothing, bills were not paid, and the local economy lurched sideways or backward.

It was common in such cases for towns, private companies, and sometimes states to print their own currency, known politely as "scrip" and less politely as "soap wrappers," "shinplasters," "doololly," and many less printable names. The idea was that issuing scrip could keep the local economy going until official currency became available again, at which point people could cash in their scrip.

The last major issue of scrip in the United States came during the Great Depression of the early 1930s. Banks were crashing right and left, and bank runs were a daily occurrence. Remember, these were the days before deposits were insured. When President Franklin Roosevelt took office early in 1933, one of his first major actions was to declare a "bank holiday" for the week of March 6–12. He closed all the banks for a week to give everyone time to relax and get their bearings.

But these were also the days before checking accounts had become widespread, when workers were paid weekly, in cash. If firms could not get to the bank, they could not pay their workers. How could the local economy react to these sorts of financial disturbances?

Each area adapted in its own way. Let's consider Atlanta. The city issued about $2.5 million in scrip, in eight different issues made during the first half of the 1930s. One of the first payments was to schoolteachers, and the city made sure that Rich's, a prominent local department store, would take the scrip at full face value. Many other stores, however, would count the scrip only at 75 percent or less of face value. Notice that by taking scrip, which it would later turn in to the city for cash, stores were effectively loaning money to the city that issued the scrip.

Such stories of scrip may sound antiquated today (though in its 1992 financial crisis, California

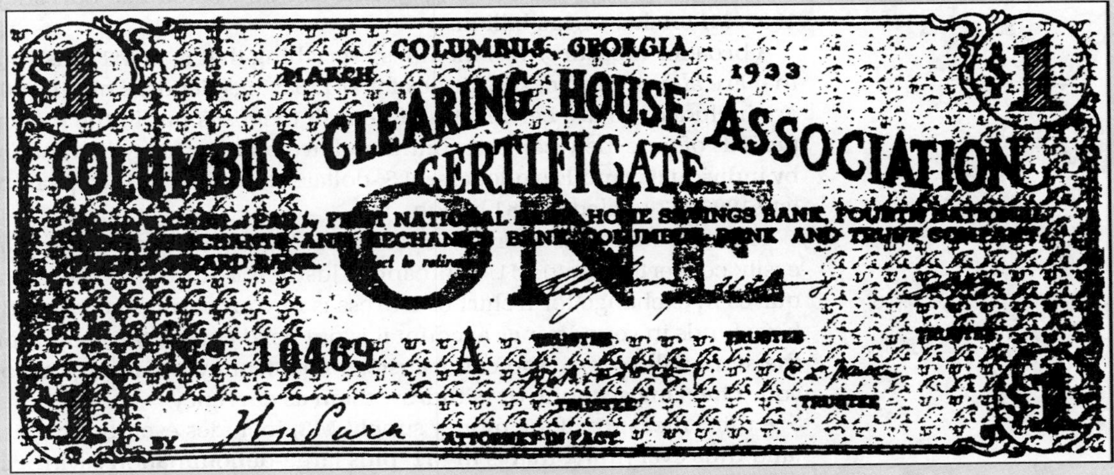

paid its workers with something akin to scrip). But they emphasize the fact that without something to serve as a medium of exchange, a yardstick for measurement, and a (short-term) store of value, an economy simply cannot function. Today the Federal Reserve acts to ensure that currency is available. But in the 1930s, issuing scrip was one thing a city could do on its own to cushion the ravages of the Great Depression.

Source: William Roberds, "Lenders of the Next-to-Last Resort: Scrip Issue in Georgia During the Great Depression," *Economic Review of the Federal Reserve Bank of Atlanta* (September–October 1990), pp. 16–30.

What exactly should be included in the money supply? A variety of items serve some of the functions of money, but not all of them. For example, the chips issued in casinos for gambling serve as a medium of exchange inside the casino and perhaps even in some nearby stores and restaurants. But no place outside the casino is obligated to take them; they are neither a generally accepted medium of exchange nor a unit of account.

The economists' measure of money begins with the currency and coins that we carry around. Economists then expand the measure of money to include other items that serve the three functions of money. Checking accounts, or **demand deposits** (so called because you can get your money back upon demand), are included in the money supply, as are some other forms of bank accounts. But what are the limits? There is a continuum here, running from items that everyone would agree should be called money to items that can work as money in many circumstances, to items that can occasionally work as money, to items that would never be considered money.

Economists have developed several measures of the money supply to take account of this variety. The narrowest, called **M1,** is the total of currency, traveler's checks, and checking accounts. In other words, M1 is currency plus items that through the banking system can be treated like currency. In late 1995, MI totaled $1,123 billion.

A broader measure, **M2,** includes everything that is in M1 plus some items that are *almost* perfect substitutes for M1. Savings deposits of $100,000 or less are included. So are certificates of deposit (deposits put in the bank for fixed periods of time, between six months and five years); money market funds held by individuals; and Eurodollars, U.S. dollars deposited in European banks. In late 1995 M2 totaled $3,781 billion.

The common characteristic of assets in M2 is that they are very *liquid,* or easily convertible into M1. You cannot just tell a store that the money it requires in exchange for a shirt or a dress is in your savings account. But if you have funds in your savings account it is not hard to turn those into something the store will accept. You can transfer funds from your savings account into your checking account, or withdraw them as currency.

A third measure of the money supply, **M3,** includes everything that is in M2 (and thus everything that is in M1) plus large-denomination savings accounts (over $100,000) and institutional money market mutual funds. M3 is just about as liquid as M2. In late 1995, M3 totaled $4,564 billion.

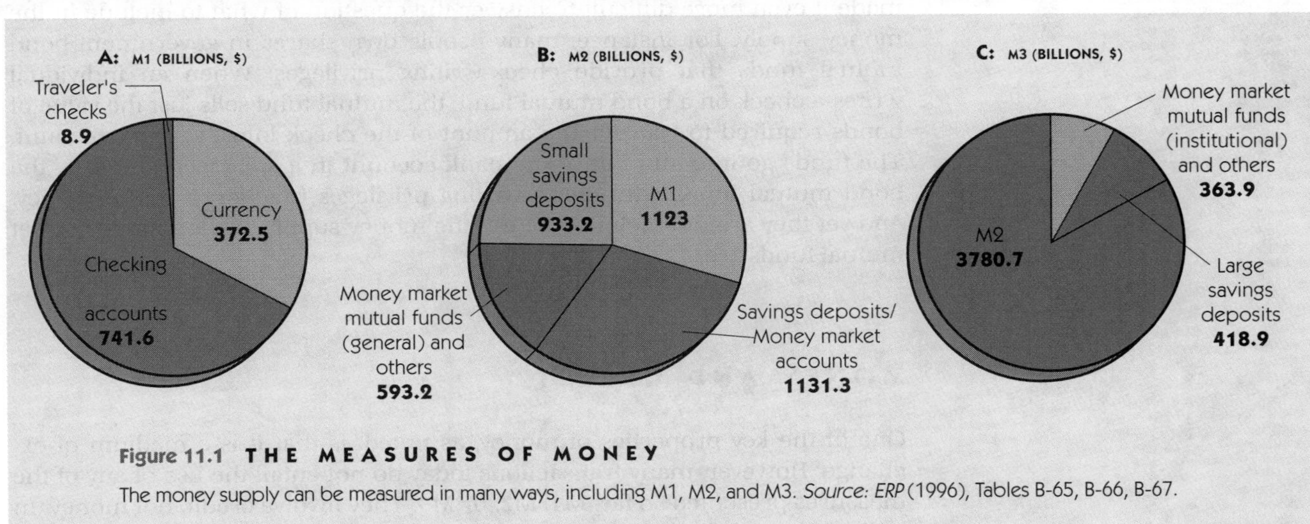

Figure 11.1 THE MEASURES OF MONEY
The money supply can be measured in many ways, including M1, M2, and M3. *Source: ERP* (1996), Tables B-65, B-66, B-67.

Figure 11.1 shows the relative magnitude of these three different measures of the money supply. Figure 11.2 shows that the different measures grow at different rates.

Recent changes in financial institutions—such as the growth of mutual

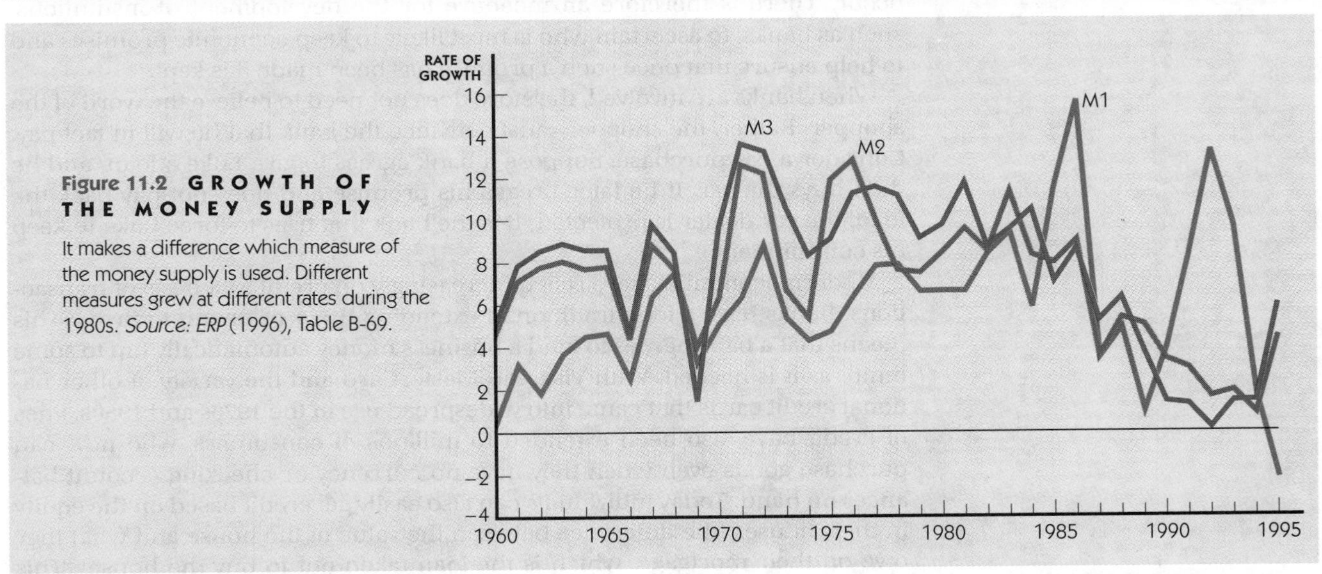

Figure 11.2 GROWTH OF THE MONEY SUPPLY
It makes a difference which measure of the money supply is used. Different measures grew at different rates during the 1980s. *Source: ERP* (1996), Table B-69.

funds, the more extensive use of credit cards, and home equity loans—have made it even more difficult to answer the question of what to include in the money supply. For instance, many people own shares in government-bond mutual funds that provide check-writing privileges. When an individual writes a check on a bond mutual fund, the mutual fund sells just the value of bonds required to transfer the amount of the check into the bank account. The funds go into and out of the bank account in a split second. Thus, the bond mutual funds with check-writing privileges function just like money. And yet they are not included within the money supply, while money market mutual funds are.

Money and Credit

One of the key properties of money, as noted, is that it is a medium of exchange. However, many transactions today do not entail the use of any of the measures presented so far: M1, M2, or M3. They involve credit, not money. In selling a suit of clothes or a piece of furniture or a car, stores often do not receive money. They receive rather, a promise from you to pay money in the future. Credit is clearly tied to money: what you owe the store is measured in dollars. You want something today, and you will have the money for it tomorrow. The store wants you to buy today and is willing to wait until tomorrow or next week for the money. There is a mutually advantageous trade. But because the exchange is not *simultaneous,* the store must rely on your promise.

Promises, the saying goes, are made to be broken. But if they are broken too often, stores will not be able to trust buyers, and credit exchanges will not occur. There is therefore an incentive for the development of institutions, such as banks, to ascertain who is most likely to keep economic promises and to help ensure that once such a promise has been made it is kept.

When banks are involved, the store does not need to believe the word of the shopper. Rather, the shopper must convince the bank that he will in fact pay. Consider a car purchase. Suppose a bank agrees to give Luke a loan, and he then buys the car. If he later breaks his promise and does not pay back the loan, the car dealer is protected. It is the bank that tries to force Luke to keep his commitment.

Modern economies have relied increasingly on credit as a basis of transactions. Banks have a long tradition of extending **lines of credit** to firms. This means that a bank agrees to lend a business money automatically (up to some limit), as it is needed. With Visa and MasterCard and the variety of other national credit cards that came into widespread use in the 1970s and 1980s, lines of credit have also been extended to millions of consumers, who now can purchase goods even when they have no currency or checking account balances on hand. Today individuals can also easily get credit based on the equity in their houses (the difference between the value of the house and what they owe on their mortgage, which is the loan taken out to buy the house). This type of credit is called home equity loans. When house prices increased

CLOSE-UP: GLOSSARY OF FINANCIAL TERMS

One of the problems in defining money is the wide variety of assets that are not directly used as a medium of exchange but can be readily converted into something that *could* be so used. Should they be included in the money supply? There is no right or wrong answer. Below are definitions of nine terms, some of which were defined in earlier chapters. Each of these assets serves, in progressively less satisfactory ways, the function of money.

Currency and coins	One-, five-, ten-, twenty-, and hundred dollar bills; pennies, nickels, dimes, quarters, and half dollars.
Traveler's checks	Checks issued by a bank or a firm such as American Express that you can convert into currency upon demand and are widely accepted.
Demand deposits, or checking accounts	Deposits that you can withdraw upon demand (that is, convert into currency upon demand), by writing a check.
Savings deposits	Deposits that technically you can withdraw only upon notice; in practice, banks allow withdrawal upon demand (without notice).
Certificates of deposit	Money deposited in the bank for a fixed period of time (usually six months to five years), with a penalty for early withdrawal.
NOW (negotiable order of withdrawal) accounts	A kind of account that breaks through legislative loopholes to allow customers to write checks on interest-bearing deposits.
Money market accounts	Another category of interest-bearing bank checking accounts, often paying higher interest rates but with restrictions on the number of checks that can be written.
Money market mutual funds	Mutual funds that invest in Treasury bills, certificates of deposit, and similar safe securities. You can usually write checks against such accounts; they are thus similar to NOW and other interest-bearing bank checking accounts.
Eurodollars	U.S. dollar bank accounts in banks outside the United States (mainly in Europe).

rapidly in the 1980s, they provided a ready source of credit for millions of home owners.

These innovations make it easier for people to obtain credit. But they have also altered the way economists think about the role of money in the economy —blurring definitions that once seemed quite clear.

THE FINANCIAL SYSTEM IN MODERN ECONOMIES

Broadly speaking, a country's **financial system** includes all institutions involved in moving savings from households and firms whose income exceeds their expenditures and transferring it to other households and firms who would like to spend more than their income allows. Here we take a closer look at the most important of these institutions.

The financial system in the United States not only allows consumers to buy cars, televisions, and VCRs even when they do not have the cash to do so. It also enables firms to invest in factories and new machines. Sometimes money goes directly from, say, a household doing some saving to a firm that needs some additional cash. For example, when Ben buys a new bond from General Motors that promises to pay a fixed amount in 90 or 180 days (or in 5 or 15 years), he is lending money directly to GM.

But most of the funds flow through **financial intermediaries.** These are firms that stand in between the savers, who have the extra funds, and the borrowers, who need them. The most important group of financial intermediaries is the banks, but there are many other groups of financial intermediaries as well, including life insurance companies, credit unions, and savings and loan associations. All are engaged in looking over potential borrowers, ascertaining who are good risks, and monitoring their investments and loans. The intermediaries take "deposits" from consumers and invest them. By putting the funds into many different investments, they diversify and thus reduce the risk. One investment might turn sour, but it is unlikely that many will. This provides the intermediary with a kind of safety it could not obtain if it put all its eggs in one basket. Financial institutions differ in who the depositors are, where the funds are invested, and who owns the institutions.

FEDERAL RESERVE SYSTEM

Just as there is a continuum—from currency and demand deposits to money market accounts—that serves in varying degrees the functions of money, so too is there a continuum of financial intermediaries that perform in varying ways the functions that banks perform. For instance, savings and loan associations (S & L's) accept deposits and make loans today in a way that is almost identical to that of banks. Financial intermediaries play an important role in our financial system. Their actions affect the supply of money (particularly money in the broader definitions, such as M2 and M3). For simplicity, the discussion here focuses on commercial banks and the narrower definition of money, M1. Traditionally, banks have been the most important way in which businesses raise capital and by which the government attempts to control the level of investment and hence the level of national economic activity.

Close-up: A Glossary of Financial Intermediaries

A variety of financial intermediaries take funds from the public and lend them to borrowers or otherwise invest the funds. Of the many legal differences between these institutions, the principal ones relate to the kinds of loans or investments they make. The following list is ranked roughly by the asset size of each intermediary.

Commercial banks	Banks chartered by either the federal government (national banks) or a state (state banks) to receive deposits and make loans.
Life insurance companies	Companies that collect premiums from policyholders out of which insurance payments are made.
Savings and loan associations (S & L's, or "thrifts")	Institutions originally chartered to receive deposits for the purpose of making loans to finance home mortgages; in the early 1980s, they were given more latitude in the kinds of loans they could make.
Credit unions	Cooperative (not for profit) institutions, usually organized at a place of work or by a union, that take deposits from members and make loans to members.
Mutual funds	Financial intermediaries that take funds from a group of investors and invest them. Major examples include stock mutual funds, which invest the funds in stocks; bond mutual funds, which invest in bonds; and money market mutual funds, which invest in liquid assets such as Treasury bills and certificates of deposit. Many mutual funds allow you to write checks against the fund.
Institutional money market mutual funds	Money market mutual fund accounts held by institutions.
CMA™ accounts (cash management accounts)	Accounts at a brokerage firm (the name was given to the first such accounts, established by Merrill Lynch) that enable people to place stocks, bonds, and other assets into a single account, against which they can write checks.

Governments today have two objectives in their involvement with the bank portion of the financial system. The first is to protect consumers: when banks go bankrupt, depositors stand to lose their life's savings. The typical saver is not in a position to audit a bank's books to see whether it is really sound. During the Depression of the 1930s, hundreds of banks closed, leaving thousands destitute. Today banks are more tightly regulated. In addition, depositors are insured by government agencies, to limit their losses should a bankruptcy occur.

The second objective of government involvement in the banking system is to stabilize the level of economic activity. We have seen the important role that the banking system plays in taking funds from savers and providing them to investors. When the banking system collapses, firms cannot obtain funds to make their investments, and the entire economy suffers. More broadly, the banking system, by its actions, affects the level of investment, and this affects the level of economic activity. Sharp declines in investment can throw the economy into a recession; sharp increases can set off an inflationary spiral.

CENTRAL BANK

Different economies have developed a variety of institutions and laws for accomplishing these twin objectives. The most important institution in each country is its **central bank.** The central bank is a bank from which other banks can borrow. But it is more than a banker's bank. It is also responsible for stabilizing the level of economic activity by controlling the money supply and the availability of credit, and for regulating the banking system to ensure its financial health. In the United States, the central bank is called the **Federal Reserve,** which was established in 1913. The Federal Reserve consists of a Board of Governors, also known as the **Federal Reserve Board,** which, with their staff, supervises a system of twelve regional **Federal Reserve banks,** and with them, monitors the operations of six thousand member banks. The collection of governors and Federal Reserve banks, often simply referred to as the "Fed," is at the heart of the **Federal Reserve System,** which includes all of the member banks.[1]

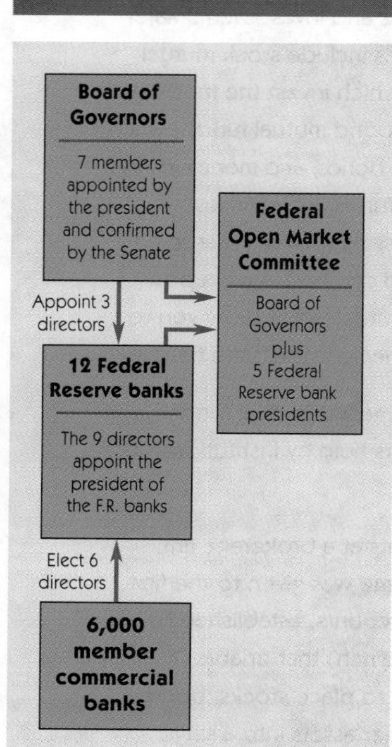

Figure 11.3 STRUCTURE OF THE FEDERAL RESERVE SYSTEM

The Federal Reserve operates at both a national level and a district level. The Board of Governors are appointed by the president; the district level includes some directors appointed nationally and some from within the district; the Open Market Committee includes the presidentially appointed governors and representatives from the district banks.

The structure of the system is depicted in Figure 11.3. The Board of Governors consists of seven members who are appointed for fourteen-year terms (although the average length of service is about seven years). While in theory each member of the Board of Governors has one vote, the chairman of the board has traditionally wielded enormous power. The chairman is appointed by the president to serve a four-year term, with that term of office intentionally set so as not to coincide with the term of the president. Once appointed, the chairman is theoretically fully independent of the president or Congress. Indeed, because the funding of the Fed comes from the profits it earns on its operations, Congress and the president cannot even threaten to reduce the Fed's funding. Still, the chairman must report regularly to Congress on the Fed's actions and budget.

CONTROLLING THE MONEY SUPPLY

The country is divided into twelve Federal Reserve districts, as shown in Figure 11.4, each with its own bank. But responsibility for stabilizing the economy through controlling the money supply is vested in a committee of the Federal Reserve called the **Federal Open Market Committee.** This commit-

[1]While the Federal Reserve banks are officially "owned" by the member banks and therefore in a technical sense are not really part of the government, most of the profits of the Fed—which generally amount to about $25 billion a year—are turned over to the U.S. Treasury.

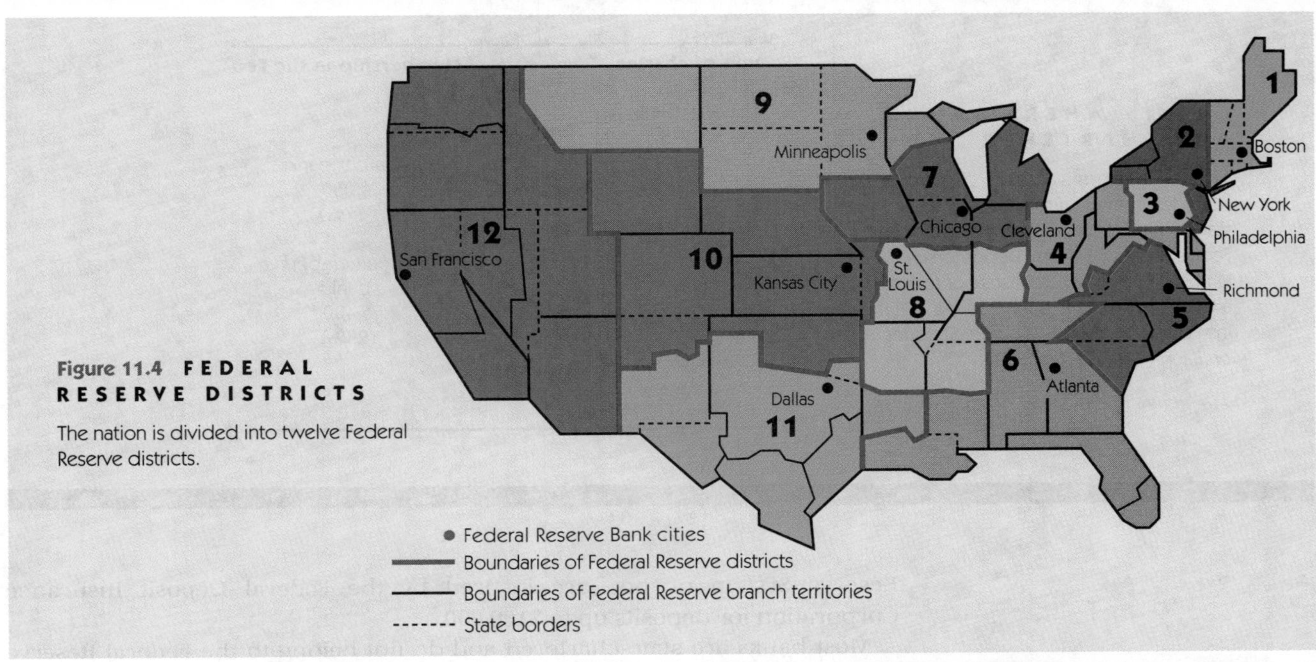

Figure 11.4 FEDERAL RESERVE DISTRICTS

The nation is divided into twelve Federal Reserve districts.

tee consists of the Board of Governors plus five of the twelve Federal Reserve bank presidents (on rotating duty). The name comes from the way the committee operates. The Fed engages in **open market operations**—so called because they involve the Fed entering the capital market directly, much as a private individual or firm would, buying or selling government bonds. (Later in the chapter, we will see how these actions translate into changes in the money supply, and look at other ways that the Fed controls the money supply.) Once the Open Market Committee has set its goals, its operations are carried out by the Federal Reserve Bank of New York, because of that bank's proximity to the huge capital markets in New York.

REGULATING BANKS

The other primary objective of central banks is ensuring the financial soundness of the other banks in the country. To open its doors, a U.S. bank must receive a charter, from either the federal government or one of the states. Figure 11.5 shows that two-thirds of all banks are state-chartered. All the federally chartered banks, and some of the state-chartered banks, belong to the Federal Reserve System; they are called **member banks,** in contrast to **nonmember banks,** which do not belong to the Federal Reserve System. Depositors in virtually all U.S. banks, whether they belong to the Federal

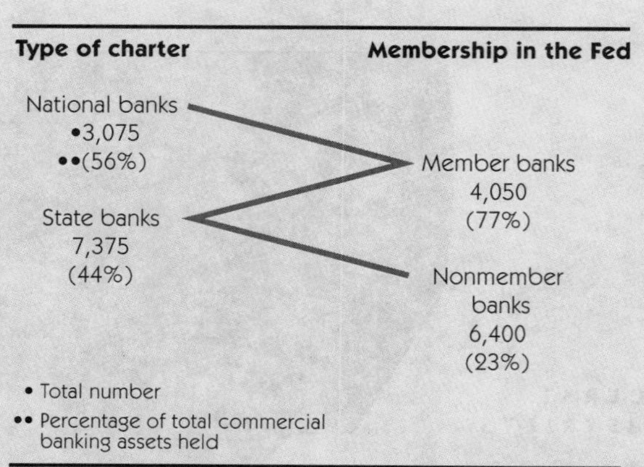

Figure 11.5 WHERE BANKS ARE CHARTERED

Two-thirds of banks are state-chartered. All federally chartered banks and some state-chartered banks are members of the Federal Reserve System. Depositors in almost all banks, whether state or federal, are insured by the Federal Deposit Insurance Corporation. *Source: Statistics on Banking* (1995), Table 104.

Reserve System or not, are insured by the Federal Deposit Insurance Corporation for deposits up to $100,000.

Most banks are state-chartered and do not belong to the Federal Reserve System. These are for the most part small banks with the important exception of large state-chartered banks in New York. A few large banks control most of the assets within the banking system; 3 percent control more than 70 percent of the assets. The smallest 60 percent control less than 8 percent of the assets. The sixteen largest banks, each with assets of over $20 billion, control one-third of the assets in the entire banking system.

The banks that are members of the Federal Reserve System are subject to three layers of regulation. The U.S. Treasury, through the comptroller of the currency, the Federal Deposit Insurance Corporation, and the Federal Reserve itself all share the job of supervision. Even so, in the late 1980s and early 1990s, a rash of bankruptcies and near bankruptcies, some in fairly large banks, raised questions about the adequacy of the banking regulations.

CREATING MONEY IN MODERN ECONOMIES

In order to understand how the Fed goes about its task of controlling the money supply, we need to know more about how a bank runs its business, particularly how banks create money. The money supply of today is created not by a mint or printing press but largely by the banking system. When you put money into the bank, the bank does not simply take the currency down to its vault, put it into a little slot marked with your name, and keep it there until

Policy Perspective: The S & L Crisis

Savings and loan associations (S & L's) have traditionally been one of America's most staid and trusted institutions—using people's savings to finance mortgages, with savings deposit accounts insured against default by the federal government. Tradition came to an abrupt halt in the mid- and late 1980s, as a major part of the S & L industry went belly up. Bank failures soared, reaching 221 in 1988, more than 20 times the number in 1980. Greed and corruption were widely cited as the cause of the problem. The solution was expensive. The government bailout which began in 1989 ultimately cost taxpayers more than $100 billion.

What really happened? Almost everyone now agrees that, though unscrupulous S & L's certainly exploited the system, the crisis had roots in Washington. In fact, the problem had been brewing since the 1970s, when the Fed suddenly began raising interest rates. S & L's were left paying far more in interest on deposit accounts than they were earning on the fixed-rate mortgages issued in years past. The government responded by relaxing the regulations governing how S & L's could use depositors' funds, and allowing S & L's to invest in higher-risk, potentially higher-return investments. Higher returns did stave off the crisis for a few years. But the downside of high-risk investments is the greater likelihood that they will go sour. And sour they went in the late 1980s—both the real estate markets and the market for high-risk bonds (sometimes called junk bonds) in which S & L's had invested heavily.

The fundamental, if unpalatable truth is that S & L managers and depositors were responding rationally to the misguided incentives built into deposit insurance. Facing bankruptcy, S & L's had little choice but to pursue the risky course—at least the high returns would enable them to continue operating—and they had little trouble obtaining the funds. After all, depositors didn't have to worry about how the S & L's handled their money (at least

up to the guarantee limit of $100,000). Those S & L's paying the highest interest rates—and taking the highest risks—attracted the most deposits.

Government regulators multiplied the problem. When the problem first arose, they should have recognized that the S & L's worsening financial situation required increased scrutiny. The S & L's were paying higher interest rates on deposits while the returns on old mortgages were fixed at low levels. Regulators should have feared the S & L's might take undue risk to bail themselves out. Instead, the government loosened the regulations. Then, as the crisis mounted in the mid-1980s, with an ever-rising number of bankruptcies they overreacted. Lest regulators be accused of regulatory laxity, they became ruthless in tightening and enforcing the regulations. Banks and S & L's responded by becoming even more conservative in their lending than the new standards required. The reduced lending contributed greatly to the economic downturn of the early 1990s.

you are ready to take it out. Instead, banks realize that not all their thousands of depositors will withdraw their money on any given day. Some will come by next week, some in two weeks, some not for a year or more. In the meantime, the bank can lend out the money deposited in its vault and charge interest. The more money the bank can persuade people to deposit, the more can be loaned out and thus the more money the bank will earn. To attract depositors, the bank pays interest on its deposits, effectively passing on (after taking its cut) the interest earned on its loans.

How much can safely be lent out? Money retained by a bank in case those who have deposited money want it back is called its **reserves.** How much needs to be kept as reserves? Should the bank keep reserves of 5 percent of deposits? 20 percent of deposits? The less it keeps as reserves, the more money it can earn, but the greater the possibility that it will not have enough funds on hand if a large number of depositors want their deposits back at the same time. To understand how these reserves work and how they affect the supply of money and credit available in the economy, we need to take a close look at the typical bank's balance sheet.

THE BANK'S BALANCE SHEET

Bankers see the world backward. Where else would loans be called "assets" and deposits be called "liabilities"? This is the perspective shown on a bank's **balance sheet.** Like any firm's balance sheet, it describes the bank's **assets** and **liabilities.** Assets are what the firm owns, including what is owed to it by others. That is why the bank's loans appear as assets on its balance sheet. Liabilities are what it owes to others. We can think of the bank's depositors as having loaned money to the bank. They can get their money back when they wish. That is why deposits are treated by the bank as liabilities.

Table 11.1 shows the balance sheet of AmericaBank. Its assets are divided into three categories: loans outstanding, government bonds, and reserves, in-

Table 11.1 **AMERICABANK BALANCE SHEET**

Assets		Liabilities	
Loans outstanding	$28 million	Deposits	$30 million
Government bonds	$ 2 million		
Reserves	$ 3 million	Net worth	$ 3 million
Total	$33 million	Total	$33 million

cluding cash in the vault. Least secure are the loans outstanding. These consist of loans to business firms, real estate loans (mortgages), car loans, house-remodeling loans, and so on. Government bonds are more secure than loans to households or firms. Most banks' holdings of government bonds are typically concentrated in Treasury bills (or T-bills), short-term bonds maturing in thirty, sixty, or ninety days after the date of issue.[2] Most secure are the reserves that are held on deposit at the "banker's bank," the local Federal Reserve bank, and the cash in the vault.

The amount of money people need to set aside for a rainy day depends (in part) on how easily they can borrow. The same is true for banks. If they can borrow easily from other banks to meet any shortfall of reserves, they need to keep very little in reserves. In the United States, the Federal Reserve banks act as the banker's bank, lending money to other banks. (Banks do not, however, have an automatic right to borrow; the Fed must concur with the request. Many central banks use this discretionary power to elicit desired behavior.) But banks need to hold reserves for an additional reason other than caution. The Fed imposes reserve requirements on banks. Today, the amount of reserves banks hold is dictated more by regulations than by the banks' own perceptions of what is prudent. After all, holding T-bills is just as safe as holding reserves with the Fed—and yields higher returns. And the level of reserves required by the Fed is designed primarily from the perspective of controlling the money supply and thereby the level of economic activity. Table 11.2 shows the current reserve requirements. This system of banking, in which banks hold a fraction of the amount on deposit in reserves, is called the **fractional reserve system.**

The liability side of AmericaBank's balance sheet consists of two items: deposits and net worth. Deposits include checking accounts, which are technically known as demand deposits, and the variety of forms of savings accounts,

[2]Long-term bonds are volatile in price, because their price changes with changes in interest rates. Banks typically hold short-term government bonds because the risk of such changes over a relatively short period of time is low, and banks wish to avoid risk.

Table 11.2 REQUIRED RESERVES

Type of deposit	Minimum reserve required (percentage of deposits)
Very large checking accounts (over $54 million)	10
Other checking accounts (under $54 million)	3
All other deposits	0

Source: Federal Reserve Bulletin (1995).

which are technically known as time deposits. The bank's net worth is simply the difference between the value of its assets and the value of its liabilities. In other words, if the bank's assets were sold and its depositors paid off, what remained would equal the net worth of the bank.

Since net worth is *defined* as the difference between the value of the liabilities and the value of the assets, the numbers on both sides of the balance sheet always balance.

How Banks Create Money

As we have seen, the coins and currency manufactured by the Treasury are a relatively small part of the money supply. Who creates the rest of the money? Banks.

To see how banks create money, let's consider all 10,450 U.S. banks as one huge superbank. Assume the Fed is requiring that reserves be 10 percent of deposits. Now suppose that a multi-multi-millionaire deposits $1 billion in currency in her account.

The bank reasons as follows. It knows it must keep a reserve-to-deposit ratio of 1 to 10, and it has a long line of loan applicants. When the bank makes a loan, it does not actually give the borrower currency. It credits him with funds in his checking account. It does this by placing an entry into its books on both the left- and right-hand side of the ledger: there is a loan on the asset side and a deposit on the liability side. If it makes $9 billion worth of loans, it liabilities will have gone up to $10 billion (the $1 billion in currency originally deposited by the millionaire plus the $9 billion worth of loans). On the asset side, the bank takes the $1 billion in currency to the Fed and is credited with the amount, so that it now has $1 billion in reserves. Thus, its reserves have increased by $1 billion, its deposits by $10 billion; it has satisfied the reserve requirement.

We can reach the same result by a slower route, as shown in Table 11.3. The

Table 11.3 SUPERBANK BALANCE SHEET

Before-deposit equilibrium			
Assets		**Liabilities**	
Loans outstanding	$ 91 billion	Deposits	$100 billion
Government bonds	2 billion		
Reserves	10 billion	Net worth	3 billion
Total	103 billion	Total	103 billion

First round (Add $1 billion deposits, $.9 billion loans)			
Assets		**Liabilities**	
Loans outstanding	$ 91.9 billion	Deposits	$101 billion
Government bonds	2 billion		
Reserves	10.1 billion	Net worth	3 billion
Total	104 billion	Total	104 billion

Second round (Add $.9 billion deposits, $.81 billion loans to previous round[a])			
Assets		**Liabilities**	
Loans outstanding	$ 92.71 billion	Deposits	$101.9 billion
Government bonds	2 billion		
Reserves	10.19 billion	Net worth	3 billion
Total	104.9 billion	Total	104.9 billion

Third round (Add $.81 billion deposits, $.73 billion loans to previous round[a])			
Assets		**Liabilities**	
Loans outstanding	$ 93.44 billion	Deposits	$102.71 billion
Government bonds	2 billion		
Reserves	10.27 billion	Net worth	3 billion
Total	105.71 billion	Total	105.71 billion

After-deposit equilibrium (Add $10 billion new deposits, $9 billion new loans to original equilibrium)			
Assets		**Liabilities**	
Loans outstanding	$100 billion	Deposits	$110 billion
Government bonds	2 billion		
Reserves	11 billion	Net worth	3 billion
Total	113 billion	Total	113 billion

[a]In each subsequent round, new deposits equal new loans of the previous round; new loans equal .9 × new deposits.

bank might reason, now that its deposits have gone up by $1 billion, that it must send $100 million to the Federal Reserve as part of its reserve requirements. But it can lend out the remaining $900 million (.9 × $1 billion). This is the first-round balance sheet that appears in the table. Deposits have increased $1 billion (compared with the initial situation), loans have increased $.9 billion, and reserves have increased $.1 billion.

For simplicity, let's assume that the lending is all made to one customer. Desktop Publishing borrows $900 million so that it can purchase new computers from ComputerAmerica. When Desktop pays $900 million for the computers, ComputerAmerica deposits the money in its account. Thus, the loan of $900 million is reflected in the addition of $900 million in deposits. This is shown on the right-hand side of the second-round balance sheet in the table, where deposits have now risen from $101 billion to $101.9 billion.

But with the $900 million additional deposits, the bank is allowed to increase its lending by .9 × $900 million, or $810 million, putting $90 million into reserves. These changes are shown in the left-hand side of the second-round balance sheet. Assume that all $810 million is lent out to various companies, each of which uses the money to purchase new goods. In each case, some other firm will sell its good and will put these new funds into the superbank. As a result, new deposits at the superbank will again grow by $810 million. As the third round begins, deposits are once again increased.

But the bank is still not in equilibrium. Because of the increase in deposits of $810 million, it can lend out .9 × $810 million = $729 million. And so the process continues. Notice that on each round, the increase in deposits is smaller than in the previous round. In the second round, the increase in deposits was $900 million, in the third round $810 million, and so on. The after-deposit equilibrium balance sheet in the last part of the table shows that the bank has increased its deposits by ten times the original deposit ($100 billion to $110 billion) and increased its lending by nine times the original deposit ($91 billion to $100 billion). The $1 billion injection into the banking system has turned into a $10 billion increase in the money supply.

In the new situation, the banking system is in equilibrium. Its reserves of $11 billion are precisely equal to 10 percent of its $110 billion deposits. It cannot lend out any more without violating the reserve requirements.

In this way, any new deposit into the banking system results in a multiple expansion of the number of deposits. This is the "miracle" of the fractional reserve system. Deposits increase by a factor of 1/reserve requirement. In the superbank example, the reserve requirement was 10 percent; 1/reserve requirement is 10. If the reserve requirement had been 20 percent, deposits would have increased by 1/.2, or 5. Note that as the deposits increased, so did the supply of outstanding loans.

In this example, there were no "leakages" outside the system. That is, no one decided to hold currency rather than put his money back into the bank, and whenever sellers were paid, they put what they received into the bank. With leakages, the increase in deposits and thus the increase in money will be smaller. In the real world these leakages are large. The ratio of M1 to reserves is only around 3, and even for M2 the ratio is only between 11 and 12. Nevertheless, the increase in bank reserves will lead to some multiple increase in the money supply. This relationship between the change in reserves and the final change in deposits is called the **money multiplier.**[3]

MONEY MULTIPLIERS WITH MANY BANKS

The money multiplier works just as well when there is more than one bank involved. Assume that Desktop Publishing and ComputerAmerica have their bank accounts in two separate banks, BankNational and BankUSA, respectively. When Desktop Publishing writes a check for $900 million to ComputerAmerica, $900 million is transferred from BankNational to BankUSA. Once that $900 million has been transferred, BankUSA will find that it can lend more than it could previously. As a result of the $900 million increase in deposits, it can lend .9 × $900 = $810 million. Suppose it lends the $810 million to the NewTelephone Company, which uses the money to buy a machine for making telephones from Equipment Manufacturing. If Equipment Manufacturing has its bank account at BankIllinois, after Equipment Manufacturing has been paid, BankIllinois will find that because its deposits have increased by $810 million, it can lend .9 × $810 = $729 million. The process continues, until the new equilibrium is identical to the one described earlier in the superbank example, where there is a $10 billion increase in the money supply. The banking system as a whole will have expanded the money supply by a multiple of the initial deposit, equal to 1/reserve requirement.

It should be clear that when there are many banks, no individual bank can create multiple deposits. Individual banks may not even be aware of the role they play in the process of multiple-deposit creation. All they see is that their deposits have increased and therefore they are able to make more loans.

The process of multiple-deposit creation may seem somewhat like a magician pulling rabbits out of a hat: it seems to make something out of nothing. But it is, in fact, a real physical process. Deposits are created by making entries in records; today electronic impulses create records on computer tapes. The rules of deposit creation are rules specifying when you may make certain entries in the books. It is these rules—in particular, the fractional reserve requirements—that give rise to the system's ability to expand deposits by a multiple of the original deposit increase.

MONEY MULTIPLIER

An increase in reserves by a dollar leads to an increase in total deposits by a multiple of the original increase.

[3]This multiplier should not be confused with the (investment) multiplier introduced in Chapter 9. That multiplier showed that an increase in investment or government expenditures leads to a multiple increase in the equilibrium level of aggregate expenditures. There are clearly similarities in the way we go about calculating the two multipliers, however.

THE INSTRUMENTS OF MONETARY POLICY

Most changes in the money supply are not the result of someone depositing a billion dollars of currency in a bank. Nor any longer do they involve someone selling gold to or depositing gold in a bank. Instead, they are the result of actions by the Federal Reserve Board. The Fed creates reserves. It does so deliberately, in order to increase the supply of money and credit. By such action, the Fed affects the level of economic activity. The connections between the actions the Fed takes and their effect on the level of economic activity are the subject of the next two chapters. Here, our concern is simply with the supply of money and credit. Money and credit, as we have seen, represent the two sides of a bank's balance sheet. When deposits (money) increase, either bank loans (credit) or bank holdings of T-bills must increase. Frequently both will. Though ultimately our concern will be with bank lending, bank lending is not directly under the control of the Fed, so it must affect bank lending through the money supply. The Fed has three tools with which it can change the money supply: reserve requirements, discount rate, and open market operations.

RESERVE REQUIREMENTS

The simplest tool available to the Fed is to alter **reserve requirements.** The Fed sets the minimum amount of money each bank is required to hold in reserves. While in principle the government could require banks to hold reserves in a variety of forms (cash, government bonds, gold), the Fed actually requires that the reserves be held as deposits with the Federal Reserve—partly because this stipulation facilitates monitoring of the reserve requirement.

Assume that banks are initially required to maintain reserves equal to 10 percent of deposits, and consider what happens if reserve requirements are lowered to 5 percent. Each bank will find that it now has **excess reserves** or **free reserves**—reserves in excess of the amount required. This means that each bank will be in a position to lend more. Where a lack of funds may have caused the bank to reject loans to projects it considered worthy, now it will make these loans. The new loans get spent, creating new deposits and allowing still further loans, and the multiplier process is once again set in motion.

DISCOUNT RATE

The second tool of monetary policy is the **discount rate.** This is the interest rate banks must pay when they borrow from the Federal Reserve banks. As explained earlier in this chapter, the Federal Reserve banks are called the banker's banks because they lend money to banks and hold their deposits.

When the discount rate is high, interest rates charged by banks tend to be high, and banks make loans less available.

Consider an aggressive bank that always keeps just the minimum amount of reserves, lending out all the rest of its funds. If a major depositor suddenly wishes to withdraw funds, the bank is forced to borrow funds to cover this withdrawal, either from other banks or from the Federal Reserve banks. When the discount rate increases, the interest rate the bank must pay for borrowing from other banks increases in tandem. The discount rate affects this bank as a direct cost of doing business. If it has to pay the Fed more to borrow itself, it must charge its own customers more.

If the bank pursues a less aggressive policy and holds more funds in the form of Treasury bills or other liquid assets, a large withdrawal causes only a minor adjustment: the bank simply sells some of its liquid assets. Raising the discount rate makes it more expensive to call upon the Fed in the event of a shortfall of funds, and this induces banks to hold more liquid assets and more T-bills, which in turn means that the bank will be lending less.

The Fed not only uses a higher discount rate to discourage banks from lending, it also rations access to the discount "window." That is, it may refuse to lend to a bank, even at the announced discount rate. This action forces the bank to take more costly remedial actions to satisfy the reserve requirements set by the Fed. Banks in good financial condition can usually borrow from each other, so today this instrument has only limited effectiveness.

The discount rate is the only interest rate the Fed directly sets. All other interest rates are set in the market, by the forces of demand and supply. But as the Fed affects banks' willingness to lend, it may at the same time indirectly affect the interest rates they charge and the rates they pay depositors. The interest rates the government pays on both short-term borrowing (T-bills) and longer-term borrowing are also determined in the market. The Fed's actions also affect these interest rates only indirectly.

The Fed often uses the discount rate, not so much for its direct effects, but as a signal of its intentions. When the Fed lowers the discount rate, the market knows the Fed is serious about making credit more available in the economy. When it raises the discount rate, the market knows the Fed means to restrict credit. But the Fed also changes the discount rate to reflect changes in interest rates that have already occurred. If market interest rates have risen but the Fed has failed to increase the discount rate in tandem, the difference between the discount rate—the rate banks have to pay to obtain funds from the Fed—and the rate they can receive on loans may be large. This will tempt banks to try to borrow excessively from the Fed. Thus, while changes in the discount rate sometimes signal a change in policy, at other times the changes just reflect the Fed's catching up with the market.

OPEN MARKET OPERATIONS

Open market operations are the most important instrument the Fed uses to control the money supply. In open market operations, the Federal Reserve enters the market directly to buy or sell government bonds. Imagine that it buys $1 million of government bonds from wealthy Joe Brown (or a thousand different Joe Brown families), paying him with a $1 million check. Joe Brown takes the check down to his bank, AmericaBank, which credits his account with $1 million. AmericaBank presents the check to the Fed, which credits the bank's account with $1 million. AmericaBank now has $1 million of new deposits (which is matched by $1 million in new reserves) and it can accordingly lend out an additional $900,000. A money multiplier goes to work, and the total expansion of the money supply will be equal to a multiple of the initial $1 million increase in deposits. And credit—the amount of outstanding loans—will also have increased by a multiple of the initial increase in deposits.

The purchase of bonds from Joe Brown by the Federal Reserve has a quite different effect from a purchase of the same bonds by a private citizen, Jill White. In the latter case, Jill White's deposit account goes down by $1 million, and Joe Brown's deposit account goes up by $1 million. The funds available in the system as a whole remain unchanged. The money multiplier goes to work only when funds enter from "outside," in particular from the Federal Reserve banks.

Thus, the Fed has three indirect ways in which it controls the money supply and credit-creating activities of banks. Through reserve requirements, it affects the amount of reserves that banks must have, relative to their deposits. Through the discount rate, it affects the cost of having too few reserves. Through open market operations, it affects the supply of reserves. By changing the required amount of reserves, the cost of not having sufficient reserves, or the supply of reserves, the Fed affects the amount that banks can lend, and the attractiveness to banks of making loans as compared with holding their assets in a liquid form, such as T-bills.

Instruments of Monetary Policy

1. Reserve requirements—the required ratio of reserves to deposits. The Fed can change the reserve requirement, the amount that banks must hold as reserves.
2. Discount rates—the rate the Fed charges for loans made to member banks. The Fed can change the discount rate and thus change the amount that banks wish to hold as reserves and the interest rate charged on loans.
3. Open market operations—by buying and selling Treasury bills, the Fed changes the supply of reserves and thus the money supply.

USING ECONOMICS: CONTROLLING THE MONEY SUPPLY

Assume, for one reason or another, the government wished to increase the money supply by $1 billion. How large of an increase in reserves will be required to generate the desired increase in money supply?

If the money multiplier is 20, then an increase in reserves of $50 million will generate an increase in money supply of $1 billion.

But what determines the money multiplier? If there is a 5 percent reserve requirement, banks hold no excess reserves, and individuals always redeposit in banks any money they receive, then the money multiplier is 20.

In practice, there is some variability in the money multiplier. As the economy goes into a recession, banks might want to *hold* excess reserves—though there are usually safe investments yielding a positive return (such as U.S. Treasury bills) so that it does not pay to leave reserves at the Fed yielding zero return. Moreover, individuals may decide to hold currency, rather than redeposit funds in the banking system. A central concern of central bankers is increasing their ability to predict changes in the money supply.

SELECTING THE APPROPRIATE INSTRUMENT

Of the three instruments, the Federal Reserve uses open market operations most frequently. Changes in discount rates and in reserve requirements are blunt tools compared with the fine-tuning that open market operations make possible. Thus, changes in reserve requirements and in discount rates are used to announce major shifts in monetary policy, but not on a regular basis. Such changes can be quite effective in signaling tighter credit (that is, changes in monetary policy that entail higher interest rates and reduced credit availability) or looser credit (that is, changes in monetary policy that have the reverse effect). Banks, foreseeing a tightening of credit, may cut back their lending, and firms may postpone investment plans.

THE STABILITY OF THE U.S. BANKING SYSTEM

The fractional reserve system explains how banks create money, and it also explains how, without the Fed, banks can get into trouble. Well-managed banks, even before the advent of the Fed and its reserve requirements, kept reserves equal to some average expectation of day-to-day needs. A bank could get into trouble in a hurry if one day's needs exceeded its reserves.

If (for good reasons or bad) many depositors lose confidence in a bank at the same time, they will attempt to withdraw their funds all at once. The bank simply will not have the money available, since most of the money will have been lent out in loans that cannot be called in instantaneously. This situation is called a **bank run.** Bank runs were as common in nineteenth-century America as they were in the old Western movies, where customers in a small town would line up at the bank while it paid out what reserves it had on a first-come, first-served basis until there was no more left. Such a run could quickly drive even a healthy bank out of business. If a rumor spread that a bank was in trouble and a few savers ran to the bank to clean out their accounts, then other investors would feel they were foolish not to run down to the bank themselves and withdraw their deposits. One vicious rumor could result in a healthy bank shutting down, and the panic setting off a run on other banks, thus destabilizing the banking system and the whole local economy.

Reducing the Threat of Bank Runs

Bank runs and panics have periodically afflicted the American banking system. In fact, one reason the Fed was set up in 1913 was to make them less likely. The last major panic occurred in the midst of the Great Depression in 1933. Since then, the modern banking system has evolved a variety of safeguards that have ended the threat of bank runs for most banks. There are four levels of protection.

First, the Fed acts as a "lender of last resort." If a bank faces a run, it can turn to the Fed to borrow funds, to tide it over. Knowing that the bank could meet its obligations means, of course, that there is no need to run to the bank. The Fed lends money when a bank faces a liquidity problem; that is, it has a temporary shortage of funds, but its assets still exceed its liabilities. It is, in other words, solvent. The objective of the next two measures is to reduce the likelihood that banks face problems of illiquidity or insolvency.

Second, the Fed sets reserve requirements. Even those bank executives who might like to live recklessly, getting along on minuscule reserves, are unable to do so.

The third level of protection is provided by the owners of the bank. Most banks are started by investors who put up a certain amount of money in exchange for a share of ownership. The net worth of the firm—the difference between the bank's assets and its liabilities—is this initial investment, augmented or decreased over time by the bank's profits or losses. If the bank makes bad investment decisions, then these shareholders can be forced to bear the cost. This cushion provided by shareholders not only protects depositors, it also encourages the bank to be more prudent in its loans. If the bank makes bad loans, the owners risk their entire investment. But if the owners' net worth in the bank is too small, the owners may see themselves in a "Heads I win, tails you lose" situation. If risky investments turn out well, the extra profits accrue to the bank; if they turn out badly, the bank goes bankrupt, but since the owners have little at stake, they have little to lose. To protect against this danger, the government requires banks to maintain certain ratios of net worth to deposits. These are called **capital requirements.** Capital requirements protect against insolvency; they mean that if the bank invests badly and many of its loans default, the bank will still be able to pay back depositors. (By contrast, reserves and the ability to borrow from the Fed protect against illiquidity; they ensure that if depositors want cash, they can get it.) On occasion —more frequently in recent years—a bank will make so many bad loans that its net worth shrinks to the point where it can no longer satisfy the capital requirements.

As a fourth and final backstop, the government introduced the Federal Deposit Insurance Corporation (FDIC) in 1933. Since then, federal banks and savings and loans have had to purchase insurance, which ensures that depositors can get all their money back, up to $100,000 per account. Since deposits are guaranteed by the federal government, depositors fearing the collapse of a bank have no need to rush to the bank. The deposit insurance thus not only protects depositors, it has an enormous impact in increasing the stability of the banking system. Simply because it exists, the threat against which it insures is much less likely to occur. It is as if life insurance somehow prolonged life.

Deposit insurance has an offsetting disadvantage, however. Depositors no longer have any incentive to monitor banks, to make sure that banks are investing their funds safely. Regardless of what the bank does with their funds, the funds are protected. Thus—to the extent that capital requirements fail to provide banks with appropriate incentives to make good loans—bank regulators must assume the full responsibility of ensuring the safety and soundness of banks.

Chapter 12 takes a closer look at the relations between monetary policy, the financial position of banks, money and credit, and the level of economic activity.

REVIEW AND PRACTICE

SUMMARY

1. Money is anything that is generally accepted in a given society as a medium of exchange, store of value, and unit of account.

2. There are many ways of measuring the money supply, with names like M1, M2, and M3. All include both currency and checking accounts. They differ in what they include as assets that are close substitutes to currency and checking accounts.

3. A buyer does not need money to purchase a good, at least not right away, if the seller or a financial institution is willing to extend credit.

4. Financial intermediaries, which include banks, savings and loans, mutual funds, insurance companies, and others, all have in common that they form the link between savers who have extra funds and borrowers who desire extra funds.

5. Government is involved with the banking industry for two reasons. First, by regulating the activities banks can undertake and providing deposit insurance, government seeks to protect depositors and ensure the stability of the financial system. Second, by influencing the willingness of banks to make loans, government attempts to influence the level of investment and overall economic activity.

6. By making loans, banks can create an increase in the supply of money that is a multiple of an initial increase in the banks' deposits. If every bank loans all the money it can and every dollar lent is spent to buy goods, purchased from other firms who deposit the check in their account, the money multiplier is 1/the reserve requirement imposed by the Fed. In practice, the money multiplier is considerably smaller.

7. The Federal Reserve Board can affect the money supply by changing the reserve requirement, by changing the discount rate, or by open market operations.

8. Reserve requirements, capital requirements, the Fed's acting as a lender of last resort, and deposit insurance have made bank runs rare.

KEY TERMS

medium of exchange
store of value
unit of account
money
demand deposits
M1, M2, M3
financial intermediaries
central bank
open market operations
reserves
fractional reserve system
money multiplier
reserve requirements
discount rate

REVIEW QUESTIONS

1. What are the three characteristics that define money?

2. What are the differences between M1, M2, and M3?

3. When consumers or businesses desire to make a large purchase, are they limited to spending only as much as the M1 money that they have on hand? Explain.

4. What is the Federal Reserve System?

5. What are the two main reasons for government involvement in the banking system?

6. What are three ways for the Federal Reserve to reduce the money supply?

7. What has the government done to make bank runs less likely?

PROBLEMS

1. Identify which of money's three traits each of the following assets shares, and which traits it does not share:
   (a) a house;
   (b) a day pass for an amusement park;
   (c) German marks held by a resident of Dallas, Texas;
   (d) a painting;
   (e) gold.

2. How might bank depositors be protected by legal prohibitions on banks' entering businesses like insurance, or selling and investing in stocks or venture capital? What are the possible costs and benefits of such prohibitions for depositors and for the government?

3. Down Home Savings has the following assets and liabilities: $6 million in government bonds and reserves; $40 million in deposits; $36 million in outstanding loans. Draw up a balance sheet for the bank. What is its net worth?

4. What factors might affect the value of a bank's loan portfolio? If these factors are changing, explain how this would complicate the job of a bank examiner trying to ascertain the magnitude of the bank's net worth. Why would the bank examiner be concerned about the value of the net worth?

5. While gardening in his backyard, lucky Bob finds a mason jar containing $100,000 in currency. After he deposits the money in his lucky bank, where the reserve requirement is .05, how much will the money supply eventually increase?

6. Why is it that if the Fed sells Treasury bonds the money supply changes, but if a big company sells Treasury bonds (to anyone other than the Fed) the money supply does not change?

7. "So long as the central bank stands ready to lend to any bank with a positive net worth, reserve requirements are unnecessary. What underlies the stability of the banking system is the central bank's role as a lender of last resort, combined with policies aimed at ensuring the financial viability of the banks—for instance, the net worth requirements." Comment.

CHAPTER 12

MONETARY THEORY

In Chapter 11 we saw the close link between the creation of money and credit (loans). This chapter explains why the money supply and the availability of credit are important to the economy. Knowing this, we can understand how monetary policy—the collection of policies aimed at affecting the money supply and the availability of credit—works.

Changes in the money supply and in the availability of credit are really two sides of the same coin. We begin by looking at the Fed's direct effects on the money supply, then turn to its effects on credit availability.

KEY QUESTIONS

1. What determines the demand for money? How and why does it depend on the interest rate and the level of income?
2. How is the demand for money equilibrated to the supply of money?
3. What are the consequences of changes in the supply of money when prices are fixed? When will it lead to a change in real output? When will it largely lead to a change in the amount of money that individuals are willing to hold?
4. What are the channels through which monetary policy affects the economy? What role is played by changes in the real interest rate? the availability of credit?
5. How does monetary policy work differently in an open economy than in a closed one?

MONEY SUPPLY AND ECONOMIC ACTIVITY

In this chapter, we continue with our assumption that the price level is fixed. (Recall that if prices are completely flexible, changes in the money supply elicit proportionate changes in the price level, leaving the real stock of money unchanged.) In the case of fixed prices, if the Fed increases the money supply, there are only two possible results. First, people who get the additional money could just hold on to it. Their bank balances would grow, but nothing would happen to the rest of the economy. In this case, monetary policy will be relatively ineffective—an outcome that is most likely when the economy is in a deep recession. Second, those who get the additional money could spend it. If the economy has excess capacity and prices are fixed, this increased spending (aggregate expenditures) will increase incomes and output.

What actually happens when the money supply is increased (assuming prices are fixed) is a combination of changed holdings of money and changed output. One of the purposes of this chapter is to understand the circumstances under which each of these effects predominates.

In Chapter 11, we learned several different ways of measuring the money supply—M1, M2, and M3. For much of our discussion, we do not have to be precise about which definition we have in mind. But it is natural to focus our attention on M1, for two reasons. First, M1 is the supply of money most directly under the control of the Fed. It is through the banking system that monetary policy has its most direct impact. M2 and M3 include such items as money market mutual fund balances which are not directly related to the banking system. Second, our primary focus here is on money's role as a medium of exchange. Money facilitates transactions. M1, which includes checking accounts and currency, is the definition of money most directly related to its use as a medium of exchange.

Within M1, we will focus on the portion most directly under the Fed's control: demand deposits and other checking-account deposits. This is also appropriate because they are the most important component of M1, accounting for more than 70 percent of the M1 total.

The Velocity of Money

The speed with which money circulates in the economy, its **velocity,** is as important to monetary policy as the money supply itself. If people keep money under the mattress for weeks after being paid, money circulates very slowly. In a bustling city, where money changes hands quickly, a given money supply supports many more transactions. The velocity of money is formally defined as the ratio of GDP to the money supply. If Y represents the real output of the economy, the quantity of goods produced in the economy, and P is a weighted average of their prices (the price level), PY is equal to nominal GDP (which, as we know, equals nominal aggregate income). Using the symbol V to denote velocity and M as the money supply, we get[1]

$$V \equiv PY/M.$$

This equation is sometimes referred to as the **equation of exchange.**

Let's use this equation of exchange to look at what happens when the money supply increases. If M increases, with the price level fixed, either V must decrease or Y must increase. This matches the possible consequences of an increase in the money supply with which we began the chapter. Individuals could simply hold the extra money, which would decrease velocity, or the amount bought, Y, may increase.

The essential problem of monetary theory is to understand when each of these outcomes will result. When the *only* effect is on money holdings, monetary policy is completely ineffective in stimulating aggregate output and employment. But if there is *some* effect on output as well, then monetary policy can be a useful instrument in stimulating the economy. It may take a large dose of the medicine—a large increase in the money supply—to achieve any desired goal, but it can be done. To answer the question of when individuals will simply be willing to hold any additional supply of money, we have to understand the determinants of the demand for money.

The Demand for Money

The velocity of money depends on how willing people are to hold, or keep, money. Because currency is an asset that bears no interest, it is like a hot potato—there are strong incentives to pass it along. Preferring to earn inter-

[1]The symbol "≡" means "is defined as" or "is identical to."

Using Economics: Calculating Velocity

To see how velocity is calculated, use the identity velocity (V) = Income (PY)/The Money Supply (M) and assume that PY = \$6 trillion per year and M = \$1 trillion. In this case, the velocity (V) is 6 per year. If producing one dollar of output required only one transaction, the average dollar would have to circulate 6 times every year to produce output (income) of \$6 trillion. If the money supply (M) were only \$500 billion, every dollar would have to circulate 12 times per year (a velocity of 12) or twice as fast.

est, people have an incentive to exchange currency for either goods or an interest-bearing asset like a Treasury bill (T-bill). The only reason to hold currency is its convenience. You can buy groceries with currency, but not with a T-bill, unless you convert your T-bill back to currency, for which there are costs (transaction costs).

The Effect of Interest Rates

People's willingness to hold money is a result of their balancing the benefits of holding money—the convenience—against the opportunity cost or the forgone interest—the interest that could have been earned if the money in their checking accounts (or the currency in their pockets) had been invested in some other asset. If checking deposits pay interest of 0 percent and very short-term government bonds (Treasury bills) pay 4 percent per year, then the cost of holding money is 4 percent per year. Today checking accounts pay interest, so the opportunity cost of holding funds in them is lower than it used to be. Nevertheless, the difference between the interest paid on checking accounts and the return to other assets of similar risk deters people from holding money. We focus on the interest rate paid on T-bills for a simple reason: they are just as safe as money. The only difference is that T-bills yield a higher interest rate, but money is better as a medium of exchange.

The demand for money is much like the demand for any other good; it depends on the price. The nominal interest rate (i) the individual could have earned on a government bond can be thought of as the price of money, since it measures the opportunity cost of holding money. As the nominal interest rate rises, the amount of money demanded declines, as shown in Figure 12.1.

The Effect of Income

The benefits of holding money are related to money's use as a medium of exchange. The more transactions people engage in, the more money they will want to hold. The demand for money arising from its use in facilitating

Figure 12.1 DEMAND CURVE FOR MONEY

The quantity demanded of money slopes down as the opportunity cost of holding funds—that is, the interest rate—increases. An increase in income causes a shift in the money demand function from *DD* to *D'D'*.

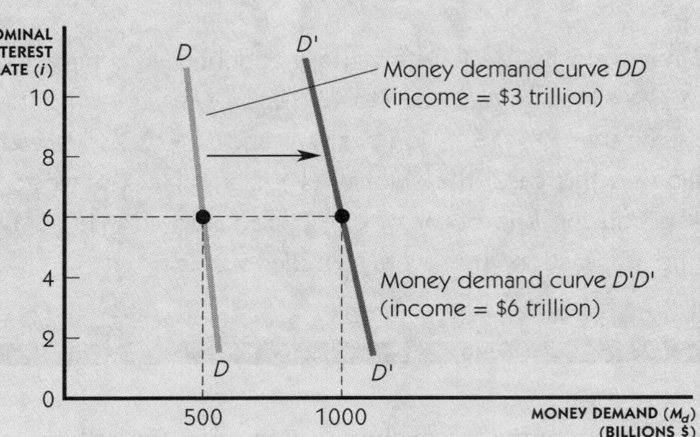

transactions is called the **transactions demand for money.** This demand for money rises with *nominal* income: higher incomes mean that the value of goods bought will be greater, which implies that the value of transactions will be greater. In fact, the demand for money increases proportionately with the nominal value of income, which equals the value of output, *PY:* if prices double, then other things being equal, people will need to have twice the amount of money to engage in the same transactions. This is illustrated in Table 12.1, which shows a hypothetical example. Figure 12.1 shows that an increase in income shifts the demand curve to the right. With an income level of $3 trillion, the demand for money is given by the curve on the left. Doubling the income level to $6 trillion shifts the demand curve for money out to the right. The table and figure illustrate the two basic properties of the demand for money. It decreases as the interest rate rises. And it increases, at a fixed interest rate, in proportion to income.

Table 12.1 DEMAND FOR MONEY

Nominal interest rate	Money demand Income: $3 trillion	$6 trillion
2%	550	1,100
4%	525	1,050
6%	500	1,000
8%	475	950
10%	450	900

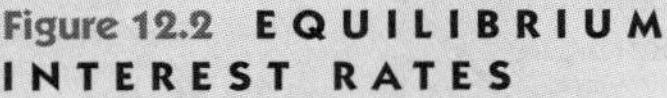
Figure 12.2 EQUILIBRIUM INTEREST RATES

The interest rate adjusts to make the demand for money equal the supply. In this diagram, a government-induced shift in the supply of money from MS_0 to MS_1 has a large effect on the interest rate, since the demand for money is relatively inelastic with respect to the interest rate.

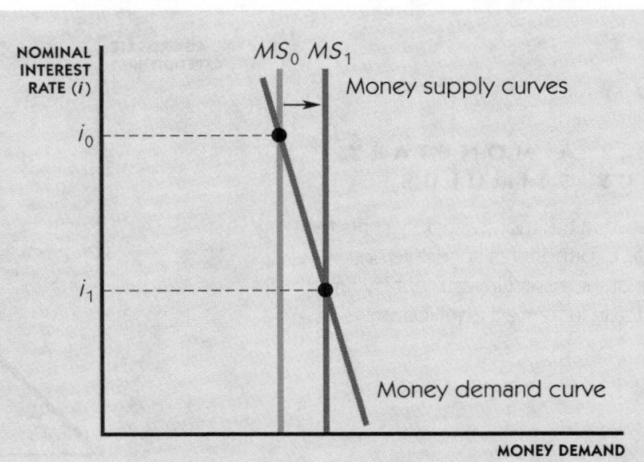

EQUILIBRIUM

In equilibrium, the interest rate adjusts to make the demand for money equal the supply. Figure 12.2 shows supply curves for money as well as a demand curve. The supply of money is controlled by the government (the Fed), through the instruments described in Chapter 11. The amount of money the government makes available does not depend at all on the interest rate. That is why the supply curves are vertical. The equilibrium interest rate with money supply MS_0 is i_0.

The principles described in this section—that the nominal interest rate is the opportunity cost of holding money, that the demand for money decreases as the interest rate rises, and that the interest rate is determined to equate the demand and supply of money—are together sometimes called **Keynesian monetary theory,** or **traditional monetary theory.** Keynes used this theory to explain how monetary policy works when it works, and why it sometimes does not work. To do this, he traced out the effects of a change in the supply of money on the interest rate, the effects of a change in the interest rate on investment, and the effects of a change in investment on the level of national income. We now take a closer look at each of the steps in this analysis.

MONETARY POLICY AND INTEREST RATES

Figure 12.2 can also be used to show how changes in the money supply can lead to changes in the interest rates. Initially, the money supply is at MS_0 and the equilibrium interest rate is i_0. When the government increases the money supply to MS_1, the interest rate falls to i_1. In the figure, the demand for money is relatively inelastic, so that an increase in the supply of money at a given level of income causes a large decrease in the interest rate. As the interest rate falls,

Figure 12.3 A MONETARY POLICY STIMULUS

An increase in the money supply shifts the aggregate expenditures schedule up, because of increased investment by firms, leading to an increased equilibrium output.

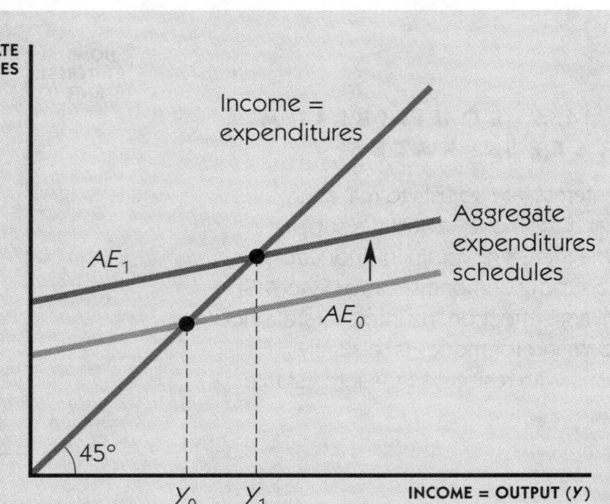

investment rises. As investment spending increases, income (which is the same as output) rises via the multiplier. (Actually, as discussed earlier, investment depends on the *real* interest rate, denoted by *r*, not the nominal interest rate. But in this part of the book, the price level is fixed, so the nominal and real interest rates are identical.)

The increase in investment shifts the aggregate expenditures schedule up, as depicted in Figure 12.3, and results in a higher equilibrium level of output. Output increases from Y_0 to Y_1.

When income increases, the money demand curve shifts to the right, as shown in Figure 12.4. Thus, the eventual equilibrium attained will involve a

Figure 12.4 SECOND-ROUND EFFECTS OF INCREASED MONEY SUPPLY

In the first round, the increased money supply led to lower interest rates (Figure 12.2), which led in turn to higher levels of national income (Figure 12.3). This higher level of income now shifts the money demand curve up (since the demand for money at each interest rate is higher). The equilibrium interest rate is i_2.

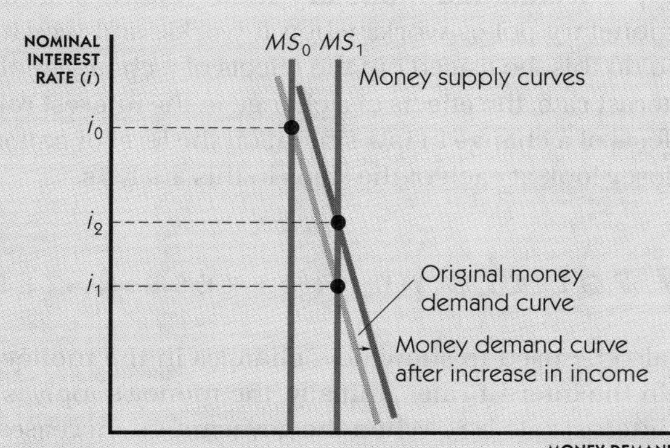

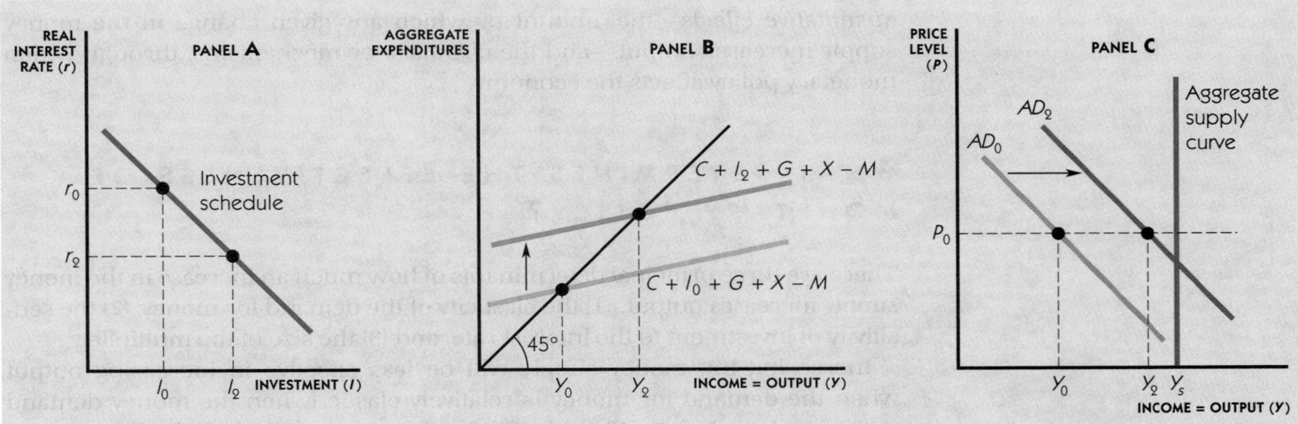

Figure 12.5 TRACING OUT THE FULL EFFECTS OF AN INCREASE IN MONEY SUPPLY

An increase in the money supply leads to a lower interest rate. Panel A shows that the lower interest rate leads to increased investment. Panel B shows that the increased investment shifts the aggregate expenditures schedule up, leading to a higher equilibrium output *at each price level.* Panel C shows that as a result, the aggregate demand curve shifts to the right.

smaller decrease in the rate of interest than i_1. The new equilibrium interest rate will lie somewhere between i_0 and i_1. In the figure, it is i_2.

We can trace out the equilibrium in the capital market at the new equilibrium interest rate: panel A of Figure 12.5 shows the level of investment, I_2, when the real interest rate is r_2 (which corresponds to the new equilibrium nominal interest rate, i_2), while panel B shows the aggregate expenditures schedule when investment is equal to I_2, and the equilibrium level of output Y_2.

The aggregate expenditures schedule assumes a particular price level. A similar effect of an increase in the money supply occurs at each price. In Chapter 9 we showed how to derive the aggregate demand curve by tracing out the intersection of the aggregate expenditures schedule with the 45-degree line at each price level. Since at each price level, the equilibrium level of output is higher, the aggregate demand curve has shifted to the right, as depicted in panel C. In this chapter, we are focusing on situations where price is fixed and there is excess capacity. We see clearly in panel C how the shift in the aggregate demand curve translates into an increase in aggregate output from Y_0 *to* Y_2.

The results of this section lead us to our twelfth point of consensus in economics:

12 Using Monetary Policy to Stimulate the Economy

When there is excess capacity and prices are rigid, increasing the money supply normally stimulates the economy, leading to higher levels of output.

While there is consensus on the conclusion that monetary policy can stimulate the economy, there is far less agreement about two other issues: The *quantitative effects*—the amount by which any given change in the money supply increases output—and the *channels,* or mechanisms, through which monetary policy affects the economy.

WHAT DETERMINES THE EFFECTIVENESS OF MONETARY POLICY?

There are three principal determinants of how much an increase in the money supply increases output: (1) the elasticity of the demand for money, (2) the sensitivity of investment to the interest rate, and (3) the size of the multiplier.

Increasing the money supply will be less effective in increasing output when the demand for money is relatively elastic (when the money demand curve is relatively flat). When the demand for money is relatively elastic, an increase in the money supply has little effect on interest rates—interest rates decrease only slightly (see Figure 12.6, panel A). *Other things being equal,* when the interest rate decreases little, there is only a small increase in investment, resulting in a small increase in GDP.

Increasing the money supply will be less effective in increasing output when investment is not very sensitive to the interest rate (investment is inelas-

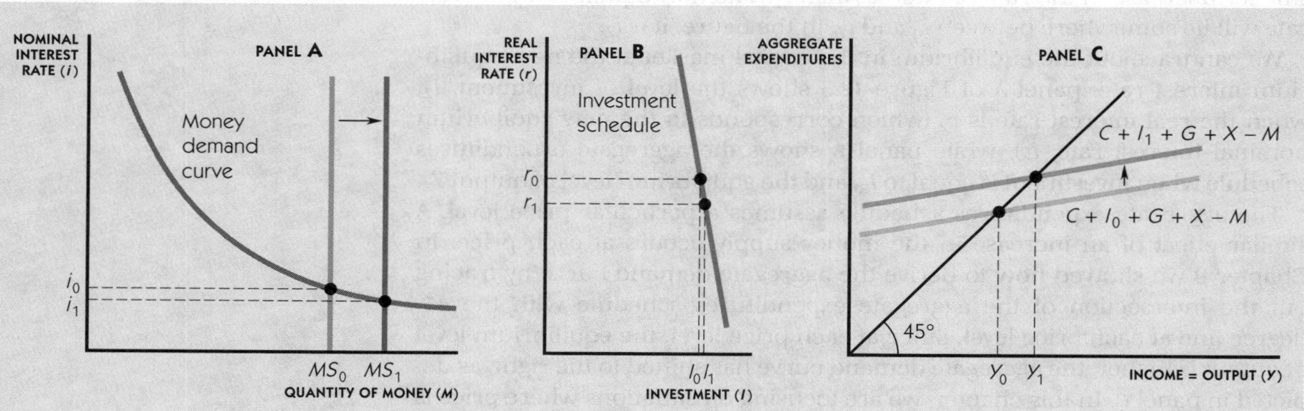

Figure 12.6 **EFFECTS OF MONETARY POLICY IN A SEVERE RECESSION**

Panel A shows that if the demand curve for money is flat, an increase in the money supply has little effect on interest rates. Panel B shows that if the investment schedule is steep, a decrease in interest rates has little effect on investment. Panel C shows that if the aggregate expenditures schedule is very flat, the multiplier is small, so that aggregate output increases very little.

tic). In this case a decrease in the interest rate resulting from an increase in the money supply will have little effect on investment, and therefore GDP (see Figure 12.6, panel B).

An increase in investment has less of an effect on output when the multiplier is small. For any given increase in investment, the smaller the multiplier, the smaller the increase in GDP. Thus, an increase in the money supply will result in a smaller increase in output when the multiplier is smaller. And, as we saw in Chapter 9, the multiplier is smaller if (1) the marginal propensity to save is large, (2) tax rates are large, or (3) the marginal propensity to import is large.

Many economists argue—as did Keynes—that when the economy is in a deep recession, monetary policy is relatively ineffective. They believe that the demand curve for money appears as in Figure 12.6A: at least at low interest rates it is relatively flat. As a result, monetary authorities have a hard time driving the interest rate down further. Exacerbating the problem facing monetary authorities is a fact that takes us beyond the model of this chapter—but is nonetheless real: in deep recessions, prices actually fall. In the Great Depression, prices fell by 25 percent. In the economic downturn in Japan in 1994 and 1995, prices fell slightly. What investors care about is *real interest rates*—the difference between the nominal interest rates and the rate of inflation. If the nominal interest rate falls, but the rate of inflation falls more, real interest rates rise. With falling prices, real interest rates exceed the nominal interest rates. If prices are falling at 10 percent a year, then even a zero nominal interest rate corresponds to a 10 percent real interest rate—by historical standards, an extremely high real interest rate.

Moreover, given investors' pessimism about economic prospects, it takes a large fall in interest rates to induce firms to invest much more. Since by definition, in a recession, there is considerable excess capacity, the marginal return from extra investment is close to zero. New machines simply add to excess capacity, not to profits. Only if the new machines are much better than the old (using so much less labor that the savings in labor more than offsets the additional capital costs) or if they are designed to make a new product, will it pay firms to make additional investments. Moreover, a lengthy period of losses will deplete a firm's cash reserves, and increase its indebtedness. Facing the threat of bankruptcy, the firm will be reluctant to undertake additional new investments, even if it could persuade banks to lend it money. As a result of these negative factors, as the economy goes into a recession, not only will the investment schedule shift down, but it also becomes relatively inelastic, that is, lower interest rates have only a small effect in inducing additional investment (Panel B, Figure 12.6).

Since increasing the money supply has a small effect on interest rates, and the decrease in interest rates has only a small effect on investment, increasing the money supply has a small effect on output, as illustrated in Figure 12.6C.

Some economists have described the ineffectiveness of monetary policy in deep recessions by saying that it is like pushing on a string. While economists differ in their judgments about how deep a recession it takes before monetary policy becomes relatively ineffective, they agree on the basic principle. This brings us to our thirteenth point of consensus in economics:

13 Monetary Policy in a Deep Recession

When the economy is in a deep recession, monetary policy is relatively ineffective in stimulating the economy to recover.

Some advocates of monetary policy claim, however, that all that matters is that there be some effect of monetary policy. A weak effect—for a given percentage change in the money supply—simply means that monetary authorities have to take more aggressive actions, by increasing the money supply by a larger percentage.

TRADITIONAL MONETARY THEORY

The nominal interest rate is the opportunity cost of holding money.
The demand for money decreases as the interest rate rises.
The interest rate equates the demand and supply for money.

TRADITIONAL THEORY OF MONETARY POLICY

When monetary policy is effective in generating increased output, it is because the policy induces a lower interest rate.

Monetary policy is ineffective in deep recessions, because

1. The money demand curve is elastic, so changes in the money supply induce only small changes in interest rates; and
2. Even large changes in the interest rate induce little change in investment and hence in aggregate demand.

MONETARISM

While there is broad agreement on the two consensus points stated above—that monetary policy can be used effectively to stimulate the economy, except when there is a deep recession—some economists, called **monetarists,** argue that the *only* effect of monetary policy is on the price level. They believe that the basic assumption underlying this chapter—that prices are fixed—is simply wrong. They argue that prices are flexible, even in the short run. Thus, *all* that happens when the money supply increases is that the price level changes with no changes in output or employment. In fact they believe that prices move approximately in proportion to the change in the money supply. They believe that the full-employment model discussed in Chapter 6 applies at all times. Some monetarists believe that even if there is unemployment, and output is below the economy's capacity, increases in the money supply are still mostly reflected in changes in the price level.

To see how monetarists arrive at this conclusion, we need to return to the equation of exchange. The equation of exchange, as presented, was a *definition* of velocity. But they make one additional assumption—velocity is constant. Thus

$$M\bar{V} = PY$$

where the bar over the V reminds us that it is fixed. If Y is assumed fixed (say at its full-employment level), then increases in M get translated into proportionate increases in P.

This equation also gives us a simple rule for the expansion of the money supply. If we want prices to be stable, and real income is increasing at say 2 percent a year, then the money supply should increase at 2 percent a year. Monetarists believe that monetary policy should focus on the monetary aggregates (the measures of the money supply), and that money supply should increase in proportion to increases in real output. Doing this will lead to stable prices.

These are the *conclusions* of the monetarists. They can, however, be simply related to the traditional monetary theory. Monetarists believe that the demand for money is just proportional to nominal output (income). It does not depend on the interest rate. Note the contrast with traditional Keynesian theory. While Keynes assumed that in deep recessions the demand curve for money was almost horizontal (the elasticity was very large), monetarists assume that the demand curve is vertical (demand does not depend on the interest rate).

$$M_d = (\text{a constant})Y_m,$$

that is, the demand for money, M_d, equals a constant times nominal income (output), Y_m. Since money demand equals money supply,

$$M_d = M_s,$$

increasing money supply increases nominal aggregate output (income) proportionately. Furthermore, since nominal income is the price level P times the real output, Y,

$$Y_m = PY,$$

if Y is *fixed*, then increasing nominal output (income) Y_m leads to an equiproportionate increase in the price level. In other words, if money supply doubles, in equilibrium, money demand must double. Money demand can

Close-up: Experimenting with a Theory—The Fed Causes a Recession

Before the late 1970s, the focus of the Federal Reserve was mainly interest rates. When the Fed thought the economy needed a boost, it decided how low it wanted interest rates to go, and expanded the money supply (for instance, by engaging in open market operations) until the interest rate reached that target. Paul Volcker, when named chairman of the Federal Reserve Board in 1979, announced that henceforth the Fed would increase the money supply at a predetermined rate, regardless of what happened to the interest rate. He shifted the "target" from controlling the interest rate to controlling the money supply. The chosen rate of expansion of the money supply was set sufficiently low to bring down the rate of inflation, which had climbed from 6.7 percent in 1977 to 9.0 percent in 1978 and 13.3 percent in 1979.

Volcker's policy was based on the theory that velocity was constant (or at least predictable). If the money supply increased at a steady pace, enough to accommodate the increased production of goods (and any anticipated change in velocity), then the price level would be steady. Recall the definition of velocity (V): $V = PY/M$.

The Fed pursued this policy vigorously. When the money supply started to increase faster than the amount targeted, the Fed engaged in open market operations, selling government bonds. Growth in the money supply was reduced, but interest rates soared to 10, then 15, then 20 percent, pushing the economy into the recessions of 1980 and 1981–82.

The Fed abandoned this policy of targeting the money supply, for two reasons. First, the rate of inflation tumbled sharply, falling to 3.8 percent in 1982. With inflation much lower and the economy in a recession, it became important to try to stimulate the economy rather than harness inflation. Second, it became increasingly evident that the velocity of circulation was not constant, and the rapidly changing financial institutions also made the appropriate definition of money less and less clear. Saying that the money supply should expand at a constant rate was one thing, but in practice did that mean M1, M2, or M3? Today the monetary authorities keep an eye on interest rates and all of the indicators of the money supply, and search for an overall feel for what these sometimes conflicting indicators are telling them.

Paul Volcker, former chairman, Federal Reserve Board

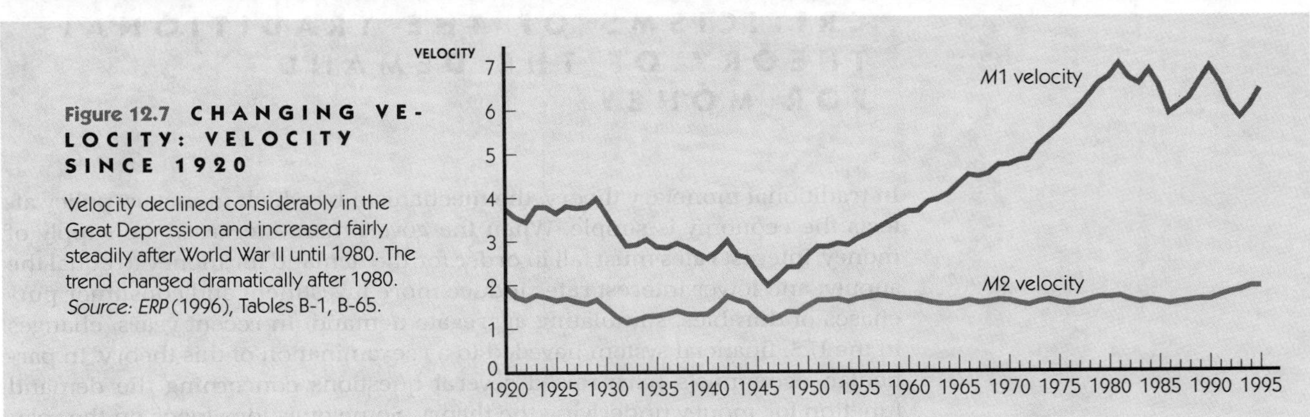

Figure 12.7 CHANGING VELOCITY: VELOCITY SINCE 1920

Velocity declined considerably in the Great Depression and increased fairly steadily after World War II until 1980. The trend changed dramatically after 1980. *Source: ERP* (1996), Tables B-1, B-65.

only double if nominal aggregate output (income) doubles, and nominal aggregate output (income) can double only if the price level doubles.

Thus, the assumption that the demand for money does not depend on the interest rate is equivalent to the assumption that velocity (PY/M) is constant. The theory that holds that because velocity is constant, increases in the money supply are reflected simply in proportionate increases in nominal income is called the **quantity theory of money.** While there have been long periods for which velocity has been nearly constant, in recent years it has changed, and often in ways that are hard to predict, as Figures 12.7 and 12.8 illustrate.

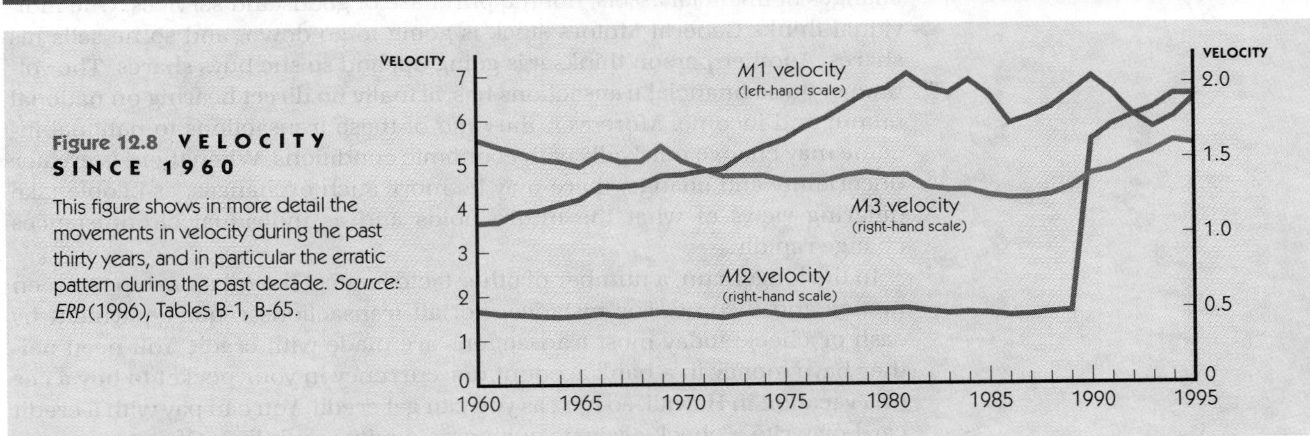

Figure 12.8 VELOCITY SINCE 1960

This figure shows in more detail the movements in velocity during the past thirty years, and in particular the erratic pattern during the past decade. *Source: ERP* (1996), Tables B-1, B-65.

CRITICISMS OF THE TRADITIONAL THEORY OF THE DEMAND FOR MONEY

In traditional monetary theory, the mechanism by which monetary policy affects the economy is simple. When the government increases the supply of money, interest rates must fall in order for the demand for money to equal the supply; and lower interest rates induce more investment and consumer purchases of durables, stimulating aggregate demand. In recent years, changes in the U.S. financial system have led to a reexamination of this theory. In particular, economists have raised several questions concerning the demand function for money underlying the theory. Some questions focus on the relationship between the demand for money and income, others on the effect of interest rates on the demand for money.

RELATIONSHIP BETWEEN MONEY AND INCOME

Earlier we saw that what particularly distinguishes money from other assets such as government Treasury bills is its role as a medium of exchange in facilitating transactions. The traditional monetary theory implies that the higher their income, the more money people will want to hold. In other words, there is a simple relationship between the volume of transactions and the level of income. This would be the case if most transactions were directly related to output—employers paying wages and buying goods from suppliers, customers buying goods from firms, and so on.

But in fact, in terms of their dollar value, most transactions are for exchanges of financial assets, not the purchase of goods and services. One individual thinks General Motors stock is going to go down, and so he sells his shares. Another person thinks it is going up, and so she buys shares. The volume of these financial transactions has virtually no direct bearing on national output and income. Moreover, the *ratio* of these transactions to national income may change markedly with economic conditions. When there is greater uncertainty and change, there may be more such exchanges, as people take differing views of what the future holds and as individual circumstances change rapidly.

In the longer run, a number of other factors affect the relationship between money and income. For instance, not all transactions require payment by cash or check; today most transactions are made with credit. You need neither have money in a bank account nor currency in your pocket to buy a car or a vacation in Hawaii, so long as you can get credit. You can pay with a credit card or write a check against your home equity credit line. Of course, some kinds of transactions are still not easily done with credit. In most cities in the

United States, for example, you still have to pay for taxis with cash. But in Australia, taxis accept Visa, MasterCard, and American Express. The transactions that require money at the point of sale represent a relatively small and shrinking proportion of all transactions in the modern economy.

Indeed, technology has altered the whole idea of the role and velocity of money. Money market mutual funds invest in Treasury bills, but often allow individuals to write checks just like a banking account. What technically happens is that the mutual fund has an arrangement with a bank upon which the check is actually written. Assume Joe writes a check to Jim. Jim takes the check to his bank. When the check arrives at Joe's mutual fund's bank to be honored, the mutual fund instantaneously transfers the required amount of money into Joe's account, from which it is instantaneously transferred out to Jim's bank, so that Jim's bank can credit Jim's account. Recall we said before that the reason that people hold money rather than T-bills is because it is a better medium of exchange. The new technologies effectively allow people to use T-bills as a medium of exchange.

Relationship between Interest Rates and the Demand for Money

This brings us to the second set of criticisms: most money, as we have seen, is in the form of demand deposits, and today—unlike fifty years ago when traditional monetary theory was first formulated—demand deposits generally bear interest. Thus, the opportunity cost of holding "money" is not the interest rate, but the *difference* between the return to holding a government bond, for example, and the interest paid on demand deposits. That difference is generally small and relates primarily to the bank's cost of running the checking account. The existence of interest-bearing checking accounts calls into question the extent to which the demand for money will rise or fall in response to changes in interest rates.

Other Criticisms of Traditional Monetary Theory

Traditional monetary theory assumed that changing the money supply affected the economy through changes in *real* interest rates. Yet there have been long periods in which real interest rates have varied very little (see Figure 10.8 on p. 265). Nominal interest rates tend to move up or down with inflation, so variations in real interest rates are far smaller than variations in nominal interest rates. Monetary policy seems to have effects that are far larger than would be indicated by the relatively small variations in real interest rates.

CRITICISMS OF TRADITIONAL MONETARY THEORY

There is no simple relationship between the demand for money and income.

- Most transactions involve not goods and services (output) but the exchange of assets. The connection between transactions related to output and those related to exchange may not be stable.
- Transactions do not necessarily need money; credit will do.
- Today, more extensive use is made of credit (credit cards) and money market funds, which effectively allow people to use T-bills as a medium of exchange.

There is no simple relationship between real interest rates and money demand and supply.

- Today, most money takes the form of demand deposits and is interest-bearing. Thus, the opportunity cost of holding money is low and is not directly related to the interest rate.
- Changes in the rate of inflation may offset changes in the nominal interest rate.

ALTERNATIVE MECHANISMS

Traditional monetary theory has thus been questioned on several fronts—both the theory of demand for money, which underlies it, and the role of interest rates. But monetary policy does seem to matter. There are several alternative mechanisms through which monetary policy exercises its influence.

CREDIT AVAILABILITY

One channel is through credit availability. In Chapter 11, we looked at the two sides of the bank's balance sheet—its deposits (the money supply) and its assets, which include loans. Various actions of the Federal Reserve reduce both deposits (the money supply) and the supply of available loans. Figure 12.9 shows the demand and supply of "credit," both a function of the interest rate. Restrictive monetary policy has the effect of reducing banks' supply of loans—shifting the loan supply curve to the left, and increasing the equilibrium interest rate at which credit is made available, while decreasing the equilibrium level of lending.

At times, banks may ration the amount of credit they make available. They typically do not simply lend to anyone willing to borrow at the interest rates

Figure 12.9 EFFECT OF MONETARY POLICY VIEWED THROUGH IMPACT ON CREDIT AVAILABILITY

Restrictive monetary policy reduces the supply of loans available at any interest rate. Thus, the equilibrium interest rate increases (from r_0 to r_1) and the quantity of loans made is reduced from L_0 to L_1. In some circumstances, interest rates appear to be rigid, and do not adjust. There will then be credit rationing, with the demand for loans exceeding the supply. In that case, the decrease in loans may even be greater, to L_2.

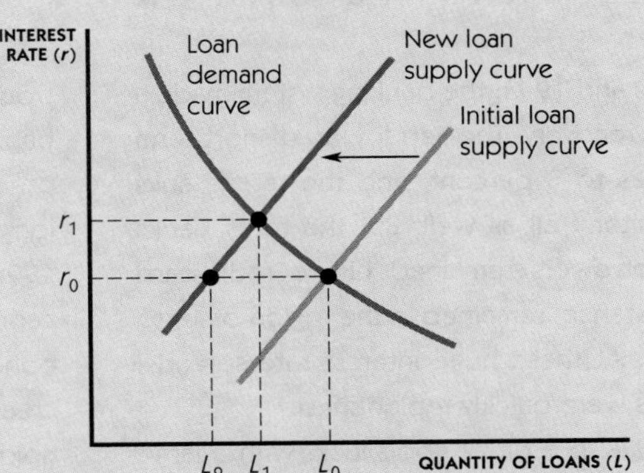

they charge. At times, they may not even extend loans to all those deemed "credit-worthy" who would like loans. They could, of course, raise the interest rate charged; but they may worry that by doing so, the best risks—those most likely to repay the loan—will go elsewhere, or decide it is not worth borrowing at such interest rates. If interest rates—like other prices—remain fixed, then a shift in the loan supply curve has an even larger effect than when interest rates adjust, as Figure 12.9 illustrates.

Even when credit is not being rationed, banks respond to a situation of tighter credit by adjusting terms of the loan contract other than the interest rate: they may, for instance, require more collateral.

In any case, the shift in the availability of credit (the shift of the loan supply curve to the left) results in lower investment, either because interest rates are higher (making it less attractive to undertake investments), because other terms of the loan contract are adjusted to make borrowing less attractive, or because funds required to undertake investments simply are not available.

PORTFOLIO THEORIES

An alternative channel by which monetary policy may affect the economy is through the price of shares and long-term bonds. At lower *nominal* interest rates, the value of long-term bonds typically increases. People feel wealthier, and because they feel wealthier, they consume more. Moreover, because bonds yield lower returns, investors turn to stocks. As the demand for stocks increases, their prices rise. Higher stock prices not only lead to increased consumption, but also to increased investment: at the higher stock prices, more firms believe that it is a good time to issue new shares, to raise additional capital, to finance new investments.

Portfolio theories argue that monetary policy affects the level of economic activity not only, or so much, through its *direct* impact on interest rates (as a

Policy Perspective: The Recovery of the Banking System

During 1992 and 1993, the banking system made a remarkable recovery. The Fed lowered short-term interest rates to 3 percent, and the rates banks paid depositors fell as well. But the rates banks charged borrowers remained high. Credit card rates, for instance, remained in the region of 16 to 20 percent. At these huge interest rate spreads, bank coffers were quickly replenished.

There was also a bit of good luck: with a large spread between long-term rates and short-term rates, many banks gambled, buying long-term government bonds. Long-term bonds yielded much higher returns than short-term bonds. Though there was no risk of default, there was a risk that the price of long-term bonds might fall, with disastrous consequences for these banks. (At the time, bank regulations only focused on default risk, not price risk.) As it turned out, the price of these long-term bonds increased substantially in late 1992 and 1993. The banks thus enjoyed a large capital gain, in addition to the higher yields of the bonds. As the economy recovered, banks increased their loan portfolios and decreased their holding of long-term government bonds. Thus, the plummeting of long-term bond prices in 1994 had relatively little impact on the banking sector.

With higher net worths, banks were willing to make more credit available. Interest rates charged on loans fell, investment increased, and the economy expanded.

result of the interaction of the demand and supply of money), but through a variety of indirect mechanisms, as individuals adjust their **portfolios,** the bundle of assets—including stocks and bonds— that they hold. These adjustments in the demands for other assets result in changes in their prices, and it is through these changes that monetary policy ultimately has its most important effects.

MONETARY POLICY IN AN OPEN ECONOMY

In today's open, international economy, one of the most important ways by which monetary policy affects the level of economic activity is by affecting the exchange rate: lowering interest rates leads to a lower exchange rate—the number of yen that can be traded for a dollar. A lower exchange rate makes American goods more attractive abroad—and foreign goods less attractive here—and thus increases exports and decreases imports. For instance, between January and April 1995 the exchange rate between the dollar and the yen fell approximately 20 percent. Thus, to a Japanese consumer, a $100 American shirt fell in price by 20 percent, from 10,000 yen to 8,000 yen. And to an American consumer, the price of Japanese goods increased by 25 percent. A computer that sold in Japan for 100,000 yen—and thus cost $1,000 in the United States—would now cost Americans $1,250. (In practice, the changes were somewhat less dramatic, since in the short run, exporters and importers "absorb" some of the variation in exchange rates.)

As exports increase and imports decrease, *net* exports increase. As Figure 12.10 illustrates, an increase in net exports leads to an increase in aggregate output. In this section, we explain in more detail how monetary policy affects the exchange rate. We begin with a review of what determines the exchange rate.

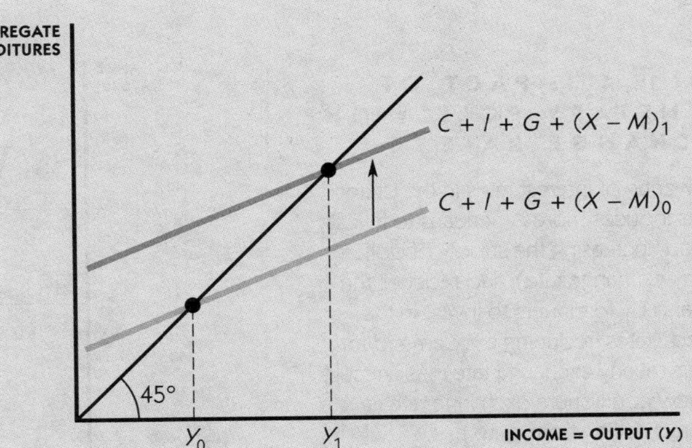

Figure 12.10 IMPACT OF AN INCREASE IN NET EXPORTS ON AGGREGATE OUTPUT

A depreciation of the exchange rate reduces the price of American goods relative to foreign-produced goods, increasing exports and reducing imports. An increase in net exports shifts the aggregate expenditures schedule up and results in an increased equilibrium level of output.

How Monetary Policy Affects Exchange Rates

In Chapter 7, we saw that the yen–dollar exchange rate (for example) is determined by the intersection of the demand and supply curves for dollars. The demand for dollars is determined in turn by Japan's demand for U.S. goods, and Japan's desire to invest in the United States. Similarly, the supply of dollars is determined by U.S. demand for Japanese goods and Americans' desire to invest in Japan. When the Fed lowers the interest rate, foreigners find it less attractive to invest in the United States, and Americans find it more attractive to invest abroad. This shifts the demand for dollars to the left and the supply of dollars to the right, as in Figure 12.11. The net result is a decrease in the exchange rate, an increase in exports, and a decrease in imports.

Why Traditional Channels of Monetary Policy May Be Less Effective in an Open Economy

While there is thus a new channel through which monetary policy exercises its influence, some of the other channels may in fact be much weaker in an open economy. One of the ways that we saw that monetary policy exercises its influence is in reducing the availability of credit. But if American firms can borrow abroad, then restricting credit from American banks simply induces borrowers to seek funds elsewhere. To be sure, not everyone has access to foreign banks. But the thousands of multinational firms do. And if enough of these firms switch their borrowing abroad, it frees up funds so American

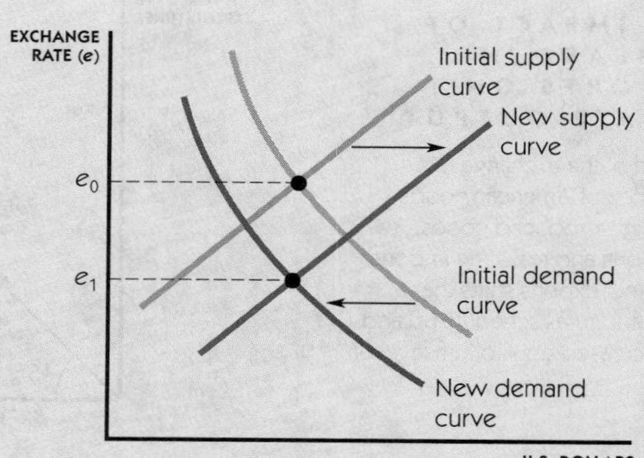

Figure 12.11 IMPACT OF MONETARY POLICY ON EXCHANGE RATES

A lowering of interest rates in the United States induces more Americans to invest abroad, increasing the supply of dollars (at any exchange rate); and reduces the demand by foreigners to invest in the United States, reducing the demand for dollars (at any exchange rate). As a result, the new equilibrium exchange rate is lowered, falling from e_0 to e_1.

banks can continue their lending to those who do not have access to foreign banks.

REVIEW AND PRACTICE

SUMMARY

1. Theories concerning the effect of monetary policy on the economy focus on the two sides of the banks' balance sheet, on money and on credit.

2. When prices are fixed, changes in the supply of money can cause changes in holdings of money or changes in output. When the economy has considerable excess capacity, normally output will increase; in deep recessions, the effect on output may be minimal.

3. Traditional theories of the demand for money focus on its dependence on the (nominal) rate of interest and on the level of income. Equilibrium requires the demand for money to be equal to the supply. Changes in the supply of money result in changes in the interest rate and, through changes in the interest rate, in the level of aggregate expenditures and equilibrium output.

4. In severe recessions, the interest elasticity of the demand for money may be high and the interest elasticity of investment is low, so monetary policy may be relatively ineffective.

5. The quantity theory of money holds that the demand for money does not depend on the interest rate, and accordingly that the velocity of money is constant. Increases in money supply then result in proportionate increases in national income. In recent years, however, velocity has not only not been constant; it has changed in relatively unpredictable ways.

6. There are many difficulties with the traditional monetary theory. Money is not used for many transactions, and many transactions involve exchanges of assets, which have little to do with income generation. Changes in technology and the structure of the economy may alter the money-income relationship. Most money bears interest, and the opportunity cost is only the difference between the interest rate it pays and the interest rate on government Treasury bills.

7. Portfolio theories stress the effect of changes in monetary policy on the demand and supply of various assets (including money) and the resulting effect on prices of assets.

8. Credit availability theories stress the effects of monetary policy on the availability of credit (the supply of loans) by banks.

9. In an open economy, monetary policy is likely to have a smaller effect on interest rates and credit availability than it otherwise would. If the Fed

attempts to restrict credit or raise interest rates, American firms can borrow from abroad.

10. In an open economy, monetary policy has effects on exchange rates: a reduction in the money supply leading to higher interest rates leads to an appreciation of the dollar, a decrease in exports, and an increase in imports.

KEY TERMS

velocity
equation of exchange
transactions demand for money
monetarists
quantity theory of money
portfolio theories

REVIEW QUESTIONS

1. What might happen in response to a change in the money supply?

2. Why does demand for money fall as the interest rate rises? What is the opportunity cost of holding money that pays interest (such as demand deposits)?

3. What might cause changes in the relationship between the demand for money and income besides changes in the interest rate?

4. Why might changes in the money supply not lead to increases in the level of investment in a severe recession?

5. What assumptions are involved in the quantity theory of money? What conclusion can be drawn on the basis of those assumptions? What is the evidence concerning the constancy of the velocity of circulation?

6. What are alternative mechanisms by which portfolio theories suggest that monetary policy affects the economy?

7. Describe how monetary policy might affect investment or consumption, *even if monetary policy has little effect at all on interest rates.*

8. How does the fact that an economy is open affect monetary policy? How do exchange rate changes affect equilibrium levels of output? How does monetary policy affect equilibrium exchange rates?

PROBLEMS

1. If GDP is $4 trillion and the money supply is $200 billion, what is velocity? How does your answer change if GDP rises to $5 trillion while the money supply remains the same? If GDP remains at $4 trillion while the money supply increases to $250 billion, how does velocity change?

2. Graph the money demand curve from the following data, with quantity of money demanded given in billions of dollars.

Interest rate	7%	8%	9%	10%	11%	12%
Money demand	900	880	860	840	820	810

How do changes in national income affect the demand curve?

3. Using money supply and demand diagrams, explain how the elasticity of the money demand curve determines whether monetary policy can have a substantial effect on the interest rate.

4. Explain how the elasticity of investment with respect to interest rates determines whether monetary policy can have a substantial effect on aggregate demand.

5. Explain how each of the following might affect the demand for money:
   (a) interest is paid on checking accounts;
   (b) credit cards become more readily available;
   (c) electronic fund transfers become common.

Would the changes in the demand for money necessarily reduce the ability of the Fed to use monetary policy to affect the economy?

6. How might an increase in national income affect the exchange rate? Before 1973 exchange rates were *fixed* by the government (with the government buying and selling dollars in order to maintain the set exchange rate). Contrast the effects of an increase in investment on equilibrium output assuming the exchange rate is fixed with the effects if exchange rates are *flexible,* that is, are allowed to vary freely to equilibrate demand and supply.

7. Describe the impact of the appreciation of the yen relative to the dollar on the Japanese economy, using the aggregate expenditures schedule.

8. In the text, we saw that if output was growing at 2 percent per year, and velocity is constant, if the government wanted stable prices, it should expand the money supply at 2 percent. In fact, velocity has been falling gradually over time. Assume that velocity in any year does not depend on the interest rate, but year after year, it falls at the rate of 1 percent per year. What does this imply about the rate at which the monetary authorities should expand the money supply if they wished to maintain stable prices?

9. Assume that banks are worried that if they raise the interest rate, they will attract borrowers who are riskier, that is, less likely to repay their loan. Borrowers who realize that there is a good chance that they will not repay their loan may be less sensitive to increases in interest rates, while borrowers who invest in conservative, safe projects will decide that at high interest rates, it simply does not pay to borrow and invest. Why might this mean that as the bank raises its interest rates, its expected return (taking into account the probability of default) might actually decrease? Assume there was an interest rate at which the expected return

was maximized, that is, further increases actually lead to a lowering of expected return. What would happen if at that interest rate, the demand for funds exceeds the supply? Would banks raise the interest rate they charged anyway?

10. Use the equation of exchange to explain the alternative possible effects of changing the money supply. (a) What happens if velocity and output are constant? (b) What happens if price and velocity are constant? (c) What does traditional monetary policy say about the normal effect of monetary policy on velocity? What does this do to the magnitude of the effect on output compared to what it would have been had velocity been constant (assuming price is constant)? (d) What does traditional monetary policy say about what happens when the economy is in a deep recession?

What do you think is the most plausible response of prices to an increase in the money supply when there is a large excess capacity and high unemployment in the economy?

11. Assume that for one reason or another, the interest rate on loans is fixed, and there is credit rationing. Show on a diagram what this implies. Assume that there are firms that rely on borrowing to finance their investment projects. They invest all of their cash flow, plus what they can borrow. What happens to investment if they have a bad year—say their sales drop because of a temporary recession in the countries to which they export goods? Show what happens to investment and GDP if as a result of monetary policy, the supply of funds at each interest rate increases? Use the diagram to explain why monetary policy may be even more effective in such situations than if the interest rate adjusts?

If the multiplier is 2, and the government increases credit availability by \$100 billion, what happens to GDP if the interest rate does not adjust. Assume that the interest rate always adjusts to equate the demand and supply of funds (a closed economy), and that the interest rate elasticity of savings is 1, so that a lowering of the interest rate from 10 percent to 9 percent lowers savings by 10 percent. Assume that initially investment (equals savings) is \$900 billion, and that as a result of monetary policy, at each interest rate, \$100 billion more funds are available for lending, but that the interest rate falls from 10 percent to 9 percent. Calculate what happens to GDP now.

APPENDIX: AN ALGEBRAIC DERIVATION OF EQUILIBRIUM IN THE MONEY MARKET

The money demand equation can be written

$$M_d = M_d(r, PY),$$

where M_d is the demand for money. If M_s is the money supply, then the equilibrium condition that the demand for money equals the supply can be written

$$M_s = M_d(r, PY). \tag{12.1}$$

From Chapter 9, we know that

$$Y = C + I + G,$$

where I (investment) depends on the interest rate, r, and G (government expenditures) is assumed to be fixed. If consumption is just $(1 - s)$ times income Y, then

$$Y = (1 - s)Y + I(r) + G,$$

or

$$Y = [I(r) + G]/s. \tag{12.2}$$

Equations (12.1) and (12.2) provide us with two equations in two unknowns (assuming that the price level P is fixed). The solution gives us the equilibrium income and interest rate. An increase in the money supply results in a new solution, with a lower interest rate and a higher level of national income.

CHAPTER 13

FISCAL AND MONETARY POLICY

There are three principal objectives of monetary and fiscal policy: maintaining full employment, promoting economic growth, and maintaining price stability. In Chapters 6 and 7, we saw that when the economy is at full employment, government policy can have significant effects on the growth rate, by affecting the level of investment. At full employment, there is a fixed size pie, and government actions affect how that pie is divided. But when there is unemployment and resources are not fully utilized, government actions can affect both the size of the pie and how it is divided. Even if a smaller share of national output goes to investment, if national output is increased enough, the level of investment will actually increase, and long-run growth will be promoted.

This chapter pulls together the insights of earlier chapters of this part to see how fiscal and monetary policy may be used to stimulate the economy and promote economic growth. We will compare the effects of monetary and fiscal policy, and analyze several issues that arise in the application of policy today. Later chapters will explore how fiscal and monetary policy relate to the problem of maintaining price stability.

KEY QUESTIONS

1. What difference does it make whether we use monetary or fiscal policy to help the economy out of a recession?
2. What are the economic effects of an increase in government expenditures accompanied by an increase in taxes of the same amount?
3. What might be the consequences of a balanced budget amendment on economic stability?

FISCAL POLICY

In Chapter 8 we defined fiscal policy as efforts to improve macroeconomic performance through changes in government expenditures and taxes. Faced with output below the full-employment level, policymakers may help restore the economy to full employment through an increase in government expenditures or a reduction in taxes. Recall our aggregate expenditures diagram from Chapter 9. An increase in government expenditures shifts the aggregate expenditures schedule up, as shown in Figure 13.1A. Equilibrium output at each price level increases, and the aggregate demand schedule shifts to the right, as illustrated in Figure 13.1B. A tax cut puts more money in the pockets of consumers, leading to an increase in consumption. This also shifts the aggregate expenditures schedule up and results in a rightward shift of the aggregate demand curve. Either way, the economy is brought closer to the full-employment level of output.

IS IT WORTH INCURRING A DEFICIT TO GET OUT OF A RECESSION?

The problem with an increase in government expenditures, or a tax cut, is that it increases the deficit. There are two concerns. First, even if the fiscal stimulus makes us better off now, future generations are saddled with debt, making them worse off. However, if government expands its investment—in infrastructure, human capital, or research—future generations may actually be better off, provided the return on those investments exceeds the interest rate. Estimated returns in many of these areas are very high. Most estimates put the return on investment in research in excess of 20 percent, and estimates of the return on investment in education greatly exceed the interest rate.

But even if increased expenditures are spent on consumption, the outcome appears favorable. Assume the government spends $1 billion in public consumption goods. As a result of the multiplier, the net increase in current income (consumption) is much higher. If the multiplier is 2, national income

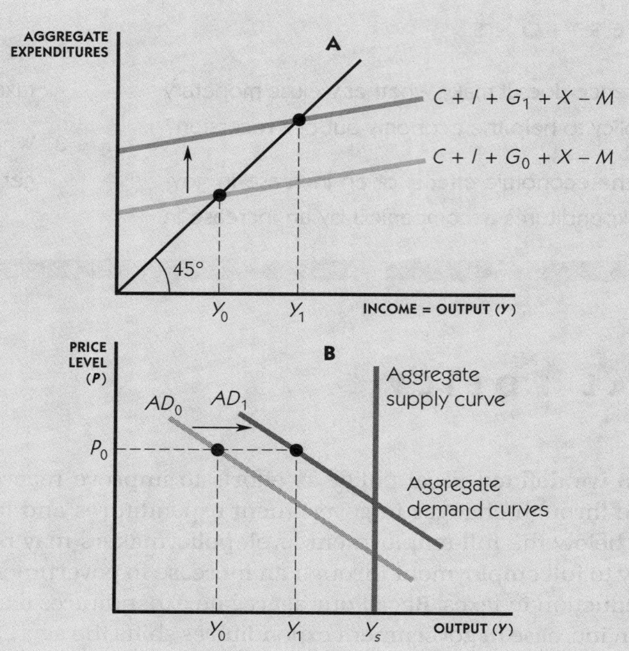

Figure 13.1 EFFECT OF INCREASED GOVERNMENT EXPENDITURES

Increased government expenditures shift the aggregate expenditures schedule up, and hence increase the equilibrium level of output at each price level. Hence the aggregate demand schedule shifts to the right—by an amount equal to the multiplier times the increase in government expenditures. At the initial fixed price level, P_0, equilibrium output increases by the amount of the shift—the multiplier times the increase in government expenditures.

increases by $2 billion. At some future date—say in the next boom—the increased indebtedness has to be paid off, with interest. But there is only $1 billion in increased indebtedness. The trade-off between an increase in national income today of $2 billion, with a reduction in consumption in the future to repay $1 billion (plus interest) in indebtedness, seems a favorable one. Indeed, the trade-off may be more favorable still, if the government has borrowed money from its own citizens. In this case, the government will simply impose a tax on some individuals, in order to repay those who purchased bonds to finance the original expenditure. Then there would be a transfer of resources from taxpayers to bondholders, but no reduction in aggregate consumption.

The trade-off from a debt-financed fiscal stimulus is slightly less favorable than this calculation since the government's dissaving (deficit) soaks up some savings that would have been available for investment. The capital stock of the economy is thus smaller, and as a result, so is future national income, making future generations worse off.

FISCAL POLICY UNDER FISCAL CONSTRAINTS

In recent years, with governments in many countries running huge deficits, increasing government expenditures in a recession to stimulate the economy has often seemed politically impossible. Thus, in the United States, Congress

Using Economics: Job Creation

In January 1993, the unemployment rate stood at 7.1 percent. There were more than 9 million unemployed. The Clinton administration proposed a stimulus package of $16 billion, to help reduce the unemployment rate. How many jobs would this have created?

Step 1. Calculate the total increase in national output. To do this we need to know the multiplier, which we will take to be 2. Thus, national output (GDP) would have increased by about $32 billion.

Step 2. Calculate the total increase in jobs associated with this increase in national output. Historically, a one percentage reduction in the unemployment rate is associated with a 2 percent increase in output. (This is called Okun's law, after the Chairman of the Council Economic Advisers under President Johnson who first identified the relationship.) In a $6 trillion economy, a 2 percent increase in output is $120 billion. Thus a $32 billion increase in GDP would be associated with a .27 percentage point reduction in the unemployment rate. With a labor force of approximately 127 million, this translates into $127 \times .0027 = 340{,}000$ jobs created.

now abides by a self-imposed constraint that it will not increase expenditures (over agreed-upon levels) unless there is an agreement to increase taxes by a corresponding amount. Such action is unlikely, given that raising new taxes is so politically unpopular, especially in an economic downturn. Similarly, the Maastricht Treaty, under which the countries of the European Union are supposed to form a common currency, calls for them to reduce their deficits to 3 percent of GDP by 1997. Achieving this goal requires cutting back on expenditures or raising taxes, but will leave little room for increasing expenditures or lowering taxes to stimulate the economy. In such situations, the government has no choice but to rely on monetary policy.

Balanced Budget Multipliers

What happens if government matches increased expenditures with increased taxes? The **balanced budget multiplier** is the increase in GDP from a dollar increase in government expenditures matched by a dollar increase in taxes. The increased taxes reduce disposable income, and thus private consumption. This largely, but not completely, offsets the expansionary effect of the increased government expenditures. To see why it only partially offsets the expansionary effect, recall that a one dollar reduction in disposable income only reduces consumption by the marginal propensity to consume times one dollar. The net effect of the increased expenditure accompanied by matching increased taxes—after the multiplier has had a chance to run itself out—is that national income rises by the amount of the increased government expenditure (rather than a multiple of that amount, as would be the case if taxes were not raised). The balanced budget multiplier is unity.

Suppose that an increase in government expenditures of \$1 billion is matched by an equal increase in taxes (ignoring, for simplicity, the dependence of taxes on income, and ignoring exports and imports). The first-round net effect is just:

$$\$1 \text{ billion} - MPC \times \$1 \text{ billion} = (1 - MPC) \times \$1 \text{ billion},$$

where *MPC* is the marginal propensity to consume. The multiplier, as we know from Chapter 9, is:

$$\frac{1}{1 - MPC}$$

so the net effect is:

$$\frac{1}{1 - MPC} \times 1 - MPC \times \$1 \text{ billion} = \$1 \text{ billion}.$$

The net effect is \$1 billion. Figure 13.2 illustrates the effect of a balanced budget increase in government expenditures. The aggregate demand curve shifts to the right by the amount of the increased government expenditures, increasing output.

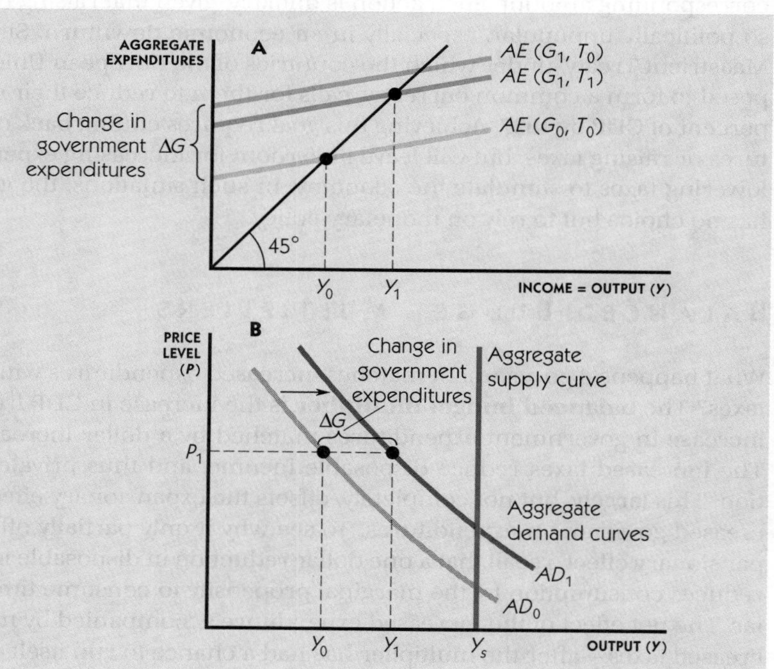

Figure 13.2 EFFECT OF INCREASED GOVERNMENT EXPENDITURES MATCHED BY TAX INCREASES

Three aggregate expenditures schedules appear in panel A. $AE(G_0, T_0)$ corresponds to aggregate expenditures before the increase in government spending and the matching tax increase. $AE(G_1, T_0)$ represents the effect of the increased government expenditures had there been no tax increase. $AE(G_1, T_1)$ shows the effect of the balanced budget increase in government spending; the balanced budget multiplier is unity, so the increase in output is equal to the increase in government spending. Panel B shows the aggregate demand curve shifting to the right by the amount of the increase in government spending.

MONETARY POLICY

In earlier chapters we have seen how monetary policy can stimulate the economy. An increase in the money supply leads to lower interest rates and increased credit availability, stimulating investment. This shifts the aggregate expenditures schedule up, and the aggregate demand schedule out, so that at any price level, aggregate output increases (see Figure 13.3). As we saw in Chapter 12, an additional mechanism is at play in an open economy: as interest rates fall, exchange rates decrease, and exports increase while imports decrease. Thus, net exports increase, and again, the aggregate expenditures schedule shifts up.

INTERACTIONS BETWEEN MONETARY AND FISCAL POLICY

So far, we have treated monetary and fiscal policy as if they were two distinct policies. In fact, there are important interactions between them. Consider the earlier discussion of a fiscal stimulus. If the monetary authorities simultaneously raise interest rates, monetary policy may partially or totally offset the expansionary effects of fiscal policy. The two are pulling in opposite directions. This happened in the early 1980s, where the restrictive monetary policy more than offset the expansive fiscal policy and the economy went into a major recession.

Sometimes the two policies work hand in hand. For instance, in 1993, the *direct* contractionary effects of deficit reduction were avoided in part by offsetting monetary policies. Unemployment actually fell. Economists sometimes refer to such monetary policies as **accommodative,** because the policies accommodate the changes in fiscal policy (or other changes in the economic environment) in ways which maintain the economy's macroeconomic performance.

Note that if the monetary authorities did nothing—that is, kept the money supply constant—in the presence of a fiscal expansion (an increase in government expenditures), interest rates would rise. The increase in national income would lead to an increase in the demand for money, and for the demand for money to equal the fixed supply, interest rates would have to rise. The rise in the interest rate would discourage investment. The increased government expenditure would have partially crowded out private investment. The net expansion in the economy is smaller—possibly far smaller—than if the monetary authorities had been more accommodative.

Figure 13.3 EFFECT OF MONETARY POLICY

An increase in the money supply leads to lower interest rates and increased credit availability, stimulating investment. This shifts the aggregate expenditures schedule up (panel A). The aggregate demand schedule shifts out, so that at any price level, aggregate output increases (panel B).

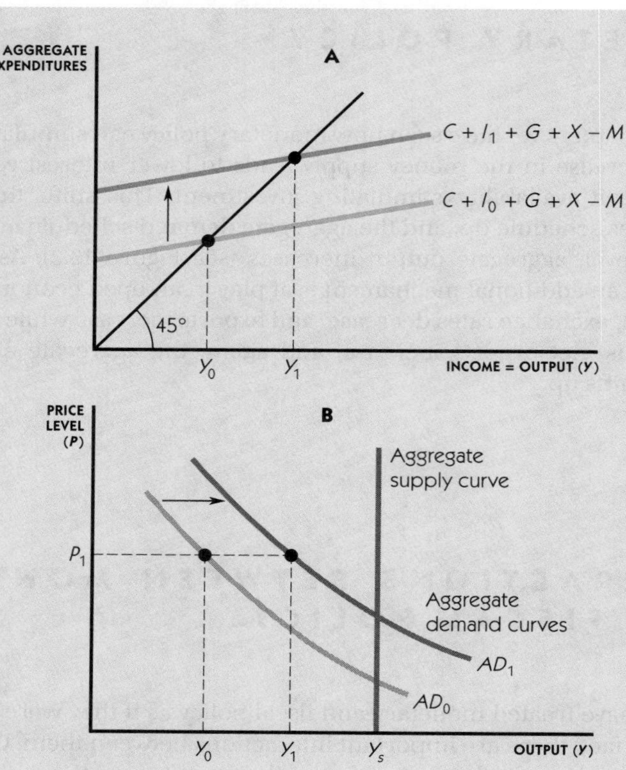

DIFFERENCES BETWEEN MONETARY AND FISCAL POLICY

There are major differences between monetary and fiscal policy, in their effects on the composition of output, their efficacy, and the lags with which their effects are felt.

EFFECTS ON THE COMPOSITION OF OUTPUT

Assume, first, that we could use either monetary or fiscal policy to stimulate the economy to the same extent. If we use monetary policy, we lower interest rates, stimulating investment. Thus, future levels of income will be higher. Using monetary policy, governments can pursue both a high-growth and a full-employment strategy. If we use fiscal policy, with a fixed money supply, as

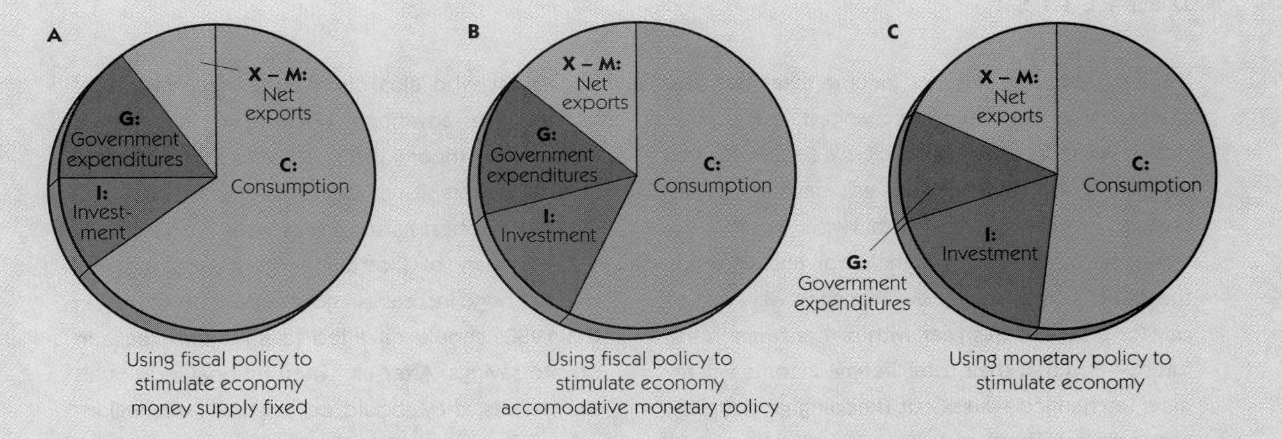

Figure 13.4 COMPARISON OF THE EFFECTS OF MONETARY AND FISCAL POLICIES

The share of investment is highest when monetary policy alone is used to restore full employment, and lowest when monetary authorities keep money supply constant, and increased government expenditures alone are used.

incomes increase, interest rates rise so that the demand for money remains equal to the supply. Figure 13.4 contrasts the composition of GDP under alternative policies, assuming part of the fiscal stimulus comes from tax cuts and part from expenditure increases. While either fiscal or monetary policy may be able to restore the economy to full employment, they have different effects on future economic growth.

But these differences become less clear if government expenditures are for investments. A substantial portion—in recent years, approximately 16 percent—of government expenditures go for physical investments, such as the construction of roads and buildings. Additionally, large amounts are devoted to investment in people (investment in human capital) and in technology, both of which serve to increase economic growth. If the government stimulates the economy by increasing public investment rather than lowering interest rates and stimulating private investment, the impact on growth will depend on the relative rates of return of these two forms of investment.

Differences in the Efficacy of Monetary and Fiscal Policy

Recall Consensus Point 13 from Chapter 12: when the economy is in a deep recession, monetary policy may be ineffective. Increases in the money supply may have little effect on interest rates, and decreases in the interest rate may have little effect on investment.

Close-up: The Public Veil and the Impact of Deficits

If the government reduces income taxes this year but keeps expenditures unchanged, the budget deficit will increase. This deficit is a liability for taxpayers. In the future, taxes will have to be increased (from what they otherwise would have been) to pay interest on the debt and to repay the debt. If taxpayers know that they will have to pay for a tax cut this year with higher taxes in the future—and that their total lifetime income will remain unchanged—a tax cut (keeping government expenditures fixed) may have no effect on consumption. Clearly, this view goes beyond the permanent income and life-cycle models introduced earlier, which said a temporary tax cut would have an effect (if small) on total lifetime wealth, and therefore have a small effect on today's aggregate consumption.

The view that whether the government finances a given level of expenditures by taxes or by borrowing makes *no* difference to current consumption—that the two are perfectly equivalent—is called the Ricardian equivalence view, in honor of David Ricardo, the nineteenth-century English economist who also discovered the principle of comparative advantage. Ricardo described the equivalence theory, then dismissed it as irrelevant. In recent years, it has been resurrected and promoted by Robert Barro of Harvard University.

The theory of Ricardian equivalence suggests that the huge increase in government borrowing in the 1980s should have led to a huge increase in private savings. After all, when rational individuals see deficits, they should expect that taxes will increase at some time in the future, and begin setting aside funds to pay the bills. But instead of increasing, private savings rates in the United States continued at their low levels in the 1980s.

There are numerous reasons why Ricardian equivalence does not hold. Many individuals do not think and act in the way envisaged in the model. Many taxpayers have little idea about the true size of the deficit and do not take into account the consequences of higher future taxes. When individuals do not fully see and respond to these consequences in ways which fully offset them, we say there is a "public veil"—just as when

they do not fully take into account what is going on inside corporations, we say there is a "corporate veil."

If the burden of repaying the public debt can be passed on to future generations—and if parents do not fully adjust bequests to their heirs to reflect this—then the tax reduction does represent an increase in the current generation's lifetime wealth, and accordingly aggregate consumption should rise for this generation.

Questions have also been raised about the efficacy of some fiscal policies. In some circumstances, a tax reduction may not stimulate much consumption. Consumers—worried about the future and thinking that the tax reduction may not be permanent—save the additional funds.[1] But if the economy has been in an extended downturn, leaving many individuals credit constrained, even temporary tax cuts are likely to be effective at increasing consumption.

Many economists worry that increased deficits—tax cuts not matched by expenditure cuts, or expenditure increases not matched by tax increases—themselves dampen the economy. Since the government will have to turn to capital markets to finance the deficit, some private investment will be crowded out. The net impact of fiscal policy must take this into account: if increased deficit-financed government expenditures crowd out an equivalent amount of private investment, there will be no stimulative effect. In the open economy of the United States, this crowding out effect is not likely to be so dramatic. Still, there may be some offsetting effects through changes in the exchange rate, but because imports and exports adjust so slowly—sometimes taking up to two years to adjust fully—the offsetting effects may not reduce by much the efficacy of fiscal policy in the very short run.

Differences in the Lags of Monetary and Fiscal Policy

Monetary and fiscal policy also differ in the speed with which they can take effect. Monetary policy stimulates the economy by lowering interest rates and increasing investment in equipment and housing. Even after firms see a decrease in interest rates, it may take some time before they place new orders for investment, and before the capital goods industry starts producing the newly ordered items. Similarly, though in the long run lower interest rates lead to increased demand for housing, it takes a while before plans are drawn up, permits are obtained, and construction starts. Typically, it takes six months or longer before the effects of monetary policy are realized. By contrast increased government expenditures have a direct and immediate effect in increasing incomes.

There is another important source of delay: governments must decide to take action. They must see that the economy is in a downturn, and that some

[1]Chapter 10 analyzed in more detail these future-oriented consumption decisions. Individuals base consumption not on their current income, but on their lifetime or permanent incomes, and a one-time, once-and-for-all, tax reduction has little effect on individual's lifetime or permanent income.

kind of stimulus is needed. These lags in taking action are often significant. The lags of government decision making are avoided through the use of **automatic stabilizers,** expenditures that automatically increase or taxes that automatically decrease when economic conditions worsen.

The economy has a number of these automatic stabilizers. Expenditures on unemployment compensation automatically go up in an economic downturn. So do other social insurance payments, as more individuals claim disability and more people retire early. Similarly, the federal income tax functions as an automatic stabilizer because of its progressive structure. A progressive tax system is one in which individuals with higher incomes pay a larger fraction of their income in taxes. As an individual's income increases, he moves into a higher tax bracket, and his average tax rate increases. Thus, when the total income (output) of the economy increases, average tax rates increase, and taxes as a fraction of GDP increase. Conversely, when the economy goes into a downturn, tax revenues would decline even if the tax rate were constant. But with a progressive tax system, they decline even more since the average tax rate declines. The fact that the tax system is progressive thus enhances its role as an automatic stabilizer.[2]

The government could, if it wanted, increase the degree of automatic stabilization. For instance, while the standard unemployment benefits last 26 weeks, during extended downturns these have been expanded to 39 or more weeks. Such extensions could be made automatic.

CONSEQUENCES OF A BALANCED BUDGET AMENDMENT

Many people have thought that it is irresponsible for government to have a deficit, reasoning that, like a business, government cannot permanently run at a loss.[3] The huge deficits of the 1980s brought the issue to a head: there was a strong political movement to adopt a constitutional amendment requiring a balanced budget, known as the **balanced budget amendment.** The proposal for such an amendment passed the House of Representatives in 1995, and failed by one vote to achieve the required two-thirds majority in the Senate.

Most economists opposed the balanced budget amendment, largely because they believed that it would eliminate the ability of automatic stabilizers to work. As we have seen, automatic stabilizers typically result in expenditures increasing and revenues falling in economic downturns, leading to deficits in recessions. But under a balanced budget amendment, the government would

[2]Before 1986, the tax system was largely unindexed, that is, it did not adjust for changes in the price level. In the 1970s, the economy experienced high unemployment together with high inflation, a condition known as stagflation. Thus, nominal GDP continued to rise even as real GDP declined. The progressivity of the unindexed tax system meant that the average tax rate increased, exacerbating the economic downturn. With indexing, average tax rates increase only when real GDP increases.

[3]A more in-depth discussion of the economic consequences of fiscal budget deficits is provided in Chapter 18.

POLICY PERSPECTIVE: DEFICIT REDUCTION AND ECONOMIC STIMULATION

When President Clinton came to office in January 1993, he faced two economic challenges: the huge deficits that had begun in 1981 and persisted since then had soared to 4.9 percent of GDP, and the economy remained in a prolonged slowdown, with unemployment still in excess of 7 percent. The two problems seemed to call for contradictory policies: increased deficits might stimulate the economy, but exacerbate the deficit problem. The Clinton administration chose to embark on a long-run deficit reduction program; it cut expenditures and increased taxes—policies which should have exacerbated the economic downturn. Yet the Clinton administration claimed its economic policies had helped turn the economy around. Did the economic policies fuel the recovery, or hinder it?

This episode demonstrates the complex relationships between monetary policy, expectations, and fiscal policy, as well as the potential importance of timing. The administration tried to structure the deficit reduction package so that more of the expenditure cuts occurred in 1995 and 1996—not so much because it wanted to postpone the political heat of expenditure cuts, but because it believed that by then, if its policies were in place, there would be an economic recovery that could withstand these expenditure cuts.

Clinton believed that the overall deficit reduction package would restore confidence in the economy—confidence that matters were being taken under control. The argument went like this. With smaller future deficits, there would be less federal debt competing for funds with private investment. Investors would anticipate this, and hence long-term interest rates would fall, even if the Fed did nothing. The lower long-term interest rates, in turn, would help stimulate the economy. (Long-term interest rates did fall.) The Fed, in turn, recognizing that the economy was less likely to become overheated as a result of excessive fiscal deficits, would maintain an easier monetary policy than it otherwise would. Indeed, it kept interest rates at 3 percent throughout 1993, not raising them until February 1994, after signs that recovery was under way.

The hope of the administration was that lower short-term interest rates induced by the Fed and lower long-term interest rates induced by increased investor confidence would more than offset the direct depressing effects of fiscal policy. The economy did indeed recover. While most economists believe that eventually the economy would, in any case, have recovered, most also think that the reduction in the deficit probably ensured that the recovery occurred faster and more strongly than otherwise would have been the case.

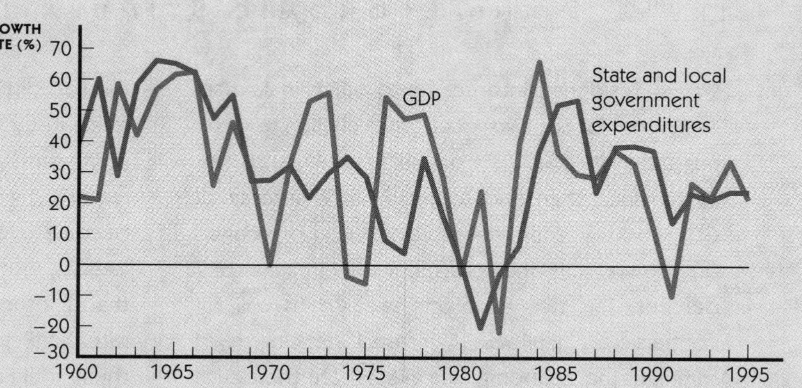

Figure 13.5 EXPENDITURES BY STATE AND LOCAL GOVERNMENTS

The figure compares the growth rate of GDP and expenditures of state and local governments. These expenditures tend to increase in booms and decrease in recessions, thus contributing to the volatility of the economy. *Source: ERP* (1995), Table B-2.

be forced to *destabilize* the economy—either raising taxes or cutting expenditures as the economy went into a recession, when just the opposite medicine is required. A look at the experience of the states, many of which have balanced budget requirements, supports this view. Figure 13.5 shows that typically, in economic booms, state expenditures increase, reinforcing the boom, and in economic downturns, they decrease, reinforcing the downturn.

With fiscal policy no longer being used to stabilize the economy—or worse, contributing to its instability—the burden of stabilization is put squarely on the shoulders of the monetary authorities. This means that interest rates will have to fluctuate more than they otherwise would, causing greater expansions and contractions in the interest-sensitive sectors (housing, durable goods, and plant and equipment). Since the lags in monetary policy—the time between when an action is undertaken and its effects are fully felt—are long and variable (typically six months or more), the economy itself will exhibit greater variability. And there are times when monetary policy is relatively ineffective in stimulating the economy (when the response of the economy to lowering interest rates is small, or smaller than anticipated), such as during the Great Depression and in the economic downturn of 1991. In such situations, the economic downturn will last longer and may be deeper than it would be if stronger automatic stabilizers were in place.

One proposal for reducing these destabilizing effects is to balance not the actual budget, but to set to zero the **full-employment deficit**—what the deficit would have been had the economy been operating at full employment. The full-employment deficit takes into account the changes in expenditures and revenues due to the current economic conditions. In a recession the full-employment deficit is smaller than the actual deficit. Most economists believe that the government is fiscally responsible so long as there is no full-employment deficit. Many argue that if there is to be a constitutional amendment regarding a balanced budget, it should be written in terms of the full-employment deficit.

Using Economics: Calculating the Full-Employment Deficit

The text described the importance of the concept of the full-employment deficit (sometimes called the structural deficit). Consider an economy which has 7 percent unemployment, when it is generally believed that the economy could operate at 5.5 percent unemployment without encountering inflationary pressures. From Chapter 4 we know that there are always some people without jobs in the economy, because of such factors as frictional and seasonal unemployment. Thus, we can assume that 5.5 percent unemployment corresponds to the full-employment level of output. Assume also that the deficit is $300 billion, output is $6 trillion, and that a 1 percentage point reduction in the unemployment rate will yield a 2 percent increase in output. What is the full-employment deficit?

Step 1. Calculate the full-employment level of output. Reducing unemployment from 7 to 5.5 percent will yield an increase in output of $180 billion.

Step 2. Calculate the extent to which tax revenues increase and expenditures decrease as output expands. Federal tax revenues increase approximately $20 for every $100 increase in GDP, while expenditures are reduced (as demands for unemployment insurance decrease, as fewer people go on disability, etc.). For simplicity, we assume those expenditures decrease by $5 for every $100 increase in GDP. Thus, the increase in GDP of $180 billion increases revenues by $36 billion and reduces expenditures by $9 billion.

Step 3. Add those amounts to the original deficit. Full-employment deficit = $300 billion – $36 billion – $9 billion = $255 billion.

Balanced Budgets and Stabilization Policy

1. An increase in government expenditure matched by an increase in tax revenues is expansionary.
2. Automatic stabilizers increase expenditures and reduce taxes automatically as the economy goes into a recession. Standard versions of the balanced budget amendment would preclude the use of automatic stabilizers as well as eliminate the possibility of using fiscal policy to stabilize the economy.
3. In practice, a balanced budget amendment would likely destabilize the economy, and force the entire burden of stabilization onto monetary policy.

REVIEW AND PRACTICE

SUMMARY

1. Increasing government expenditure (without increasing taxes) stimulates the economy, but generates a deficit. If the government spends the additional funds on investments which yield returns in excess of the interest rate, then increased government expenditure can make the economy stronger both today and in the future.

2. Increases in government expenditure matched by increases in taxes can still stimulate the economy, but there will be no multiplier effects.

3. Monetary policy stimulates the economy by increasing investment and net exports. Thus, stimulating the economy through monetary policy has a more positive effect on economic growth than doing so through fiscal policy unless the increased government expenditures are spent on investments. In deep recessions, however, monetary policy may not be very effective.

4. The lags associated with monetary policy may be longer than those associated with fiscal policy.

5. Automatic stabilizers help to stabilize the economy, without any policymaker making an active decision.

6. Most versions of a balanced budget amendment would circumscribe the operation of automatic stabilizers and thus serve to destabilize the economy. All the burden of stabilization would be placed on monetary policy.

KEY TERMS

balanced budget multiplier
accommodative monetary policy
automatic stabilizers
balanced budget amendment
full-employment deficit

REVIEW QUESTIONS

1. How does an increase in government expenditure shift the aggregate expenditures schedule and the aggregate demand curve? How does monetary policy shift the aggregate expenditures schedule and the aggregate demand curve?

2. If the economy is in a recession, describe the trade-off between today and the future associated with an increase in government expenditures. How does what the government spends its increased expenditures on affect the trade-off? If the government spends the funds on investments that yield high returns, is there still a trade-off? Even if the government spends the funds on public consumption, why might the trade-off still appear attractive?

3. What is the effect of an increase in government expenditure matched by an increase in taxes?

4. Compare the effects of monetary and fiscal policy on the level of investment and the composition of output.

5. What other factors are important in the choice between monetary and fiscal policy?

6. What effect might a balanced budget amendment have on the stability of the economy?

7. What are automatic stabilizers, and why are they important?

PROBLEMS

1. Show how a decrease in the price level leads to an increase in aggregate demand and equilibrium output if money supply remains unchanged and there is excess capacity in the economy.
   (a) Use the demand and supply curves for money to show the effect on interest rates.
   (b) Use the investment function to show the effect on investments.
   (c) Use the aggregate expenditures schedule to show the effect on equilibrium output.

2. Show the differences in the effect of an increase in government expenditure when monetary authorities (a) keep the money supply constant, and (b) expand the money supply to keep the interest rate constant. Trace out the effects on (a) the demand and supply curves for money and the equilibrium interest rate; (b) the level of investment; (c) the aggregate expenditures schedule and the equilibrium level of output at any fixed price; and (d) the aggregate demand curve.

3. Assume you are in charge of monetary policy. The economy is $60 billion below capacity, or 1 percent of its $6 trillion capacity. (a) You are told the government does not plan to increase government expenditures or change tax rates at all. How much must you increase the money supply? Assume: money demand has an interest elasticity of .8, an income elasticity of 1; investment elasticity is .8 and investment amounts to 10 percent of GDP ($540 billion); and the multiplier is 2. (b) In some countries, such as the United Kingdom, the monetary authorities are more directly under control of the government than in the United States. Assume the government says

that it plans to increase government expenditures to restore full employment, but it wants the monetary authorities to keep interest rates constant. By how much must they increase the money supply? (Use the same assumptions as in part a). Assuming the multiplier is 2, by how much must government expenditure be increased. (c) Now assume the monetary authorities are independent, and have announced that they will not change the money supply. By how much will interest rates rise if the government is successful in restoring the economy to full employment? How will that affect investment? What does this imply for the required magnitude of increase in government expenditure?

4. When individuals become wealthier they consume more. If prices fall, the *real value* of wealth which is denominated in monetary terms—like money and government bonds—increases. Would you expect this effect to be large or small? Assume government bonds and money represent 10 percent of national wealth, and that an increase in real wealth of 10 percent leads to a .6 percent increase in consumption. Assume consumption represents 90 percent of GDP and the multiplier is 2. Assume prices fall by 5 percent. By approximately what percent will GDP increase? Assume the economy is 10 percent below capacity. How long would it take the economy to be restored to full employment if prices continued to fall at the rate of 5 percent per year?

5. The economy is $60 billion below capacity, or 1 percent of its $6 trillion capacity. The government contemplates stimulating the economy by alternative policies. Assume the multiplier is 2, and that investment is completely interest inelastic. Calculate the required increase in government expenditures. Calculate the required increase in government expenditures if the government increases taxes in tandem. Can monetary policy be used to stimulate the economy?

6. Consider the extreme case where the individuals and firms within a country can borrow (or lend) abroad as much as desired at a fixed real interest rate. Can monetary authorities affect the level of real investment? Assume that as the monetary authorities try to raise interest rates, funds flow in from abroad; as they flow in, they bid up the exchange rate. Trace through the effects: (a) of the increased demand for U.S. dollars by foreign investors wishing to invest in the U.S. on the exchange rate; (b) the effect of the exchange rate on the aggregate expenditures schedule and on GDP.

7. Several European countries are scheduled to form a European Monetary Union (EMU), in which they would have a single currency. Effectively, this means that exchange rates between the countries would be fixed, and there would be a single interest rate for all the countries. The governments have agreed that certain criteria must be met to join the EMU. These include reducing the fiscal deficit as a share of GDP to below 3 percent. What might be the macroeconomic effects of this deficit reduction (a) if each country's monetary authorities do not adjust interest rates? (b) if interest rates are reduced? Why might the simultaneous reduction of

deficits by all the countries lead to a larger reduction in output than if only one country reduced its deficit, if interest rates do not fall? Use diagrams to illustrate your answer.

8. Assume that after the European Monetary Union is established, interest rates will be the same in all countries within the Union. Assume that unemployment in one country within the Union, say France, increases. What can the government do to restore full employment?

Contrast what might be done about unemployment in France within the European Monetary Union with what might be done about unemployment in California. In what ways will the situation be similar? How will they differ?

9. Compare the effects on longer term economic growth of using monetary rather than fiscal policy to stimulate an economy when capital flows freely internationally with the effects within a closed economy.

PART FOUR

DYNAMICS AND MACRO POLICY

So far, we have discussed two of the three key macroeconomic problems: growth and unemployment. We now turn to the third, *inflation*. What causes it? Why is it a problem? What can government do about it?

This part of the book does more, however, than just round out our discussion of the three key macroeconomic problems. It also describes and explains the *dynamics of wage and price adjustments*. Part Two focused on full-employment economies; Part Three on economies with unemployment. We emphasized that the key distinction between the two were assumptions about adjustments. In Part Two, wages and prices adjusted quickly so that the labor market was always in equilibrium. In Part Three, wages and prices were fixed. We were taking a snapshot of the economy, before the dynamic process unfolded. We recognized that when the demand for labor was less than the supply at the current wages, or when the demand for goods was less than the supply at the current price level, there were pressures for wages and prices to fall. But the adjustments do not occur instantaneously. Similarly, if initially the economy's resources were fully employed, and there was a rightward shift in the aggregate demand curve, there would be excess demand for goods at the going price level. This creates upward price pressure, but again, prices do not adjust instantaneously.

The fact that wages and prices do not adjust instantaneously—that they are sticky—means that after any disturbance, there will be at least a period in which demand does not equal supply. If at current prices and wages demand is less than supply, output is limited by aggregate demand, so that an increase in aggregate demand—say as a result of increased government expenditure—increases output and employment.

Understanding why unemployment persists and why prices may rise, not just once, but year after year entails understanding the dynamics of adjustment. In this part, we will *describe* observed regularities in wage and price adjustments and *explain* both the consequences of these observed patterns and the sources of wage and price stickiness.

Part Four consists of three chapters. Chapter 14 provides the basic description of wage and price dynamics. It explains the major determinants of the rate of inflation. Chapter 15 takes a closer look at the labor market, to see why wages in particular often exhibit rigidities. Finally Chapter 16 brings together the insights of Parts One, Two, and Three to discuss some of the central policy issues in macroeconomics and the controversies surrounding them. Should the government intervene? And if so, what is the most effective form of intervention?

CHAPTER 14

INFLATION: WAGE AND PRICE DYNAMICS

It is an axiom of political rhetoric that inflation is bad. Popular sentiment runs so strongly against inflation that it is usually taken for granted that the government should do something about it. But if the government needs to do something about inflation, we need to know what causes it. How do we explain why some countries have higher inflation rates than others? Why does the United States have a lower inflation rate today than it did fifteen years ago?

If inflation is so disliked, why don't governments simply get rid of it? The answer is that, normally, inflation can only be reduced at a cost—only if the unemployment rate is allowed to increase. This chapter looks at the trade-off between inflation and unemployment, and how this trade-off can be changed. Many economists believe that in the long run, there is no trade-off: attempting to reduce unemployment to too low a level is a chimera. Not only does inflation increase, but it increases at a faster and faster rate, until inflation, not unemployment, becomes viewed as the central economic problem. This chapter explains these critical debates which underlie so much of current policy discussions.

KEY QUESTIONS

1. What are the costs of inflation? Why does it make a difference whether inflation is anticipated? How can the costs be ameliorated?
2. What is the trade-off between inflation and unemployment? How do expectations about inflation affect the level of inflation associated with any level of unemployment?
3. Why might inflation accelerate if the unemployment rate is kept at too low a level? How do these considerations affect government policies?
4. What are the factors that affect the critical unemployment rate below which inflation starts to increase? How has this critical unemployment rate changed over time?
5. Why is it that once inflation starts, it tends to persist?
6. What role does monetary policy play in initiating or perpetuating inflation?
7. What are some of the reasons for wage and price rigidities?

THE COSTS OF INFLATION

We identified growth, unemployment, and inflation as the three key macroeconomic problems. Part Two discussed issues of growth, and Part Three of unemployment. Here we focus on inflation and the relationship between inflation and unemployment. While the costs of unemployment are apparent—not only is there a loss in output, but the misery of those who cannot secure gainful employment is palpable—the costs of inflation are more subtle, and over the years have been greatly ameliorated.

People sense there is something wrong with the economy when there is high inflation. Workers worry that their paycheck will not keep pace with increases in the price level, and thus their living standards will be eroded. Investors worry that the dollars they receive in the future will be worth less than the dollars they invested, leaving them with less than enough to live comfortably in their old age.

When inflation is anticipated, many of its economic costs disappear. Workers who know that prices will be rising by 10 percent this year, for example, may negotiate wages that rise fast enough to offset the inflation. Lenders know that the dollars they will be repaid will be worth less than the dollars they lent, and they take this into account when setting the interest rate they charge or when deciding whether to make the loan.

But even when inflation is not perfectly anticipated, workers and investors can immunize themselves against the effects of inflation by having wages and returns **indexed** to inflation. For instance, when wages are perfectly indexed, a 1 percent increase in the price level results in a 1 percent increase in wages.

In recent years, Social Security payments and tax rates have both been indexed. Many countries, including the United Kingdom, Canada, and New Zealand, sell indexed government bonds so that savers can put aside money knowing that the returns will not be affected by inflation. In May 1996, the U.S. government announced its intention to begin selling indexed bonds.

WHO SUFFERS FROM INFLATION?

While indexing softens the effects of inflation, it is far from complete. So who suffers today from inflation? Many people may suffer a little, since indexing does not fully protect them, but some are more likely to suffer than others. Among the groups most imperfectly protected are lenders, taxpayers, and holders of currency.

Lenders Since most loans are not fully indexed, increases in inflation mean that the dollars that lenders receive back from borrowers are worth less than those they lent out. Many people put a large part of their savings for their retirement into bonds or other fixed-income securities. These people will suffer if an inflationary bout comes between them and their nest eggs. The extent to which they will suffer depends in large measure on whether the price changes were anticipated. After World War II, many people bought bonds yielding a 3 or 4 percent annual return. They did not anticipate much inflation. When inflation reached double-digit levels in the late 1970s, the rate of interest they received did not even come close to compensating them for the reduced value of the dollars they had invested. In real terms, they received a negative return on their savings.

Taxpayers Our tax system is only partially indexed, and inflation frequently hurts investors badly through the tax system. All returns to investment are taxed, including those that do nothing more than offset inflation. Consequently, real after-tax returns are often negative. Consider a rate of inflation of 10 percent and an asset that yields a return of 12 percent before tax. If the individual has to pay a 33 percent tax on the return, his after-tax yield is 9 percent—not enough to compensate him for inflation. His after-tax real return is minus 1 percent.

Holders of Currency Inflation also makes it expensive for people to hold currency because as they hold it, the currency loses its value. Since currency facilitates a variety of transactions, inflation interferes with the efficiency of the economy by discouraging the holding of currency. The fact that inflation takes away the value of money means that inflation acts as a tax on holding money. Economists refer to this distortionary effect as an **inflation tax.**

This distortion is not as important in modern economies, where checking accounts are frequently used instead of cash, and checking accounts typically pay interest. As the rate of inflation increases, the interest rate paid on checking accounts normally increases as well. Even in Argentina in the 1970s, when prices were rising at 800 percent a month, bank accounts yielded more than

Close-up: Hyperinflation in Germany in the 1920s

Following World War I, Germany was required by the victorious Allied nations to make substantial "reparation" payments. But the sheer size of the reparations, combined with the wartime devastation of German industry, made payment nearly impossible. John Maynard Keynes, then an economic adviser to the British government, was among those who warned that the reparations were too large. To finance some of Germany's financial obligations, the German government started simply printing money.

The resulting increases in both the amount of circulating currency and the price level can be seen in the figure. From January 1922 to November 1923, the average price level increased by a factor of almost 20 billion.* People made desperate attempts to spend their currency as soon as they received it, since the value of currency was declining so rapidly. One story often told by Keynes was how Germans would buy two beers at once, even though one was likely to get warm, for fear that otherwise, when it came time to buy the second beer, the price would have risen.

At an annual inflation rate of 100 percent, money loses half its value every year. If you save $100 today, in five years it will have buying power equal to only 3 current dollars. It is possible for nominal interest rates to adjust even to very high inflation rates. But when those high inflation rates fluctuate in unanticipated ways, the effects can be disastrous.

Periods of hyperinflation create a massive redistribution of wealth. If an individual is smart or lucky

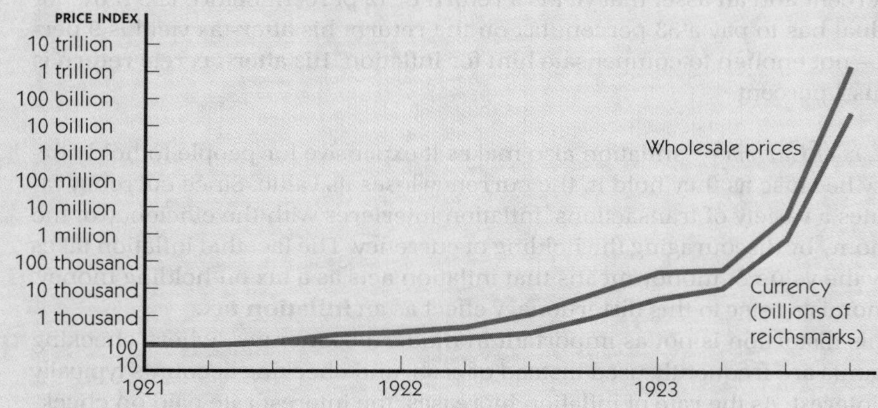

Inflation in Germany during the 1920s reached levels that may seem unbelievably high. At the end of 1923, prices were 10 billion times higher than they were two years earlier.

enough to hold assets in a form such as foreign funds or land, then the hyperinflation will do little to reduce that person's actual wealth. Those who cannot avail themselves of these "inflation-proof" assets will see their wealth fall.

*Thomas Sargent, "The Ends of Four Big Inflations," in Robert Hall, ed., *Inflation* (Chicago: University of Chicago Press, 1982), pp. 74–75.

800 percent a month. Still, poorer individuals who do not have checking accounts—and therefore must hold much of what little wealth they have in the form of currency—are adversely affected.

The Economy There are two costs of inflation to the economy as a whole. The first has to do with relative prices. Because price increases are never perfectly coordinated, increases in the rate of inflation lead to a greater variability of relative prices. If the shoe industry makes price adjustments only every three months, then in the third month, right before its price increase, shoes may be relatively cheap, while right after the price increase, shoes may be relatively expensive. On the other hand, the prices of groceries might change continually throughout the three-month period. Therefore, the ratio of the price of groceries to the price of shoes will continually be changing. When the average rate of inflation is only 2 or 3 percent per year, this does not cause much of a problem. But when the average rate of inflation is 10 percent per month, inflation causes real distortions in how society allocates its resources. When inflation gets very high, economies tend to allocate considerable resources to avoid the costs of inflation and to take advantage of the discrepancies in prices charged by different sellers. Rather than carrying money, which quickly erodes in value, people rush to deposit their money in interest-bearing bank accounts.

The second economy-wide cost of inflation arises from the risk and uncertainty that inflation generates. If there were perfect indexing, the uncertainty about the rate of inflation would be unimportant. But as indexing is not perfect, the resulting uncertainty makes it difficult to plan. People saving for their retirements cannot know what to put aside. Business firms borrowing money are uncertain about the price they will receive for the goods they produce. Firms are also hurt when they build wage increases into multiyear contracts to reflect *anticipated* inflation. If for any reason a firm finds that the prices it can charge increase less rapidly than anticipated in the contract, the employer suffers.

Misperceived Costs of Inflation

We have discussed the significant costs of inflation, but much of the aversion to inflation comes from a variety of forms of misperceptions. If a poll were conducted asking people whether they were hurt or helped by inflation, most would say they were hurt. Much of this is simply *perception*. People "feel" price increases much more vividly than they do the corresponding income increases. They "feel" the higher interest rates they have to pay on loans more than they do the decrease in the value of the dollars with which they repay lenders. A closer look at who benefits and who loses from unanticipated inflation suggests that there are probably more gainers than there are losers. This is simply because there are probably more debtors than lenders, and debtors benefit from unanticipated inflation.

In many inflationary episodes, many individuals not only *feel* worse off, they *are* worse off—but inflation itself is not the culprit. The oil price increases of 1973 set off a widespread inflation in the United States. The higher price of oil also made the United States poorer than it had previously been, because it was an oil importer. Someone's standard of living had to be cut, and inflation did the cutting. Frequently those whose incomes were cut—unskilled workers, whose wages did not keep pace with prices—cited as the *cause* of their lower incomes the inflation that accompanied the oil price increases. However, generalized price inflation was only a symptom. The underlying cause of that particular inflation, and of the reduced real incomes, was a sharp rise in the price of oil.

It is clear that the costs of inflation are different, and undoubtedly lower, than they were before indexing was so extensive. Today economists do not agree on the *magnitude* of the adverse effects of inflation. There is considerable evidence that high rates of inflation have strongly adverse effects on economic performance. But there is little evidence that at the moderate rates of inflation that the United States has experienced in recent years there are any significant adverse effects.

Costs of Inflation, Actual and Perceived

Real costs
- Variability in relative prices
- Resources devoted to mitigating the costs of inflation and taking advantage of price discrepancies
- Increased uncertainty

Misperceptions
- Failing to recognize offsetting increases in income
- Blaming inflation for losses in real income that occur during inflationary episodes but are caused by other factors

INFLATION AND UNEMPLOYMENT

While there is some debate about the *magnitude* of the costs of inflation, if it were costless to reduce inflation, clearly governments would do so. But lower inflation can typically be obtained only through higher unemployment. In this section, we analyze the relationship between inflation and unemployment.

In the previous two parts of the book, we examined two different models of the economy: the full-employment and unemployment models. These models are based on opposite assumptions about prices and wages. In the full-employment model, we assumed that prices and wages are perfectly flexible. In the unemployment model, we assumed that prices and wages are fixed. The full-employment model gives us a useful picture of the economy in the long run. Eventually, prices and wages do adjust so that the economy returns to the full-employment level of output. The unemployment model is a closer picture of the economy in the very short run, in which prices and wages adjust very little, if at all. Our objective now is to understand the middle ground between the very short run of the unemployment model (with fixed wages and prices), and the long run of the full-employment model.

In Part Three we focused on the case when at the current price level, P_0, aggregate demand fell short of aggregate supply, as illustrated in Figure 14.1 by the aggregate demand curve AD_1. As we know, in this situation, output (Y_1) is limited by aggregate demand. When the economy is below the full-employment level of output, policymakers may attempt to shift the aggregate demand curve to the right, increasing output and reducing unemployment. But if the aggregate demand curve is shifted too far to the right, say to AD_2, at the current price level P_0, aggregate demand exceeds aggregate supply; upward price pressure is injected into the economy, and inflation rears its ugly head. On the other hand, if the initial situation is represented by AD_2, upward price pressure may be diminished by leftward shifts of the aggregate demand curve. If this is taken to extremes, the level of output may fall below the full-employment level.

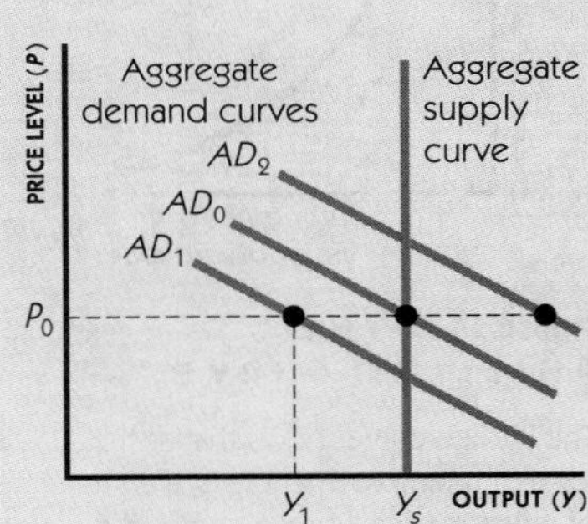

Figure 14.1 SHORT-RUN EQUILIBRIUM

When aggregate demand is less than aggregate supply at the current price level, output will be limited by aggregate demand (Y_1), and there will be involuntary unemployment. When aggregate supply is less than aggregate demand at the current price level, output will be limited by aggregate supply and there will be upward price pressure.

The problems of inflation and unemployment lie on opposite sides of the aggregate supply curve. When aggregate demand exceeds aggregate supply at the current price level, the economy will experience inflation (rising prices) as it moves to the future equilibrium level. On the other hand, when aggregate demand is less than aggregate supply at the current price level, unemployment becomes the problem. In both cases, the size of the effects on the rates of inflation and unemployment will depend on the size of the gap between aggregate supply and aggregate demand; the larger the gap, the larger is the effect. This interconnection between inflation and unemployment is the key to understanding the dynamics of adjustment—the middle ground between the full-employment and unemployment models we have studied thus far.

The challenge for economists and policymakers is threefold: (1) to determine the state of the economy at any given time; (2) to determine how policy

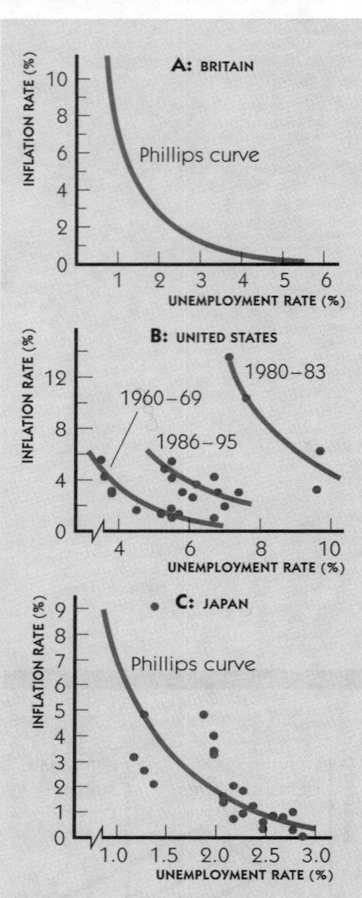

Figure 14.2 THE PHILLIPS CURVE

The Phillips curve shows that as the level of unemployment falls, the rate of inflation rises. Panel A shows the curve A. W. Phillips actually plotted in 1958 for the British economy. Panel B depicts the Phillips curve relationship for U.S. data in the 1960s, early 1980s, late 1980s, and early 1990s. Panel C gives the Phillips curve for Japan for 1970–1995. *Source: ERP* (1995), Tables B-40, B-63, B-110, B-111.

can change the state of the economy favorably; and (3) to determine how inflation and unemployment are likely to change in the future. Two of the key factors they look at in assessing the state of the economy are the unemployment rate—a measure of the "tightness" of the labor market—and the rate of change of wages. Economists and policymakers also examine conditions in the product and capital markets, but for various reasons, unemployment and wages are an especially good gauge of where the economy is and where inflation is heading.

THE PHILLIPS CURVE

The framework for thinking about the rate of change of wages is the same as that used for thinking about the rate of change of prices. Just as the greater the gap between demand and supply at the current price level, the more pressure there is for prices to increase, and so the *faster* will be the rate of price increases, so too in the labor market: the "tighter" the labor market, the faster we expect the price of labor—wages—to rise. This kind of relationship has been verified in a number of instances, as illustrated in Figure 14.2. The relationship is called the **Phillips curve** after A. W. Phillips, a New Zealander who taught economics in England in the 1950s.

The different panels of Figure 14.2 show Phillips curves for different countries and periods. In every case, the unemployment rate at which inflation is zero is positive. There are several reasons for this. In the economy, not every worker is qualified to do every job. There may be unemployment of autoworkers and excess demand for computer programmers. If wages respond upward to excess demand more strongly than they respond downward to excess supply, average wages will be rising even when the excess demand for one type of labor equals the excess supply of the other. Similarly, there may be unemployment in Detroit and vacancies in Seattle. But unemployed autoworkers in Detroit cannot simply walk into jobs making airplanes in Seattle. By the same token, there will always be some workers moving between jobs; in Chapter 4 we referred to this as frictional unemployment.

THE EXPECTATIONS-AUGMENTED PHILLIPS CURVE

In the 1970s, the stable relationship between unemployment and inflation seemed to disappear. The economy experienced high unemployment with high inflation. There was a simple explanation for this: the rate at which wages increase at any level of unemployment depends on expectations concerning inflation. If workers expect prices to be rising, they will demand offsetting wage increases; and employers will be willing to grant those higher wage increases, because they believe that they will be able to sell what they produce at higher prices.

Inflationary expectations ran high in the 1970s, resulting in higher rates of inflation coexisting with higher unemployment. This is represented diagrammatically in Figure 14.3. The Phillips curve shifts up, incorporating the inflationary

Figure 14.3 THE EXPECTATIONS-AUGMENTED PHILLIPS CURVE

The position of the Phillips curve depends on inflationary expectations. Increased expectations concerning inflation shifts the Phillips curve up. U^* is the natural or non-accelerating inflation rate of unemployment (NAIRU). At U^*, if expected inflation is π_1, actual inflation is π_1; when expected inflation is π_2, actual inflation is π_2. At lower umemployment rates, inflation exceeds inflationary expectations, and eventually the Phillips curve shifts up still more. At higher unemployment rates, inflation is less than the expectations concerning inflation, and the Phillips curve shifts down.

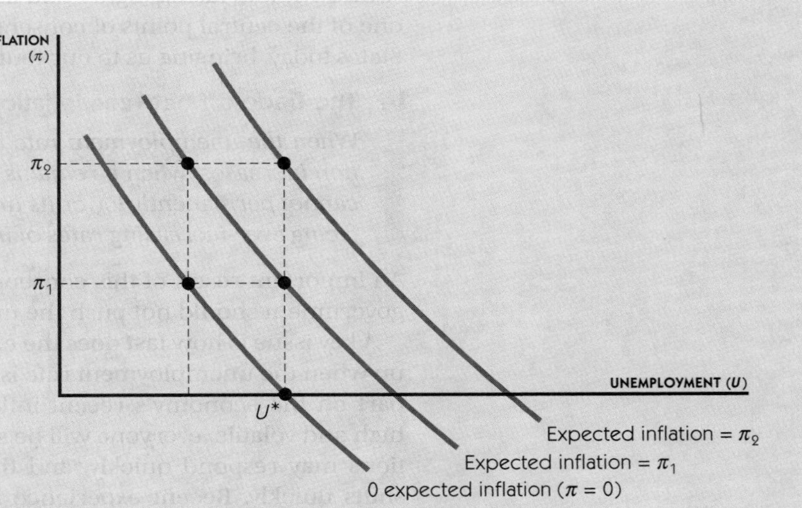

expectations. Because it includes inflationary expectations, the newly positioned Phillips curve is called the **expectations-augmented Phillips curve.** The Phillips curve shifted up successively during the 1970s, until it stabilized in the early 1980s. The Phillips curve stabilizes when actual inflation equals expected inflation. This occurs at a special level of unemployment sometimes called the **natural rate of unemployment,** indicated by U^* in Figure 14.3.

To better understand the role of the natural rate of unemployment, consider how expectations about inflation are affected both by recent experience and anticipated changes in policy and economic conditions. Take the simple case where expectations are simply adaptive, that is, they respond or adapt to recent experience. Assume the economy was initially in a situation where prices had been stable for an extended period of time. Given this historical experience, workers expect zero inflation, represented in Figure 14.3 by the Phillips curve labeled $\pi = 0$. Suppose the government reduces unemployment below the rate U^* (where inflation equals expected inflation), and keeps it at the lower rate. This induces an increase in the inflation rate. As the inflation rate increases, the expectations-augmented Phillips curve shifts up, so that there will be higher rates of inflation at each level of unemployment. If the government continues to maintain the unemployment rate below U^*, this will fuel higher expected inflation, resulting in another upward shift of the expectations-augmented Phillips curve. Thus, if the government attempts to maintain the unemployment rate below the natural rate, the inflation rate will continue to increase. As expectations adapt to each successive increase in the inflation rate, inflation increases still more. Accordingly, today, the natural rate is generally known as the **non-accelerating inflation rate of unemployment,** or NAIRU for short.

An economy cannot *permanently* lower its unemployment rate below the NAIRU without facing higher and higher rates of inflation. This has emerged as one of the central points of consensus among macroeconomists in the United States today, bringing us to our fourteenth consensus point.

14 The Trade-off between Inflation and Unemployment

When the unemployment rate remains below the NAIRU the rate of inflation increases; when it remains above the NAIRU it decreases. An economy cannot permanently lower its unemployment rate below the NAIRU without facing ever-increasing rates of inflation.

An important result of this consensus is an emerging belief about policy: the government should not push the unemployment rate below the NAIRU.

A key issue is how fast does the expectations-augmented Phillips curve shift up when the unemployment rate is below the NAIRU? The answer depends in part on the economy's recent inflationary experience: if inflation has been high and volatile, everyone will be sensitized to inflation, inflationary expectations may respond quickly, and the expectations-augmented Phillips curve shifts quickly. Recent experience in the United States, where inflation has been low and stable, suggests a rather sluggish response: if the unemployment rate is kept below the NAIRU by 2 percentage points for one year, then the inflation rate will increase by 1 percentage point. Conversely, to bring the inflation rate down by 1 percentage point requires keeping the unemployment rate *above* the NAIRU by 2 percentage points for one year (or by 4 percentage points for six months). The amount by which the unemployment rate must be kept above the NAIRU for one year to bring down inflation by 1 percentage point is called the **sacrifice ratio.** In 1996, the sacrifice ratio for the United States was believed to be about 2.

SHIFTS IN THE NAIRU

Though the *concept* of the NAIRU is now well accepted, economists do differ in their estimate of what the critical level of unemployment is below which inflation begins. This is because the NAIRU itself may vary over time. In the late 1980s, most economists thought that the NAIRU was around 6 percent, or slightly higher. As the unemployment got pushed down to 5.8 percent, and then to 5.6 percent, and hovered in that range throughout 1994 and 1995, more and more economists believed the NAIRU had decreased. In its annual report issued in February 1995, President Clinton's Council of Economic Advisers concluded that the NAIRU had deceased to somewhere in the range of 5.5–5.8 percent. By February of 1996, they suggested that the range was probably even lower. Other economists worried that inflation would appear, but only with a long lag. Today, few economists believe that the evidence is strong enough to suggest a precise number for the NAIRU; the best that can be done is to identify a range of plausible values.[1]

[1]In Europe, the large structural changes that have occurred in the last fifteen years have increased the uncertainty surrounding the value of the NAIRU. Many economists in Europe believe that the uncertainty is so large as to make the concept of little use in policymaking.

Using Economics: Calculating the Sacrifice Ratio

In the late 1980s, it was believed that the NAIRU was around 6.0 to 6.2 percent. The unemployment rates from 1987 to 1990 are given in the table below. During this period the inflation rate increased from 4.4 to 6.1 percent. Let us show that this data is consistent with a sacrifice ratio of 1.4, assuming a NAIRU of 6.2.

We add up the successive experiences of each year. In 1987 the unemployment rate was 6.2 percent, equal to our assumed value of the NAIRU, so no increase in inflation was caused. (Though unemployment varied from month to month, we take the difference between the *average* unemployment for the year and the NAIRU, and divide it by the sacrifice ratio. The sacrifice ratio gives the increase in unemployment above the NAIRU for one year required to bring down the inflation rate by one percentage point, so the reciprocal of the sacrifice ratio gives the increase in the inflation rate from holding the unemployment rate below the NAIRU by one percentage point for one year.) The 1988 experience added one-half percentage point to the inflation rate ($.7 + \frac{1}{1.4} = .5$), the 1989 experience, slightly less than 0.7 percentage point, and the 1990 experience, one-half percentage point. Thus, the experience from 1987 to 1990 is indeed consistent with a sacrifice ratio of 1.4.

Year	Unemployment Rate	Inflation Rate
1987	6.2	4.4
1988	5.5	4.4
1989	5.3	4.6
1990	5.5	6.1

Source: ERP (1996), Tables B-38, B-60.

Some of the changes in the NAIRU are predictable. There is always some frictional unemployment, people moving from job to job. Such movement is more common among new entrants into the labor force; in the 1970s, there were many new entrants, as the baby boomers reached working age and as more women entered the labor force. As a result the NAIRU increased. In the 1990s, these trends reversed themselves, partially accounting for the decline in the NAIRU. Government policies to help workers move quickly from one job to another may lower the NAIRU. Similarly, competitive pressures have increased, and unionization has decreased, so that wages more frequently fall, and are slower to rise. This too has helped lower the NAIRU.

The Long-Run Phillips Curve

The relationship between unemployment and the inflation rate *in the long run* is called the long-run Phillips curve, shown in Figure 14.4. The long-run Phillips curve is vertical at the level of unemployment that we have identified as the NAIRU. An economy cannot *permanently* lower its unemployment rate below the NAIRU without facing faster and faster inflation. It cannot "buy" a

Figure 14.4 A VERTICAL LONG-RUN PHILLIPS CURVE

Assume initially there is no inflation, and that the government decides to "buy" less unemployment by allowing increased inflation. For a short time, unemployment is reduced to U_0, but then the inflationary expectations shift the expectations-augmented Phillips curve up, so that at π_1, unemployment increases back to U^*. If the government again attempts to lower the unemployment rate below U^*, it can only do so by allowing inflation to increase further, to π_2. But this raises the Phillips curve yet again. If it kept inflation fixed at π_2, unemployment would rise again to U^*. Only by allowing the inflation rate to continue to increase can an unemployment rate below U^* be sustained. The only unemployment rate that can be sustained with a fixed rate of inflation is U^*: the long-run Phillips curve is vertical.

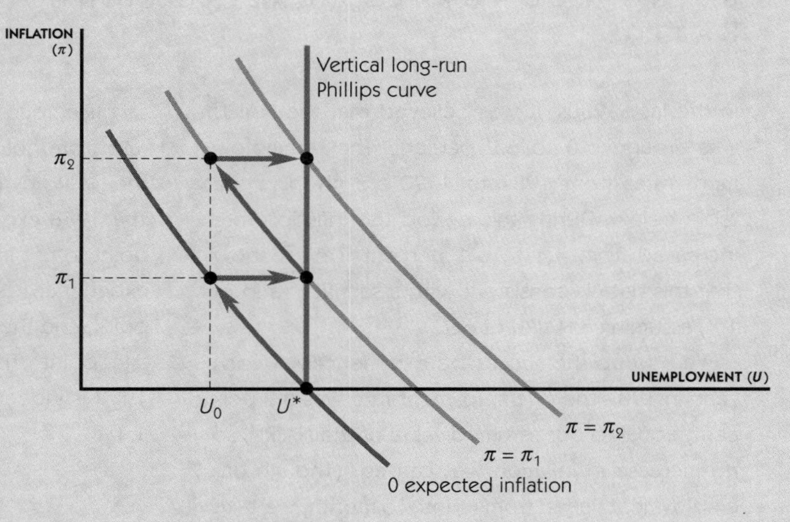

lower unemployment rate by accepting just a slightly higher inflation rate. But there is still a short-term trade-off. In the short term, the economy may be able to obtain lower unemployment at the price of higher inflation.

RATIONAL EXPECTATIONS

In the example given above, the expectations-augmented Phillips curve shifts up gradually over time, as market participants experience higher inflation rates, and build those expectations into their wage bargains. Their expectations are assumed to *adapt* to what they actually experience; when expectations are formed in that way, they are said to be **adaptive.**

In path-breaking work done in the 1970s that earned him the Nobel Prize in 1995, Robert Lucas suggested that the upward shift in the expectations-augmented Phillips curve could occur much more rapidly. Market participants did not have to wait until inflation actually occurred to build it into their expectations. They could *rationally anticipate* it. If, for instance, the government tried to stimulate the economy by expanding the money supply, firms and workers would rationally expect that prices would increase, and they would build that expectation into their behavior. These expectations, based on an understanding of the structure of the economy, are referred to as **rational expectations.**

There is one very strong implication of rational expectations. Assume the government announced it was going to keep the unemployment rate below the NAIRU by expanding the money supply. Workers and firms would antici-

BASICS OF INFLATION AND UNEMPLOYMENT

PHILLIPS CURVE: Shows the relationship between inflation and unemployment; the lower the unemployment rate, the higher the inflation rate.

INFLATION EXPECTATIONS-AUGMENTED PHILLIPS CURVE: The level of inflation associated with any level of unemployment depends on expectations concerning inflation; the higher inflationary expectations, the higher the level of inflation associated with any level of unemployment. As inflationary expectations increase, the inflation expectations-augmented Phillips curve shifts up.

NAIRU: The NAIRU (non-accelerating inflation rate of unemployment) is the unemployment rate at which actual inflation equals expected inflation and both remain constant. It is positive. If the unemployment rate remains below the NAIRU level, the rate of inflation will continue to accelerate. To reduce the rate of inflation requires keeping the unemployment rate below the NAIRU.

LONG-RUN PHILLIPS CURVE: The relationship between the inflation rate and unemployment in the long run, with full adjustment of inflationary expectations. It is generally believed to be vertical.

pate the increased inflation, and this would instantaneously shift up the expectations-augmented Phillips curve. Indeed, if the impact of the faster expansion of the money supply was fully anticipated, prices would rise proportionately; there would be no increase in the real money supply, and hence no effect on the level of economic activity. In this case the vertical long-run Phillips curve applies even in a relatively short time span, possibly even less than a year.

How quickly expectations adjust depends on economic circumstances. When inflation has been stable for an extended period of time, households and firms are likely to take the inflation rate as given. They will change expectations only gradually. But in economies which have experienced high and variable inflation, households and firms realize the importance of forming accurate predictions of inflation, and in that case, expectations are more likely to be highly responsive to changes in government policy.

There is one curious aspect of highly responsive expectations. While the government cannot reduce unemployment below the NAIRU level without inflation increasing very rapidly, there may also be little cost to the government reducing the inflation rate. If firms and households believe that the government

Policy Perspective: Indexed Bonds

In May 1996, Secretary of the Treasury Robert Rubin announced the United States' intention to join the small band of countries that issue indexed bonds. Such bonds guarantee a *real return,* independent of the rate of inflation. If an indexed bond promised to pay one percent real, and the inflation rate is 4 percent, it pays 5 percent total; if the inflation rate is 2 percent, it pays a total return of 3 percent.

Indexed bonds have a number of other important virtues. One is saving for retirement. Currently, people have no way of investing completely safely for their retirement. A bondholder faces significant risk from increases in the inflation rate. If a bond pays 7 percent, and inflation turns out to be 10 percent, the retiring individual may find himself much less well off than he had thought. Many pension funds provide pensions that rise with inflation. But individuals have no way of putting aside money to insure themselves against a high rate of inflation.

Yet another advantage would be a likely reduction in the government's cost of borrowing. Since individuals and pension funds dislike bearing the inflation risk, they would be willing to pay extra for inflation insurance, and the government is in a better position to bear this risk than anyone else.

There is a final advantage to policymakers and economic researchers. Looking at the difference in returns between indexed and nonindexed bonds can yield important information concerning inflationary expectations. For instance, if the interest rate on unindexed bonds increases by 1 percent, and the price of indexed bonds remains unchanged, we may infer that investors' expectations concerning inflation have increased by 1 percent.

Secretary of the Treasury Robert Rubin

will reduce the inflation rate, inflationary expectations can be brought down almost overnight, with the consequent downward shift in the expectations-augmented Phillips curve. The trick, of course, is for the government to convince others that it will succeed in getting the inflation rate down. It may be difficult to establish such credibility, and the "price" may be high—running the economy at a high unemployment rate over an extended period of time.

INFLATION, AGGREGATE DEMAND, AND AGGREGATE SUPPLY

The previous section focused on the labor market—on unemployment—and described how the level of unemployment combines with inflationary expectations to determine the rate of inflation. Because wages and prices move in tandem, by studying the determinants of wage inflation, we are in fact studying the determinants of overall inflation. In this and the next section, we take a closer look at the linkage between labor and product markets. This will enable us to see more closely the relationship between the dynamic analysis that we have just described, focusing on the rate of change of wages and prices, and the static analysis of Parts Two and Three, which used the tools of the aggregate supply and demand curves.

AGGREGATE SUPPLY

We begin by focusing in on the product market, on aggregate demand and supply. In earlier chapters, we described the economy's potential GDP, Y_s, the amount of output it could produce using the available labor supply and stock of plant and equipment. For simplicity, we assumed that labor supply was inelastic. As a result, changes in the price level did not draw more people into the labor force, and thus the economy's potential output was not sensitive to the price level.

Another way of thinking of the economy's aggregate supply is that it is the level of output that would be produced if wages and prices were perfectly flexible, so that labor was always fully employed. Because of this assumption that wages and prices can adjust fully to ensure full employment, economists sometimes call the vertical aggregate supply curve the **long-run aggregate supply curve.**

Firms may not be willing to hire all the available workers if the price they receive for the goods is low *relative* to the wages they pay workers. The **short-run aggregate supply curve** assumes that wages are fixed—they do not fall to ensure that there is full employment. It asks: How much are firms willing to supply at each price level? Typically, it has the shape depicted in Figure 14.5. The curve has three parts. If there is excess capacity, then there can be large increases in output with little or no increase in the price level—the horizontal portion. If the economy is using all of its resources fully, then no increase in the price level can elicit an increase in output—the vertical portion. And in between, there is an upward-sloping portion, where higher prices can coax producers to work their machines harder.

The relationship between the vertical portion of the short-run aggregate supply curve, the long-run (vertical) aggregate supply curve, and the NAIRU requires some discussion. In the short run, as we saw in Chapter 4, the economy can operate at more than 100 percent of normal capacity, as maintenance

Figure 14.5 SHORT-RUN AGGREGATE SUPPLY CURVE

The short-run aggregate supply curve gives the level of output that will be produced at each price level, given a particular level of wages. By contrast, the long-run aggregate supply curve gives the level of output that will be produced when wages are flexible, and so labor and capital are working at what might be viewed a "normal" level of full capacity. Because for short periods of time, capital and labor can work more beyond this level, at high prices, short-run aggregate supply can exceed long-run aggregate supply.

The short-run aggregate supply curve has three portions: a flat portion where there is a large amount of excess capacity, a vertical portion when there is no spare capacity, and an upward-sloping portion in between.

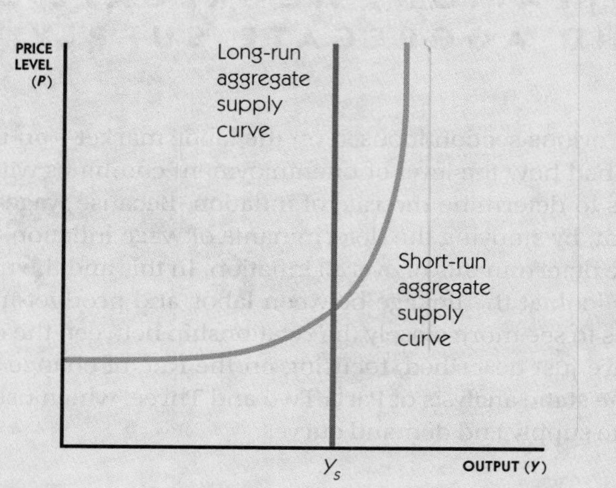

on machines is deferred. Moreover, for short periods of time workers may be induced to work overtime, and additional workers may be brought into the labor force temporarily. But it is not possible in the long run to defer maintenance or to induce workers to work, say, additional shifts. To the extent that one can work workers and machines "overtime" the vertical portion of the short-run aggregate supply curve lies to the right of the long-run aggregate supply curve, as depicted in Figure 14.5. The position of the long-run aggregate supply curve represents the *normal* capacity of the economy. When the economy is operating beyond normal full capacity, there will be upward pressure on prices, and when it is operating below normal full capacity, there will be downward pressure on prices. Thus, the output of the long-run aggregate supply curve is that corresponding to the NAIRU; at that unemployment rate, the inflation rate is neither increasing nor decreasing.

SHORT-RUN EQUILIBRIUM

We can now see how equilibrium output *(in the short run)* depends on the price level. When the price level is very high, as in Figure 14.6A, aggregate demand is less than aggregate supply—the familiar case of Part Three. Firms only produce what they can sell. Output is equal to aggregate demand.

Panel B illustrates a case where at the current price, P_1, the short-run aggregate supply exceeds the long-run aggregate supply, but aggregate demand is larger still. Output is determined by the short-run aggregate supply curve.

The general principle here is: the short side of the market always dominates.

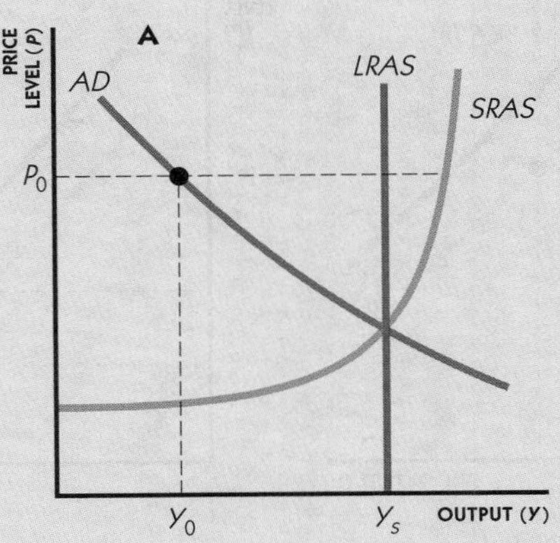

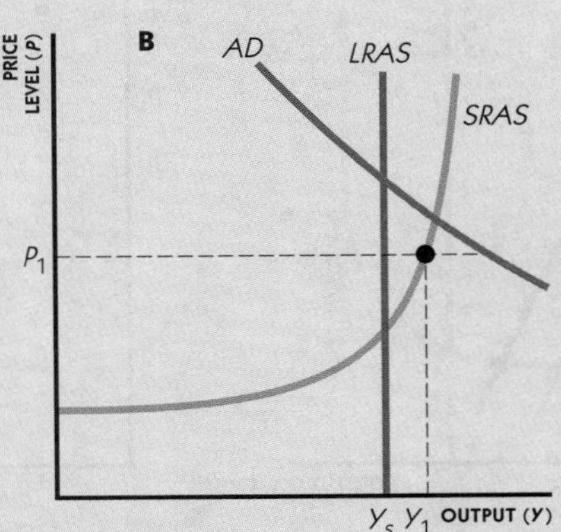

Figure 14.6 **SHORT-RUN OUTPUT DETERMINATION**

The graphs in panels A and B show aggregate demand *(AD)*, long-run aggregate supply *(LRAS)*, and short-run aggregate supply *(SRAS)* curves. In panel A, at P_0, aggregate demand is less than aggregate supply. Output equals Y_0. In panel B, at the current price, P_1, the short-run aggregate supply exceeds the long-run aggregate supply, but aggregate demand is larger still. Output is determined by the short-run aggregate supply curve.

SHIFTS IN AGGREGATE DEMAND CURVES

We can use this framework to show the consequences of shifts in the aggregate demand curves on inflationary pressures. There are three situations. Panel A of Figure 14.7 shows the aggregate demand curve initially intersecting

SHORT-RUN OUTPUT DETERMINATION

When the price level fails to adjust to equate aggregate demand and aggregate supply, the short side of the market dominates:

(a) If at the given price level, aggregate demand is less than aggregate supply, the actual output will be given by aggregate demand.

(b) If at the given price level, the short-run aggregate supply is less than aggregate demand, the actual output will be given by the short-run aggregate supply.

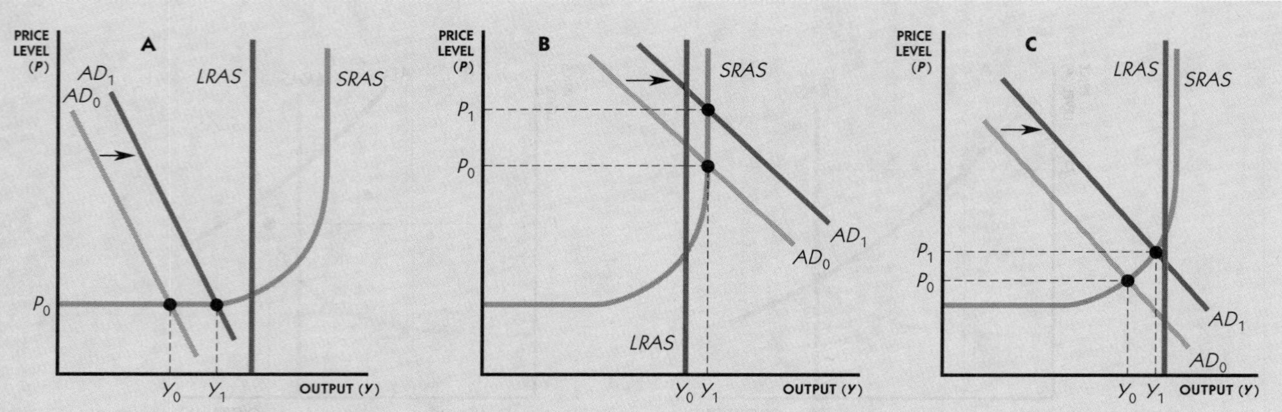

Figure 14.7 SHIFTS IN THE AGGREGATE DEMAND CURVE

The graphs in panels A, B, and C show aggregate demand *(AD)*, long-run aggregate supply *(LRAS)*, and short-run aggregate supply *(SRAS)* curves. Panel A. The initial equilibrium is along the horizontal portion of the short-run aggregate supply curve, so that rightward shifts in the aggregate demand curve lead to increased output but no upward price pressure. Panel B. The initial equilibrium is along the vertical portion of the aggregate supply curve, so that rightward shifts in the aggregate demand curve lead to no increased output, but considerable upward price pressure. Panel C. The initial equilibrium is along the upward-sloping portion of the aggregate supply curve. Rightward shifts in the aggregate demand curve lead to upward pressures on prices. If nothing else changed, eventually equilibrium would be restored with aggregate demand equaling aggregate supply at P_1, and with output higher than before.

the short-run aggregate supply curve along the horizontal portion of the aggregate supply curve. The initial price level is P_0 and the initial output is Y_0. There is large excess capacity. A rightward shift in the aggregate demand curve leads to a new equilibrium output, Y_1. At Y_1, there is no excess demand for goods. There is no upward price pressure. Because there is so much excess capacity, the increase in aggregate demand has not resulted in any inflationary pressure.

Panel B shows the aggregate demand curve initially intersecting the short-run aggregate supply curve along the vertical portion of the aggregate supply curve. We assume initially that the price is P_0, so again, in the initial situation, aggregate demand just equals aggregate supply. Now, however, a rightward shift in the aggregate demand curve leads to no change in aggregate output—after all, the economy is already operating at full capacity. But there is large upward pressure on prices. Inflation that starts with a rightward shift in the aggregate demand curve is referred to as **demand-pull inflation.**

The situation depicted in Figure 14.7B occurred in 1965. At the time, the economy was operating at close to capacity. President Johnson wanted to fight a war in Vietnam, but did not want Americans to know how costly such a war might be. As a result, he decided not to raise taxes, at least not enough to pay for the war. In addition, he did not want to cut other government expenditures, including his War on Poverty. With the initial equilibrium along the vertical portion of the aggregate supply curve, the increased government expen-

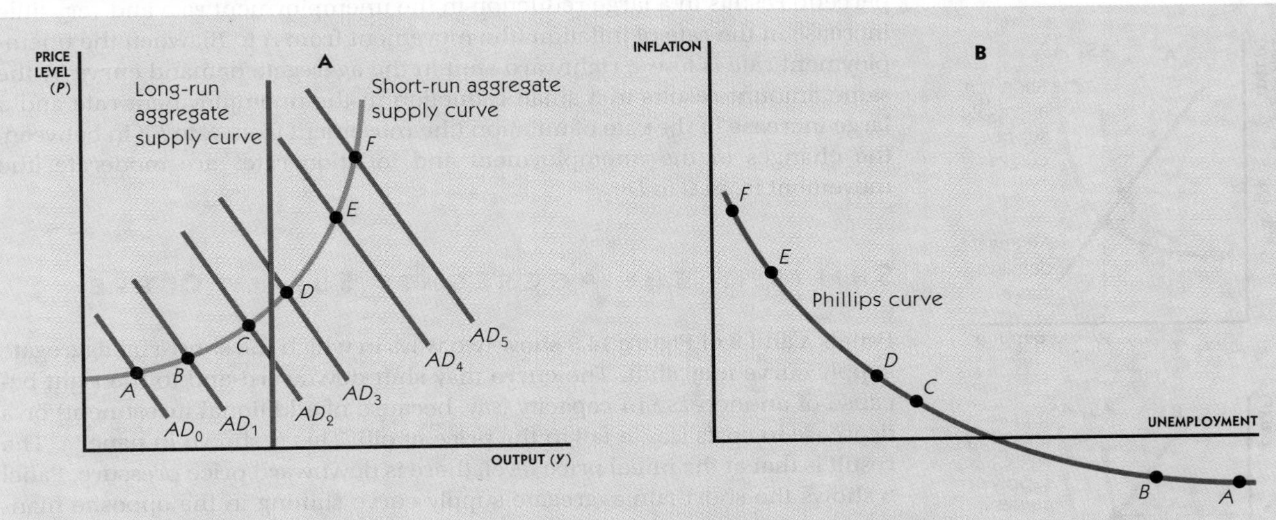

Figure 14.8 THE SHAPE OF THE PHILLIPS CURVE: TRANSLATING STATIC SHIFTS IN THE AGGREGATE DEMAND CURVE INTO MOVEMENTS ALONG THE PHILLIPS CURVE

When there is large excess capacity—when the unemployment rate is high—shifts in the aggregate demand curve result in large reductions in the unemployment rate and small increases in the inflation rate—the movement from *A* to *B*. When unemployment is very low, shifts in the aggregate demand curve result in small reductions in the unemployment rate and large increases in the inflation rate—the movement from *E* to *F*. In between, shifts in the aggregate demand curve result in moderate reductions in the unemployment rate and increases in the inflation rate—the movement from *C* to *D*.

ditures shifted the aggregate demand curve to the right, giving rise to inflationary pressures. The inflation rate, which had been running at an annual rate of between 1 and 2 percent in the early 1960s, climbed to the then staggering rate of almost 6 percent by 1970.

Panel C shows the aggregate demand curve initially intersecting the short-run aggregate supply curve along the upward-sloping portion of the aggregate supply curve. Again, we assume initially the price is P_0, where aggregate demand equals aggregate supply. Again, a rightward shift in the aggregate demand curve gives rise to upward price pressure; but now, as the price level increases, output actually increases, since the aggregate supply curve (in this region) is upward sloping.

Thus, the extent to which the shift in the aggregate demand curve gets reflected in increased prices or increased output depends on the slope of the short-run aggregate supply curve: when it is horizontal, output increases and there is no price pressure; when it is vertical, output cannot increase but there are large upward pressures on price; and when it is upward sloping, output increases *and* there is upward price pressure. This static picture translates into the shape of the typical Phillips curve shown in Figure 14.8. When the unemployment rate is high, a given rightward shift in the aggregate

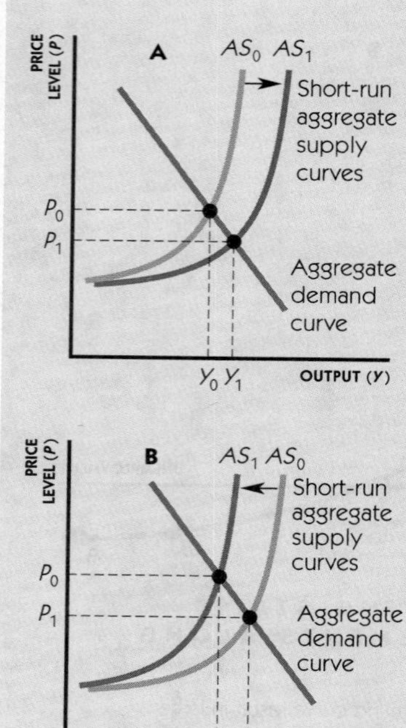

Figure 14.9 SHIFTS IN THE SHORT-RUN AGGREGATE SUPPLY CURVE

The short-run aggregate supply curve may shift downward and to the right, due to increases in capacity or decreases in costs, or upward and to the left, due to decreases in capacity or increases in cost. Panel A shows the shift downward and to the right from AS_0 to AS_1, resulting in downward pressure at the original price level. As prices fall, output will increase. Panel B shows the shift upward and to the left from AS_0 to AS_1, resulting in upward price pressure at the original price level.

demand curve (say, increasing aggregate demand at a given price level by 1 percent) results in a large reduction in the unemployment rate and very little increase in the rate of inflation (the movement from *A* to *B*); when the unemployment rate is low, a rightward shift in the aggregate demand curve by the same amount results in a small reduction in the unemployment rate and a large increase in the rate of inflation (the movement from *E* to *F*); in between, the changes in the unemployment and inflation rates are moderate (the movement from *C* to *D*).

SHIFTS IN THE AGGREGATE SUPPLY CURVE

Panels A and B of Figure 14.9 show two ways in which the short-run aggregate supply curve may shift. The curve may shift downward and to the right because of an increase in capacity (say, because of additional investment) or a decrease in costs (say, a fall in the price of oil). This is shown in panel A. The result is that at the initial price level, there is downward price pressure. Panel B shows the short-run aggregate supply curve shifting in the opposite manner, upward and to the left. This may be caused by an increase in costs, such as occurred in the 1970s when oil prices rose dramatically. The result is upward price pressure at the initial price level, leading to inflation. Inflation that arises from this type of shift in the aggregate supply curve is called **cost-push inflation.**

In 1973, the Organization of Petroleum Exporting Countries (OPEC), consisting mainly of nations in the Middle East, decided to impose an embargo on the shipment of oil to certain Western nations, including the United States. Even after the embargo was lifted, OPEC restricted oil production, so that the price of oil rose dramatically. For the U.S. economy as a whole, the higher oil prices raised costs of production. The short-run aggregate supply curve shifted upward and to the left, resulting in inflationary pressures.

SHORT-RUN AGGREGATE SUPPLY

The short-run aggregate supply curve has three portions: a vertical segment, where the economy is operating at full capacity; a horizontal segment, along which output can be increased with little or no increase in the price level; and an upward-sloping portion joining the two.

Shifts in the aggregate supply curve result either from increased capacity (new investment), shifting the curve to the right; or changes in costs of production, for instance, as a result of increases in the price of imported oil, shifting the curve up, or technological change, shifting the curve down.

Figure 14.10 THE OIL PRICE SHOCK AND THE END OF THE VIETNAM WAR

The end of the Vietnam War shifted the aggregate demand curve to the left, from AD_0 to AD_1. If nothing else had happened, this would have put downward pressure on prices. But at the same time, the oil price shock shifted the short-run aggregate supply curve up, from $SRAS_0$ to $SRAS_1$. At the old price p_0, output was reduced, while upward price pressure persisted.

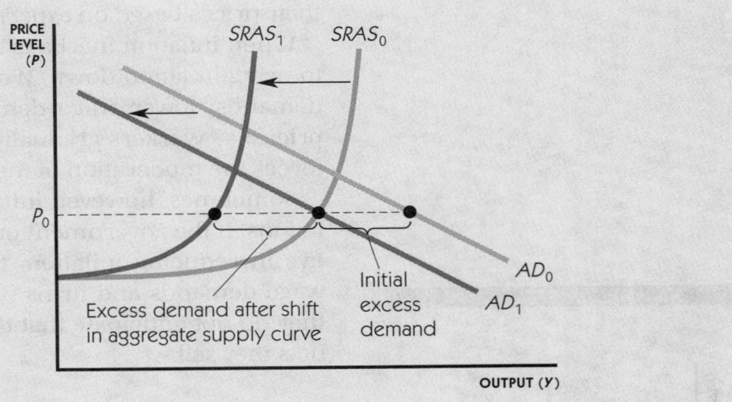

The timing could not have been worse. As we saw earlier, the increased government expenditure to finance the Vietnam War had ignited inflation. As the Vietnam War wound down, reduced government expenditures would have led to a leftward shift in the aggregate demand curve, resulting in downward price pressure. But the upward shift in the short-run aggregate supply curve more than offset this effect, and the economy had **stagflation**—inflation went up as unemployment went up. This is illustrated in Figure 14.10. The inflationary episode that had begun with a rightward shift in the aggregate demand curve as a result of the Vietnam War was carried forward with an upward shift in the aggregate supply curve as a result of the oil embargo. Moreover, as we saw earlier, inflationary expectations were raised during the period, exacerbating the inflationary episode.

INFLATION INERTIA

Earlier in the chapter, we described how if the unemployment rate remains at the NAIRU level, inflation will simply continue at a given rate. This tendency of inflation to persist is referred to as **inflation inertia.** Inflation inertia occurs because higher wages lead to higher prices (and expectations of higher prices), which in turn lead to higher wages. At the higher prices, firms are willing to pay, and workers demand, higher wages. And at higher wages firms demand higher prices, which consumers are willing to pay.

It makes little difference how inflation is started—whether through a shift in the aggregate demand curve that gives rise to demand-pull inflation or through a shift in the aggregate supply curve that gives rise to cost-push inflation. Once started, wage increases give rise to price increases which give rise to further wage increases, in a continuous cycle.

Expectations help to maintain inflation inertia. Workers base their demand for wage increases on their *expectations* of price increases; and firms may set their prices based on *expectations* of increases in wages and other costs.

When inflation inertia is strong, it can take long periods of unemployment to bring inflation down. With high unemployment, workers' moderate wage demands; lower wage demands translate into slower rates of increase in prices; as workers gradually realize that inflation is slowing down, this reinforces the moderation of their wage demands.

Sometimes, however, inflation can be stopped quickly, by reversing expectations. If the government puts into place policies that are thought to be effective in reducing inflation, then, for instance, workers may moderate their wage demands and firms will not be willing to grant increased wages since they do not anticipate that they will be able to get higher prices for the products they sell.

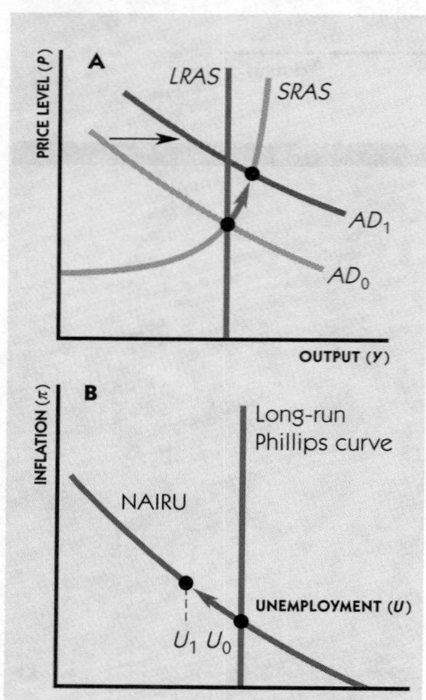

Figure 14.11 EXCESSIVELY EXPANSIONARY MONETARY POLICY SETS OFF INFLATION

Increasing the money supply shifts the aggregate demand curve to the right (panel A). There is upward price pressure. As prices rise, output increases along the short-run aggregate supply curve. As output increases, so does employment. In panel B the unemployment rate falls below the NAIRU level, and as a result inflation accelerates.

MONETARY POLICY

Inflation is often viewed as essentially a monetary phenomenon. In Part Two, where prices were perfectly flexible, we saw that this was the case. Increases in the money supply translated into increases in the price level, with no real effect on the economy. On the other hand, in Part Three, where prices were perfectly rigid, by assumption monetary policy did not have an *immediate* effect on inflation, but it did have an effect on output. In this part, which bridges the discussion between perfectly flexible and perfectly rigid prices, we will see that in general monetary policy has an effect both on output and inflation.

Figure 14.11A shows that an increase in the money supply shifts the aggregate demand curve to the right. Assume that initially aggregate demand equaled (both short-run and long-run) aggregate supply, and that initially there was no inflation. The shift in the aggregate demand curve leads at the current price level to upward price pressure, and, as we have seen, this upward price pressure gradually translates into higher prices. With higher prices, output increases along the short-run aggregate supply curve. As output increases, so does employment. Panel B shows that the unemployment rate falls below the NAIRU level, and as a result inflation sets in. Thus, an increase in the money supply can begin an inflationary episode.

Monetary policy may also play a role in sustaining inflation inertia. If the money supply is allowed to increase in tandem with prices, inflation can persist. However, with restrictive policies, inflation can be reduced.

Whether monetary policy is being restrictive depends to a large extent on the rate of increase in the money supply. In Chapter 12, we saw that normally the demand for money (at any interest rate) increases with *nominal* income. If the economy's real growth is, say, 2 percent, and prices are increasing at 3 percent, then if the money supply is increased at the rate of 5 percent per year, the increased supply of money will just equal the increased demand at an unchanged interest rate. If the money supply increases less rapidly, inter-

INFLATION INERTIA AND MONETARY POLICY

Inflation once started perpetuates itself:

- Increases in prices lead to increases in wages, which in turn lead to further increases in prices
- Expectations of inflation get built into wage formation

Monetary policy can dampen or accelerate inflation

est rates must rise for demand to equal supply, reducing investment. The aggregate demand curve shifts to the left and inflationary pressures are reduced.

EXPECTATIONS AND FOREIGN EXCHANGE RATES

In Chapter 12, we saw that there were two channels through which monetary policy affects the economy: it affects interest rates, and thus investment, and, in an open economy, it affects exchange rates, and thus net exports. In our earlier analysis, we noted that a decrease in the interest rate makes financial investment in the country less attractive, decreasing the demand for its currency and thereby decreasing the exchange rate. The lower exchange rate makes the country's goods more attractive abroad—increasing exports—and makes other countries' goods more expensive—decreasing imports. The result is an increase in net exports, shifting the aggregate demand curve to the right. The same logic applies to a restrictive monetary policy. Higher interest rates lead to a higher exchange rate and a decrease in net exports, shifting the aggregate demand curve to the left.

This analysis ignores one critical ingredient in the determination of exchange rates, a wild card which makes predicting the effect of monetary policy on exchange rates difficult: expectations. If American investors hold yen, and the dollar *appreciates,* they make a capital loss. Consider Jack who spent $1,000 to buy yen in April 1995, when the exchange rate was 80 yen to the dollar. He received 80,000 yen. Four months later, the exchange rate was 100 yen to the dollar. If he cashed in his yen, he would have received $800, for a 20 percent loss in only four months. If investors expect the dollar to appreciate, they sell yen and buy dollars, so the demand for dollars increases. Hence, the exchange rate rises—confirming their expectations. It is easy to see how a spiral of increasing exchange rates can emerge, as—at least up to a point—each rise of the dollar reinforces beliefs that the dollar will rise further.

How investors and speculators form their expectations—and how monetary policy affects those expectations—is a complicated matter that is not completely understood. But inflationary expectations are an important determinant. If the price level in the United States is expected to rise faster than the price level of Japan, investors will believe that *in the long run* the dollar must decline in value relative to the yen.

Expectations reinforce the dampening effect of tighter monetary policy when tighter monetary policy leads to an appreciation of the dollar because of its effects on inflationary expectations: if investors believe that the monetary authorities are taking actions to dampen the economy—and hence reduce inflation—they will expect the dollar to increase in value relative to the yen (compared to what it otherwise would have been), and this expectation of an increased value leads to higher demand for dollars today—and a higher exchange rate. The higher exchange rate makes imports more attractive to Americans, while Japanese consumers find American goods more expensive, and so the United States will export less.

CAUSES OF WAGE AND PRICE RIGIDITIES

We have *described* in this chapter how wages and prices adjust—how, for instance, wages increase faster the lower the unemployment rate. These empirical regularities make sense; after all, the tighter the labor market, the more likely employers will be scrambling to hire workers, and the more wages will rise. But to economic theorists, these explanations are not fully satisfactory. Why don't wages and prices adjust faster than they do? If they did, unemployment might not be able to persist as long. Economists have identified three key reasons why wages and prices adjust slowly—adjustment costs, risk and imperfect information, and imperfect competition that gives rise to kinked demand and labor supply curves.[2]

ADJUSTMENT COSTS

The first explanation for price rigidities emphasizes the costs of changing prices. When firms change their prices, they must print new menus and price lists or otherwise convey the change in prices to their customers. Changing prices costs money, and these costs are referred to as **menu costs.** Menu costs may be large, but advocates of the menu-cost explanation of price rigidities, who include Gregory Mankiw, George Akerlof, and Janet Yellen, point out

[2]In some cases, these explanations seem to explain too much—they suggest that under some circumstances, prices and wages will not adjust at all to, say, small changes in demand or costs. But the economy consists of many firms in different circumstances. Some may be in a situation where they do not respond at all, while others may respond fully. The *average* for the economy will reflect a slow response. In the next chapter, we consider a set of explanations that pertain particularly to the labor market.

that even small costs can have big effects. If each firm in the economy is slow to adjust its prices because of menu costs, even if these costs are small, the cumulative effects could still be significant. There could be powerful aggregate price rigidities.

Still, when firms face a shift in the demand curves for their products, as in Figure 14.12, they must choose whether to adjust quantity or price. While there are costs of adjusting either prices or quantity, the costs of adjusting quantity are almost always much greater. Facing such choices, firms will adjust prices rather than quantities. Accordingly, *in most instances* the direct costs of making adjustments do not provide a convincing explanation of price rigidities.

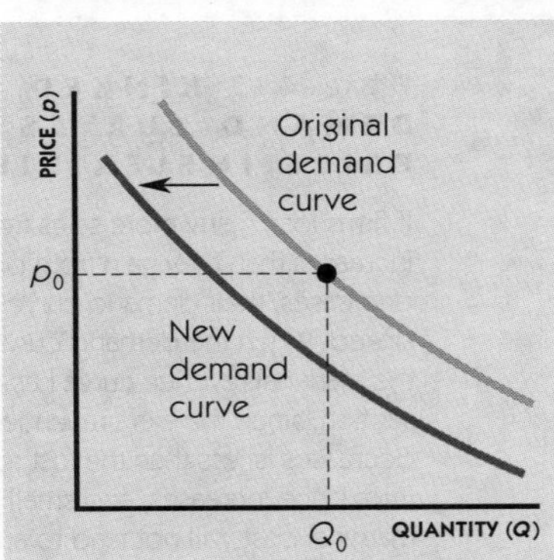

Figure 14.12 ADJUSTMENT COSTS

Shifts in the demand curve facing a firm necessitate adjustments in either the price charged or the quantity produced. How the firm adjusts depends in part on the costs of adjusting each and the risks associated. If the costs or risks of adjusting prices are high, and of adjusting quantities are low, then the firm will leave price unchanged, and lower quantity: there will be price rigidity.

RISK AND IMPERFECT INFORMATION

Risk and imperfect information provide important reasons for price and wage rigidities. Firms experience a great deal of uncertainty about the consequences of price and wage changes. When a firm lowers its price, whether sales increase or not depends on how other firms in the industry respond and how its customers respond. If rivals respond by lowering their prices, the firm may fail to gain market share, and its profits simply plummet with the decline in prices. If rivals fail to respond, the firm may gain a competitive advantage. Customers may think that this is just the first of several price decreases, and decide to postpone purchases until prices get still lower; thus a decrease in price might even result in reduced sales. Similarly, the consequences of a firm lowering its wages depend on how its workers and rival firms respond. Other firms might leave wages unchanged, and use the opportunity to try to recruit the firm's best employees. Alternatively, they might respond by lowering wages in a corresponding manner. In one case profits would fall, in the other, they would rise.

The uncertainty associated with wage and price changes is often much greater than that associated with changing output and employment. When a firm cuts back on its production, provided it does not cut back too drastically, its only risk is that its inventories will be depleted below normal levels, in which case it simply increases production next period to replace the lost inventories. If production costs do not change much over time, there is accordingly little extra risk to cutting back production. Similarly, there is little risk to a firm decreasing its employment simply by not hiring new workers as older workers leave or retire—much less risk than associated with lowering wages.

Since firms like to avoid risks, they try to avoid making large changes to prices and wages; they would rather accept somewhat larger changes in quantities—in the amount produced or in the hours worked. As a result wages and prices are sticky.

KINKED DEMAND CURVES

A third group of explanations attribute price rigidities to the shape of demand curves facing firms under imperfect competition. Recall that with perfect competition, a firm faces a horizontal demand curve. With imperfect competition,

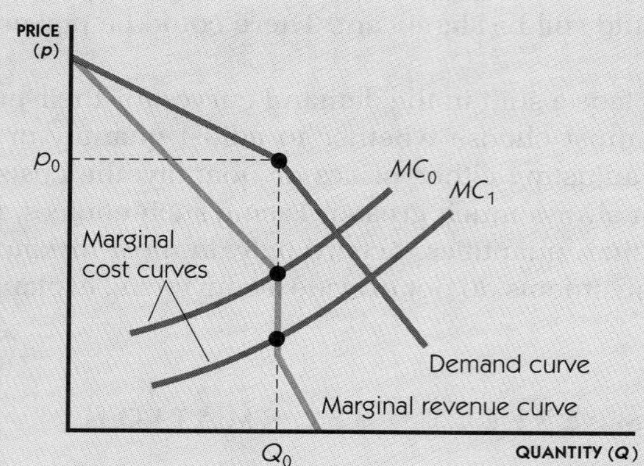

Figure 14.13 KINKED DEMAND CURVES AND PRICE INFLEXIBILITY

If firms lose many more sales from price increases than they gain from price decreases, their demand curve will be kinked. When the demand curve is kinked, the marginal revenue curve has a vertical section, since the extra revenue from price decreases is less than the lost revenue from price increases, and small changes in marginal cost will not lead to any change in price or output.

a firm faces a downward-sloping demand curve; in particular, the demand curve may have a kink, as illustrated in Figure 14.13. The kink means that firms lose many more sales when they raise prices above the current price, p_0, than they gain when they lower prices below p_0.

There are two reasons why the demand curve may be kinked—that is, why there are very different responses to price increases and price decreases. First, companies believe that if they raise their prices, their own customers will immediately know it and will start searching for stores selling the good at a lower price. But if they lower their prices without heavy expenditures on advertising, customers at other stores may not find out about their lower prices, so they gain few new customers.

Second, firms worry that if they raise their prices their rivals will not match the increase, and hence they will lose customers from their relatively uncompetitive prices. But if they lower their prices, rivals will view this as a threat and will match the decrease and the firm will gain little from the attempt to beat the market.

Kinked demand curves have one dramatic implication: small changes in marginal costs may have no effect on the price firms charge. Even if the com-

SOURCES OF WAGE AND PRICE RIGIDITY

Adjustment costs

Risks associated with wage and price adjustments

Imperfect competition with kinked demand or labor supply curves

pany's costs go down, it will continue to charge the price at the kink, p_0 in Figure 14.13. Firms worry, for instance, that if they cut their price in response to the lower marginal cost, other firms will simply match them and they will be no better off. Thus, kinked demand curves give rise to price rigidities: small changes, such as those resulting from a fall in wages, have no effect on either the output or pricing decisions of the firm.

A similar analysis applies to labor, in markets where firms have to pay higher wages to obtain more workers with required skills. There may be *different* responses to a firm's lowering or increasing its wages. If a firm raises wages, rival firms may match the increase out of fear of losing their best workers; but if a firm lowers wages, the rival firms may not respond, taking advantage of their higher wages to attract the best workers. Thus, the consequences of lowering wages may be costly.

REVIEW AND PRACTICE

SUMMARY

1. The costs of inflation increase with its level, the variability in its rate, whether it is anticipated, and the extent of indexation. Among the costs are the resources devoted to mitigating its effects and those associated with increased uncertainty. Increased indexation has lowered many of the costs.

2. Some of the antipathy to inflation is based on misperceptions, such as blaming inflation for losses in real incomes that occur during inflationary episodes but are caused by other factors.

3. *Other things equal,* lower levels of inflation are associated with higher levels of unemployment. This relationship is called the Phillips curve.

4. The level of inflation associated with any particular level of unemployment will increase as expectations of inflation increase. As a result, if the government tries to maintain unemployment at a very low rate, the inflation rate will continually increase, as each increase in inflation is built into individuals' expectations. The Phillips curve that reflects the effects of inflationary expectations is called the expectations-augmented Phillips curve.

5. The unemployment rate at which the inflation rate is stable—at which actual inflation is equal to expected inflation—is called the NAIRU, the non-accelerating inflation rate of unemployment.

6. The NAIRU can change because of changes in the structure of the labor force, and increasing competition in labor and product markets, which puts downward pressures on wages and prices.

7. With rational expectations, changes in policy can be reflected directly into inflationary expectations; the expectations-augmented Phillips curve can shift up immediately upon the announcement of a policy change.

8. The short-run aggregate supply curve gives the amount that firms are willing to supply at each price level (given current wages). It has three portions: a horizontal portion (with excess capacity, there can be large increases in output with little or no changes in price), a vertical portion (representing the full capacity of the economy), and an upward-sloping portion.

9. When at the current price level aggregate demand is greater than aggregate supply, there is upward pressure on prices. But wages and prices do not adjust instantaneously to clear labor and product markets. The rate of change in prices or wages is related to the magnitude of the gap between supply and demand.

10. There is considerable inflation inertia. Once started, inflation can persist, as increases in wages lead to increased prices, and increases in prices lead to increased wages.

11. Monetary policy may allow the money supply to increase in tandem with prices—and thus help perpetuate inflation; or, by restricting the rate of increase of the money supply, it may dampen inflation.

12. Prices and wages may be slow to adjust for three reasons. Firms may face large costs of adjustments. Firms may adjust output and employment rather than prices and wages because the uncertainties associated with changing prices and wages may be greater. And firms may face kinked demand and labor supply curves.

Key Terms

indexing
inflation tax
Phillips curve
expectations-augmented Phillips curve
natural rate of unemployment
non-accelerating inflation rate of unemployment
adaptive expectations
rational expectations
long-run aggregate supply curve
short-run aggregate supply curve
demand-pull inflation
cost-push inflation
menu costs

Review Questions

1. What are the costs, actual and perceived, of higher inflation? How has indexing affected the costs of inflation? What difference does it make whether inflation is anticipated or unanticipated, and why?

2. Why is there a trade-off between inflation and unemployment in the short run?

3. What role do changes in expectations play in shifting the Phillips curve? What difference does it make whether expectations are adaptive or rational?

4. What is the NAIRU? Why, if unemployment is kept below the NAIRU, will the rate of inflation accelerate? Why might the long-run Phillips curve be vertical?

5. What factors affect the NAIRU?

6. What is the shape of the typical short-run aggregate supply curve?

7. What is the relationship between the dynamic analysis of the Phillips curve and the static analysis of aggregate demand and supply curves?

8. What is inflation inertia? What factors contribute to its existence?

9. How does monetary policy affect inflation? What difference does it make whether there are rational expectations? whether the economy is open?

10. What are some explanations for wage and price rigidities?

PROBLEMS

1. Priscilla earns $40,000 per year, but her wages are not indexed to inflation. If over a period of three years inflation is at 5 percent and Priscilla receives raises of 2 percent, how much has the actual buying power of her income changed over that time?

2. Patrick receives a gift of two $100 bills for his birthday. Because he likes having the bills around to admire, he does not spend them for a year. With an inflation rate of 6 percent, what inflation tax does he pay? If he put them into a bank account paying 4 percent, what is the real value of his $200 at the end of the year? If he puts them into a money market fund paying 8 percent, what is the real value at the end of the year?

3. "It is unfair to tax capital gains—the increases in the value of stocks and bonds—at the same rate as ordinary income in inflationary situations." Discuss this statement, paying particular attention to a comparison of capital gains and interest income.

4. There have been proposals to increase Social Security benefits with the wages received by current workers, so that retired individuals do not fall behind those who are employed. What would be the consequences of increasing Social Security benefits *both* to compensate for increases in the price level and to match salary increases of the currently employed?

5. Social Security payments are currently indexed to the consumer price index (CPI). There is a widespread belief that the CPI overstates the true rate of inflation, because, for instance, it does not correctly account for improvements in quality. Assume that the overstatement is approximately

.5 percent per year. Discuss whether Social Security payments should be indexed to the CPI—.5 percent.

6. Why might the inflation effect of a onetime increase in a tax rate on final goods be different from other events that might start an inflationary spiral?

7. The sacrifice ratio measures the number of "unemployment years" required to bring down inflation by 1 percent. Thus, if the sacrifice ratio is 2, then one can bring down the inflation rate by .5 percent either by increasing the unemployment rate by .5 percent for two years, or by increasing the unemployment rate by 1 percent for one year, or by 2 percent for a half year. If the sacrifice ratio is 1, then how long will it take to bring down the inflation rate by 2 percent?

8. Assume the government maintained the unemployment rate above the NAIRU by 1 percent for 2 years, and the inflation rate increased by 1 percentage point, from 3 to 4 percent. Assume the costs to bringing down inflation are identical to the benefits (lower unemployment) associated with the increase in inflation. What must the government do to decrease the inflation rate to its original level? What is the sacrifice ratio?

9. If you were in the position of the Fed in 1994, with unemployment approaching 6 percent, and other indicators suggesting the economy had relatively little excess capacity, but had shown no strong signs of incipient inflation, would you have raised interest rates? Why or why not?

10. "If expectations adjust quickly to changes in economic circumstances, including changes in economic policy, then it is easy to start an inflationary episode. But under the same conditions, it is also easy to stop inflation." Discuss. If true, what implications might this finding have for economic policy?

11. Use aggregate supply and demand curves to explain whether (and when) the following events might trigger inflation:
   (a) an increase in business confidence;
   (b) an increase in the discount rate;
   (c) the development of important new technologies;
   (d) an increase in the price of imports;
   (e) an increase in government spending.

12. What would be the effect on the Phillips curve of an announcement that OPEC—the cartel of oil-producing countries—had fallen apart, and thus the price of oil was expected to fall dramatically?

13. While playing around with old economic data in your spare time, you find that in 1963, unemployment was 5.5 percent and inflation was 1.3 percent; in 1972, unemployment was 5.5 percent and inflation 3.2 percent; in 1979, unemployment was 5.8 percent and inflation 11.3 percent; in 1988, unemployment was 5.5 percent and inflation 3.6 percent. Does this evidence necessarily imply anything about the shape of the short-run or long-run Phillips curve? How might you interpret this data?

CHAPTER 15

UNEMPLOYMENT: UNDERSTANDING WAGE RIGIDITIES

Large numbers of people collecting unemployment insurance, huge lines at firms that are hiring workers, plants closing down and laying off workers—all are symptoms of an economy in a recession. Even more than lost output and reduced profits, the human misery that results from unemployment is a poignant reminder of the political commitment to limit both the extent and the costs of unemployment in the economy. But if we are to understand how to reduce unemployment, we must first understand its causes.

Although unemployment represents a situation where the supply of labor exceeds its demand, the macroeconomics of unemployment in Part Three looked at the product rather than the labor market. The reason is simple. Variations in output underlie most variations in employment. And variations in aggregate demand underlie most variations in output. Still, one important fact remains, which we emphasized in Chapter 6. No matter what the source of variation in the aggregate demand for labor, if real wages adjusted, full employment could be sustained. Unemployment is fundamentally a labor market phenomenon. It reflects a failure of real wages to adjust to changes in economic circumstances. The last chapter gave several reasons why wages and prices may be sticky. This chapter focuses on special features of the labor market that may contribute to rigidities in wages, particularly in *real wages.*

KEY QUESTIONS

1. What are the reasons that wages may not fall even when there is excess supply of labor?
2. What policies might reduce either the extent of unemployment or the costs borne by those who are thrown out of work?
3. What are some of the problems facing the unemployment insurance system?

THE WAGE-EMPLOYMENT PUZZLE

It is difficult to reconcile observed changes in employment (or unemployment) and wages with the basic competitive model. If we applied the basic model to the labor market, we would predict that when the demand for labor goes down, as in a recession, the real wage also falls, as illustrated in Figure 15.1. A leftward shift in the demand for labor results in lower wages. If the supply of labor is unresponsive to wage changes (that is, the labor supply curve is inelastic), as depicted by the steepness of the line in the figure, the reduction in the real wage is large.

In the real world it doesn't seem to happen this way. In the Great Depression, for example, when the demand for labor fell, real wages in manufacturing actually rose. One estimate shows that while unemployment increased from 5.5 percent in 1929 to 22 percent in 1934, real wages *rose* by more than

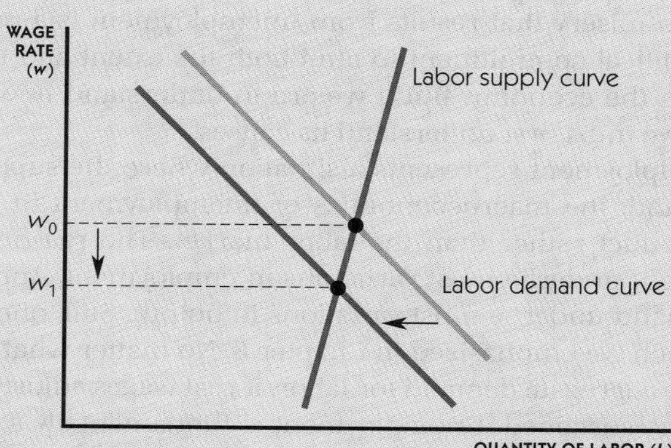

Figure 15.1 CHANGES IN THE DEMAND FOR LABOR AND REAL WAGES

Traditional theory predicts that when the demand curve for labor shifts to the left, real wages fall.

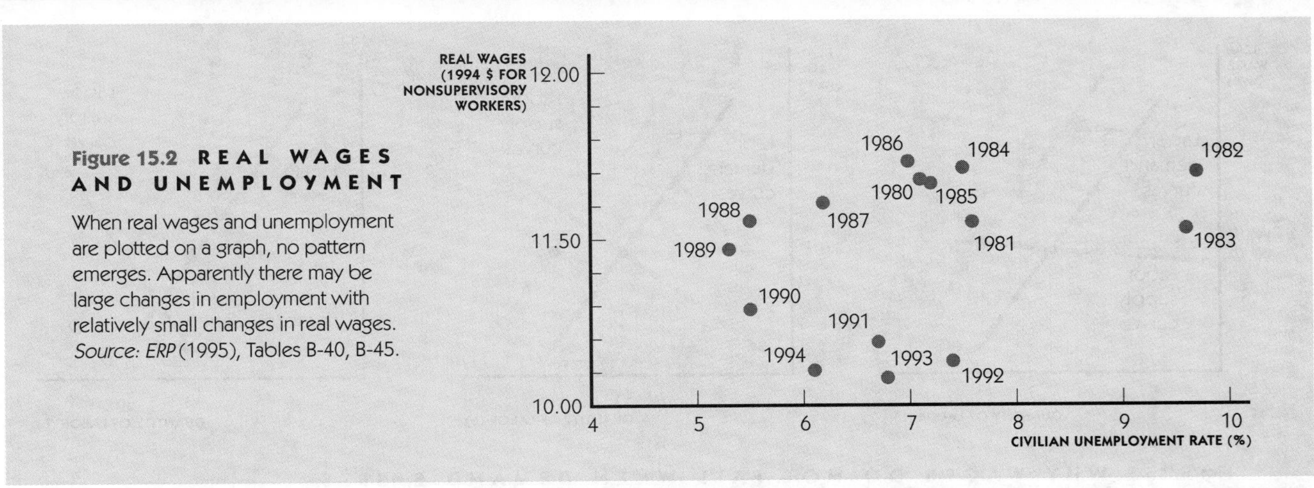

Figure 15.2 REAL WAGES AND UNEMPLOYMENT

When real wages and unemployment are plotted on a graph, no pattern emerges. Apparently there may be large changes in employment with relatively small changes in real wages. *Source: ERP* (1995), Tables B-40, B-45.

20 percent. In the 1980s, a much more recent example, real wages again rose as the unemployment rate increased, from 5.2 percent to 9.5 percent.

Figure 15.2 shows the real wage and unemployment rates during the 1980s and early 1990s. Real wages have not been much affected by changes in unemployment. There are three possible explanations. The first is that the supply curve for labor is horizontal and the demand curve for labor has shifted, as shown in Figure 15.3A. In this case, the labor market has moved along the labor supply curve to a new point of equilibrium. Almost all economists reject this interpretation, because of the huge amount of evidence suggesting that the labor supply curve is relatively inelastic (steep), not flat.

The second possible interpretation is that there are shifts in the labor supply curve that just offset the shifts in the labor demand curve, as depicted in panel B. The shifting demand and supply curves trace out a pattern of changing employment with little change in the real wage. Again, the labor market winds up at an equilibrium point. The reduced employment in the Great Depression was, in this view, due to a decreased willingness to supply labor—in other words, an increased desire for leisure. As we learned in Chapter 8, there have been marked changes in the supply of labor, as women and baby boomers have joined the labor force. But most economists do not see any persuasive evidence that the supply curve for labor shifts much as the economy goes into or comes out of a recession, let alone to the extent required in Figure 15.3B. And they see no reason why shifts in the demand curve for labor would normally be offset by shifts in the supply curve.

The third interpretation is that there has been a shift in the demand curve for labor, with no matching shift in the supply curve *and no corresponding change in the real wage,* depicted in Figure 15.3C. The labor market is stuck in disequilibrium. At the wage w_0/P, the amount of labor that workers would like to supply remains at L_0. But as the demand for labor shifts, the number of

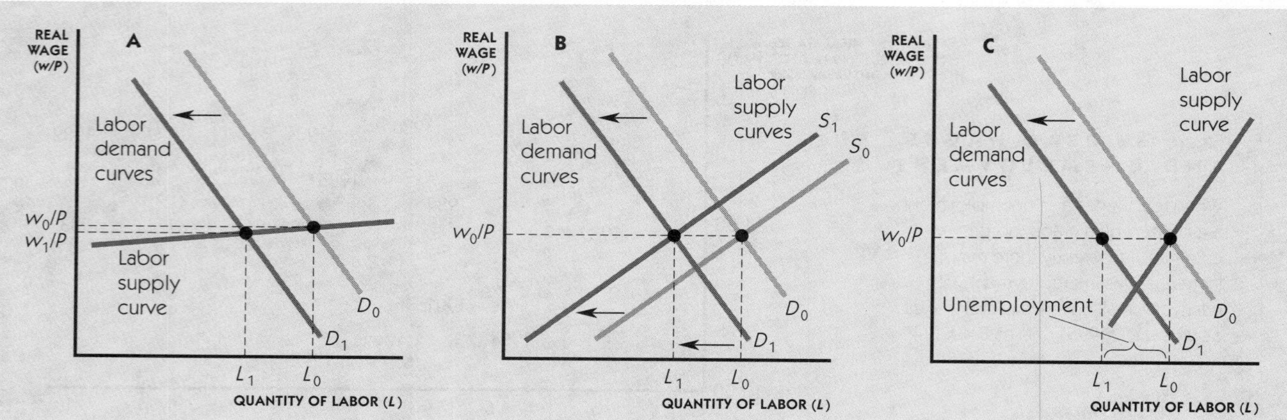

Figure 15.3 WHY WAGES DO NOT FALL WHEN DEMAND SHIFTS

Panel A shows a very elastic labor supply curve. A leftward shift in demand for labor from D_0 to D_1 will decrease employment without affecting wages. Panel B shows a shift in both supply and demand curves. Although the shift in demand for labor from D_0 to D_1 would reduce wages by itself, it is offset by a shift in the supply of labor from S_0 to S_1, leaving the wage level unchanged. In panel C, the demand for labor shifts from D_0 to D_1, but wages do not fall for some reason. Involuntary unemployment results.

workers hired at w_0/P falls from L_0 to L_1. The difference, $L_0 - L_1$, is the level of unemployment. If the wage does not fall, most economists—and virtually all of the general public—would say the unemployment is involuntary. People are willing to work *at the going wage,* but the work is not there. The same argument holds even if there is a slight shift in the labor supply curve and a slight change in the wage. The adjustment in the wage is too small to align demand with supply.

The question posed by panel C is fundamental to macroeconomics. How do we explain the apparent fact that wages do not fall in the face of a shift in the demand curve for labor? Reasons abound, as we will see in the following sections.

EXPLANATIONS OF WAGE RIGIDITIES

Why don't wages fall enough to eliminate unemployment quickly? We looked at several explanations in the previous chapter. Two possibilities are important for the current discussion. First, firms may not be allowed to lower wages, because of union pressure or government legislation. Second, the efficient wage for the firm (i.e., the wage at which profits are maximized) may be at the current wage level. It may not pay the firm to reduce wage levels, even if the supply curve for labor changes. The reasons for wage stickiness may vary from industry to industry and may overlap.

Unions, Contracts, and Government Regulations

One reason real wages may not decline as employment declines is that contracts and regulations are in place that keep them from doing so. In effect, there are wage floors, like the price floors we encountered in Chapter 3. The most conspicuous example is union contracts.

Union Contracts Labor union power explains wage rigidities in some industries. High wages in the U.S. steel industry, for example, undoubtedly contributed to the high costs of production in that industry, especially in the 1970s and 1980s—and to the decline of American companies in the world steel market in that period. Average wages in the steel industry in 1982 were $13.96 per hour, 64 percent more than the going wage in all manufacturing industries. (They fell sharply relative to average manufacturing wages after that.)

Unions and management share the blame when the high wages called for in their contracts make an industry uncompetitive. In many instances, unions have insisted on high wages even in the face of declining employment. Management has sometimes found it easier to pay the unions what they ask—even if doing so may not be good for the long-term health of the firm—rather than suffer the aggravation of a protracted negotiation or a strike.

It may even be in the interests of those currently employed in unionized industries to demand wages so high that they significantly reduce the demand for workers. If a union demands ever-higher wages, the employer will have an incentive to reduce the work force. But if the decline in the work force is slow enough, it can be accomplished by natural attrition (that is, by workers who choose to retire or quit). In that case, the job security of those still employed is not threatened. Nonunion workers who would be willing to work for less money are shut out by the union contract and have no way of offering to work for a lower wage.

Unions occasionally accept wage cuts in severe recessions. During the recession of the early 1980s, for example, unions in the airline, automobile, and steel industries accepted wage cuts rather than drive their firms into bankruptcy.

Economists do not agree about whether or not unions can obtain higher wages for their members over the long run than would be the case in a competitive labor market. But there is little doubt that unions slow the pace of wage adjustments. The first reason is that union contracts are for a fixed period—three years is typical. If the contract is signed just before an economic downturn, it may be more than two years before any wage adjustment, even if workers agree to one at that time. And if the economy is back on the road to recovery by the time the contract comes up for renewal, the workers' wages will have been largely insulated from the economic downturn.

The second reason union contracts may slow the adjustment process is through cost-of-living adjustment (COLA) clauses. In periods when there is high and variable inflation, union contracts frequently build in clauses that tie wage increases to the rate of inflation. Real wages are, in consequence, relatively unaffected by the rate of inflation or unemployment.

The final reason is that, to the extent that unions are sensitive in their collective bargaining to the unemployment rate, average union wages adjust slowly to changes in unemployment, since different contracts expire at different months and different years.

Union contracts, however, cannot provide the full explanation of rigid wages in the United States. There was high unemployment before unions became important, and there has been high unemployment recently, despite the steady decline of unions over the past thirty years. As the economy went into the Great Depression in 1929, only 7 percent of the labor force was unionized. In the recession of 1982, only 18.8 percent of the work force belonged to unions and the unemployment rate hit 10 percent.

UNION CONTRACTS

May reduce employment in unionized sectors.

May slow down real wage adjustment, thus contributing to cyclical unemployment.

Do not cover enough of the labor force to fully explain unemployment trends.

Implicit Contract Theory Union-contract-style wage rigidities may come about even in the absence of a union or an explicit labor contract. This is because the relations between an employer and her employees are governed by a host of implicit understandings developed over time between the firm and its workers. These implicit understandings are referred to as an **implicit contract.**

Workers are generally risk averse. Many have fixed financial commitments like monthly rent or car payments. They do not want their wages to fluctuate with every change in the demand and supply of labor. Firms can bear these market fluctuations more easily. First, the owners of firms tend to be wealthier, with a larger cushion for adjusting to variations in income. Second, in the event of a temporary shortfall of funds, companies can borrow more easily than can most workers.

Given that firms are less vulnerable to economic fluctuations than individual workers, it pays companies to provide at least some indirect "insurance" to their workers. Workers will be willing to work for a dependable firm that pays a steady wage, even if that wage is lower on average than the highly varying wages they could get elsewhere. Such a firm provides a form of insurance to its workers through an implicit contract—an understanding that the wages will not vary with the month-to-month, or even year-to-year, variations in the labor market. That is, the firm behaves *as if* it had a contract with its workers guaranteeing the wage. It is called an implicit contract because it is an understanding, not a formal or explicit contract. In these circumstances, the wage workers receive can be thought of as consisting of two parts: the "market" wage (the wage the worker could receive elsewhere) plus an adjustment for the implicit insurance component. When the market wage is relatively low, the wage received by the worker may be higher than the market wage. The worker is receiving a benefit on the implicit insurance policy. When the market wage is high, the wage received by the worker may be lower than the market wage. The difference is the premium the worker pays for wage stability.

For many industries in which long-term employment relations are common, implicit contract theory provides a convincing explanation of why wages do not vary much. But it does not explain layoffs. The risk of most concern to workers is the complete cessation of their income. Thus, implicit contract theory seems to predict that rather than laying people off, firms will engage in **work sharing;** they will reduce the hours each person works. Some firms have in fact experimented with work sharing, but it is not common. Layoffs are.

Proponents of the implicit contract theory try to explain layoffs in two ways. Both explanations are ultimately unsatisfactory. The first focuses on the fixed costs of employment and the idea that productivity shrinks more than proportionately with changes in the length of the workday. If a worker needs the first half-hour to settle into work, the last half-hour to get ready to leave, and a one-hour lunch break, then a six-hour day will lose the same two hours as an eight-hour day. So a firm seeking to cut its labor bill by 25 percent, by cutting its workday from 8 to 6 hours, would find its productivity reduced by 33 percent. This does not, in fact, explain layoffs, however, because the work sharing could simply take the form of fewer days a week rather than fewer hours a day.

The second explanation for layoffs given by implicit contract theorists is that unemployment insurance encourages layoffs. In most places, individuals are not eligible for unemployment compensation in the event of a layoff unless they work full time. (Some European countries now allow unemployment compensation for those who face reductions in their work week.) If a company trims the work week, it and its workers share the cost. If the company lays off workers instead, the government shares the cost. This is an unsatisfactory explanation because it once again only suggests a different form of work sharing—one in which there are short-term layoffs that take the form of job rotations. One group might be laid off for two months, the next group for the next two months, and so on. Job rotations such as these, in fact, are vary rare in the real world.

But the most telling criticism of implicit contract theory is that it does not really explain why wages of job seekers should fail to decline when there is unemployment. Even in the deepest recession, the labor market is like a revolving door, with people quitting jobs and some firms hiring new workers. Even if implicit contract theory could explain why some workers are laid off, it does not explain why employers do not pay new employees lower wages than they pay to their existing work force. If the wages paid to new employees fell sufficiently, presumably there would be no unemployment.

Insider-Outsider Theory Seeking an explanation for why firms faced with recessionary conditions do not pay lower wages to new employees, economists have devised what is known as **insider-outsider theory.** Insiders in this case are those with jobs at a particular firm. Outsiders are people who want jobs at that firm.

Insider-outsider theory focuses on the importance of training costs. Each firm needs a labor force trained in the special ways that it operates. Most of the training is done by current employees, the insiders. The insiders recognize that by training new employees, outsiders, they are reducing their bargaining position with the firm. The company can promise to continue to pay them higher wages than the newcomers, but the insiders know this promise could be broken. In future bargaining situations, the employer can use the availability of the lower-wage workers to exert downward pressure on the wages of the other employees. Knowing this, the insiders refuse to cooperate with training the outsiders, unless the new employees' interests are made coincidental with their own. The firm can accomplish this only by offering similar pay. This results in wage stickiness and unemployment persists.

Insider-outsider theory holds, further, that even if the current employees were to train new, lower-paid workers, the firm should not take the new workers' willingness to work at a low wage seriously. For once an outsider has been trained, she becomes a trained insider able to extract from the firm higher wages.

Wage systems in which new workers are paid less than established workers doing the same job are called **two-tier wage systems.** Firms do not seem to like two-tier wage systems. Most such experiments—such as the contract between Ford and its workers signed in 1982, which provided that new workers be paid 85 percent of what previously hired workers received—are relatively short-lived. The Ford experiment was abandoned in 1984.

Minimum Wages A minimum wage set by the government may result in unemployment. The minimum wage is a government-enacted price floor. To the extent that workers would accept and firms would offer wages below the minimum if they were allowed to, the minimum wage keeps the demand for labor from equaling supply. Most workers in the United States earn considerably more than the minimum wage, so minimum wage legislation has little effect on unemployment for these workers. However, many economists believe that minimum wage legislation probably does contribute *some* to the unemployment of unskilled workers, including teenagers just entering the labor force. This effect may not be strong, however. When, in 1990, the government set a special, lower minimum wage for teenagers, for example, relatively few firms availed themselves of this opportunity. They paid their teenaged employees wages that were in excess of the new minimum wage. Still, it is worth noting that in recessions, unemployment rates among unskilled workers and teenagers often increase much more than for the population as a whole.

EFFICIENCY WAGE THEORY

Even in a world without contracts, explicit or implicit, wages may not fall enough to eliminate unemployment because firms may find they make more profits by paying a wage higher than the one at which the labor market would clear. If paying higher wages leads to higher productivity, then higher wages may improve a firm's profits.

In Chapter 1, we learned that when Henry Ford opened his automobile plant in 1914, he paid his workers more than double the going wage. He wanted his workers to work hard. He knew that his new technique of production—the assembly line—when combined with motivated workers, would increase his profits. Many modern companies apply the same philosophy.

WHY DOES PRODUCTIVITY DEPEND ON WAGES?

Economists have identified three main reasons why firms may benefit if they pay high wages: wages affect the quality of the work force, the level of effort, and the rate of labor turnover. Each of these reasons has been extensively studied. In each, productivity may depend not just on the wage paid, but also on the wage paid relative to that paid by other firms and on the unemployment rate.

Quality of the Labor Force It is all too common for companies to discover after a wage cut that they have lost the best of their workers. Indeed, this is the reason frequently given by firms for not cutting wages. This is an example of adverse selection: the average quality of those offering to work for a firm is affected adversely by a lowering of the wage.[1] If a firm lowers wages, its best workers will most likely find a new job at the old (higher) wage and therefore will most likely leave.

Level of Effort We can easily see that it would not pay any worker to make any effort on the job if all firms paid the market-clearing wage. A worker could reason as follows: "If I shirk—put out a minimal level of effort—I will either be caught or not. If I don't get caught, I get my paycheck and have saved the trouble of making an effort. True, if I am unlucky enough to be caught shirking, I risk being fired. But by the terms of the basic competitive model, I can immediately obtain a new job at the same wage. There is, in effect, no penalty for having been caught shirking."

Firms that raise their wages above the market-clearing level will find that they have introduced a penalty for shirking, for two reasons. First, if their workers are caught shirking and are fired, they will have to take the lower wage being offered by other firms. Second, if many firms offer higher-than-market-clearing wages, unemployment will result, since at the higher wages firms as a whole will hire fewer workers. Now a worker who is fired may have to remain unemployed for a time.

[1]It should be clear that we have now moved away from the assumption that all workers are identical.

Close-up: Efficiency Wages in Tanzania

One of the implications of efficiency wage theory—that employers may be able to get work done more cheaply by *increasing* wages—can lead to some topsy-turvy implications. Or as Alfred Marshall, a famous economist of the late nineteenth and early twentieth centuries put it: "Highly paid labour is generally efficient and therefore not dear labour; a fact which though it is more full of hope for the future of the human race than any other that is known us, will be found to exercise a very complicating influence." The first chapter of this book gave the example of Henry Ford taking advantage of efficiency wage theory by paying higher wages in the automobile industry. But the theory can have striking implications in less developed countries too.

Consider the experience of the east African nation of Tanzania, formed by the union of Tanganyika and Zanzibar in 1964. When the area now known as Tanzania achieved independence in 1961, most wage earners worked on large plantations. Most of the workers were migrants, as is commonly the case in Africa, returning from the plantations to their home villages several times each year. The workers had low productivity and were not paid much. After independence, the government decreed that wage rates for the plantation workers would triple. Plantation owners predicted disaster; such a massive increase in the price they paid for labor, they thought, could only drive them out of business. But the government responded with predictions based on efficiency wage theory, that higher wages would lead to a more productive and stable work force.

The government predictions turned out to be correct. Sisal, for example, is a plant cultivated because it produces a strong white fiber that can be used for cord or fiber. Overall production of sisal quadrupled under the efficiency wage policy. This occurred not because of a change in the overall physical capital available, but because more motivated and highly skilled workers were better employed by the plantation owners. Over several years following the wage increase, however, employment in Tanzania's sisal industry fell from 129,000 to 42,000, thus illustrating how efficiency wages can increase unemployment.

Sources: Mrinal Datta-Chaudhuri, *Journal of Economic Perspectives* (Summer 1990), pp. 25–39; Richard Sabot, "Labor Standards in a Small Low-Income Country: Tanzania," Overseas Development Council (1988).

Consider a wage just high enough that workers are induced not to shirk. We know this wage must exceed the wage at which the demand for labor equals the supply. If one of the unemployed workers offers to work for a lower wage at a particular firm, he will not be hired. His promise to work is not credible. The firm knows that at the lower wage, it simply does not pay the worker to exert effort.

The no-shirking view of wages also provides a gloomy forecast for the consequences of well-intentioned unemployment benefits offered by government. Assume the government, concerned about the welfare of the unemployed, increases unemployment benefits. Now the cost of being unemployed is lower; hence the wage a firm must pay to induce workers to work—that is, not to shirk—is higher. As a result, wages are increased, leading to a lower level of employment. The higher unemployment benefits have increased the unemployment rate.

Higher wages may lead to higher levels of effort for another reason. They may lead to improved worker morale. If workers think the firm is taking advantage of them, they may reciprocate by taking advantage of the firm. If workers think their boss is treating them well—including paying them good wages—they will reciprocate by going the extra mile.

Rate of Labor Turnover Lowering wages increases the rate at which workers quit. Economists refer to this rate as the **labor turnover rate.** It is costly to hire new workers, to find the jobs that best match their talents and interests, and to train them. So firms seek to reduce their labor turnover rate by paying high wages. The lower the wages, the more likely it is that workers will find another job more to their liking, either because it pays a higher wage or for some other reason. Thus, while firms may save a little on their direct labor costs in the short run by cutting wages in a recession, these savings will be more than offset by the increased training and hiring costs incurred as demand rises again and they have to replace lost workers. We can think of what workers produce net of the costs of hiring and training them as their *net* productivity. Higher wages, by lowering these turnover costs, lead to higher net productivity.

DETERMINING THE EFFICIENCY WAGE

If, as we have just seen, net productivity increases when a firm pays higher wages, then it may be profitable for an employer not to cut wages even if there is an excess supply of workers. This is because the productivity of the employer's work force may decline enough in response to a wage cut that the overall labor costs per unit of production will actually increase.

The employer wants to pay the wage at which total labor costs are minimized, called the **efficiency wage.** The wage at which the labor market clears —the wage at which the supply of labor equals the demand for labor—is called the market-clearing wage. There is no reason to expect the efficiency wage and the market-clearing wage to be the same. **Efficiency wage theory** suggests that labor costs may be minimized by paying a wage higher than the market-clearing wage.

If the efficiency wage is greater than the market-clearing wage, it will still pay any profit-maximizing firm to pay the efficiency wage. There will be unemployed workers who are willing to work at a lower wage, but it will not pay firms to hire them. At the lower wage, productivity will decline enough to more than offset the lower wage.

If productivity depends on wages because effort increases with the wage—the shirking view of wages—the efficiency wage *must* exceed the market-clearing level. But if productivity depends on wages for some other reason, the efficiency wage can be less than the market-clearing wage. In that case, competition for workers will bid up the wage to the competitive, market-clearing level. Firms would like to pay the lower, efficiency wage, but at that wage they simply cannot hire workers. In efficiency wage theory, the market-clearing wage thus forms a floor for wages.

In general, the efficiency wage for any firm will depend on two factors: the wage paid by other firms and the unemployment rate. The wage paid by other firms matters because if other companies pay a lower wage, a firm will find that it does not have to pay quite as high a wage to elicit a high level of effort. Workers know that if they are fired, the jobs they are likely to find will pay less. Thus, the cost of being fired is increased, and this spurs employees on to working harder. The wage paid by other firms matters for other reasons as well. If wages paid by other firms are low, then the firm will lose fewer workers to other firms if it lowers its wages, and thus the "cost" of lowering wages—increased turnover rate—will be lower. Also, firms will find it easier to hire high-quality workers at any wage if the wages paid by competitors are lower.

The unemployment rate comes into play because as it increases, firms will again find that they do not have to pay quite as high a wage to elicit a high level of effort. The workers know that if they are fired, they will have a harder time getting a new job.

Efficiency wage theory also suggests a slow adjustment process for wages. Each firm is reluctant to lower its wages until others do, for several reasons. The company worries that its best workers will be attracted by other firms. It worries that the morale of its workers, and thus their productivity, will be impaired if they see their wage is below that of similar firms. No company wants to be the leader in wage reductions. Each therefore contents itself with reducing its wage slowly, and never much below that of other firms. Gradually, as wages in all firms are lowered, employment is increased and unemployment reduced.

These patterns are in contrast to the basic competitive model, which predicts that with a relatively inelastic supply curve for labor, there will be large and quick changes in wages in response to changes in the demand for labor. It is these wage changes that prevent unemployment.

WHY ARE THERE LAYOFFS?

Efficiency wage theory also helps explain why, if the economy needs a 25 percent reduction in labor supplied, workers don't simply work thirty hours rather than forty, and save jobs for the 25 percent of their colleagues who otherwise would be laid off.

According to efficiency wage theory, the reason workers do not just work

Policy Perspective: Minimum Wages

To many Americans, it has long seemed that if you work full time fifty-two weeks a year at some job, you ought to earn enough to support yourself and your family. During the Great Depression of the 1930s, Congress gave force to that feeling by enacting the Fair Labor Standards Act of 1938. Among the provisions of the act was a requirement that most businesses pay at least a *minimum wage* to all workers. Since then, Congress has raised the minimum wage as the cost of living in the economy has increased. Because of these increases, the minimum wage has generally been about half the average wage for all workers. But during the 1980s, the minimum wage was not increased, and as it slipped to a near all-time low, it was increased with bipartisan support in 1991. But by the mid-1990s, it had again fallen to a near forty-year low. Whether it should be raised again became a heated political subject in 1996.

Economists had long opposed minimum wages, on the grounds that raising any price—including the price of labor—above the market-determined level introduced distortions; they worried that raising the minimum wage would increase unemployment among low-skilled workers. But studies conducted in the early 1990s, especially by Professors David Card and Alan Krueger of Princeton University, called into question these views. They looked for a natural experiment, two neighboring states in similar economic circumstances, but with different levels of the minimum wage. In 1992 New Jersey raised its minimum wage (but neighboring Pennsylvania did not). Focusing their attention on low-paid restaurant workers, they found no significant adverse effects. These and other studies have led to considerable agnosticism: it appears that a modest minimum wage is unlikely to have significant employment effects.

One reason suggested that employment effects might be small is the efficiency wage theory: higher wages lead to higher productivity, largely offsetting the additional costs of the higher wages. Indeed, during discussions over raising the minimum wage from $4.25 to $5.15 (over two years), it was estimated that at least 3 million workers earning between $5.15 and $5.75 an hour would also receive a pay raise. The fact that employers who do not have to raise wages *choose* to do so suggests that labor markets are not like the markets for ordinary commodities like steel; employers do worry about the impact of wages on productivity. Raising the minimum wage raises "norms" of how workers should be treated, and generates a ripple effect.

Many economists had also opposed minimum wage increases, believing that it was not a very effective way of targeting help to the poor. It used to be that many minimum wage workers were teenagers or secondary workers in families which were not poor. But increasingly, minimum wage workers have become the primary source of incomes for their families. Today, the average share of household income earned by a minimum wage worker is one-half.

A further advantage of raising the minimum wage is that it increases the incentives to work, by increasing the difference between what someone on welfare receives and what a worker gets.

Source: David Card and Alan Krueger, *Myth and Measurement,* (Princeton: Princeton University Press, 1995).

thirty hours rather than forty is that by reducing work proportionately among its workers, a firm will in effect be reducing overall pay proportionately. The company will fall back into the traps outlined above. If it lowers overall pay, it may lose a disproportionate fraction of its better workers. These workers can obtain offers of full-time work and full-time pay, and they will find this more attractive than a job with 80 percent of full-time work and 80 percent of the pay. (They may enjoy the extra leisure, but it will not help meet the mortgage payments.) Furthermore, workers now working part time will find that their incentives to exert high levels of effort decline. If they get fired, losing a part-time job is not as serious as losing a full-time job. This ability to explain concentrated layoffs is one feature that sets efficiency wage theory apart from some of the alternative views of wage rigidity.

THE IMPACT OF UNEMPLOYMENT ON DIFFERENT GROUPS

One striking aspect of unemployment in the United States is that it affects different groups in the population very differently. In competitive markets, wages will adjust to reflect productivity. Groups with higher productivity will have commensurately higher wage rates, while groups with lower productivity will have lower wage rates. But people in both groups will have jobs. There would be no reason for different groups to have different unemployment rates. Thus, we must go beyond the basic model of competitive markets to understand why unemployment affects different groups differently.

The efficiency wage theory argues that there may be some kinds of laborers—such as part-time workers or those with limited skills—who, at any wage, have sufficiently low productivity that it barely pays a firm to hire them. To put it another way, while they may receive a low wage, the wage is only just low enough to offset their low productivity. Paying higher wages would not increase productivity enough to offset the wage increase. And paying lower wages would reduce productivity, making that option unworkable as well.

It is these groups, who lie right at the margin of the firm's hiring decision, who will bear the brunt of the fluctuations in the demand for labor. Teenagers and young workers not only have higher average unemployment rates, they bear more than their proportionate share of the burden of variations in employment.

LIMITS OF EFFICIENCY WAGE THEORY

Efficiency wage theory may provide a significant part of the explanation for wage rigidities in a number of different situations: where training and turnover costs are high; where monitoring productivity is difficult; and where differences in individuals' productivity are large and important, but it is difficult to ascertain them before hiring and training them. But efficiency wage considerations are likely to be less important in situations where workers are paid piece rates on the basis of how much they produce, or in situations where training costs are low and monitoring is easy. These situations may indeed exhibit greater wage flexibility, at least if there are no union pressures, implicit contracts, or insider-outsider considerations.

OKUN'S LAW AND DISGUISED UNEMPLOYMENT

As high as the unemployment statistics sometimes climb, they still may not fully reflect the underutilization of labor. Firms find it costly to hire and train workers. When they have a temporary lull in demand, they may not even lay workers off, for fear that once laid off, the workers will seek employment elsewhere. Thus, firms keep the workers on the job, but may not fully utilize them. This is **labor hoarding,** and can be thought of as a form of disguised unemployment. Employees are not really working, though they are showing up for work. Like open unemployment, it represents a waste of human resources.

The importance of disguised unemployment was brought home by Arthur Okun, chairman of the Council of Economic Advisers under President Johnson. He showed that as the economy pulls out of a recession, output increases more than proportionately with employment; and as the economy goes into a recession, output decreases more than proportionately with the reduction in employment. This result is **Okun's law.** In Okun's study, for every 1 percentage point decrease in the unemployment rate, output increased by 3 percent. Today, most economists still think output increases more than proportionately with employment, though not as much as Okun suggested. Current estimates predict that a 1 percentage point increase in the unemployment rate will correspond to a 2 to 2.5 percent decrease in output (a 2 percent decrease in output is the rule of thumb used elsewhere in this text). This was a remarkable finding, for it seemed to run contrary to one of the basic principles of economics—the law of diminishing returns—which would have predicted that a 1 percentage point decrease in the unemployment rate would have less than a proportionate effect on output. The explanation for Okun's law, however, was simple. Many of those who were working in a recession were partially idle. As the economy heated up, they worked more fully, and this yielded the unexpected increase in output.

ALTERNATIVE EXPLANATIONS OF WAGE RIGIDITIES

1. Unions with explicit and implicit contracts prevent wages from falling. Insider-outsider theory explains why firms do not pay newly hired workers a lower wage. Minimum wages explain why wages for very low skilled workers do not fall.
2. Efficiency wage theory suggests that it is profitable for firms to pay above-market wages. This is because wages affect the quality of the labor force, labor turnover rates, and the level of effort exerted by workers.

POLICY ISSUES

This chapter has explored possible reasons why wages do not fall to the level where the demand for labor equals the supply. The truth involves a combination of all the explanations. Minimum wages may play a role among very low skilled workers. Unions play a role in some sectors of the economy. And in some jobs, firms do not cut wages because of efficiency wage considerations.

But wages do sometimes fall, as in the Great Depression. But what are important for firm decisions are wages *relative to* prices. Wages do not fall *fast enough* to equilibrate demand and supply. And all the reasons given in this chapter play a role, not only in explaining why wages do not fall, but also in helping us to understand why, when they fall, they fall slowly.

When the labor market does not clear and involuntary unemployment results, there may be an economic role for government. It is worth reviewing government policies designed to overcome failures in the labor market. Such policies have included increasing wage flexibility; reducing the costs of unemployment by providing replacement income to the unemployed; and increasing the efficiency of the labor market through reemployment programs.

INCREASING WAGE FLEXIBILITY

Those who see wage rigidities as a major cause of unemployment and believe that they are created by unions or implicit contracts have sought ways of increasing wage flexibility. In Japan, for example, large companies have long-term (lifetime) implicit contracts with their workers, but workers receive a substantial fraction of their pay in the form of annual bonuses. In effect, this means that the wage a worker receives varies from year to year depending on the fortunes of the firm. Unemployment in Japan is considerably less variable than in the United States, and many economists believe that flexible wages are an important part of the reason. In his book *The Share Economy,* Martin Weitzman of Harvard University has advocated that U.S. firms adopt a similar system.

Two features make wage flexibility unattractive to workers. First, workers would have to bear more risk in income fluctuations. Under the current U.S. system, workers who have considerable seniority, and who often dominate union negotiations, face little risk of being laid off during hard times. Their incomes are relatively secure, both from year-to-year variation and from the threat of complete cessation. With the bonus system, however, all employees, including the more senior ones, would face considerable risk. And as the discussion of implicit contracts pointed out, the firm is generally in a better position than the worker to bear the risk of economic fluctuations.

Second, workers worry that the firms most likely to be willing to give large profit shares to their employees in exchange for wage concessions may be those firms that expect the smallest profits. By giving up a share of the profit, they are giving the least away. In effect, when the workers' pay depends on the profits of the firm, workers become much like shareholders—what they receive depends on how well the company does. It does no good to own a large share in the profits of a firm that makes no profits.

This second reason makes it clear why unions do not trust wage flexibility systems. Their concern that firms without profits will be the most willing to offer to share them with their workers proved justified in 1985, when employees of Eastern Airlines actually accepted a pay reduction in return for a share of the profits. The airline went into bankruptcy soon after.

Still, the fact is that large segments of Japanese industry employ a system with greater wage flexibility, and that system seems to give rise to less variability in employment. Japan appears to have overcome the obstacles to making wages vary with profits. How this happened, whether it is possible for the United States to move to a system with more flexible wages, and what role government should play in encouraging such a move, remain questions of debate among economists.

REDUCING THE COSTS OF UNEMPLOYMENT

During the past half century, governments have made it their responsibility not only to reduce the level of unemployment but also to reduce the costs borne by those unfortunate enough to be unemployed. The difficulty is, how do we do this without giving rise to further economic problems?

UNEMPLOYMENT INSURANCE

The unemployment insurance program is the most important one for reducing the cost to the worker of being unemployed. It was started in the midst of the Great Depression with passage of the Social Security Act in 1935. Unemployment insurance programs are run by the states, within federal guidelines, and vary by state. The typical program pays up to 50 percent of a person's former salary for twenty-six weeks. In a number of instances, when the unemployment rate has increased, coverage has been extended to thirty-nine weeks or longer. To be eligible for the maximum, workers must have worked for a minimum number of weeks—forty out of the previous fifty-two, for example. Thus, new workers are not covered by unemployment insurance.

Critics of the program worry that it reduces the incentive of unemployed workers to search for jobs. There is some evidence for this. The number of people who get jobs just as their unemployment benefits expire is far greater than can be accounted for by chance. Others worry that when generous unemployment insurance is available, workers have less incentive to exert effort at any given level of wages and unemployment because the threat of being fired is not as fearsome as it would otherwise be. To restore the incentives of efficiency wages, firms must pay higher wages, but when they do, the higher cost of labor induces them to hire fewer workers. By this logic, high unemployment insurance actually contributes to increasing the unemployment rate.

What we have here is another illustration of a familiar basic trade-off. Economic arrangements that diminish risk also diminish incentives. A person who is guaranteed a job will have little incentive to work. If unemployment insurance were sufficiently generous that it fully replaced whatever income he lost if he were fired, a worker would not find any economic incentives for working. And a worker who is laid off would have no incentive to look for a new job. Thus, some critics of the current unemployment insurance system argue that we have gone too far in reducing risk—and reducing incentives.

Other critics argue that the current U.S. unemployment system is targeted to the wrong groups—that it does not provide enough support for either the long-term unemployed or new entrants into the labor force, but provides too much for the short-term unemployed. Insurance for unemployment periods of six or eight weeks may be unnecessary in the eyes of many economists. They argue that people should be able to finance these short-term spells out of savings or by borrowing. One recent study calculated that requiring an unemployed worker to wait two weeks before receiving any unemployment payments would save $1.1 billion a year in lower unemployment benefits, while still assuring a steady stream of income to the longer-term unemployed. These economists believe that in general, insurance should be designed to cover *large* losses, against which individuals cannot self-insure.

THE U.S. REEMPLOYMENT SYSTEM

In 1994 Secretary of Labor Robert Reich (who formerly taught at Harvard's Kennedy School) proposed redirecting America's unemployment system to create a "reemployment system," focusing on providing both incentives and resources to encourage more rapid transitions from one job to another. The objective of this system is to increase the efficiency of the labor market. A nationwide system of "one-stop job centers" would provide both job search and training information. Training would be directed toward available job opportunities. And to be eligible for extended unemployment insurance benefits (beyond the basic twenty-six weeks), workers would have to enroll in active training and job search programs.

REVIEW AND PRACTICE

SUMMARY

1. Involuntary unemployment exists when the supply of labor exceeds the demand for labor at the prevailing market wage. This happens when demand for labor at each wage level falls but real wages do not decline.

2. Explanations for why firms may be unable to reduce wages and thus unemployment include union contracts or implicit contracts, insider-outsider theory (which explains why firms do not pay lower wages to new hires), and minimum wage laws.

3. Reducing wages may actually lead to an increase in labor costs, because (a) it may result in a lower average quality of workers as the best workers leave; (b) it may result in lower effort; and (c) it may result in higher turnover costs.

4. Firms often do not fully utilize their labor force in economic downturns. This labor hoarding means that as the economy expands, output increases more than in proportion to increases in employment.

5. Making wages depend more on firm profits might result in less variability in employment. But workers would risk income reductions in hard times, and would worry that the firms most likely to give large profit shares to employees are those with the smallest profits to share.

6. Unemployment insurance reduces the costs to workers of being laid off, but it also reduces workers' incentives to work hard or to search for a new job. Firms' responses may lead to higher rather than lower unemployment.

Key Terms

implicit contract
work sharing
insider-outsider theory
labor turnover rate
efficiency wage
Okun's law

Review Questions

1. What gives rise to involuntary unemployment?

2. List reasons why firms may be unable or unwilling to reduce wages.

3. True or false: "The prevalence of unions and minimum wage laws is the primary reason for wage stickiness, and therefore for unemployment, in the U.S. economy." Discuss your answer.

4. If an implicit contract is not written down, why would a firm abide by it? Why would a worker?

5. Why does implicit contract theory predict that work sharing is more likely than layoffs?

6. Give three reasons why productivity may depend on the level of wages paid.

7. How does an efficiency wage differ from a market-clearing wage?

8. How does efficiency wage theory help explain why different groups may have very different levels of unemployment?

9. What trade-off does society face when it attempts to expand economic security for workers with higher unemployment benefits or greater job security?

PROBLEMS

1. In 1996, Congress passed legislation increasing the minimum wage in two steps from $4.25 per hour to $5.15 per hour. Explain why efficiency wage theory suggests that the effect on employment may be relatively small.

2. Would you be more or less likely to observe implicit contracts in industries where most workers hold their jobs for only a short time? What about industries where most workers hold jobs a long time? Explain.

3. A number of businesses have proposed a two-tier wage scale, in which the wage scale for new employees is lower than the wage scale for current employees. Using the insights of insider-outsider theory, would you be more or less likely to observe two-tier wage scales in industries where a lot of on-the-job training is needed than in those where not much is needed?

4. The following figures represent the relationship between productivity and wages for the Doorware Corporation, which makes hinges.

Wage per hour	$ 8	$10	$12	$14	$16	$18	$20
Hinges produced per hour	20	24	33	42	52	58	60

Graph the productivity-wage relationship. From the graph, how do you determine the efficiency wage? Calculate output per dollar spent on labor for the Doorware Corporation. What is the efficiency wage?

5. Would you be more or less likely to see efficiency wages in the following types of industries?
   (a) industries where training and turnover costs are relatively low;
   (b) industries where it is difficult to monitor individual productivity;
   (c) industries that have many jobs where individual differences in productivity are relatively large.

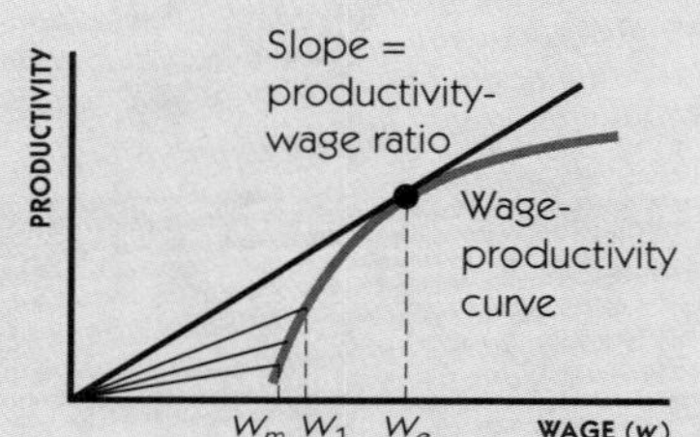

Figure 15.4 THE RELATIONSHIP BETWEEN PRODUCTIVITY AND WAGES

As wages rise, productivity increases, at first quickly and then more slowly. The efficiency wage is the wage at which the ratio of productivity to wage is highest. It is found by drawing a line through the origin tangent to the wage-productivity curve.

APPENDIX: DERIVATION OF THE EFFICIENCY WAGE

Figure 15.4 depicts a curve that represents one possible relationship between productivity and wages. We refer to this curve as the **wage-productivity curve.** Productivity here can be thought of as "the number of pins produced in an hour," or any similar measure of output. There is a minimum wage, w_m, below which the firm will find it difficult, if not impossible, to obtain labor. At a very low wage, w_1, the company can only hire the dregs of the labor market —those who cannot get jobs elsewhere. Worker morale is low, and effort is low. Workers quit as soon as they can get another job, so labor turnover is high.

As the firm raises its wage, productivity increases. The company earns a reputation as a high-wage firm, attracting the best workers. Morale is high, turnover is low, and employees work hard. But eventually, as in so many areas, diminishing returns set in. Successive increases in wages have incrementally smaller effects on productivity. The firm is concerned with wage costs per unit of output, not wage costs per employee. Thus, it wishes to minimize not the wage but the wage divided by productivity.

This can be put another way. The company wishes to maximize the output per dollar spent on labor (we are assuming that all other costs are fixed). Since productivity is defined as output per unit of time (pins per hour), and the wage is labor cost per unit of time (dollars per hour), dividing productivity by the wage produces the equation

$$\frac{\text{productivity}}{\text{wage}} = \frac{\text{output/unit of time}}{\text{dollars/unit of time}} = \frac{\text{output}}{\text{dollars spent on labor}}.$$

Thus, a decision to make the ratio of output to dollars spent on labor as high as possible is mathematically equivalent to a decision to make the ratio of productivity to wages as high as possible. To tell what level of wages will accomplish this goal, Figure 15.4 shows the productivity-wage ratio as the slope of a line from the origin to a point on the wage-productivity curve. The slope of this line is the ratio of productivity (the vertical axis) to the wage (the horizontal axis).

As we draw successive lines from the origin to points on the wage-productivity curve with higher wages, the slope first increases and then decreases. The slope is largest for the line through the origin that is just tangent to the wage-productivity curve. The wage at this point of tangency is the wage at which labor costs are minimized: the efficiency wage, w_e.

Figure 15.5 shows that changes in unemployment rates may shift the wage-

Figure 15.5 SHIFTING THE PRODUCTIVITY-WAGE RELATIONSHIP

If unemployment is low, workers have many alternative job possibilities. With the threat of being fired reduced, at each wage workers work less hard, so productivity is lower. In the case shown here, the efficiency wage will be lower when there is high unemployment than when there is low unemployment.

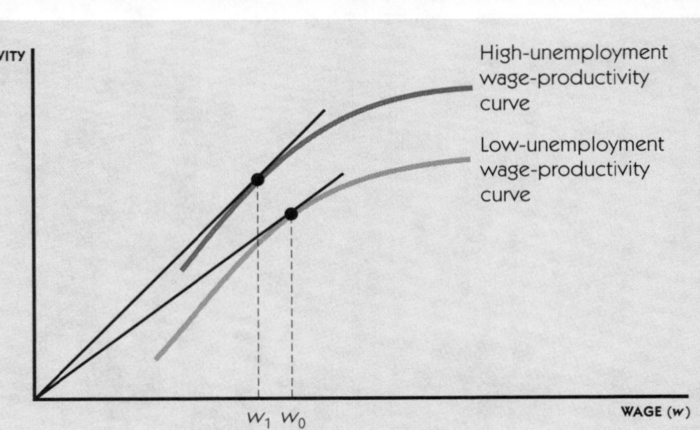

productivity curve. At each wage, the productivity of the labor force is higher at the higher unemployment rate. Also, the efficiency wage—the wage at which the ratio of productivity to the wage is maximized—is lowered slightly. It falls from w_0 to w_1. The change in the efficiency wage may be relatively small, even if the shift in the curve relating productivity to wages is relatively large.

CHAPTER 16

Inflation vs. Unemployment: Approaches to Policy

Making economic policy can be like walking a tightrope. Lean too far one way, and unemployment increases. Lean too far the other way, and prices rise. It is even possible to have the worst of all worlds: simultaneous inflation, unemployment, and slow growth.

Many of the basic macroeconomic problems stem from variability in the level of economic activity. When the economy is dragging along, a jump start may be required to reignite it. But when the economy is racing, inflation may loom. Both unemployment and inflation cause economic hardship. Unemployment particularly affects the young, who have no cushion of accumulated savings to fall back upon, as well as blacks, Hispanics, and unskilled workers. Inflation takes its toll among those retired people whose incomes do not rise commensurately with inflation.

After briefly reviewing these costs, this chapter focuses on the major policy issues: Should the government intervene to stabilize the economy? If so, how? With monetary or fiscal policy? It then illustrates some of the basic issues by a historical review of the major policy debates over the past three decades.

KEY QUESTIONS

1. What are the key issues facing policymakers as they decide whether to stimulate (or dampen) the economy? What are the costs, actual and perceived, of inflation? Of unemployment?
2. What are the alternative explanations of the pronounced fluctuations in the level of economic activity in the economy? Why does the economy periodically experience a downturn in which unemployment is high, growth slows down, and output actually falls?
3. Why do some economists believe the government should not intervene to stabilize the economy? Why do they believe that such intervention is unnecessary, ineffective, or more likely to do harm than good? And why do other economists believe that intervention can be helpful?
4. How can government attempt to dampen economic fluctuations and reduce the NAIRU, below which inflation starts to accelerate?
5. What have been some of the major policy debates over the past three decades? How do they illustrate general principles?

THE IMPACT OF INFLATION AND UNEMPLOYMENT

When should policymakers act to stimulate or dampen the economy? Each decision involves a trade-off. Consider the problem facing U.S. policymakers in 1994 and 1995, as the unemployment rate decreased from 7 percent to 6 percent to 5.4 percent. Everyone agreed that at some point, inflationary pressures would set in. The question was, when? If, for instance, the Fed acted too early and raised interest rates too much, the recovery could stall, throwing the economy back into recession. If it waited too long, inflation would increase. How much would it cost to bring inflation down? What would be the costs of a higher level of inflation?

THE BASIC TRADE-OFFS

The discussions of earlier chapters have set the scene for how policymakers approach these decisions: the costs of high unemployment—including the loss in output—are apparent. Typically, lowering the unemployment rate by 1 percentage point (say from 7 to 6 percent) increases output by 2 percent. In a $10 trillion economy, this translates into $200 billion per year.

Inflation too has its costs, though the discussion of Chapter 14 suggested that at the low levels of inflation that have prevailed in the United States during the past fifteen years, some of those costs are more perceived than real.

Chapter 14 also clarified the trade-offs. Today, the focus is not so much on trading a little more inflation for a temporary lowering of the unemployment rate. Governments recognize that they cannot permanently run the economy at a rate lower than the NAIRU without inflation accelerating, and most do not seem even willing to take advantage of the short-run gains from reduced unemployment, which typically occur earlier than the inflation costs, which are felt only with a lag. Today, the debate focuses more on risk: if there is uncertainty about the NAIRU, how aggressive or conservative should government be? How willing should it be to risk an increase in inflation, at the cost of failing to use the economy's resources as fully as they might be used? But in assessing these risks, economists continue to evaluate the costs of inflation and of unemployment. Not surprisingly, those who worry more about unemployment argue for more aggressive policies, while those who worry about inflation argue for conservative policies.

DIFFERENT VIEWS OF TRADE-OFFS

Key in understanding these different positions is the recognition that unemployment and inflation impact different groups. Low-wage workers and other disadvantaged groups are the most likely to benefit from low unemployment policies. Since they have little savings, they bear little of the costs of inflation. The costs of *unanticipated* increases in inflation are typically borne most by those who hold long-term bonds—who see the value of those bonds decrease as nominal interest rates increase, as typically happens when inflation increases.

It is thus not surprising that unions typically push for more aggressive macroeconomic policies, and that Wall Street bondholders push for more conservative policies. Since more aggressive policies typically entail the Fed's lowering interest rates—a major cost for firms who typically borrow to finance inventories and purchases of plant and equipment—and lead to higher levels of output, both of which are good for business, it is also not surprising that businesses, such as the National Association of Manufacturers, also typically support more aggressive policies. The split in views is often characterized as a difference in views between Main Street and Wall Street.

PERSPECTIVES ON FLUCTUATIONS AND MACROECONOMIC POLICY

There is widespread agreement on the desirability of high growth, low unemployment, and low and stable inflation. But economists disagree about the role and means of government in pursuing these objectives. Some economists believe that government attempts at intervention have little effect, or worse, only destabilize the economy. Others argue that government interventions are generally successful.

For simplicity, we can split economists into two broad groups on these issues—interventionists and non-interventionists. Non-interventionists tend to have great faith in markets and little faith in government. Believing the economy adjusts quickly and efficiently to disturbances, non-interventionists see little role for government action. Interventionists argue that because markets adjust slowly, there may be extended periods of unemployment, and government policies can restore the economy to full employment faster than the market would do on its own.

Figure 16.1 shows the rate of change of output over the past 125 years. The figure illustrates the central challenge in "managing" the economy: its variability. It is not as if there is an isolated episode in which the aggregate demand curve shifts to the left, resulting in unemployment. The prescription then would be simple: use monetary or fiscal policy to shift the aggregate demand curve back to the right. The problem is that the economy is always changing, always fluctuating. Some non-interventionists accept that markets may adjust slowly, but argue that government efforts do more harm than good. There is a real fear that because of the length of time it takes for policies to be put into effect, the government will be stimulating the economy just when it should be dampening it, and vice versa. There are some economists

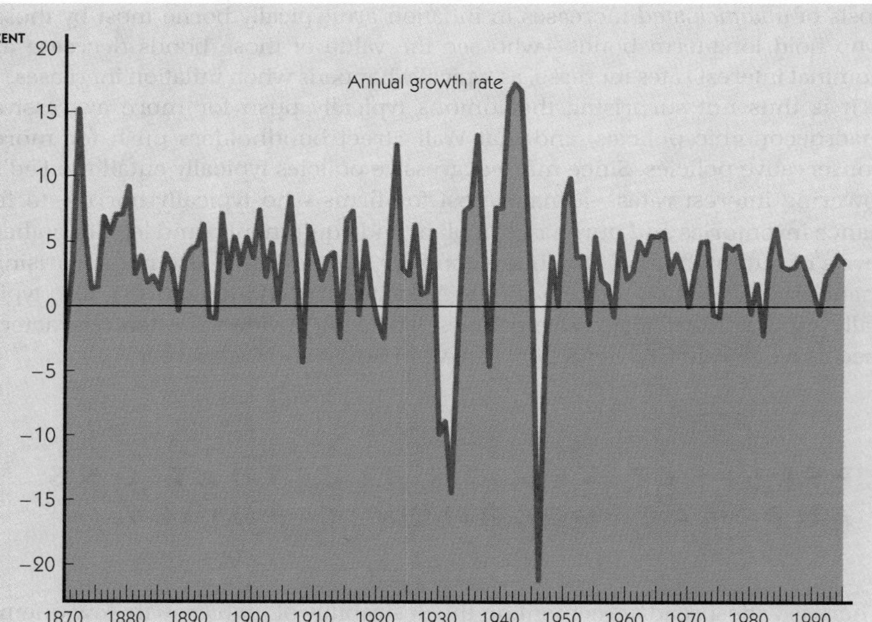

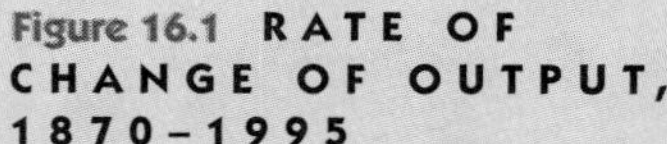

Figure 16.1 RATE OF CHANGE OF OUTPUT, 1870–1995

Output growth has varied markedly over the past 125 years, but appears to have been more volatile before World War II than after, when the government actively tried to stabilize the economy. *Sources:* Angus Maddison, *Dynamic Forces in Capitalist Development,* Oxford University Press, 1991; *ERP* (1996).

who think that government policies have actually contributed to the economy's fluctuations. Views concerning whether government should or should not intervene depend strongly on views concerning the origins and nature of the economy's fluctuations.

ECONOMIC FLUCTUATIONS

Figure 16.2A shows the movement of U.S. economic output over the past forty-five years. A smooth line has been drawn through the data, tracing out the path the economy would have taken had it grown at a steady rate. This line represents the economy's **long-term trend.** The economy is sometimes above the trend line and sometimes below. Panel B shows the percentage by which the economy has been below or above trend for the past sixty-five years. It also shows the unemployment rate, to illustrate the negative correlation between these deviations of output from trend and unemployment. The term "recession" is reserved for periods in which output actually declines, but even growth at a substantially lower rate represents an economic slowdown, with significant consequences.

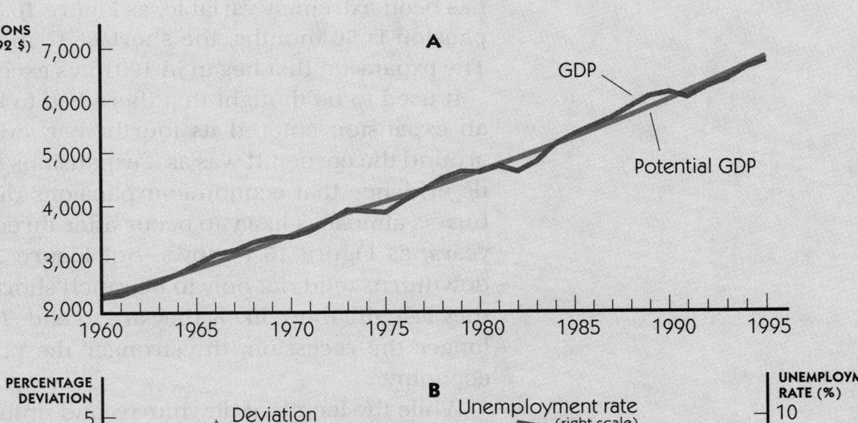

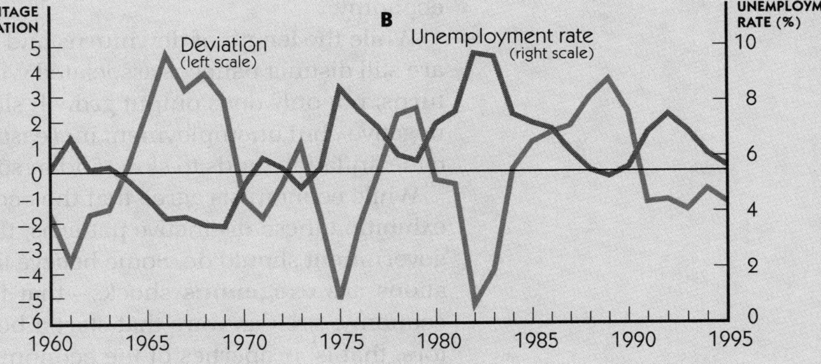

Figure 16.2 ECONOMIC FLUCTUATIONS: OUTPUT

Panel A shows how real output has moved above and below a long-term trend line over the past forty-five years. Panel B compares the deviation of GDP from its long-term trend with the unemployment rate. Notice that when GDP is above its long-term rate, unemployment tends to be low; and when GDP is below its long-term rate, unemployment tends to be higher. *Source: ERP* (1995), Tables B-1, B-40, B-116.

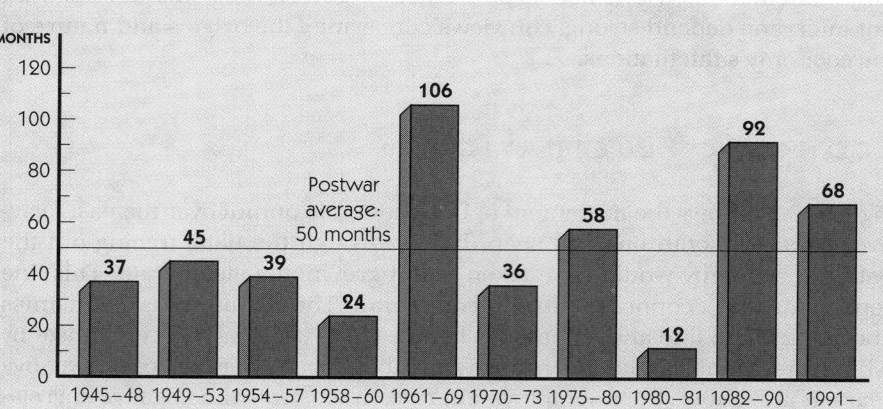

Figure 16.3 THE DURATION OF ECONOMIC EXPANSIONS

Over the past fifty years, there has been a high variability in the length of time that economic expansions have lasted. The average is 50 months, the shortest 12 months, and the longest 106 months. As this book goes to press, the expansion that began in 1991 has lasted more than 68 months. *Source: ERP* (1996), Chart 2-11.

At one time, economists thought there was a certain inevitability to these economic fluctuations—they were so regular that they were called business cycles. But at least since World War II, the length of time between recessions has been extremely variable, as Figure 16.3 shows. Average duration of an expansion is 50 months, the shortest 12 months, and the longest 106 months. The expansion that began in 1991 has exceeded the postwar average.

It used to be thought that there *had* to be a downturn every four years. As an expansion entered its fourth year, everyone looked toward a recession around the corner. It was as if expansions *had* to die of old age. But there is little evidence that economic expansions die of old age—an economic downturn is almost as likely to occur after three years of an expansion as after five years, as Figure 16.4 shows. But Figure 16.4 also illustrates that economic downturns tend not only to be much shorter than expansions, but the longer they last, the more likely they are to end. The reason for this is partly that the longer the recession, the stronger the pressure for action to stimulate the economy.

While the length of downturns and upturns has been highly variable, there are still distinct patterns associated with the economy's fluctuations. In downturns, not only does output growth slow down (and sometimes even become negative), but unemployment increases. Hours worked per worker tend to decline, inflation tends to slow, and in some cases, prices even start to fall.

While economists agree that the economy has been marked by fluctuations exhibiting these distinctive patterns, they disagree about the *causes* and what government should do. Some believe that the underlying sources of the fluctuations are **exogenous** shocks—that is, disturbances originating outside the economy, such as wars that start a boom. Others focus on **endogenous** factors, that is, properties of the economy itself, such as a tendency of the economy to become overconfident in expansions, leading to overinvestment (including overinvestment in inventories), leading in turn to a downturn as

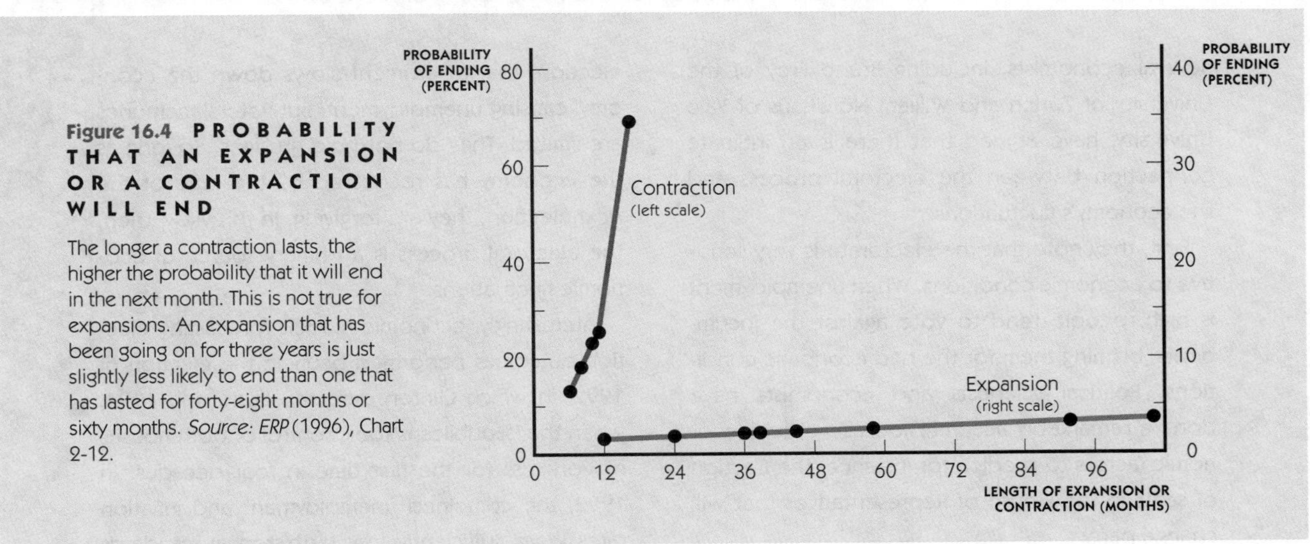

Figure 16.4 PROBABILITY THAT AN EXPANSION OR A CONTRACTION WILL END

The longer a contraction lasts, the higher the probability that it will end in the next month. This is not true for expansions. An expansion that has been going on for three years is just slightly less likely to end than one that has lasted for forty-eight months or sixty months. *Source: ERP* (1996), Chart 2-12.

investment slows down once the overinvestment is recognized. Today, most economists think economic fluctuations involve a mixture of exogenous and endogenous factors: an external shock (such as an increase in the price of oil) may hit an economy, but endogenous factors may sometimes amplify the initial effects and make them more persistent.

Some of the variation in economic activity is an inevitable consequence of people's inability to predict the future perfectly. There will be times in which firms overestimate demand and produce too much. When production exceeds sales, inventories build up. As inventories build up, firms are induced to cut back on their production. And by the same token, government interventions designed to stabilize the economy may not do so, and may even exacerbate the fluctuations, because government cannot predict perfectly where the economy is going. Indeed, in many cases, it may not even know with much precision where the economy is today. Data gauging the health of the economy become available only with a lag.

Most economic downturns in the postwar period in the United States have been associated with large increases in interest rates by the Fed; but these increases in turn have been motivated by evidence of actual or incipient inflation. In some cases, such as the oil price shock of 1973, exogenous shocks played a role in accelerating inflation. In other cases, the natural buoyancy of the economy has led aggregate demand to outpace aggregate supply. Economists disagree whether monetary policy could have more finely tuned the economy: By a timely raising of interest rates, could it have kept aggregate demand moving precisely in step with aggregate supply, so that inflation did not pick up, and so that the Fed could have avoided "slamming on the brakes"? Or, having failed to stop the inflation, could it have slowed down the economy

Close-up: The Political Business Cycle

Several economists, including Bruno Frey of the University of Zurich and William Nordhaus of Yale University, have argued that there is an intimate connection between the electoral process and the economy's fluctuations.

First, they note that the electorate is very sensitive to economic conditions. When unemployment is high, people tend to vote against the incumbents, blaming them for the bad economic conditions. Political scientists and economists have done a remarkably accurate job using these economic factors to predict, for instance, the fraction of seats in the House of Representatives that will change party.

Second, these economists note that politicians are aware of this. Since politicians like to get reelected, they plan for economic policies to be favorable at the time of election.

The third part of the theory maintains that the electorate is shortsighted. These economists argue that it pays politicians to overstimulate the economy as elections approach, even though this may (and systematically does) have adverse effects after the election. The overheated economy generates inflation; to quell the inflation, after the election, the government slows down the economy, causing unemployment. But voters' memories are limited. They do not hold grudges. So long as the economy has recovered by the time of the *next* election, they are forgiving. In this view, then, the electoral process is a primary source of economic fluctuations.

Interestingly, economic models forecasting election outcomes performed badly in the election of 1992, in which Clinton defeated Bush, and 1994, when the Republicans took control of both houses of Congress for the first time in four decades. In 1992, the combined unemployment and inflation rates were sufficiently low by historical standards that Bush should have been re-elected, according to most of the models. In 1994, the economic conditions, as measured by those two variables, were at a three-decade high, so incumbents should have done extremely well. But in both 1992 and 1994 incumbents were defeated. One explanation sometimes made was that in both cases, voters were expressing dissatisfaction. Though macroeconomic statistics were favorable, real incomes of many Americans had stagnated—or even declined—from the early 1970s to the early 1990s.

President George Bush on the campaign trail in July 1992

more gradually, and thus avoided as deep a recession at the same time that it lowered inflation?

Interventionists believe that appropriate policies can both reduce the endogenous forces that either give rise to or help sustain fluctuations—for instance by strengthening the automatic stabilizers discussed in Chapter 13—and increase the likelihood that interventions actually stabilize the economy.

THE NON-INTERVENTIONIST PERSPECTIVE

Those who share the view that government should not intervene to stabilize the economy differ in their reasons. Some believe that the economy is efficient, so that there is little that government can add; others believe that government action is ineffective; while still others believe that governments do have significant effects—but more often make matters worse. We now take a closer look at each of these perspectives.

REAL BUSINESS CYCLE THEORY: INTERVENTION IS UNNECESSARY

Intervention is clearly unnecessary if the economy always operates efficiently, at full employment. **Real business cycle** theorists attribute the economy's fluctuations to exogenous shocks, such as the 1973 and 1979 oil price increases, but believe that markets adjust quickly—prices and wages are sufficiently flexible that full employment will be restored quickly—and certainly more quickly than it would take government to recognize a problem, take actions, and have an effect. Since the economy typically operates at full employment, government need only worry about inflation. But recall from our discussion of Part Two that when the economy is at full employment, prices tend to increase with the money supply. Price stability—and full employment—can be attained if the monetary authorities let the money supply expand at the rate of increase in real GDP.

NEW CLASSICAL MACROECONOMICS: INTERVENTION IS INEFFECTIVE

Some non-interventionists claim that the government cannot even have an effect on output in the short run, because the private sector largely undoes any government action. Thus, if the government increases the money supply, with rational expectations, all market participants recognize that this will simply have an effect on the price level. Price levels adjust instantaneously, so that the *real* money supply is unchanged. The expansionary effects of the increase in money supply are thus completely counteracted, and monetary policy has no *real* effects. Similarly, an increase in the government deficit is perfectly offset by an increase in private savings as households foresee the need for higher taxes in the future.

The view that policies are largely ineffective, and to the extent that they are effective, it is only in the very short run—with no permanent gains—was strongly advanced by the **new classical economists,** led by Robert Lucas of the University of Chicago.

INTERVENTION IS COUNTERPRODUCTIVE

Faith in markets is one thing; faith in the ability of government to improve on markets is another. Some non-interventionists see more shortcomings in markets than do real business cycle theorists and new classical economists, but nonetheless have little confidence in the ability of government to improve macroeconomic performance. Indeed, some hold the view that intervention is counterproductive, for two reasons.

First, they recognize that there are important **lags**—between the time the government recognizes a problem and takes action, and between the time the action occurs and its macroeconomic effects are fully realized. By the time the effects are fully realized, the action may no longer be appropriate. Lags by themselves would not be a problem if the government could accurately forecast where the economy is going and the exact effects of policy on the economy. But everyone—including the government—sees the future with a cloudy crystal ball, and as a result, governments risk taking the wrong action. In recent years, governments have become much more sensitized to the problem of timing. One of the reasons given for President Bush's reluctance to take strong actions to stimulate the economy in the midst of the economic downturn in 1991, was a worry that, given the shallowness of the recession, the economy might quickly recover on its own, making any extra government expenditures or reductions in taxes unnecessary and potentially harmful.

Second, critics of strong interventionist policies argue that there are systematic political reasons that interventions are often misguided. Politicians want the economy to be strong before an election. They thus tend to overheat the economy, with gains in employment showing up before the election, but costs, in terms of inflation, showing up (hopefully) only after the election.

RULES VS. DISCRETION: THE NON-INTERVENTIONIST PERSPECTIVE

Critics of intervention claim that historically, whether because of political motivations, or simply because of the lags described earlier, the government has actually exacerbated the economy's fluctuations. When the government attempts to dampen a boom, its policies reducing demand take effect just as the economy is weakening, reinforcing the downward movement. Conversely, when the government attempts to stimulate the economy, the increase in demand kicks in as the economy is strengthening on its own, thereby igniting inflation. Thus, critics of government action, such as Nobel Prize–winning economist Milton Friedman, now at Stanford's Hoover Institution, and formerly of the University of Chicago, conclude that economic policy should be based on simple *rules* rather than the *discretion* of government policymakers. For example, **monetarists** like Friedman believe the government should expand the money supply at a constant rate, rather than adjusting the money supply in response to specific economic events or conditions. According to Friedman and others, by sticking to such rules, the government would eliminate a major source of uncertainty and instability in the economy: uncertainty about future government policy.

Furthermore, they believe not only that government should pursue certain rules, but that it should have its hands tied, so that it has no choice. The reason for this is that even if the government today promised to follow certain rules—such as not trying to stimulate the economy should there be a downturn—it will not (or politically, cannot) follow those rules. The problem of whether the government will actually carry out a promised course of action is called the problem of **dynamic consistency.** The government may announce that a particular tax change is permanent—and it might even deceive itself into believing that the tax change is permanent. But when circumstances change, policies will change. And the fact that policies will change—and that individuals and firms expect them to change—has enormous consequences for the behavior of individuals and firms. In 1981, for instance, new legislation gave special tax breaks to the real estate industry. These breaks were intended (by the legislation) to be permanent. A real estate boom resulted. The boom is partly attributed to builders rushing to take advantage of the tax break which they believed would eventually be repealed. They were right: the tax advantages were repealed in 1986.

THE INTERVENTIONIST PERSPECTIVE

The most compelling case for intervention is based on the belief that without intervention, recovery may take an unconscionably long time and that there are interventions which on balance can reduce the economy's fluctuations. As a practical matter, governments *must* intervene: political pressures will not allow them to sit idly by if the economy goes into a deep recession. In any case, the Fed must make decisions constantly about what to do. Even to keep the money supply constant, or to increase it at a fixed rate, requires decisions: forecasts about what the money supply would be in the absence of Fed action, and judgments about the consequences of particular actions.

The underlying assumption of the non-interventionists is that markets adjust quickly and so unemployment is, at most, a short-term affair. There have been periods in which this assumption seems unpersuasive: in the Great Depression, high unemployment persisted for many years. Unemployment rates in some European countries have exceeded 10 percent for more than a decade. Earlier chapters have explained both the reasons for, and consequences of, wage and price stickiness. As a practical matter, when unemployment rates are high, governments are under enormous pressures to reduce them.

Today, the leading school of thought of economists who believe that government can and should intervene to stabilize the economy is called **New Keynesianism.** They share Lord Keynes's view that unemployment may be persistent, and that though there may be market forces which restore the economy to full employment, those forces work so slowly that government action is required. The New Keynesian theories differ from older Keynesian analyses in their emphasis on microeconomics—they share, for instance, with many real business cycle and new classical economists, a view that the economy consists largely of profit-maximizing competitive firms, though they typically believe that markets often deviate significantly from the *perfectly* *competitive* ideal assumed by real business cycle and new classical theories. But they have identified a variety of reasons—such as costs of adjustment and imperfections of information—why markets do not adjust quickly to disturbances.

Moreover, they agree that while there are forces which enable the economy to dampen and absorb exogenous shocks, there are also endogenous forces which sometimes amplify shocks and make them more persistent. Noninterventionists emphasize the former forces. As firms cut back production in response to an inventory buildup, wages and prices fall. At these low prices and wages, firms decide it is a good time to buy new machines; households may decide it is a good time to buy durables and new houses. These decisions help raise aggregate demand, offsetting the dampening effect of the excess inventories.

By contrast, New Keynesian economists emphasize the forces within the economy which amplify fluctuations and help make those fluctuations persist. Thus, the fall in the price of oil in 1985 might have been viewed as a good thing for the economy—the reverse of the increase in the price of oil in 1973 and 1979. But the unanticipated fall in the price of oil led to massive disruptions and bankruptcies in oil-producing states; these in turn weakened the real estate market and banking system in those states, leading to an overall contraction of economic activity. The impacts were felt well beyond the oil industry, and in the process of being disseminated through the region, seemed to be amplified.

THE MULTIPLIER-ACCELERATOR

The most widely discussed of the systematic endogenous forces that amplify fluctuations is called the multiplier-accelerator. We already encountered the multiplier: an upturn in exports is amplified by the multiplier, so that the increase in GDP may be two or more times the increase in exports. But matters do not stop here: the increase in GDP leads firms to want to invest more to meet the increased demand for goods. Typically, it takes around $2 to $3 of capital to produce $1 of GDP. Thus, if firms expect output to increase by, say, $100 billion, they will want to increase their capital stock by $200 to $300 billion. This is called the **accelerator.** As firms increase their investment, GDP grows even more. Increased investment of $200 billion results in a further increase of GDP by $400 billion, if the multiplier is 2. But this increase in GDP may give rise to a further increase in the demand for investment. Thus, the multiplier and accelerator help to amplify and propagate what was initially an exogenous shock—an increase in exports.

Not only does the structure of the economy serve to amplify and propagate external shocks, it may also, on its own, convert an expansion into a downturn. To see how this occurs, consider what happens as the economy continues to expand. Eventually, it hits constraints. For example, shortages of labor may impose a limit on the expansion of the economy. Once these constraints are hit, the economy stops expanding, or at least stops expanding as fast. But when the economy expands at a slower rate, the demand for investment decreases. And because of the multiplier effects, this reduces aggregate demand. A downturn in the economy thus begins. As output declines, investment drops lower, further accentuating the decline. Investment comes to a standstill. But eventually the old machines wear out or become obsolete. Even to produce the low level of output associated with the recession, new investment is required. This new investment stimulates demand, which in turn stimulates investment; the economy turns up.

OTHER SOURCES OF AMPLIFICATION

There are other reasons that the internal structure of the economy may amplify fluctuations. For instance, firms rely heavily on profits as a source of funds for investment. They may face constraints on the amounts they can borrow and they may find it impossible to raise funds by issuing new shares, or feel that the cost of doing so is so unattractive, that they would prefer to rely on internally generated funds. As the economy goes into a downturn, profits fall; decreased profits lead to decreased investment, exacerbating the economic downturn.

While New Keynesians agree that adjustments in interest rates and prices may *partially* offset these destabilizing influences—lower interest rates providing greater impetus for firms to invest, for instance, in a recession—these adjustments are simply too weak to offset them fully.

Schools of Thought in Macroeconomic Policy

NONINTERVENTIONISTS

Real business cycle theorists believe fluctuations in economic activity are due to exogenous shocks and that markets respond quickly to economic disturbances. Government intervention is unnecessary.

New classical economists think that policies can have no long-run effect because the private sector anticipates the effects of policy and undoes them. Policies can only have a real effect in the short run, and then only if prices do not respond quickly.

Others believe that even though markets adjust slowly, discretionary macroeconomic policies make matters worse rather than better because of lags in determining the need for policy and then implementing it.

INTERVENTIONISTS

New Keynesians think markets respond slowly, so periods of unemployment can be extended. Discretionary macroeconomic policy can be effective.

Business cycles may be endogenous phenomena and forces exist that amplify fluctuations. Governments should both engage in discretionary macroeconomic policies and design built-in stabilizers that make the economy more stable.

POLICIES TO IMPROVE ECONOMIC PERFORMANCE

Interventionists claim not only that markets, by themselves, do not ensure full employment, but that government interventions can *and have* contributed to the stability of the economy. While there *are* instances in the past in which government actions may have exacerbated an economic downturn, they believe that by and large the government's record is a positive one, as evidenced, for instance, by Figure 16.1. In the period before World War II, government did not systematically try to stabilize the economy; it appears that the variability of output was higher—with many more episodes when not only did growth slow down, but output actually decreased.

While academic economists often debate *whether* government should intervene, most policy debates center around *when* and *how*. There are three sets of policies designed to improve the economy's economic performance.

First, government should attempt to change the structure of the economy to make it more stable. Automatic stabilizers (discussed in Chapter 13), which automatically lead to increased government expenditures when the economy goes into a downturn, are the most important example.

Second, it should use *discretionary* policy to stimulate the economy when output is low and unemployment high, and to dampen the economy when inflation is strong.

Third, it should attempt to lower the NAIRU, so that price stability (stable inflation) can be attained at a lower level of unemployment.

RULES VS. DISCRETION: AN INTERVENTIONIST PERSPECTIVE

Interventionists argue that discretionary macroeconomic policy can and has helped stabilize the economy. They also argue that the historical record shows why it is not possible to follow simple rules. Consider, for instance, the simple rule discussed earlier—that the money supply should simply increase at a constant rate, the rate of increase of *real* GDP. Since the monetary authorities do not directly control the money supply, this still entails some discretion: they must forecast what will be happening to the economy and, on the basis of that, make judgments concerning what policies to undertake so that the money supply will expand at the desired rate. While such policies enjoyed enormous popularity at the end of the 1970s and in the early 1980s, at least some of their consequences were viewed unfavorably. In the United States, under Fed chairman Paul Volcker, the seemingly single-minded pursuit of this policy led interest rates to soar—to over 17 percent—and to the worst recession in half a century. Furthermore, as we saw in Chapter 12, the marked changes in the relationship between the monetary aggregates (money supply) and output which have occurred during the past two decades removed the theoretical underpinnings of this approach. Inevitably, central banks must use discretion, if only to judge whether there has been a change in the structure of the economy.

INFLATION–UNEMPLOYMENT TRADE-OFFS

What should the government do when it intervenes actively? The analysis of Chapter 14 provides the analytic basis for these decisions. Clearly, we would like to have both low rates of inflation and low rates of unemployment. But is there a trade-off? Can we get, say, lower rates of unemployment only by allowing the inflation rate to increase?

In the years immediately following the discovery of the Phillips curve, most economists thought that there was a trade-off. Those economists who thought the costs of inflation were high argued for a high unemployment rate, while those who thought the benefits of low inflation paled in comparison with the costs of unemployment argued for somewhat lower unemployment rates. Thus disagreements about policy largely hinged upon disagreements about the *costs* of inflation and unemployment. Economists who focused on the hardship that unemployment imposed on workers advocated low unemployment policies; those who focused on the impact of inflation on investors (including retired individuals who depend on interest payments to live) advocated low inflation policies.

But in the 1970s, as the unemployment rate and inflation rate increased together and as economists became more aware of the importance of inflationary expectations and inflation inertia there developed an increasing consensus that the economy could not enjoy a sustained level of unemployment below the NAIRU, without ever-increasing inflation.

There still remained two elements of disagreement about the nature of the trade-off. First, while there was agreement that the long-run Phillips curve was (at least close to) vertical, some economists thought that in the short run—for a period of perhaps several years—the economy could experience lower unemployment while inflation increased only moderately. Others worried that with rational expectations, even short periods of low unemployment—unemployment below the NAIRU—could give rise to high levels of inflation. They saw the economy as standing on a precipice: leaning toward too low a level of unemployment quickly leads to soaring inflation.

The experience within the United States over the past fifteen years strongly suggests that those worries were unfounded. Slight deviations above or below the NAIRU seem to lead to slight increases or decreases in the rate of inflation. The economy does not stand on a precipice.

The second disagreement concerned the costs of "disinflation"—the name given to reducing the inflation rate. Assume policymakers made a mistake, and pushed the unemployment rate below the NAIRU. Inflation increased slightly. What would it take to reduce inflation? Clearly, the economy would have to operate for a while at a higher level of unemployment—at a level above the NAIRU. Those who advocated a cautious policy—making sure that

Policy Perspective: The 1995 Bumpy Soft Landing

From 1992 to 1994 the economy recovered gradually from the 1991 recession. The unemployment rate fell slowly from 7.6 percent to 5.4 percent. As unemployment approached what was then viewed as the NAIRU of around 6 percent, the Fed became worried about an overheated economy. It started to raise interest rates. Beginning in 1994 it raised interest rates six times, for a total increase of 3 percent. The hope was for a "soft landing"—a smooth transition from recovery to sustained growth without an overshooting that would lead to inflation—which in turn would lead to higher interest rates, which in turn would lead to a new economic downturn. (See the figure below for a depiction of a soft landing versus the more typical overshooting pattern.)

Later, however, as the economy's unemployment rate gradually fell in 1996, to a low of 5.1 percent and growth increased, it appeared in retrospect that the Fed had achieved a landing, which if not perfect, was as smooth as any in recent decades. In fact, the Fed did not forecast correctly where the economy was going; indeed, because data became available with a lag, it did not even have an accurate picture of where the economy was at the time it acted. Critics argued vociferously against the interest rate hikes of December 1994 and February 1995, saying that they saw weaknesses in the economy down the road. The Fed ignored these warnings. Revised data issued in January 1996 showed that even as the Fed was increasing interest rates in February 1995, growth had stalled out—in the first quarter of 1995 it was less than one-half of one percent. As data came in through the spring of 1995 and worries about an economic slowdown mounted, the soft landing had been converted into a "bumpy soft landing."

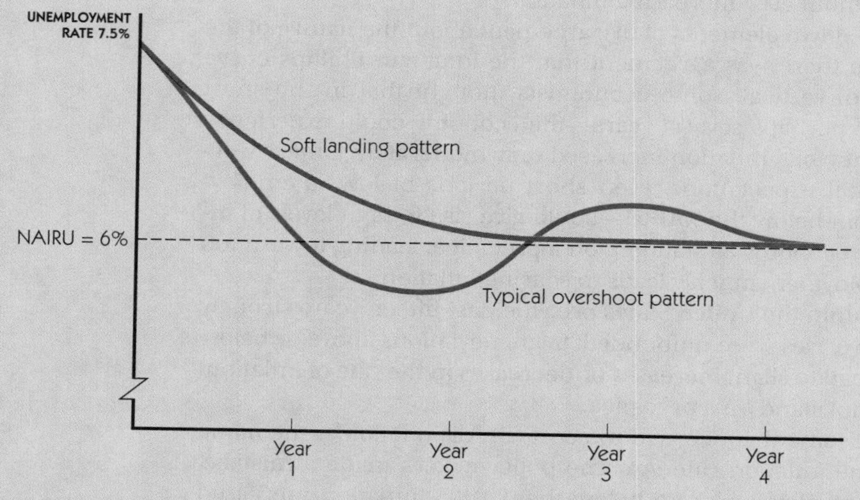

the unemployment rate never fell below the NAIRU—worried that the costs of reducing inflation were very high. In particular, they looked to the experience of the 1970s and 1980s: to wring the inflationary expectations of the 1970s (when inflation hit double-digit levels) out of the economy, the United States had to go through a deep recession.

But the evidence from attempts to reduce more moderate inflation suggests that the costs are low. Indeed, the loss in output and employment from "killing" inflation are matched by the gains in output and employment during the period in which unemployment remained below the NAIRU.

CONTROVERSIES IN MACROECONOMIC POLICY

Evaluating the Costs of Inflation and Unemployment

- How large are the costs of moderate inflation?
- How large are the costs of unemployment?
- Since the costs of inflation and the costs of unemployment are borne by different individuals, how do we "value" these different costs?

Trade-offs

- How quickly will attempts to lower unemployment below the NAIRU lead to increases in prices and price expectations? How quickly will runaway inflation set in? Does the economy sit on a precipice?
- Are there large costs associated with disinflation? What is the relationship between these costs and the benefits that the economy achieved in the period during which unemployment was lower than the NAIRU?

IMPLEMENTING POLICIES: TARGETS

So far, we have focused our discussion on *what are the trade-offs* and *what should be the objectives of macroeconomic policy.* But even when there is agreement about the objectives of macroeconomic policy, there may be disagreements about how best to achieve those objectives. For instance, the government might believe that the NAIRU is 5.6 percent, and might wish to keep the unemployment rate at that level, but it does not directly control the unemployment rate. The Fed might want to keep the inflation rate at 3 percent, but it does not directly control the inflation rate. Over the years, economists have come up with a variety of "targets"—intermediate variables, not necessarily of interest for their own sake, but which are easier to control than the variables of real interest, and which are (or were thought at the time to be) closely related to the variables of real concern. Thus, in the late 1970s and early 1980s, many central banks focused on the **monetary aggregates,** the statistics

Using Economics: Calculating the Risks of Pursuing Aggressive Full-Employment Policies

Throughout the 1990s a central problem facing the Fed has been the uncertainty about the NAIRU. The Fed must assess the risks—the costs and benefits—associated with "overshooting" versus those of setting one's sights too low.

In 1994, for instance, some economists thought that the NAIRU was at 6.0 percent, while others thought that it had been lowered to around 5.6 percent. What if the Fed has assumed the NAIRU was 5.6 percent, when it was actually 6.0 percent? In Chapter 14, we learned that the sacrifice ratio gives the amount by which the unemployment rate has to be maintained above the NAIRU for one year to lower the inflation rate by 1 percentage point. It is conventionally estimated at around 2. Conversely, lowering the unemployment rate for a full year by .4 percentage points below the NAIRU increases the inflation rate by .2 percentage points. (If a 1 percent increase in inflation is associated with a 2 percentage point increase in unemployment, a 1 percentage point increase in unemployment will be associated with a .5 percentage point increase in inflation, and a .4 percentage point increase in unemployment will be associated with a .2 percentage point increase in inflation.) The cost of the Fed's error would be that inflation would have increased by .2 percentage points.

On the other hand, if the Fed assumed that the NAIRU had remained at 6.0 percent, when it had fallen to 5.6 percent, the economy would have suffered a higher level of unemployment than was necessary to maintain stable prices. What is the lost value of output—assuming that the Fed had persisted in maintaining the higher unemployment rate for a year? According to current estimates, Okun's law says that reducing unemployment by 1 percentage point increases output by 2 percent. Accordingly, maintaining the unemployment rate at a level that is .4 percent "too high" costs the economy .8 percent of GDP. In a $6 trillion economy, this translates into $48 billion per year—a fairly steep price to pay.

describing the money supply (M1, M2, etc.). Controlling these would, it was believed, stabilize the inflation rate. It was believed that there was a stable relationship between the money supply and nominal income. If the money supply increased by 3 percent, nominal income would increase by only 3 percent. And since most of the advocates of this theory believed that the economy normally operated at full employment, if the economy's full-employment output was growing at 3 percent, that would imply that there would be no inflation. (The rate of increase of nominal income is the rate of increase of real income plus the rate of increase of prices.) But just as the theory came to be widely believed, the empirical relationship fell apart, as we saw in Chapter 12. The ratio of the money supply (say M1) to nominal income appeared to vary in ways that were hard to predict. Thus, controlling the money supply was not a good target. At other times, central banks have focused on variables such as the real interest rate, the rate of inflation, or the unemployment rate. Today, in the United States, the Fed takes an eclectic approach, incorporating data about all of these variables (including the monetary aggregates) into its analysis.

STRUCTURAL POLICIES: REDUCING THE NAIRU

Discretionary monetary and fiscal policy, no matter how aggressively and well pursued, will never completely eliminate the economy's fluctuations. Governments therefore try to improve the structure of the economy, to dampen the fluctuations and to reduce the NAIRU, so that the economy can have lower unemployment rates without the threat of increasing inflation. The major set of policies aimed at dampening fluctuations are the automatic stabilizers, discussed in Chapter 13, which automatically reduce taxes and increase expenditures as the economy slows down. Here, we focus on policies aimed at lowering the NAIRU.

Government has tried to lower the NAIRU in several ways: by increasing labor mobility, increasing the competitiveness of the economy, controlling directly the increase in wages and prices, and moral suasion.

INCREASING LABOR MOBILITY

By reducing the time that it takes for people to move from job to job the government can reduce frictional unemployment and thus lower the NAIRU. Policies that facilitate labor mobility include one-stop job centers, which not only enable individuals to ascertain quickly vacancies for which they might be suited, but also provide information about training opportunities. A central part of Sweden's active labor policies are training programs that provide those who have lost their jobs the skills required for the new jobs being created. In December 1994, President Clinton proposed a broad program of "skill grants"—vouchers that those who have lost their jobs could use to obtain training at the school of their choice.

Some government policies, particularly in Europe, have probably reduced labor mobility—and thus increased the NAIRU. There is concern that legislation intended to increase workers' job security (by making it more difficult for employers to fire them) has had the side effect of making employers more reluctant to hire new workers, and thus has impeded the process of job transition. Changing these laws may lower the NAIRU.

MAKING THE ECONOMY MORE COMPETITIVE

A second approach, which received considerable attention in the late 1970s and early 1980s, entails shifting the aggregate supply curve down and to the right, as illustrated in Figure 16.5. This increases output, and thus reduces inflationary pressure. One way of shifting the aggregate supply curve down and to the right is by reducing regulations that inhibit competition.

These and other measures making the economy more competitive may lower the NAIRU: a more competitive economy—particularly one that is more open to international competition—will have less pressure to increase prices and wages, even when the unemployment rate is low. Workers worry, for instance, that if they demand significant wage increases, the products they produce will not be able to compete with foreign imports, demand for what they produce will decrease, and they will face a risk of losing their jobs.

Figure 16.5 EFFECTS OF REDUCED INDUSTRIAL REGULATION

Reduced regulation that restricts competition is represented as a shift down and to the right of the short-run aggregate supply curve, from AS_0 to AS_1. Output increases and inflationary pressures are reduced.

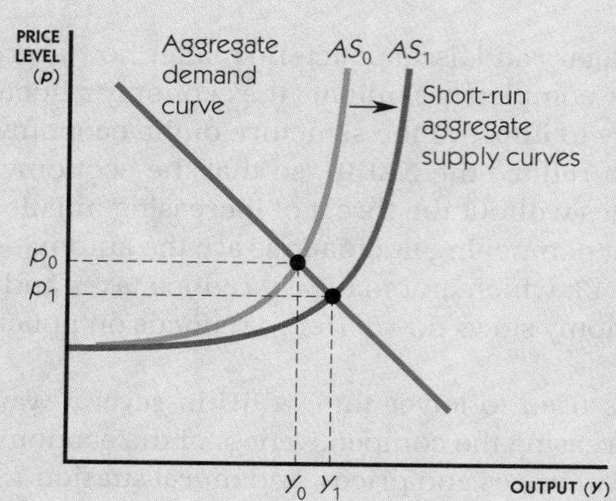

WAGE AND PRICE CONTROLS AND MORAL SUASION

In the 1950s and 1960s, many believed that competition—market forces—were insufficient to control price and wage increases. Large unions could demand—and get—large wage increases, regardless of the unemployment rate; and industries, like steel, which were dominated by a few large producers could—and would—raise their prices, even when there was large excess capacity. In a number of instances, governments tried to reduce the inflationary pressures—at any level of unemployment—by imposing direct controls on wages and prices. Such controls, by interfering with how the price system serves to allocate resources, impose high costs on the economy and tend to be effective only for short periods of time. When the price controls are removed, prices increase rapidly, largely undoing any benefits from the lower rates of price increases while controls were in place. Today, few economists advocate price and wage controls as a way of lowering the NAIRU.

A less intrusive way that some governments have tried is "moral suasion" or jawboning, in which they try to *persuade* firms and workers not to raise prices and wages. The government sets wage and price guidelines, with which it hopes workers and firms will voluntarily comply. The government often has considerable leverage beyond its appeal to moral rectitude, because it can threaten not to buy from firms that violate its suggestions. There have been some dramatic episodes where such jawboning appears to have worked. President Kennedy, concerned that a proposed increase in prices by U.S. Steel would set off an inflationary spiral, successfully jawboned the company into rolling back the price increases. Today, however, most economists are skeptical about the power of moral suasion to have any long-term effect on price setting.

A BRIEF HISTORY OF MACROECONOMIC POLICY

The historical record, illustrated in Figure 16.1, shows clearly that fiscal and monetary policy has not been able to eliminate the economy's fluctuations. But fluctuations appear smaller today than before World War II, and government policy may have played a role. In the following sections, we review briefly the major policy debates of the past thirty years.

THE HEYDAY OF DISCRETIONARY FISCAL POLICY: THE 1960S

The heyday of discretionary fiscal policy occurred during the Kennedy and Johnson administrations. In 1963, with a weak economy, Kennedy's economic advisers—all dedicated Keynesians—argued for a tax cut to stimulate the economy. The tax cut was enacted, and worked just in the manner predicted. Later, in 1968, as the Vietnam War expenditures led to an overheating of the economy, President Johnson's advisers recommended the imposition of a surtax, to dampen slightly the economy.

THE ERA OF INFLATION AND ANTI-INFLATIONARY POLICY

As inflation increased markedly in the 1970s, macroeconomics increasingly became focused on reducing inflation. The fact that inflation and unemployment both increased—an effect that became known as stagflation—cast doubt on the traditional concept of the Phillips curve, with a stable trade-off between inflation and unemployment. As we have seen, new classical economists focused attention on the role of expectations, which could change quickly. This meant that bad economic policy could quickly give rise to inflation, but it also meant that good economic policy could quickly bring inflation under control.

The failure of government policy to provide a stable macroeconomic environment provided renewed interest in rules-based policy. Adopting rules-based policies would bring an immediate reward: the *expectation* that inflation would thereby be controlled would immediately bring down the inflation rate. In particular, monetarism, which sought to bring inflation under control by fixing the rate of growth of the money supply, enjoyed a brief moment of popularity in many industrialized economies—before becoming discredited as the relationship between money supply and national income became unstable. In the United States, tight monetary policy succeeded in bringing inflation down dramatically, from 12 percent per year in 1979 to 3 in 1983—but at a high cost, with unemployment soaring to over 10 percent at the depth of the recession. Economists still debate whether a more gradual policy would have succeeded in reducing inflation—with less drastic costs.

With rapid inflation, the problem did not seem to be lack of aggregate demand. Economists, who naturally think about markets in terms of demand and supply, thus turned more of their attention to aggregate supply. Indeed, a major cause of the inflationary episode were supply shocks, especially the increases in oil prices in 1973 and 1979. President Reagan wanted to reduce taxes *and* reduce inflation. Reducing taxes shifts the aggregate demand curve to the right, as consumers' disposable income rises. Reducing taxes may also shift the aggregate supply curve to the right, *if* as a result individuals are willing to work harder and firms invest more. In addition to these tax changes, President Reagan continued the process of *deregulation,* reducing the regulations which restricted competition in industries like airlines and natural gas, which President Carter had initiated. These reductions in taxes and regulations give rise to *supply-side* effects. If the supply-side effects exceed the demand-side effects, then inflation would be reduced; if demand-side effects dominate, a tax cut is inflationary. Some of President Reagan's economic advisers believed that the supply-side effects would dominate. Most economists were skeptical about the *magnitude* of the effects: in the short run, the shifts in the supply curve would not be large. The evidence appeared to confirm these predictions. Inflation was brought under control because of monetary policy; increased interest rates (soaring to 17 percent) more than offset the expansionary fiscal policy, shifting the aggregate demand curve far to the right.

POLICY IN THE 1990S

The tax reduction of 1981, unaccompanied by corresponding expenditure cuts, left a major legacy: huge deficits. The national debt quadrupled in twelve years and the deficit-GDP ratio reached more than 5 percent.

MACROECONOMIC POLICY IN A HIGH DEFICIT ENVIRONMENT

A consensus emerged in the early 1990s that the deficit had to be reduced. This had an important implication for macroeconomic policy: it virtually eliminated the scope for discretionary fiscal policy. When President Clinton took office in January 1993, he faced a dilemma. Although he was elected on a commitment to reduce unemployment, the necessity of reducing the deficit, would, in traditional macroeconomic theory, have imposed a huge drag on the economy, as the aggregate demand curve shifted to the left. But between 1992 and 1996 the deficit was reduced from $290 billion to $107 billion, and yet the economy expanded, with unemployment falling from over 7 percent to below 5.5 percent. There was a simple answer to this puzzle: reduced deficits lead to reduced interest rates. It was *as if* monetary and fiscal authorities had coordinated their policies, with monetary expansion more than offsetting fiscal contraction. Moreover, because bond markets seemed to believe that the deficit reduction was credible, long-term interest rates fell—even before the deficit reduction was fully implemented. This gave a big boost to interest-sensitive sectors, such as housing. Administration advocates argued that, as important as the deficit reduction was in allowing interest rates to fall, equally important was an economic environment that was conducive to business. This included efforts to make the product sector more competitive by aggressively pursuing antitrust policies, by opening up markets at home and abroad to international competition (see Chapter 19), and by reforming regulations, especially in telecommunications (where a new law passed in 1996 replaced the sixty-year-old regulatory regime which had ruled the industry).

MONETARY POLICY AND UNCERTAINTY OVER NAIRU

The major debate of the 1990s focused on *how* expansionary monetary policy should be. This debate hinges on uncertainty over NAIRU and the risks of aggressive versus conservative policies. In the early 1990s, the prevalent view was that the NAIRU was around 6 percent. As the unemployment rate reached 5.4 percent in 1995, and there was no evidence of inflationary pressures, many economists became convinced that the NAIRU was lower, and that interest rates should remain low to encourage the continuation of the expansion. Others worried that there were long lags—the evidence of incipient inflation would only turn up months later. The Fed, aware that it took six months or more before its policies had full effect, and worried that the economy would become overheated, gradually increased interest rates from 3 percent to nearly 6 percent between 1994 and 1995. The economy continued to expand (though at a more moderate pace), with unemployment continuing to fall until it reached 5.4 percent—with still no evidence of increasing inflation. The debate over whether there should be continued monetary easing continued through 1995 and 1996. Monetary conservatives, while lowering their estimate of the NAIRU, were convinced that further decreases in the unemployment rate would ignite inflation. Some argued that as long as the bond market believed that inflation would ignite, the Fed could not do much to lower the unemployment rate; even if it left short-run interest rates unchanged, long-term rates would rise, dampening the economy. Others advocated a gradual exploration of lower unemployment rates, to see whether the economy might operate at 5.3, 5.2, or even 5.1 percent—or lower—without starting inflation. All parties recognized that there was uncertainty about the NAIRU. The critical issues were the costs and benefits of conservative policies—temporarily missing the opportunity for more rapid growth and higher output until more evidence mounted, versus the risk of temporarily higher inflation should it turn out that the NAIRU was in fact 5.5 percent or higher.

ECONOMIC SECURITY

While the overall macroeconomic performance of the economy in the mid-1990s was strong (the sum of the unemployment and inflation rates, known as the misery index, was the lowest it had been in three decades), there were many individuals whose enthusiasm over the economy did not match the economic statistics. Many workers felt insecure. Economists traced this sense of insecurity to two trends.

First, in the face of competitive pressures, many American industries had been forced to restructure and to "downsize." One widely noted instance came in early 1996, when AT&T announced that it was letting 40,000 of its employees go. While there was no strong evidence that the overall rate of job dislocation—the chance that a worker who had been employed at a job for three or more years would lose it—had increased substantially, the rate for white-collar and older workers—groups which previously had been relatively secure in their jobs—was up dramatically.

Second, beginning in 1973, there had been a marked increase in wage inequality. Not only did the ratio of the wages at the bottom to those at the top fall, but the *real wage* of those at the bottom—the lower 40 percent—fell. Though by the mid-1990s there was evidence that the *trend* had slowed or slightly reversed itself, real wages at the bottom remained lower than they had been two decades earlier. This increased inequality meant that those who lost their jobs saw a real threat to their standard of living; even if they got another job, it was not as good. On average, dislocated workers who found a full-time job had their wages reduced by 10 percent; and even three years after having lost their jobs, a quarter had not regained employment. (Of these, half simply left the labor force.)

Joseph Schumpeter, a famous economist of the early twentieth century who emphasized the role of innovation, described the market economy as a process of creative destruction: jobs were always being destroyed at the same time that new jobs were being created. The AT&T layoffs referred to above illustrate this: while employment at AT&T was reduced, overall employment in the telecommunications sector was increased as a result of the vast array of new products that came about from enhanced competition in the sector. While the economy as a whole may benefit, particular individuals—those who lose their jobs—are worse off.

Those economists referred to earlier as "interventionists" believe not only that government should actively try to reduce the magnitude of economic fluctuations, but also that it should reduce the costs of unemployment and transitions. While non-interventionists argue that unemployment is at most a temporary phenomenon, and that individuals should cope with it on their own (for instance, by putting aside savings), interventionists believe that the government-run unemployment insurance program has made an important contribution in enhancing economic security. (This is true even if it may have, at the same time, led to higher unemployment rates because it reduced individuals' incentives to search for a new job.)

A variety of policies have been proposed to address the recent concerns about economic insecurity. Most important, low levels of unemployment imply that a worker who loses a job has a better chance of finding another. And a good "safety net"—including good unemployment insurance benefits—helps reduce the risks borne by workers. One of the main anxieties facing workers who lose their jobs is loss of health insurance. In their 1996 budget, the Clinton administration proposed extending unemployment benefits to include health insurance, but to date, the proposal has not been passed by Congress.

Three sets of proposals have been put forward to facilitate transitions from

POLICY PERSPECTIVE: THE MCJOBS DEBATE

The success of the United States in creating new jobs in recent years contrasted markedly with that of Europe, as the following chart illustrates. Almost all of the eight million jobs created in the G-7 (the seven major industrialized countries) from 1994 to 1996 were in the United States—and over 90 percent of those created in the United States were in the private sector. In April 1996, the economic leaders of the G-7 nations met in Lille, France, to discuss the employment situation. President Chirac of France, aware of the dismal jobs performance of Europe, but concerned about the quality of the jobs created in America—labeled McJobs, in reference to hamburger flippers—called for a "third way." The Americans pointed out that this portrait of job creation in the United States was simply wrong. To be sure, a large number of the newly created jobs were in the service sector; after all, America was undergoing a transition from an economy based on manufacturing to one based on services, just as it had transformed from an agricultural economy into a manufacturing economy in the nineteenth and early twentieth centuries. But the service sector included high-technology and high-paying sectors, including finance and computer services. A more refined analysis showed that the majority (more than 60 percent) of new jobs were in industries and occupations with median salaries exceeding the median for the economy as a whole.

Moreover, the number of individuals who were working part time because they could not find full-time employment had been consistently declining, while the number of individuals who held multiple jobs had remained roughly unchanged at around 6 percent. While some of these variations are part of cyclical patterns (typically in an economic recovery, more individuals decide to hold multiple jobs, simply because they are easier to obtain), the overall pattern did not support the charge that America had failed to create good-quality full-time jobs.

Source: Bureau of Labor Statistics, Department of Labor.

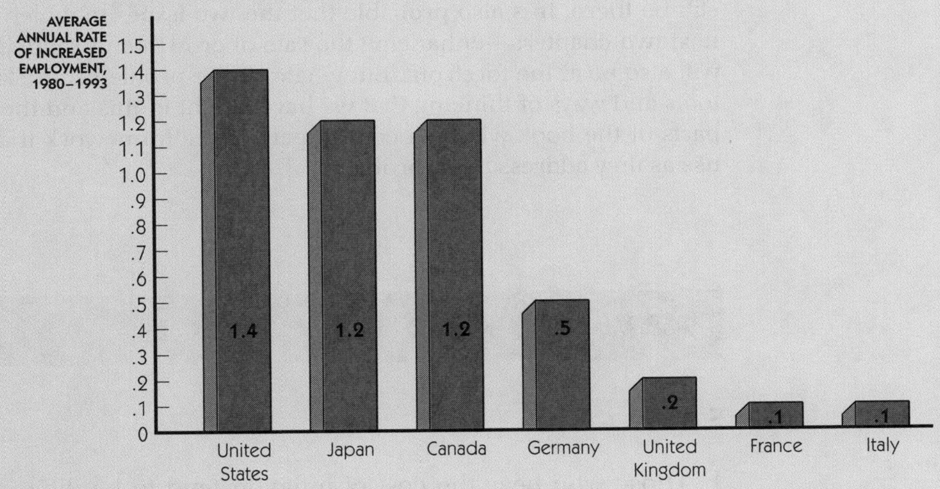

one job to another. Since educated workers make transitions more easily, concern about transitions has provided another rationale for strong support of education. The active labor market policies discussed earlier in the chapter are aimed at providing the training and information required to move workers from one job to another. To signify the importance of these efforts, Secretary of Labor Robert Reich proposed renaming the unemployment insurance system the "reemployment system."

The final set of proposals were concerned with pensions and health insurance. Many insurance policies had provisions that excluded coverage for conditions that members of the family had before the new job began. Proposals were put forward enhancing the "portability" of health insurance and pensions. In July 1996, Congress passed major legislation enchancing health insurance portability.

While these are examples of the kinds of proposals intended to address concerns about economic anxiety, there is far less agreement about what to do about the increased disparity in wages and incomes. Again, since low-skilled individuals are those that suffer most from an economic slowdown, maintaining a high level of employment is not only good macroeconomic policy; it is also good distribution policy.

Economic Challenges of the Twenty-First Century

As we have seen, every period has its own economic problems. Just as it is difficult to predict the performance of the economy a year or two from now, it is hard to predict the central problems and controversies that will be facing the economy in five or ten years. It is probable that the challenges we have discussed in this chapter—maintaining full employment with stable prices and addressing the concerns of dislocated and low-wage unskilled workers—will still be there. It is also probable that the two issues to which we turn in the next two chapters—enhancing the rate of growth and reducing the deficit—will also be at the forefront. But whatever the problems, the kinds of analytic tools and ways of thinking that we have taught in this and the preceding two parts of the book will be a central part of the framework that policymakers use as they address those problems.

Review and Practice

Summary

1. Those who bear the cost of inflation tend to be different from those who bear the cost of unemployment. The latter costs tend to be concentrated especially among the unskilled.

2. The economy is constantly subjected to fluctuations. The fluctuations are partially generated exogenously, by disturbances from the outside, and partially endogenously, by the structure of the economy. The structure of the economy may also amplify exogenous shocks, resulting in effects which persist long after the initial disturbance. Economic expansions have varied greatly in their duration, and contractions in their depth. Still, there are marked similarities among fluctuations in the manner in which different variables (like output, employment, and hours) move together.

3. Those who criticize active intervention argue that markets adjust quickly, so that unemployment is only short-lived. Attempts by government to intervene are not only unnecessary, but are largely ineffective, since they are offset by actions of the private sector. And to the extent that they do have effects, such policies often exacerbate fluctuations, because of the long lags and limited information of government and because political pressures result in its overheating the economy before elections.

4. Most governments believe that they should intervene to help stabilize the economy. Without government intervention, there may be long periods of high and persistent unemployment. While policymakers recognize that there are often long lags, and that policy is made with imperfect information (so that at times, policy may be ill-timed or counterproductive) on average, policy can be and has been stabilizing.

5. Critics of discretionary policy believe governments should tie their hands, using fixed rules. But critics of fixed rules argue not only that this represents giving up on an important set of instruments, but that fixed rules never work well, because they fail to respond to the ever-changing structure of the economy.

6. Current policy discussions recognize that the economy cannot be kept at unemployment rates below the NAIRU for long. The debate is over: (a) What is the level of the NAIRU and have changes in the structure of the economy lowered it? (b) What are the risks and rewards of aggressive policies trying to keep the unemployment rate right at the NAIRU, versus more cautious policies, which lower the unemployment rate only after more evidence that the NAIRU is lower has mounted?

7. Those who argue for aggressive policies believe that the costs in lost output and economic insecurity from the failure to keep unemployment as low as possible without giving rise to large inflationary risks are significant, while the real costs of low inflation are small, especially when there is indexing. They also believe that it is not too costly to correct "mistakes," that is, by pushing the unemployment rate below the NAIRU for a short period of time. Those who argue for more cautious policies worry that once started, inflationary episodes are hard to bring under control, typically requiring extended periods of high unemployment. They think not only that the costs of inflation are high, but also that the short-run benefits of reduced unemployment are more than offset by the risks of higher unemployment, should inflation be ignited and the Fed "forced" to disinflate.

8. Governments can pursue policies both to stabilize the economy (automatic stabilizers) and to lower the NAIRU (by improving labor mobility, increasing competitiveness of markets, and moral suasion).

9. Each period in our economy's history has had its own economic problems, such as avoiding overheating the economy in the years of the Vietnam War, controlling inflation and avoiding stagflation in the 1970s, recovering from the deep recession of 1981–83 or the far shallower recession of 1991–92. In the mid-1990s, with inflation under control, unemployment rates low, and the fiscal deficit reduced, concerns focused on stimulating economic growth, reducing wage inequality—or at least increasing real wages at the bottom—enhancing economic security, and reducing the deficit further.

KEY TERMS

exogenous
endogenous
real business cycle
monetarists
dynamic consistency
New Keynesianism
monetary aggregates

REVIEW QUESTIONS

1. How do inflation and unemployment affect different groups differently, and how do these differences affect views concerning macroeconomic policy?

2. What are the alternative explanations of the sources of the economy's fluctuations? What is the relationship between views about the nature of these fluctuations and views about the role of government?

3. What are some of the controversies today in macroeconomic policy? What are some of the disagreements concerning the risks asociated with pursuing an aggressive policy, maintaining the economy at a rate of unemployment as close to NAIRU as possible?

4. Why do some economists believe that active government intervention in an attempt to stabilize the economy is either unnecessary or undesirable? What are the counterarguments?

5. Describe the rules versus discretion debate.

6. What steps may the government take to lower the NAIRU?

7. How was it possible for the government to increase taxes and reduce expenditures in 1993, and yet stimulate the economy, helping bring it out of a recession?

8. Describe the principal macroeconomic problems of the past four decades.

9. What are some of the major macroeconomic challenges currently facing the country?

PROBLEMS

1. Describe the actions of the private sector that might offset the following actions of government. In which cases do you think the actions will *fully* offset the government actions?
   (a) The government increases the money supply.
   (b) The government attempts to increase aggregate demand by increasing government expenditures without increasing taxes.
   (c) The government increases Social Security payments to the elderly in an attempt to make them better off. (Assume that the elderly currently receive some financial support from their children; or that the individuals save for their retirement needs, with the level of savings determined in order to attain a certain standard of living in retirement.)
   (d) The government attempts to reduce inequality by taxing inheritances.

2. In parliamentary governments, such as the United Kingdom, the prime minister can announce a change in taxation or expenditure, and implement the change almost immediately. (A failure to ratify the proposal of the government would constitute a vote of no-confidence, and bring down the government.) How might this fact affect the balance between the use of monetary and fiscal policy?

3. Some critics of indexed bonds have argued that indexation will reduce government's resolve to fight inflation. Compare the *real* costs to government of an increase in inflation when the government has used, say, long-term indexed bonds and when it has used conventional long term bonds to finance indebtedness. Compare the real costs to bondholders of an increase in inflation in the two circumstances. Do you think that indexation will increase or decrease the resolve to fight inflation?
   Other critics of indexed bonds have argued that indexation imposes a huge risk on the government, because if inflation increases, the government will have to pay more interest. Proponents suggest that indexation reduces the risk faced by the government, because there is less variability in the *real* payments made by government. Assume the rate of inflation in the future may be either 5 percent or 15 percent (with equal probability). Compare the risks associated with an indexed bond paying 2 percent real interest and a nominal bond paying 12 percent. Which form of bond do you think is less risky from the government's perspective?

4. If the economy is in a boom, why might a multiplier-accelerator model predict that it will eventually slow down? If the economy is in a recession, why might the multiplier-accelerator model predict that it will eventually speed up?

5. In the traditional multiplier-accelerator model, an increase in GDP of $100 billion gives rise to an increased demand for additional capital. If the desired ratio of capital to output is 2, and if the $100 billion increase in output is believed to be permanent, what is the increase in the desired level of capital? Assume firms try to fill this gap in one year. What then is the increase in desired investment? If prices of capital goods rise in booms and fall in economic downturns, why might increases in output give rise to smaller increases in the demand for investment in booms and larger increases in economic downturns? What happens to the demand for investment if firms believe that the economic expansion will not be sustained?

6. A decision tree outlines the consequences of each decision depending on how some uncertainty is resolved. Below is a decision tree for the Fed's decision to pursue an aggressive or a cautious unemployment/inflation policy. The NAIRU is either 5 percent or 6 percent, but the Fed is uncertain about the real value of the NAIRU. Under the aggressive strategy, the Fed will set the unemployment rate at 5 percent; under the cautious strategy, unemployment is set at 6 percent. Each strategy has different consequences, depending on the real value of the NAIRU. These are outlined in the decision tree.

Strategy	NAIRU	Outcome
Agressive Strategy: set unemployment at 5 percent	NAIRU = 6 percent	Outcome?
	NAIRU = 5 percent	Outcome?
Cautious Strategy: set unemployment at 6 percent	NAIRU = 6 percent	Outcome?
	NAIRU = 5 percent	Outcome?

Fill in the outcomes for each branch of the decision tree under the following assumptions: (a) it takes two years to discover the true NAIRU (if the Fed chooses the aggressive strategy when the NAIRU is actually 6 percent, higher inflation will occur in two years, indicating the real value of the NAIRU); (b) keeping the unemployment rate 1 percentage point below (above) the NAIRU for one year increases (decreases) the inflation rate by 1 percentage point; (c) decreasing (increasing) the unemployment rate by 1 percentage point increases (decreases) output by 2 percent; (d) GDP is initially at $10 trillion; (e) after the real NAIRU is discovered, the Fed changes the unemployment rate so as to return the inflation rate to its original level over a two-year period; and (f) ignore any indirect effect of inflation on output. What happens to output and inflation during the four-year period for each policy option? Evaluate the trade-offs between the aggressive and cautious policies.

PART FIVE

ISSUES IN MACROECONOMIC POLICY

Unemployment and inflation, the subjects of Parts Three and Four, are not the only economic concerns that make the news. Deficits in the United States, starvation in Ethiopia, the economic crises in the formerly Communist countries of the Soviet Union and Eastern Europe, are among other events that have grabbed headlines in the past decade. In this part of the book, we use the principles and insights developed in the preceding chapters to take a look at these and other current public policy issues.

Chapter 17 discusses a major problem facing the United States: the slowdown in its rate of economic growth. The country is growing neither as fast as it did in earlier decades nor as fast as some of its major economic rivals. We ask, what causes economic growth, and what can be done to stimulate it?

Chapter 18 focuses on the fiscal deficit, which has been at the center of public concern now for more than a decade. We learn how the deficit impacts the economy, and what can be done about it.

U.S. economic policy emerges within an international context, which is why we consider so many international topics throughout this book. In Chapter 19, we focus on international trade policy, including barriers to trade, fair trade laws, and international trade agreements such as GATT and NAFTA.

The collapse of the Soviet empire is undoubtedly one of the biggest events of the twentieth century, just as its rise was. In the aftermath of World War I, the Soviets established an alternative economic system that they believed would eventually dominate capitalism. In Chapter 20, we look at what the system's basic tenets were, why it failed, and the problems these countries face today in making a transition to capitalism.

Most of the world lives in countries where incomes are but a fraction of those in the United States, Western Europe, Japan, and the other developed countries. By the standards in these less developed countries, referred to as the Third World, most people who consider themselves poor in the more developed countries are indeed well off. In Chapter 21, we learn some of the major differences between the developed and less developed countries. We also ask, what are some of the major issues facing these poorer countries as they struggle to grow and raise themselves out of the mire of poverty in which they have remained for centuries?

CHAPTER 17

Growth and Productivity

The changes that have taken place in the U.S. standard of living during the past century are hard to comprehend. In 1900, Americans' level of consumption was little higher than the average citizen's in Mexico or the Philippines today. Life expectancy was low, in part because diseases like smallpox, diphtheria, typhoid fever, and whooping cough were still common. You were fifteen times more likely to catch measles in 1900 than you would be today. The abundance of land meant that relatively few Americans were starving, but luxuries were scarce. People worked as long as they could, and when they could no longer work, they became the responsibility of their children; there was no easy retirement.

During the nineteenth century, the standard of living in England and a few other European countries was perhaps slightly higher than that of the United States. These countries' standard of living was the highest in the world, but even within Europe, there were famines. In the most famous of these, the Irish potato famine of 1845–48, more than a tenth of the population died, and more than another tenth migrated to the United States. For those living in Asia, Africa, and Latin America, as the vast majority of people did then and do now, life was even harder.

KEY QUESTIONS

1. What are the principal determinants of growth in the economy?
2. What factors might account for the slowdown of growth in the United States? What, for instance, might explain the low savings rate or the low investment rate?
3. Are there policies available to the government that might stimulate economic growth?

Higher standards of living are reflected not only in higher incomes and longer life expectancies, but also in shorter working hours and higher levels of education. Improved education is both a benefit and a cause of higher living standards. Table 17.1 compares the United States in 1900 and 1995, indicating stark contrasts in standards of living. Underlying all these differences is an increase in the output for each hour worked, what Chapter 4 identified as productivity. One major goal of this chapter is to understand what causes productivity to increase. A second is to understand the slowdown in growth that has taken place during the last two decades.

The rate of growth of the economy depends on two factors: the rate of increase in the number of hours worked, and the rate of increase in the output per hour worked, the *productivity* of the labor force.

Table 17.1 THE UNITED STATES IN 1900 AND 1995

	1900	1995
Population	76 million	263 million
Life expectancy	47 years	77 years
GNP (in 1995 dollars)	$420 billion	$7,250 billion
GNP per capita (in 1995 dollars)	$5,500	$27,500
Average hours worked each week in manufacturing industry	59 hours	42 hours
Average hourly pay in manufacturing industry (in 1995 dollars)	$4.40	$12.35
Total telephones in country	1.3 million	>200 million
Percentage of those age 5–19 enrolled in school	51 percent	93 percent

Sources: Economic Report of the President (1996); *Statistical Abstract of the United States* (1995).

Rate of growth of economy = rate of increase in the number of hours worked + the rate of increase in the output per hour worked:

$$g_Q = g_H + g_P$$

where

g_Q = rate of growth of output

g_H = rate of increase in number of hours worked

g_P = rate of increase in productivity (output per hour)

During the 1990s, both of these have been markedly lower than they were in the 1960s. To understand why, we need to understand better the underlying forces giving rise to increases in the labor force and productivity.

EXPLAINING PRODUCTIVITY

For almost a century, the United States has been at the center of the technological advances that have changed the world. The telegraph, telephone, laser, transistor, airplane, assembly line, jet engine, atomic energy . . . the list of U.S. technological achievements goes on and on. Beyond these path-breaking developments are countless smaller improvements: new as well as better products, less expensive ways of making old products. The country has reaped a huge reward. Levels of productivity and living standards increased continually and rapidly. Today, productivity and standards of living in the United States are higher than in any other major country.

Figure 17.1 shows, however, that the rate of growth of productivity—per capita income—slowed considerably in the seventies and early eighties, and has remained low. (Productivity tends to vary markedly with business fluctuations. As the economy recovers from a recession, output increases faster than employment, and productivity soars; when the economy goes into an economic downturn, output decreases faster than employment, and productivity falls. Consequently, economists measure long-run productivity growth from one business cycle peak to the next [points where resources are being fully used] or over sufficiently long periods of time that the cyclical fluctuations become small relative to the long-term trends. Figure 17.1 takes this approach, measuring productivity growth over the previous decade. Cyclical effects are apparent: the low productivity growth for 1982 is in part attributable to the severe recession of that year.)

Does it make much difference if the average rate of productivity growth falls from about 2 percent to 1 percent? What's so important about a difference of

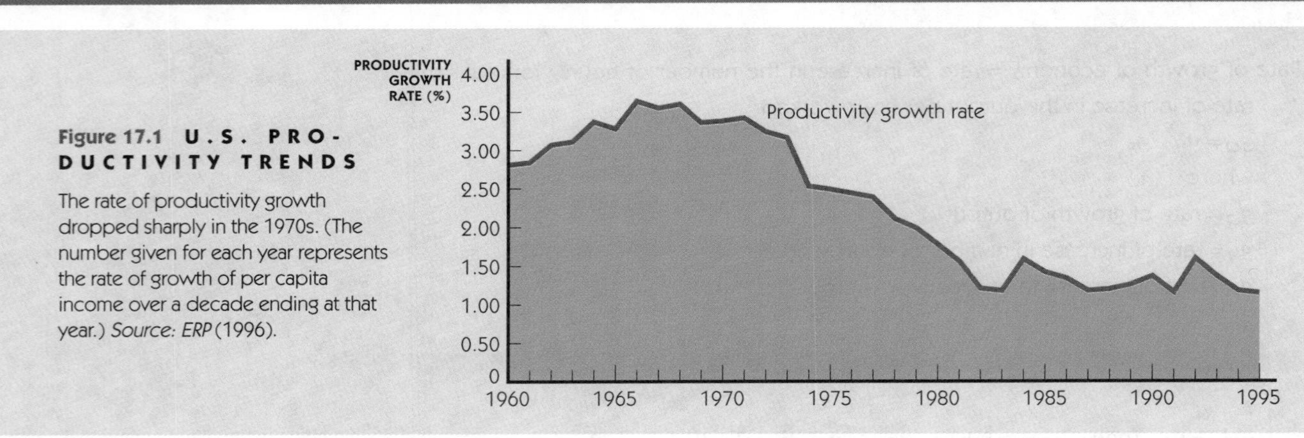

Figure 17.1 U.S. PRODUCTIVITY TRENDS

The rate of productivity growth dropped sharply in the 1970s. (The number given for each year represents the rate of growth of per capita income over a decade ending at that year.) *Source: ERP* (1996).

1 percentage point? In fact, it makes a great deal of difference, because the differences compound over time. Consider this simple calculation. Two countries start out equally wealthy, but one grows at 1 percent a year while the other grows at 2 percent a year. The difference in productivity would be barely perceptible for a few years. But after thirty years, the slower-growing country would be only three-quarters as wealthy as the faster-growing one. America's lower growth compared with the growth of other developed countries in the last two decades explains why many countries have almost caught up to the United States, as shown in Figure 17.2.

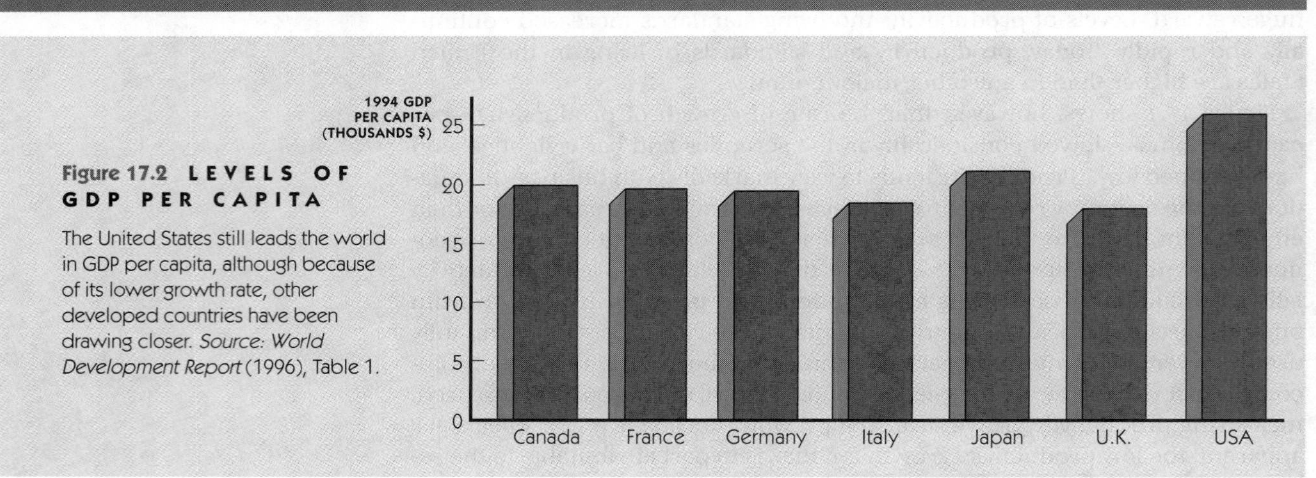

Figure 17.2 LEVELS OF GDP PER CAPITA

The United States still leads the world in GDP per capita, although because of its lower growth rate, other developed countries have been drawing closer. *Source: World Development Report* (1996), Table 1.

Lower growth in productivity means lower growth in standards of living. On average, people will have less of everything—from smaller houses, to poorer health care, to less travel, and fewer government services than otherwise. Many families have been able to sustain increases in their income, but only with both spouses working—and the reduced leisure puts strains on the families and represents a lowering of living standards.

To understand what may have contributed to the productivity slowdown, we need to understand what causes increases in output per hour in the first place. There are four key factors: savings and investment; education and the quality of the labor force; reallocating resources from low- to high-productivity sectors; and research and development. The next sections discuss these factors in turn.

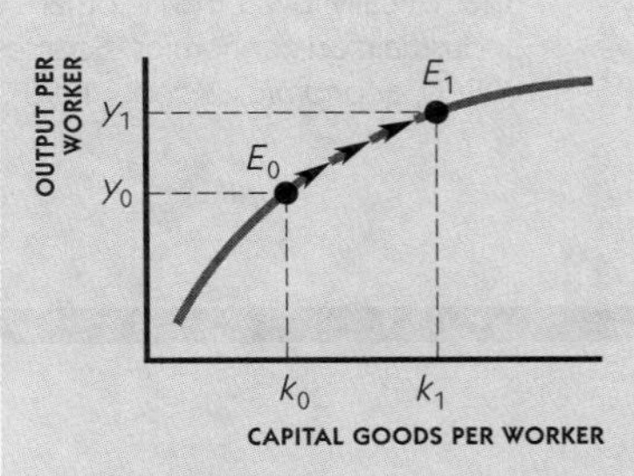

Figure 17.3 INVESTMENT AND PRODUCTIVITY

An increase in the investment rate (the ratio of investment to GDP) results in capital deepening. As capital per worker increases, output per worker increases.

SAVINGS AND INVESTMENT

Workers today are more productive than they were twenty or one hundred years ago because they have more and better machines. An American textile worker can produce far more than a textile worker in India, partly because of differences in the equipment they use. Many textile workers in India still use handlooms, similar to those used in America two hundred years ago.

Higher levels of investment relative to GDP result in more capital per worker. Economists call this **capital deepening.** As capital per worker increases, output per worker increases. Suppose an economy has an investment rate of 10 percent of GDP, and a low level of capital per worker. Increasing its investment rate to 15 percent will raise the level of capital per worker, and thus productivity. This is illustrated in Figure 17.3. Increasing capital per worker from k_0 to k_1, raises output per worker from y_0 to y_1.

In Chapters 6 and 7 we discussed the relationship between savings and investment. In a closed economy, savings equal investment, as illustrated in Figure 17.4. In the figure, we assume that savings do not depend on the interest rate. A reduction in savings leads to higher interest rates, and higher interest rates lead to lower investment.

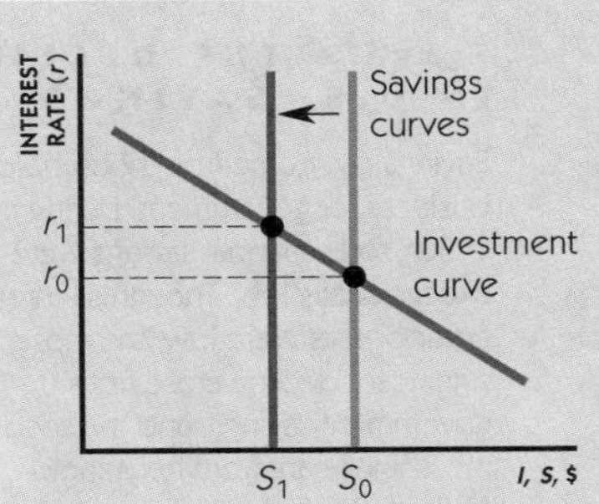

Figure 17.4 SAVINGS AND INVESTMENT

Lower savings rates lead to higher interest rates and lower levels of investment.

In an open economy, matters are more complicated. Domestic savings need not equal investment, because the country can finance investment from abroad. (If this is done, gross national product (GNP)—the measure of output that nets out payments of interest and dividends to foreigners—will increase less than GDP, which is simply the amount produced within a country; citizens of the country will have to share the benefits of higher productivity with foreigners. But even though the U.S. economy is open, U.S. savings and investment tend to move together, with a reduction in national savings of $100 leading to a reduction of investment of between $35 and $50.

Figure 17.5 compares the savings rates in developed countries. Both in relation to other countries and historically, U.S. savings rates in recent years have been low. For example, the U.S. savings rate has been less than one-seventh that of Japan. Because of its adverse effects on investment, the low savings rate may underlie some of the slowdown in productivity.

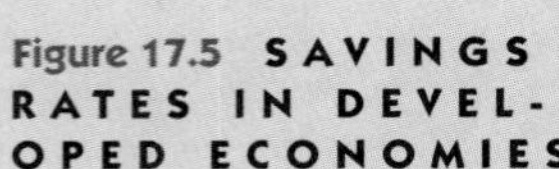

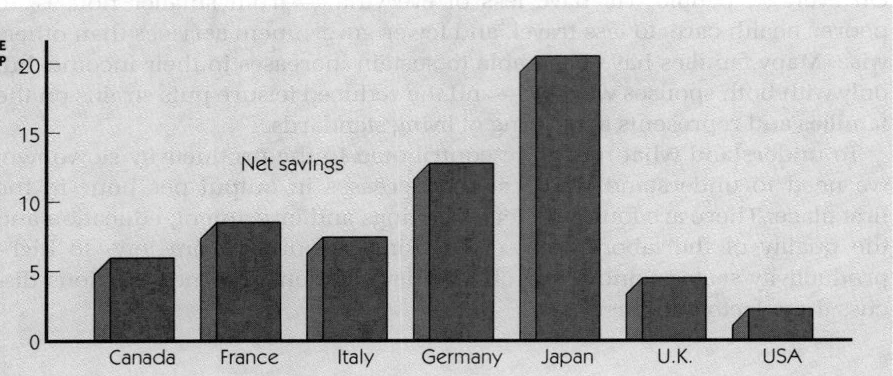

Figure 17.5 SAVINGS RATES IN DEVELOPED ECONOMIES

During the 1980s and 1990s, the United States savings rate was dramatically lower than in other industrialized economies. *Source:* OECD, *Economic Outlook* (1990).

WHY ARE U.S. SAVINGS SO LOW?

To see why U.S. savings are so low, it is useful to break down savings into three components: personal (or household) savings, business savings, and government savings (the fiscal surplus, when the government has one). Figure 17.6 shows how each of these as well as total savings has changed over time. The figure makes clear that the low level can largely be attributed to the huge gov-

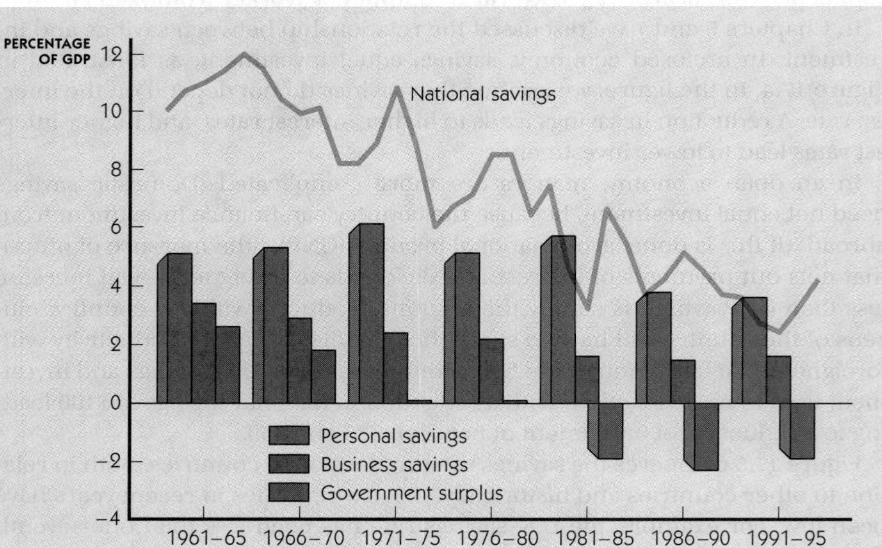

Figure 17.6 THE DECLINE IN U.S. SAVINGS

Savings can come from households, business, or government. During the 1980s, total national savings were exceptionally low. Though all three components were low, the most significant decline arose from government savings, and the second most significant from household savings. The federal deficit worsened in 1991 and 1992, but following the passage of the 1993 deficit reduction act and the economic recovery, the federal deficit improved markedly. *Source: ERP* (1996), Table B-28.

ernment deficits and a low level of household savings. Beginning in 1993, the federal government succeeded in reducing the deficit, from almost 5 percent of GDP in 1992 to under 2 percent in 1996. But at the same time, personal savings decreased slightly, moderating the overall increase in national savings. Here, we focus on household savings; Chapters 7 and 18 address government deficits.

We can use the basic framework for consumer choice introduced earlier (Chapter 5) to analyze the determinants of savings. Prices (here, the interest rate) and preferences affect the desire for consumption in the future versus consumption today. People save for future needs—for retirement (life-cycle savings); to buy a home, pay for their children's college education, or to meet certain other needs (target savings); for emergencies, for periods in which their incomes may be low, say because they are laid off from their job or in which their needs are high, or because they require medical attention (precautionary savings); and people save to leave something to their children (bequest savings).

During the past two decades, virtually all of the motives and incentives for saving changed in a way to discourage saving. Improved Social Security (particularly during the 1970s) reduced the need for private savings for retirement; improved capital markets and insurance—provided by both government and employers—meant that people did not have to save as much for emergencies; improved capital markets also meant that people did not have to save as much for a down payment on a house; and improved government student-loan programs meant that parents did not have to save as much for their children's education.

But one change should have stimulated savings: an increase in the real after-tax return. In the 1980s, taxes on the return to capital, particularly for upper-income levels, plummeted—from 70 percent in 1980 to 28 percent in 1986—and real before-tax returns soared. Nevertheless, savings fell. This should not come as too much of a surprise: we also learned in Chapter 5 that the effect of changes in real after-tax interest rates on savings, while positive, is probably small.[1]

But the changes discussed so far, by themselves, do not seem to account fully for the low levels of savings. Accordingly, economists have looked elsewhere for an explanation.

The **life-cycle theory of savings** emphasizes that savings will differ in different parts of an individual's life cycle. The 45–65 age group are typically high savers; no longer facing the burden of children, they recognize the necessity of setting aside money for their retirement. The percentage of the population in this group has been low since the mid-1970s, but has begun to increase in the 1990s. This should provide an impetus for an increased personal savings rate.

Some economists argued that the huge increase in real estate prices in the 1980s meant that more individuals were saving in the form of home equity; these savings were not recorded in the national income accounts. Though the

[1]There, we saw that while the *substitution* effect leads to increased savings, the *income* effect results in reduced savings. While on theoretical grounds the *net* effect is ambiguous, the evidence supports a small positive effect.

explanation seemed plausible at the time, it suggested that when real estate prices leveled out, or fell, as they did in the late 1980s and early 1990s, savings rates would increase. They did not.

Finally, some economists attribute the decline in savings rates to a change in values: the "Now" generation wants its consumption now, and puts less money aside for its children.

Whatever the explanation for low savings, those who believe that increasing savings is necessary to stimulate productivity feel stymied: microeconomic instruments to stimulate household savings, such as tax preferences, are likely to have at most small effects. Thus, economists have increasingly seen macroeconomic policies—particularly the reduction in the deficit—as the main way by which the government can enhance investment: by borrowing less, interest rates will be reduced and investment stimulated. Reducing the deficit increases national savings. This was the strategy for increasing national savings adopted by the Clinton administration in 1993. (At the same time, *how* the deficit is reduced matters. If high-return public investments, such as in infrastructure, education, and research, are reduced, overall investment may fall, and productivity growth may be slowed. We will look at these factors shortly.)

EXPLANATIONS OF LOW SAVINGS

Improved Social Security
Improved insurance markets
Improved capital markets
Change in values: less future-oriented behavior

INFRASTRUCTURE

Most discussions of the low level of investment in the United States focus on low *private* investment. But government investment is also important. These investments include roads, bridges, airports, and harbors, called **infrastructure.** Without adequate infrastructure, the private sector cannot perform effectively. During the 1980s, not only did the deficit soar, but infrastructure investment declined. In many cases, even maintenance activities were forgone, so that by 1992, the nation's infrastructure was in worse shape than it was a decade earlier. While the public capital stock amounted to 50 percent of GDP in 1970, by 1990, it amounted to only about 40 percent. This declining public capital stock has exerted a drag on the economy's productivity, though there are no precise estimates of the magnitude.

POLICIES TO STIMULATE SAVINGS AND INVESTMENT

Government has only limited tools to stimulate savings and investment. Reducing the fiscal deficit increases national savings, and in a closed (or not perfectly open) economy, this leads to increased investment. Reducing the deficit by cutting back on infrastructure investment (or other forms of investments such as in education) may, however, be counterproductive; overall investment (public plus private) may decline, and the public investment may yield as high or higher returns than the induced private investment.

When the economy is at full employment, in a closed economy investment subsidies have little or no effect on aggregate investment. With given government expenditures and consumption, the Fed simply has to raise interest rates to ensure that aggregate demand equals the full-employment level of output. Since savings is relatively insensitive to interest rates, investment (equal full-employment savings) will be relatively unaffected. In an open economy, investment subsidies induce more investment and more borrowing from abroad. If the subsidies lower the before-subsidy marginal return to investment to the point where it is below the cost of capital from abroad, the country (at the margin) is actually worse off as a result of the additional investment. GDP—what is produced in the United States—increases, but GNP—netting out what has to be paid to foreigners (so what Americans can actually spend)—actually decreases.

GDP can be increased if savings can be increased (and consumption reduced). The apparent unresponsiveness of savings to the real interest rate has made most economists skeptical about the potential use of tax policy to encourage savings. There is some evidence that IRAs (individual retirement accounts) have had some effect, largely because banks and other financial institutions have used them as the basis of advertising campaigns to obtain deposits.

WHY LOWER SAVINGS AND INVESTMENT IS NOT THE WHOLE STORY

As important as the low savings and investment rates are in explaining the low rates of growth of productivity, they are not the whole story. As we have seen, capital accumulation leads to increases in output per worker—in productivity. However, this effect is limited to the short run. After an increase in the rate of savings and investment, the economy eventually reaches a new ratio of capital to worker. This is capital deepening. At the new level of capital to worker, the economy is indeed operating at a higher level of productivity, but the productivity *increase* has run its course. This is illustrated in Figure 17.7, which uses a hypothetical time series for real output to display the economy's growth path. Three segments of the growth path are evident. The first segment (*AB*) represents the economy's growth before the increase in the rate of savings and investment. The steep segment that follows (*BC*) represents the period of capital accumulation arising from the increase in the rate of savings and investment; as capital per worker increases, so does productivity and the growth rate of the economy. But once the new, higher level of capital per worker is reached, the economy resumes its original growth rate, represented by the third segment (*CD*).

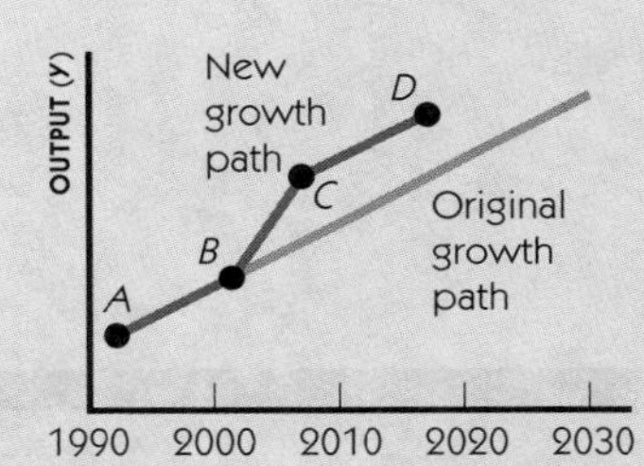

Figure 17.7 SHORT-RUN AND LONG-RUN EFFECTS OF CAPITAL DEEPENING

Capital deepening increases output per worker (productivity), and therefore economic growth, but the effects on the rate of growth of productivity (as opposed to the level of productivity) are limited to the short run. The graph shows three segments of a hypothetical growth path. *AB* represents the economy's growth before an increase in savings and investment. *BC*, the steep segment, represents the period of capital accumulation arising from an increase in savings and investment. Once the new, higher level of capital per worker is reached, the economy resumes its original growth rate, represented by the third segment, *CD*.

Figure 17.8 DIMINISHING RETURNS TO CAPITAL

With a given production function, the increase in capital goods per worker from k_2 to k_3 would result in a smaller increase in productivity than the corresponding increase from k_1 to k_2.

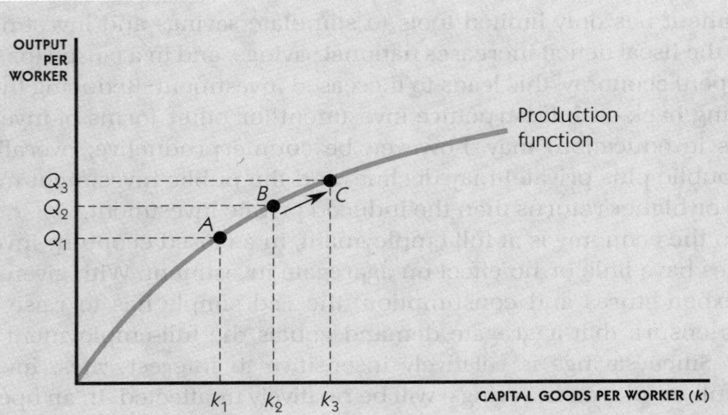

This analysis may suggest that repeated increases in the rate of savings and investment, generating continuous capital deepening, will result in a long-run increase in the rate of productivity increase and therefore a long-run increase in the rate of economic growth. This is *not* the case because of the law of diminishing returns, which says that as the amount of capital goods per worker continues to increase, successive increments of capital increase output per worker by less and less. Eventually, further increases in capital per worker will yield almost no increase in output per worker. Figure 17.8 shows that as the economy increases capital per worker from k_2 to k_3, the increase in output per worker is much smaller than when the economy increases capital per worker by a similar amount from k_1 to k_2.

Yet in fact, productivity growth did not diminish during periods of rapid capital accumulation. Figure 17.9 shows productivity growth in the United States in twenty-year periods since 1880. Productivity growth actually increased from 1900 to 1970 during a period of enormous accumulation of capital goods. Similar patterns have been observed elsewhere. Japan, for example, has had steadily increasing productivity growth along with large increases in capital goods per worker for the past quarter century.

The reason that productivity growth can continue over long periods is that capital deepening is not the only, or even the primary, source of productivity increases. If we are to understand why the rate of productivity growth has decreased, we need to look at the other sources, to which we now turn.

Figure 17.9 LONG-RUN U.S. PRODUCTIVITY GROWTH

Productivity growth increased sharply during the first part of the twentieth century, a period of rapid capital goods accumulation, before declining in the last few decades. *Source:* Angus Maddison, *Dynamic Forces in Capitalist Development,* 1991.

HIGHER QUALITY OF THE LABOR FORCE

A second major source of productivity growth, which today is even more important than increased capital per worker, is a higher-quality labor force. Running a modern industrial economy requires a well-educated labor force. In addition, an economy on the cutting edge of technological change needs trained engineers and scientists to discover and shape those innovations.

Spending money on education and training improves workers' skills and productivity. These expenditures are investments—just like investments in machines and buildings. And just as expenditures on plant and equipment result in physical capital, we say that expenditures on education result in **human capital.** Thus, increases in human capital are one of the major sources of economic growth.

One nationally representative survey found that establishments with more educated work forces had significantly higher productivity: increasing years of education by 10 percent increased productivity by 8.6 percent. Indeed, returns to education have increased markedly—even as the number of educated has increased: by 1994 the median full-time worker with at least a bachelor's degree earned 74 percent more per week than one with only a high school diploma—up from 36 percent in 1979. Though some of this difference may be attributed to the fact that those who graduate from college are more able (and hence would have earned higher incomes even if they had not gone on to college), even accounting for factors such as family background or high school performance, the returns to education appear significant. Just a year of college has been estimated to increase earnings by 5 to 10 percent, or more.

THE STRENGTHS OF THE U.S. EDUCATIONAL SYSTEM

In recent years, there have been significant increases at least in the "quantity" of education in the United States. More students are finishing high school. The drop-out rate fell from 14.1 to 11 percent between 1973 and 1993. More high school students are attending and completing college. The percent of high school graduates enrolling in college after graduation increased from 49 percent in 1980 to 62 percent in 1993. As the new, more highly educated workers have replaced older workers, the share of the work force with a college degree has nearly doubled, from 16 percent in 1973 to 29 percent in 1993. And enrollment in graduate schools has increased even more than undergraduate enrollment.

A particular strength of America's educational system has been its egalitarianism. While other countries have made decisions on whether a particular child is suitable for a college education at early ages (sometimes as young as eleven), in the United States such decisions are made much later, and students typically get repeated chances. Early sorting, based on test scores, gives a distinct advantage to children with more educated parents.

Another great strength is the U.S. system of junior colleges and state universities, many of which provide a high-quality education to those who could not afford to go to private schools or who may not have performed well in high school. In many countries, such students would have been precluded from further education. (Ironically, while in many respects the American educational system is more egalitarian than those of other developed countries, in one respect it is less so. Most European countries charge virtually no tuition to students who are admitted to their universities, and some actually pay all or part of students' living costs.)

Still another strength is America's universities, which number among the greatest in the world. Students from virtually every other country come to the United States to study, as both undergraduates and graduate students. The discoveries and innovations flowing out of the universities' research laboratories have been an important basis of America's technological superiority.

SYMPTOMS OF A U.S. HUMAN CAPITAL PROBLEM

While there is thus great strength within the U.S. educational system, there are symptoms of some problems that may be contributing to the slowdown of U.S. productivity. The concern is that while on quantitative measures the U.S. looks good, with high levels of expenditure and high levels of enrollment, the quality of U.S. education is low. On a number of standardized tests particularly in areas of science and mathematics, American students perform below students from many other countries—even countries which have until recently been classified as less developed, such as Korea and Taiwan (see Figure 17.10). Of course, standardized tests are imperfect and limited; one of the many problems with them is that they do not measure creativity. But the tests do measure success in certain objectives of education, such as mastery over basic skills. The poor performance of American students is thus disturbing.

Similarly, while America remains unique in the large fraction of its youth that goes to college, a smaller proportion of U.S. college students choose to study science and engineering, in comparison to students from some other countries, such as Japan and Korea. Evidence suggests that the fraction of the work force that are engineers and scientists is a major determinant of rapid economic growth.

Finally, a significant fraction of America's population is deprived of the opportunity to realize their full potential. The role of family background in determining educational achievement has increasingly been recognized. Children who grow up in poverty are less likely to attain an education commensurate with their ability. Yet the number of children in poverty has in-

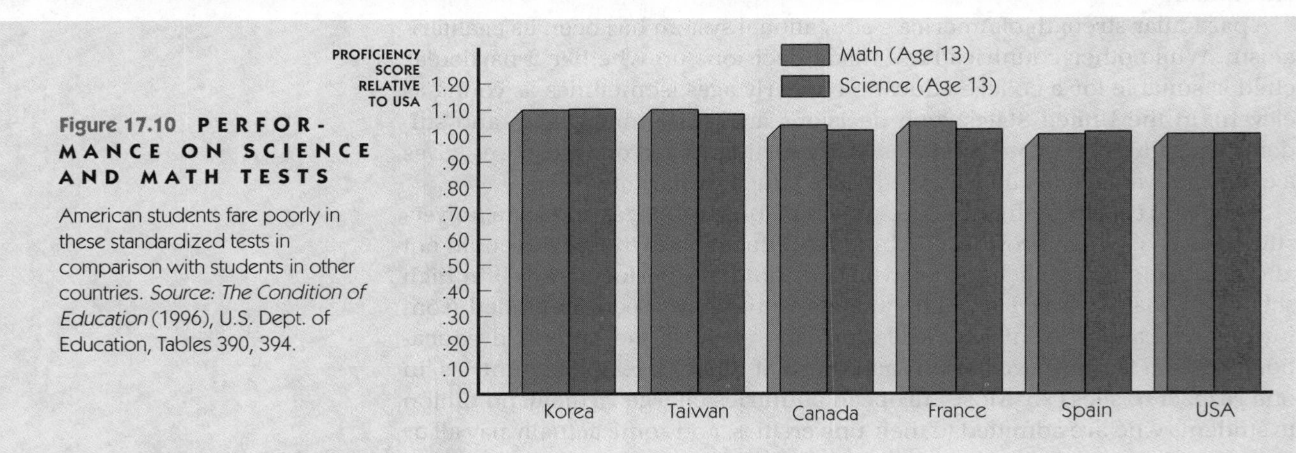

Figure 17.10 PERFORMANCE ON SCIENCE AND MATH TESTS

American students fare poorly in these standardized tests in comparison with students in other countries. *Source: The Condition of Education* (1996), U.S. Dept. of Education, Tables 390, 394.

creased markedly in recent decades, from 15 percent in 1970 to 21 percent in 1992. With the flight to the suburbs that began in the 1950s, and with increasing violence and drugs in inner city high schools, those left in inner cities are less likely to get a quality education. Moreover, a college education has become less affordable for children from poor families. Tuitions at public and private colleges and universities have increased at rates far exceeding increases in the cost of living; real incomes of poorer families have fallen; and the real value of government grant and loan programs (such as Pell grants) has declined. Not surprisingly, the gap between the fraction of children from poor families and rich families going on to higher education has increased.

REALLOCATING RESOURCES FROM LOW- TO HIGH-PRODUCTIVITY SECTORS

During the past century, the United States has evolved from an agricultural economy to an industrial economy to a service economy. Figure 17.11 shows this dramatic structural change. The service sector, broadly defined, includes not only traditional services such as haircuts and restaurant meals but also the more sophisticated services provided by doctors and lawyers, educational institutions, and computer programmers, among others. The medical sector alone has grown to the point where today it accounts for more than 14 percent of GDP.

The movement out of agriculture and into industry explains some of the productivity increase in the early part of the century. While the level of productivity in agriculture was increasing rapidly, it remained lower than in industry. Thus, as workers shifted out of low-productivity jobs in agriculture into high-productivity jobs in manufacturing, average productivity in the economy increased. With almost all labor now out of agriculture—and with agricultural productivity increased to the point where incomes in that sector are comparable to those in the rest of the economy—this kind of shift can no longer be a source of overall productivity growth. But there remain other opportunities. Productivity in the telecommunications and export sectors is substantially higher than in other parts of the economy. Telecommunications deregulation will facilitate the movement of resources into that sector. And recent international trade agreements (see Chapter 19) will open up new opportunities for export growth. Both should contribute to the overall increase in productivity.

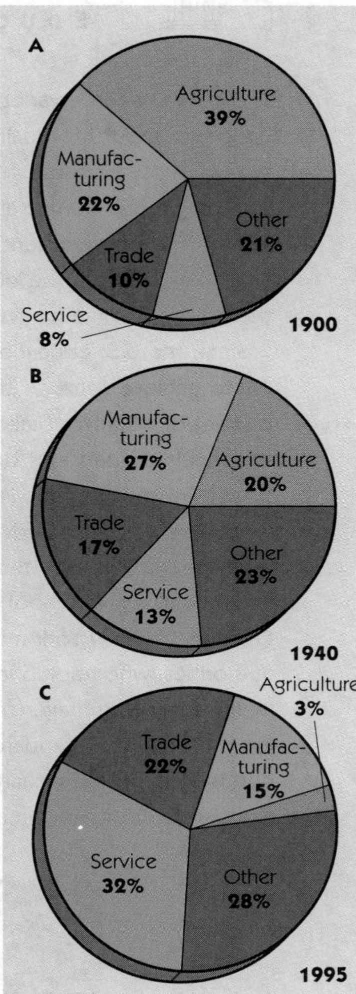

Figure 17.11 SECTORAL SHIFTS

Employment in the U.S. economy shifted from agriculture to manufacturing industries in the first half of this century and from manufacturing to services in the second half. *Sources: Historical Statistics of the United States* (1975); *ERP* (1996), Table B-42.

TECHNOLOGICAL CHANGE

This final source of productivity growth may be the most important. Indeed, prior to 1973, as much as two-thirds of all increases in productivity were due to technological progress. One of the major differences between the economy today and in 1900 is the routine nature of change in the modern economy. The prototype of the nineteenth- and early twentieth-century inventors were people like Thomas Edison and Alexander Graham Bell—lone individuals,

Policy Perspective: Improving the U.S. Education System

There have been a variety of policy responses to concerns about the quality of the U.S. education system. Most of these have not entailed simply spending more money: already, the United States spends on a per student basis more than almost any other country. The question is, how to make the dollars spent more productive.

Since the U.S. educational system is clearly failing to achieve some of the goals expected of it, one set of initiatives (called Goals 2000) attempts to articulate goals and define performance measures. Given the mobility of Americans, there would be significant advantages to defining national standards—so that an employer would know what a high school diploma in Mississippi or California or New York meant. But state and local authorities, who traditionally have had responsibility for education, have strongly resisted establishing such national standards. Thus, federal legislation has encouraged each state to set up its own goals and performance measures.

There are also numerous proposals for reforming the ways in which elementary and high school education is organized. Most of these entail greater decentralization, that is, giving more autonomy to the school, as opposed to the school district. Voucher proposals—in which parents are given a certain amount of money to spend on the education of their children, and they can choose which school to attend—have been advocated by those who believe that vouchers would induce greater competition, and hence quality, in education. But critics have worried that such proposals would lead to the end of the public schools, would increase social segregation in education, and would be ineffective in improving quality, particularly in communities with less educated parents, who will be less able to make informed choices and less effective in influencing school policies than parents in communities with more highly educated parents.

Some of the programs that help the disadvan-

taged, including Head Start, appear to have yielded substantial economic payoffs. Head Start—which provides pre-school help—has been shown to give a persistent boost to academic achievement: compared to similar children who have not participated in the program, those who have are less likely to be held back in school and more likely to graduate from high school.

Recently the federal government has attempted to devise programs to facilitate the transition of high school graduates to the workplace. Germany has long had a successful apprenticeship program for similar students, and the new School to Work program has encouraged states to set up similar partnerships with industry.

working by themselves or with a small number of collaborators. Small entrepreneurs and innovators continue to play a role in developing new products, particularly in the computer industry. But the prototype of a modern research effort, like the U.S. program to put an astronaut on the moon, has thousands of scientists working together to accomplish in a few short years what would have been almost unimaginable earlier. Technological change in the modern economy is a large-scale, systematic effort. Modern research is centered in huge laboratories, employing thousands of people. While some of these laboratories are run by the government—such as the Brookhaven, Argonne, and Lawrence laboratories, which carry out research in basic physics—many are private, like Bell Labs (part of AT&T), where the transistor and laser were developed. Indeed, most major firms spend about 3 percent of their gross revenues on research and development.

The current level of technological progress has become so expected that it is hard to believe how different the view of reputable economists was in the early 1800s. Real wages of workers were little higher than they had been five hundred years earlier, when the bubonic plague destroyed a large part of the population of Europe and thereby created a great scarcity of labor. After half a millennium of at best slow progress, Thomas Malthus, one of the greatest economists of that time, saw population expanding more rapidly than the capacity of the economy to support it. What was missing from his dismal forecast was technological change.

EXPENDITURES ON R & D

A major determinant of the pace of technological progress is the level of expenditures on R & D. These expenditures are a form of investment—expenditures today yield returns in the future.

While overall expenditures on R & D, as a percentage of GDP, are relatively high in the United States—only Japan and Germany are higher—much of this has been for defense purposes, as illustrated in Figure 17.12. Government nondefense R & D in the United States plays a relatively small role. Figure 17.13 shows how government and private R & D expenditures, as a percentage of GDP, have changed over the last twenty years. Federal expenditures on nondefense R & D have actually fallen. As Japanese and German scientists and engineers devote their efforts to building better consumer products, a disproportionate

Figure 17.12 INTERNATIONAL COMPARISON OF R & D EXPENDITURES

While total U.S. R & D expenditures are comparatively high, a larger proportion of U.S. expenditures goes to defense. *Source:* National Science Foundation, "Science and Engineering Indicators" (1993), Tables 4-3, 5-39.

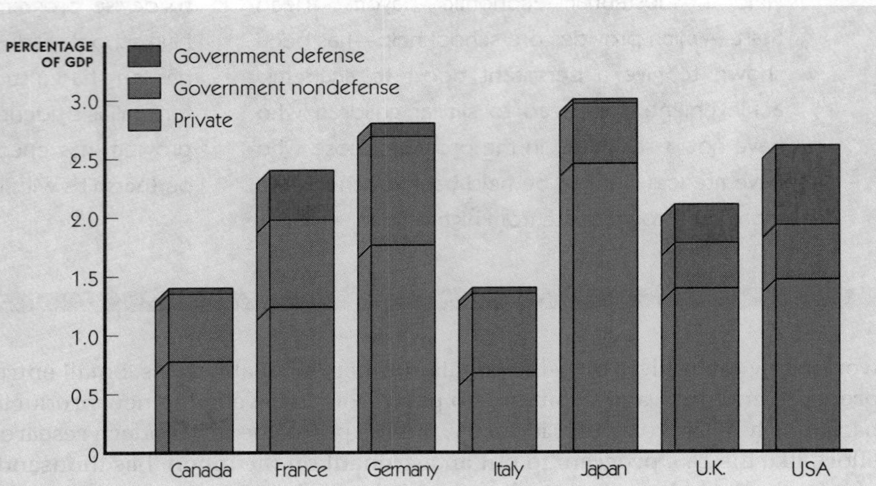

Figure 17.13 U.S. R & D EXPENDITURES AS A PERCENTAGE OF GDP

Total U.S. R & D expenditures have increased slightly since 1972, though in recent years there has been a slight decline. Overall increases in private R & D expenditures have offset the drop in total federal R & D expenditures. Federal nondefense R & D expenditures have remained low, dropping from .6 percent of GDP in 1972 to .4 percent of GDP in 1994. *Source: Statistical Abstract of the United States* (1995), Table 979.

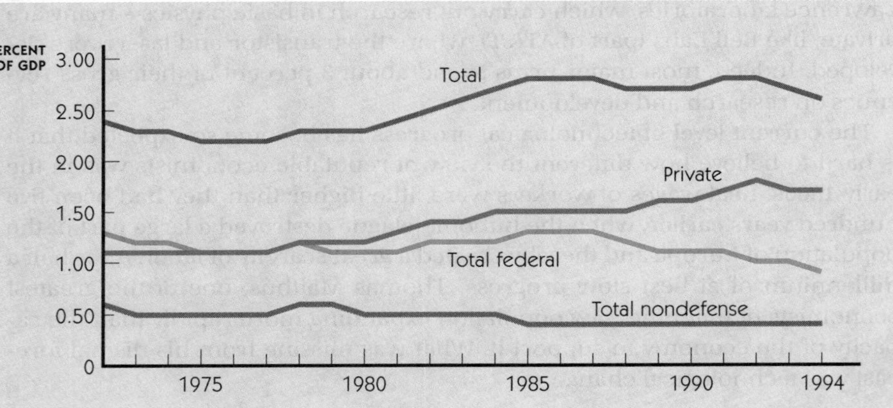

fraction of America's scientists and engineers devote their efforts to building better bombs, missiles, and other weapons.

This underinvestment in R & D is reflected in the U.S. record on patents. Figure 17.14 shows that today, relative to the size of the population, the United States is performing more poorly (by this indicator) than Japan, the United Kingdom, and Germany.

The high rates of return on R & D expenditures support the view that there is underinvestment in research: some estimates put the private returns at over 25 percent, and since many of the returns accrue to firms other than

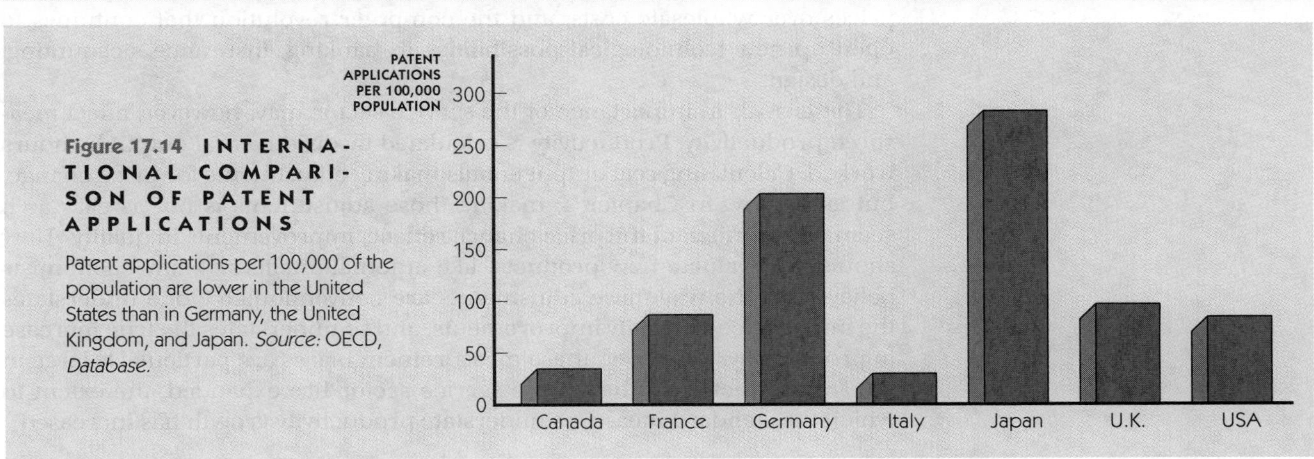

Figure 17.14 INTERNATIONAL COMPARISON OF PATENT APPLICATIONS
Patent applications per 100,000 of the population are lower in the United States than in Germany, the United Kingdom, and Japan. *Source:* OECD, *Database.*

those undertaking the research, social returns are estimated to be even higher. High risk, combined with limitations on the ability to borrow to finance R & D, provide part of the explanation for the seeming underinvestment in R & D.

Some economists, however, even while agreeing with the evidence concerning underinvestment in R & D, have raised questions about the importance of R & D in explaining the *current* productivity slowdown. It normally takes years for the effects of R & D to show up in productivity statistics. To the extent that the productivity slowdown in the 1970s was due to decreased expenditures on research, it would have been due to a decrease in expenditures in the 1950s and 1960s. But the 1960s in particular was a period of high spending on research.

OTHER POSSIBLE FACTORS

There may be other factors contributing to the slowdown in the pace of technological progress. Two that have received prominence in recent years relate the productivity slowdown to the increased importance of the service sector and the unexpected increase in energy prices in the 1970s.

Service Sector Some economists, such as William Baumol of New York and Princeton Universities, contend that the decline in heavy industry—in steel, automobiles, and manufacturing in general—and growth in the service sector help explain the recent slowdown in productivity growth. In fact, in recent years, productivity growth in manufacturing has been quite robust, even higher than in the 1960s. Those worried about the potential for technological change in services cite such examples as haircutting: the only major innovation in the field in the past hundred years has been the electric hair clipper. But other economists are more hopeful. They cite the development by McDonald's of more efficient ways of delivering "fast food," improvements by many of the country's major retailers that have reduced the markup of retail prices over wholesale costs, and the computer revolution that continues to open up new technological possibilities in banking, insurance, accounting, and design.

The growth in importance of the service sector may, however, affect *measured* productivity. Productivity is calculated by dividing *real* output by hours worked. Calculating real output entails making adjustments for price change; but as we saw in Chapter 4, making those adjustments is not as easy as it seems. How much of the price change reflects improvements in quality? How should we evaluate new products, like automatic tellers? Many economists believe that the way these adjustments are conventionally done understates the importance of quality improvements, and so understates the true increase in productivity. Moreover, these measurement biases are particularly large in the service sector, so that as the service sector has expanded, the extent to which the standard measures understate productivity growth has increased.

The Energy Crisis There are other factors that may have contributed to the slowdown of technological change. Some economists focus on the fact that the slowdown seems to have occurred around 1973, when oil prices soared. Much of the existing capital was designed for a world of cheap energy, and much of the investment in the subsequent years went not to capital deepening, but to replacing the old capital with more energy efficient machines and buildings. In this perspective, the standard procedures overestimate net investment since 1973. Moreover, firms diverted more of their research budgets to looking for ways of saving on energy, again at the expense of research that might have increased overall productivity. Other economists question the importance of the run-up in energy prices, since the real price had declined to earlier levels by the mid-1980s. In any case, energy constitutes a small percentage of GDP.

THE POLICY DEBATES OF THE 1990S

Policy discussions have focused on both corporate and public R & D expenditures. Because of the importance of spillovers or externalities—those undertaking research reap only a fraction of the total returns—there is widespread agreement that government should support R & D through preferential tax treatment (such as the incremental R & D tax credit, under which government in effect pays 25 percent of the increase in R & D expenditures).

Far more controversial, however, have been direct government expenditures to develop new technologies or to subsidize corporations doing so. Critics label such subsidies as *industrial policies*—an attempt by government to intervene in the markets' allocation of resources. They claim government is notoriously bad at picking winners, that is, areas with a high likelihood of success. In their view, firms driven by the profit motive are more likely to make good decisions than the government.

Technology advocates contend that there are important spillovers from technological research, that there is clear evidence of underinvestment in advanced technology (as one would expect, given the spillovers, and limitations of firms' ability to obtain funds to finance risky research), and that the govern-

CLOSE-UP: ENDOGENOUS GROWTH THEORY

Technological change is the primary cause of increases in standards of living. Recent theories of economic growth, with major contributions by Karl Shell of Cornell University and Paul Romer of University of California, Berkeley, have emphasized that the pace of technological change is at least partly endogenous, that is, a consequence of investment expenditures by private firms and government in R & D. To be sure, there is a certain unpredictable aspect to innovations: science fiction writers may speculate about the discoveries of the next century, but who at the beginning of the nineteenth century could have predicted the transistor, the laser, superconductivity, atomic energy, and the myriad of other breakthroughs that have lead to improvements in productivity? Still, by and large, if more money is spent on research, there will be more discoveries. Research is like drilling for oil: you can't be sure where you will find oil, but with a well-designed exploration strategy, there is a high likelihood that the more you spend on exploration, the more oil you will find. At least for a long while, increased expenditures on R & D can sustain increased rates of growth in productivity.

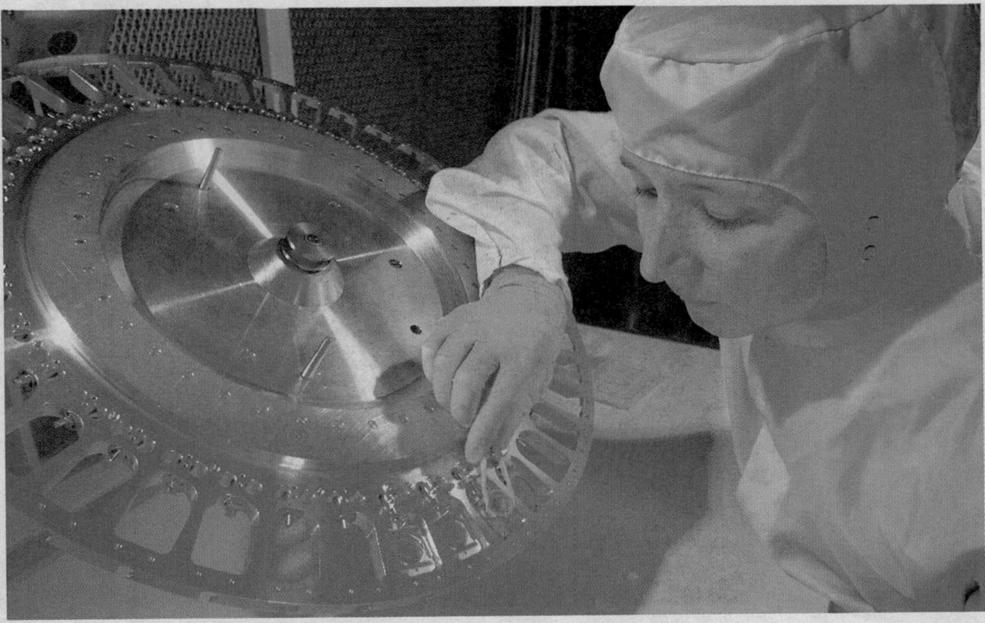

ment has had a credible record of picking winners—including, in recent years, the development of computers, the Internet, and the support of the computer chip industry. Furthermore, recent technology programs have introduced reforms to enhance the likelihood of success, including requiring recipients to put up a considerable amount of their own capital and subjecting applicants to a stiff competitive process in which independent experts are used to judge the likely significance of any spillovers.

POLICY PERSPECTIVE: FLAT PANEL DISPLAYS

Flat panel displays are the kinds of screens used in laptop computers. There are compact and have a myriad of uses, both civilian and military. In 1994 the Department of Defense announced its first major dual-use technology initiative, the support of production and research in flat panel displays in the United States. At the time, almost all such displays were imported from Japan. The Department of Defense worried that without a domestic source of these important high-technology components, the U.S. defense industry could be at a disadvantage. But while an important component in military computers, they also have obvious civilian uses. It made no sense simply to support the technology for the military.

Needless to say, the initiative received a mixed reception. Critics worried that it opened the door to a more aggressive industrial policy. Since much of modern technology had military uses, did this mean that the U.S. government was opening the door to support of any segment of the industry that failed the test of international competition? Advocates welcomed the explicit recognition that defense and civilian technologies are closely related, and that the most cost-effective way of providing for the military may be by providing broader-based civilian support.

Indeed, advocates of technology expenditures argue that the government has long had a policy of supporting technology—in effect an industrial policy—under the guise of the Defense Department. The issue, from their perspective, is whether, with the end of the Cold War, there should be a redeployment of expenditures toward research with more explicit nondefense benefits.

Another major policy debate has centered around the extent to which R & D should be cut, either to finance deficit reduction or tax cuts. Advocates say that deficit reduction and tax cuts will spur economic growth, while critics say that such policies are likely to be counterproductive, given the high returns to R & D and its crucial role in economic advances.

FACTORS CONTRIBUTING TO PRODUCTIVITY GROWTH

Savings and Investment (capital accumulation)
Improved quality of labor force
Reallocation of labor from low-productivity sectors to high-productivity sectors
Technological progress

TOTAL FACTOR PRODUCTIVITY

Low and declining rates of savings and investment, low and declining quality of U.S. education, and low and declining levels of government investment in civilian R & D may have all contributed to the low and declining rates of productivity growth in the United States. Economists have asked, can we quantify the roles of different factors? To do this, they have used a methodology called **total factor productivity analysis,** in which they ask, if there had been no technological change, based on what we know about the returns to and increases in the supply of capital (human and physical) and labor, how much would productivity have increased?

Suppose the share of capital in output—the amount of output attributable to capital (the total returns to capital divided by GDP)—is 20 percent, and the growth of capital is 10 percent. The share of capital in output (20 percent) multiplied by capital growth (10 percent) gives us the amount that capital growth contributes to the growth of output (2 percent).[2] The same logic applies to

[2]To see this, consider the change in output, ΔQ, "attributable" to an increase in capital by an amount ΔK, if r is the return to capital,

$$\Delta Q = r\Delta K.$$

The percentage increase in Q is just

$$\frac{\Delta Q}{Q} = \frac{r\Delta K}{Q}.$$

Multiplying the numerator and the denominator of the expression on the right-hand side by K, we obtain

$$\frac{\Delta Q}{Q} = \frac{rK}{Q}\frac{\Delta K}{K}.$$

labor. But capital and labor do not account for all of growth. The part of growth which cannot be explained by increases in capital and labor is called the increase in total factor productivity. The rate of total factor productivity increase is calculated as follows:

$$\text{TFP} = g_Q - (S_K \times g_K) - (S_L \times g_L)$$

where

S_K = share of capital in GDP
S_L = share of labor in GDP
g_Q = rate of growth of output
g_K = rate of growth of capital
g_L = rate of growth of labor.

The increase in total factor productivity reflects the increasing efficiency with which an economy's resources are used. Some of this is the result of research and development, but at least prior to 1973, much of the increase in total factor productivity could not be easily explained. The part that could not be explained was referred to as the **residual**—the part of growth that was "left over" after all the systematic sources of growth were taken into account. The spread of new production techniques, such as replaceable parts in the nineteenth century, the assembly line in the early twentieth century, and just-in-time inventory management techniques in recent years, are all examples of technological advances that bear little relationship to R & D expenditures, and thus form part of this "residual."

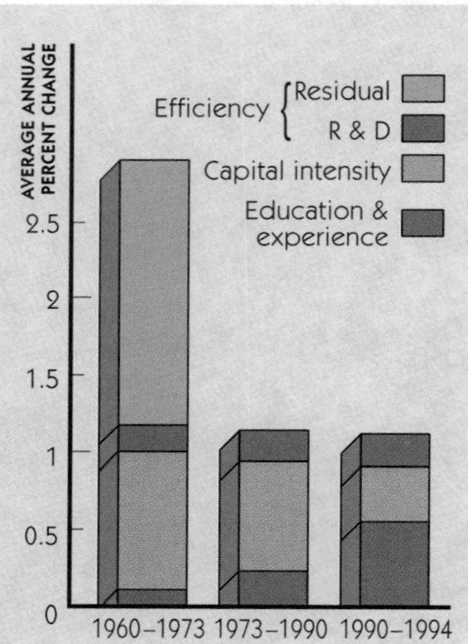

Figure 17.15 **GROWTH ACCOUNTING**

Over half of the decline in productivity growth since 1973 is left unexplained after accounting for changes in the education and experience of the work force, capital stock, and investments in R & D.

Figure 17.15 uses the methodology described earlier to analyze the sources of increase in productivity for three different time periods—1960 to 1973, 1973 to 1990, and 1990 to 1994.

Several conclusions emerge from the chart. First, the overall rate of productivity growth was much higher before 1973 than after—the slowdown in productivity growth to which we referred earlier. Second, since 1973 almost all productivity growth can be explained by increases in inputs (including research and development), while before 1973, there was a large residual. It is the decrease in the residual that appears to account for most of the slowdown in productivity. Third, since 1973, increases in capital have contributed less to economic growth, but increases in human capital (education and experience) have contributed more.

These results—and especially the fact that the unusually high rate of productivity growth in the 1950s and 1960s cannot be easily explained—pose major problems for those involved in long-term forecasting. Was the rapid growth of productivity in the 1950s and 1960s an aberration, a result of almost two decades of depression and war, with the consequent postponement of the introduction of new innovations into the economy? Or are the 1970s and

rK/Q is just the share of capital in GDP (rK is the total return to capital, and Q is output). Hence the percentage increase in output attributable to the increase in K is the percentage increase in capital times the share of capital.

USING ECONOMICS: CALCULATING TOTAL FACTOR PRODUCTIVITY

Between 1990 and 1994, it is estimated that GDP went up by 7.3 percent, the capital stock increased by 6.6 percent, and the labor force—adjusted for improvements in education—by 5.4 percent. If the share of capital in output is 30 percent and labor is 70 percent, what is the percent increase in total factor productivity over this period?

Start with the formula for total factor productivity (see p. 454):

$$\text{TFP} = g_Q - (S_K \times g_K) - (S_L \times g_L).$$

The percent increase in total factor productivity equals the growth in national output (g_Q) minus the growth in output attributable to capital ($S_K \times g_K$) minus the growth in output attributable to labor ($S_L \times g_L$). Substituting the data for the period from 1990 to 1994:

$$\text{TFP} = 7.3 - (.3 \times 6.6) - (.7 \times 5.4)$$
$$= 1.54.$$

Over the period, total factor productivity increased 1.54 percent.

1980s an aberration—a period of adjustment as fundamentally new technologies, such as computers, became more widely used, their full benefits only to be reaped in future decades?

GROWTH OF THE LABOR FORCE

Earlier in the chapter, we noted that the total growth rate of the economy equaled the growth in hours worked plus the growth in output per hour worked (productivity).

Slow growth in the mid-1990s was partially attributable to the slow pace of productivity, but it was also partially attributable to the slow growth of hours worked. In 1995, for instance, while the unemployment rate hovered around a relatively low 5.5 percent, hours worked increased by only around 1 percent, as compared to an average of 2.3 percent in the 1960s.

Growth in the labor force is driven by two factors: demographics and participation rates. In the Depression, birthrates declined, and then soared immediately after World War II (the baby boomer generation). Thus, as the baby boomers reached working age in the late 1960s and 1970s, the labor force increased markedly. At various times in the United States, immigration has also contributed substantially to the increase in labor force.

The decision whether to work—labor force participation—is affected by a variety of economic and noneconomic factors. There has been a marked increase in female labor force participation over the past quarter century, partially offset by a decrease in male labor force participation. Changes in attitudes

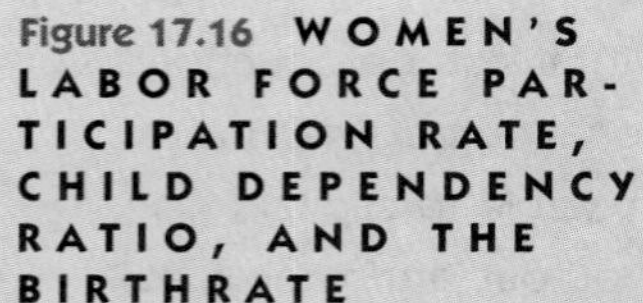

Figure 17.16 WOMEN'S LABOR FORCE PARTICIPATION RATE, CHILD DEPENDENCY RATIO, AND THE BIRTHRATE

The growth of female labor force participation has tapered in the 1990s, following rapid growth in the 1970s and 1980s. This trend appears to be associated with the leveling off of the child dependency ratio for women. By the 1990s, the affect of the reduced dependency ratio on labor force participation may have run its course. *Source: ERP* (1996), Chart 2-4.

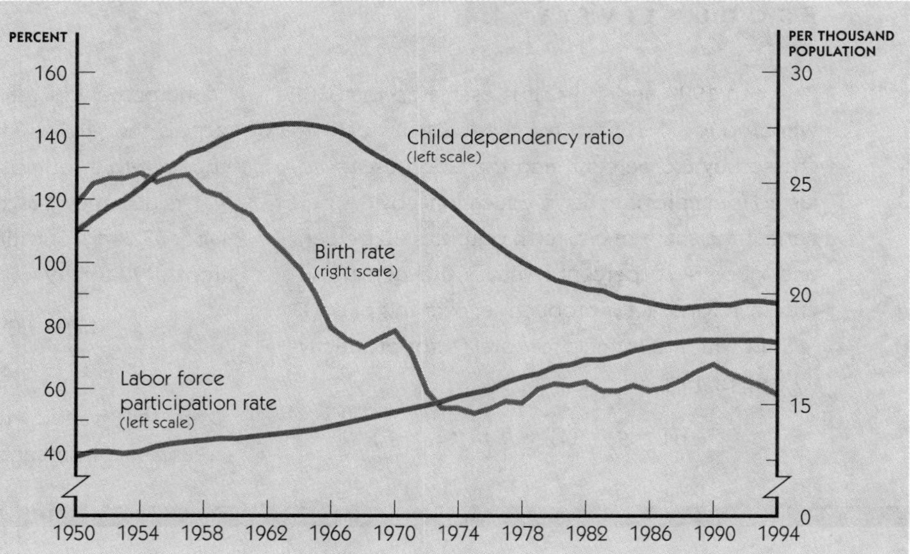

toward women working, especially when they have children, as well as changes in desired family sizes, reduced discrimination, and increased educational opportunities for women have all contributed to increased female participation. Improved Social Security and pension benefits have, on the other hand, led many men to retire earlier.

The lower than expected rate of growth of the U.S. labor force in the 1990s has been attributed largely to a slowing down of the rate of growth of female labor force participation. (See Figure 17.16.) One factor that may help explain this is changes in the number of dependents. As women postponed having children until they were older and as they chose to have smaller families, the number of dependents per working age woman declined. This decline appears to be associated with an increase in female participation. Now, this "dependency ratio" has leveled off, and so too has the increase in labor force participation.

Slower growth in the labor force caused by slower growth of the population has a markedly different effect than slower growth caused by lower productivity. The latter is associated with slower increases in standards of living. By contrast, faster population growth may give rise to congestion and place higher demands on the environment. On the other hand, some economists believe that the rapid expansion of the economy as it seeks to adapt to the increased labor force gives rise to a dynamism which generates increased productivity: increased labor force growth (at least to a point) helps cause increased productivity growth. But the causation also works in reverse: economic slowdowns, such as the Great Depression, lead to low birthrates.

THE COSTS OF ECONOMIC GROWTH

Faith in the virtues of economic progress is widespread. Few openly embrace the alternative of economic stagnation and lower standards of living. Yet not everyone benefits from changes in technology. In the early 1800s, English workmen destroyed labor-saving machinery rather than see it take over their jobs. They were referred to as **Luddites,** after their leader Ned Ludd, whose role may have been largely mythical. Concerns about workers thrown out of their jobs as a result of some innovation are no less real today.

What needs to be kept in mind, and has already been stressed earlier in the book, is that technological progress creates jobs as it destroys them. Of course, it can be hard to teach an old dog new tricks, so a middle-aged or older worker who loses her job may have real difficulty in getting another that is even nearly as good.

Not surprisingly, technical progress frequently meets with resistance. While there is growing acceptance that such resistance is futile—change will eventually come—and that the benefits of progress exceed the costs, there is also increasing recognition of the role of government in assisting individuals who are displaced by technological change in their transition to alternative employment. Such assistance can be thought of as a form of insurance. Most workers face the possibility that their jobs will be made technologically obsolete. Knowing that if they are thrown out of work for this reason they will be at least partially protected adds to a sense of security, something most workers value highly.

More generally, we saw in Part Two that in the long run, with flexible wages, the economy will create enough jobs to match the supply. In Part Three, we saw that in the short run, wage and price rigidity may lead to significant unemployment, but that there are government policies that can help ensure that the economy remains close to full employment. To the extent that government employs such policies, there will be fewer worries about jobs. There will be less resistance to new technologies that lead to job loss, as workers become more confident that the economy will at the same time generate new job opportunities.

ARE THERE LIMITS TO ECONOMIC GROWTH?

In the early 1800s, the famous British economist Thomas Malthus envisioned the future as one in which the ever-increasing labor force would push wages down to the subsistence level, or even lower. Any technological progress that occurred would, in his view, raise wages only temporarily. As the labor supply increased, wages would eventually fall back to the subsistence level.

Over the past century, there has been a decrease in the rate of population growth, a phenomenon perhaps as remarkable as the increase in the rate of technological progress. One might have expected improved medicine and health conditions to cause a population explosion, but the spread of birth control and family planning has had the opposite effect, at least in the more developed countries. Today family size has decreased to the point where in many countries population growth (apart from migration) has almost halted. Those who worry about the limits to growth today believe that *exhaustible* natural resources—like oil, natural gas, phosphorus, or potassium—may pose a limit to economic growth as they are used up in the ordinary course of production.

Most economists do not share this fear, believing that markets do provide incentives for wise use of most resources—that as any good becomes more scarce and its price rises, the search for substitutes will be stimulated. Thus, the rise in the price of oil led to smaller, more efficient cars, cooler but better insulated houses, and a search for alternative sources of energy like geothermal and synthetic fuels, all of which resulted in a decline in the consumption of oil.

Still, there is one area in which the price system does not work well—the area of externalities. Without government intervention, for example, producers have no incentive to worry about air and water pollution. And in our globally connected world, what one country does results in externalities for others. Cutting down the rain forest in Brazil, for example, may have worldwide climatic consequences. The less developed countries feel that they can ill afford the costs of pollution control, when they can barely pay the price of any industrialization. Most economists do not believe that we face an either/or choice. We do not have to abandon growth to preserve our environment. Nevertheless, a sensitivity to the quality of our environment may affect how we go about growing. This sensitivity is building a new consensus in favor of **sustainable development,** that is, growth not based simply on the exploitation of natural resources and the environment in a way that cannot be sustained. In many cases, policies can be devised that improve economic efficiency, and thus promote economic growth, at the same time that they decrease adverse environmental effects. These include elimination of energy subsidies and certain agricultural subsidies that induce farmers to use excessive amounts of fertilizers and pesticides.

THE PROGNOSIS

Though this century has been marked by large increases in productivity, the rate of productivity growth has not been steady. There have been periods of relative stagnation as well as periods in which the economy has burst forth with energy and growth. Is the decline in productivity growth in the United

States just a passing phase? Or were the high rates of productivity growth during the 1950s and 1960s the aberration?

The analysis of this chapter suggests grounds for both pessimism and optimism. There is no quick or easy reversal of many of the factors hampering productivity growth, such as the low rate of private savings. But some of the factors hampering productivity growth are more easily altered. These include the failure of government to improve the economy's infrastructure, the large fiscal deficit, and the low level of expenditures on research and development, at least expenditures directed at improving the economy's productivity rather than increasing military prowess.

Most economists think it unlikely that the United States will ever again be in the position of technological dominance it held for so long. But there is widespread optimism that the U.S. economy can return to a higher level of productivity growth, provided the right government policies are pursued.

REVIEW AND PRACTICE

SUMMARY

1. The United States experienced a marked slowdown in the rate of productivity growth in the early 1970s, compared with the preceding two decades. Even seemingly small declines in the rate of increase in productivity will have a powerful adverse effect on the standard of living over a generation or two.

2. There are four major sources of productivity growth: increases in the accumulation of capital goods (investment); a higher quality of the labor force; greater efficiency in allocating resources; and technological change. Since 1973 almost all of the increase in productivity can be attributed to increases in capital, improvements in human capital, and expenditures on research and development. In recent years, the relative role of human capital has increased and the role of physical capital has decreased.

3. The rate of savings in the United States has declined in recent years. Some of the reasons are improved government retirement programs, more extensive insurance coverage and greater ease in borrowing, and changes in social attitudes.

4. Because private savings does not respond much to after-tax rates of return (the interest elasticity is low), it is difficult to increase savings by providing tax incentives. Reducing the government deficit—such as occurred beginning in 1993—may be more effective.

5. Increases in human capital—improved education—are a major source of productivity increases. There are large returns to investments in education. While the U.S. educational system has important strengths,

there are serious concerns about the quality of education American students are receiving in preparation for the labor force and about the number of scientists and engineers being trained.

6. The twentieth century has been marked by shifts in the U.S. economy from an agricultural base to an industrial base and more recently to a service base. Some economists think that the potential for technological progress is less in the service sector than in the industrial sector, and this accounts for part of the productivity slowdown.

7. Improvements in technology, partly as a result of expenditures on research and development (R & D) are a major source of increases in productivity. Government supports R & D through both direct spending and tax incentives, though direct support for R & D that is not defense-related has actually declined during the past quarter century.

8. Some of the changes in the rate of growth of the economy are a result of changes in the rate of growth of the labor force. This is partly a result of demographics—changes in the number of children born in different years—and partly a result of decisions to participate in the labor force. There has been an overall trend for decreased labor force participation by men and increased labor force participation by women.

9. There has long been concern that certain natural resources (like oil) will someday run out, causing economic growth to halt. However, most economists would argue that the price of resources will increase as they become more scarce, and this will encourage both greater conservation and a search for substitutes.

10. Sustainable development requires growth strategies that use resources and the environment in ways that do not jeopardize future potential growth.

Key Terms

capital deepening
life-cycle theory of savings
infrastructure
total factor productivity analysis
Luddites
sustainable development

Review Questions

1. True or false: "Since growth-oriented policies might have an effect of only a percent or two per year, they are not worth worrying much about." Explain.

2. What are the four possible sources of productivity growth?

3. What are the various explanations of the slowdown of the rate of increase in productivity?

4. What are the components of overall U.S. savings, and how did they change in the 1980s?

5. What are some reasons for the decrease in the savings rate in recent years?

6. Will government policies to raise the rate of return on savings, such as exempting interest from taxes, necessarily lead to much increased savings?

7. What is the link between changes in savings and changes in investment in a closed economy, in a small open economy, and in a large open economy like the United States? What is the link between changes in the capital stock (investment) and the rate of growth of productivity in the short run? What is the link between changes in the capital stock and the *level* of productivity (output per worker) in the long run? What is meant by capital deepening?

8. What policies might the government use to increase investment in R & D?

9. What is total factor productivity and how is it measured?

10. What are some costs of economic growth? Short of seeking to restrain growth, how might government deal with these costs?

11. What are some of the concerns about limits to economic growth? How have they been overcome in the past?

PROBLEMS

1. Will the following changes increase or decrease the rate of household savings?
   (a) The proportion of people in the 45–64 age bracket increases.
   (b) Government programs provide secure retirement benefits.
   (c) Credit cards become much more prevalent.
   (d) The proportion of people in the 21–45 age bracket increases.
   (e) Government programs to guarantee student loans are enacted.

2. Explain how the following factors would increase or decrease the average productivity of labor:
   (a) successful reforms of the educational system;
   (b) the entry of new workers into the economy;
   (c) earlier retirement;
   (d) high unemployment rates during a recession.

3. Suppose a firm is considering spending \$1 million on R & D projects, which it believes will translate into patents that it will be able to sell for \$2.5 million in ten years. Assume that the firm ignores risk. If the interest rate is 10 percent, is the firm likely to attempt these R & D projects? If the government offers a 20 percent R & D tax credit, how does the firm's calculation change?

4. Explain why a rapid influx of workers might result in a lower output per worker (a reduction in productivity). Would the effect on productivity depend on the skill level of the new workers?

5. Explain, using supply and demand diagrams, how a technological change such as computerization could lead to lower wages of unskilled workers and higher wages of skilled workers.

6. Using the model of Chapter 6, discuss the effect on the level of investment for an open economy of (a) an increased government deficit; (b) an increased government expenditure, financed by taxes on households that reduce their disposable income; (c) an investment tax credit. How will such policies affect future living standards of those living in the country?

CHAPTER 18

Deficits and Deficit Reduction

We saw in Chapter 7 that beginning in 1981, the United States began to run high fiscal deficits. The increased deficits led to increasing debt, and an increasing burden on the government simply to pay interest on the debt. Beginning in 1993 the deficit was finally reduced not only as a percentage of GDP but in absolute terms—with the debt/GDP ratio leveling off and finally beginning to decline—and in 1995 there emerged a bipartisan consensus on working toward a balanced budget. Still there remained debates about how deficit reduction should be accomplished, and whether even the most aggressive proposed actions addressed the long-term problems of the country.

This chapter reviews the origins of the deficit problem and the debate about the consequences of deficits and how the deficit problem should be addressed. The final section addresses the long-term problems facing the United States and most other industrialized countries.

KEY QUESTIONS

1. What gave rise to the fiscal deficit? And why is it so difficult to reduce?
2. What are the central economic issues in the debate about how deficits should be reduced?
3. What are the procedural reforms that have been proposed to ensure that deficits do not emerge in the future, and what are the problems with these reforms?
4. What are the long-term problems facing the United States and other industrialized countries that if not adequately addressed are likely to result in a deficit problem emerging in the future, even if the deficit is reduced now?

THE SOURCES OF THE CURRENT U.S. DEFICIT PROBLEM

The current U.S. deficit problem began around 1981. As we saw in Chapter 7, federal budget deficits soared in the 1980s and early 1990s, with the real deficit peaking at more than $290 billion in 1992. Figure 18.1 tells the same story in terms of the ratio of the deficit to GDP. The deficit as a percentage of GDP rose to a peacetime record of 6.3 percent in 1983, hovering between 3 and 5 percent for most of the remainder of the decade, and gradually decreasing from 4.9 percent in 1992 to around 2 percent by the mid-1990s.

A good way to pose the question of what caused the soaring budget deficit is to ask: What changed between the 1970s (and earlier decades) and the 1980s? There are five main answers to this question.

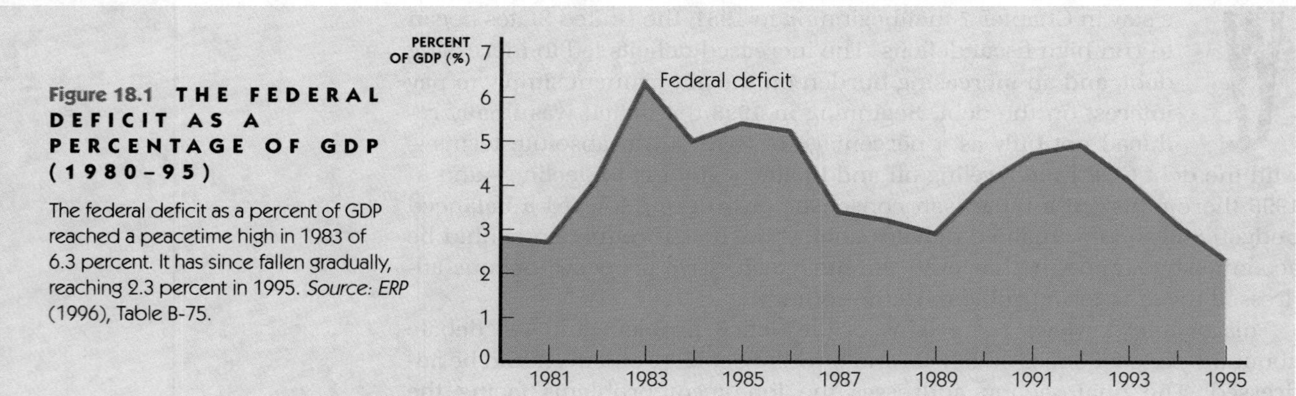

Figure 18.1 THE FEDERAL DEFICIT AS A PERCENTAGE OF GDP (1980–95)

The federal deficit as a percent of GDP reached a peacetime high in 1983 of 6.3 percent. It has since fallen gradually, reaching 2.3 percent in 1995. *Source: ERP* (1996), Table B-75.

Reduced Federal Taxes During the 1970s, federal taxes usually collected between 18 and 19 percent of GDP. In 1980 and 1981 that percentage climbed to over 20 percent. (Remember, 1 percent of a multitrillion-dollar economy will be tens of billions of dollars.) Tax cuts enacted early in the Reagan presidency pushed the federal tax take back down to its historical range of 18–19 percent of GDP. The slight increase in taxes in 1993 has not altered this basic picture.

Higher Defense Spending Federal defense spending fell during the 1970s, as the Vietnam War came to an end, from 8.4 percent of GDP in 1970 to 4.9 percent of GDP in 1979. In 1979, though, the Soviet Union invaded Afghanistan, and President Carter called for a large defense buildup. After Ronald Reagan was elected president in 1980, he followed through on these plans. From 1983 to 1988, defense spending exceeded 6 percent of GDP. With the end of the Cold War, there has been a reduction in defense spending to under 4 percent of GDP. Though the threat of small wars in various parts of the world has kept the "peace dividend" smaller than many had hoped, the reduction in defense spending as a percentage of GDP played an important part in the deficit reductions after 1993.

Higher Social Spending on the Elderly As the elderly population in the United States has grown, not only absolutely but as a proportion of the population, federal expenditures on programs like Social Security and Medicare (providing health care to the aged) have expanded dramatically. These programs averaged 5.0 percent of GDP in the 1970s, but increased to over 6 percent of GDP by 1980 and close to 7 percent by 1982. By the mid-1990s they constitute 7 percent of GDP.

Increasing Health Care Expenditures Through Medicare and Medicaid (the government program providing health care to the poor), the government has assumed an increasing share of total health care expenditures, to the point where today, the federal government alone pays 30 percent of all health care expenditures. Health care expenditures themselves have soared. Through the 1980s and early 1990s these expenditures were increasing at close to 12 percent per year, doubling every six years. A number of initiatives undertaken during the Bush and Clinton administrations have brought the rate of increase down to between 8 percent and 10 percent, a number still far higher than the rate of income growth.

Higher Interest Payments Like other borrowers, the federal government pays interest. During the 1970s, federal interest payments were about 1.5 percent of GDP. But from 1983 to 1990 they exceeded 3 percent of GDP. The main reason was the increasing deficit. If the debt in 1995 were the same as it had been at the start of the Reagan era in 1981 (after adjusting for inflation), the government would be running a balanced budget, rather than a deficit of $160 billion. Deficits, through interest payments, feed on themselves.

Factors Not Contributing to the Deficit Problem In a sense, any expenditure can be thought of as contributing to the deficit problem—if that expenditure were reduced, other things equal, the deficit would be reduced. But some factors

Close-up: Measuring the Budget Deficit—What's Large, What's Real, and What's Right?

The deficits of the 1980s and 1990s have been huge. At its peak in 1992 the dollar figure was $290 billion. By 1996 it had been brought down to $117 billion. But are dollar amounts the right way to measure the size and importance of deficits? Shouldn't we take into consideration the effects of inflation and the growth of the overall economy?

Robert Eisner of Northwestern University argues for focusing on the overall increase in the *real* debt—that is, the debt adjusted for changes in the price level. With total debt outstanding to the public of approximately $3.6 trillion, an inflation rate of 3 percent implies a reduction of the real value of the debt of $108 billion per year. This decrease in the real value of the outstanding debt, in Eisner's view, should be subtracted from any increase in debt due to the deficit. In fiscal 1996, this inflation-adjusted deficit was only $9 billion, compared to the measured deficit of $117 billion.

According to this definition, the Carter administration actually ran an inflation-adjusted surplus due to the effects of inflation on the value of the debt. By contrast, the relatively low rates of inflation during the Reagan and Bush administrations were not enough to offset the large deficits due to expenditures far exceeding revenues.

The full-employment or structural deficit takes into account the level of economic activity in the economy, as we saw in Chapter 13. It asks, what would the deficit have been had the economy been operating at full employment? For instance, in 1991, as the economy was in recession, the deficit was officially $269 billion—the largest in history up to that point—but the structural deficit was $191 billion, still large by any standards, but $78 billion less than the actual deficit. But the Reagan years look particularly bad from this perspective, since, except during wars, the economy had never previously run large structural deficits.

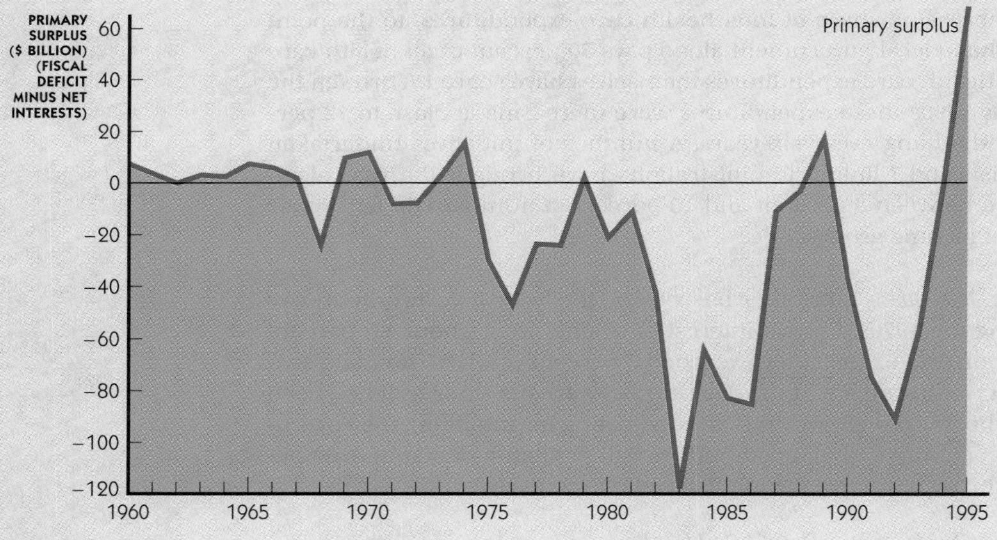

In recent years, as well as in the years immediately following World Wars I and II, the U.S. government was saddled with a huge debt. The interest payments on this inherited debt make it particularly difficult to attain a balanced budget. The primary deficit asks what the deficit would have been had there been no inherited debt; that is, it subtracts interest payments from the deficit. If the government is running a primary surplus, it means that revenues more than cover current expenditures. The government ran a primary surplus for only the second time since 1979 in 1995 (see figure above).

Source: ERP (1996), Table B-76.

commonly given credit for the deficit problem do not deserve the blame they receive. For instance, polls suggest that many Americans believe welfare payments and foreign assistance are at fault. Yet, general welfare payments, such as aid to families with dependent children (AFDC) and food stamps, are less than 4 percent of the federal budget, and their share of the federal budget has decreased in recent decades. Under the AFDC program, benefits per family fell by 55 percent from 1970 to 1993. Similarly foreign assistance is minuscule—about 1 percent of the federal budget. Reducing welfare payments and foreign assistance would still leave a substantial deficit.

FACTORS CONTRIBUTING TO THE DEFICIT PROBLEM

Reduced taxation
Increased defense spending
Higher social spending on elderly
Increased public health costs
Higher interest payments

CONSEQUENCES OF GOVERNMENT DEFICITS

When the government runs a deficit, it must borrow to pay the difference between its expenditures and its revenues. When it runs a deficit year after year, it must borrow year after year. The cumulated value of these borrowings is the *federal debt*—what the government owes. Figure 18.2 shows the soaring federal debt. The immediate consequence of the soaring federal debt is that

Figure 18.2 THE FEDERAL DEBT

The debt represents the accumulation of previous deficits. Panel A shows the federal debt (in real dollars) soaring enormously in the 1980s; by the early 1990s it had far exceeded the previous record set in World War II. Panel B shows the debt as a percentage of GDP. While the real debt continued to increase in the mid-1990s, as a percentage of GDP it had finally begun to stabilize.

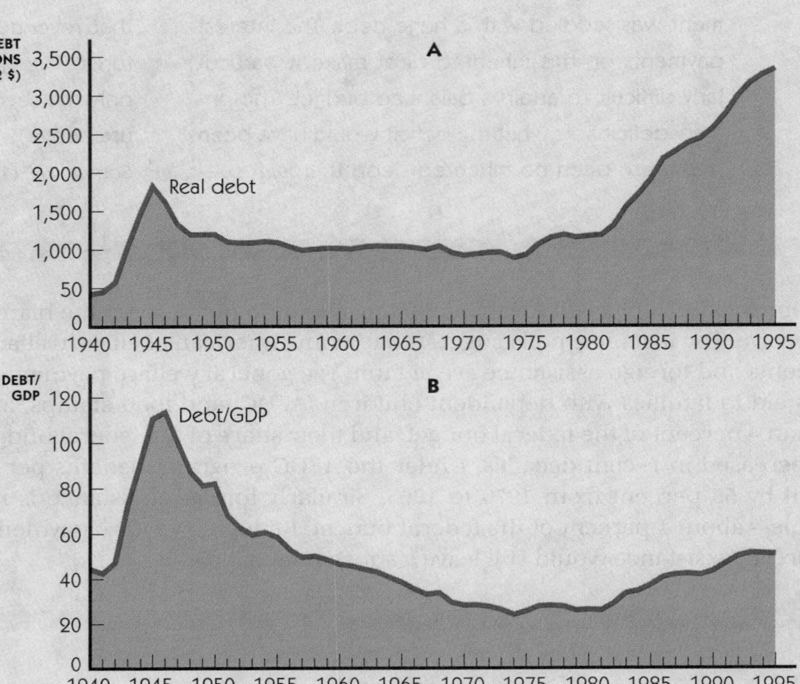

the government has to pay out more and more in interest—one of the factors that we identified earlier as contributing itself to the deficit.

Economists have traditionally argued that government borrowing, just like individual borrowing, makes sense or does not make sense according to the purpose for which the money is used. It makes sense to borrow to buy a house that you will live in for many years or a car that you will drive for several years. In that way, you spread out paying for the item as you use it. It makes economic sense to borrow money for an educational degree that will lead to a higher-paying job in the future. But if you are paying this year for the vacation from two years ago, maybe you should chop up your credit cards!

Countries are in a similar situation. Borrowing to finance a road, school, or industrial project that will be used for many years may be quite appropriate. Borrowing to pay for projects that are never completed (or perhaps are never even started) or borrowing to finance this year's government salaries poses real problems. Many governments have taken on more debt than they could comfortably pay off, forcing them to raise taxes sharply and reduce living standards. Others have simply failed to repay, jeopardizing their ability to borrow in the future.

Financing government expenditures by borrowing rather than by raising taxes results in higher levels of consumption in the short run (since disposable income is higher). When the economy is at full employment, higher consumption implies there is less room for investment. To maintain the economy at full employment without inflation, the Federal Reserve Board has to increase interest rates. Deficit financing leads to lower investment, and thus, in the long run, to lower output and consumption.

Reducing the deficit has the opposite effect: it allows interest rates to fall, stimulating investment, and thus promoting economic growth and better future living standards.

How Future Generations Are Affected by the Deficits

By borrowing, the government places the burden of reduced consumption on future generations. The U.S. government partly financed World War II by borrowing rather than raising taxes. Suppose that the bonds it issued were purchased by forty-year-old workers. Then thirty years later, as these forty-year-olds enter retirement, the government decides to pay off the bonds by raising taxes on those who are then in the labor force. In effect, the government is transferring funds from these younger workers to those who *were* the workers during the war, who are now seventy and retired. Thus, part of the cost of the war is borne by the generation who entered the work force *after* the war. The lifetime consumption of those who were forty during the war is little affected. They might otherwise have put their savings into stocks or bonds issued by firms; the war (to the extent it is financed by debt, or bonds) affects the form of their savings, but not the total amount they have to spend over their lifetime.

Alternative Perspectives on the Burden of the Debt

Though the discussion so far represents the current dominant views, some believe that these views overstate the burden of the debt. Two different reasons are given.

The "Debt Does Not Matter Because We Owe It to Ourselves" Argument

It used to be argued in the United States that the fiscal deficit does not matter because we simply owe the money to ourselves. The budget deficit was compared to the effect of one brother borrowing from another on the total welfare of the family. One member of the family may be better off, another worse off, but the indebtedness does not really matter much to the family as a whole. Financing government expenditures by debt, it was argued, could lead to a transfer of resources between generations, but this transfer would still keep all the buying power in the hands of U.S. citizens.

We now recognize that this argument is wrong on three counts. First, even if we owe the money to ourselves, the debt affects investment and thus future wages and productivity, as noted. And second, today we do not in fact owe the money to ourselves. The United States is borrowing abroad and becoming indebted to foreigners. The consequences of the country spending beyond its means are no different from those of a family spending beyond its means. Eventually it has to pay the price of the consumption binge. In the case of a national consumption binge, it is future generations that have to pay the price.

Third, simply to pay interest on the debt requires high levels of taxes, and taxes introduce distortions into the economy, discouraging work and savings. (There is some disagreement among economists about the *quantitative* significance of this effect.

RICARDIAN EQUIVALENCE

There is a more recent argument that, in the face of increased deficits, individuals save more. Robert Barro of Harvard University—developing an argument made (and later rejected) by David Ricardo, one of the nineteenth century's greatest economists—believes that individuals care so much about their children that they increase their bequests when they see their offspring faced with future indebtedness caused by government deficits. To be able to be more generous in their bequests, they increase their household savings by exactly the amount of the increase in the deficit: national savings does not change. The increased government dissaving is fully offset. This view is called **Ricardian equivalence** because it contends that taxation and deficits are *equivalent* means of financing expenditures.

The evidence does not support Barro's theoretical contention. Increased government deficits may lead to slightly higher household savings, but far too little to offset fully those deficit increases. In the late 1980s and early 1990s, when the deficit was running at more than 5 percent of GDP, the household savings rate was only 3 to 4 percent. If Barro's theory were correct, then in the absence of the government deficit, household savings rates would have been an implausibly low number between minus 1 and minus 2 percent.

CONSEQUENCES OF GOVERNMENT DEFICITS

1. Some of the burden of current expenditures is shifted to future generations directly.
2. Issuing bonds may decrease investment and thus make future generations worse off indirectly.
3. Foreign indebtedness may increase, reducing future standards of living.
4. Government dissaving has not been offset by private savings.

ADDRESSING THE DEFICIT PROBLEM

At one level of analysis, reducing the deficit is a simple matter: either increase taxes or reduce expenditures. Currently, there appears limited public taste for tax increases, even on the wealthy. Thus discussions have focused on improving the efficiency of government or cutting back on government programs.

All through the years that the deficit was rising, politicians were arguing that both of these should be done; and yet remarkably little progress was made until 1993. The question is why?

CUTTING BACK ON GOVERNMENT PROGRAMS

Understanding how government spends money helps explain why reducing expenditures proved so difficult during the 1980s. There are two basic types of government expenditures: **discretionary** and **nondiscretionary.** Discretionary expenditures—which include expenditures on military, government operation, and most education and training programs—are decided on an annual basis. Each year, Congress and the president have the *discretion* to change their levels. By contrast, nondiscretionary spending is made up of interest payments on the national debt and **entitlements,** where the law specifies certain benefits—such as Social Security, Medicare, and food stamps—to which individuals who meet certain criteria are *entitled,* and expenditure is then determined simply by the cost of those entitlements.

THE FAILURES OF THE 1980s

President Reagan had made a commitment not to cut Social Security and to increase expenditures on defense. With these commitments, to eliminate the deficit would have required drastic—and seemingly unacceptable—cutbacks in other programs. The total of all nonmilitary discretionary expenditures was less than $300 billion, so that it was essentially impossible to eliminate a $200 billion deficit—which by 1992 had increased to close to $300 billion—simply by cutting back on these programs.

The challenge of reducing the deficit and keeping it low remains much the same today: as Figure 18.3 shows, nondefense discretionary expenditures represent a relatively small fraction of total government expenditures. Entitlement expenditures, especially those directed at the aged—Social Security, Medicare, and large parts of the Medicaid program—are large and anticipated to increase markedly as the baby boomers reach retirement. Unless these programs are reformed, there will be continuing pressures on other parts of the budget. If it is assumed that taxes cannot be increased and defense expenditures cannot be decreased, then the burden of adjustment falls on nondefense discretionary expenditures.

Figure 18.3 THE CHALLENGE OF REDUCING FEDERAL SPENDING

A large proportion of federal spending is devoted to three areas: defense, entitlement programs, and interest payments. To reduce federal spending, large cuts must be made in at least some of these categories, since other areas of spending are simply not large enough to make much difference. *Sources: ERP* (1995), Chart 2-12; *ERP* (1996), Table B-77.

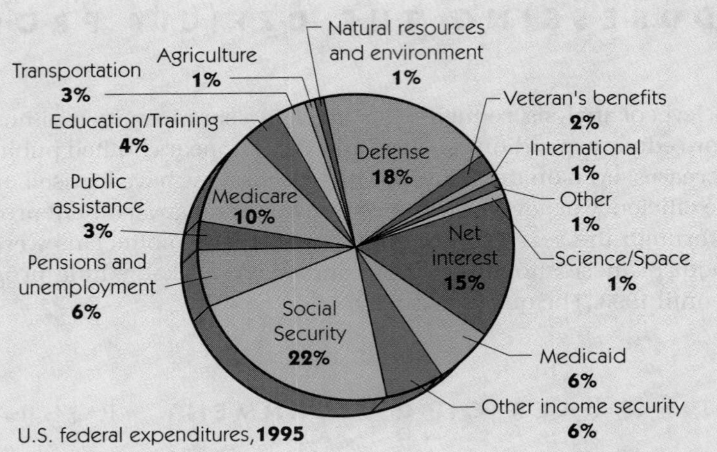

Ongoing Issues in Deficit Reduction

By late 1995, a bipartisan consensus had been reached that the deficit should be eliminated within a few years. Between 1992 and 1996, the deficit was in fact reduced by 60 percent, and in real terms, and as a percentage of GDP, the reduction was even more dramatic. The deficit reduction debate really became a debate over the size of government. One side argued that expenditures and taxes should be reduced; reduced taxes, especially on capital gains, would stimulate economic growth. The other argued that these further cuts in expenditures would jeopardize investments in human capital and technology, which had high returns, and accordingly would be counterproductive—growth might actually be retarded. They argued further that while it was clear that the benefits of capital gains tax reduction went disproportionately to the wealthy—who had already received most of the benefits from economic growth over the past two decades—it was not clear that there would be significant growth benefits. There was little evidence linking variations in a capital gains tax to either savings, investment, or economic growth.[1] Indeed, because some forms of investment would, with a capital gains tax reduction, receive preferential tax treatment, the allocation of resources would be distorted and economic efficiency, and possibly growth, impaired.

While there was a wide consensus on the desirability of deficit reduction, there remained some who argued that tax reduction was more important than deficit reduction. Thus, even if one could not reduce expenditures, the beneficial effects of lower taxes (increased incentives to work and save) exceeded the detrimental effects of the resulting increased deficits. Most

[1]Earlier discussions noted that the savings rate was not very sensitive to returns.

Using Economics: Calculating the Impact of Deficit Reduction on Growth

Deficit reduction is supposed to make room for more private investment, and thus stimulate economic growth. The question is, by how much? Consider the consequences of reducing a $150 billion deficit to zero. The lower deficit will reduce interest rates, increase investment, reduce foreign borrowing, and perhaps lower domestic savings. Assuming that savings are not interest elastic, we noted earlier that increasing national savings by $100—say by reducing the deficit—increases investment by $50. Accordingly, reducing the deficit by $150 billion increases investment by $75 billion. If the capital stock is around $15 trillion, this represents a .5 percent increase in the capital stock.* If the share of capital is .2, an increase in the capital stock by .5 percent should increase output by .1 percent. This may seem like a small number—but cumulated over a large number of years, it can make a large difference.

*Recall the discussion of Chapter 17, where we showed that the increase in growth (percent increase in output) attributable to an increase in the capital stock was equal to the share of capital times the percent increase in the capital stock.

economists remained skeptical of these so-called **supply siders**, who emphasized the increased inputs of capital and labor from lower taxes. Critics of the supply-siders argued that there was little statistical evidence in support of such large supply responses, and that the "Reagan" experiment of lowering tax rates (the top tax rate was brought down from 70 percent to 50 percent in 1981, and then to 31 percent in 1986) had proven itself a failure, leading to huge deficits.

Improving the Budgetary Process

The persistence of the deficit led many to argue that there should be a change in the way budgets are adopted. In this section, we consider two such changes. One of these has already been implemented; the other remains under discussion.

Budget Enforcement Act and Scoring

In 1990 Congress passed the Budget Enforcement Act, designed to reduce the likelihood of runaway deficits. Whenever Congress passes a new program, it is required to provide new taxes to pay for it, or to find offsetting expenditure

Policy Perspective: Scoring the Clinton Deficit Reduction Package

The Congressional Budget Office (CBO) has had a long reputation for being nonpartisan. The director of the CBO at the time that Clinton was introducing his managed health care reforms was Bob Reischauer, a Democrat; yet because he said that the evidence on the extent to which managed care would reduce health care costs was not clear, he refused to credit the programs with much savings. The nonpartisan nature of the CBO was reaffirmed when, under the new director, June O'Neill, appointed when the Republicans gained control of the House and Senate, the CBO refused to credit the Republican managed health care reforms with as much savings as they would have liked.

On other issues, however, critics worried whether the CBO was departing from its traditional nonpartisan view. Consider the question: How much would interest rates fall as a result of deficit reduction? Presumably, as government expenditures decreased, interest rates would fall, as the Fed took actions to ensure that the economy remained at full employment. To be sure, how much interest rates would fall was problematic, since it depended on the interest elasticity of investment (the percentage increase in investment resulting from a 1 percent decrease in the interest rate), of which economists had markedly different estimates. Still, she concluded that interest rates would fall by approximately 1.7 percentage points. But, the CBO refused to give the Clinton deficit reduction package *any* credit for interest rate reduction, since in their estimates, the Clinton budget deficit reduction package did not *fully* achieve a balanced budget. Critics of the CBO argued that, while they might disagree with the CBO assessment of the magnitude of the expenditure cuts, the cuts were sufficiently severe that there should have been *some* interest rate reductions—roughly in proportion to the reductions in the expenditures.

Other critics pointed out that even the CBO's estimate of the magnitude of the deficit (apart from interest rate reductions) was problematic, since these estimates were more conservative than not only those of the Clinton administration, but also of the consensus of business forecasters; and that its estimate of the rate of increase of health care costs failed to incorporate recent changes in trends in those variables, and was higher than those of the career actuaries who had for years collected the data and provided the estimates. But supporters of the CBO pointed out that in using those numbers, the CBO was simply continuing to use numbers similar to those that it had used under Democratic leadership. If there was a fault, it was not with partisan leadership, but with the longstanding methods of the CBO.

cuts. The Congressional Budget Office (CBO)—ostensibly a nonpartisan group of professionals—"scores" the program—that is, calculates how much it will cost. Inevitably, there are issues of judgment involved. Thus, in recent debates on health care reform, the CBO argued that managed care would, in the short run, result in only limited savings. Had they scored managed care as generating large savings, it might have been far easier to adopt health care reforms.

CAPITAL BUDGETS

Businesses emphasize the distinction between expenditures to buy machines—capital expenditures—and other expenditures. Investments enhance the firm's ability to produce in the future. We argued earlier that there was a marked difference between borrowing to make an investment and borrowing to buy a vacation. Government accounting systems do not make a distinction, though businesses do. Not only do businesses distinguish between the kinds of expenditure in their annual reports, but they maintain capital accounts which show their assets (including machines) and liabilities.

Some have argued that government should have a capital budget, which would identify expenditures on investments. While some countries have done so, the United States has not, partially because of the political problems of defining investments. Most capital budgets only include investments in physical objects, like roads; and education advocates have worried that such a capital budget would divert resources away from human capital formation, from education and research. Similarly, health advocates argue that providing good health care for children is an investment in their future, raising their productivity and lowering future expenditures on medical care.

OTHER STRATEGIES

Two other suggestions for improving the budgetary process have been widely discussed. One, the **line item veto,** gives the president the right to veto particular expenditures within a budget bill. It went into effect in January 1997. Previously, he could only accept or reject the entire bill. He was loathe to veto a large bill for, say, national defense, simply because of some small wasteful expenditure that goes to benefit the constituents of some Congressman. (See Policy Perspective box.) The other is a constitutional amendment, called the **balanced budget amendment,** requiring Congress to adopt a balanced budget. We discussed this earlier, in Chapter 13. Such an amendment has come within a few votes of passing several times. Advocates say it would (by definition) force fiscal responsibility; the government would have to come up with a balanced budget. Critics point out the severe problems of implementation: What happens if Congress fails to comply, for instance because revenues fall short because of an economic recession? Balancing the budget on the basis of prospective expenditures and revenues requires someone to make estimates. Who should do that, and how can one ensure that it is done in a nonpolitical way? Many economists criticize the balanced budget amendment because it takes away one of the main tools of economic stabilization; it will make it more difficult to maintain the economy at full employment, putting almost all of the responsibility on monetary policy. Those who are less confident of the ability of monetary policy to counter quickly a severe recession are particularly worried about such amendments. Some of the proposals—though not the ones that have come close to passage by Congress—have included escape clauses in the event of a recession.

Policy Perspective: The Line Item Veto

Another proposal designed to reduce expenditures is the line-item veto, giving the president the right to veto particular expenditure items within the appropriations bills sent to him by Congress. Members of Congress frequently put into such bills "pork" provisions—such as new courthouses in their districts—and the line item veto is designed to allow the president to ferret out such expenditures.

Several states have such provisions. The evidence suggests that expenditures in states with the line item veto are no less than in states without it. One reason may be that governors are then brought into the "deals" which are inevitably put together to enable legislation to get passed.

While many members of Congress promised to support the line item veto, they have been worried that doing so would increase the president's power. In 1996, Congress passed and the president signed into law the line item veto.

The Long-Term Problem: Entitlements and the Aged

Even if the United States is able to eliminate its deficit over the next few years, the long-term problem will persist: entitlement expenditures for Medicare and Social Security are likely to soar in the coming decades. The reasons are twofold. First, the number of elderly in the U.S. population will increase dramatically, vastly increasing the number of eligible recipients for Social Security and Medicare. Second, health care costs for the elderly may continue to increase.

The Growing U.S. Elderly Population

The twenty years following World War II saw a huge increase in births in the United States, giving rise to the generation commonly known as the baby boomers. During the early decades of the twenty-first century, the baby boomers will reach retirement age. At the same time, life expectancy will also be skyrocketing. In 1935, when the Social Security system was adopted, life expectancy at age sixty-five was only 12.6 years; by 1995, it had increased by almost 50 percent to 17.2 years; by 2040, it is expected to increase to 19.1 years, with some calculations predicting an even greater increase to 21 years. These population trends will have dramatic consequences. The number of elderly

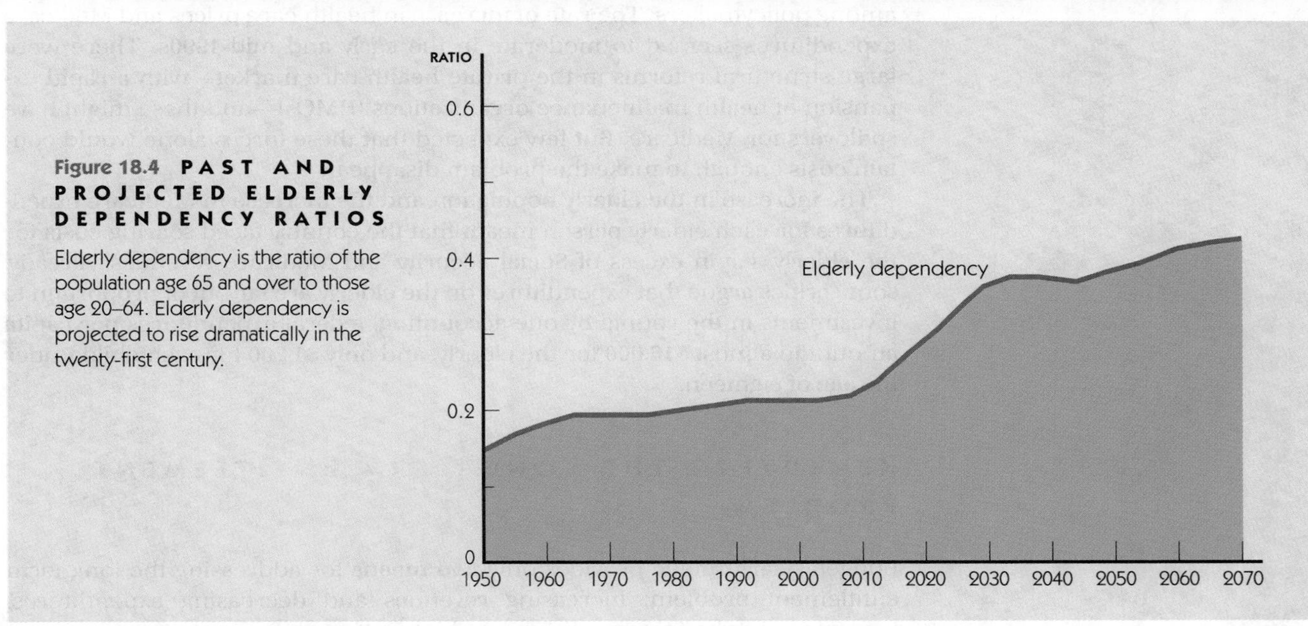

Figure 18.4 PAST AND PROJECTED ELDERLY DEPENDENCY RATIOS
Elderly dependency is the ratio of the population age 65 and over to those age 20–64. Elderly dependency is projected to rise dramatically in the twenty-first century.

will increase by 38 to 44 million by 2040, and there will be more Social Security beneficiaries to be supported by each working-age member of the population, as illustrated in Figure 18.4.

The increase in the number of beneficiaries has, of course, been anticipated. Social Security and Medicare tax rates have been set so that revenues today exceed expenditures, and the difference has been put in a government trust fund, to be used as the baby boomers reach retirement age. The problem is that the amount set aside has not been large enough. As of 1996, projections were that the Medicare trust fund would run out of funds in 6 years. In the case of Social Security, expenditures would exceed revenues in 2020, starting the depletion of the trust fund; it would be fully depleted in 2030.

INCREASING HEALTH CARE COSTS FOR THE ELDERLY

Trends in the costs of health care only exacerbate the problem. In the 1980s and early 1990s health care prices have increased at a pace far in excess of the increase in the cost of living. During the same time, health care costs for each elderly person have increased even more, with Medicare expenditures increasing at a rate of more than 10 percent per year. Looking ahead to the next century, such spending increases appear unsustainable.

The evolution of increasing health care costs has attracted some debate among policymakers. The rate of increase in health care prices and Medicare expenditures seemed to moderate in the early and mid-1990s. There were large structural reforms in the private health care market—with a rapid expansion of health maintenance organizations (HMOs)—and these might have spillovers for Medicare. But few expected that these forces alone would contain costs enough to make the problem disappear.

The increase in the elderly population and the increase in Medicare expenditures for each elderly person meant that the country faced soaring costs for the elderly, far in excess of Social Security and Medicare revenues. Already, some critics argue that expenditures on the elderly are far out of proportion to investments in the young: by one accounting, federal expenditures per capita amount to almost $16,000 for the elderly, and only $1,200 for each child under the age of eighteen.

Remedying the Long-Term Entitlement Problem

Budgetary arithmetic provides only two means for addressing the long-term entitlement problem: increasing revenues and decreasing expenditures. Revenues may be increased through higher tax rates or increased incomes (resulting from greater productivity). Expenditures are reduced when government programs are eliminated or downsized, and when the number of beneficiaries for entitlements are reduced. The recent political climate offers little optimism for those who propose higher tax rates, even though the magnitude of the tax increases required to bring the Social Security fund into balance are relatively modest—an increase in the payroll tax rate of less than 3 percent would probably do the trick.

Another line of attack is to change the benefit structure of entitlements in ways which reduce expenditures. For instance, increased life expectancy, along with a decline in the relative importance of physical labor in the workplace and improved health of the elderly, provides a rationale for restructuring Social Security. Many sixty-five-year-olds could continue to work. Indeed, the Social Security reforms of 1983 increased the normal retirement age to sixty-seven, and there have been proposals to link the normal retirement age to longevity—as life span increases, so would the retirement age.

There have also been proposals to invest portions of the Social Security trust fund in equities. Historically, equities have yielded a far higher return than government bonds (in which trust funds are currently invested). If equities continue to yield the same high returns, then the solvency of the trust fund can be extended, possibly even permanently, without reducing benefits or increasing taxes. Critics worry about the variability of the returns to the stock market, arguing that there is a chance that matters would be made even worse than they are today. They worry too that with the Social Security system buying fewer government bonds, the government would have to pay higher interest rates to finance its debt, exacerbating the deficit problem. At this point, there is no agreement about the likely magnitude of the increase in interest rates, and therefore about the quantitative significance of this concern.

The increases in public health care costs for the aged represent a more serious problem, and there is consensus that somehow these costs need to be brought under control. A seemingly easy way is simply to reduce the reimbursement rate for hospitals and doctors. However, critics of such proposals argue that there is a limit to this strategy—below some point, providers will either not provide services or there will be a decrease in the quality of services provided—and we may be near that point. Another way to control public health care costs is to force the aged to pay a larger fraction of their costs, but besides being politically unpopular, putting much of an additional burden on the elderly would force many of them into poverty. Introducing more means testing—making those who can afford it pay more—while helpful in reducing the deficit, would not address the more fundamental structural problems.

Structural reforms have focused on two strategies: improved consumers' incentives, and improved management of care. Most individuals have most of their serious health care costs paid for by insurance, and thus have no incentive to economize. Those who focus on incentives argue for more extensive use of deductibles, encouraging major medical and catastrophic insurance policies, which cover individuals for large bills only. Proposals for medical savings accounts would allow individuals to set aside money in a tax-exempt account to meet the expenses that they would then have to bear. Critics point out that most of the explosion of health care costs is associated precisely with these major medical expenses, and hence these reforms would not address the central issue. Moreover, medical savings accounts would do little to decrease government's costs, since individuals would opt for the catastrophic and major medical policies when they are healthy, but transfer to standard programs when they become sick—which is when most of the costs are incurred anyway.

Other structural reforms focus on **managed care.** These reforms recognize that most decisions about health care utilization are effectively made by doctors. The problem is to provide doctors with appropriate incentives. The fee-for-service system, in which doctors are paid for every service they perform, has incentives for doctors to provide more services than needed (especially since typically, insurance firms and government bear the costs, not the patient). Under managed care, the health care provider (typically an HMO) receives a fixed fee per year per patient. It thus has an incentive to ensure that they receive, for instance, cost-effective preventive care. Medicare reforms in 1983 resulted in hospitals receiving a fixed fee for each incidence of illness they treated; earlier they had been reimbursed on the basis of services performed. The new arrangement provided incentives for them to lower treatment costs. Unfortunately, it also provided an incentive for hospitals to get patients out of the hospital as soon as possible. Not surprisingly, post-hospital care costs ballooned. One widely discussed structural reform would make hospitals responsible for hospital and post-hospital care, providing them an incentive to manage overall costs, not only costs within the hospital.

Some critics of all of these proposals say that America will not be able to solve its health care cost problem until it faces up to the underlying cause: rapid changes in technology, which have enhanced the ability to extend life span, but at a high cost. The changes in technology, themselves, are a result of misdirected incentives: since life-prolonging innovations will get adopted, almost regardless of costs, researchers have little incentive to focus on costs (unlike other areas, in which costs are crucial). Research needs to be more cost conscious, and more of it needs to be redirected to reducing costs of health care.

Finally, society needs to ask fundamental questions: how much of its resources should be devoted to prolonging life, and how much should be spent on other uses, such as increasing the productivity of the young? Is a $20,000 hip replacement for a ninety-year-old with a life expectancy of a few years the most valuable use of society's resources? These are difficult and unpleasant questions, but as long as society as a whole bears the brunt of these costs, through its Medicare and Medicaid programs, there is no way of avoiding them.

REVIEW AND PRACTICE

SUMMARY

1. The early 1980s were marked by a surge in the size of federal budget deficits. There are five main causes for the increase: lower taxes, higher defense spending, higher spending on support for the elderly, higher health care expenditures, and higher interest payments.

2. Government borrowing can be an economic burden for future generations in several ways. First, future generations may have to bear the burden of paying off the borrowing; there is a transfer from one generation to another. Second, government borrowing can crowd out investment, which will reduce future output and wages. Third, when the money is borrowed from foreign investors, then Americans as a whole must pay some of their national income each year to foreigners just for interest, resulting in lower standards of living.

3. Government dissavings (deficits) have not been offset by private savings, as Ricardian equivalence would have suggested; and it is not true that "the debt does not matter, because we only owe it to ourselves."

4. Growing entitlement expenditures, growing interest expenditures from increasing federal indebtedness, and continuing commitments to defense all make reducing the deficit, or keeping it under control, difficult. Discretionary nondefense expenditures represent a relatively small fraction of all government expenditures. Without cutbacks in entitlements or defense, attaining and maintaining a zero deficit will entail huge cutbacks in these expenditures.

5. Current debates focus on the size of government, with some arguing for tax cuts financed by further expenditure cuts, while others argue that if high-return public investments in education, research, and infrastructure are reduced, growth will be impaired. Supply siders argue that tax cuts, even if unaccompanied by expenditure cuts, will stimulate the economy; and that their beneficial effects outweigh the costs of any increased deficit.

6. Earlier attempts to reform the budgetary process have met with only limited success. Requiring new expenditures to be paid for by new taxes or reduced expenditures has (apart from the ongoing increase in the cost of entitlements) curtailed the growth of the deficit, but not reduced it. Other proposals for reforming the budgetary process include the balanced budget amendment, capital budgeting, and the line-item veto.

7. Entitlements—such as increased Social Security and public health care expenditures—represent a major long-run deficit problem. Factors contributing to the entitlement problem are the aging population, increased life spans, earlier retirement ages, and soaring health care costs.

8. Among the proposals for containing the growth of government health care costs are those which provide increased incentives for consumers to economize in their use of health care services and those which provide improved incentives and responsibilities for doctors to manage care more efficiently.

Key Terms

Ricardian equivalence
discretionary spending
nondiscretionary spending
entitlements
supply siders
line item veto
balanced budget amendment
managed care

Review Questions

1. What happened to the size of the budget deficits in the 1980s? Had there ever been such large deficits in peacetime?

2. Name five fiscal changes that contributed to the large budget deficits of the 1980s.

3. What is the relationship between the deficits and the U.S. government debt?

4. What are the consequences of an increased deficit in a closed economy? in an open economy? How can borrowing from abroad affect future generations for the better? How can it affect future generations for the worse?

5. What is the argument that "the debt doesn't matter, since we owe it to ourselves"? What is wrong with this argument?

6. Since it is politically difficult to cut defense spending, entitlement programs, and interest payments, why can't federal spending be cut substantially by focusing on all the other federal programs?

7. How has the budgetary process been changed in order to control the deficit? Has it been successful? What further changes have been proposed? What are the problems with these proposals?

8. What role do entitlements play in the growth of the deficit? What accounts for the growth of entitlement spending? What can be done about it?

PROBLEMS

1. True or false: "Government borrowing can transfer resources from future generations to the present, but it cannot affect the overall wealth of the country." Discuss.

2. Explain how reducing the budget deficit would contribute to long-term growth in a closed economy, using the savings-investment identity. Use the savings-investment diagram introduced earlier to contrast the effects in an open and closed economy.

3. Suppose a certain country has private savings of 6 percent of GDP, foreign borrowing of 1 percent of GDP, and a balanced budget. What is its level of investment? If the budget deficit is 1.5 percent of GDP, how does your answer change?

4. The real value of the debt (in 1995 dollars) in 1995 was $3.6 trillion and in 1980 was $1.3 trillion. Assume that 50 percent of this buildup in the debt would have gone into investment, so that the capital stock would have been $1.15 trillion larger in 1995. Assume that the capital stock in 1995 was $15 trillion. By how much lower was GDP in 1995 as a result of the displaced investment, if the share of capital is .2? (Hint: use the results of Chapter 17, relating increases in outputs to increases in inputs.)

5. One proposal to contain the deficits is a balanced budget amendment to the constitution, that would require the government to maintain a balanced budget every year.

(a) Explain why if the economy goes into a downturn, this would either force the government to raise taxes or reduce expenditures.

(b) What would be the consequences of raising taxes or reducing expenditures under these circumstances?

(c) How might you design a balanced budget amendment that would not force the government to cut back expenditures or raise taxes in an economic downturn?

(d) Explain why if interest rates are increased to dampen the economy the balanced budget amendment might force the government to cut back other expenditures (or raise taxes). More generally, describe the interaction between monetary and fiscal policy under a balanced budget amendment.

6. Should expenditures on health care for children be considered an "investment" in a capital budget? What other expenditures might legitimately be classified as "investment"?

7. Assume the government sells some of the land it currently rents out for grazing. Should the revenues received be counted as reducing the deficit? How would the transaction be treated under a capital budget?

8. "The resources that were spent fighting World War II were spent during the period 1940–1945. Hence, the generations that were alive and paying taxes during that period are the generations that bore the burden of the cost of the war, regardless of how it was financed." Discuss.

9. Why does the way government achieves deficit reduction make a difference for economic growth?
   (a) Assuming the government raises taxes on interest income, what is the total impact on national savings, taking into account both deficit reduction and changes in private savings? What is the impact on investment? (Hint: how does your answer depend on the interest elasticity of savings?)
   (b) Assuming the government raises taxes on wage income, what is the impact on GDP in the short run? (Hint: how does your answer depend on the elasticity of labor supply?) What is the impact on the deficit and on investment?
   (c) Assume the government reduces expenditures on investments in technology and education, which yield a return of 15 percent, while the marginal return on private investment is 7 percent.

CHAPTER 19

TRADE POLICY

Go into any Gap or other clothing store and look at the labels: while some items are made in the U.S.A., others come from Hong Kong, Malaysia, China, Taiwan, the Philippines, or India. Today, Americans enjoy products produced around the world, and those in other countries travel in American jets, take American medicines, and watch American-made movies. In Chapter 2, we saw that there are gains for all countries when they produce and trade according to their comparative advantage.

In spite of the gains from trade, countries have imposed a variety of barriers to trade. Over the past fifty years, the United States has worked with other countries to lower these barriers to trade. This chapter explores both the barriers to trade and the major initiatives to remove these barriers.

KEY QUESTIONS

1. Why and how do countries erect barriers to trade?
2. What is meant by fair trade laws? What is dumping, and why are economists often critical of antidumping laws?
3. Why are government subsidies to industries considered a barrier to trade? To what extent do countervailing duties correct this problem?
4. Why is protection so popular? Who are the winners and losers from free trade?
5. What are some of the institutions and agreements through which trade barriers have been reduced?

COMMERCIAL POLICY

Countries that have *no* barriers to trade are said to practice **free trade,** but most countries engage in some form of **protectionism,** that is, in one way or another they restrict the importation of goods. Policies directed at affecting either imports or exports are referred to as **commercial policies.** This and the next section take up the forms trade barriers take, their economic costs, and their economic and political rationale; the next section explores international attempts to reduce these trade barriers.

There are four major categories of trade barriers—tariffs, quotas, voluntary export restraints and other **nontariff barriers,** and a set of laws called "fair trade laws" that, by and large, actually serve to impede trade rather than promote fair trade.

TARIFFS

Tariffs are simply a tax on imports. Since a tariff is a tax that is imposed only on foreign goods, it puts the foreign goods at a disadvantage. It discourages imports.

Figure 19.1 shows the effect of a tariff. The figure shows a downward-sloping demand curve for the product, and an upward-sloping domestic supply curve. For simplicity, we consider the case of a country sufficiently small that the price it pays for a good on the international market does not depend on the quantity purchased. In the absence of a tariff, the domestic price is equal to this international price, p^*. The country produces Q_s, consumes Q_c, and imports the difference, $Q_c - Q_s$. With a tariff, the price consumers have to pay is increased from p^* to $p^* + t$, where t is the tariff. Domestic production is increased (to Q_s')—producers are better off as a result. But consumers are

Figure 19.1 EFFECT OF TARIFFS

A small country faces a horizontal supply curve for a good at the international price, p^*. In the absence of tariffs, the price in the country will be p^*. The country will produce Q_s (the quantity along the supply curve corresponding to p^*), consume Q_c (the quantity along the demand curve corresponding to p^*), and import $Q_c - Q_s$. A tariff at the rate t increases the price in the country to $p^* + t$, lowers aggregate consumption to Q_c' (the quantity along the demand curve corresponding to $p^* + t$), and increases domestic production to Q_s' (the quantity along the supply curve corresponding to $p^* + t$). Domestic producers are better off, but consumers are worse off.

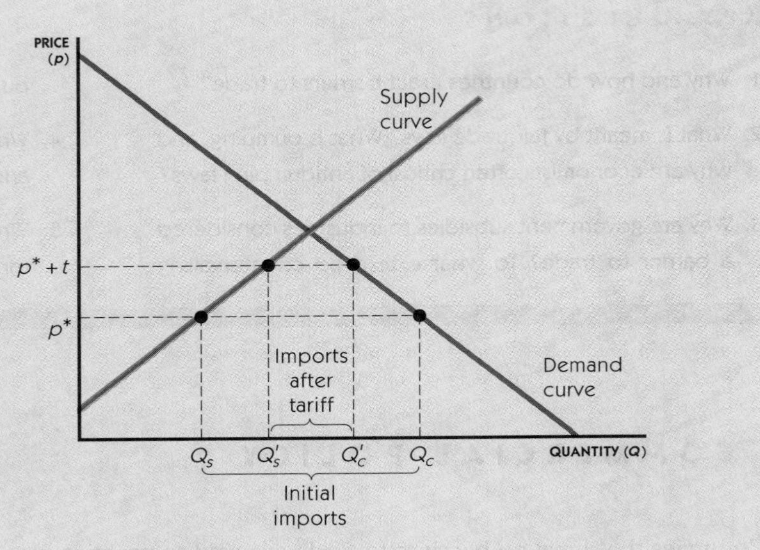

worse off, as the price they pay is increased. Their consumption is reduced to Q_c'. Since production is increased and consumption reduced, imports are reduced: the domestic industry has been protected against foreign imports.

QUOTAS

Rather than setting tariffs, many countries impose **quotas**—limits on the amount of foreign goods that can be imported. For instance, in the 1950s, the United States imposed a quota on the amount of oil that could be imported, and strict quotas still control the import of textiles.

Producers often prefer quotas. With limitations on the quantity imported, the domestic price increases above the international price. With quotas, domestic producers know precisely the magnitude of the foreign supply. If foreigners become more efficient or if exchange rates change in favor of foreigners, they still cannot sell any more. In that sense, quotas provide domestic producers with greater certainty than do tariffs, insulating them from the worst threats of competition.

Quotas and tariffs both succeed in raising the domestic price above the price at which the good could be obtained abroad. Both thus protect domestic producers. There is, however, one important difference: with quotas, those who are given permits to import get a profit by buying goods at the international price abroad and selling at the higher domestic price. The government is, in effect, giving away its tariff revenues. These profits are referred to as **quota rents.**

Using Economics: Quantifying the Losses to Society from Tariffs

We can quantify the net loss to society from imposing tariffs. The difference between the amount consumers are willing to pay and what they have to pay is called consumer surplus. For the last unit consumed, the marginal benefit exactly equals the price paid, and so there is no consumer surplus. But for the first units consumed, individuals typically would be willing to pay far more—reflected in the fact that the demand curve is downward sloping in the figure below. In the initial situation, the consumer surplus is given by the triangle *ABC*, the area between the demand curve and the price line, p^*. After the price increase, it is given by the triangle *ADE*. The net loss is the trapezoid *BCED*.

But of this loss, the rectangle *BDHF* represents increased payments to producers (the increased price, *BD*, times the quantity that they produce), and *HFGE* is the tariff revenue of the government (imports, *HE*, × the tariff). Of the increased payments to domestic producers, some is the cost of expanding production. The rest represents a difference between price and the marginal cost of production—increased profits. This is the area *BIHD*. Thus, the societal loss is represented by two triangles, *EGC* and *HFI*. The triangle *EGC* is similar to the loss to consumers arising from a monopolist's raising his price. The triangle *HFI* is the waste of resources resulting from the fact that as the economy expands production because of the tariff, the cost of domestic production exceeds the costs of purchasing the good abroad.

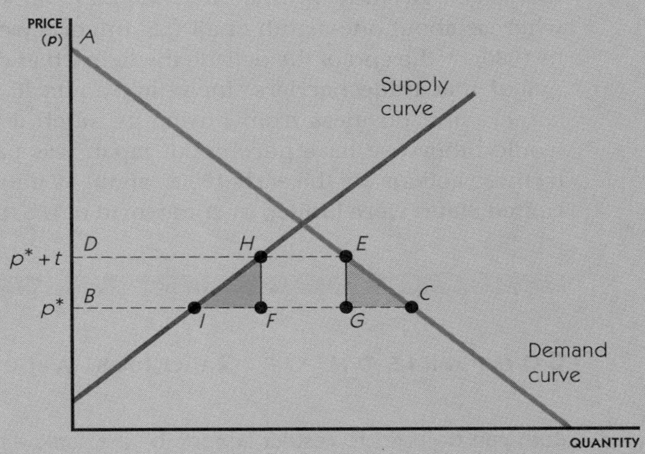

Voluntary Export Restraints

In recent years, international agreements have reduced the level of tariffs, and restricted the use of quotas. Accordingly, countries have sought to protect themselves from the onslaught of foreign competition by other means. One that became popular in the 1980s was **voluntary export restraints** (VERs). Rather than limiting imports of automobiles, for example, the United States persuaded Japan to limit its exports.

There are two interpretations of why Japan might have been willing to go along with this VER. One is that they worried the United States might take stronger actions, like imposing quotas. From Japan's perspective, VERs are clearly preferable to quotas, because with VERs, the quota rents accrue to Japanese firms. A second interpretation is that VERs enabled Japanese car producers to act collusively. It might have been in their self-interest to collude to reduce production and raise prices, but such collusion would have been illegal under antitrust laws. The VER "imposed" on the Japanese car producers output reductions they would have chosen themselves if they had been permitted to under the law. No wonder, then, that they agreed to go along! The cost to the American consumer of the Japanese VER was enormous. American consumers paid more than $100,000 in higher prices for every job created.

VERs and quotas are the clearest nontariff barriers. But today they are probably not the most important. A host of regulations have the same effect of imposing barriers to trade. For instance, health-related regulations have been abused in ways that restrict trade. When, in 1996, Russia threatened to halt U.S. exports of chickens for failure to satisfy health regulations, U.S. chicken exporters were faced with a nontariff barrier. Various types of regulations have been used to establish nontariff barriers.

During the 1980s, as tariff barriers were being reduced, nontariff barriers increased. A study by the International Monetary Fund concluded that, whereas about one-eighth of all U.S. imports were affected by protectionism in 1980, by the end of the decade the figure had risen to one-quarter. It is estimated that trade barriers (including nontariff barriers) may prevent consumers and business from buying as much as $50 billion in imports they would otherwise have purchased. Japan was particularly adversely affected by these actions. By the early 1990s, about 40 percent of Japan's exports to the United States were limited by some form of U.S. protectionism.

Comparison of Quotas and Tariffs

Both can be used to restrict imports by the same amount, with the same effect on consumers and domestic producers.

With quotas, the difference between domestic price and international price accrues to the importer, who enjoys a quota rent.

With tariffs, the difference accrues to government as tariff revenues.

VERs (voluntary export restraints) are equivalent to quotas, except that the quota rents are given to foreign producers.

"FAIR TRADE" LAWS

Most people believe in competition. But most people believe that competition should be fair. When someone can undersell them, they suspect foul play. The government has imposed a variety of laws to ensure that there is effective and fair competition domestically. Laws have also been enacted by most countries to ensure "fair competition" in international trade. But most economists believe that in practice they are protectionist measures, reducing competition and restricting imports. To ensure fair competition, economists argue that the same laws which apply domestically should be extended internationally—that is, there should not be two standards of fairness, one applying domestically, one internationally. New Zealand and Australia, in their trade relations, have applied the same laws to trade between themselves that they do domestically. But elsewhere, progress has been limited.

There are three important "fair trade" laws, applying to dumping, countervailing duties, and market surges.

ANTIDUMPING LAWS

Dumping refers to the sale of products overseas at prices that are below cost and lower than those in the home country. Normally, consumers greet discounted sales with enthusiasm. If Russia is willing to sell aluminum to the United States at low prices, why should we complain? One reason that might be of concern is predatory pricing. By selling below cost, the foreign companies hope to drive the American firms out of business. Once they have established a monopoly position, they can raise prices. In such a case, American consumers gain only in the short run. In competitive markets, however, predation simply cannot occur, for in such markets, firms have no power to raise prices. In almost all of the cases where dumping has been found, markets are sufficiently competitive that predation is not of concern.

As administered, the antidumping laws are more frequently used as a protectionist tool. If dumping is discovered, a duty (tariff) is levied equal to the difference between the (calculated) cost of production and the price. Under the criteria employed, most American firms could be charged with dumping. Critics of the dumping laws worry that other countries will imitate American practices. If so, just as the international community has eliminated tariff barriers, a whole new set of trade barriers will have been erected.

SUBSIDIES AND COUNTERVAILING DUTIES

A second trade practice widely viewed as unfair is for governments to subsidize domestic firms' production or exports. For example, the government may give certain domestic industries tax breaks or pay a portion of the firms' costs. These subsidies give companies receiving them an unfair advantage. Trade is

Policy Perspective: Surrogate Countries and Canadian Golf Carts

Question: How, if Canada did not produce golf carts, could the cost of Canadian golf carts be used to accuse Poland of dumping? Answer: The United States sometimes achieves wonders when its markets are at stake.

The standard criterion for judging whether a country is dumping is whether it is selling commodities on the U.S. market at prices below those for which it sells them at home or elsewhere, or at prices below the costs of production. For nonmarket economies, the Department of Commerce formulated a special criterion—below what it would have cost to product the good in a "comparable" (or "surrogate") country.

The case of the Canadian golf cart and Poland is a real case. Poland was accused of dumping golf carts on the U.S. market at a time when Canada was not even making comparable golf carts. Commerce asked the question: What would it have cost for Canada to produce these golf carts, had it chosen to do so? Not surprisingly, the resulting cost estimate was higher than the price the real golf carts were being sold for in the United States, and Poland was found guilty of dumping. Similar charges have been made on similar grounds against Russian sales of natural resources.

For years, Western countries had preached to the Soviet Union and the other socialist countries the virtues of the market. Beginning in 1989, with the demise of communism, former iron-curtain countries sought to transform their economies into market economies. Under the old regime, these countries had traded mainly with themselves, and generally engaged in barter. In the new era, they sought to enter international markets, like any other market economy.

Though the design and production quality of many of its manufactured goods made them unsuitable for Western markets, Russia had a wealth of natural resources—including uranium, aluminum, and other products—that it could produce on a competitive basis. Moreover, with the reduction of defense expenditures—good news from virtually every perspective—Russia's demand for many of these raw materials was greatly reduced. It sought to enter international markets for these commodities at an unfortunate time, however, since the recession in Western economies

had resulted in low demand, and hence low prices, for these commodities. The increase in supply from Russia exacerbated these problems.

American producers attempted to discourage Russian exports by filing, or threatening to file, dumping charges. Though Russia was probably not selling these commodities at prices below those prevailing at home or elsewhere, or at prices below costs of production, the "surrogate" country criterion made the dumping charges a very real threat. Russia agreed to a cutback in aluminum production in 1994, to be matched by cutbacks in other countries.

To the Commerce and State Departments, this may have seemed a reasonable way to avoid trade conflict. But consumers paid a hidden high price, in terms of higher prices for aluminum and products using aluminum. In April of 1994, the Justice Department announced an investigation to see if the agreement and actions violated antitrust laws.

Meanwhile, since it was clear that the old dumping laws did not deal adequately with the problems of economies in transition, at summit meetings between Presidents Clinton and Yeltsin during 1993 and 1994, Clinton promised reform. A proposal was submitted to Congress, but failed to pass. Until such legislation is adopted, market access by these countries will continue to be a source of tension. They rightly claim that market economies fail to practice what they preach—the virtues of free markets.

determined not on the basis of comparative advantage, but of relative subsidy levels.

The usual logic of economics seems to be reversed. If some foreign government wants to subsidize American consumers, why should they complain? Presumably, only if the subsidies are part of a policy of predation—if the subsidies are used to drive American firms out of business and establish a monopoly position, after which prices will be raised. Most foreign subsidies do not fall into this category.

Opposition to these subsidies arises from the companies who see their businesses hurt. While the gains to consumers outweigh the losses to businesses, the gain to each consumer is small, and consumers are not well organized. Producers, being far more organized, are able and willing to bring their case to Washington. In response, Congress has passed laws allowing the U.S. government to impose **countervailing duties,** that is, taxes that offset any advantage provided by these subsidies.

While governments preach against other countries providing subsidies, however, they engage in the practice themselves, most commonly with export subsidies. At various times, the U.S government has subsidized the export of wheat, pork, peaches, and a host of other commodities.

Market Surges

The final category of "fair trade" law is not really concerned with *unfair* trade, but with the consequences of rapid economic changes—in particular **surges** of imports—which may have strong adverse effects on particular industries.

Policy Perspective: Japan as a Trading Partner

Economic relations between Japan and the United States (as well as many other countries) have been tense for years. Underlying the tension is Japan's huge trade surplus (see figure below) and a variety of practices which have the effect of reducing access to the Japanese market. In response to these concerns, in early 1993 Japan and the United States signed an agreement, a so-called framework for addressing problems of market access. Discussions focused on several major areas, including procurement, insurance, and automobiles.

Underlying the discussions were several major differences in viewpoints. First, Japan emphasized that the trade surplus was largely a macroeconomic phenomenon, a result of its high savings rate. We saw in Chapter 7 that

$$X - M = S_d - I$$

that is, the trade surplus is just equal to the difference between domestic savings (including government savings) and investment. Japan's trade surplus would only be reduced if it increased its investment or reduced its savings. Since Japan's interest rates were already low—by 1995, they were less than 1 percent per year—it could not do much in that way to stimulate investment, and it did not want to discourage savings.

The United States argued that the Japanese government should direct actions to stimulate imports: fiscal actions to stimulate its economy—increased expenditures and reduced taxes—would result in increased imports. They also argued for reduced nontariff barriers—such as regulations which kept out U.S. parts from the automobile market and anticompetitive practices which limited Japanese firms' purchases from foreign competitors.

To ensure that Japan actually reduced these impediments to imports, the United States argued for

quantitative targets. In previous negotiations, Japan had promised to reduce trade barriers, but nothing had happened. The United States was concerned that without quantitative measures of progress, nothing would happen. Japan, for its part, argued that setting quantitative targets was equivalent to managing trade—and that violated basic principles of free trade. A compromise eventually was reached whereby a range of quantitative indicators measuring progress would be looked at, but no strict quotas for trade would be set.

A third set of issues revolved around the responsibility of government for lack of market access. Each side had a wealth of anecdotes. U.S. cars had made little headway in Japan, simply because American car manufacturers only made cars with steering wheels on the left-hand side. This was symptomatic of failing to pay attention to the realities of the marketplace.

But the Americans cited a host of government regulations—and the manner in which they were applied—which served as barriers to market access. When U.S. financial companies wanted to introduce new financial instruments into the Japanese market, for example, they were precluded from doing so—allegedly because Japanese regulators had to look at their "safety." During the delay, Japanese firms positioned themselves to enter the market. Thus, American firms lost the competitive advantage they would have had with earlier entry.

There is, in fact, a grain of truth in both sides' contentions: the basic trade imbalances are a result of macroeconomic imbalances, the surplus of savings over investment in Japan and of investment over savings in the United States. On the other hand, nontariff barriers impede access of foreigners to Japanese markets, keeping consumer prices there high, and probably discouraging Japanese consumption of imports. Even if eliminating these nontariff barriers did not redress the trade imbalance, it would at least make clear that the reason for these trade imbalances was not "unfair" trade practices.

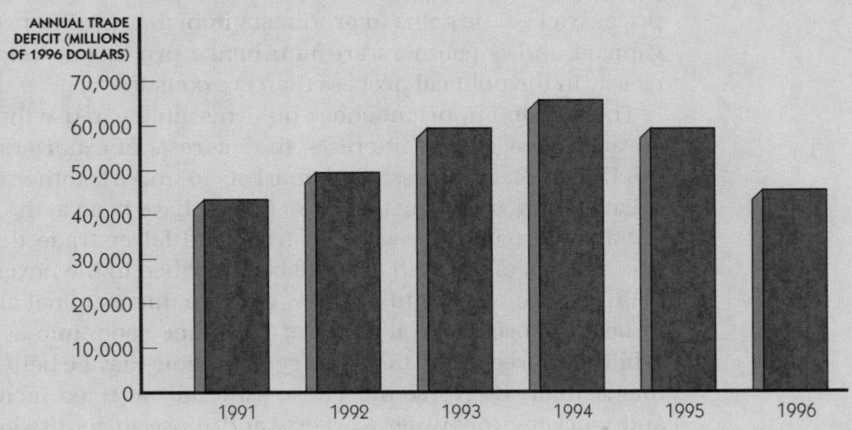

THE U.S. TRADE DEFICIT WITH JAPAN

The United States has had a huge trade deficit with Japan. In 1995, it began to decline. The trade deficit for 1996 is projected from data for the first nine months of the year. *Source:* Department of Commerce, Report FT-900.

The market surge laws are intended to provide temporary protection to give the industry time to adjust. In practice, the protection provided by antidumping laws is so much more effective that little reliance is placed on the market surge laws.

UNFAIR TRADE LAWS

Dumping
Countervailing duties
Market surges

POLITICAL AND ECONOMIC RATIONALE FOR PROTECTION

Chapter 2 showed how free trade, by allowing each country to concentrate production where it has a comparative advantage, can make all countries better off. Why, in spite of this, is protection so popular? The basic reason is simple: protection raises prices. While the losses to consumers from higher prices exceed the gains to producers in higher profits, producers are well organized and consumers are not; hence producers' voices are heard more clearly in the political process than are consumers'.

There is an important check on firms' ability to use the political process to advance their special interests: the interests of exporters, who realize that if the United States closes off its markets to imports, other countries will reciprocate. Thus, exporting firms like Boeing have been at the forefront of advancing an international regime of freer and fairer trade through international agreements, of the kind that will be described in the next section.

But before turning to a review of these international agreements, we need to take a closer look at some of the other economic aspects of protection. While with free trade, the country as a whole may be better off, certain groups may actually be worse off. Those especially affected include displaced firms and workers, low-wage workers, and those in industries in which without free trade, competition is limited.

DISPLACED FIRMS AND WORKERS

China has a comparative advantage in inexpensive textiles while the United States has a comparative advantage in manufacturing complex goods, like advanced telephone exchanges. If the United States starts to import textiles from

China, U.S. textile manufacturers may be driven out of business, and their workers will have to find work elsewhere. More than offsetting these losses are the gains to the export industries. In principle, the gainers in those industries could more than compensate the losers, but such compensation is seldom made: hence the opposition of the losers to opening trade.

Typically, economists shed few tears for the lost profits of the businesses who are hurt by opening trade. After all, that is just one of the risks that businesses face, and for which they are typically well compensated. New innovations destroy old businesses: the introduction of the automobile hurt the carriage trade. But barring the door to new technologies—or cheaper products from abroad—is bad economics—and bad economic policy.

There is, however, often more sympathy toward workers affected by trade—though there is no reason why there should be greater concern for workers displaced by opening trade than by new innovations. When the economy is running at close to full employment, workers who lose their jobs typically do find new employment. But they often go through a transition period of unemployment, and when they eventually do find a new job, there is a good chance that their wages will be lower (in the United States, in recent years, a worker who is successful in finding full-time employment experiences on average a 10 percent wage decline). While these particular laborers are worse off, workers as a whole are better off, because those who get newly created jobs in the export industries are paid far more (on average 13 to 15 percent more) than the average for the economy. Concern about the transitional costs borne by displaced workers has motivated Congress to pass laws for special assistance for these workers to help them find new jobs and obtain the requisite training.

Sensitivity to the problems of displaced workers is particularly strong when unemployment is high because those who lose a job cannot easily find alternative employment. Auto workers in Michigan who see their jobs lost as a result of imports of Japanese cars view the Japanese as "stealing" their jobs. Indeed, in such situations, trade is *blamed* for the high unemployment rate. If we restrict imports, it is argued, we will keep jobs in America.

Beggar-Thy-Neighbor Policies

In Chapter 8 we saw that output may be limited by aggregate demand. Aggregate demand depends on consumption, investment, government expenditures, and net exports. Net exports equal exports minus imports. Increasing imports thus reduces net exports—reducing aggregate demand, national output, and employment. Policies that attempt to increase national output by reducing imports are called **beggar-thy-neighbor policies,** because the jobs gained in one country are at the expense of jobs lost in another. If America imports less, foreigners export less. Restricting imports into the United States may *initially* have a positive effect on U.S. output. But the gains are typically a mirage. Other countries will import from us only if they can sell goods to us. Even without retaliatory measures by other countries, if the United States restricts imports, typically exports fall in tandem. Without exports to the United States, other countries' income falls, and with the fall in income, they import

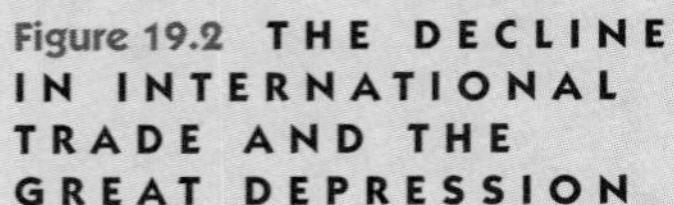

Figure 19.2 THE DECLINE IN INTERNATIONAL TRADE AND THE GREAT DEPRESSION

U.S. exports and imports fell dramatically during the Great Depression. One contributing factor to the decline in trade was the Hawley-Smoot Tariff Act introduced in 1930.

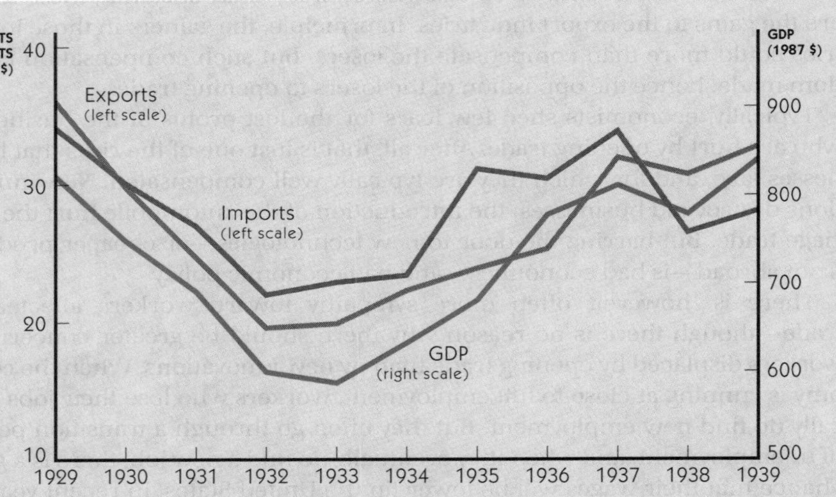

less, including from the United States. Moreover, when other countries see reduced exports as a result of active policies by other countries to restrict imports, they tend to respond by retaliating, by playing tit-for-tat.

The worst instance of these beggar-thy-neighbor policies occurred at the onset of the Great Depression, when, in 1930, the United States passed the Hawley-Smoot Tariff Act, raising tariffs on many products to a level which effectively prohibited many imports. Other countries retaliated. As U.S. imports declined, incomes in Europe and elsewhere in the world declined. As incomes declined and as these countries imposed retaliatory tariffs, they bought less from the United States. U.S. exports plummeted, contributing further to the economic downturn in the United States. With incomes in the United States plummeting further, U.S. imports declined even more, contributing still further to the decline abroad, which then fed further into the decline in U.S. exports. The downturn in international trade that was set off by the Hawley-Smoot Tariff Act, charted in Figure 19.2, is often pointed to as a major contributing factor in making the Great Depression as deep and severe as it was.

INTERNATIONAL TRADE AND JOBS

Opposition to imports is strongest when the economy is in a recession, but restricting imports as a way of creating jobs tends to be counterproductive.

Wages in Impacted Sectors

Beyond these short-run problems of transition and unemployment, there may be long-run problems facing workers in impacted sectors. The United States has a comparative advantage in producing goods such as airplanes and high-tech products which require highly skilled workers. As the United States exports more of these goods, the demand for these skilled workers increases in the United States, driving up the wage of skilled workers. Similarly, the United States has a comparative disadvantage in producing goods which require a high ratio of unskilled labor, such as lower quality textiles. As imports compete against these U.S. industries and their production decreases, the demand for unskilled labor decreases. This drives down the wages of unskilled workers.

These decreased wages for unskilled workers are often blamed on imports from third world countries like China, where wages are but a fraction of those in the United States. The consensus among economists who have looked closely at the matter is that international trade explains a relatively small part of the decline in wages—perhaps 20 percent. Nonetheless, those who see their meager livelihood being threatened are among the most ardent advocates of trade restrictions. Again, economists argue that the appropriate response is not to restrict trade, but to increase skills: not only are the workers receiving the skills better off, as their wages rise commensurate with the increase in their productivity; but as more workers become skilled, the remaining supply of unskilled workers is reduced; and with a smaller supply of unskilled workers, the real wages of the remaining unskilled workers increases, offsetting the adverse effects of trade.

Increased Competition

International trade also has other adverse effects in industries where competition is limited. With limited competition, firms enjoy monopoly or oligopoly profits. Some of these extra profits are often passed on to workers. Particularly when those industries are unionized, workers may receive wages far higher than workers of comparable skill working elsewhere in the economy.

Effects of Trade on Wages

International trade may lower wages of unskilled U.S. labor and those working in industries where competition is limited.

International trade raises wages of skilled U.S. workers.

International trade introduces more competition; with the increased competition, monopoly and oligopoly profits get competed away. Firms are forced to pay competitive wages—that is, the lowest wage that they can for workers with the given skill.

The Infant Industry Argument

While job loss and decreased wages and profits from international competition provide much of the political motivation behind protection, economists have asked, are there any *legitimate* arguments for protection. That is, are there circumstances where protection may be in the *national* interest, and not just in the interests of those being protected? Two arguments have been put forward.

The first is the **infant industry argument.** Costs in new industries are often high, coming down as experience is gained. The infant industry argument is that, particularly in less developed countries, firms will never be able to get the experience required to produce efficiently unless they are protected from foreign competition.

Economists have traditionally responded to this argument skeptically. If it pays to enter the industry, eventually there will be profits. Thus, the firm should be willing to charge today a price below cost to gain the experience, because today's losses will be more than offset by the future profits. But more recently, the infant industry argument has found more favor. Firms can only operate at a loss if they can borrow funds. If capital markets do not work well, firms may not be able to borrow even if their eventual prospects are reasonable. This is a particular danger in less developed countries.

This may be a legitimate argument. But it is not an argument for protection. It is an argument for assistance, which can take the form of loans or direct subsidies. Economists argue for direct assistance rather than protection because the assistance is transparent. Everyone can see that it is a subsidy to producers. Economists criticize protection because it is a hidden tax on consumers, with the proceeds transferred to producers. The lack of transparency encourages what is referred to as rent seeking[1]: industries spend resources to persuade government to impose these hidden taxes which benefit themselves.

Strategic Trade Theory

Another argument for protection is that protection can give a country a strategic trade advantage over rivals by helping reduce domestic costs. There may be economies of scale: the larger the level of production, the lower the mar-

[1]Rents refer to payments to a factor of production that are in excess of what is required to elicit the supply of that factor. In the absence of entry, protection would result in higher prices, yielding returns to the industry that are above their competitive levels; these higher returns are rents. The irony is that typically, the higher returns do attract entry, and the additional entry dissipates the rents—though prices remain high.

ginal costs. Protection ensures a large domestic sales base, and therefore a low marginal cost. The instances in which **strategic trade theory** might provide a rationale for protection appear relatively rare. Even then, they tend to be effective only when foreign governments do not retaliate by taking similar actions.

INTERNATIONAL COOPERATION

Recognizing both the temptation of shortsighted trade policy and the gains from trade, nations large and small have since World War II engaged in a variety of efforts to reduce trade barriers. At the global level, the prominent effort is known as the **General Agreement on Tariffs and Trade (GATT).** On a slightly smaller scale, regional trading blocs have also been developed.

GATT AND THE WTO

After World War II, the countries of the world realized that there was much to be gained from establishing an international economic order in which barriers to trade were reduced. They established the GATT. In 1995, this was replaced by the **World Trade Organization (WTO).**

GATT was founded on three guiding principles. The first was *reciprocity:* if one country lowered its tariffs, it could expect other countries in GATT to lower theirs. The second was *nondiscrimination:* no member of GATT could offer a special trade deal that favored only one or a few other countries. The third was *transparency:* import quotas and other nontariff barriers to trade should be converted into tariffs, so their effective impact could be ascertained.

GATT has proceeded in a number of stages, called **rounds** (the Kennedy Round, completed in 1967, the Tokyo Round, completed in 1979, and most recently, the Uruguay Round, completed in 1993). Collectively, the rounds have reduced tariffs on industrial goods markedly. The average tariff on manufactured goods was 40 percent in 1947. By 1992, they had been reduced to 5 percent, and the Uruguay Round reduced them still further.

The Uruguay Round was remarkable for two achievements. It began the process of extending the principles of free and fair trade to a number of much more difficult areas. There were, for instance, agreements to reduce agriculture subsidies, particularly export subsidies, and to ensure that intellectual property rights—patents and copyrights—were respected. Secondly, it created the WTO to help enforce the trade agreements. Previously, a country that believed that it was suffering from an "unfair trade" practice could bring a case to a GATT panel that would examine the evidence. Even if the panel was unanimous, however, in finding that an unfair trade practice had occurred, there was little in the way of effective enforcement. Under the WTO, a country injured by an unfair trade practice will be authorized to engage in retaliatory actions.

REGIONAL TRADING BLOCS

GATT and WTO have made some progress in reducing trade barriers among all countries. But the difficulties of reaching agreements involving so many parties have made progress slow. In the meantime, many countries have formed **trading blocs,** agreeing with their more immediate neighbors not only to eliminate trade barriers, but also to facilitate the flow of capital and labor. Perhaps the most important of these is the **European Union,** the successor to the **Common Market,** which now embraces most of Europe. The **North American Free Trade Agreement, NAFTA,** will result eventually in a free trade zone within North America—that is, an area within which goods and services trade freely, without tariffs or other import restrictions. There are also many smaller free trade zones, such as those between New Zealand and Australia, and among groups of countries in Latin America and in Central America.

While the gains from internationally coordinated reductions in trade barriers are clear, the gains from regional trading blocs are more controversial. Reducing trade barriers within a region encourages trade by members of the trading bloc. Lowering barriers among the countries involved results, of course, in **trade creation.** But it also results in **trade diversion.** Trade is diverted away from countries that are not members of the bloc, who might, in fact, have a comparative advantage in the particular commodity. Under these conditions, the global net benefits will be positive if the trade creation exceeds the trade diversion. Typically, when trade blocs are formed, tariffs against outsiders are harmonized. If the external trade barriers are harmonized at the lowest common level (rather than at the average or highest levels) at the same time that internal trade barriers are lowered, it is more likely that the trade creation effects exceed the trade diversion effects.

Expanding regional trading blocs to cover investment flows raises particular anxieties, especially when the bloc includes countries with very different standards of living. In the NAFTA debate, Ross Perot used the metaphor of a giant sucking sound: Mexico would suck up huge amounts of investment that otherwise would have occurred in the United States. The accusation was not just that goods produced today in Mexico would cost Americans jobs. It was also that American firms would move down to Mexico, to take advantage of low-wage labor, and the capital that flowed down to Mexico would not be available for investment in the United States.

Such arguments are based on an important misconception. They fail to take account of the fact that capital markets are already global. The United States is not limited in its investment to savings in the United States. Capital will flow to good investment opportunities wherever they are. If there are good investment opportunities in the United States, capital will flow there, regardless of how much Americans invest in Mexico. Investment barriers impede this flow of capital to its highest productive use, thus lowering world economic efficiency.

The "Perot" argument is based on a "zero sum" view of the world—that what

Mexico gains must come at the expense of the United States. Perot's argument is similar to the one that says when a country imports, it loses jobs: the gains to foreigners from their exports are at the expense of domestic firms, which otherwise would be creating these jobs. In Chapter 2, we saw what was wrong with this argument: the theory of comparative advantage says that when countries specialize in what they produce best, *both* countries are better off. Workers gain higher wages when they move into those sectors where their productivity is highest; and consumers gain from the lower prices. So too with investment. When investment flows to where its return is highest, world output is increased. Since the return to capital is increased when it is efficiently allocated, savings rates may also increase, so that the overall supply of funds will be higher. Higher savings rates and more efficient use of available savings will combine to give a higher world economic growth rate.

But just as not everyone necessarily gains from trade according to comparative advantage, so too not everyone will necessarily gain from the flow of capital to Mexico. There will be some investment diversion from other countries to Mexico, as Mexico becomes more attractive to investors throughout the world because of its improved access to the huge American market. Most economists believe that the net effect on investment in the United States will be negligible, and could even be positive. Industries within the United States that see their opportunities expand by selling more to Mexico will invest more, more than offsetting the reduced investment from firms that decline in the face of competition from Mexican imports.

In fact, investment flows augment the gains from trade which would occur in their absence because there are important trade-investment links. American companies producing abroad tend to use more parts from America, just as French companies producing abroad tend to use more French parts. Thus, flows of investment often serve as a precursor to exports.

Trade-offs between Regional and International Agreements

The potential economic trade-off between increased trade within the region and the expense of reduced trade outside the region has led some economists, such as Jagdish Bhagwati of Columbia University, to oppose regional trade agreements. There is also concern about political trade-offs. Should the U.S. government spend the limited political resources it has to overcome protectionist antitrade sentiment focusing on regional or worldwide agreements? Recent U.S. governments have pursued a pragmatic policy. Their ultimate objective is to eliminate economic barriers everywhere, by means of international approaches coordinated through the WTO. At the same time, they are aggressively pursuing regional trade agreements involving broad removal of barriers within the Western Hemisphere and between the United States and the countries of the Pacific Rim. They view this as the most practical way to achieve economic integration. Agreements may be easier to obtain among a limited set of often similar partners than among all the countries of the world.

CLOSE-UP: MERCANTILISM—OLD AND NEW

Mercantilism is the name of the school of thought that was prevalent in Europe between about 1500 and 1800 and focused on building up the power and wealth of the state through aggressive pursuit of exports. They also discouraged imports and thought that a country's strength was related to its store of gold and silver. Josiah Child, one of the better-known mercantilists, wrote in 1693: "Foreign trade produces riches, riches power; power preserves our trade and religion."

To have lots of products left over to export, the nation had to produce more than it consumed, so citizens were exhorted to work hard for low wages.

Adam Smith, the father of modern economics, recognized the fallacies in mercantilism. A country's wealth, he argued, was not measured by its gold and silver, but by the productivity of its resources. Smith pointed out that even from the standpoint of national power, a nation's army does not run on gold and silver, but on physical products like ships, food, clothing, and weapons.

The world has changed dramatically in the more than two centuries since Adam Smith formulated his attack on mercantilism. But the mercantilist spirit remains alive—and the criticisms of the new mercantilist arguments are direct descendants of Smith's analysis.

Modern mercantilists view exports as desirable today, not because they lead to the accumulation of gold, but because they lead to job creation. By the same token, imports are viewed poorly, both because they lead to job loss and dependency on foreigners.

Some countries, such as Japan and Korea, have successfully pursued strong export-oriented policies; and most economists believe that these policies have contributed to their economic success. But the reason is quite different from that of the older mercantilist theories that focused on the accumulation of riches. Japan and Korea did accumulate capital rapidly, but this was because of their extraordinarily high savings rates. Their export-oriented policies were important because to be successful in international markets, their industries had to be efficient and adopt high standards of production. Their export-oriented policies helped their industries become more competitive and adopt advanced technologies.

Today, in the United States, we recognize that trade is important, not because it creates jobs—if the Federal Reserve Board does its job, the economy will operate at or close to full employment most of the time—but because it leads to higher standards of living, as Americans can specialize in producing those goods in which it has a comparative advantage, and because competition from abroad forces American firms to become more efficient. These are essentially the same reasons that Smith put forward for why, though protection may benefit businessmen, free trade would be beneficial for society as a whole.

This is especially true in relation to complicated issues such as investment and regulations. The U.S. government also believes that a successful regional strategy will bring to bear pressures which will hasten fully international agreements.

AREAS OF INTERNATIONAL COOPERATION

Multilateral trade agreements—WTO
- Based on principles of reciprocity, nondiscrimination, and transparency
- Uruguay Round extended trade liberalization to services and agricultural commodities and helped establish intellectual property rights

Regional trade agreements—NAFTA, European Union
- Risk of trade diversion rather than trade creation
- But may be better able to address complicated issues, such as those involving investment

REVIEW AND PRACTICE

SUMMARY

1. Countries protect themselves in a variety of ways besides imposing tariffs. These nontariff barriers include quotas, voluntary export restraints, and regulatory barriers. Quotas and voluntary export restraints are now banned by international agreement. While in recent decades there have been huge reductions in tariff barriers, there has been some increase in nontariff barriers.

2. While all countries benefit from free trade, some groups within a country may be adversely affected. In the United States, unskilled workers and those in industries where, without trade, there is limited competition, may see their wages fall. Some workers may lose their jobs, and may require assistance to find new ones.

3. Laws nominally intended to ensure fair trade—the dumping, countervailing duty, and market surge laws—often are used as protectionist measures.

4. Concern about imports is particularly strong when unemployment is high. But beggar-thy-neighbor policies, which attempt to protect jobs by limiting imports, tend to be counterproductive.

5. The World Trade Organization, which replaced the GATT, provides a framework within which trade barriers can be reduced. It is based on reciprocity, nondiscrimination, and transparency. The Uruguay Round of

the GATT extended trade liberalization to new areas, including agriculture and intellectual property, and established the World Trade Organization.

6. Difficulties at arriving at trade agreements involving all of the nations of the world have resulted in broader regional agreements, including NAFTA. There is a risk that these regional agreements may give rise to trade diversion offsetting the benefits from trade creation.

Key Terms

protectionism
nontariff barriers
quotas
voluntary export restraints
dumping
countervailing duties
market surges
beggar-thy-neighbor policies
infant industry argument
strategic trade theory
General Agreement on Tariffs and Trade (GATT)
World Trade Organization (WTO)
North American Free Trade Agreement (NAFTA)
trade creation
trade diversion

Review Questions

1. What are the various ways in which countries seek to protect their industries against foreign imports?

2. How do tariffs and quotas differ?

3. Why are consumers worse off as a result of the imposition of a tariff?

4. What are the laws designed to ensure fair international trade? How have they worked in practice?

5. What are nontariff barriers to international trade?

6. How is it possible that while there are gains to free trade, some groups are adversely affected? Which are the groups in the United States that are most adversely affected?

7. What are beggar-thy-neighbor policies? What are their consequences?

8. What do GATT and the WTO do? What are their basic underlying principles? What have been GATT's achievements? What further advances were accomplished under the Uruguay Round?

9. What is NAFTA? What are the advantages of regional free trade agreements?

10. What is meant by trade diversion versus trade creation?

PROBLEMS

1. Suppose that Japanese products go out of fashion in the United States. How would this affect Japan's exports? What would happen to the exchange rate? What would happen to national income in Japan, on the assumption that the Japanese government did not undertake offsetting actions? What effect would this, in turn, have on U.S. exports? On U.S. national income, again with the assumption that the U.S. government did not undertake offsetting actions? Use the diagrammatic techniques learned in earlier chapters to answer these questions.

2. Explain why the balance of trade between Japan and the United States would worsen as Japan goes into a recession, if at the same time, the United States is recovering from a recession.

3. Explain why, if the United States succeeded in getting Japan to remove some of its trade barriers, the exchange rate between the yen and the dollar might change, but the trade balance might not be affected much. Why would the removal of these trade barriers still be beneficial for the United States?

4. During 1993, the price of aluminum fell, partly because of the worldwide recession, which affected raw materials like aluminum particularly adversely, partly because new techniques allowed aluminum cans to be produced using about 10 percent less aluminum, and partly because Russia, no longer using the aluminum to make airplanes, began exporting it. The U.S. aluminum companies threatened to file dumping charges against Russia, although Russia was selling the aluminum at world prices. What do you think might have been the consequences if the dumping charges had actually been filed? (Some background facts that might be relevant: Japan is a major importer of aluminum; some U.S. aluminum companies are major owners of non-U.S. producers.)

5. If you were a government intent on discouraging imports, how might you use regulatory policies to further your objective?

6. If Mexican workers receive a third of the wages that U.S. workers do, why don't all American firms move down to Mexico?

7. If Mexico becomes a more attractive place to invest, is the United States helped or hurt?

8. Should the U.S. treat foreign-owned firms producing cars in the United States (like Mazda) differently from American firms? Should Ford, Chrysler, and GM be allowed to form a research consortium, excluding these producers? Should the U.S. government give money to a research consortium that excludes these firms? Should they be eligible for research funds themselves on a equal basis?

9. How should the government prioritize its efforts on opening markets to U.S. firms? By the impact on U.S. workers? Impact on U.S. companies?

Impact on U.S. investors? How would you prioritize the following four examples: (a) opening up the Japanese market to allow Toys-R-Us to open retail stores in Tokyo, selling toys made in China; (b) opening up the Japanese securities markets to ensure that Goldman Sachs and other U.S. investment firms can sell securities to Japanese pension funds; (c) opening up the Japanese car market to enhance the ability of GM, Ford, and Chrysler to sell U.S. cars in Japan; and (d) opening up the Chinese car market to enhance the ability of Toyota and Mazda to sell American-made cars to China?

CHAPTER 20

ALTERNATIVE ECONOMIC SYSTEMS

The Soviet Union has dissolved, and formerly Communist countries all over Eastern Europe and the Baltic areas are overhauling their economic systems, making them more market based. Even the most populous country in the world, China—though retaining communism as its *political* system—has committed itself to using markets in its economic life. Such an enormous change makes it difficult to remember the days of rivalry between the Soviet Union's Communist economy and the mixed capitalist economies of Western Europe and the United States. As recently as the 1970s, many Western observers, including reputable economists, considered it only a matter of time before the Soviet Union would draw even and eventually win the economic race.

Today the formerly Communist countries look to their Western European neighbors and see much higher living standards. This chapter contrasts Soviet-style economies with those of Western countries, highlighting the major differences that might account for their divergent growth paths and standards of living. Toward the end of the chapter, we will learn about the two major versions of socialism that differed from that of the former Soviet Union: the workers' cooperatives of the former Yugoslavia and the attempts by Hungary and China to incorporate elements of a market into socialism.

Studying these alternative economic systems is not only important in providing insights into the major economic and political conflict of the twentieth century. Understanding why socialism and communism have failed provides us insights into what makes markets work.

KEY QUESTIONS

1. What were the economic conditions that gave rise to the socialist idea?
2. What were the central characteristics of Soviet-style socialism? How did it differ from the market system in the way it allocated resources?
3. Why did it fail?
4. What are some of the principal reforms of Soviet-style socialism that have been tried, and how did they fared?
5. What problems do the former socialist economies face in making the transition to a market economy?

TERMINOLOGY

Several terms are useful in describing alternative economic systems. Under **socialism,** the government owns and operates the basic means of production—the factories that make cars and steel, the mines, the railroads, the telephone system, and so on. Under **communism,** the government essentially owns all property—not only the factories, but also the houses and the land. In practice, no government has abolished all private property. People still own the clothes they wear and durable consumption goods like cars and television sets.

The term "communism" is used to describe the economic system in countries that came under the domination of the Soviet Union and China in the years after World War II. These countries shared an economic system that involved not only state ownership of assets but also considerable central control of economic decisions. Because of the important role played by central planning, these economies are referred to as **planned economies.** These countries also had a political system that did not allow free elections, free speech, or a multitude of other rights found in democracies.

The economies of the United States and Western Europe, in contrast, are commonly referred to as capitalist economies, because of the important role played by private capital. They are also called mixed economies, since government plays a large role, and market economies, because of their heavy reliance on firms and households interacting in markets. Table 20.1 compares living standards in the Soviet-style economies just before the revolutionary events of 1989–91 with those in the rest of the world.

Table 20.1 COMPARISON OF LIVING STANDARDS BETWEEN PLANNED AND MARKET ECONOMIES

	GNP per capita (1988 $)	Annual GNP growth rate (%) 1965–1988	Life expectancy at birth	Adult illiteracy (%)
Soviet-style economies:				
USSR	2,660	4.0	70	<5
China	330	5.4	70	31
Hungary	2,460	5.1	71	<5
Market economies:				
U.S.A.	19,840	1.6	76	<5
India	340	1.8	58	57
Italy	13,330	3.0	77	<5
Egypt	660	3.6	63	56
Sweden	19,300	1.8	77	<5

THE ORIGINS OF SOCIALISM AND COMMUNISM

The eighteenth and nineteenth centuries produced the industrial revolution, and with it a dramatic change in the structures of the economies and societies it touched. New technologies resulted in development of the factory system and increased movement of workers from rural to urban areas. In the fast-growing cities, workers often lived in squalid conditions. In order for families to eke out a living, children went alongside their parents to work in the factories, where they worked long hours in unhealthy conditions. Periodically economies faced a recession or depression. Workers were thrown out of their jobs and forced to beg, steal, or starve. Life for the unlanded peasants in the rural sectors was hardly more idyllic. In Ireland in the 1840s, for instance, a fifth of the population (half a million people) starved to death.

While the vast majority of people thus lived on the edge of survival, a few had considerable wealth, often inherited. Between the very wealthy and the poor was a small but growing middle class, mainly commercial and professional. (By contrast, today in Europe and America, it is the middle class, consisting of professionals, businesspeople, and high-wage workers, that is dominant.)

Were these conditions inevitable? Could they be changed? If so, how? These questions preoccupied numerous social thinkers from the late eighteenth century on. Many saw the capitalist economic system as the culprit. The most influential critic of the capitalist system was a German man living in England named Karl Marx.

Marx believed that the force of history had led the economy inevitably to evolve from medieval feudalism to capitalism, and that the economy, just as inevitably, would evolve from capitalism to socialism and eventually to communism. Not only would there be no private property, the state would make all allocation decisions. "From each according to his ability," wrote Marx, "and to each according to his needs."[1] Clearly Marx's vision of socialism provided different answers from the market economy to the basic economic questions of what to produce and in what quantities, how to produce it, for whom it should be produced, and who makes the decisions. The state, *not* the market, would decide what, how, and for whom.[2]

Among those who found Marx's ideas particularly attractive was a Russian revolutionary, Vladimir Ilyich Lenin. In October 1917, the Bolsheviks—the party of Lenin, with Marxism as its official ideology—seized the government. The first "Communist" government was established. Translating Marx's ideology into a program for running a populous, poor, and largely undeveloped and rural country was no easy task. It was ironic that Russia, hardly touched by capitalism at the time of the revolution, became the first to try to implement Marx's ideas. Since Marx had predicted that countries would have to pass through the capitalist phase *on the way* to socialism, he had expected socialism to arise first in countries such as Britain or France.

Indeed, the economic system that we know today as communism is as much due to how Lenin and his successor, Joseph Stalin, adapted Marx's ideas to the situation they found in Russia as it is to Marx's original ideas. What Marx's reaction would be to what evolved there one can only guess, but a hint is provided by his comment on the ideas of the French Marxists: "As for me, I am not a Marxist."

Disillusionment with Markets

In the United States and other developed countries today, there is widespread confidence in markets and in the efficiency with which they allocate resources. To be sure, there are market failures, periods of unemployment, and pockets of poverty. But we have seen in this book how markets by and large allocate resources efficiently. We have seen as well how selective government interventions can remedy the market failures and, if there is the political will, at least partially address the problem of the inequality of income generated by the market.

But this confidence has not always been present; neither is it universal now. When the United States went into the Great Depression in 1929, not to recover

[1]*Critique of the Gotha Program* (1875).

[2]In Marx's view, socialism and communism were transitional stages to an eventual time when the state would wither away. How production would be organized—how the basic decisions of what to produce, how to produce it, and for whom it should be produced would be made—in this eventual period was left unclear.

Close-up: Marxist Economics

Of the many writers in the nineteenth century who advocated socialism, none was more influential than Karl Marx. His ideas not only influenced how socialism developed within the Soviet Union, they gave rise to the Marxist school of economics. Like any major school, ideas evolve, as do disagreements among its members. Following are a few of the major ideas.

One important idea concerns what determines, or should determine, prices. The answer given by the basic economic model is the law of supply and demand. Marx, by contrast, made use of what was called the labor theory of value, a set of ideas developed earlier by the British economist David Ricardo. The labor theory of value argued that the value of any good should be attributed to the workers who made it. A good that required more labor should be valued more highly, and vice versa. Marx considered the difference between what a good was sold for and the labor costs that went into making the good—the profits of the firm and the return to capital—as exploitation of workers. By contrast, in market economies profits are viewed as providing firms with incentives, and capital is seen as a scarce factor—like any other scarce factor, such as land or labor—that will be efficiently allocated only when it fetches a return.

Another important strand in Marxist thought is that the economic system affects human nature. This book has taken the preferences of individuals as given. The demand curves for candy and CDs, for example, have been based on the trade-offs that people are willing to make. And we have not asked why workers may shirk if they are not provided incentives.

Many Marxists believe that under a different social system, people would be less materialistic, more concerned about helping one another, more committed to their jobs. During wartime, we often see changes in attitudes and behavior. Whether human nature is sufficiently mutable that *some* social system might achieve these idealistic goals over long periods of time remains debatable. What is clear is that none of the Soviet-style economies succeeded.

A third strand of Marxist thought emphasizes the link between politics and economics. Marxists claim that the answer to the question of "for whom" is provided by power—the economic power of monopolies and the political power of the wealthy. The wealthy use government to gain for themselves what they cannot achieve in the marketplace. Marxists cite instances of governments spending hundreds of billions of dollars to fight a war to preserve business interests, while claiming insufficient money to finance the rebuilding of urban ghettos or to provide free college education to the poor. The debate on the validity of these claims, as always with moral issues and other value judgments, takes us beyond the boundaries of economics.

Marx may have been correct in his emphasis on the importance of economic factors in determining the evolution of society. In an ironic twist of history, though, economic forces appear to have injured socialism more than capitalism. It is the economic successes of the capitalist systems of the industrialized world, combined with the economic failures of the Soviet-style socialist economies, that led to the reaction against socialism in Eastern Europe and the Soviet Union.

fully until World War II, millions of Americans were thrown out of jobs. The capitalist economic system did not seem to be functioning well. Today, to the billions of people still living in abject poverty in India, elsewhere in Asia, and in Africa and South America, markets have failed to meet their rising aspirations. And even within the industrialized countries, there are many who have not partaken of the general prosperity. For them the market system does not seem to have worked well.

It is not surprising, then, that many have sought an alternative economic system, which would generate faster sustained economic growth at the same time as it promoted greater equality. Throughout much of the twentieth century, many saw socialism as the answer. They believed that if the government controlled the economy, not only would recessions be eliminated, so too would what they saw as the chaos of the marketplace, for instance the excess expansion of capacity in one industry accompanied by shortages in another industry.

HOW SOVIET-STYLE SOCIALIST ECONOMIES WORK

Private property, prices, and the profit incentive play a central role in market economies. If these are abandoned in a Soviet-style socialist economy, what replaces them? Three major components are central planning, force, and political controls and rewards.

In Soviet-style economies, decision making, including coordination of economic activity, was to be done by government ministries, through central planning. Five-year plans were drawn up, with detailed targets—how much steel production was to be increased, how much food production, and so on. Individual plant managers were told not only what they were to produce, but how they were to produce it.

Market incentive schemes were also sometimes replaced by force. We saw in earlier chapters that some incentive schemes take the form of the carrot, some of the stick. The Soviet Union under Joseph Stalin preferred the stick. Those who did not meet their targets were rewarded with a sojourn in Siberia.

Political controls and rewards also helped replace the lack of economic incentives. Key positions in the economy went to faithful members of the Communist party. In the early days of the revolution, these included many who really believed in socialism as an alternative, superior form of economic organization. Given their ideological commitment, economic incentives to work hard to meet the goals were relatively unimportant. And to the extent that incentives were important, they were provided by the potential for promotion. But as the years went by, membership in the party came to be seen as the vehicle for getting ahead, not as a matter of belief. Under Leonid Brezhnev, who was the first secretary of the Communist party from 1964 to 1982, (a term used to describe the actual head of the party), this cynical attitude spread. The party faithful not only received good jobs but enjoyed other benefits, including access to special stores at which goods not generally available could be acquired.

A basic aspect of market economies, competition, was shunned. Just as the Communist party had a monopoly in the political sphere, no competition with government enterprises was allowed, and the government enterprises did not compete with one another. They did not, of course, eliminate all competition: there was still competition to be promoted to top positions and thus receive higher incomes and access to desirable goods. But success in this competition was not based on how efficiently you produced the goods that consumers wanted, or how innovative you were in devising new products. Rather, success was measured by how well you complied with the bureaucratic targets and requirements and how well you performed in the politics of the bureaucracy and party.

The planned economy or central planning failed miserably in replacing markets. The central planners simply did not have the requisite information. Workers, for instance, were often mismatched with jobs. They were given job security, but this reduced their economic incentives. Pay, and even promotion, were generally not related to performance, and thus the incentives were undermined. Without economic incentives, workers often exerted the minimal level of effort that they could get away with.

Similarly, firms had no incentive to produce beyond the quotas assigned to them. Indeed, they had an incentive not to do so. If they showed that they could produce more with fewer inputs, in subsequent years their quotas would be increased. In the absence of a price system, shortages often developed, not only of consumer goods, but also of inputs into production. Hence, firms squirreled away any extra raw materials they could get their hands on.

The absence of prices and profits had further debilitating effects. In market economies, returns to investment are the signals that determine how capital should be allocated. The quest for profits provides the incentive for entrepreneurs; equally important, losses are a signal for firms to close down. In socialist economies, with the state owning all firms and therefore all profits, profits provide little incentive. And losses are seldom used as a basis for shutting down establishments. If a firm makes a loss, the government meets the deficit. János Kornai, a Hungarian economist who teaches both in his native land and at Harvard, refers to this phenomenon as **soft budget constraints,** to contrast them with the harsh reality of budget constraints facing firms in a market economy. For the firm in a socialist system, there is no penalty for making losses, and no incentive to conserve on resources or to innovate.

In a way, it made sense for the Soviet government not to pay too much attention to profits, since the prices firms received for what they produced and the prices they paid for the inputs they used (including labor and capital) were not market-clearing prices. They did not represent the scarcity value of the resources used or of the goods produced. Thus, the profits were not a good measure of the benefits or costs of the firm's production. By the same token, since prices were not set at market-clearing levels, they did not reflect true scarcity. Hence returns to investment—measured in rubles—were not a sound guide for allocating investments. Prices and wages provided little guidance for whether firms should try to economize more on labor or capital or other inputs.

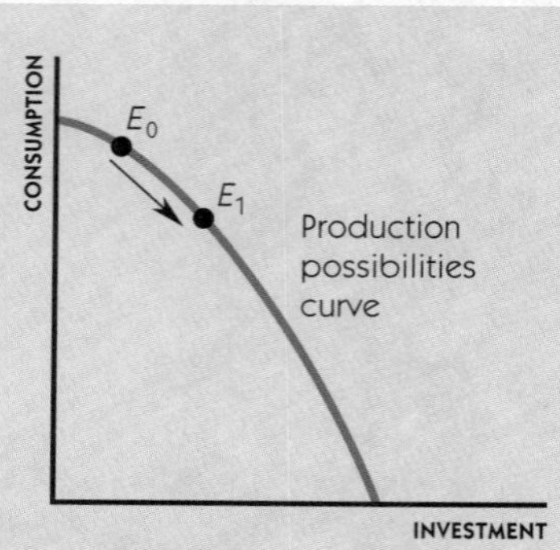

Figure 20.1 RAPID INDUSTRIALIZATION: MOVEMENTS ALONG THE PRODUCTION POSSIBILITIES CURVE

Soviet-style socialists believed that rapid growth of heavy industry was desirable, so they increased investment. But as the production possibilities curve shows, this can only be done at the expense of consumption. Central planners tried to move the economy toward a point such as E_1, with a high output of investment goods and a low output of consumption goods.

It is perhaps no accident that the fields in which the Soviet Union achieved its greatest success—military research, space technology, and mathematics and physics—were all fields in which markets play a limited role even in capitalist economies. In the absence of prices and interest rates to guide investment, decisions were made on beliefs about the "correct" path of development. Stalin had two basic ideas. First, he recognized that resources that were not allocated to consumption could be given to investment. In terms of the production possibilities curve depicted in Figure 20.1, his first objective was to reduce consumption and move the economy from a point such as E_0 to E_1. One of the aims of the collectivization of agriculture was to do just that, to squeeze the farmers as much as possible. But urban workers' wages were also kept low. By keeping wages low and the supply of consumer goods limited, the Soviet planners in effect "forced" the economy to have high savings.

His second idea was to focus investment on heavy industry. Stalin considered huge factories, such as steel mills, the central symbol of modern economies, which distinguished them from less developed, agrarian economies. He therefore invested primarily in heavy industry, providing little support for agriculture, consumer goods, or housing. The two ideas were in a sense intertwined. With low wages and low consumption, there was little need to invest in industries to provide consumption goods.

Soviet-Style Socialism and Inequality

The Soviet government, through its planning ministry, not only decided what was to be produced and how. It also provided the answer to the "for whom" question. In answering this question, three aspects of Soviet ideology played an important role. First, Soviet-style economies were committed to heavy industrialization and a de-emphasis on agriculture. Not surprisingly, then, a large part of the burden of the costs was borne by agriculture. Forced collectivization in agriculture kept agriculture wages low. In effect, there were high taxes on agriculture.

Second, the program of high savings and low consumption could be interpreted as putting an emphasis on consumption of future generations at the expense of consumption of the current generation.

Third, an attempt was made to reduce the inequality in society, at least according to the rhetoric of the leaders. The government determined everyone's wages. It decided how much more a skilled worker got than an unskilled worker. Some goods it allocated directly, such as markets for housing and medical care.

Whether or to what extent Soviet-style socialist systems were successful in reducing inequality remains debated. On the one hand, after confiscating all land and other property, there were no longer any very rich people. Also, free medicine and highly subsidized food and apartments provided a "safety net" for the poor. Moreover, one of the major sources of poverty—unemployment—was eliminated. But on the other hand, differences in life-style between the worst-off members of society and high party officials remained enormous. Whole families of ordinary citizens lived crowded together in one room. And though no one starved, they spent long hours in lines to obtain the barest necessities of life. By contrast, high party officials enjoyed vacations along the beaches of the Black Sea, could buy goods unavailable elsewhere at stores reserved for party members, and had chauffeur-driven cars and other powers and perquisites enjoyed by relatively few within the capitalist world. Large wage differentials, commensurate with those observed in capitalist economies, also existed, though they may have translated into smaller differences in living standards, given the many things provided cheaply by the state.

Even the most vaunted achievement of socialism, prevention of the abject extremes of poverty, has in recent years been thrown into doubt. In the period of 1960–61 in China, for example, demographers now estimate that as many as 20 million Chinese starved to death. In the democracies, a free press would have presumably ensured that a calamity like this could not have occurred. Something would have been done. In China, it went almost unnoticed.

THE BASIC ECONOMIC QUESTIONS UNDER SOVIET-STYLE SOCIALISM

1. What is produced?
   - Heavy industrial goods
   - Other goods as the state sees fit
2. How are goods produced?
   - With technologies and inputs decided upon by the state (often capital-intensive technologies)
3. For whom are they produced?
   - For future generations (high forced savings rates)
   - For present generations according to the wages set by government (high "taxes" on agriculture)
   - For government officials, who get high rewards
4. Who makes the decisions?
   - Central planning authorities

FAILURE OF SOCIALISM

For several decades, Stalin's program appeared successful. He was able to force net investment rates up to almost unprecedented levels, more than 23 percent of net national product in 1937, for example. Many factories were built. The official statistics suggested a path of rapid industrialization and growth. There is growing doubt about the reliability of the statistics, but there is little doubt that any gains were accompanied by political repression. The USSR's economic progress was interrupted by World War II, in which 20 million Russians are believed to have died, and the economy was greatly disrupted.

The period after World War II saw the spread of Soviet-style socialism to Eastern Europe—Poland, Czechoslovakia, East Germany, Hungary, Romania, Bulgaria, Yugoslavia, and Albania—and, in 1949, to China.[3] In the case of the Eastern European countries, at least, the spread was hardly voluntary. It was the price they paid for being liberated from the Germans by Soviet troops at the end of the war. Before the war, some Eastern European countries had enjoyed reasonably high standards of living. Others, such as Albania, had been extremely poor and backward.

The ensuing decades witnessed several changes in attitudes toward the Soviet-style socialist experiment. At first, the "efficiency" virtues of the system were lauded. The planning mechanism replaced the perceived chaos of the marketplace. Investment could be directed in a rational way. Resources could be quickly mobilized. Moreover, the government could force the high levels of savings required for a successful development program. Textbooks as well as popular writings talked about a trade-off between growth and development on the one hand and freedom on the other. Strong central control was thought to be necessary for rapid growth. Moreover, it was thought that Soviet-style socialism could raise the quality of life to a level the market economy had not been able to attain. Basic human services like health and education could be brought to the masses.

But as economies like Czechoslovakia and Hungary, which had been prosperous before the war, fell behind other European countries, concerns about the efficiency of the system were raised. Such systems could force their citizens to save more because they could repress consumption, but could they allocate resources efficiently? It became increasingly clear that the countries were not growing as fast as one would have thought. The higher savings rates did little more than offset the higher levels of inefficiency.

By the mid-1970s, inklings of an impending economic crisis became more and more apparent. While agricultural productivity in the United States and Western Europe had boomed, in the Soviet-style socialist countries it had stagnated. Nikita Khrushchev, who led Russia from the death of Stalin until he was replaced by Brezhnev in 1964, recognized the problems in agriculture and directed more of the country's investment there. But in 1973, the Soviet Union began buying massive amounts of wheat from the United States and other Western countries to feed its people.

As Mikhail Gorbachev came to power in 1985 the magnitude of the problems the country faced became even clearer. It became evident that many of the statistics on industrial production had been more exaggerated than even

[3]Mongolia had adopted Soviet-style socialism much earlier, in 1924. Cuba adopted a variant much later, under Castro in 1959. North Korea and North Vietnam both adopted Soviet-style socialism as soon as their governments were established.

Close-up: Environmental Damage in the Soviet Union

One of the alleged advantages of centrally controlled economies was that unlike ruthless capitalists, socialist firms would take into account the costs and benefits to all members of society. In the area of environmental protection, that promise was not kept. In fact, in the words of one recent study, "When historians finally conduct an autopsy on the Soviet Union and Soviet Communism, they may reach the verdict of death by ecocide."

Market economies often have difficulty dealing with pollution externalities. But in attempting to grow faster, Soviet central planners often made pollution problems worse. For example, oil and energy prices were held deliberately low, as a form of assistance to manufacturers who used oil as an input. But lower prices encouraged wasteful use of energy. When combined with a lack of antipollution measures, this produced literally sickening air pollution. Today in the industrial center of what was called Magniogorsk, nine out of ten children become ill with pollution-related diseases like bronchitis, asthma, and cancer.

Highly intensive farming, in a situation where no one had a property right to the land and an incentive to protect it, led to massive pesticide use and soil erosion. Three-quarters of the surface water in what used to be the Soviet Union is now badly polluted, either from industrial or agricultural sources.

Perhaps the most publicized result of all was the explosion at the Chernobyl nuclear power station in 1986, which exposed perhaps 20 million Soviet citizens to excessive radiation. If that nuclear power plant had been forced to use safety equipment to avoid that externality, it might well have been shut down years earlier.

Rather than correcting the market failures that led to pollution, Soviet central planners had magnified them into ecological disasters.

Sources: "Rubbishing of a Superpower," *The Economist,* April 25, 1992, pp. 99–100; M. Feshbach and A. Friendly, *Ecocide in the USSR* (New York: Basic Books, 1992).

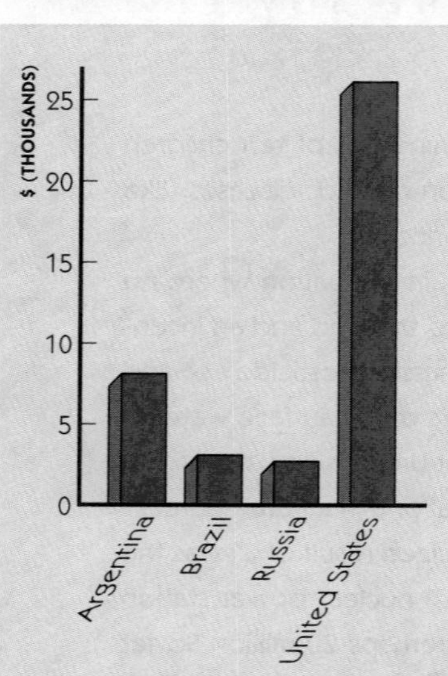

Figure 20.2 THE RUSSIAN STANDARD OF LIVING

Today, after decades of socialism, the average standard of living in Russia is close to that of Brazil, Argentina, and other less developed nations. *Source: World Development Report* (1996), Table 1.

many skeptics had thought. Indicators of well-being, such as infant mortality statistics, had similarly been distorted.

In most economists' judgment, the Soviet-style socialist experiment was a failure. Today, more than seventy years after the Soviet-style socialist experiment began in Russia, income per capita is a tenth of what it is in the United States. Russia finds its standard of living close to that of Brazil, Argentina, and other countries considered to be underdeveloped, as illustrated in Figure 20.2. The Soviet-style socialist experiment had remarkable achievements, like the Sputnik satellite, but a productive and growing economy was not among them.

REASONS FOR THE FAILURE

The continued success of the capitalist system and the failure of Soviet-style socialist economies can be attributed to incentives and markets, or the lack of them.

The socialists failed to recognize the importance of incentives. Workers, both in collective farms and in manufacturing firms, had no incentive to do more than was required. Managers similarly had no incentives. Firms could not keep any profits they made, and managerial pay in any case did not depend on the profitability of the enterprise. There was no competition, and the soft budget constraints—the fact that losses would be made up by the government—further attenuated managerial incentives.

Equally important, there was no incentive for innovation and growth. The increases in productivity of the labor force in capitalist economies over the past century, with the concomitant increases in wages, are in no small measure the result of the innovative efforts of entrepreneurs. These entrepreneurs almost surely did not succeed out of the desire to enhance the welfare of their workers; they were motivated by the lust for profits and the desire for returns to their savings. But as Adam Smith said, such motives provide a far surer guide to the enhancement of a nation's wealth than any other.

Socialists wanted to replace the market mechanism for allocating resources with central planning. But they encountered two further problems. First, the bureaucrats did not have the requisite information to know how to allocate resources efficiently. Managers of firms had no incentive to tell the central planners what the minimum inputs required to meet their production goals were. Rather, they had every incentive to claim they needed more than they really did. This made their job easier. And they had no incentive to exceed their goals; for if they did, the planners would raise their targets for the next year.

Second, planners could not perfectly monitor the various firms in the economy, to ensure that resources were used in the way intended. And firms had only limited incentives to comply with the planners' directives. They were not rewarded, and they knew they were only imperfectly monitored. Sometimes the managers could divert resources meant for the firm to their own private use. Their disdain for the planners was enhanced by the fact that the planners often put impossible demands on them, such as asking them to produce outputs without providing them the requisite inputs. To fulfill their quota, firms had to acquire the inputs from a "gray" market outside the planning system.

The socialists did not understand the importance of capital markets, interest rates, and profits. As this text has emphasized, capital is a scarce resource. It must be allocated efficiently. Prices provide the signals that make this possible. Because the Soviet-stlye socialist economies set prices by command rather than through markets, prices did not provide the necessary signals. Try as they might to use the planning mechanism to replace the market mechanism, socialist government planning boards simply did not have the requisite information to allocate investment efficiently.

Given the scarcity of capital, the Soviet strategy of heavy industrialization probably did not make much sense. It would have made more sense to focus attention on industries that require less capital.

The failure of worker incentives, the failure of planners to allocate resources efficiently, and the failure of firms to use resources efficiently largely accounted for the inefficiency of the system. But there were other factors as well. The drabness of life, the lack of opportunity afforded by the system, the long hours spent in lines trying to get rotten vegetables or a small portion of meat, all contributed to social malaise, evidenced by a high incidence of alcoholism, which impaired worker productivity. The worker under Soviet-style socialism seemed truly alienated from his work.

CAUSES OF THE FAILURE OF SOVIET-STYLE SOCIALISM

1. Failure to provide adequate incentives to workers and managers
   Lack of competition, soft budget constraints, and lack of incentives to stimulate innovation and growth were major factors.
2. Failure of planning mechanism to replace markets
   Planners lacked the requisite information to allocate resources efficiently.
   Planners lacked the ability to monitor firms and make sure resources were used in the ways intended.

REFORMS IN THE SOVIET-STYLE SOCIALIST ECONOMIES

As the failures of Soviet-style socialism became more evident, a variety of reforms were discussed. Three courses of action were possible: try harder to make the socialist system work; give up on socialism and move to a market-based system;

or find a third way, which would be neither capitalism nor socialism. For three decades, beginning with Khrushchev, the Soviet Union tried the first strategy. Workers were exhorted to work harder. Money poured into agriculture but left little traces of enhanced productivity. Campaigns—including one against vodka—were launched to increase worker productivity.

During 1990 and 1991, there was much debate over whether or not the first strategy should be abandoned. In October of 1990, Gorbachev announced that the Soviet Union would be converted to capitalism in five hundred days. He soon dropped this program, whereupon the economists who had been advising him on the market strategy resigned. It appeared as if there would be another attempt to make socialism work. But then, following the attempted coup in August 1991 and the dissolution of the Soviet Union, directions were changed again: most of the newly created republics seemed committed to adopting some form of market system.

People looking for a third solution sought ways of combining what they saw as the strengths of capitalism with those of socialism. Hungary made some attempt to do this. But perhaps the most successful experiment was in China, where the so-called responsibility system in agriculture essentially allowed farmers to sell most of what they produced in markets and to keep the proceeds. As a result, agricultural production skyrocketed during the late 1970s and early 1980s. The annual growth rate of grain production in the six years after the responsibility system was adopted (1978–1984) was 5 percent, compared with 3.5 percent in the thirteen years before the new system (1965–1978).

MARKET SOCIALISM

An important idea behind several of the reform movements was market socialism, which argued that an economy could combine the advantages of market mechanisms with public ownership of the means of production. Oskar Lange—who was a professor of economics at the University of Chicago before returning to Poland after World War II, eventually to become a vice-president of that country's Communist government—was a leading advocate.

Under market socialism, prices would serve the same allocative role that they do in capitalist economies. Prices would be set so that demand equaled supply. Firms would act like competitive price takers. They would maximize their profits at the prices they faced. They would produce up to the point where price equaled marginal cost. They would hire labor up to the point where the value of the marginal product of labor was equal to the wage. But since government owned all machines and buildings, it would take responsibility for all investment decisions. These decisions would be made according to a national plan, which defined the nation's priorities. The planning process would entail close interaction between the government planners and the firms, with the firms informing the planners of what was required to meet various production goals.

In the 1930s, there was a great debate between the advocates of market socialism, including Oskar Lange, and a group of Austrian economists, including Ludwig von Mises and Nobel laureate Friedrich von Hayek. The Austrians did not believe that government could have the information required to efficiently allocate investment. They thought the task of allocating resources, or even setting market-clearing prices, was simply too complicated to be done by a government bureau. (As it turned out, they were largely correct.) And they did not believe government-owned firms would act like private firms. In their view, market socialism was doomed to failure. The advocates of market socialism emphasized the fact that there were, in modern terms, pervasive market failures. Capital and risk markets were imperfect. There were externalities. Competition was imperfect. The market gave rise to great inequality. And capitalist economies seemed prone to periodic chronic illnesses—to recessions and depressions. Pointing out these failures, of course, does not prove that market socialism can do any better, or even as well as capitalism.

PROBLEMS WITH MARKET SOCIALISM

Market socialism faces two key problems: obtaining the requisite information to set prices and providing managers with incentives.

Information to Set Prices In order to set prices at market-clearing levels, planners have to know, in effect, both demand and supply curves. They have to know an enormous amount about what consumers want as well as firms' capabilities. But they seldom have this information, partly, as noted, because firms have no incentive to tell planners their capabilities. Even with good information, it is extraordinarily difficult for a government bureaucracy to set prices at market-clearing levels. In Lange's time it was still plausible to hope, as he did, that faster computers would solve the problem. But as better and better computers have been developed, it has become increasingly clear that the problems of setting simultaneously the prices of the millions of goods produced in a modern market economy cannot be solved by a computer, however advanced.

Indeed, it has become clear that while prices play a central role in how the market economy functions, they are only part of the market's incentive systems. Customers also care about the *quality* of the goods they purchase. For instance, for firms, having inputs delivered on time is essential. Consider producing nails in a socialist economy. Given a directive to produce so many nails, the nail factory produces short, stubby nails. When the directive is modified to include a specification for a longer nail, the factory responds by producing a nail with the cheapest steel it can get hold of; the result is that the nail splits when hit too hard. When told that the steel should not be too brittle, the firm finds a kind of steel that bends too easily to make it useful for many purposes.

In market economies, firms will not produce at the market price unless they know they can sell the goods. In a socialist economy, the producer simply delivers the goods to another government enterprise, whose problem it is to sell the good. When China set too high a price for fans, for example, the factories produced more fans than could be sold. Meanwhile, there were huge shortages of most other consumer goods.

While setting prices wrong for consumer goods causes inconvenience, setting prices wrong for producer goods impairs the entire production process. If a firm producing an intermediate good cannot get some input it needs, it will not be able to provide its product to the firms that need it. A shortage at one critical point can have reverberations through other parts of the economy.

Incentives Under market socialism, managers often lack incentives. When the enterprise makes a profit, they cannot keep the profit. And when the enterprise makes a loss, the government makes up the deficit. Market socialism therefore does not resolve the problem of soft budget constraints. Furthermore, competition, which lies at the heart of the market's incentive system, is absent, and this lack of competition is reflected in all aspects of behavior, including the incentive to produce goods that reflect what customers want.

Some aspects of the experiments with market socialism have been successful, at least as compared with Soviet-style socialism. As was noted, the responsibility system of agriculture in China has resulted in huge increases in agricultural productivity. But overall, the success of most of the experiments is more debatable. To some, market socialism lacks the best features of both capitalism and socialism: it lacks the market's incentive structure and traditional socialism's other mechanisms of economic control. Within Hungary, for example, which had gone the farthest along the road to market socialism before 1989, a consensus developed against market socialism.

In 1992, China embarked on further reforms, in which prices and investment were increasingly placed in the hands of individual enterprises. What distinguished this form of market socialism from capitalism was the ownership of enterprises. Most were either state owned, or owned by villages and townships, or were cooperatives. The system, which had evolved gradually since 1979, had produced remarkable results—growth rates which averaged in excess of 10 percent for almost two decades.

WORKERS' COOPERATIVES IN YUGOSLAVIA

Yet another type of socialist experiment occurred in Yugoslavia. Marshal Tito, a communist who led the fight against the Nazis in Yugoslavia and became the country's leader after World War II, broke with Stalin in 1948. In the ensuing years, decentralization and decision making by firms became an important part of the Yugoslavian economy. Ownership of firms was turned over to the workers, who were responsible for choosing their own managers. (In practice, the Communist party exercised considerable influence both in the choice of managers and in the decisions made.)

The idea of worker-owned and -managed firms—cooperatives—has a long history throughout Europe and in the United States. Even today in the United States, there are some enormously successful worker-owned firms—Amana, which makes refrigerators; Avis, the country's second largest car rental company; and W. W. Norton, the publisher of this book. Ulgar, a successful household appliances firm, began as a worker cooperative in Mondragón, Spain.

Today, with thousands of workers located in many separate plants, it is still run as a cooperative.

A major argument for cooperatives is that because the worker is also part owner, she has a greater commitment to the firm and more incentive to work hard. While this argument seems valid for cooperatives involving relatively few workers, it does not apply as well to large enterprises. And this proved to be a problem in Yugoslavia. Managers elected by a vote of the workers may be as remote as managers chosen by a board of directors. In cooperatives with thousands of workers, each worker gets back a negligible amount of any extra profits that result from anything he does. The most successful cooperatives thus are often the smaller ones.

In Yugoslavia, the cooperatives encountered another problem—lack of incentive to hire new workers. If new workers have the same rights as old workers, the profits of the enterprise must be divided more ways. Whether for this or other reasons, Yugoslavia was plagued with high unemployment rates.

Investment posed still a third problem. When Yugoslavian workers left their cooperative, they received nothing. There was therefore little interest in investing, at least in the long term, or otherwise increasing the market value of the enterprise. Workers did not have an incentive to make investments that yielded returns beyond the date of their retirement.[4]

Some of these problems are not *inherent* in cooperatives. For instance, in cooperatives in the United States and Europe, when a person retires or leaves the cooperative for any other reason, he takes his capital out. He is viewed as a part owner of the enterprise; the share he owns depends on the rules of the cooperative, typically how long he has been with the cooperative and in what positions he has served. By the same token, when a worker joins a cooperative, she has in effect to buy a share. (The company may loan her the money, so her take-home pay may be reduced until she has contributed her capital share.) The better the cooperative does, the more she will be able to receive when she leaves. This provides an obvious incentive for the cooperative to make good investment decisions.

TRANSITION TO MARKET ECONOMIES

Many former socialist countries, including Hungary, the Czech Republic, and Poland, are today committed to becoming market economies. Others, such as Bulgaria, Romania, and Albania, want *some* market reforms, but how many and how fast remains uncertain. The following discussion describes key problems facing countries as they move toward a market economy.

[4]This list of problems that Yugoslavia faced is not meant to be exhaustive. There were others: lack of competition among people who purchased farmers' produce, for instance, meant that farmers received lower prices for their goods, and this discouraged farmers' production.

These problems of transition are exacerbated by the economic chaos in the former Soviet Union—the main trading partner of the Eastern European countries. As these countries face the problems of transition, they face the additional burden of finding new markets to replace sales to the Soviet Union, which have plummeted. To make matters worse, the kinds of goods they produced for the Soviet Union are not the high-quality goods consumers in Western Europe, Japan, and the United States want. Not only must they find new markets. They must also reorient their production.

MACROECONOMIC PROBLEMS

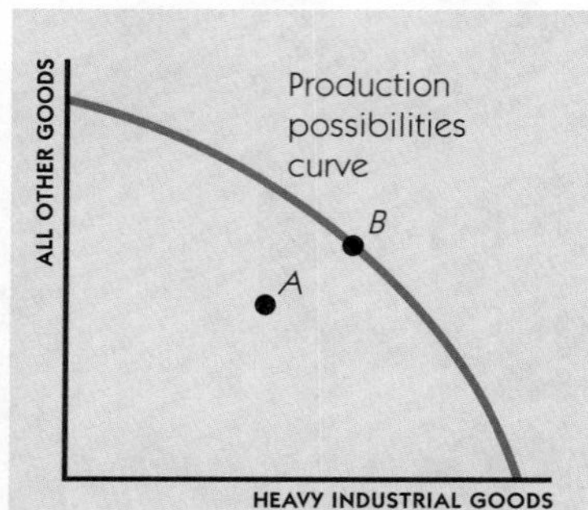

Figure 20.3 INEFFICIENCIES UNDER SOCIALISM

The Soviet-style socialist economies seemed to use their resources inefficiently, so that they operated substantially below the production possibilities curve, such as at point *A*. Moving the economy from *A* to a point like *B*, on the production possibilities curve, will entail substantial improvements in efficiency.

The first transition hurdle Eastern European economies face is a period of disruption in which living standards, at least for some, fall below even the low level that they had been under socialism.

A central problem with socialism was that resources were inefficiently allocated. If the economy is to move from a point inside its production possibilities curve (such as *A* in Figure 20.3) to a point on the curve, resources will have to be reallocated. Factories will have to be shut down. Workers will have to be let go. These disruptions will be reflected in high transitional unemployment. Transitional unemployment is like frictional unemployment—the unemployment that occurs as workers move between jobs—magnified many times over. Poland, the first country to attempt the transition, experienced unemployment rates estimated at 25–35 percent. In Romania, miners, seeing their real wages cut by a third, rioted and succeeded in bringing down the market-oriented prime minister. The new prime minister, however, was an economist even more committed to market reforms.

Unemployment is particularly serious in Eastern European countries, because they do not have the same kinds of safety nets that protect people forced out of jobs in Western Europe and the United States. This is not surprising, since under the previous regime unemployment was not a problem. Firms retained workers even when they were no longer needed; they had no profit motive, no budget constraint. But now, in the transition, firms do face budget constraints. Moreover, since capital markets are not yet working well, new firms are not being created and old firms are not expanding production to absorb the workers who have been laid off.

Inflation receives considerable attention in Eastern Europe these days, partly because it is felt by everyone, partly because typically wages do not keep pace with prices (so that living standards fall). But the fall in living standards is not really caused by the inflation. It is caused by the economic disruption of the transition process, which simultaneously reduces output, leads to inflation, and lowers living standards. In Russia inflation was not brought under control until 1994—and even then it proceeded at the rate of 18 percent per year.

The reason inflation always seems to arise in the transition is easy to see. The Soviet-style economies were run with prices below market-clearing levels. In Russia, indeed, the price of bread was kept so low that farmers found it cheaper to buy bread to feed their pigs than grain. Shortages were endemic. Hence, once prices were freed, price increases were inevitable. A onetime price increase is not the fundamental worry, however. The danger is that it will lead to inflationary expectations which, once established, perpetuate inflation.

Huge government deficits contribute to inflationary pressures. As the government's control over the economy weakens, its revenue sources often diminish. Under socialism, it could simply seize corporate profits. If it wanted to increase profits and thus its revenues, government could just increase the prices charged or reduce the wages paid. As government abandoned its role in wage and price setting, it lost its ability to raise revenues in this way. But cutting back on expenditures seems no easier in Eastern Europe than elsewhere. Food subsidies are a major drain on the budget, but government threats to reduce them have met with stiff opposition. As profits shrank, and, for huge numbers of enterprises, turned into losses, the economies in transition faced a dilemma. They could subsidize those enterprises making losses, or shut them down. With limited revenues, subsidies required deficit financing; and the debt contributed to inflationary pressures. If they were shut down, unemployment increased. Poland chose unemployment. Throughout much of the early 1990s, Russia seemed to choose inflation, with the unemployment rate remaining relatively low. Some countries got a large dose of both.

PRIVATIZATION AND COMPETITION

Private property and competition are at the center of the market economy. *Allowing* competition is easy. The government can simply say that anyone who wants to set up a firm and has the necessary resources can do so. Generating and sustaining competition are more difficult.

One important way for Eastern European countries to promote competition is through trade liberalization—opening up the economy to competition from abroad. But while most economists believe that trade liberalization will enhance economic efficiency in the long run, some are concerned about those who lose out in the competition, including people who lose their jobs. They give a variant of the infant industry argument, which goes like this. Enterprises in the former socialist economies have been insulated from competition for decades. It is unfair to suddenly subject them to competition and make their survival depend on this market test. They need time to learn how to compete.

Another way to promote competition is to sell off different parts of existing state enterprises to private entrepreneurs. There are few problems in selling off small businesses—barbershops, retail stores, restaurants. The real difficulties come in selling large enterprises like automobile or cement factories. Selling them to foreigners raises a host of thorny problems. No country likes to see its factories owned by foreigners. And if a country sells the factories to buyers abroad at too low a price, it is as if the country is giving away its hard-earned savings to foreigners. In Eastern Europe, there is a further problem. People with the most money include former party bosses. There is a bitter irony in seeing those who exploited the system under the

Communist government for their own advantage retain their advantageous position, this time as capitalist bosses.

Different countries have approached the problem of privatization differently. The Czech Republic first privatized stores, restricted purchases of the stores to citizens (and prohibited their resale to foreigners for two years), and accepted the grim fact that many of the hated Communist bosses would now become capitalist bosses. Economic efficiency, in the minds of Czech reformers, was more important than revenge. The country distributed vouchers to all citizens, which the citizens used to bid for shares in the larger, privatizing firms. Thus, in one stroke, the Czech Republic hoped both to privatize and to establish a viable stock market. With the widely distributed ownership of firms, they hoped to establish a people's capitalism. The next problem the Czechs face is that with no shareholders having a large stake in a firm, managers will run the firm with little outside check on their behavior. There have been proposals to deal with this problem, such as the establishment of holding companies or investment banks, but no consensus has emerged.

Hungary, by contrast, has taken the view that the advantages of foreign ownership—in particular, the advantage of foreigners' expertise—outweigh the disadvantages. Government officials point out that almost 40 percent of Belgian firms are foreign owned with no adverse effects. They envisage a similar role for foreign ownership within their own economy.

Russia, like the Czech Republic, used vouchers, but a large fraction of the shares were distributed to the workers and managers of each enterprise, raising questions about the extent to which managers will be subject to outside control.

SPEED OF TRANSITION

The pace of privatization has also varied greatly across countries and sectors. In Russia, by 1995, 55 percent of the large enterprises (outside of certain key sectors, such as energy) had been privatized. In the Czech Republic, 70 percent had been privatized. But in Romania and Bulgaria, privatization is proceeding at a very slow pace.

The former Soviet-style socialist economies face a difficult problem in deciding how fast to make the transition to capitalism. One approach is "cold turkey" or shock therapy. Make the plunge, live through a short nightmarish period, and then enjoy a future prosperity. The other approach calls for a more gradual transition and considers political as well as economic issues. For instance, will the pain caused by cold turkey be so great that support for the market will erode?

Poland tried the cold turkey approach, at least with respect to its macroeconomic adjustment. Inflation was brought under control, but at the expense of a drastic drop in output and employment, and the defeat of the government that undertook the plan. And even after the macroadjustments are made, the microeconomic problems—for instance, making factories more efficient, reallocating labor and capital—remain. Most of the other countries have moved more cautiously.

POLICY PERSPECTIVE: SHOCK THERAPY

The debate about the speed of transition has been heated—both inside the countries and from foreign commentators. Those advocating a quick transition have cited the famous aphorism, "You can't jump across a chasm in two steps." Advocates of a slower transition pointed out that "It takes nine months even to produce a baby," to which the advocates of fast transition replied, "But you can't be half pregnant."

What is at issue involves both economics and politics. If a fast transition results in high levels of unemployment, political disillusionment can set in, and political pressures may halt the reform process. When the reformers lost the Russian elections in December 1993, Strobe Talbott, who headed U.S. Russian policy (he subsequently became Deputy Secretary of State) criticized the "shock therapy" of rapid transition by saying there was too much shock and too little therapy. He seemed to be suggesting that he thought that the transition had proceeded too rapidly, without sufficient attention to those hurt by it.

There was a quick response from market reformers, who argued that the problem was too slow, not too rapid, transition. In a sense, both were correct. The slow transition was evidenced in low unemployment rates and low rates of privatization. But the rapid rates of inflation had left many older people (whose pensions did not increase with inflation) with a rapidly decreasing standard of living. In the rush to engage in economic reforms, too little attention may have been placed on the safety net.

Even those countries that managed to arrest and reverse the decline in GDP during transition faced a problem of increasing inequality.

The problem is that the success of market economies depends on a host of long-established institutions, not just on the abstract concept of markets. And all these institutions have to be functioning reasonably well if the economy is to prosper. There must be credit institutions to sort out potential loan applicants, to monitor the loans, and to see that funds go where they are most productive and are used in the way promised. There must be a legal structure that ensures contracts will be enforced and determines what happens when one party cannot fulfill its contract (bankruptcy). There must be an antitrust policy that ensures firms compete against one another.

Beyond that, the more advanced countries have developed a set of safety nets to help certain segments of society, such as the unemployed. Since unemployment was not a problem in socialist economies, these societies do not have such safety nets. There may be a huge human toll if the transition, with its attendant unemployment, proceeds before the safety nets are in place. Yet the budgetary problems facing all of these governments make it hard to institute such programs quickly.

Those who advocate a more gradual transition to market economies believe that the long-run success of these economies will be enhanced by thinking through each of the components, trying to design the best possible institutions, adapting to the particular situations in which they find themselves, and borrowing where appropriate from the United States, Western Europe, and Japan.

Today, almost all the countries of the former Soviet empire pay lip service to a commitment toward market reform. In some, the pace is so gradual as to be, to date, almost imperceptible. In Ukraine, market reforms were resisted as long as possible. But as inflation rates soared to over 100 percent per month and as the economy became unable to pay for its imports of energy—leading to factories threatened with closure, homes unheated, and farms unable even to get oil to run their tractors—a set of reforms was put into place in 1994. In other countries, such as the Czech Republic, the reforms have been rapid.

Even with rapid reforms, for most of the countries in transition it will take years, perhaps decades, to overcome the problems bequeathed by their Communist systems.

REVIEW AND PRACTICE

SUMMARY

1. Socialism grew out of the grave economic problems that characterized nineteenth-century industrial economies—severe recessions and depressions, unemployment, and bad working and living conditions.

2. Soviet-style socialism used central planning, under which government bureaucrats made all major decisions about what would be produced, how it would be produced, and for whom it would be produced. Competition was banned. Prices, set by the government, often did not reflect relative scarcities. Private property was restricted.

3. In socialist economies, firms and workers lacked incentives. Firms had little incentive to make profits since profits went to the state, and little incentive to avoid losses since the government would meet any deficits. Firms thus faced soft budget constraints. Similarly, socialism protected workers against layoffs. The trade-off was that this greater security created a lesser incentive for efficiency and hard work.

4. In Soviet-style economies, the government used force to impose high savings rates (which meant low consumption) and decided where investment funds went, pushing heavy industrialization. Government often lacked the requisite information to make informed decisions concerning how to allocate resources. Central planning was not able to replace markets.

5. The Soviet-style socialist experiment is today considered a failure by most economists. Russia's standard of living is no higher now than that of many underdeveloped countries.

6. Three possible reforms have been proposed for Soviet-style socialist economies: try harder to make socialism work; give up on socialism and

move to a market-based system; find a third alternative between socialism and markets. Today the focus is on the latter two strategies.

7. Among the problems faced by countries in their transition to a market economy are unemployment and inflation. These countries also do not have in place a safety net to protect those hurt in the transition process.

8. Privatizing state-controlled firms has proved difficult in many countries, given the reluctance of governments to sell factories to foreigners or former party bosses, who are often the only ones with sufficient resources to buy the enterprises. Still, in many countries, there has been substantial progress in privatization, expecially where voucher schemes have been employed.

Key Terms

socialism
communism
planned economies
soft budget constraints

Review Questions

1. What were some of the problems that motivated Karl Marx's criticism of capitalism?

2. What are some of the central characteristics of Soviet-style socialism?

3. How is the rate of national savings determined in a socialist economy, as opposed to a capitalist economy? How is the allocation of capital determined in a socialist economy, as opposed to a capitalist economy? Who determines what goods are produced in a socialist economy?

4. Why are budget constraints "soft" in socialist countries and "hard" in market economies?

5. What is market socialism? What did its advocates claim? What are the main problems it faces?

6. What are workers' cooperatives? What did its advocates claim for them? What were the problems of workers' cooperatives in Yugoslavia?

7. What are the central problems facing countries trying to move from Soviet-style socialism to market economies? Why are inflationary pressures common in a socialist country that is moving toward a market economy? Why is rising unemployment common?

8. What benefits do socialist economies hope to gain from privatization? What are some of the problems facing privatization programs?

9. What are the advantages and disadvantages of the "cold turkey" approach for a socialist economy in transition?

PROBLEMS

1. Explain how each of the following incentives is different in a socialist and a market economy:
   (a) the incentive of a manager to make wise decisions;
   (b) the incentive of workers to exert their best effort;
   (c) the incentive of a bank manager to screen prospective borrowers carefully.

2. Queues (lines) form when there is a shortage of goods. Use a supply and demand diagram to explain why socialist price controls tend to lead to queues.

3. Are the problems of soft budget constraints unique to socialist economies?

4. Why did the Soviet-style socialist economies have almost no safety nets of unemployment and welfare benefits?

5. In the Soviet-style socialist economies, housing was very scarce, and much of it was controlled by firms. What consequences might this have for labor mobility?

6. If you were a top official in a country that practiced Soviet-style socialism, would you rather have a very high income or access to a special store where all items are guaranteed to be in stock? Why?

7. Imagine that you are sixty years old and you work for a workers' cooperative in Yugoslavia. If you consider only your own self-interest, are you likely to support hiring more workers? Would you support long-term investments in capital?

CHAPTER 21

Development

Three-quarters of the world's population live in **less developed countries,** or **LDCs.** In the United States, one of the world's wealthier nations, the idea of "less developed" is often applied to rural areas, or to urban areas where houses and businesses are run down. Life in the LDCs poses far more serious problems. It is not that houses are run down, but that a large percentage of the population have no housing at all; not that people's diet is limited, but that they are starving to death; not that medical care is far off or costly, but that it is simply unavailable. The contrast between life in some LDCs and life in the United States is significantly greater than the contrast between life in America today and two centuries ago.

The LDCs pose some of the most poignant problems in economics. There are no simple answers, no easy formulas that, if followed, will ensure successful solutions. Still, as this chapter explains, economists have learned a lot during recent decades about the process of economic development.

KEY QUESTIONS

1. In what ways, besides their grinding poverty, do the developing countries differ from the United States, Japan, and the countries of Western Europe?

2. What are the impediments to growth in developing countries?

3. What policies can these countries pursue to improve their standards of living?

BACKGROUND

Statistics cannot convey the full measure of what it means to live in a less developed country, but they can provide a start. In the United States, life expectancy at birth is about 77 years. In Peru, it is 65 years; in India, 61 years; in Nigeria, 52 years. In the United States, 8 infants die for every 1,000 live births; in Brazil, 57; in Pakistan, 95; in Ethiopia, 122. The average American completes 12 years of schooling, while the average African gets only 5 years. India, with a population three and a half times larger than that of the United States, has a GDP roughly one-fifth that of the United States. This means that per capita income in India is about 5 percent of that in the United States.

The statistics connect to one another in a vicious cycle. Little or no education, malnutrition, and poor health care reduce productivity and thus incomes. With low incomes, people in the LDCs cannot afford better education, more food, or better health care. Life is hard in LDCs. In many African countries, whose standards of living were already low, population has been growing faster than national income, so that per capita income is falling. Life is getting worse, not better.

The United Nations and the World Bank (a bank established by the major industrialized countries after World War II that provides loans to LDCs) group countries into three categories: low-income countries, with GNP per capita of $725 or less in 1994; high-income countries, with GNP per capita above $8,955; and middle-income countries, with GNP per capita in between. The low-income countries are the LDCs. The high-income countries are referred to as **developed countries.** Because the basis of their higher level of income is their higher level of industrialization, they are also referred to as the **industrialized countries.** Figure 21.1 shows countries in the various income categories. In the Western Hemisphere, hardly 200 miles apart, lie one of the richest countries, the United States, with a per capita income of $25,880 in 1994, and one of the poorest, Haiti, with a per capita income of $230.

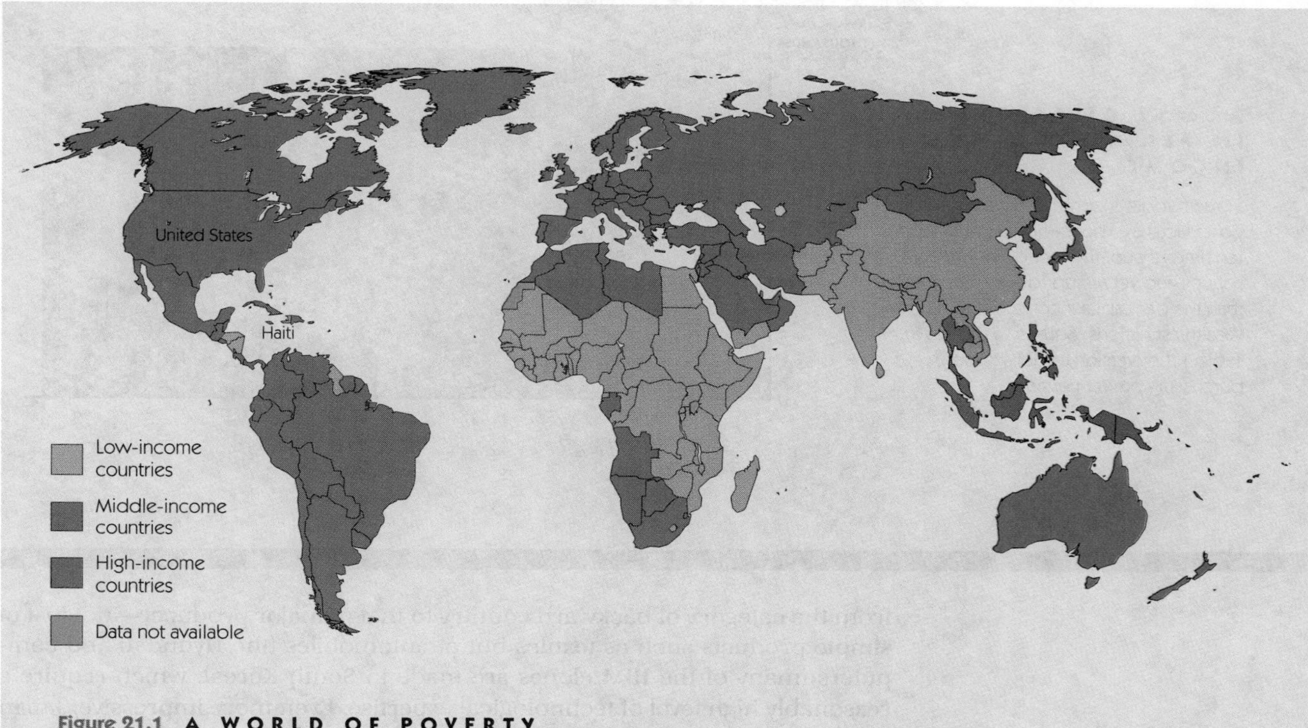

Figure 21.1 A WORLD OF POVERTY

This map shows the less developed countries (LDCs), here labeled "low-income countries," as well as the middle-income and developed countries. Most of the world lives in low-income countries. The developed countries consist mainly of those in Western Europe, the former colonies of Great Britain (Canada, Australia, New Zealand), the United States, and Japan. *Source: World Development Report* (1996).

The income gap among the high-income countries, including the countries of Western Europe, the United States, Canada, Japan, Australia, and New Zealand, has narrowed considerably over the past hundred years, but the gap between the high-income countries and the low-income countries has not. Figure 21.2 shows per capita income in several LDCs, ranging from $100 in Ethiopia to $720 in Egypt. Note that U.S. per capita income in 1994 was $25,880, compared to Ethiopia and Egypt that is 250 and 35 times as large, respectively. However, there are signs that change is possible. Some countries have made notable progress in recent years.

First, several countries have moved from the circle of LDCs to the ranks of middle-income countries. These are referred to collectively as **newly industrialized countries,** or **NICs** for short. These success stories include the "gang of four": South Korea, Taiwan, Singapore, and Hong Kong. Just thirty years after the devastating Korean War, for instance, South Korea has moved

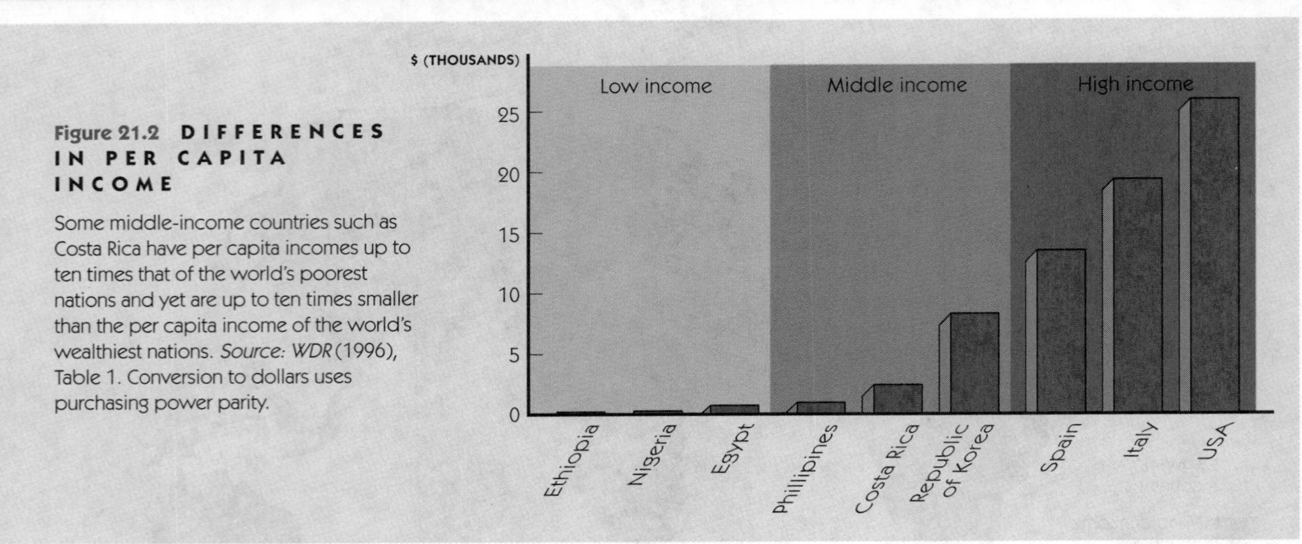

Figure 21.2 DIFFERENCES IN PER CAPITA INCOME

Some middle-income countries such as Costa Rica have per capita incomes up to ten times that of the world's poorest nations and yet are up to ten times smaller than the per capita income of the world's wealthiest nations. *Source: WDR* (1996), Table 1. Conversion to dollars uses purchasing power parity.

from the category of backward country to that of major producer—not just of simple products such as textiles but of automobiles (the Hyundai) and computers (many of the IBM clones are made in South Korea), which require a reasonably high level of technological expertise. Even more impressive, Japan has moved from the ranks of middle-income countries to one of the most prosperous in the world.

Second, there have been pockets of remarkable progress *within* the less developed countries. In the early 1960s, agricultural research centers around the world (funded largely by the Rockefeller Foundation) developed new kinds of seeds, which under correct conditions increase the yields per acre enormously. The introduction and dissemination of these new seeds, accompanied by enormous improvements in agricultural practices—known as the **green revolution**—led to huge increases in output. India, for example, finally managed to produce enough food to feed its burgeoning population, and now sometimes exports wheat to other countries.

Third, even the grim statistics for life expectancy—57 in Bangladesh and 52 in sub-Saharan Africa (compared to 77 in the United States)—represent improvements for many countries. But these improvements have a darker side in some countries—a population explosion reminiscent of the Malthusian nightmare. Malthus envisioned a world in which population growth outpaced increases in the food supply. In Kenya during the early 1980s, for instance, improved health conditions enabled the population to grow at the remarkable rate of 4.1 percent a year, implying a doubling of the population every eighteen years, while output increased only at the rate of 1.9 percent a year. Output increases do nothing to improve per capita income when the population grows even faster.

The 1980s was a particularly hard decade for some of the poorest countries,

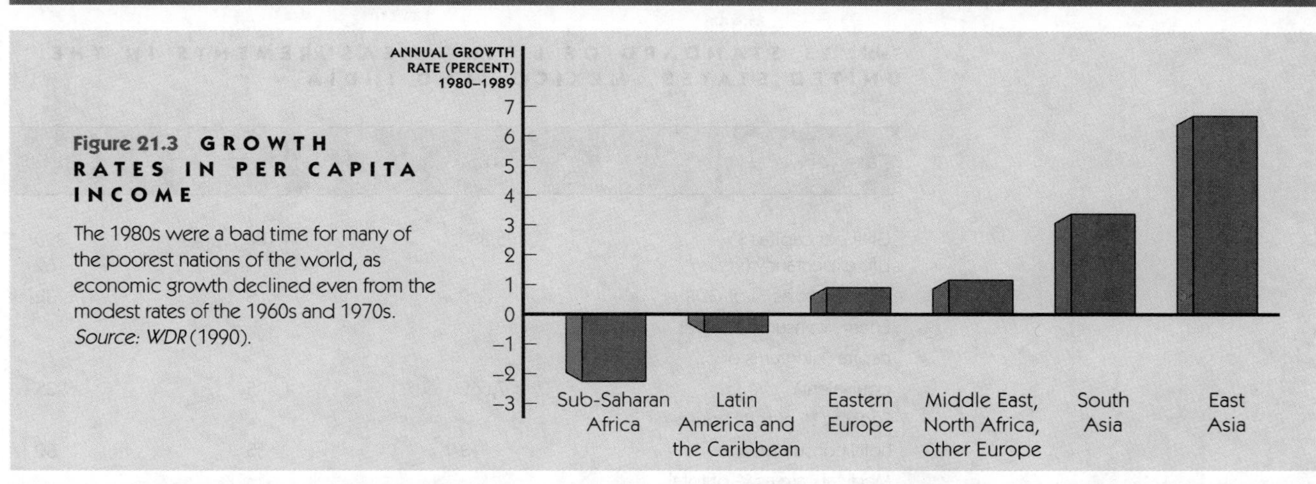

Figure 21.3 GROWTH RATES IN PER CAPITA INCOME

The 1980s were a bad time for many of the poorest nations of the world, as economic growth declined even from the modest rates of the 1960s and 1970s. *Source: WDR* (1990).

as Figure 21.3 shows. Sub-Saharan Africa[1] had basically stagnated for the previous quarter century. But during the 1980s per capita income actually fell by 2.4 percent per year. Latin America had grown at a little more than 2 percent a year in per capita income for the previous quarter century. During the 1980s per capita income there fell by .7 percent a year.

LIFE IN AN LDC

Just as there are large differences between the LDCs and the industrialized countries, so too are there large differences among the LDCs. The largest LDC of all, China, has a Communist government. The second largest, India, has an avowedly socialist government, but also functions as the world's largest democracy. Literacy standards in Costa Rica rank with those of the industrialized countries. But more than half of the adult population in sub-Saharan Africa is illiterate. One must be careful in generalizing about LDCs. Still, certain observations are true for *most* of them.

Table 21.1 summarizes some of the most important dimensions of living standards—contrasting the United States, a high-income country; Mexico (its nearest neighbor to the south), a middle-income country; and India, a low-income country. Incomes and life expectancies in most LDCs are low. A large fraction of the population lives in the rural sector and is engaged in agriculture. Lacking modern equipment like tractors, they work on small plots (an acre or two, compared to more than a hundred acres in the United States). In many cases, they even lack the resources to buy productivity-increasing inputs like fertilizer and pesticides—averaging less than half the fertilizer per acre used in more developed countries. In many countries, most farmers are

[1]All of Africa south of the Sahara except South Africa.

Table 21.1 **STANDARD OF LIVING MEASUREMENTS IN THE UNITED STATES, MEXICO, AND INDIA**

Category	U.S.	Mexico	India
GNP per capita ($)	25,880	4,180	320
Life expectancy (years)	77	71	62
Agriculture as % of GDP	2	8	32
Energy consumption per capita (kilograms of oil equivalent)	7,662	1,525	235
Food as % of total household consumption	13	35	52
Medical care as % of total household consumption	14	5	3
Average annual inflation (GDP deflator): 1984–94	3.3	40.0	9.7
Average annual growth of population (%): 1980–94	1.0	2.0	2.0
Infant mortality rate (per 1,000 live births)	8	35	70
Population per physician	420	1,242	2,460
Population in cities of 1 million or more as % of total population	43	28	9

Source: World Development Report (1991–1996). Data are for the most recent year available, in most cases 1994.

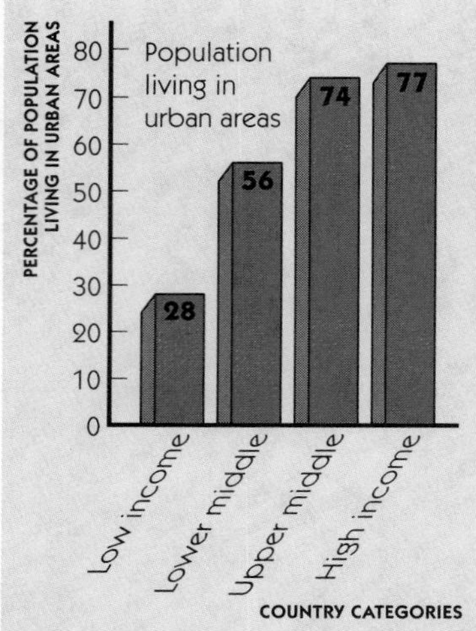

Figure 21.4 **RATES OF URBANIZATION**

The percentage of the population living in urban areas tends to be higher in developed countries than in LDCs. *Source: WDR* (1996), Table 9.

landless, tilling the landlord's land under **sharecropping** arrangements, in which the landlord gets half the output. In several countries, **land reform** has redistributed land to the peasants. Such land reforms were a precursor to the remarkable growth in Taiwan and Japan. In other countries, such as the Philippines and Peru, the land reforms have been only partially successful.

Over the past fifty years, most LDCs have experienced gradual urbanization (see Figure 21.4). Those who live in the cities have a much higher standard of living, including access to better education and health facilities. The marked differences between the cities and rural areas have led some to refer to these economies as **dual economies.** While there are large income disparities between rural and urban sectors, there are equally large disparities within the urban sectors, with government workers and those few lucky enough to get jobs in manufacturing earning many times average wages. These high wages attract migrants from the rural sector, often resulting in high urban unemployment. Rates in some cities exceed 20 percent.

IMPORTANT DIFFERENCES BETWEEN DEVELOPED AND LESS DEVELOPED COUNTRIES

	DEVELOPED COUNTRIES	LDCs
Per capita income	Over $9,000	Less than $725 per year
Production/Employment	Less than 10% of the work force is in agriculture	More than 70% of the work force is in agriculture
Urbanization	Less than 30% live in rural areas	More than 60% live in rural areas
Population growth rate	Less than 1.0%	Often more than 3.0%

EXPLANATIONS OF UNDERDEVELOPMENT

Part of LDC poverty arises from lack of resources. They have less physical capital per capita and less human capital, with high illiteracy rates and low average years of schooling. The lower levels of physical capital per capita are not the result of low savings rates—in fact savings rates of most are considerably higher than that of the United States (see Figure 21.5). Their high population growth rates mean that they have to save a lot just to stand still.

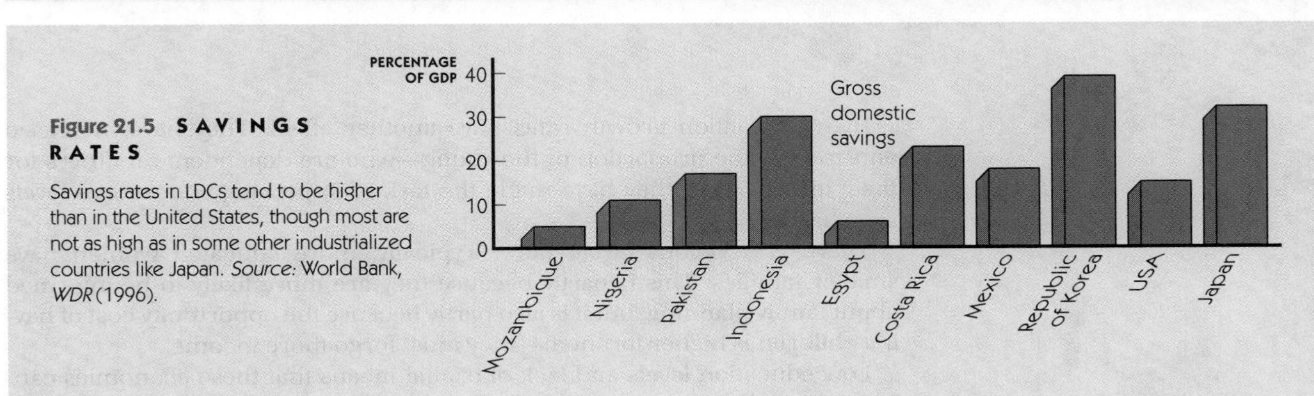

Figure 21.5 SAVINGS RATES
Savings rates in LDCs tend to be higher than in the United States, though most are not as high as in some other industrialized countries like Japan. *Source:* World Bank, *WDR* (1996).

USING ECONOMICS: THE MAGIC OF COMPOUNDING

The central challenge facing less developed countries is to increase living standards, or income per capita. There are two parts of a strategy to do this: faster growth in GDP and slower growth in population. Often policies seem to have a small effect: the rate of growth of GDP might be increased from 2 percent to 4 percent, and the rate of growth of population might be slowed from 3 percent to 1.5 percent. But because of the magic of compounding these slight differences can have cumulatively large effects over a span of a few decades.

For instance, with a 4 percent growth rate, output doubles every 18 years, while with a 2 percent growth rate, output doubles every 36 years. This means that in the relatively short horizon of 72 years, if two countries initially had the same output, the country with the higher growth rate has an output *four times* as great. In 144 years, a little less than a century and a half, the difference has magnified to sixteen times. (To derive these results, you can use what is sometimes called the rule of 72: something growing at the rate of g doubles in a period of time equal to 72 divided by the growth rate, g.*)

By the same token, a country with a population growth rate of 3 percent doubles its population every 24 years, while with a 1.5 percent growth rate, the population doubles in 48 years. If two countries had initially the same population, in 144 years, the faster growing country would have a population 8 times as large.

If the faster growing economy also had the slower growing population, output per capita would be 128 times as large.

Of course, there really is no magic in compounding: a faster growth rate today means that the economy is larger tomorrow, so that *base* from which further growth takes place is that much larger. The power of compounding is, however, real: fifty years ago, Korea had a slightly lower per capita income than India. Through growing slightly faster, year after year, today Korea has a per capita income that is eight times that of India.

*Formally, if GDP grows at the rate of g percent per year, GDP in t years will have grown by a factor e^{gt}. $e^{.72} = 2$, so GDP will have doubled when $gt = .72$. If $g = .02$, $t = .72/.02 = 36$. If $g = .04$, $t = .72/.04 = 18$.

High population growth rates have another effect. They have increased enormously the proportion of the young—who are dependent on others for their income. And they have made the task of improving educational levels even harder.

There is a vicious circle here. Typically, more educated women have smaller families. This is partly because they are more likely to be informed about family planning, but it is also partly because the opportunity cost of having children is higher for them—they must forgo more income.

Low education levels and lack of capital means that these economies cannot avail themselves of much of the most advanced technologies. With important exceptions,[2] they specialize in low-skill *labor-intensive* industries (products which require much labor relative to the amount of equipment they employ), like textiles.

Importance of Capital

How much of the difference between developed and less developed countries can actually be attributed to lack of capital as opposed to inefficient use of capital? If a shortage of capital in LDCs were the major difference between the developed and less developed countries, the law of diminishing returns would predict that the return to capital in the industrialized countries would be much lower than the return in LDCs. The more capital a country has relative to its population, the lower is the output per machine and the lower the marginal return to capital. In other words, the shortage of capital in LDCs should make the return to capital greater. This difference in returns would naturally result in a movement of capital from the more developed to the less developed countries, as business firms searched out profitable investment opportunities.

The evidence shows some differences in the return to capital. But these differences are too small to demonstrate that a capital shortage is the major problem faced by the LDCs. Moreover, if a capital shortage were the major problem, the LDCs would use what capital they have very intensively. But this does not typically happen. For example, factories run extra daily shifts more often in developed countries than in LDCs.

A much more important impediment to growth in many less developed countries is the lack of efficiency in how scarce funds are used. In Venezuela, which tried to invest its oil dollars as fast as they came in during the 1970s, output increased by 10 cents for every dollar invested in capital equipment. In contrast, in the United States and other developed countries, each extra dollar of investment results on average in an output increase of between 30 and 50 cents—three to five times higher. In many LDCs, greater investment simply does not lead to much increased output.

There are a number of reasons for this. Some economists, such as Walter Rostow of the University of Texas, have argued that at any moment a country has only a limited absorptive capacity for more capital. LDCs lack the human capital, the experience, and technological know-how to pursue many projects simultaneously. The absorptive capacity is most limited in the poorest countries. When investments are pushed beyond absorptive capacity, they yield very low returns.

Many economists, however, believe that there are two more fundamental reasons for the low returns to capital: lack of developed capital markets to allocate capital efficiently, and well-intentioned government interventions which nonetheless support low-return projects. At least in the past, many

[2]There is, for instance, a large highly educated elite in India, which has become a center for the development of computer software.

Close-up: Transnational Corporations as a Source of Capital

Less developed countries lack capital, both to get the machines needed for greater production and to increase the human capital of their population. But where is that capital to come from?

LDCs can, through savings, provide some capital themselves. Countries like Mexico, Brazil, and South Korea have shown a capacity to save more than 20 percent of GDP per year. By world standards, those countries are fairly well off. The poorest countries, like many in Africa or Asia, save only about 7 percent of GDP.

The other alternatives all involve investment capital coming in from abroad, whether through foreign aid, private bank loans, or direct foreign investment. The problem with depending on foreign aid is that there is not enough. For example, in one recent year the total foreign aid received by all LDCs was perhaps 1 percent of their combined GDP.

Another possibility is private financial capital, commonly in the form of bank loans. This was tried with a vengeance in the 1970s. But after the experience of countries like Brazil, Argentina, and Mexico not being able to repay their loans on time in the 1980s, U.S. banks are not eager to plunge into a massive new round of lending. They put their toes in the water again in the early 1990s, only to be burned again with the Mexican peso crisis of 1995.

The final possibility is direct foreign investment, more commonly known as investment by multinational or transnational corporations. This method has some obvious advantages. The transnational company has an interest in looking after its investment and managing it carefully, which means that the money is less likely to be spent inefficiently. The company, not the country, takes the risk. Moreover, the company doing the investment will often send new technology to the LDC and train workers there.

The main disadvantage of direct investment is political. The governments of LDCs often prefer loans or grants that they can spend as they wish over investment controlled by foreign business executives. In the past, LDCs often passed laws that discouraged foreign companies from investing. But as the options for obtaining capital from other sources dwindled, transnational corporations looked better as an alternative. The current level of direct foreign investment in LDCs is only about $10 billion. How-

ever, according to a recent United Nations report:

> In an era of large international capital flows and rapid technological change, developing countries will increasingly look to transnational corporations for economic stimulation. For their part, transnational corporations will frequently be in a position to provide significant long-term benefits to many developing countries. An important component in the next generation of development policies is that this mutuality of interest continues to grow.

Source: United Nations Center on Transnational Corporations, *Transnational Corporations in World Development* (New York: United Nations, 1988), pp. 10–11.

countries thought that a symbol of development was having a steel mill or some other big factory, even if such a factory was unsuitable for the economic conditions of the country.

INEQUALITY

Many LDCs are also marked by high levels of inequality. Thousands of homeless people sleep in the streets along which the wealthy travel in expensive cars. Some of this inequality is simply due to the law of supply and demand. There is an abundance of unskilled labor and a scarcity of skilled labor and entrepreneurs, so that unskilled wages are low and those who have skills do well.

Indeed, earlier theories suggested that inequality contributed to economic growth. Sir Arthur Lewis, who received the Nobel Prize for his work on development economics, argued that what he called the **surplus of labor** kept wages low and profits high. Workers earning subsistence wages could not save, but capitalists could, so that the higher profits contributed to a higher savings rate. In this view, there was a trade-off between growth and equality.

Today, many economists believe that growth and equality are really complementary, as evidenced by the East Asia miracle discussed later in the chapter.

FACTORS CONTRIBUTING TO UNDERDEVELOPMENT

Lack of physical capital
Lack of education
Lack of technology
Lack of developed capital markets
Government interventions that impair efficient resource allocation
Extreme income inequality

CLOSE-UP: THE INTERNATIONAL DEBT CRISIS

Borrowing from abroad can make sound economic sense. For instance, much of the development of the American railroad network in the nineteenth century was financed by bonds issued in Europe. Over the past two decades, many firms and governments of less developed countries have borrowed billions of dollars from banks in the United States and other developed countries, as the table here shows. But while the nineteenth-century U.S. railroad companies were able to repay investments, it became apparent in the 1980s that some of the countries that had borrowed heavily—particularly Brazil, Argentina, and Mexico—could not repay what they owed. The resulting crisis threatened the economic prospects of the LDCs and the financial viability of many American banks.

The immediate cause of the problem was simple. In the 1970s, real interest rates were low, and banks were flush with "petro dollars"—dollars that oil producers, particularly in the Middle East, had earned from selling their oil at the high prices that prevailed beginning in 1973—and wanted to invest or deposit them abroad. Both borrowers and lenders were optimistic that the loans would create economic growth, and repayment would be easy.

Then three things happened. First, nominal and real interest rates soared in the late 1970s. The interest payments rose far beyond any level that the borrowers had imagined. Second, the world entered a recession in the early 1980s, and the worldwide slowdown in growth made it even more difficult for the LDCs to pay back what they owed. Third, oil prices fell in the early 1980s. Some of the largest borrowers had been oil producers, like Mexico and Indonesia, and they had intended to repay their loans by selling oil.

But bad luck is not the only culprit. The banks are also to blame for failing to take into account the risks associated with the loans they were making. They should have realized, for instance, that prices for goods like oil are volatile. The banks also placed too much trust in the assurance of foreign governments that the loans would be invested productively. Much of the money was invested in projects that were probably not economically viable from the start. By contrast, some better-managed countries like the Republic of Korea borrowed heavily but invested the money wisely and have been able to repay it.

Massive defaults on loans were avoided only by debt rescheduling. As a payment came due, the banks lent the country more money, in effect postponing the date at which repayment was to occur. As a condition for this rescheduling, the lenders insisted that the borrowers "put their houses in order"—cutting back, for instance, on their huge budget deficits. But this strategy of squeezing the LDCs to pay had its own problems. The only way the countries could repay was for them to grow more. But growth required additional capital, which foreign lenders were reluctant to provide. The only way out was to forgive some of the debt and then count on the rest being repaid.

Debt forgiveness, which amounts to a gift to the debtor countries, also has its problems. For example, will forgiveness encourage countries to borrow more in the future than they have the capacity to repay? Is Brazil more deserving of such a multibillion-dollar gift than many poorer countries in Latin America or Africa, just because it borrowed more?

Country	Public or publicly guaranteed external debt in 1989	1994
Brazil	$84 billion	$151 billion
Mexico	$76	128
India	$54	99
Argentina	$51	77
Indonesia	$41	97
Egypt	$40	33
China	$37	101
Poland	$35	42
Turkey	$35	66
Nigeria	$32	34
Venezuela	$25	37
Algeria	$24	30
Philippines	$23	39
Morocco	$19	23
Korea	$17	55

Source: *World Development Report* (1996).

FAILED GOVERNMENT POLICIES

Most of the countries of Asia and Africa were colonies of the European powers until World War II. As they got their independence in the aftermath of the war, the new governments took upon themselves the responsibility of promoting economic development. Almost all believed that strong government action would be required, with some, such as India, taking an avowedly socialist strategy. These ideas were partly in revulsion to what they saw as the exploitive capitalism of their colonial masters, partly a reflection of the seeming success of the Soviet Union's rapid industrialization.

PLANNING

In many LDCs, the government attempted to direct the overall course of the economy by planning. A "Ministry of Planning" would draw up a detailed plan, typically for five years, specifying how much each sector of the economy would grow, how much investment would occur in each sector, where the output of each sector would go, and where each sector would receive its inputs. The Ministry of Planning had enormous powers, among them allocating investment funds and the foreign exchange required to import raw materials from abroad.

In many LDCs, the government undertook some of the investments itself, but it also gave powerful inducements to private firms to conform to the dictates of the government's plan—for example, by restricting access to needed foreign exchange only to approved investment projects or by making credit more readily available for approved investment projects.

In the last decade, there has been considerable disillusionment with planning—a disillusionment that set in even before the failures of the Soviet-style system became evident. Planned economies like India have done worse than unplanned economies like Hong Kong. There are good reasons for this. The 1960s' views on the need for planning ignored the extensive planning that goes on in all economies. For example, when U.S. Steel decided to build a steel mill on the southern shores of Lake Michigan in the early twentieth century, it made sure that there were sources of inputs and the transportation facilities to deliver these inputs—limestone from southern Indiana, coal and coke from Illinois, and iron ore from Minnesota. It also made sure there was a source of demand. The issue is not whether planning is needed—it surely is—but whether the most effective place to do the planning is in a government centralized bureau or at the level of the firm. Today most economists are skeptical about the ability of a centralized bureau to do effective planning.

One of the main arguments for centralized planning was its presumed greater ability to coordinate. But the experience of the past quarter century has shown that centralized planning offices generally do not do a good job at coordination. One reason is that they often lack the requisite information. Another is that firms can more easily deal with the details of investment projects—deciding what kind of plant to construct, how to construct it, making sure that it is constructed in an efficient way, and so on—than can government bureaucrats. And these details, more than anything else, determine the success of the projects.

TILTING THE ECONOMY

The purpose of planning, of course, was to do more than just substitute for the markets' role in coordinating economic activity. It was also at least to tilt the economy in ways that would enhance growth.

Some ideas on how this might be done were borrowed from the Soviet Union, such as an emphasis on capital-intensive industries like steel. Many countries pursued a policy known as **import substitution,** stressing the substitution of domestically produced goods for goods previously imported. In this view, the hallmark of a developed country is modern industry. Rather than importing steel, automobiles, TV sets, computers, and other such products, a nation should produce them itself in order to develop the skills necessary for modernization. It should produce, in other words, all the goods it had previously imported from the industrialized economies. This is the road to development that most of the larger LDCs, including India, China, and Brazil, undertook in the years after World War II. At times, each of these countries has taken import substitution to extremes, insisting, for example, on domestically produced computers even when they might not be able to perform the functions of imported computers.

India, like many other LDCs, has also placed a heavy emphasis on domestically owned businesses. At least 50 percent of each company must be owned by citizens of India. When Coca-Cola refused to disclose the secret of its closely guarded formula to its Indian-controlled subsidiary, the government shut down Coca-Cola. At times, it seemed as if "Indian-made cola for Indians" would become a rallying point for Indian nationalism, just as "Buy American" campaigns have been a rallying point for protectionism in America.

But the import substitution approach has disadvantages of its own. Trade barriers set up to protect domestic firms can end up protecting inefficient producers. The absence of foreign competition means that there is an insufficient spur to innovation and efficiency. The profits to which trade barriers frequently give rise provide a source of government corruption. And the trade barriers remain years after they are introduced.

In some cases, the value added of the protected industry is actually negative. Consider an LDC car producer. Many of the car parts have to be imported. The value added of the car manufacturer is not the total value of the car, but only the difference between the value of the car and the value of the imported components. Assume that because of sloppy manufacturing, a significant fraction of the imported parts are damaged. It might be cheaper for the country to import the entire car than import the components and assemble the car. Of course, with protection, the LDC car manufacturer may still be making profits. Consumers suffer, because they have to pay higher prices.

The problems are even worse when the protected industry is one like steel, whose product is used in other industries. An LDC car manufacturer might be profitable if it could only purchase steel at international prices. But if it is forced to pay inflated prices to buy domestically produced steel, it cannot compete with foreign producers. The government might try to offset this by subsidizing the car manufacturers. A subsidy or trade protection in one sector thus grows into a complex of subsidies and trade protection in other sectors.

Although trade protection to stimulate import substitution generally leads to massive inefficiencies, it has proved successful for a time in some countries—such as Brazil, which enjoyed several decades of rapid growth before the debt crisis of the 1980s tainted that picture. Also, supporters of import substitution note that many of the most rapid bursts of growth of the current developed countries occurred in wartimes, when the economy was inwardly directed, not export oriented. These same supporters, looking at the experience of Japan, argue that at least for industrial goods, import substitution—the development of a domestic market—must precede exports. Before Japan was able successfully to sell cars abroad, it first had to develop a market for Japanese cars at home.

When Government Becomes the Problem

Sometimes government has actually impeded the development process. It has done this both by allocating inefficiently those resources over which it has direct control and by interfering in the function of markets so that *they* could not efficiently allocate resources. Countries following the Soviet model attempted to imitate not only its reliance on planning but also its pattern of development, with heavy emphasis on industries such as steel—whether such a pattern of industrialization was appropriate for those countries or not.

Mao Tse-tung, perhaps because he saw that wheat was the predominant grain consumed in the more developed countries, directed that vast areas of China be converted from rice to wheat. This land was not suited for wheat, and agricultural productivity suffered. The conversion to wheat fields actually depleted the land of its fertility, so that when it was eventually returned to growing rice, productivity was lower.

There are flops in the private sector as well, like the Edsel or the nicotine-free cigarette—mistakes that cost the companies making them hundreds of millions of dollars. But the firm (its owners) bears the costs of these mistakes, and has a strong incentive to avoid making them. A company that makes a mistake cannot finance itself indefinitely. When the Ford Motor Company discovered that the Edsel was a mistake, it quickly discontinued production, cutting its losses. It knew, and acted upon, the basic lesson that such costs should be treated as bygones.

The government, by contrast, can support an unprofitable firm for many years. Also, the scale of mistakes governments make sets them apart from the mistakes of private firms. If a single farmer mistakenly decides to grow wheat rather than rice, the costs he faces are not comparable to the costs borne by China when Mao made his mistake.

Mao's mistake was an honest mistake of judgment, not a consequence of his pursuit of private interests. But some problems facing the LDCs arise from governmental corruption, and here private interests conflict with public ones. Corruption is often associated with the large role government plays in an LDC, particularly in restricting foreign trade. When the government imposes a high tariff or otherwise protects an industry, the protected firms can raise their prices and increase their profits. If there are only one or two such firms, they will be tempted to share some of the resulting profits with the government official responsible for the protection. And the government official, knowing this, has a strong incentive to ask the private firms to share some of the profits.

These problems arise in all countries. The building inspectors in New York have periodically been charged with accepting bribes to speed approvals, for instance. However, these problems are more likely to arise in countries where government salaries are low relative to the size of the bribes being offered, where institutions like a free press that might closely monitor this kind of corruption do not exist, and where government regulations are more pervasive.

Between honest mistakes and corruption lies a third category: rent-seeking activities. If government has the power to confer special benefits, people will seek those benefits for themselves. Firms will try to persuade government that they deserve protection from foreign competition, knowing that such protection will increase their profits. They may give outright bribes, or they may simply spend funds to help elect officials who are sympathetic to their views.

Critics of an activist role for government in development—such as Anne Krueger of Stanford University, formerly vice-president of the World Bank—see these problems as casting serious doubt on the wisdom of government planning. We might *imagine* a government's improving on the market, they argue, but if we look more closely at how governments actually behave, and take into account the natural incentives for counterproductive behavior on the part of government bureaucrats (as opposed to the incentives for efficiency on the part of private firms), we see that government activity can and often does impede development.

THE EAST ASIA MIRACLE

As the development strategies based on planning, import substitution, and heavy industrialization were failing, the countries of East Asia had been pursuing a different set of strategies and achieving growth rates of 7 percent or more year after year. At these growth rates, GDP doubles every ten years.

Several ingredients were essential to their success. Governments in these countries also took an active role. But they pursued market-oriented policies which encouraged development of the private sector. They sought to augment and "govern" the market, not to replace it. A key policy was to ensure the macroeconomic stability of the economy, avoiding for the most part high inflation. As part of this strategy, governments maintained a high level of fiscal responsibility, eschewing the huge budget deficits that characterize many LDCs.

They sought to augment all the ingredients to growth, including fostering high savings rates—often in excess of 25 percent. (See Figure 21.5.) In Japan, more than a third of these savings went into accounts at the postal savings banks established by the government. These provided a secure and easy way, particularly for those in the rural sector, to save. In Singapore, the government established a provident fund, to which all workers were required to contribute 40 percent of their income. The money went not only to finance their retirement, but also to purchase homes. More than 70 percent of all Singaporeans now own their own homes—in a country which, at independence in 1959, had an unemployment rate of more than 30 percent and negligible home ownership.

Many of the countries in East Asia began their growth spurt with a high level of literacy. But they pushed it even further, enhancing the opportunities particularly for women. These countries realized that if they were to become developed, they had to bridge the technological gap. Many countries, including Taiwan and Korea, sent thousands to the United States to study science and engineering. And they devoted huge resources to establishing quality universities within their own countries.

These governments also influenced the allocation of capital in a myriad of ways. Banks were discouraged from making real estate loans and loans for durable consumption goods. This helped to increase private savings rates and discouraged real estate speculation, which often serves to destabilize the economy. As a result, more funds were available for investment in growth-oriented activities, like new equipment.

In addition, governments established development banks, to promote long-term investment in activities like shipbuilding, steel mills, and the chemical industry. These interventions have been more controversial and their success has been mixed. The steel firms in Taiwan and Korea are among the most efficient in the world. But soon after the chemical industry was established in Korea, the price of oil, an essential ingredient, soared, and the industry suffered losses for almost two decades. With the decline in oil prices, it is now doing better. Proponents of these initiatives argue that they have technological benefits for other sectors and are necessary as part of a long-run growth strategy.

The Japanese government took a variety of other initiatives to promote certain industries. Among its most noted successes were its entry into the computer chip market. By the early 1980s, Japan looked as if it would completely dominate that market, before Intel and other American producers reasserted American leadership. The dangers of government intervention are often symbolized by the Japanese government's failed attempt to discourage Honda (a manufacturer of motorcycles) from entering the auto market, arguing that there were already too many producers.

EXPORT-LED GROWTH

One factor that distinguished the countries of East Asia from less successful LDCs was their emphasis on exports. A growth strategy focusing on exports is called **export-led growth,** in contrast to the import substitution policy described earlier. Firms were encouraged to export in a variety of ways, including being given increased access to credit, often at subsidized rates.

In export-led growth, firms produce according to their long-term comparative advantage. This is not current comparative advantage, based on current resources and knowledge. It is dynamic comparative advantage, based on acquired skills and technology, and recognition of the importance of learning by doing—of the improvement in skills and productivity that comes from production experience. With exports, demand for the goods produced by an LDC is not limited by the low income of its citizens. The world is its market.

Advocates of export-led growth also believe that the competition provided by the export market is an important stimulus to efficiency and modernization. The only way a firm can succeed in the face of keen international competition is to produce what consumers want, at the quality they want, and at the lowest possible costs. This keen competition forces specialization in areas where low-wage, less developed countries have a comparative advantage, such as labor-intensive products. It also forces firms to look for the best ways of producing. International firms often take a role in helping to enhance efficiency. For instance, the clothing store chain Benetton has developed production techniques that combine large production runs with rapid adaptability in style and color. In this way, the firm has been able to take advantage of low-wage LDCs by producing most of what it sells in these countries.

Finally, export-led growth has facilitated the transfer of advanced technology. Producers exporting to developed countries not only come into contact with efficient producers within those countries, they also learn to adopt their standards and production techniques. They come to understand better, for instance, why timeliness and quality in production are important.

Fostering Equality

Another distinctive aspect of East Asia's development strategy is its emphasis on equality. We have already noted several aspects of these egalitarian policies: Singapore's home ownership program; the almost universal provision of elementary and secondary education, which includes women; and the land redistribution programs that were the precursor of growth in several of the countries, including Taiwan and Japan. In many of these countries, government has also tried to curb excessive wage inequality and to discourage conspicuous consumption by the rich.

Their experience has shown that one can have high savings rates without either the oppressiveness of Soviet-style governments or vast inequalities. The equality measures actually have promoted economic growth. The land reforms have resulted in increased agricultural production—the sharecropping system previously in place had had the effect of a 50 percent tax on output. The high education levels have increased productivity directly and facilitated the transfer and adoption of more advanced technology. And more education for women, as we have noted, is associated with declining rates of population growth.

But the greatest boon of equality for development may be through its political effects. Inequality frequently gives rise to political instability, and political instability has strong adverse effects on the economic climate. In such an atmosphere, both domestic and foreign firms will be reluctant to invest. The countries of East Asia not only managed to have remarkable political stability, but as their incomes grew, there was a strong trend toward democratization.

One of the policies these countries did *not* engage in was large-scale food subsidies. These are often justified as promoting equality, but in fact their effect is more problematic. This is because the food subsidies typically benefit mainly those in the urban sector, and are often paid for out of taxes (or suppressed prices) in the agricultural sector. Since those in the urban sector are on average far better off than those in the rural sector, this type of redistribution takes from the very poor to give to the poor. Food subsidies also can be a major budgetary drain on the government, reducing funds for growth-oriented investments.

REDEFINING THE ROLE OF GOVERNMENT

The central question many LDCs are asking today is, what can we learn from the success of the East Asian countries and the failures elsewhere? What can governments do, or refrain from doing, to effectively facilitate economic growth? Today, there is widespread consensus on the main elements of a successful development strategy.

Macroeconomic Stability Governments need not only maintain macroeconomic stability, but constrain expenditures in line with their revenues.

Positive Investment Climate A favorable climate for investment, including foreign investment, enhances growth not only by increasing the stock of capital, but also by facilitating the transfer of valuable technology.

Population Policy High rates of growth of population put a strain on almost any economy, but especially poor economies. Savings must be devoted to housing the growing population and providing capital to the new entrants to the labor force, leaving little for capital deepening, which would enhance productivity. Today, knowledge about contraception is widespread; but knowledge about the means to control population is not enough. People have to want to reduce family size. In the absence of a social insurance system, parents often rely on large families to ensure that there is someone to take care of them in their old age. The benefits of having children are of course more than economic. The evidence suggests that one of the most reliable ways of controlling population is to increase the cost—the opportunity cost—of having children; educating women does exactly that. That is why female education not only has a direct benefit, in increased productivity, but an indirect benefit, in reduced population growth.

Provide More and Better Education Education increases the productivity of the labor force and enables the economy to adopt more advanced technologies.

Provide an Institutional Infrastructure Some examples of this type of infrastructure are an effective legal system, strong competition laws, and a regulatory system supporting a safe and sound financial system.

Provide a Physical Infrastructure In this area, the direct role of government versus the private sector has been evolving. Many countries have discovered that parts of the infrastructure—like toll roads—can be provided privately, relieving the government of both fiscal and managerial burdens.

Avoid Protectionism Avoid policies, such as protectionism, which reduce competition, leading to increased costs and prices.

While there is widespread consensus on these elements of a development strategy, some elements are more contentious. Most of the countries of East Asia actively promoted exports and the transfer and adaptation of modern technology. And most analysts of the East Asia experience give these policies considerable credit for their economic success. Yet critics worry that in other countries, these attempts by government to "direct" the development of the economy have been singularly unsuccessful; the programs have been captured by special interests, and used to enhance the profits of these special interests rather than to promote economic growth.

THE ROLE OF THE ADVANCED COUNTRIES

What can the advanced countries do to help? Direct foreign assistance, especially from the United States, has been declining in importance. In 1995, U.S. assistance as a percentage of GDP was lower than any other major industrialized country, and even in absolute dollars, was surpassed by France, Germany, and Japan. Even this does not tell the full story, since a disproportionate part of U.S. aid goes to Israel and Egypt.

Today, international capital markets are far better developed than they were fifty years ago, with funds investing in "emerging markets" becoming hot-ticket items on Wall Street. Countries, like China and Thailand, that provide an investment-friendly atmosphere have little trouble attracting funds. Still, for the poorest countries, especially in Africa, there is a huge need for development assistance. And for all of the developing countries, there is a need for technical assistance and help in areas like education and health in which the private sector is not particularly interested.

There is an ongoing debate about how effective such assistance has been. There have been huge successes, some supported by private foundations as well as by government. The development of high-yielding crops with the support of the Rockefeller Foundation and the dissemination of the seeds and new technologies throughout the developing world has resulted in a "green revolution." Countries like India have become self-sufficient in food. But there have also been failures. Food aid sometimes depresses local prices, hurting farmers and discouraging domestic production. Some large projects have been criticized for damaging the environment and resulting in increases in crop yields that were insufficient even to pay the interest on the loans.

Today, an increasing fraction of aid is distributed through multilateral development banks—the World Bank, the regional banks in Asia, Africa, and Latin America, and the EBRD, the European Bank for Reconstruction and Development, which focuses on the economies of Eastern Europe and the former Soviet Union.

Although support for foreign aid in the United States has been waning, many economists continue to emphasize the importance of trade for LDCs and developed countries alike. Giving less developed economies access to the

Policy Perspective: The Mexican Peso Crisis

In January 1995, the Mexican peso crashed, losing a quarter of its value (relative to the dollar) in a single day, and in the span of a couple weeks, more than 40 percent of its value. The U.S. government, other governments, and the International Monetary Fund (IMF) were called to the rescue. While the IMF pledged $7.7 billion in credits, the United States lent more than $20 billion to Mexico.

To the media and much of the public, the crash of the peso seemed like a shock. But many economists, such as Rudiger Dornbush of M.I.T., had anticipated the crisis. The Mexican government had made extremely impressive economic reforms under President Salinas, and the signing of NAFTA was a positive step for Mexico's economic future. But the Mexican government's macropolicies had been less sound. They had run moderate deficits over a number of years, which they had financed with short-term borrowing denominated in dollars. They had also worked hard to sustain the value of the peso—despite the much higher rate of inflation in Mexico than elsewhere. Thus, by late 1994, the peso was overvalued by at least 25 percent. Economists within the Mexican government realized this, but the government was unwilling to allow the peso to depreciate before the presidential election. The new Mexican government took only three weeks to recognize that it could not sustain the value of the peso. But it could not engineer a smooth reduction.

Many lost millions as a result of the decrease in the value of the peso. Still more millions were lost as the Mexican stock market crashed. Finally, those who had invested in Mexican bonds worried that the government would not be able to pay off bondholders when the debt became due. The U.S. government worried that the emerging turmoil would spread to other emerging markets, disrupting their growth plans. It also worried that an economic downturn in Mexico could lead to a flood of immigrants to the United States. These were among the reasons cited in favor of the Mexican bailout.

Critics of the bailout argued that the main beneficiaries were investors, who should have realized the risks they faced. The devalued peso would be good for the Mexican economy, as it promoted exports and discouraged imports. In fact, the Mexican trade deficit which had swelled over the past few years was reversed to a trade surplus in the first months of 1995.

The subsequent events did not fully resolve the question of whether the bailout should have

taken place. Mexico went through a deep economic downturn, with unemployment and interest rates soaring. By the middle of 1996, the economy had shown signs of a slow recovery, though the banking system remained fragile; still, Mexico was able to repay half of its loans from the U.S. government.

Even with the bailout, other countries like Argentina were hit hard by the "contagion" effect, resulting from the loss of investor confidence. It is difficult to ascertain how much harder these countries would have been hit had there not been a bailout.

But both within the United States and abroad, a consensus emerged that the Mexico experience should not be repeated. In a meeting of the leaders of the industrialized countries held in June 1995 in Halifax, Nova Scotia, they set in motion reforms which would increase the surveillance by the International Monetary Fund of the economies of the world, so that markets would be better informed concerning the risks that they face, and which would increase the funds available for lending in the event of a crisis. And discussions were begun on the development of "work-out arrangements" for countries, analogous to those available to firms in the event of bankruptcy. Whether these initiatives will suffice to avoid a similar crisis remains to be seen.

U.S. markets is a "win-win" policy. American consumers win by having a greater variety of goods at lower prices. The less developed country benefits by having a huge market for its goods. The United States has a system of preferential treatment for poor countries, called GSP (general system of preferences). Of course, as always with trade, some U.S. producers and their workers complain about the loss of jobs to these low-cost competitors. As argued in Chapter 2, the total benefits to trade generally outweigh the losses to certain groups.

THE PROSPECTS

The enhanced means of production that resulted from the industrial and scientific revolutions of the past two centuries have meant ever-rising living standards for most of those lucky enough to live in the developed countries of Europe and North America. And the past fifty years have extended the benefits of development to an increasing number of countries—in full measure to Japan, and more moderately to middle-income countries such as Singapore, South Korea, and Taiwan.

There are pockets of success elsewhere as well. The area around São Paulo in Brazil has the look and feel of prosperity. India, as noted above, has become self-sufficient with regard to food. Thailand has been having a boom. Success often seems precarious; for instance, for many of these countries, the debt crisis of the 1980s was a major setback, with growth stalling, and in some cases, incomes actually declining. Still, the outstanding lesson of recent decades is that success is possible. There is the real prospect that more and more of these countries, if they pursue wise policies and enjoy political stability, will be able to pull themselves out of the cycle of poverty in which they have lived for centuries.

But for the most unfortunate countries, such as sub-Saharan Africa—which lack human and physical resources and have burgeoning populations that consume much of whatever gains they are able to obtain—the prospects are less optimistic. Lack of hope contributes to political instability, making economic progress all the more difficult.

An Agenda for Development

How the developed countries can help
- Reduce trade barriers
- Increase foreign aid
- Facilitate foreign investment

Growth-oriented policies for LDCs
- Reduce population growth
- Increase quantity and quality of education
- Provide a basic infrastructure (roads, ports, a legal system)
- Provide a favorable climate for investment, including foreign investment
- Facilitate development of capital markets (financial intermediaries)
- Spend more government revenues on investment rather than consumption, such as food subsidies
- Develop a competitive export sector

Policies that may inhibit growth
- Trade protection
- Regulations, licensing

Review and Practice

Summary

1. In less developed countries, or LDCs, life expectancies are usually shorter, infant mortality is higher, and people are less educated than in developed countries. Also, a larger fraction of the population lives in the rural sector, and population growth rates are higher.

2. In recent years, newly industrialized countries (NICs) such as South Korea, Singapore, Hong Kong, and Taiwan have managed to improve their economic status dramatically. Other LDCs, like India, have expanded food production considerably. But the standard of living in some of the poorest LDCs, such as many African nations, has actually been declining, as population growth has outstripped economic growth.

3. Among the factors contributing to underdevelopment are lack of physical capital, lack of education, lack of technology, and lack of developed capital markets. The factors interact: low education levels impede the transfer of advanced technology; low incomes make it difficult to invest heavily in education.

4. Central planning has not been effective in LDCs. Governments lack the requisite information and often misdirect resources.

5. Import substitution policies have often been implemented through protectionist policies, which have raised domestic prices, often give rise to inefficiencies, and, when applied to intermediate goods like steel, have adverse effects on those industries that use the input.

6. The success of the countries of East Asia is based on activist government policies, which include helping develop and using markets rather than replacing them; promoting high levels of investment and savings, and strong support for education; improving capital markets, which facilitate an efficient allocation of scarce capital; promoting exports; and fostering equality.

7. Effective development policies include maintaining macroeconomic stability (including sound fiscal policies), creating a positive investment climate (including for foreign investors), controlling population, providing more and better education, providing an institutional infrastructure (including an effective legal system, competition laws, and a sound financial system), and ensuring that there is the necessary infrastructure (roads, electricity), which may be provided either publicly or privately.

8. Advanced countries can help LDCs through the provision of aid (capital assistance), technical assistance, and opening markets to trade.

KEY TERMS

less developed countries (LDCs)
developed or **industrialized countries**
newly industrialized countries (NICs)
green revolution
dual economies
import substitution
export-led growth

REVIEW QUESTIONS

1. List some important ways in which LDCs differ from more developed countries.

2. What are the most important factors inhibiting growth in the LDCs? Why is capital shortage *alone* not the most important factor? What can be done to help overcome the problem of capital shortage? How do some of the factors interact with each other?

3. How does rapid population growth make it more difficult to increase a country's standard of living?

4. Why has centralized government planning failed? Does planning occur in market economies?

5. How and why have governments sometimes tried to tilt the economy, interfering with how markets by themselves would allocate resources? Compare import substitution and export promotion strategies. Why have export promotion strategies, by and large, been more successful than import substitution strategies?

6. What are some of the factors that contributed to the East Asia miracle?

7. Why might fostering equality promote economic growth?

8. What are some of the roles that government can play in promoting economic development and growth?

9. What are some of the roles that the advanced countries can play in promoting economic development among the LDCs?

PROBLEMS

1. In the United States, the economy grew by 2.6 percent per year (in real terms) during the 1980s. In India, the economy grew by 5.3 percent during the 1980s. However, population growth in the United States was .8 percent annually, while population growth in India was 2.1 percent annually. Which country increased its standard of living faster for the average citizen? By how much?

2. Nominal GNP in Kenya was 9 billion shillings in 1967 and 135 billion shillings in 1987. The price level in Kenya (using 1980 as a base year) rose from 40 in 1967 to 200 in 1987. And the population of Kenya increased from 10 million to 22 million in those twenty years. What was the total percentage change in real GNP per capita in Kenya from 1967 to 1987?

3. True or false: "LDCs do not have much capital because their rates of saving are low. If they saved more or received more foreign aid, they could rapidly expand their economic growth." Discuss.

4. How might each of the following hinder entrepreneurs in LDCs?
   (a) lack of functioning capital markets;
   (b) pervasive government control of the economy;
   (c) lack of companies that offer business services;
   (d) a tradition of substantial foreign control of large enterprises.

5. What is the economist's case for having the government be responsible for providing infrastructure? (Hint: You may wish to review the concept of a public good.)

6. If many LDCs simultaneously attempted to pursue export-led growth, what would be the effect in world markets on the quantities and prices of products mainly sold by LDCs, like minerals, agricultural goods, and textiles? What effect might these quantities and prices have on the success of such export-led growth policies?

7. Explain how the idea of import substitution conflicts in the short run with the idea of comparative advantage. Need the two ideas conflict in the long run? Why or why not?

8. Why might a family in an LDC feel economic pressure to have more children than a family in a developed country?

Glossary

absolute advantage: a country has an absolute advantage over another country in the production of a good if it can produce that good more efficiently (with fewer inputs)

accelerated depreciation: a provision of the tax code which allows for deductions from income for purposes of calculating tax liability for the depreciation of machines (that is, for their wearing out and obsolescence) which are in excess of the true decrease in value. This may entail, for instance, the use of a shorter life span than the actual life span of the machine or building

accelerator: the effect on GDP of the increase in investment that results from an increase in output. For instance, the greater output leads a firm to believe the demand for its products will rise in the future; the resulting increase in investment leads to growth in output and still further increases in investment, accelerating the expansion of the economy

accommodative monetary policies: monetary policies which accommodate changes in fiscal policy (or other changes in the economic environment) in ways which maintain the economy's macroeconomic performance

acquired endowments: resources a country builds for itself, like a network of roads or an educated population

adaptive expectations: expectations based on the extrapolation of events in the recent past into the future

adverse selection: principle that says that those who most want to buy insurance tend to be those most at risk, so charging a high price for insurance (to cover those at high risk) will discourage those at less risk from buying insurance at all; similar phenomena occur in credit, labor, and product markets

aggregate consumption function: the relationship between aggregate consumption and aggregate income

aggregate demand curve: a curve relating the total demand for the economy's goods and services at each price level, given the level of wages

aggregate expenditures schedule: a curve that traces out the relationship between expenditures—the sum of consumption, investment, government expenditures, and net exports—and national income, at a fixed price level

aggregate supply: the amount of goods that firms would be willing to supply, given their plant and equipment, assuming wages and prices are flexible and adjust so that the labor force is fully employed

aggregate supply curve: a curve relating the total supply of the economy's goods and services at each price level, given the level of wages

appreciation: a change in the exchange rate that enables a unit of currency to buy more units of foreign currencies

asset: any item that is long-lived, purchased for the service it renders over its life and for what one will receive when one sells it

automatic stabilizers: expenditures that automatically increase or taxes that automatically decrease when economic conditions worsen, and which therefore tend to stabilize the economy automatically

autonomous consumption: that part of consumption that does not depend on income

average costs: the total costs divided by the total output

balanced budget amendment: a proposed amendment to the Constitution which would require that the federal government have a balanced budget (that is, that prohibits deficits)

balanced budget multiplier: the increase in GDP from a dollar increase in government expenditures matched by a dollar increase in taxes

balance sheet: the accounting framework that shows a firms assets, liabilities, and net worth

bank run: a rush on a bank by its depositors to withdraw their funds, as they lose confidence in the bank's finances

barter: trade that occurs without the use of money

basic competitive model: the model of the economy that pulls together the assumptions of self-interested consumers, profit-maximizing firms, and perfectly competitive markets

beggar-thy-neighbor policies: restrictions on imports designed to increase a country's national output, so-called because they increase that country's output at the same time that they hurt the output of other countries

bilateral trade: trade between two parties

black market: an illegal market in which proscribed trades occur. For instance, in war time, when coupons are required to buy certain basic commodities, it may be illegal to buy and sell coupons; black markets typically develop in which these coupons are in fact traded

boom: a period of time when resources are being fully used and GDP is growing steadily

budget constraint: the limitations on consumption of different goods imposed by the fact that households have only a limited amount of money to spend (their budget). The budget constraint *defines* the opportunity set of individuals, when the only constraint that they face is money

business cycle: the fluctuations in the level of economic activity in the economy. At one time, it was thought that these fluctuations were extremely regular; today, the term is used to refer to fluctuations even when they have no regular periodicity

capital: funds used for investment; the term is also used for the value of an individual's investment or a firm's capital stock

capital deepening: an increase in capital per worker

capital gains: the increase in the value of an asset

capital goods: the machines and buildings firms invest in, with funds obtained in the capital market

capital goods investment: investments in machines and buildings (to be distinguished from investments in *inventory,* in *research and development,* or in *training* (human capital)

capital goods markets: the markets in which capital goods are traded

capital inflow: the inflow of capital (money) from abroad, to buy investments, to be deposited in U.S. banks, to buy U.S. government bonds, or to be lent in the United States for any reason

capital loss: a capital loss occurs when an asset is sold at a price below the price at which it was purchased; the difference is the magnitude of the capital loss

capital market: the various institutions concerned with raising funds and sharing and insuring risks; it includes banks, insurance markets, bond markets, and the stock market

capital outflows: the outflow of capital (money) to abroad

capital requirements: the capital that the government requires of banks (defined as a certain ratio of net worth to deposits) to ensure their financial viability

causation: the relationship that results when a change in one variable is not only correlated with but actually causes a change in another variable; the change in the second variable is a consequence of the change in the first variable, rather than both changes being a consequence of a change in a third variable

central bank: the bank that oversees and monitors the rest of the banking system and serves as the bankers' bank

centralization: organizational structure in which decision making is concentrated at the top

central planning: the system in which central government bureaucrats (as opposed to private entrepreneurs or even local government bureaucrats) determine what will be produced and how it will be produced

centrally planned economy: an economy in which most decisions about resource allocation are made by the central government

chain-weighted real GDP: the method of calculating real GDP in which the percentage increase in output from each year to the next is calculated by comparing the value of output of both years in the earlier year's prices

circular flow: the way in which funds move through the capital, labor, and product markets between households, firms, the government, and the foreign sector

classical economists: economists prevalent before the Great Depression who believed that the basic competitive model provided a good description of the economy and that if short periods of unemployment did occur, market forces would quickly restore the economy to full employment

classical unemployment: unemployment that occurs as a result of too-high real wages; it occurs in the supply-constrained equilibrium, so that rightward shifts in aggregate supply reduce the level of unemployment

closed economy: an economy that neither exports nor imports

commercial policies: policies directed at affecting either imports or exports

Common Market: the predecessor of the European Union

communism: an economic system in which the government owns all property and in which it is responsible for most economic decision making

comparative advantage: a country has a comparative advantage over another country in one good as opposed to another good if its *relative* efficiency in the production of the first good is higher than the other country's

competitive equilibrium price: the price at which the quantity supplied and the quantity demanded are equal to each other

competitive model: the basic model of the economy, in which profit-maximizing firms interact with rational, self-interested consumers in competitive markets, in which all participants are price takers (that is, they assume that prices are unaffected by their actions)

complement: two goods are complements if the demand for one (at a given price) decreases as the price of the other increases

compound interest: interest paid on interest; a savings account pays compound interest when, say, interest is credited to the account every day, so that on subsequent days, interest is earned not only on the original principal, but also on the credited interest

constant returns: a production function has constant returns when increases in an input (keeping all other inputs fixed) increase output proportionately

constant returns to scale: a production function has constant returns to scale when equiproportionate increases in all inputs increase output proportionately

consumer price index: a price index in which the basket of goods is defined by what a typical consumer purchases

consumption function: the relationship between disposable income and consumption

correlation: the relationship that results when a change in one variable is consistently associated with a change in another variable

cost-push inflation: inflation whose initial cause is a rise in production costs

countervailing duties: duties (tariffs) that are imposed by a country to counteract subsidies provided to a foreign producer

coupon rationing: a system of rationing (often used in wartime) in which, in order to buy some commodity, such as a pound of sugar, a coupon is required, in addition to the dollar price. Each individual or household is issued so many coupons for certain essential commodities each month

credit constraint effect: when prices fall, firms' revenues also fall, but the money they owe creditors remains unchanged; as a result, firms have fewer funds of their own to invest. Because of credit rationing, firms cannot make up the difference; accordingly, investment decreases

credit rationing: credit is rationed when no lender is willing to make a loan to a borrower or the amount lenders are willing to lend to borrowers is limited, even if the borrower is willing to pay more than other borrowers of comparable risk who are getting loans

crowding out: a decrease in private investment resulting from an increase in government expenditures

cyclical unemployment: the increase in unemployment that occurs as the economy goes into a slowdown or recession

debt: capital, such as bonds and bank loans, supplied to a firm by lenders; the firm promises to repay the amount borrowed plus interest

decentralization: organizational structure in which many individuals or subunits can make decisions

deficit: see **fiscal deficit**

deficit spending: the situation that exists when government expenditures are greater than revenues

deflation: a persistent decrease in the general level of prices

demand curve: the relationship between the quantity demanded of a good and the price, whether for an individual or for the market (all individuals) as a whole

demand-constrained equilibrium: the equilibrium that occurs when prices are stuck at a level above that at which aggregate demand equals aggregate supply; output is equal to aggregate demand

demand deposits: deposits that can be drawn upon instantly, like checking accounts

demand-pull inflation: inflation whose initial cause is aggregate demand exceeding aggregate supply at the current price level

demand shocks: unexpected shifts in the aggregate demand curve

demographic effects: effects that arise from changes in characteristics of the population such as age, birthrates, and location

depreciation: (a) the decrease in the value of an asset; in particular, the amount that capital goods decrease in value as they are used and become old; (b) a change in the exchange rate that enables a unit of one currency to buy fewer units of foreign currencies

depreciation allowance: the provision of the tax code which allows for deductions from income for purposes of calculating tax liability for the depreciation of machines (that is, for their wearing out and obsolescence)

deregulation: the lifting of government regulations to allow the market to function more freely

devaluation: a reduction in the rate of exchange between one currency and other currencies under a fixed exchange rate system

developed or industrialized countries: the wealthiest nations in the world, including Western Europe, the United States, Canada, Japan, Australia, and New Zealand

diminishing returns: the principle that says that as one input increases, with other inputs fixed, the resulting increase in output tends to be smaller and smaller

discount rate: the interest rate charged to banks when they wish to borrow from the central bank

discouraged workers: workers who would be willing to work but have given up looking for jobs, and thus are not officially counted as unemployed

discretionary expenditures: government expenditures which are decided on an annual basis

disposable income: income after paying taxes

dissaving: negative savings; an individual is dissaving when consumption exceeds income

division of labor: dividing a production process into a series of jobs, with each worker focusing on a limited set of tasks; the advantage of division of labor is that each worker can practice and perfect a particular set of skills

double coincidence of wants: one individual has what the other individual wants; required in order for barter to work

downward rigidity of wages: the situation that exists when wages do not fall quickly in response to a shift in the demand or supply curve for labor, resulting in an excess supply of labor

dual economy: the separation in many LDCs between an impoverished rural sector and an urban sector that has higher wages and more advanced technology

dumping: the practice of selling a good abroad at a lower price than at home, or below costs of production

durable goods: goods that produce a service over a number of years, such as cars, major appliances, and furniture

dynamic consistency: a government promise (or plan) is dynamically consistent if the government actually carries out the proposed course of action

econometrics: the branch of statistics developed to analyze the particular kinds of problems that arise in economics

economics: the social science that studies how individuals, firms, governments, and other organizations make choices, and how those choices determine the way the resources of society are used

efficiency wage: the wage at which total labor costs are minimized

efficiency wage theory: the theory that paying higher wages (up to a point) lowers total production costs, for instance by leading to a more productive labor force

elastic: see **relatively elastic**

elasticity of labor supply: the percentage change in labor supplied resulting from a 1 percent change in wages

elasticity of supply: see **price elasticity of supply**

endogenous factors: properties of the economy itself, such as a tendency of the economy to become overconfident in expansions, which tend to generate or exacerbate economic fluctuations; more generally, an endogenous variable in a model is any variable that is determined within the model itself

entitlements: programs that provide benefits automatically to individuals meeting certain criteria (such as age)

entrepreneurs: people who create new businesses, bring new products to market, and develop new processes of production

equation of exchange: the equation relating velocity, the value of output, and the money supply (MV = PY)

equilibrium: a condition in which there are no forces (reasons) for change

equilibrium price: see **competitive equilibrium price**

equilibrium quantity: the quantity demanded (which equals the quantity supplied) at the equilibrium price, where demand equals supply

equity, shares, stock: terms that indicate part ownership of a firm; the firm sells these in order to raise money, or capital

equity capital: capital, such as shares (or stock), supplied to a firm by shareholders; the returns received by the shareholders are not guaranteed but depend on how well the firm does

European Union: the agreement among most of the countries of Western Europe not only to remove trade barriers but also to allow the free flow of labor and capital; it succeeded the Common Market

excess demand: the situation in which the quantity demanded at a given price exceeds the quantity supplied

excess or **free reserves:** reserves that banks hold in excess of what are required

excess supply: the situation in which the quantity supplied at a given price exceeds the quantity demanded

exchange rate: the rate at which one currency (such as dollars) can be exchanged for another (such as marks, yen, or pounds)

exit the market: a consumer exits the market when he decides that at that price, he would prefer to consume none of the product in that market

exogenous shocks: disturbances to the economy originating outside the economy (such as wars or floods)

expectations-augmented Phillips curve: a Phillips curve relationship (that is, a relationship between inflation and unemployment) which takes into account the impact of inflationary expectations; as inflationary expectations increase, the inflation associated with any level of unemployment increases

expected return: the average return—a single number that combines the various possible returns per dollar invested with the chances that each of these returns will actually be paid

experimental economics: the branch of economics which analyzes certain aspects of economic behavior in a controlled, laboratory setting

export-led growth: the strategy that government should encourage exports in which the country has a comparative advantage to stimulate growth

exports: goods produced domestically but sold abroad

externality: a phenomenon that arises when an individual or firm takes an action but does not bear all the costs (negative externality) or receive all the benefits (positive externality)

federal debt: the cumulative amount that the federal government owes

federal governmental structure: a system in which government activity takes place at several levels—national, state, county, city, and others

Federal Open Market Committee (FOMC): the committee of the Federal Reserve System which sets monetary policy

Federal Reserve banks: banks that belong to the Federal Reserve system

Federal Reserve Board (Fed): the government agency responsible for controlling the money supply and interest rates

Federal Reserve system: the major banking system of the United States, consisting of the Federal Reserve Board, the regional Federal Reserve banks, and the member banks

fiat money: money that has value only because the government says it has value and because people are willing to accept it in exchange for goods

final goods approach to measuring GDP: the approach to measuring GDP which adds up the total dollar value of goods and services produced, categorized by their ultimate users/purchasers (consumption by households, investment by firms, investment by government, and net exports)

financial intermediaries: institutions that form the link between savers who have extra funds and borrowers who desire extra funds

financial investments: investments in stocks, bonds, or other financial instruments; these investments provide the funds that allow investments in *capital goods* (physical investments)

financial system: that part of the economy which includes all the institutions involved in moving savings from savers (households and firms) to borrowers, and in transferring, sharing, and insuring risks; it includes banks, insurance markets, bond markets, and the stock market

firm wealth effect: lower prices or lower demand cause firms' profits and net worth to fall, and this makes them less willing to undertake the risks involved with investment

fiscal deficit: the gap between government expenditures and its revenues from sources other than additional borrowing

fiscal policies: policies that affect the level of government expenditures and taxes

fiscal stimulus: an attempt by the government to stimulate the economy (increase aggregate demand) through fiscal policy, that is, a reduction in taxes or an increase in expenditures

fixed costs: the costs resulting from fixed inputs, sometimes called **overhead costs**

fixed exchange rate system: an exchange rate system in which the value of each currency is fixed in relationship to other currencies

flexible or **floating exchange rate system:** a system in which exchange rates are determined by market forces, the law of supply and demand, without government interference

flows: variables such as the output of the economy *per year;* stocks are in contrast to flows; flows measure the changes in stocks over a given period of time

flow statistics: measurements of a certain rate or quantity per period of time, such as GDP, which measures output per year

fractional reserve system: the system of banking in which banks hold a fraction of the amount on deposit in reserves

free reserves: see **excess reserves**

free-rider problem: the problem that occurs when someone thinks he may be able to enjoy something without paying for it, and so fails to contribute to the cost; free-rider problems arise in the provision of public goods

free trade: trade among countries which occurs freely, without barriers such as tariffs or quotas

frictional unemployment: unemployment arising from the "friction" associated with people moving from one job to another, or moving into the labor force

full-employment deficit: the budget deficit that would have prevailed if the economy were at full employment, thus with higher tax revenues and lower public assistance expenditures

full-employment level of output: the level of output that the economy can produce under normal circumstances with a given stock of plant and equipment and a given supply of labor

full-employment or **potential output:** the level of output that would prevail if labor were fully employed (output may exceed that level if workers work more than the normal level of overtime)

gains from trade: the benefits that each side enjoys from a trade

GDP deflator: a weighted average of the prices of different goods and services, where the weights represent the importance of each of the goods and services in GDP

GDP per capita: the value of all goods and services produced in the economy divided by the population

General Agreement on Tariffs and Trade (GATT): the agreement among the major trading countries of the world that created the framework for lowering barriers to trade and resolving trade disputes; established after World War II, it has now been succeeded by the World Trade Organization (WTO)

general equilibrium: the full equilibrium of the economy, when all markets clear simultaneously

green GDP: a measurement of national output which attempts to take into account effects on the environment and natural resources

green revolution: the invention and dissemination of new seeds and agricultural practices that led to vast increases in agricultural output in less developed countries during the 1960s and 1970s

gross domestic product (GDP): the total money value of the goods and services produced by the residents of a nation during a specified period

gross national product (GNP): a measure of the incomes of residents of a country, including income they receive from abroad but subtracting similar payments made to those abroad

human capital: investments in people (such as through education and training)

imperfect information: a situation in which market participants lack information (such as information about prices or characteristics of goods and services) important for their decision making

implicit contract: an unwritten understanding between two groups involved in an exchange, such as an understanding between employer and employees that employees will receive a stable wage throughout fluctuating economic conditions

import function: the relationship between imports and national income

imports: goods produced abroad but bought domestically

import substitution: the strategy that focuses on the substitution of domestic goods for goods that were previously imported

incentive-equality trade-off: in general, the greater the incentives, the greater the resulting inequality

income approach to measuring GDP: the approach to calculating GDP that involves measuring the income generated to all of the participants in the economy

income effect: the reduced consumption of a good whose price has increased that is due to the reduction in a person's buying power, or "real" income; when a person's real income is lower, normally she will consume less of all goods, including the higher-priced good

income-expenditure analysis: the analysis that determines equilibrium output by relating aggregate expenditures to income

indexing: the formal linking of any payment to a price index

industry: the collection of firms making the same product

inelastic: see **relatively inelastic**

infant industry argument: the argument for protection that new industries need to be protected; as they learn from experience, their production costs will fall, and they can then compete fairly with more established firms in the developed countries

infinite elasticity of demand: the situation that exists when any amount will be demanded at a particular price, but nothing will be demanded if the price increases even a small amount

infinite elasticity of supply: the situation that exists when any amount will be supplied at a particular price, but nothing will be supplied if the price declines even a small amount

inflation: the rate of increase of the general level of prices

inflationary spiral: a self-perpetuating system in which price increases lead to higher wages, which lead to further price increases

inflation inertia: the tendency of inflation to persist

inflation tax: the decrease in buying power (wealth) that inflation imposes on those who hold currency (and other assets, like bonds, the payments for which are fixed in terms of dollars)

infrastructure: the roads, ports, bridges, and legal system that provide the necessary basis for a working economy

inputs: the various material, labor, and other factors used in production

insider-outsider theory: the theory that firms are reluctant to pay new workers (outsiders) a lower wage than current workers (insiders), because current workers will fear being replaced by the new, low-wage workers and will not participate in cooperating with and training them

interest: the return a saver receives in addition to the original amount she deposited (loaned), and the amount a borrower must pay in addition to the original amount he borrowed

interest elasticity of savings: the percentage increase in savings resulting from a one percent change in the interest rate

interest rate effect: the situation that exists when lower interest rates (resulting from an increase in the money supply or a fall in the price level) induce firms to invest more

intertemporal trades: trades that occur *between* two periods of time

investment: from the national perspective, an increase in the stock of capital goods or any other expenditure designed to increase future output; from the perspective of the individual, any expenditure designed to increase an individual's future wealth, such as the purchase of a share in a company. (Since some other individual is likely selling the share, that person is disinvesting, and the net investment for the economy is zero.)

investment function: the relationship between the level of real investment and the value of the real interest rate; also called the *investment schedule*

investment schedule: the relationship between the level of investment and the (real) rate of interest

investment tax credit (ITC): a provision of the tax code in which the government reduces a company's tax bill by an amount equal to a percentage of its spending on investment

investors: those who supply capital to the capital market (including individuals who buy shares of stock in a firm or lend money to a business)

involuntary unemployment: the situation that occurs when the supply of those willing to work at the going market wage exceeds the demand for labor

Keynesian monetary theory: see **traditional monetary theory**

Keynesian unemployment: unemployment that occurs as a result of insufficient aggregate demand; it arises in the demand-constrained equilibrium (where aggregate demand is less than aggregate supply), so that rightward shifts in aggregate demand reduce the level of unemployment

labor force participation rate: the fraction of the working-age population that is employed or seeking employment

labor hoarding: a situation where (in an economic downturn) firms keep workers on the job, though they do not fully utilize them

labor market: the market in which labor services are bought and sold

labor turnover rate: the rate at which workers leave jobs

lags: the difference in time between two events, such as between the time the government recognizes a problem and takes action, and between the time the action occurs and its macroeconomic effects are fully realized

land reform: the redistribution of land by the government to those who actually work the land

law of supply and demand: the law in economics that holds that *in equilibrium* prices are determined so that demand equals supply. Changes in prices thus reflect shifts in the demand or supply curves

leakages: income generated in one round of production that is not used to buy more goods produced within the country

learning by doing: the increase in productivity that occurs as a firm gains experience from producing, and that results in a decrease in the firm's production costs

legal entitlement: a right (or entitlement) granted by law; for instance, rent control laws may grant current occupants the right to continue to occupy an apartment for life at a pre-specified rent

less developed countries (LDCs): the poorest nations of the world, including much of Africa, Latin America, and Asia

liabilities: what a firm owes to others

life-cycle savings: savings that is motivated by a desire to smooth consumption over an individual's lifetime and to meet special needs that arise in various times of life; saving for retirement is the most important aspect of life-cycle savings

life-cycle theory of savings: the theory of savings which emphasizes the importance of life-cycle savings, and that savings will differ in different parts of an individual's life cycle

linear demand curve: a demand curve that is a straight line, that is, in which demand is a linear function of price

line item veto: the right of the president (or a governor) to veto a particular item (line) within a bill, without vetoing the entire bill

lines of credit: an agreement by a bank to lend a business automatically (up to some limit), as it is needed

liquidity: the ease with which an asset can be sold

long-run aggregate supply curve: the aggregate supply curve that applies in the long run, when wages and prices can adjust fully to ensure full employment

long-term bonds: bonds with a maturity of more than ten years

Luddites: early nineteenth-century workmen who destroyed labor-savings machinery rather than see it take over their jobs

M1, M2, M3: measures of the money supply: M1 includes currency and checking accounts; M2 includes M1 plus savings deposits, CDs, and money market funds; M3 includes M2 plus large-denomination savings deposits and institutional money-market mutual funds

macroeconomics: the top-down view of the economy, focusing on aggregate characteristics

managed care: a health care system in which the health care provider, in return for a fixed fee per year, manages the care of the individual, including decisions about whether a specialist is required

marginal benefit: the extra benefits resulting, for instance, from the increased consumption of a commodity

marginal cost: the additional cost corresponding to an additional unit of output produced

marginal costs and benefits: the extra costs and benefits that result from choosing a little bit more of one thing

marginal propensity to consume: the amount by which consumption increases when disposable income increases by a dollar

marginal propensity to import: the amount by which imports increase when disposable income increases by a dollar

marginal propensity to save: the amount by which savings increase when disposable income increases by a dollar

marginal rate of transformation: the amount of extra production of one good that one obtains from reducing the production of another good by one unit, moving along the production possibilities curve

marginal revenue: the extra revenue received by a firm for selling one additional unit of a good

market clearing: the situation that exists when supply equals demand, so there is neither excess supply nor excess demand

market demand: the total amount of a particular good or service demanded in the economy

market demand curve: the total amount of a particular good or service demanded in the economy at each price; it is calculated by "adding horizontally" the individual demand curves, that is, at any given price, it is the sum of the individual demands

market economy: an economy that allocates resources primarily through the interaction of individuals (households) and private firms

market failure: the situation in which a market economy fails to attain economic efficiency

market for risk: the market (the institutions and arrangements) in which risks are transferred (exchanged), transformed, and shared

marketplace: the place where, in traditional societies, goods were bought and sold. In today's economy, only in the case of a few goods and services is there a well-defined marketplace

market risks: risks that arise from variations in market conditions, such as changes in prices or demand for a firm's product

markets: places where goods or services (including labor) are bought, sold, and traded. The term is used today metaphorically; there is no single marketplace where any particular good is bought and sold; the collection of all the places where exchanges take place is thought of as "the market." See also **capital market**

market supply: the total amount of a particular good or service that all the firms in the economy supply

market supply curve: the total amount of a particular good or service that all the firms in the economy together would like to supply at each price; it is calculated by "adding horizontally" the individual firm's supply curves, that is, it is the sum of the amounts each firm is willing to supply at any given price

market surplus: there is a market surplus (or surplus for short) if at the going price, the amount firms are willing to produce exceeds the amount households demand

medium of exchange: an item that can be commonly exchanged for goods and services throughout the economy

menu costs: the costs to firms of changing their prices

microeconomics: the bottom-up view of the economy, focusing on individual households and firms

missing market: when there is a good or service which individuals would like to purchase (at a price at which that good could be profitably produced) but which is not available in the market, the market for that good or service is said to be missing

mixed economy: an economy that allocates resources through a mixture of public (governmental) and private decision making

model: a set of assumptions and data used by economists to study an aspect of the economy and make predictions about the future or about the consequences of various policy changes

monetarists: economists who emphasize the importance of money in the economy; they tend to believe that an appropriate monetary policy is all the economy needs from government, and market forces will otherwise solve any macroeconomic problems

monetary aggregates: the statistics which describe the various measures of the money supply (M_1, M_2, and so forth)

monetary policies: policies that affect the supply of money and credit and the terms on which credit is available to borrowers

money: any item that serves as a medium of exchange, a store of value, and a unit of account

money multiplier: the amount by which a new deposit into the banking system (from the outside) is multiplied as it is loaned out, redeposited, reloaned, etc., by banks

monopolist: the single firm in a monopoly, that is, in an industry in which there is a single firm

monopolistic competition: the form of imperfect competition in which the market has sufficiently few firms that each one faces a downward-sloping demand curve, but enough that each can ignore the reactions of rivals to what it does

monopoly: a market consisting of only one firm

monopsonist: the single buyer of a good or service

moral hazard: the principle that says that those who purchase insurance have a reduced incentive to avoid what they are insured against

multilateral trade: trade between more than two parties

multiplier: the factor by which a change in a component of aggregate demand, like investment or government spending, is multiplied to lead to a larger change in equilibrium national output

multiplier-accelerator model: a model that relates business cycles to the internal working of the economy, showing how changes in investment and output reinforce each other; the central ingredients of the model are the multiplier and the accelerator

myopic expectations: expectations are myopic when they are "short sighted," for instance, simply assuming that today's prices will continue into the future

nationalization: the process whereby a private industry is taken over by the government, whether by buying it or simply seizing it

natural endowments: a country's natural resources, such as good climate, fertile land, or minerals

natural rate of unemployment: the rate of unemployment at which the rate of inflation is zero

negative public savings: a fiscal deficit, where expenditures exceeds revenues

negative sloped curve: a curve in which as the variable measured along the horizontal axis is increased, the variable measured along the vertical axis decreases

net capital inflows: total capital inflows minus total capital outflows

net domestic product (NDP): GDP minus the value of the depreciation of the country's capital goods

net export function: a curve that gives the level of net exports at each level of income

net exports: total exports minus total imports

neutrality of money: a situation where an increase in the money supply simply increases prices proportionately, and has no real effects on the economy

new classical economists: economists who, beginning in the 1970s, built on the tradition of classical economists and believed that by and large, market forces; if left to themselves, would solve the problems of unemployment and recessions

new growth economists: economists who, beginning in the 1980s, sought to understand better the basic forces that led the economy to grow fast at one time and slower at another, or some countries to grow faster than others

new Keynesian economists: economists who, beginning in the 1980s, built on the tradition of Keynesian economists and focused attention on unemployment; they sought explanations for the failure of wages and prices to adjust to make labor markets and possibly other markets clear

newly industrialized countries (NICs): nations that have recently moved from being quite poor to being middle-income countries, including South Korea, Taiwan, Singapore, and Hong Kong

nominal GDP: the value of gross domestic product in a particular year measured in that year's prices

nominal interest rate: the percentage return on a deposit, loan, or bond; the nominal interest rate does not take into account the effects of inflation

nonaccelerating inflation rate of unemployment (NAIRU): the level of unemployment at which actual (realized) inflation equals inflationary expectations; below this rate of unemployment, the rate of inflation increases; above it, it decreases

nondiscretionary: expenditures that are determined automatically, such as interest payments and expenditures on entitlements

nontariff barriers: barriers to trade that take forms other than tariffs (such as regulations which disadvantage foreign firms)

normative economics: economics in which judgments about the desirability of various policies are made; the conclusions rest on value judgments as well as facts and theories

North American Free Trade Agreement (NAFTA): the agreement between Canada, the United States, and Mexico that lowered trade and other barriers among the countries

Okun's law: the observation that as the economy pulls out of a recession, output increases more than proportionately to increases in employment

oligopoly: the form of imperfect competition in which the market has several firms, sufficiently few that each one must take into account the reactions of rivals to what it does

open economy: an economy that is actively engaged in international trade

open market operations: central banks' purchase or sale of government bonds in the open market

opportunity cost: the cost of a resource, measured by the value of the next-best, alternative use of that resource

opportunity sets: a summary of the choices available to individuals, as defined by budget constraints and time constraints

output per capita: a nation's output divided by the number of individuals in the country

outputs: the goods and services that are produced by firms

overhead costs: the costs a firm must pay just to remain in operation. They do not depend on the scale of production

Pareto efficient: a resource allocation is said to be Pareto efficient if there is no rearrangement which can make anyone better off without making someone else worse off

peak: the top of a boom

perfect competition: a situation in which each firm is a price taker—it cannot influence the market price; at the market price, the firm can sell as much as it wishes, but if it raises its price, it loses all sales

perfectly elastic: infinite elasticity; a demand or supply curve is perfectly elastic if it is horizontal

perfectly inelastic: zero elasticity; a demand or supply curve is perfectly inelastic if it is vertical, so the demand or supply is completely insensitive to price

perfectly mobile capital: capital that responds quickly to changes in returns in different countries

permanent home hypothesis: the theory that individuals base their current consumption levels on their permanent (long-run average) income

Phillips curve: the trade-off between unemployment and inflation such that a lower level of unemployment is associated with a higher level of inflation

physical capital: investments in plant and equipment; the term is used to distinguish these investments from investments in people, called human capital

planned economy: economies in which the government takes central responsibility for economic decision making, including developing plans for economic growth

planned and unplanned inventories: planned inventories are those firms choose to have on hand because they make business more efficient; unplanned inventories result when firms cannot sell what they produce

policy ineffectiveness proposition: the proposition that government policies are ineffective—policies aimed at stimulating aggregate demand at most change the price level

portfolio theories of monetary policy: theories that argue that monetary policy affects output through its effect on prices of various assets, in particular the prices of stocks

positive economics: economics that describes how the economy behaves and predicts how it might change—for instance, in response to some policy change

positively sloped curve: a curve in which as the variable measured along the horizontal axis is increased, the variable measured along the vertical axis increases

potential GDP: a measure of what the value of GDP would be if the economy's resources were fully employed

present discounted value: how much an amount of money to be received in the future is worth right now

price: the price of a good or service is what must be given in exchange for the good

price ceiling: a maximum price above which market prices are not legally allowed to rise

price elasticity of demand: the percentage change in quantity demanded of a good as the result of a 1 percent change in price (the percentage change in quantity demanded divided by the percentage change in price)

price elasticity of supply: the percentage change in quantity supplied of a good as the result of a 1 percent change in price (the percentage change in quantity supplied divided by the percentage change in price)

price floor: a minimum price below which market prices are not legally allowed to fall

price index: a measure of the level of prices found by comparing the cost of a certain basket of goods in one year with the cost in a base year

price level: some measure of the average prices in the economy; when analyzing the product market as a whole, the equilibrium *price level* is given by the intersection of the aggregate demand curve and the aggregate supply curve

price makers: firms that affect, or make, the price as a result of their actions, especially as a consequence of their level of production

price system: the economic system in which prices are used to allocate scarce resources

price takers: firms that take the price for the good or service they sell as given; the price is unaffected by their level of production

principal: the original amount a saver deposits in a bank (lends) or a borrower borrows

principle of consumer sovereignty: the principle that holds that each individual is the best judge of what makes him better off

principle of substitution: the principle that holds that in general there are large possibilities for substitution, both by consumers and by firms, so that an increase in the price of say an input will lead the firm to substitute other inputs in its place

private property: ownership of property (or other assets) by individuals or corporations; under a system of private property, owners have certain property rights but there may also be restrictions on the use of property, such as zoning restrictions which limit the use of property to specified purposes, such as residential or commercial purposes

privatization: the process whereby functions that were formerly undertaken by government are delegated instead to the private sector

producer price index: a price index that measures the average level of producers' prices

product differentiation: the fact that similar products (like breakfast cereals or soft drinks) are perceived to differ from one another and thus are imperfect substitutes

production-facilitating function of inventories: the role of inventories in facilitating production, for instance, by avoiding costly stoppage of production as a result of an interruption of supplies

production possibilities: the combination of outputs of different goods that an economy can produce with given resources

production-smoothing function of inventories: the

role of inventories in allowing production to continue at a steady level, in the face of fluctuations in demand

product liability: the obligation of a producer to compensate victims of a defective product that has injured them

product market: the market in which goods and services are bought and sold

production possibilities curve: a curve that defines the opportunity set for a firm or an entire economy and gives the possible combinations of goods (outputs) that can be produced from a given level of inputs

productivity, or **GDP per hour worked:** how much an average worker produces per hour, calculated by dividing real GDP by hours worked in the economy

property rights: the rights of an owner of private property; these typically include the right to use the property as she sees fit (subject to certain restrictions, such as zoning) and the right to sell it when and to whom she sees fit

protectionism: the policy of protecting domestic industries from the competition of foreign-made goods

public good: a good, such as national defense, that costs little or nothing for an extra individual to enjoy, and the costs of preventing any individual from the enjoyment of which are high; public goods have the properties of nonrivalrous consumption and nonexcludability

pure public good: a good which possesses the property of nonexcludability (in which it is *impossible* to exclude any individual from enjoying the benefits of the good) and nonrivalrousness (the consumption or enjoyment of the good by one individual does not subtract at all from that of other individuals)

quantity theory of money: the theory that velocity is constant, so that changes in the money supply lead to proportionale changes in nominal income (which also equals the value of output)

quota rents: profits that accrue to firms which are allocated the rights to import a good subject to quotas that result from the artificially created scarcity

quotas: limits on the amount of foreign goods that can be imported

rational choice: a choice process in which individuals weigh the costs and benefits of each possibility, and in which the choices made are those within the opportunity set that maximize net benefits

rational expectations: expectations are rational when people make full use of all relevant available past data in their formation of an expectation

rationed goods: when individuals get less of a good than they would like at the terms being offered, the good is said to be rationed

rationing by queues: allocating scarce resources on the basis of who is most willing and able to wait in line the longest

rationing system: any system of allocating scarce resources, applied particularly to systems other than the price system. Rationing systems include rationing by coupons and rationing by queues

real balance effect: as prices fall, the real value of people's money holdings increases, and they consume more

real business-cycle theorists: a school of economists who contend that the economy's fluctuations have nothing to do with monetary policy but are determined by real forces

real exchange rates: exchange rate adjusted for changes in the relative price levels in different countries

real GDP: the real value of all final goods and services produced in the economy, measured in dollars adjusted for inflation

real income: income measured by what it can actually buy, rather than by the amount of money; income adjusted for inflation

real interest rate: the real return to saving, equal to the nominal interest rate minus the rate of inflation

real wage: the nominal wage divided by the (consumer) price level

recession: two consecutive quarters of a year during which GDP falls

relatively elastic: a good is said to be relatively elastic when the price elasticity of its demand is greater than unity

relatively inelastic: a good is said to be relatively inelastic when the price elasticity of its demand is less than unity

relative price: the ratio of any two prices; the relative price of apples and oranges is just the ratio of their prices

reservation wage: the wage below which an individual chooses not to participate in the labor market

reserve requirements: the minimum level of reserves that the central bank requires be kept on hand or deposited with the central bank

reserve: money kept on hand by a bank in the event that those who have made deposits wish to withdraw their money

residual: that part of the growth of the economy that cannot be explained by increases in inputs

retained earnings: that part of the net earnings of a firm that are not paid out to shareholders, but retained by the firm

risk premium: the additional interest required by lenders as compensation for the risk that a borrower may default; more generally, the extra return required to compensate an investor for bearing risk

sacrifice ratio: the amount by which the unemployment rate must be kept above the NAIRU for one year to bring down inflation by 1 percentage point

scarcity: term used to describe the limited availability of resources, so that if no price were charged for a good or service, the demand for it would it exceed its supply

search: the process by which consumers gather information about what is available in the market, including prices, or by which workers gather information about the jobs that are available, including wages

seasonal unemployment: unemployment that varies with the seasons, such as that associated with the decline in construction in winter

shadow price: the true social value of a resource

sharecropping: an arrangement, prevalent in many less-developed countries, in which a worker works land, giving the landowner a fixed share of the output

shortage: a situation where, at the going market price, demand exceeds supply

short-run aggregate supply curve: the relationship between aggregate supply (what firms are willing to produce) and the price level that prevails in the short run; in particular, it is not assumed that wages adjust fully to ensure full employment (see long-run aggregate supply curve)

short-run production function: the relationship between output and employment in the short run, that is, with a given set of machines and buildings

short-term bonds: bonds that mature within a few years

simple interest: a savings account pays simple (rather than compound) interest when interest is paid only against the original principal (deposit)

Smith's "invisible hand": the idea that if people act in their own self-interest, they will often also be acting in a broader social interest, as if they had been directed by an "invisible hand"

socialism: an economic system in which the means of production are controlled by the state

social science: a branch of science which studies human social behavior; the social sciences include economics, political science, anthropology, sociology, and psychology. As a science, these disciplines explore human behavior systematically, involving both the formulation of theories and the examination of data

soft budget constraints: budget constraints facing a firm in which the government subsidizes any losses

stagflation: a situation in which high inflation is combined with low growth and high unemployment

static expectations: the belief of individuals that today's prices and wages are likely to continue into the future

sticky prices: prices that do not adjust or adjust only slowly toward a new equilibrium

sticky wages: wages that are slow to adjust in response to a change in labor market conditions

stocks: variables like the capital stock or the money supply stock, that describe the state of the economy (such as its wealth) at a point of time; they are contrasted by flows

stock statistics: measurements of the quantity of a certain item at a certain point in time, such as capital stock, the total value of buildings and machines

store of value: something that can be accepted as payment in the present and exchanged for items of value in the future

strategic trade theory: the theory that holds that protection can give a country a strategic advantage over rivals, for instance by helping reduce domestic costs as a result of economies of scale

structural unemployment: long-term unemployment that results from structural factors in the economy, such as a mismatch between the skills required by newly created jobs and the skills possessed by those who have lost their jobs in declining industries

substitute: two goods are substitutes if the demand for one increases when the price of the other increases

substitution effect: the reduced consumption of a good whose price has increased that is due to the changed trade-off, the fact that one has to give up more of other goods to get one more unit of the high-priced good; the substitution effect is associated with a change in the slope of the budget constraint

sunk cost: a cost that has been incurred and cannot be recovered

supply curve: the relationship between the quantity supplied of a good and the price, whether for a single firm or the market (all firms) as a whole

supply-constrained equilibrium: the equilibrium that occurs when prices are stuck at a level below that at which aggregate demand equals aggregate supply; in a supply-constrained equilibrium, output is equal to aggregate supply but less than aggregate demand

supply shocks: unexpected shifts in the aggregate supply curve, such as an increase in the international price of oil or a major earthquake that destroys a substantial fraction of a country's capital stock

supply siders: economists who emphasize the importance of aggregate supply, in particular the responsiveness of supply to lower taxes and regulations; some argue that lowering tax rates leads to such large increases in inputs of capital and labor that total tax revenues may actually increase

surges: unexpected large increases in imports

surplus: the magnitude of the gain from trade, the difference between what an individual would have been willing to pay for a good and what she has to pay. See also **market surplus**

surplus labor: a great deal of unemployed or underemployed labor, readily available to potential employers

sustainable development: development that is based on sustainable principles; sustainable development pays particular concern to environmental degradation and the exploitation of natural resources

technological risks: risks facing a firm associated with technology, such as whether a new technology will work or be reliable

theory: a set of assumptions and the conclusions derived from those assumptions put forward as an explanation for some phenomena

time constraints: the limitations on consumption of different goods imposed by the fact that households have only a limited amount of time to spend (twenty-four hours a day). The time constraint *defines* the opportunity set of individuals if the only constraint that they face is time

time value of money: the fact that a dollar today is worth more than a dollar in the future is called the time value of money

total factor productivity analysis: the analysis of the relationship between output and the aggregate of all inputs; total factor productivity growth is calculated as the difference between the rate of growth of output and the weighted average rate of growth of inputs, where the weight associated with each input is its share in GDP

trade creation: new trade that is generated as a result of lowered tariff barriers

trade deficit: the excess of imports over exports

trade diversion: trade that is diverted away from outside countries as a result of lowering tariffs between the members of a trading bloc

trade-offs: the amount of one good (or one desirable objective) that must be given up to get more of another good (or to attain more of another desirable objective)

trading blocs: groups of countries that agree to lower trade and other economic barriers among themselves

traditional monetary theory: the theory (first developed by John Maynard Keynes, and therefore sometimes referred to as Keynesian monetary theory) that the nominal interest rate is the opportunity cost of holding money, that the demand for money decreases as the interest rate rises, and that the interest rate is determined to equate the demand and supply of money

transactions demand for money: the demand for money arising from its use in buying goods and services

transplants: plants constructed in one country by firms based in another. United States factories producing Mazdas and Toyotas are Japanese transplants

trough: the bottom of a recession

two-tier wage system: wage systems in which newly hired workers are paid lower wages than established workers are paid

unemployment rate: the fraction of those seeking employment that cannot get jobs

unitary price elasticity: a demand curve has unitary price elasticity if the demand for the commodity decreases by one percent when the price increases by one percent. If demand has unitary elasticity, then expenditures on the good do not depend at all on price. A supply curve has unitary price elasticity if the supply of the commodity increases by one percent when the price increases by one percent

unit of account: something that provides a way of measuring and comparing the relative values of different goods

value-added: the value added in each stage of production is the difference between the value of the output and the value of the inputs purchased from other firms

value-added approach to measuring national output: in the value added approach to measuring national output, the value-added of each of the firms in the economy are added up

value of the marginal product of labor: the value of the extra output produced by an extra unit of labor; it is calculated by multiplying the marginal product of labor times the price of the good that is being produced

variable costs: the costs resulting from variable inputs

velocity: the speed with which money circulates in the economy, defined as the ratio of income to the money supply

voluntary export restraints (VERs): restraints on exports that are "voluntarily" imposed by an exporting country, though often in response to a threat that if such constraints are not imposed, the importing country will impose import quotas

voluntary unemployment: a situation in which workers voluntarily drop out of the labor force when the wage level falls

wage-productivity curve: the curve that depicts the relationship between wages and productivity

wholesale price index: a price index that measures the average level of wholesale prices

work sharing: reducing all employees' hours by equal amounts rather than firing some workers

World Trade Organization (WTO): the organization established in 1995, as a result of the Uruguay round of trade negotiations, replacing GATT, designed to remove trade barriers and settle trade disputes

zero elasticity of demand: the situation that exists when the quantity demanded will not change, regardless of changes in price

zero elasticity of supply: the situation that exists when the quantity supplied will not change, regardless of changes in price

Credits

p. 6, courtesy Chrysler Corporation, Auburn Hills, MI; **p. 15,** Bettmann; **p. 44,** ©Mike Dobel/Masterfile; **p. 51,** courtesy Intel Corporation; **p. 85,** Corel CD-ROM, image #506048; **p. 112,** ©Dick Hemingway; **p. 140,** Corel CD-ROM, image #29026; **p. 169,** ©1994 Ken Stratton/The Stock Market; **p. 184,** Reuters/Corbis-Bettmann; **p. 206,** The Detroit Free Press, Photo Department; **p. 258,** courtesy Jim Mairs; **p. 261,** ©C. P. George/H. Armstrong Roberts; **p. 267,** courtesy Simmons Mattress Co., **p. 281,** courtesy Federal Reserve Bank of Atlanta; **p. 291,** UPI/Bettmann; **p. 318,** UPI/Corbis-Bettmann; **p. 324,** Neil Ryder Hoos; **p. 340,** courtesy Tom McCarthy; **p. 343,** Corbis-Bettmann; **p. 354,** Warder Collection; **p. 364,** Reuters/Corbis-Bettmann; **p. 390,** ©Lynn McLaren/The Picture Cube; **p. 410,** Reuters/Corbis-Bettmann; **p. 446,** ©Dick Hemingway; **p. 451,** Corel CD-ROM, image #506050; **p. 452,** courtesy IBM Corporation; **p. 490,** courtesy Golf Carts Fore You, Hudson, FL; **p. 492,** Bettmann; **p. 517,** ©TASS/Sovfoto; **p. 540,** Corbis-Bettmann; **p. 552,** Corbis-Bettman.

INDEX